Making a Diff...
for America's Children
Speech-Language Pathologists in Public Schools

Second Edition

Barbara J. Moore and Judy K. Montgomery

With a foreword by Kathleen Whitmire, Ph.D.

Edited by Dale Ducworth, MCD, CCC-SLP

Thinking Publications® • Greenville, South Carolina

Library of Congress Cataloging-in-Publication Data

Moore, Barbara J., 1957-

   Making a difference for America's children : speech-language

pathologists in public schools / Barbara J. Moore and Judy K. Montgomery;

with a foreword by Kathleen Whitmire. -- 2nd ed.

      p. cm.

   Includes bibliographical references and index.

   ISBN 978-1-58650-855-5 (alk. paper)

   1. Speech therapy for children--United States. 2. Communicative

disorders in children--United States. 3. Children with

disabilities--Education--United States. I. Montgomery, Judy K., 1947-

II. Title.

   LB3454.M66 2007

   371.91'42--dc22

                                2007043193

Printed in the United States of America

Cover Design by Sharon Webber

Photos by Sharon Donnelly (pp. 4, 59, 68, 80, 99, 195, 263 [bottom], 267, 291, 305 [middle], 310, 348, 381, 407 [bottom], 412, 420)

A Division of Super Duper® Inc.

P.O. Box 24997 • Greenville, SC 29616-2497 USA
1.800.277.8737 • Fax 1.800.978.7379
www.superduperinc.com

To my dad, for your unconditional love and support always; throughout my life you have quietly demonstrated what it means to make a difference in someone's life—you are my model and my hero.

Barb

To my husband Ken for his patience and silent pride that such a volume could finally be completed; and to my many colleagues and students who gave me inspiration and ideas to pass along in this professional community.

Judy

Contents

#TP-29703 Making a Difference - 2nd Ed. • ©2008 Thinking Publications® • www.thinkingpublications.com • 1-800-277-8737

List of Figures and Tables

Figures

Tables

#TP-29703 Making a Difference - 2nd Ed. • ©2008 Thinking Publications® • www.thinkingpublications.com • 1-800-277-8737

Foreword

The profession of speech-language pathology is influenced by a multitude of factors in a fascinating way. We are affected by the contexts in which we practice and the individuals for whom we provide services. As our communities, our nation, and the world change, so does our profession. Societal, political, medical, demographic, and technological shifts reverberate throughout our workplaces and our practice. And who could have predicted the magnitude of these changes over the past several years? From fundamental legislative and regulatory changes to unprecedented shifts in our nation's demographics, from speed-of-light growth in technology to the globalization of the workforce—the world is not the same today as it was when the first edition of this book was published in 2001. And thus, our profession is not the same. Those of us who have been in this field for more than a few years have come to know the demands and excitement that accompany such rapid societal and professional changes. The challenge for all of us is to constantly update our skills and knowledge in order to provide the supports needed by children with communication differences, difficulties, and disorders to succeed in school and prepare for a productive and satisfying future. Fortunately, this publication helps us do that.

The first edition of *Making A Difference: Speech-Language Pathologists in Public Schools (2001)* and its companion piece *Making a Difference in the Era of Accountability: Update on NCLB and IDEA 2004 (2005)* offered excellent guidance to speech-language pathologists and provided a comprehensive overview of the delivery of services in the schools. Building on that foundation, this second edition provides the updates needed to help us navigate the changing waters—not only to keep our clinical skills current but also to help school-based speech-language pathologists take the leadership roles they can and should assume in moving our schools through educational reform. With our unique understanding of the relationships among language, literacy, and learning, and our solid training in data-driven decision making for instruction and intervention, speech-language pathologists bring critical expertise to the table when schools design and implement programs that benefit *all* children.

Current educational reform is the result of several factors including an increased emphasis on literacy, particularly early literacy; a sharpened focus on evidence-based practice; an increasingly diverse population (including English learners); and a growing concern about our students' inability to compete in the global workforce. Federal legislative changes reflect these factors with a heightened demand for accountability in our nation's schools. All of this is happening at the same time that the response to intervention (RtI) movement is sweeping through our schools with the potential to overhaul both general education and special education. Speech-language pathologists are coming to understand the importance of their workload rather than caseload through their work both with and on behalf of students. Authors Judy Montgomery and Barbara Moore must be commended for the way they have masterfully woven together all these issues. This second edition is impressive in its scope and breadth, yet remains readable and accessible for students and seasoned practitioners alike. The authors skillfully move back and forth between explaining the "big picture" and providing practical hands-on information, making this a valuable resource for today's clinicians.

Judy and Barbara have made significant contributions to the practice of speech-language pathology in the schools over the years, and this publication continues that legacy. The readers of this book are the lucky beneficiaries of Judy and Barbara's years of experience, commitment to the schools, passion for our profession, and diligence in remaining informed and current. Their collaborative spirit and sharp intellect shine throughout this publication. Those who read this comprehensive and useful edition will indeed be prepared to step into the leadership roles needed to move our profession and our nation's schools forward to meet the needs of *all* students.

— Kathleen A. Whitmire, Ph.D., CCC-SLP

ASHA Fellow

Board Recognized Specialist in Child Language

Director, RTI Action Network,
    National Center for Learning Disabilities, Inc.

Former Director, School Services in Speech-Language
    Pathology, American Speech-Language-Hearing Association

Preface

In the late 1990s, our dear friend, Nancy McKinley, approached us with an idea: a comprehensive text on the delivery of speech-language pathology services in public schools. We were intrigued by this idea, and the result was a book entitled *Making a Difference for America's Children: Speech-Language Pathologists in Public Schools (2001)*. In our first writing endeavor of such magnitude, we found an exciting venue to compile information about the incredibly diverse practice of speech-language pathologists in public schools.

Much has happened since 2001 when the first edition was published. In the preparation of the second edition, we were astonished with the realization of how much has changed in a short six year span. The overhaul to the educational system has been dramatic during this time period, starting at the end of 2001 with the passage of No Child Left Behind. The significant changes in the legislative and research/evidence base of our field has enabled our profession to be responsive, to grow, and to expand.

In this 2008 edition, our purpose is the same as it was in 2001:

> The intent of the book is to provide a framework for an expanded working situation and to create a vision of the possibilities for children and professionals within legal guidelines and requirements. Public education, the profession of speech-language pathology, and the students and families we serve are constantly changing (Moore-Brown & Montgomery, 2001, p. xiv).

The educational work setting provides ongoing challenges and opportunities for the speech-language pathologists and audiologists who choose it as their professional home. It is our belief, and our message, that these practitioners not only have unique skills and talents to serve students, but that they also can and should be involved with the reform efforts underway in all schools and districts. As leaders in these efforts, speech-language pathologists and audiologists can influence system improvements and impact the lives of many more children than just those on their immediate caseloads.

We believe that the synergistic collaboration of professionals is critical to professional success and improved student achievement. We also believe that it is vital for speech-language pathologists and audiologists to be in the forefront of school reform efforts, as well as to stay current with the evidence base and changing practices. We believe that how we collectively respond to these critical issues will impact the future of the professions.

The period of time between 2001 and 2008 has been replete with educational issues and reforms at unprecedented rates. As a result of these influences, all educators, including speech-language pathologists and audiologists, are being asked to revamp their practice accordingly. The reader will find discussions of these reforms reflected in this updated text. These include:

- The reauthorization of the Elementary and Secondary Education Act, known as No Child Left Behind (NCLB, 2001).

- The reauthorization of the Individuals with Disabilities Education Improvement Act (2004).

- The evolution of evidence-based/scientifically based practice as a standard of care in speech-language pathology, audiology and educational fields.

- The insightful changes brought about by International Classification of Disability (ICD) and International Classification of Functionality (ICF) from the World Health Organization (WHO).

- The overwhelming impact of autism spectrum disorders (ASDs) on special education services, specifically speech-language pathology.

- The development of a workload approach (ASHA, 2002a) to better consider and reflect the work demands of speech-language pathologists in public schools.

- The creation of a prereferral prevention-intervention process known as response to intervention (RtI).

- The elimination of the use of the discrepancy model for eligibility determination of specific learning disabilities.

- The inclusion of five areas of reading instruction (phonemic awareness, phonics instruction, *[reading]* fluency, vocabulary development, and text comprehension) in two federal laws, NCLB and IDEA 2004.

- Dealing with an increase in the demands for services during a time of persistent personnel vacancies (e.g., shortages) in many parts of the country.

- Evolution of new roles and responsibilities related to school reform issues.

One additional area that we addressed in this text is the work of educational audiologists, who are fewer in number than speech-language pathologists in schools, but nevertheless play a vital role in providing services to children with communication impairments. To the best of our ability, we have featured their work, which we believe is noteworthy and important.

We have been grateful to the many people throughout the country over the course of the past six years who have taken the time to provide us comments and feedback about the first edition of *Mak-*

ing A Difference: Speech-Language Pathologists in Public Schools (2001) as well as the companion *Making a Difference in the Era of Accountability: Update on NCLB and IDEA 2004 (2005)*. Not only is it exciting when someone takes the time to approach you and comment on your work, but we have taken your comments and suggestions to heart and have tried to reflect them in this updated edition. Your enthusiasm for school-based services is what fueled our own excitement about the need for this updated project.

Throughout the text we have attempted, as before, to provide a resource which will be of use to both students and working professionals. The world of schools is exciting and ever changing. The complexity of issues and mandates stimulates and challenges our work daily. We often do not pause to consider how far we have traveled to incur evolution as a discipline, in our practice or as a system. Mostly we contend with the current issue at hand and try to consider how to best deal with that issue. Our intention is that this text can provide perspective on the current issues facing not only school-based speech-language pathologists and audiologists, but the entire educational system. Our belief and premise is that our services exist within a system and are intended to be designed to support the students and the public education system itself. As we have learned from Friedman (2007), what we do in one place has a dramatic impact somewhere else, quite far away. The world—and therefore education—is flat.

We are grateful to again have had the opportunity to work together and honor the work of school-based speech-language pathologists and audiologists. As we often say, the work done by these professionals "knocks our socks off." We hope that this book will provide information and understanding about where we are heading as an educational system and a profession. We are enthused, inspired, and encouraged by what speech-language pathologists and audiologists do every day, and how they truly make a difference for America's children.

> We must not, in trying to think about how we can make a big difference, ignore the small daily differences we can make which, over time, add up to big differences that we often cannot foresee.
>
> — Marian Wright Edelman

Acknowledgements

Many conversations, acts of kindness, and serendipitous moments occur on the way to publishing a book, and this one is no different. The road to this second edition began three years ago with the changes in the federal laws. Not only do education reforms occur, life happens to each of us along the way. So, to begin, we acknowledge those who understood that life's rewards and challenges can, and do, ebb and flow with the publishing of a book.

There are a few individuals who provided us stalwart assistance and constant encouragement during this writing effort. They include:

- Kathleen Whitmire, Susan Karr, and Roseanne Clauson of the ASHA office who were always available, and always delivered on the promise of "whatever you need."

- Celeste Roseberry-McKibbin and Janna Smith Lang for 12 hour turn around on needed information.

- Susan Brannen, who told Barbara that it was okay not to finish the book, and then provided a quote when we did.

- Clint Johnson, who remained calm and positive throughout.

- Thomas and Sharon Webber, who staunchly moved the project along.

- Dale Ducworth, who has been a focused and skillful editor, and now is a lifelong friend.

Additionally, we would like to acknowledge those who cheer from the sidelines and teach us so much. They include:

- The many committed, supportive, and dedicated professionals with whom we met as we traveled the country talking about speech-language and hearing services in public schools. We listened to you and learned from you, and we believe that your work is reflected in this text.

- Professional colleagues in our state who are really the best friends we could have: Beth Nishida, Melissa Jakubowitz, Dee Parker, Barbara Hoskins, Claudia Dunaway, Jennifer Shubin—you are the best!

- Perry Flynn, Nancy Kuhles, Judy Rudebusch, and Maureen Staskowski for providing forms, miscellaneous information and encouragement

- The speech-language pathologists, psychologists, and program specialists of Anaheim Union High School District, California who demonstrate daily how to work in a collaborative manner, make a difference for children, and thus energize our work.

- The attorneys from whom Barbara has learned—Jeff Riel, Karen Gilyard, Darin Barber, and Howard Fulfrost. Each of you has influenced our perspective of law from a student-centered approach.

Finally, we again honor the memory of Nancy McKinley, who conceived the original idea for this text. We continue to miss you.

CHAPTER 1

Speech-Language and Audiology Services in the Educational System: Trends and Considerations

IN THIS CHAPTER

This chapter introduces the issues surrounding the educational system within which school-based speech-language pathologists work, including the impact of school reform for both general and special education; characteristics of children and families of the twenty-first century; and incidences of children with disabilities who are identified as needing special education (e.g., speech-language) services in the schools. The chapter concludes with a consideration of predictions about school reform and the changing roles of professionals.

1. How has the role of the school-based speech-language pathologist evolved since the implementation of special education in this country?

2. What is meant by "educational reforms"? Why is it important for speech-language pathologists in public schools to be aware of general and special education reforms?

3. How have school reform movements affected the delivery of speech-language services in schools?

4. Discuss why the information presented about children and their environments is important to speech-language pathologists in schools.

5. Discuss how educational trends will influence your work.

Speech-Language and Audiology Services in Public Schools

Many people work together to make the American educational system successful for children. Among the talented and dedicated people who make a difference for children in America's public schools are speech-language pathologists and audiologists, who specialize in speech, language, and communication development and disorders. The discipline of communication sciences and disorders is comprised of two professions—speech-language pathology and audiology. The primary focus of this book will be on the practice and contributions of speech-language pathologists providing services in America's public schools and the difference that these services, and those who provide them, make for children whose communication needs hinder their accomplishments in reading, writing, listening, and speaking. We also have made every attempt to include information about the valuable work of educational audiologists and the critical role that they play in public education.

Speech-language and audiology services in public schools serve vital functions for students with COMMUNICATION DISORDERS, and the provision of such services has grown and evolved significantly over the past 30 plus years. Accordingly, the roles of speech-language pathologists and audiologists in public schools are nearly unrecognizable compared to the work of speech-language pathologists and audiologists in the late 1960s and early 1970s. This change is due to a combination of factors. First, schools, as institutions, are not the same as they were 30 years ago. Public expectations and demands placed upon the educational system are greater now than at any time in the history of the country. This is most dramatically illustrated in the legislative mandates placed upon schools and their employees. Second, the children of the twenty-first century have different needs and bring more diverse life experiences to the school setting. Third, the professions of speech-language pathology and audiology have evolved, along with our scientific research base, which consequently impacts our practice. For speech-language pathologists and audiologists to work effectively in the public school setting, they must not only be competent in the treatment of communication disorders, delays, and disabilities, but also understand the educational system in which they work.

In the past, university programs for communication disorders taught that speech-language pathologists and audiologists in the school setting were predominantly segmented and separated from the general education system that employed them. Such segmentation is no longer true for speech-language pathologists in schools. Educational systems (used here to refer to public school systems) are increasingly dynamic and interactive institutions. Speech-language pathologists and audiologists, in either preservice or in-service situations, must be able to view their work within the context of the larger dynamic, interactive, and responsive educational system. The educational system of the twenty-first century is not segmented. Thus, the work of all professionals working with children is meaningfully connected.

Educational Reforms That Shaped the Profession

The United States and Europe have a long history of programs for certain types of communication disabilities, such as deafness (Hardman, Drew, & Egan, 2007), although such programs were generally found only in special schools. School programs to address the issue of "stammering" were first introduced into public education in 1910. Teachers of English literature were frequently given some training to provide "speech correction" to their students, and between the 1920s and 1940s, university programs for specialists in the area of "speech improvement" or "speech correction" developed. Legislation was passed in 45 states to provide funding for speech and hearing programs by the mid-1960s. Since then, speech-language programs have evolved as a vital part of public school services.

From the early titles of "speech teacher" or "speech correctionist," a variety of titles have since been used to describe the professional who is responsible for the treatment of communication disorders in schools: *speech-language specialist, communication specialist, speech therapist, and speech-language pathologist.* The title speech-language pathologist will be used in this book to refer to a specialist who operates a speech-language program addressing communication disorders in a public school setting.

The professional organization of speech-language pathologists and audiologists is the AMERICAN SPEECH-LANGUAGE-HEARING ASSOCIATION (ASHA). School-based speech-language services have received increasing recognition within ASHA since 1925, when the organization was founded under the original name of the American Society of Speech Correction. The 2005 ASHA membership data reported that 54.5 percent of members were speech-language pathologists working in schools (ASHA, 2006c).

Speech-language services in schools are provided as part of the continuum of SPECIAL EDUCATION services, which exist through the mandates created by state and federal legislation during the wave of civil rights reforms in the

1970s. Special education is designed to support the general education program. Consequently, special education programs have been affected by the long history of educational reforms that have unfolded with increasing intensity since the early 1980s. As these reforms are reviewed, the reader should keep asking the question "How do these changes affect speech-language services?"

General and Special Education Reforms

Institutional change is a part of American culture in nearly every segment of society, responding to forces on many levels: economic, demographic, political, and social. Educational reforms reflect change in these areas as well, reacting to issues that occur inside and outside the school system (Fullan, 2001). In a classic example, the nation was caught off guard in the 1950s when the Soviet Union launched Sputnik, the first satellite, into space. The United States reacted by dramatically increasing the focus on science education in the early 1960s. Thus, politics, economics, and world public opinion influence educational reform in the United States.

Current reform movements in general education began with the infamous report from the National Commission on Excellence in Education in 1983 entitled *A Nation at Risk: The Imperative for Educational Reform*. This report announced the dismal performance of America's children on reading, writing, and math testing compared to their peers from other countries. The report rocked the educational system and set off waves of reform movements in every state legislature, school district, and neighborhood school (Evans & Panacek-Howell, 1995). Since the 1980s, business leaders have pointed to the nation's public schools and criticized them for failing to prepare an adequate workforce. Education has continued to receive increasing national attention, and has been part of the political forefront under the last three presidential administrations. Consequently, significant changes have occurred in how school systems are governed, how instruction is delivered and measured, and how business is conducted in schools across the country.

Reforms have occurred in both general and special education but for different reasons. While the reform of general education programs was prompted by national concerns about the skills and potential competitiveness of American students in a global economy, the reform of special education programs occurred as part of the ongoing mission to provide students with disabilities access to general education. Historically, general and special education reform movements have evolved and changed independently. Separate parallel reform efforts in funding streams, administrative structures, accountability demands, curricula, personnel, certification requirements, and even separate facilities have existed, but facilities have dramatically changed through legislation.

In 1986, the REGULAR EDUCATION INITIATIVE (REI)—led by Madeline Will, Assistant Secretary for Special Education and Rehabilitative Services, with her report *Educating Students with Learning Problems: A Shared Responsibility*—criticized the dual system of general and special education and contained a set of proposals that called for general and special educators to share responsibilities for the education of students with disabilities. In the late 1980s and 1990s, the REI evolved into the INCLUSION MOVEMENT, which reflects a philosophy that students with special needs should be fully integrated into general education classrooms, and not removed from the classroom to receive supports and services necessary for their educational success (Friend & Bursuck, 2002). By the late 1990s, the original goal of special education, to provide access to general educational services, had been successfully implemented (IDEA 1997).

There are many commonalities in the reform movements of general and special education on which a unified system can be built. The call is to work together and resolve the differences, not as general or special educators, but as educators of all children. As speech-language pathologists and audiologists provide services within school settings, understanding the issues of reform (see Chapter 2) and the demands of the educational system is necessary to support students within the context of reform programs. To this end, the U.S. Department of Education (1999) reported to Congress:

> Joint participation and leadership of general and special educators in curriculum and standards development, professional development, resource allocation, and instruction are critical in helping students with disabilities access the general education curriculum and acquire skills that will better prepare them for life after school (p. ii).

Education plays a unique role in the transmission and perpetuation of values that seek to rectify political and social inequalities. Even though the early reform movements of general education did not address children with disabilities, this is vastly different under current reform movements. Schools have the opportunity to demonstrate how educators and students can live in a world of diversity.

Standards-Based Reform and Accountability

During the 1990s, educational reforms began to have greater concerns for all students who were at risk for educational failure, including students with disabilities. Legislative mandates reflected a movement towards standards-based education (see Chapter 2) and accountability, which established expectations for what students need to learn and know at a certain grade level. In a standards-based system, all students and teachers of any given grade level, anywhere in the district or state, work toward common educational goals. This system reduced variability between classrooms and teachers in terms of the content that was taught, and also provided for consistency from one grade level to the next. In addition, in a standards-based system, students, parents, and the public are aware of the requirements of each grade level. Many districts have also established pacing-guides so that teachers know how to pace their lessons to ensure that the information is covered in a consistent manner in all classrooms. Each state has adopted its own set of standards for all grade levels. Schools are held accountable for what students are expected to learn through statewide assessment systems. Under these systems, state tests are designed to assess what has been taught. In order to make the systems work together, standards, curriculum, and testing must all be aligned.

Nolet and McLaughlin (2000) describe standards-based reform as follows:

> Standards-based reform is a policy response to the dissatisfaction with the performance of American schools that

has been growing in both the public and private sectors for a number of years. Major elements of standards-based reform are (a) higher content standards, (b) the use of assessments aimed at measuring how schools are helping students meet the standards, and (c) an emphasis on holding educators and students accountable for student achievement (p. 2).

Standards-based reform relies on a philosophy of having a systematic method of measuring student achievement. Standards were meant to apply to all students. In terms of students with disabilities, this approach represented a significant shift in the educational system's thinking about student learning and programming. Special education was built on the design of an individualized plan for each student—an INDIVIDUALIZED EDUCATION PROGRAM (IEP). The INDIVIDUALS WITH DISABILITES EDUCATION ACT (IDEA) 1997 called for a shift from access to quality education. Sitting in a classroom with nondisabled peers was no longer considered enough for students with disabilities. Until this time, there were no expectations or requirements that students with disabilities would master the same curriculum as their general education peers, or that the educational system should realize quantifiable educational results for these students. Under the new system, these students must learn and the system must be responsible for ensuring that this learning takes place. In a system seeking results, individualized performance was no longer the only consideration for

students with disabilities. The performances of special education students alongside other learners in the school were considered.

For special educators, expanding their view to include the bigger picture of the educational system is no small task. Speech-language pathologists and audiologists must realize how the philosophy of standards-based reform will shape their own view of the task they undertake when working with students. To this end, speech-lan-

guage pathologists must consider their role as professionals who are knowledgeable in language development and disorders, as well as knowledgeable in the curriculum.

Curriculum and instruction are the core of the educational process. Real change in education comes with changes in the content and in the instructional methods that teachers use. Both curriculum and instruction in turn are shaped by expectations about the kinds of educational outcomes that students should manifest by the time they graduate from high school. (See Chapter 2 for further discussion.)

The late 1990s, known as the Era of Standards-Based Instruction, evolved into the current Era of Accountability. With this shift in focus, for the first time, schools and districts were held accountable—by law—for student learning as measured by statewide testing of standards. Students with disabilities were, and still are, expected to perform like all other students in terms of results. Chapter 2 fully describes the accountability systems established under the federal laws, NO CHILD LEFT BEHIND (NCLB, 2001) and the INDIVIDUALS WITH DISABILITIES EDUCATION IMPROVEMENT ACT of 2004. This high stakes environment has brought special education into the forefront of discussions about instructional improvement and change. Additionally, it has blended the reform movements of general and special education.

The implications for speech-language pathologists, audiologists, and special and general educators were apparent. We must all work toward effective practices which positively impact student learning. Accountability in this era is not only for students; it is for educators as well, and will significantly impact our practice. Notably, literacy, curriculum, and statewide testing, are now the tools of the speech-language pathologist. Our practice will need to be educationally relevant in order to meet the needs of our clientele, as well as the requirements of the law. The rest of this text will focus on these changes, and how speech-language pathologists and audiologists play a key role in advancing the educational reforms of standards-based instruction and accountability.

Children and Families in the Twenty-First Century

In the early decades of television, the traditional nuclear family was frequently portrayed as two parents and two children, usually one boy and one girl. Not surprisingly, educators often came to expect that children in their classes came from such a family. The realities of children and families in the twenty-first century have changed; not only has the family structure changed, but the circumstances of families have changed as well. Modern-day families no longer have only one member of the family serving as the breadwinner, as was often characterized by television shows like *Ozzie and Harriet* or *The Brady Bunch*. And perhaps more importantly, the economic conditions of families are different in the early part of the twenty-first century.

Indicators of Children's Well-Being

Despite media characterizations, even in 1950, only 47 percent of children in the United States lived in traditional families in which the father worked full-time and the mother was not in the workforce; by 1990, this number had shifted to a mere 17.9 percent. A difference also existed between White and Black families. In the 1940s to 1960s, 45 to 50 percent of White children and less than 30 percent of Black children lived in traditional families. These numbers shifted to only 20 percent for White children and only 5 percent for Black children in 1990 (U.S. Department of Commerce, 1993).

The National Center for Education Statistics (NCES, 2003) provides this information about the conditions of children in the United States:

- Between 1979 and 2001, the percentage of children's parents who had at least completed high school increased from 76 percent to 88 percent, but parents of Black and Hispanic children continue to have less education than the parents of their White peers.

- The poverty rate of school-age children is 17 percent and did not change between 1976 and 2001, although the percentage of children classified as "nonpoor" (twice the poverty rate) increased. Black and Hispanic children are more likely to be impoverished than White children.

- The highest proportion of children living in poverty (24 percent) is in school districts located in large metropolitan central cities, followed by children living in school districts located in midsize metropolitan areas (20 percent).

- The percentage of two parent households decreased from 83 percent in 1976 to 68 percent in 2001.

- The percentage of children speaking a language other than English at home increased from 8 percent in 1976 to 17 percent in 1999. This is primarily due to the increase in the Hispanic population. Of these families, 71 percent of Hispanic children spoke a language other than English at home in 1999, as compared to 4 percent of White or Black children.

- The number of 5- to 24-year-olds who spoke a language other than English at home more than doubled between 1979 and 1999. In 1999, among these young people who spoke a language other than English at home, one-third spoke English with difficulty (i.e., less than "very well"). Spanish was the language most frequently spoken among those who spoke a language other than English at home.

An awareness of the conditions of the families in a community and in the country is important for speech-language pathologists and other educators, especially when school teams are asked to consider children's learning challenges. Consider the information reported by the Federal Interagency Forum on Child and Family Statistics (2007) in the sidebar on pp. 10–11. When reviewing the statistics in the sidebar, think of the impact each condition might have on normal child development, including language that affects learning.

Profiling America's Children: Selected Key Indicators of Well-Being

Population and Family Characteristics

- In 2006, there were 73.5 million children in the United States, 1.3 million more than in 2000. This number is projected to increase to 80 million and represent 24 percent of the population in 2020 (p. 4).

- The number of children under 18 represents about 25 percent of the population and has decreased since 1964 at the end of the baby boom when children represented 36 percent of the population (p. 4).

- The proportion of children under age 18 living with two married parents fell from 77 percent in 1980, to 73 percent in 1990, to 69 percent in 2000, and 66 percent in 2006. Among children under age 18 in 2005, 23 percent lived only with their mothers, 5 percent lived with only their fathers, and 4 percent lived with neither parent (p. 4).

- In 2005, 61 percent of children age 6 and under who were not yet enrolled in kindergarten received some form of nonparental childcare on a regular basis, while 39 percent were cared for only by their parents (p. 5).

Children as a Proportion of the Population

- Children ages 0–17 represent 25 percent of the total population, the same as in 2003 (p. 14).

- In 2004, 58.9 percent of U.S. children were White, non-Hispanic; 15.5 percent were Black, non-Hispanic; 19.2 percent were Hispanic; 3.9 percent were Asian and 4.1 percent were all other races (p. 14).

Difficulty Speaking English

- In 2005, 20 percent of school-age children (ages 5–17) spoke a language other than English at home. Five percent of children ages 5–17 had difficulty speaking English (p. 14).

Economic Security Indicators

- In 2004, the number and percentage of children living in families with incomes below their poverty thresholds were 12.5 million and 17 percent, respectively, both unchanged from 2003 (p. 6).

- Poverty among children varies greatly by family structure. In 2004, children living in female-householder families with no husband present continued to experience a higher poverty rate (43 percent) than children living in married-couple families (9 percent) (p. 6).

Continued

#TP-29703 Making a Difference - 2nd Ed. • ©2008 Thinking Publications® • www.thinkingpublications.com • 1-800-277-8737

Profiling America's Children – *Continued*

• In 2004, 89 percent of children ages 0–17 had health insurance coverage; 30 percent had government health insurance coverage; 5 percent of children ages 0–17 have no usual source of health care (p. 7).

Health Indicators

• The percentage of children ages 0–17 in very good or excellent health is 82 percent (p. 8).

• The health of the Nation's children has improved in many areas, including vaccination coverage, teen birth rates, and child mortality. However, the increasing prevalence of overweight children and low birth weight infants is of concern (p. 8).

• The increasing percentage of overweight children is a public health challenge. In 1976–1980, only 6 percent of children ages 6–17 were overweight. By 1988–1994, this proportion had risen to 11 percent, and it continued to rise to 15 percent in 1999–2000. In 2001–2002, 17 percent of children were overweight, most recently in 2003–2004, this proportion was 18 percent. Black, non-Hispanic girls were at particularly high risk of being overweight (25 percent) compared with White, non-Hispanic and Mexican-American girls (16 percent and 17 percent, respectively) (p. 8).

• In 2004, 8 percent of children ages 5–17 were limited in their activities because of one or more chronic health conditions (p. 15).

• The percentage of infants born with low birth weight was 8.2 percent in 2005, up slightly from 8.1 percent in 2004 (p. 16).

Education Indicators

• In 2005, 60 percent of children ages 3–5 were read to daily by a family member, an increase from 53 percent in 1993. White, non-Hispanic and Asian children were more likely than their Hispanic and Black, non-Hispanic peers to be read to daily in 2005. Children living in families below their poverty thresholds were less likely to be read to daily than their peers in nonpoor households (p. 12).

• Fifty-seven percent of children ages 3–5 who were not yet in kindergarten were enrolled in center-based early childhood care and education programs in 2005. This percentage was higher than in 1991 (53 percent), but lower than the percentage in 1999 (60 percent). In 2005, Hispanic children were the least likely to be enrolled in center-based programs; 43 percent of Hispanic children were enrolled, compared with 70 percent of Asian children, 67 percent of Black, non-Hispanic children, and 59 percent of White, non-Hispanic children (p. 12).

Source: Federal Interagency Forum on Child and Family Statistics (2007), pp. 4–8, 12, 14–16

Significance of Child and Family Statistics

Why should speech-language pathologists and audiologists attend to statistics such as these? Simply put, language and other learning issues that arise out of the conditions mentioned above strongly influence which children are more likely to be referred for special education services. Concerns were raised by Congress during the reauthorization of IDEA (1997) about the rate of increase in the number of racial and ethnic minority students who were identified as requiring special education services. Between 1980 and 1990, the rates of special education identification grew 53 percent for Hispanic children, 13.2 percent for Black children, and 107.8 percent for Asian children. This compared to an increase of 6 percent for White children.

Despite the attention given in 1997, IDEA 2004 focuses greater attention and mandates toward overidentification of minority children in special education. In the latest reauthorization, Congress included a new section on "overidentification and disproportionality" (IDEA 2004, Section 1412 [c][24]) due to finding that Black children were identified disproportionately with mental retardation and emotional disorders, and that in general, minority children in schools with predominantly White students and teachers are disproportionately placed in special education. Children and family statistics help educators understand conditions which may contribute to learner challenges, and may or may not necessarily require special education, but likely will need extra attention and/or assistance from the public education system.

A child's upbringing can significantly affect classroom performance. Language growth and development depend on many factors, both constitutional (nature) and experiential (nurture). Cognitive development, working memory, and vocabulary size all influence success in the classroom (Biemiller, 1999; Montgomery, 2007). Oral language development, which begins in infancy, lays the foundation for reading, writing, and other school experiences. Speech-language pathologists in schools must understand the implications of differences in the language development experiences of children from all types of backgrounds and experiences (Langdon, 2000).

Referencing several studies, Biemiller (1999) noted that children from low-income families had been found to have "smaller vocabularies and less advanced language development than their more advantaged peers" (p. 13). In a longitudinal study of the language and achievement differences between advantaged and disadvantaged children, Hart and Risley (as cited in Biemiller, 1999) found that "advantaged children were found to have twice the vocabulary of welfare children and were adding vocabulary at twice the rate" (p. 14). Intriguingly, Hart and Risley (1995) reported:

> A child's upbringing can significantly affect classroom performance. Language growth and development depend on many factors, both constitutional (nature) and experiential (nurture).

The longitudinal data showed that in the everyday interactions at home, the average (rounded) number of words children heard per hour was 2,150 in the professional families, 1,250 in the working-class families, and 620 in the welfare families... Given the consistency we saw in the data, we might venture to extrapolate to the first 3 years of life. By age 3, the children in professional families would have heard more than 30 million words, the children in working-class families 20 million, and the children in welfare families 10 million (p. 132).

Children who come to school with a primary language other than English or from a different cultural background will also bring different linguistic experiences. These experiences can be varied, from realizing the benefits of bilingualism to having limited opportunities to develop language skills and school-type experiences. The linguistic abilities that a child brings to school lay the foundation on which the child will build his or her academic knowledge.

Condition of Education

In order to appreciate the broader institution in which speech, language, and audiology services are provided, information about the education system as a whole will be presented throughout this text. The National Center for Educational Statistics (NCES) is charged with reporting to Congress information about the condition and progress of education in the United States. The following information was reported in their 2003 report, and adds to the profile of children who come to school every day in the United States:

- The difference in children's reading skills and knowledge, often observed in later grades, appears to be present when children enter kindergarten and persist or increase throughout the first two years of school (p. iii).

- The resources that children possess when they began kindergarten, such as their early literacy skills and the richness of their home literacy environment, were related to their reading skills and knowledge upon entering kindergarten and their gains in reading achievement by the end of kindergarten and first grade (p. iii).

- Public elementary and secondary enrollment was projected to reach 47.9 million in 2005, decrease to 47.6 million in 2010, and then increase to 47.7 million in 2012. The West will experience the largest increase in enrollments of all regions in the country (p. iv).

As members of a building, district, or regional support team, speech-language pathologists will be called on to build strong schoolwide programs that will help to develop the linguistic, cognitive, academic, and behavioral skills of students with and without disabilities. Speech-language pathologists are in a unique position to work as members of multidisciplinary teams that serve children schoolwide in order to help children develop the language and communication skills needed for school success. Increasingly, audiologists are being consulted about the hearing environment of schools, including consideration of acoustical conditions of classrooms.

Incidence of Children With Disabilities

IDEA 2004 requires that services be provided to children who are identified as having a disability from birth to 21 years of age. Annually, the U.S. Department of Education (USDE) reports to Congress on the latest issues and information about the children served under IDEA. The most recent report was in 2004, reflecting data from the 2001–2002 school year. Over six million children received services under IDEA 2004. The percentage of students receiving services in public schools under this law has increased from 8.7 percent in 1976–77 to 13.7 percent in 2003–2004 (National Center on Educational Statistics [NCES], 2006). The eligibility categories of specific learning disability and speech-language impairment represent the two largest eligibility categories (48.3 percent and 18.7 percent) nationally (USDE, 2004b). In 1994, the number of infants and toddlers (ages 0–2) who received services was 165,351. By fall 2002, that number rose to 268,331, representing a 62.3 percent increase in the number of infants and toddlers served in that eight year span. The NCES states the following regarding the growth in special education numbers:

> Slowly, increasing numbers and proportions of children are being served in programs for the disabled. During the 1993–94 school year, 12 percent of students were served in these programs compared with 13.7 percent in 2003–04. Some

of the rise since 1993–94 may be attributed to the increasing proportion of children identified as having speech or language impairments, which rose from 2.3 percent of enrollment to 3.0 percent of enrollment; other health impairments (having limited strength, vitality, or alertness due to chronic or acute health problems, such as a heart condition, tuberculosis, rheumatic fever, nephritis, asthma, sickle cell anemia, hemophilia, epilepsy, lead poisoning, leukemia, or diabetes), which rose from 0.2 to 1.0 percent of enrollment; and autism and traumatic brain injury, which rose from 0.1 to 0.4 percent of enrollment (p. 1).

The statistics and numbers reported here, both in terms of the conditions in which children live and the identified number of children served through special education programs, give a sense of the sometimes daunting nature of the issues that are faced and must be considered by school-based speech-language pathologists. Throughout the training program in communication disorders and throughout a speech-language pathologist's or audiologist's working career, it will be critical to have refined clinical skills in all areas of the field. However, when working with children in a school setting, one of the foremost tasks is to understand the circumstances in which a child lives. Speech-language pathologists and audiologists must seek information regarding a student's living situation, and then understand the ecological impact this has on his or her language and learning devel-

> One of the foremost tasks is to understand the circumstances in which a child lives.

opment in order to design appropriate diagnostic practices, intervention protocols, or both. This awareness marks the beginning of seeing the student as a whole child and as a member of a family, classroom, and school community.

Predictions for the Future

This first chapter presents a broad view of the issues facing educational systems, particularly as they apply to the education of children with disabilities and the provision of special education, specifically speech-language services, in the public schools. While reading the chapters in this book, consider the application of points of law or the provision of assessment and intervention services within the context of the forces and issues that affect the educational system and the children and families served. Also consider the evolving roles for speech-language pathologists and audiologists in schools, and how these roles embrace system change and invite speech-language pathologists and audiologists to be a part of building the systems of the future while providing services to students and working in concert with educators and interested others.

Schools are dynamic and changing institutions. Change is constant, which can be energizing and frustrating. System change, however, is vital as we respond to new research and the needs of society and legislative requirements. In

order to consider the future as it is currently defined, consider the following information as it relates to all educators.

Twenty-First Century Learners

Just as educators and parents have become familiar with standards and accountability, our world continues to change. In education, we can focus on the current reform movements, while always keeping an eye out for the latest trends and issues that are on the horizon. Importantly, our work is to consider the future that students will be facing when they leave our school buildings. Our mission is to ensure that students are prepared to enter the world of work in a future that is undefined. In the work world of the Digital Age, workers will need to have twenty-first century skills that extend beyond the mastery of standards. The base competency that workers will need to compete in a global economy and a digital world is more sophisticated and technological than it has ever been. The NCREL/Metiri Group (2007)

describes the importance of educational systems preparing students for the future:

> In order to thrive in a digital economy, students will need Digital Age proficiencies. It is important for the educational system to make parallel changes in order to fulfill its mission in society, namely the preparation of students for the world beyond the classroom. Therefore, the educational system must understand and embrace the following 21st century skills (shown in Figure 1.1) within the context of rigorous academic standards (p. 2):
>
> 1. Digital-age literacy
> 2. Inventive thinking
> 3. Effective communication
> 4. High productivity

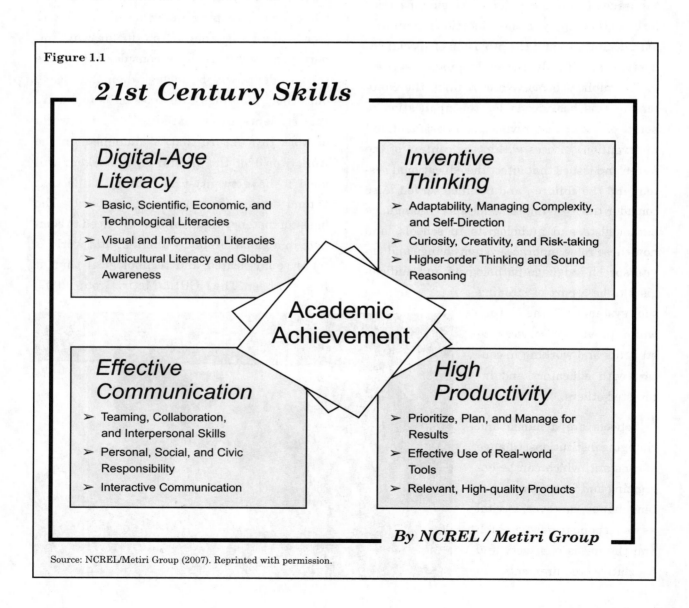

Figure 1.1

21st Century Skills

Digital-Age Literacy
- Basic, Scientific, Economic, and Technological Literacies
- Visual and Information Literacies
- Multicultural Literacy and Global Awareness

Inventive Thinking
- Adaptability, Managing Complexity, and Self-Direction
- Curiosity, Creativity, and Risk-taking
- Higher-order Thinking and Sound Reasoning

Academic Achievement

Effective Communication
- Teaming, Collaboration, and Interpersonal Skills
- Personal, Social, and Civic Responsibility
- Interactive Communication

High Productivity
- Prioritize, Plan, and Manage for Results
- Effective Use of Real-world Tools
- Relevant, High-quality Products

By NCREL / Metiri Group

Source: NCREL/Metiri Group (2007). Reprinted with permission.

These skills will be further defined and discussed in Chapter 10, but as speech-language pathologists and audiologists work with children and students in schools, it is critical to remember the ultimate goal—for these children to have the skills to compete in a global economy. Children with disabilities, like all children, must be prepared by the educational system for their role in the future. The NCREL/Metiri Group also makes this observation:

> In this Digital Age, intellectual capital drives progress, so political, social, and economic advances in the 21st century will be possible only if the intellectual potential of America's youth is well developed. To accomplish this, we must meet the changing learning needs of all students (p. 1).

What's Hot in Literacy Education

The International Reading Association identified the following areas of practice as the "hot" topics in literacy education.

Extremely Hot:
- Adolescent literacy

Very Hot:
- Direct/explicit instruction
- English as a second language; English learners (EL)
- Fluency
- High-stakes assessment
- Informational text
- Literacy coaches/reading coaches
- Scientific evidence-based reading research and instruction (Cassidy & Cassidy, 2007)

Speech-language pathologists will increasingly be working in collaborative and RESPONSE TO INTERVENTION (RtI) models (see Chapter 5), and each of these topics in literacy education will involve their active participation. The more that professionals know about these topics, the better.

Top Trends in Special Education

For speech-language pathologists and audiologists, the future work that we will do in schools will be driven by the same forces that are creating change in general education. Assessment and intervention trends are identified as follows:

Assessment will be:
- Based on RtI models.
- Performance-based.
- Curriculum driven.
- Considerate of the demands of statewide and classroom assessments.
- Limiting use of standardized measures.

Intervention will be:
- Focused on assisting students to master curriculum—the work of school.
- Focused on outcomes and student achievement.
- Provided through blended service delivery models.
- Provided within networks.

As you consider the twenty-first century skills that students need, the trends in reading and literacy and the trends in assessment and intervention for special education, it is clear that speech-language pathologists and audiologists will be in the center of building stronger schools and more effective programs for students. Speech-language pathologists and audiologists working in public schools will be a part of the realizations toward these trends and ask "What role will I play?" and "How will these programs, initiatives, movements, and predictions influence my work?" While speech-language pathologists and audiologists in public schools all over the country consider these questions, let us say, "Welcome to the public schools!"

CHAPTER 2

Legislative Foundation of Special Education

IN THIS CHAPTER

This chapter provides an overview of the legislative history of special education in the United States for struggling and disabled learners; describes the foundations of the laws; reviews the development of special education legislation for these populations; discusses the impact and interface of the No Child Left Behind Act (NCLB, 2001) and the Individuals with Disabilities Education Improvement Act (IDEA 2004), including the implications of standards-based reform and accountability. This chapter introduces the cornerstone concepts of free appropriate public education (FAPE) and least restrictive environment (LRE) and discusses the relevance of these for speech-language and audiology services in schools.

CHAPTER QUESTIONS

1. Explain how the legislative history of special education led to laws that are considered to be civil rights protections.

2. Discuss how the concepts of free appropriate public education (FAPE) and least restrictive environment (LRE) apply to speech, language, and hearing programs.

3. Review some of the significant changes in IDEA 2004. Discuss why you think these changes are now required in federal law.

4. Discuss the impact of No Child Left Behind (2001) on general and special education.

5. Consider what knowledge speech-language pathologists and audiologists will need in order to assist students in accessing standards and core curriculum.

Legislative History of Education for Struggling Learners

Special education and other educational programs are governed by a combination of federal, state, and local laws and regulations. Both general and special education laws are extensive and encompass broad requirements. At the federal level, a framework is set forth of what is required. The law is then interpreted and administered by the U.S. Department of Education (USDE), which sets forth federal rules, known as the CODE OF FEDERAL REGULATIONS. States then pass legislation that incorporates their interpretation of the federal law and regulations. Counties, administrative units, and school districts can adopt detailed procedures directing their implementation of state and federal laws. State laws may grant greater rights to children and their parents than federal laws do, but they must at least meet the federal requirements. In some cases, the federal law leaves procedures to be set by states and local entities.

Chapter 1 described how the reform issues of general and special education historically existed in parallel, but not in a coordinated fashion. To some degree, this was reflected in the legislation that was put forth during these times. Currently, the laws of general and special education are intended to be coordinated and encompass all learners in the United States. The history of our democracy is deeply rooted in equal opportunity, which is grounded in the public education system. The role of the federal government in education has been historically questioned, yet is now firmly established. The central focus of the educational system in the United States is at the heart of ensuring that all citizens have access to the American Dream. To this end, significant legislation governs education, particularly as it applies to individuals who may not have the advantages of others in reaching their full educational potential. These learners include children who are underprivileged economically or those with educational disabilities.

General Education

The role of the federal government has expanded significantly over the past 100 years, and certainly in the last 30. In 1965, as part of the War on Poverty and the Civil Rights movement, President Lyndon B. Johnson signed into law the Elementary and Secondary Education Act (ESEA) which broadened both the federal influence and the legislative intent for educational programs in the United States. Title I of ESEA was specifically intended to support economically underprivileged children, and to address the inequalities in the educational system experienced by these children, particularly those in poor and rural areas (Wright, Wright, & Heath, 2003).

As with special education, the laws of general education have gone through considerable revisions since the original enactment. This is reflected in reform movements and is the result of public and political pressure. While parents and teachers of children with disabilities were fighting for programs and the right to an appropriate education for these children, others were concerned about the overall educational picture for all children in the United States.

On January 8, 2002, ESEA was reauthorized by P.L. 107-110, known as the NO CHILD LEFT BEHIND ACT of 2001 (NCLB). Prior to the implementation of NCLB, speech-language pathologists, audiologists, and special educators had infrequently attended to ESEA's remedial programs for students who were economically disadvantaged, the largest of which was Title I. NCLB completely revamped all educational programs under its purview and expanded the scope of its role beyond any previously realized (Robelen, 2005). Most importantly to speech-language pathologists, audiologists, and other special educators, NCLB now includes requirements for students with disabilities, forging stronger bonds between general and special education. This new piece of legislation, along with the reauthorization of the INDIVIDUALS WITH DISABILITIES EDUCATION IMPROVEMENT ACT of 2004 (IDEA 2004), represents the living reality of "the call... to build on the commonalities and resolve the differences, not as general or special educators, but as educators of all children" (Moore-Brown & Montgomery, 2001, p. 12).

Special Education

On December 3, 2004, President George W. Bush signed into law the reauthorization of IDEA 2004. The most current updating of the nation's special education law again reaffirmed the legislative and political commitment to the education of children with disabilities, strongly emphasizing the need for aligning special education practices and outcomes with those of general education and NCLB. The road to this ceremony in room 350 of the Dwight D. Eisenhower Office Building was long, beginning before the implementation of the EDUCATION FOR ALL HANDICAPPED CHILDREN ACT (EAHCA) in 1975, which established the framework for special education as it is known today. In his signing statement, President Bush acknowledged this embattled history as he set the vision of what the law would mean for children with disabilities:

> America's schools educate over 6 million children with disabilities. In the past, those students were too often just shuffled through the system with little expectation that they could make significant progress or succeed like their fellow classmates. Children with disabilities deserve high hopes, high expectations, and extra help.

The history of special education has been characterized by controversy encountering debate ranging from philosophical to fiscal issues. Critics of special education, including general educators and politicians, have become increasingly vocal about their concerns regarding expense (see "Funding" in Chapter 9), lack of adequate results (see "Including Children with Disabilities in Assessments, Performance Goals, and Reports to the Public" on p. 33), and a dual system for disciplining students (see "Behavior and Student Discipline" in Chapter 8).

IDEA 2004 strongly established that the national mandate regarding the education of students with disabilities includes academic achievement at the same level as expected for children in general education. This agenda can be seen with the statement of findings in the introduction to the bill (see sidebar on pp. 24–25). Congress acknowledged the impressive history that led to the establishment of special education and not only emphasized that these issues should not be forgotten, but also presented the challenge to educators and those involved with students with disabilities to improve educational results for these children. Speech-language pathologists and audiologists and other special educators who work under IDEA 2004 should understand the long battle and historic events that led to the current special education system.

Until the mid-to-late 1960s, the federal government played virtually no role in the education of children with disabilities, with the exception of providing some assistance between the 1820s and 1870s in creating special schools for children who were blind, deaf, or mentally ill (Friend & Bursuck, 2002). Most of the responsibility for educating children with disabilities previously fell to states or to private individuals and organizations.

According to the Council for Exceptional Children (CEC, 1997b), by 1911, a United States Bureau of Education survey found "6% of cities reporting special classes (i.e., 11% for gifted; 25% for backward; 10% for physically exceptional [non-English speaking]; and 17% for morally exceptional, delinquent, and incorrigible" [p. 11]).

In 1930, "the White House Conference on Special Education reported the following statistics of handicapped *[sic]* children in the United States: 300,000 crippled; 18,212 deaf; 3,000,000 hard of hearing; 14,000 blind; 50,000 partially seeing; 1,000,000 defective speech; 450,000 mentally retarded; and 1,500,000 gifted" (CEC, 1997b, p. 20).

After both World War I and World War II, the U.S. government recognized the need for vocational-type training for veterans, especially those who returned with disabilities from war. Federal involvement in the education of children with disabilities was slow to follow. Some states provided education to students who entered public education with a variety of difficulties, including mental retardation. Notably, states such as Illinois, New York, Florida, California, and Wisconsin implemented programs that followed functionally based (called *occupational* or *vocational education*) curricula, focusing on job skills, community skills, living skills, and some academically related skills. The need for federal involvement in mandating and regulating the education of children with disabilities began to emerge with a growing parent movement and with the assistance of President John F. Kennedy, who established the President's Committee on Mental Retardation in the early 1960s (CEC, 1997b; Friend & Bursuck, 2002).

In 1958, President Dwight D. Eisenhower signed P.L. 85-926, the Education of Mentally Retarded Children Act, which was a bill that provided financial assistance to colleges educating teachers of children with mental retardation. The first direct subsidy for services to special populations, including children with disabilities, came in 1966, the second year of the Elementary and Secondary Education Act (ESEA, P.L. 89-10). This act established the system of remedial education for economically disadvantaged students, known as Title I, and provided some entitlements to state-supported or state-operated schools "for the handicapped *[sic]*" (Martin, Martin, & Terman, 1996, p. 27).

IDEA 2004 Statement of Findings

(c) FINDINGS. Congress finds the following:

(1) Disability is a natural part of the human experience and in no way diminishes the right of individuals to participate in or contribute to society. Improving educational results for children with disabilities is an essential element of our national policy of ensuring equality of opportunity, full participation, independent living, and economic self-sufficiency for individuals with disabilities.

(2) Before the date of enactment of the Education for All Handicapped Children Act of 1975 (P.L. 94-142), the educational needs of millions of children with disabilities were not being fully met because—

  (A) the children did not receive appropriate educational services;

  (B) the children were excluded entirely from the public school system and from being educated with their peers;

  (C) undiagnosed disabilities prevented the children from having a successful educational experience; or

  (D) a lack of adequate resources within the public school system forced families to find services outside the public school system.

(3) Since the enactment and implementation of the Education for All Handicapped Children Act of 1975, this title has been successful in ensuring children with disabilities and the families of such children access to a free appropriate public education and in improving educational results for children with disabilities.

(4) However, the implementation of this title has been impeded by low expectations, and an insufficient focus on applying replicable research on proven methods of teaching and learning for children with disabilities.

(5) Almost 30 years of research and experience has demonstrated that the education of children with disabilities can be made more effective by—

  (A) having high expectations for such children and ensuring their access to the general education curriculum in the regular classroom, to the maximum extent possible, in order to—

Continued

IDEA 2004 Statement of Findings – *Continued*

(i) meet developmental goals and, to the maximum extent possible, the challenging expectations that have been established for all children; and

(ii) be prepared to lead productive and independent adult lives, to the maximum extent possible;

(B) strengthening the role and responsibility of parents and ensuring that families of such children have meaningful opportunities to participate in the education of their children at school and at home.

Source: IDEA (2004 § 601[c])

Roots of Special Education in Civil Rights Legal Action

The lack of federal assistance was not just apparent in the education of children with disabilities, but also in terms of other educational issues. The Supreme Court case that changed all of this was *Brown v. Board of Education* (1954). The Supreme Court ruled unanimously that the doctrine of "separate but equal" was inherently unequal and therefore unconstitutional. While *Brown* specifically dealt with racial segregation, it laid the foundation for the education of children with disabilities and other groups because the right-to-education issue was argued on the principles of equal protection under the law for all citizens.

Brown clarified that although the U.S. Constitution never once refers to public education, the principles of equal protection and due process under the FIFTH and FOURTEENTH Amendments apply to public education. For all groups who have experienced segregation or discrimination, the foundation of *Brown* is solid. Equal opportunity, equal protection, and the right to an education are founded in the Constitution and apply to all groups, regardless of race, color, creed, gender, disability, or national origin. In this decision, the court established that "integration into public education was the only way in which student's constitutional rights to equal opportunity could be protected when diverse student groups learned together" (Friend & Bursuck, 2002, p. 7).

Equal protection and due process have continued to be critical to special education law. Two major court cases solidified the connection between equal protection and due process under the Fourteenth Amendment: *Pennsylvania Association for Retarded Children (PARC) v. Com-*

monwealth of Pennsylvania and *Mills v. D.C. Board of Education.*

The *PARC* case (1971) challenged a state law in Pennsylvania that allowed public schools to deny an education to children whom examiners determined to be below the mental age of five. *PARC* was settled on a consent decree that (1) provided full access to an education for children with mental retardation, (2) established the standard of appropriateness, and (3) established a standard for LEAST RESTRICTIVE ENVIRONMENT (LRE).

On the heels of the *PARC* case, *Mills v. D.C. Board of Education* (1972) was a case brought by students with varying types of disabilities who had been excluded from school and denied an education in the District of Columbia schools. The basis of their exclusion from school was due to the disabilities of these children. In their ruling the District Court ordered the following:

- The District of Columbia shall provide to each child of school age a free and suitable publicly supported education regardless of the degree of the child's mental, physical, or emotional disability or impairment. Furthermore, defendants shall not exclude any child resident in the District of Columbia from such publicly supported education on the basis of a claim of insufficient resources.

- Defendants shall not suspend a child from the public schools for disciplinary reasons for any period in excess of two days without affording him a hearing pursuant to the provisions of Paragraph 13.f., and without providing for his education during the period of any such suspension.

With the strength of *Brown, PARC,* and *Mills,* court cases continued to be brought forward, yet estimates showed that millions of children with disabilities still were not receiving a public education. Most states had some form of special education programs, but these varied dramatically from state to state. Ultimately, during the 1970s, states joined with existing advocacy groups to seek federal legislation that would provide financial assistance and guidance for the provision of education to children with disabilities (Martin, Martin, & Terman, 1996; Friend & Bursuck, 2002).

Legislative Response: Special Education as a Federal Mandate

In 1970, Congress passed the EDUCATION OF THE HANDICAPPED ACT (EHA, P.L. 91-230). This law established minimum requirements for states to follow to receive federal assistance. Following *PARC* and *Mills*, Congress acted by passing laws in the area of nondiscrimination and funding. In Section 504 of the REHABILITATION ACT of 1973 (P.L. 93-112), discrimination against those with disabilities was prohibited in any system that received federal funding (see "Parental Notification and Involvement" in Chapter 8). Additional federal financial assistance for states came in the amendments to the Elementary and Secondary Education Act of 1974 (ESEA, P.L. 93-380).

These dramatic changes to the ESEA clearly laid the foundation for what was soon to come. In 1975, Congress amended the EHA by passing the Education for All Handicapped Children Act (EAHCA, P.L. 94-142). This law established special education as it is known today, with requirements for the provision of services, procedural safeguards, and funding mechanisms to support the programs. The federal mandate for special education has been revised and updated several times since 1975. The 1990 amendments (P.L. 101-476) renamed the law to be the "Individuals with Disabilities Education Act" commonly referred to as IDEA, which is how the law is now known. In addition, the AMERICANS WITH DISABILITIES ACT (ADA, P.L. 101-336) was signed into law by President George Bush in 1990, further expanding the scope of discriminatory practices identified as illegal in all public accommodations. The 2004 reauthorization of IDEA kept the acronym IDEA, but added the word "improvement" to the full name of the law, so that it is known as P.L. 108-446, the Individuals with Disabilities Education Improvement Act of 2004 (IDEA 2004).

Federal mandates, including those for special education, provide guidance through legislation, but then require states to develop their own programs to implement the federal regulations. It is for this reason that the provision of services may look different from state to state. Monitoring how states implement their special education programs is the responsibility of the Office of Special Education Programs (OSEP). OSEP works closely with the STATE EDUCATIONAL AGENCIES (SEAs) to ensure that federal requirements are being met in each state, and uses a continuous improvement monitoring model that focuses on student outcomes.

States work hard to maintain their own identity in the provision of special education services. Issues such as provision of FREE APPROPRIATE PUBLIC EDUCATION (FAPE), LEAST RESTRICTIVE ENVIRONMENT (LRE), student discipline, funding, and SERVICE DELIVERY to students in correctional facilities have provided arenas for the struggle between state and federal interpretations of special education procedures. The history of special education shows a recurring pattern of a series of legal cases, followed by revisions to the law, followed by another series of legal cases that interpret the revisions.

The Education for All Handicapped Children Act (EAHCA)

In 1975, the EAHCA put into place the system under which special education has operated since its origination. The act described a complex set of procedures designed to rectify the issues that had been brought forward by the courts, parents, educators, and states. Congress was concerned with the number of children who remained unserved by the public school systems, so CHILD FIND, a mandate that LOCAL EDUCATIONAL AGENCIES (LEAs) be proactive in finding children with disabilities, was instituted as an important requirement under this new law. The history of court decisions leading up to the establishment of the EAHCA was reflected in the law's key components including:

- Providing federal funding for special education programs.

- Establishing procedures to ensure the provision of special education services.

- Establishing conceptual parameters under which the procedures were to be followed, including free appropriate public education, least restrictive environment, procedural safeguards, and zero reject.

- Requiring the provision of services to children ages 0–21, identified through child find activities, resulting in an evaluation process and qualifying for services according to certain ELIGIBILITY criteria.

Following the passage of EAHCA in 1975, states were allowed three years to establish a state plan for the implementation of the law. The federal law gave the outline of a process for developing an INDIVIDUALIZED EDUCATION PROGRAM (IEP) that would be based on an evaluation to determine the child's eligibility for the program (see Chapter 4 for a full description of IEP processes and procedures including eligibility requirements).

One of the most critical features of the EAHCA (1975) was the institution of procedural safeguards or due process protection for children and parents, which provided full partnership for parents in the decision-making processes in special education. When used in special education, due process refers to the procedural rights, protections, and safeguards for parents and children, and also refers to procedures involving hearings and mediation. Procedural safeguards provide (1) timelines for evaluations, (2) access to and review of records, (3) parental involvement and consent, (4) parental input into program development, and (5) procedures for complaints and disagreements. If parents and school districts are unable to agree on identification, evaluation, or any other aspects of the IEP program or placement (including GOALS and SHORT-TERM OBJECTIVES or BENCHMARKS), then either party may request a DUE PROCESS HEARING. A due process hearing involves presentation of evidence by both parties before an impartial hearing officer. Prior to the hearing, mediation may be requested or required. (See Chapter 8 "Resolution Sessions, Mediation, Due Process Hearings, and State IDEA Complaints.")

Over the years, several amendments have been added to the EAHCA (1975), increasing the requirements under this law. Two important changes occurred in 1986: the PRESCHOOL AMENDMENTS TO THE EDUCATION OF THE HANDICAPPED ACT (P.L. 99-457) and the addition of Part H (currently Part C), which extended the age of eligibility to include infants and toddlers who qualified for services under less intensive eligibility criteria. This change came as a result of professionals and parents lobbying Congress to fund early intervention services, with the belief that early intervention would prevent or reduce the need for lifelong special services. The other significant addition to the law came in 1986 with the passage of the HANDICAPPED CHILDREN'S PROTECTION ACT (known as the Attorneys' Fees Bill, P.L. 99-372). This act authorized awarding attorneys' fees to families who prevailed in lawsuits under the due process provisions of the law (see "Impartial Due Process Hearings" in Chapter 8).

The Individuals With Disabilities Education Act (IDEA): EAHCA 1990 and 1997 Revisions

Understanding the evolution of legislative mandates under the law is important, as it demonstrates how legal requirements are implemented as a response to societal and political circumstances and advances in research. In this way, change becomes an ever-occurring situation in schools, as educators must adjust to the latest changes in the law. It takes time to implement changes that occur in the law. However, when legislation is enacted, the time to implement is typically short, challenging school districts to bring their systems quickly into compliance, even if the new requirements are not philosophically or fiscally easy to implement. The lesson for practitioners in schools is this: Expect change to occur on a regular basis.

The 1990 revisions to the 1975 EAHCA included a new name: the INDIVIDUALS WITH DISABILITIES EDUCATION ACT (IDEA). This name reflected the consciousness of the "People First" movement, which emphasized that persons with disabilities should be recognized as individuals first, replacing the label as a name (see sidebars on pp. 30–31).

The following modifications to EAHCA (1975) in IDEA (1990) provisions reflected further changes in the communities of persons with disabilities and special education:

- The addition of two new eligibility categories: traumatic brain injury (TBI) and autism. Children with these conditions were certainly eligible for special education previously, but were usually identified under other categories that did not fully describe the disability. By 1990, medical technology enabled higher survival rates from accidents, evidenced by an increase in students with TBI in schools. These children showed a different pattern of recovery, in that their special needs did not result from a developmental condition as did all other eligibility areas. Identifying these students under the categories of speech or language impairment, mental retardation, and/or other health impairment did not accurately identify the learning needs of these students. By 1990, much controversy existed regarding the education of students with autism. Again, identification under categories such as speech and language or mental retardation did not accurately describe characteristics that were unique to children with autism. Therefore, autism was added to the list of eligibility categories.

- Inclusion of a requirement for TRANSITION planning beginning at the age of 16. This requirement came out of findings that most students who had been receiving special education and related services were not successful in the world of work. It became apparent that as part of their special education services, IEP teams needed to specifically address the development of skills that students needed to master to hold a job. As a result, a statement of needed transition services, often called an INDIVIDUALIZED TRANSITION PLAN (ITP), was required for students beginning at the age of 16 (changed to age 14 under IDEA [1997] and then back to 16 under IDEA 2004).

- A renewed focus on students with severe disabilities and on the integration of these students into their communities and schools. This focus was consistent with the REGULAR EDUCATION INITIATIVE (REI) and the INCLUSION MOVEMENT (discussed in "Educational Reforms That Shaped the Profession" in Chapter 1) that fought against the isolation and segregation of students with disabilities. The new requirements under IDEA (1990) called for greater integration of students with even the most significant disabilities.

- The clarification that ASSISTIVE TECHNOLOGY (AT) devices should be considered as part of a student's IEP. This requirement mandated consideration and purchase of assistive technology devices if the IEP team found that the student was in need of such services.

American Psychological Association's (APA's) Guidelines for "People First" Language

The guiding principle for "nonhandicapping" language is to maintain the integrity of individuals as human beings. Avoid language that equates persons with their condition (e.g., *neurotics, the disabled)*; that has superfluous, negative overtones (e.g., stroke *victim);* or that is regarded as a slur (e.g., *cripple)*....Use *disability* to refer to an attribute of a person [e.g., child with a learning disability] and *handicap* to refer to the source of limitations, which may include attitudinal, legal, and architectural barriers as well as the disability itself (e.g., steps and curbs handicap people who require the use of a ramp [and severe visual impairment is a handicap to drivers])....As a general rule, "person with _____," "person living with _____," and "person who has _____" are neutral and preferred forms of description.

From *Publication Manual of the American Psychological Association* (5th ed., p. 69), by the American Psychological Association (APA), 2001, Washington, DC: Author. ©2001 by the APA.

"People First" Language

- Person with a disability
- Speech of children with language impairment
- Child who has autism
- Person who has quadriplegia
- Persons who stutter

- Individual without speech
- Man with cerebral palsy
- Person with Down syndrome
- Person who uses a wheelchair
- Children with normally developing speech

Sources: Folkins (1999); Parent Advocacy Coalition for Educational Rights (PACER) Center (1989)

Requirements of IDEA (1997)

With the reauthorization of IDEA in 1997, Congress identified the lack of positive educational results as a major concern for the education of students with disabilities. IDEA shifted the focus of special education from educational access to accountability for educational results. According to Cernosia (1999), new requirements reflected this significant shift in the law with four main themes:

1. Strengthening parental participation in the educational process.

2. Accountability for student's participation and success in the general education curriculum and mastery of IEP goals/objectives.

3. Remediation and disciplinary actions addressing behavior problems at school and in the classroom.

4. Responsiveness to the growing needs of an increasingly more diverse society (p. 1).

While acknowledging that the mandate for special education had resulted in progress, Congress (IDEA 1997) stated that there was a need to do much more. In order to accomplish this, reauthorization focused on five areas (OSERS, 1999).

1. **Raising expectations for children with disabilities**

IDEA (1997) procedures contain several requirements for describing how the student accesses the general education curriculum and how the student's disability affects his or her ability to be successful in the curriculum. For speech-language pathologists and audiologists, this requirement clearly points to the necessity of knowing and understanding the demands of the curriculum at all grade levels and across school, district, and state requirements (see Chapter 4 for specific regulations). For the first time, legislation required that students were to participate in state testing and demonstrate that they are making progress in the general education curriculum. Accommodations for a student's disability could not be allowed to water down the curriculum or slow the pace of learning. The goal of achieving general education expectations challenged special educators to identify methods that would allow students to access the curriculum.

2. Increasing parental involvement in the education of their children

The parents of a child with a disability are expected to be equal participants along with school personnel, in developing, reviewing, and revising the IEP for their child. IDEA (1997) called for even greater parent involvement. This implies an active role in which the parents (1) provide critical information regarding the strengths of their child and express their concerns for enhancing the education of their child;

(2) participate in discussions about the child's need for special education and related services and supplementary aids and services; and (3) join with the other participants in deciding how the child will be involved in and progress in the general curriculum, how the child will participate in district- and statewide assessments, and what services the agency will provide to the child as well as the setting of those services.

Working with parents as partners in the IEP process can be both rewarding and challenging. Speech-language pathologists and audiologists of the future must have well-developed skills in many different areas to work with parents, both as participants in the IEP and evaluation processes, and as partners in the intervention for identified children.

3. Ensuring that general education teachers are involved in planning and assessing children's progress

IDEA (1997) clarified for the first time the critical role that general education teachers held in the education of students with disabilities, requiring that these teachers must participate in the development, review, and revision of IEPs. General education teachers play a central role in the education of children with disabilities and have important expertise regarding the general curriculum and the general education environment. With the emphasis on involvement and progress in the general curriculum added by the IDEA Amendments of 1997, regular education teachers have a critical role (together with special education and related services personnel) in implementing FAPE for most children with disabilities. IDEA (1997) instituted the following for the participation of general education teachers in the IEP process:

- The student's teachers must have access to the IEP document.

- Teachers must be informed of their specific responsibilities related to implementing the IEP.

- Teachers must be informed of the specific modifications and supports that must be provided to the student.

- Teachers must participate in the development, review, and revision of the IEP, including assisting in developing positive behavioral interventions and determining supplementary aids, services, and program modifications.

- Services to assist the teacher, such as consultation or training, may be included under supplemental aids and services.

- Attendance and participation of a regular education teacher is required if the student is, or may be, participating in the regular education environment.

The intent of these regulations is to guarantee that special education is not a "place," or a separate system, but rather a support to general education. Consequently, speech-language pathologists and audiologists must know the workings of the general education classroom and the expectations for teachers and students, in order to provide support to both.

> **The services provided by the SLP, audiologist, or any other special educator must be designed to assist the child in benefiting from the core curriculum.**

The requirement for participation of general education teachers on IEP teams brought a new dimension to the IEP. This provision reinforced the reality that children with IEPs are part of a school system. The services provided by the speech-language pathologist, audiologist, or any other special educator must be designed to assist the child in benefiting from the core curriculum. The general education teacher brings this focus to the IEP team. General education teachers need guidance in terms of their role and responsibilities as team members and at IEP meetings. Chapters 5, 6, and 7 offer ideas that may help the general education teacher be prepared to participate on an IEP team.

4. Including children with disabilities in assessments, performance goals, and reports to the public

Students with disabilities were typically excluded from statewide assessments until the mid-1990s, when reform movements in both general and special education called for educational systems to be responsible and accountable for the learning of all students. Under IDEA (1997), states were required to include students with disabilities in district- and statewide assessment programs. In addition to including students with disabilities in the district- and statewide accountability program, IDEA (1997) also required states to have performance goals and indicators established for children with disabilities. These goals were required to be consistent to the maximum extent appropriate with the performance goals and standards for children without disabilities.

5. Supporting quality professional development for all personnel who are involved in educating children with disabilities

IDEA (1997) recognized that professional development would be required for individuals working with children with disabilities. Professional development may be provided in a variety of different ways. Among these are workshops, conferences, specialized trainings, mentoring, staff meetings, professional study groups, professional journals, and others. Individuals may obtain professional development from professional associations, such as the AMERICAN SPEECH-LANGUAGE-HEARING ASSOCIATION (ASHA) or state-level speech and hearing associations, local education agencies (LEAs), or from other agencies that provide workshops and trainings. These trainings might focus on an identified need area in the school or district. State and regional trainings could also be available to both general and special education professionals.

Aligning IDEA With NCLB

The President's Commission on Excellence in Special Education (2002; a commission appointed by President George W. Bush to determine needs to address in the impending reauthorization of IDEA) made strong recommendations for changes in IDEA and alignment with NCLB. Commission members made three major (broad) recommendations that form the foundation of the report:

1. Focus on results, not on process.

2. Embrace a model of prevention, not a model of failure.

3. Consider children with disabilities as general education children first.

The Commission posed this final challenge:

The Commission is optimistic that our nation can build on the success of the past and do even better in meeting the needs of special education children and their families. But we will do so only through a focus on educational achievement and excellence, teacher quality and support, and rigorous research. We will succeed if we work to create a culture of high expectations, accountability, and results that meet the unique needs of every child. Only then can the promise of no child left behind truly be fulfilled (pp. 8–9).

Source: President's Commission on Excellence in Special Education (2002)

Selected NCLB Terminology

Adequate Yearly Progress—A school or school district has met target goals for test scores, attendance, and/or graduation.

Annual Measurable Objectives—A set of state-established benchmarks for monitoring changes in performance among and across student subgroups, schools, and districts. States must establish the objectives as part of the adequate yearly progress (AYP) report required by No Child Left Behind. These objectives apply to all groups, with some slight variations depending on a school's grade span.

High Objective Uniform State Standard of Evaluation (HOUSSE)—An optional method of documenting subject matter competency in core academic subject(s) for a teacher who is not new to the profession, in order to meet the definition of highly qualified teacher.

Highly Qualified Teacher—Teachers must hold the appropriate state certification in the core area(s) they are teaching. Special education teachers are considered highly qualified if the teacher passed the state special education examination or met alternate achievement standards. All special education teachers must hold at least a bachelor's degree.

Supplemental Services—Under NCLB, eligible students attending schools that have not met performance targets for three consecutive years have a right to free tutoring and other "supplemental services."

The Interface of General and Special Education Requirements: NCLB and IDEA 2004

No Child Left Behind (NCLB)

The impact of No Child Left Behind (NCLB, 2001) has resounded throughout every school building across the United States. Prior to NCLB, the influence of the ESEA was felt mainly by schools that served students from low socioeconomic backgrounds. NCLB has clearly established a strong federal role in education and has set the bar high for educators and students. The law has ignited widespread reform in instructional programs. Most importantly, NCLB, along with the subsequent reauthorization of IDEA 2004, put accountability for the learning of students with disabilities in the forefront by establishing requirements which tracked the progress of these students. Prior to this, general and special educators were not truly being held accountable for producing results with target populations, including students with disabilities.

Key Principles and Programs of No Child Left Behind

The U.S. Department of Education (USDE, 2002a) summarizes the four key principles of NCLB as "stronger accountability for results; greater flexibility for states, school districts, and schools in the use of federal funds; more choices for parents of children from disadvantaged backgrounds; and an emphasis on teaching methods that have been demonstrated to work" (p. 2). In addition, NCLB increased the emphasis on reading instruction, training of high-quality teachers, and language instruction for English learners. Revisions of the Elementary and Secondary Education Act (ESEA) created by NCLB apply to several different programs. NCLB is organized into ten sections called "titles." Each title establishes the requisites of a program or set of programs. Some of the most commonly known are listed in Table 2.1.

School districts (i.e., local education agencies) with a high proportion of students who are economically disadvantaged are eligible for Title I funds. Funding flows to school districts and buildings based upon complex formulas (which will not be described here). Funds may be used for either schoolwide programs, such as before or after school programs or summer programs, or targeted assistance programs, such as instruction in reading or math (USDE, 2002a).

Special education programs and the programs funded through NCLB are considered "categorical" programs (see "Funding" in Chapter 9). This means that dollars allocated to these programs must be spent for the specific purposes intended under each category. In years past, students who met the criteria for both special education and Title I were only allowed to participate in one program or the other, due to strict spending requirements. However, in recent years, greater flexibility has been built into the funding systems in order to extend services of both programs to eligible students. Title I resources are used by school districts to provide a variety of extra and expansive services to students in general or special education. In fact, co-mingling of funds under these two programs is encouraged by the federal government.

Table 2.1	**NCLB Programs at a Glance**
Section	**Example Programs**
Title I Improving the Academic Achievement of the Disadvantaged	Local Education Agencies, Reading First, Early Reading First, Even Start Migrant Education Program, Even Start Family Literacy
Title II Preparing, Training, and Recruiting High Quality Teachers and Principals	Teacher and Principal Training and Recruiting Enhancing Education through Technology
Title III Language Instruction for Limited English Proficient and Immigrant Students	Language Instruction for Limited English Proficient and Immigrant Students
Title IV 21st Century Schools	Safe and Drug-Free Schools and Communities 21st Century Community of Learning Centers
Title V Promoting Informed Parental Choice and Innovative Programs State and Local Innovative Programs	Public Charter Schools Public School Choice Magnet Schools Innovation in Education
Title VI Flexibility and Accountability	Improving Academic Achievement Rural Education Initiative
Title VII Indian, Native Hawaiian, and Alaska Native Education	Indian Education Native Hawaiian Education Alaska Native Education
Title VIII Impact Aid Program	Impact Aid
Title IX General Provisions	Consolidated Planning and Administration Unsafe Schools Choice
Title X Repeals, Redesignations, and Amendments to Other Statutes	McKinney-Vento Homeless Education

Source: U.S. Department of Education (2002a, 2004b)

NCLB Assessment and Accountability

To achieve the purpose of and comply with the requirements of NCLB, states are required to adopt challenging academic content and performance standards in math, reading, and science.

As stated in the legislation,

> The purpose of this title is to ensure that all children have a fair, equal, and significant opportunity to obtain a high-quality education and reach, at a minimum, proficiency on challenging State academic achievement standards and State academic assessments (NCLB § 1001).

States must describe what students are expected to know in order to achieve performance levels of advanced, proficient, or basic, and then administer annual academic assessments in these areas. State assessments were required to be aligned with the academic content and performance standards of the state by the 2005–2006 school year. (The requirements for science standards went into effect in 2005–2006; statewide assessment in science began in the 2006–2007 school year.)

All students are required to reach proficiency on the academic standards assessments by the year 2013–2014. Each state's accountability system must establish set targets to measure schools' and districts' progress toward this goal and establish a system to report annual performance. Every district and school must show continuous improvement in student performance, known as adequate yearly progress (AYP) (34 C.F.R. § 200.13). States and school districts must report the progress of each of the following groups:

1. All public school students

2. Students in each of the following subgroups:

   a. Economically disadvantaged students

   b. Students from major racial and ethnic groups

   c. Students with disabilities

   d. Students with limited English proficiency (34 C.F.R. § 200.13 [7][i][ii])

States are required to use their data from the year 2001–2002 as the baseline year (34 C.F.R. § 200.16 [a]). Using that baseline, each state must establish intermediate goals for annual progress between the base year and the target year of 2013–2014 (34 C.F.R. § 200.17). Annual measurable objectives (AMO) must also be established by states, identifying a minimum percentage of students that must meet or exceed the proficient level of academic achievement on state assessments annually (34 C.F.R. § 200.18). Schools must also test at least 95 percent of students in each of the above identified groups in order to meet criteria for AYP (34 C.F.R. § 200.20 [c][1][i]).

Schools and districts that fail to achieve AYP for two consecutive years are identified for school improvement (34 C.F.R. § 200.32 [a]). When a school or a district is designated for school improvement, parents have the option to transfer their child to another school or eligible children may receive state-approved supplemental educational services (34 C.F.R. § 200.32 [c][2][i][ii]). A percentage of funds from the district's Title I allocation must be set aside to pay for these services and/or transportation. Supplemental educational services are not to be confused with special education services provided through an individualized education program (IEP). Supplemental educational services are provided outside the school day and are intended to give additional academic assistance to eligible students (Moore-Brown, 2004b). The STATE EDUCATION AGENCY (SEA) must maintain and distribute a list of approved providers of supplemental educational services.

Both NCLB and IDEA 2004 require the participation of students with disabilities in state-wide assessments and standards-based programs. NCLB specifically tracks performance of students with disabilities to monitor annual progress. A limited number of students are allowed to take alternate assessments. These are generally students with significant cognitive impairments. Initially, the number of students whose scores from alternate assessment would be excluded from the state's AYP was capped at 1 percent. An April 2005 modification to the policy allowed an additional 2 percent of students to take alternate assessments (USDE, 2005a) (see Table 2.2).

The rationale for why students with disabilities are included in accountability systems is described in the background section of the Code of Federal Regulations for No Child Left Behind/Title I (see sidebar on pp. 41–42). All educators need to understand the rationale for this, and it is succinctly described in the language of the law. It is notable that the rationale for including students with disabilities in the accountability system is justified in the law for general education. For further information for speech-language pathologists and other special educators on the practice implications of including students with disabilities in large scale assessments, see Chapter 3.

Highly Qualified Staff

NCLB contains requirements for teachers and paraprofessionals to be HIGHLY QUALIFIED (HQ). These requirements mean that teachers must hold the appropriate state certification in the core academic area(s) they are teaching. Core academic subjects are identified as English, reading or language arts, mathematics, science, foreign languages, civics and government, economics, arts, history, and geography. Teachers may establish that they are highly qualified through a process known as High Objective Uniform State Standard of Evaluation (HOUSSE), which allows for documentation of activities considered sufficient to prepare a teacher as highly qualified. Additionally, NCLB requires that all paraprofessionals in Title I programs have two years of postsecondary education, in addition to a high school diploma or its equivalent (USDE, 2002a). The National Education Association (NEA, 2004) and the National Association of State Directors of Special Education (NASDSE, 2004) point out "it is critical to note that the new NCLB paraprofessional qualifications apply to *all* paraprofessionals with instructional duties who are employed in a school that receives schoolwide Title I program funds" (p. 24). Although NCLB requirements do not specifically apply to special education teachers, IDEA 2004 requires that special education teachers be both NCLB HQ as well as IDEA HQ. In other words, special education teachers must hold credentials that establish their qualifications under both laws.

The provisions for highly qualified teachers under NCLB reflected the concerns from teacher education, school districts, and advocacy

Table 2.2

Type and Characteristics of Assessment Methods

	Assessment Methods	Foundation for Content Assessed	How Performance is Evaluated	Who Can Participate	Caps on Using Proficient Scores for AYP
Tests Based on Grade-level Achievement Standards	1. Regular assessment based on grade-level achievement standards	State's academic grade-level content standards	Grade-level achievement standards	Open to all students, including any student with a disability	None
	2. Regular assessment with accommodations based on grade-level achievement standards	State's academic grade-level content standards	Grade-level achievement standards	Any student with a disability. Some states make this option available to other students as well.	None
	3. Alternate assessment based on grade-level achievement standards	State's academic grade-level content standards	Grade-level achievement standards	Any student with a disability. Some states make this option available to other students as well.	None
Tests Based on other Achievement Standards	4. Assessment based on modified achievement standards*	State's academic grade-level content standards	**Modified** achievement standards	Student with a disability who can make progress toward, but may not reach grade-level achievement standards in the same time frame as other students and who may need changes in the breadth or depth of the assessment to appropriately reflect his or her proficiency †	Proficient scores may be counted for AYP subject to a cap of 2.0 percent of all students assessed at the state and district levels; no limit on number who can participate in this option †
	5. Alternate assessment based on alternate achievement standards ‡	State's academic grade-level content standards	**Alternate** achievement standards that promote access to the general curriculum based on professional judgment of high expectations	Student with the most significant cognitive disabilities	Proficient scores may be counted for AYP subject to a cap of 1.0 percent of all students assessed at the district or state level; no limit on number who can participate in this option

*Some states may choose not to use modified achievement standards.

† No final regulations had been established at the time this paper was released.

‡ Some states may choose not to use alternate achievement standards.

Source: OSEP (2006, April)

Including Children With Disabilities in State Assessment Programs

The Individuals with Disabilities Education Act (IDEA 2004), Section 504 of the Rehabilitation Act of 1973, and Title I require inclusion of all students with disabilities in the State assessment system. Title I further requires that the assessment results for all students (and all students with disabilities, among other groups) who have been enrolled in a school for a full academic year be used in calculating AYP for the school, and that the assessment results of students who have been in a district for a full academic year be used in calculating AYP for the district and the State. System accountability should be just that—accountability for everyone in the system. Students with disabilities are a part of the student body. Most of these students spend the majority of their time in general education classrooms, and receive instruction from regular classroom teachers. Regardless of where students receive instruction, all students with disabilities should have access to, participate in, and make progress in, the general curriculum. Thus, all students with disabilities must be included in the measurement of AYP toward meeting the State's standards.

Several critical elements in Title I as amended by the NCLB Act ensure that schools are held accountable for educational results, so that the best education possible is provided to each and every student. Three critical elements—academic content standards, academic achievement standards, and assessments aligned to those standards—provide the foundation for an accountability system ensuring that students with disabilities reach high standards. State assessments are the mechanism for determining whether schools have been successful in teaching students the knowledge and skills defined by the content standards. States are required to hold all students to the same standards except that these regulations permit States to measure the achievement of students with the most significant cognitive disabilities based on alternate achievement standards.

Only by including all students in accountability measures will certain unintended negative consequences be avoided. For example, we know from research that when students with disabilities are allowed to be excluded from school accountability measures, the rates of referral of students for special education increase dramatically. (See National Center on Educational Outcomes Synthesis 26: http://cehd.umn.edu/nceo/onlinepubs/Synthesis26.htm). In addition, students with disabilities accrue positive benefits when they are included in school accountability systems. Educators realize that these students also count, just like all other students; they understand that they need to make sure that these students reach high levels of learning, just like other students. When students with disabilities are part of the accountability system, educators' expectations for these students are more likely to increase.

Continued

Including Children With Disabilities – *Continued*

One State explains the instructional benefits of including students with the most significant cognitive disabilities in its assessment: "Some students with disabilities have never been taught academic skills and concepts, for example, reading, mathematics, science, and social studies, even at very basic levels. Yet all students are capable of learning at a level that engages and challenges them. Teachers who have incorporated learning standards into their instruction cite unanticipated gains in students' performance and understanding. Furthermore, some individualized social, communication, motor, and self-help skills can be practiced during activities based on the learning standards."

Too often in the past, students with disabilities were excluded from assessments and accountability systems, and the consequence was that they did not receive the academic attention they deserved. Access and exposure to the general curriculum for students with disabilities often did not occur, and there was no systemwide measure to indicate whether or what they were learning. These regulations are designed to ensure that schools are held accountable for the educational progress of students with the most significant cognitive disabilities, just as schools are held accountable for the educational results of all other students with disabilities and students without disabilities.

Source: USDE (2003)

groups that the most qualified teachers typically did not work with the neediest children, yet those were the children who specifically needed the most qualified teachers. By requiring school districts to have highly qualified (HQ) teachers and paraprofessionals, the law created a situation where schools and districts were required to ensure that all children would have the opportunity to learn because their teachers and aides were qualified.

Focus on What Works and Reading First

NCLB requires the use of scientifically based educational practices. Funds are directed only to programs that support effective teaching methods that will lead to improved student learning and achievement (USDE, 2002a). Funds for professional development are available under NCLB, especially through Title I and Title II.

To further assist teachers, the United States Department of Education's Web site (http://www.ed.gov) contains resources for teachers, including lesson plans and classroom resources for planning scientifically based instruction. USDE also provides the What Works Clearinghouse (http://www.whatworks.ed.gov), where reviews of studies on intervention effectiveness are available. (See the sidebar on p. 44 for an extended list of useful Web sites and the information that they contain.)

Effective reading instruction is a focus for NCLB. A national effort to deal with reading issues is regulated through the Reading First programs and provides grants to states. Reading First is designed to assist schools and districts reach NCLB's goal of ensuring that every child can read at grade level or above by the year 2013–2014. Reading First incorporates funds for professional development of teachers and administrators, who learn how to use instructional strategies based on scientifically based reading research methods. Reading First programs are built upon the research completed by the National Reading Panel (2000) and reported in the book *Put Reading First* (Armbruster & Osborn, 2001), which identifies five essential areas of reading development (see sidebar on p. 45).

Early Reading First grants are available to address the needs of young children entering kindergarten, and Even Start Family Literacy Program grants are available to establish programs for low-income families (USDE, 2002a). Speech-

language pathologists should inquire about the programs available in their schools, participate in staff development opportunities, and coordinate their services for students with disabilities who will likely be receiving instruction through these initiatives.

NCLB notably requires that instructional methods be based upon scientifically based research, which is defined as "research that involves the application of rigorous, systematic, and objective procedures to obtain reliable and valid knowledge relevant to education activities and programs (NCLB § 9101 [37]). Such prescriptive language reflects increasing control of education through federal rules. In the fields of communication disorders and reading research, the term EVIDENCE-BASED PRACTICE (EBP) refers to this same reliance upon data to make intervention decisions. For all educators, including speech-language pathologists, this focus means that the interventions and instructional methods that we use in our daily work with children must be based on sound evidence and not based on what feels good or what materials are avail-

able. Nye, Schwartz, and Turner (2005) suggest: "The use of EBP to treat communication disorders requires clinicians to use the best available scientific evidence in combination with their professional experiences and judgment to guide their clinical decisions" (p. 6).

Conflicts Between NCLB and IDEA Requirements

When NCLB was enacted in 2002, special educators and policymakers became concerned about conflicts between the mandates of NCLB and IDEA (1997) (Moore-Brown, 2004b). NCLB established broad sweeping changes that, in certain areas, appeared to be in conflict with the requirements of IDEA (1997). Consequently, IDEA 2004 incorporated some of the NCLB mandates, but certain conflicts remain. The disparity between the requirements of these two laws arises mainly from the all-inclusive provisions of NCLB. Although the reforms of general and special education are no longer separate or parallel, understanding the conflicts that existed between the requirements of NCLB and

---

Web Sites for Helpful Information

United States Department of Education http://www.ed.gov

What Works Clearinghouse http://www.whatworks.ed.gov

Reading Rockets http://www.readingrockets.org

Read Write Think http://www.readwritethink.org

100 Best Books for Kids http://www.teachersfirst.com/100books.cfm

International Reading Association http://www.reading.org

Family Read-Aloud http://www.bookitfamilies.com/

American Speech Language Hearing Association (ASHA) http://www.asha.org

Council for Exceptional Children (CEC) http://www.cec.sped.org

Office of Special Education and Rehabilitative Services
http://www.ed.gov/about/offices/list/osers/programs.html

National Reading Panel
http://www.nationalreadingpanel.org/Publications/Publications.htm

National Institute for Literacy
http://www.nifl.gov/partnershipforreading/publications/reading_first1.html

---

Essential Components of Reading Development

Phonemic Awareness – the ability to notice, think about, and work with the individual sounds in spoken words (p. 2)

Phonics Instruction – teaches children the relationships between the letters (graphemes) of written language and the individual speech sounds (phonemes) of spoken language (p. 12)

Fluency – the ability to read a text accurately and quickly (p. 22)

Vocabulary – listening, speaking, reading, or writing vocabulary (p. 34)

Text Comprehension – comprehension is the purpose for reading; text comprehension must be purposeful and active (p. 57)

Source: Armbruster & Osborn (2001)

IDEA 2004 is important. Part of the reason for the conflict between the laws is that they are intended for two fundamentally different purposes, which lay in the establishment of entitlement under each law. IDEA 2004 provides individual entitlement, such as individualized assessment, individualized instruction, and individualized education programs, while NCLB establishes group entitlement, such as ensuring all children will read at grade level, regardless of disability or English proficiency, social-economic status, or living conditions (Moore-Brown, Powell, & Nishida, 2005).

Assessment of students with disabilities and the inclusion of their scores in the reporting system is required. Educational systems must be responsible and held accountable for the growth and progress of students with disabilities. Many educators, researchers, and parents are concerned about statewide testing of these students and the application of AYP mandates for proficiency for all students by the year 2013–2014. Students with disabilities are allowed to take statewide assessments with the accommodations and modifications that are already in their individualized education programs (IEPs), but states vary in their interpretations and allowances. In fact, it is important to understand that, as with all federal laws, NCLB implementation is variable from state to state (Power-de-Fur, 2004).

The definition of "in need of special education" appears to conflict with the expectation for AYP. Most students receiving special education services are identified due to an academic deficiency resulting from their disability. If these students were performing at or near grade level, they would not be identified for special education services. Related to this, the turnover of students in the disability subgroup means that new, lower performing students will be added to the disability group as higher performing students are dismissed from special education. Once students approach grade-level skills (i.e., near the proficient range), they are most likely dismissed from special education, as they should be. New students who are struggling academically enter special education and are counted in the disability subgroup's performance. This is one of the major conflicts between the requirements of NCLB and IDEA 2004. Policymakers and educators continue to discuss possible adjustments in this system. One of the promising proposals is the development of a growth model which could track the progress of individual students toward standards, rather than measuring them against a standard they will not meet by definition of their eligibility. The core of the conflict between NCLB and IDEA 2004 can best be summarized as this:

- NCLB requires that all students must progress at the same rate and achieve the same outcomes, and progress is defined only by achieving proficiency on statewide tests.

- IDEA 2004 requires that individual decisions are made for students by a multidisciplinary assessment team and an IEP team, and that the team develop an individualized education program (IEP) to address the student's individualized learning needs. The conflict appears to be how to treat everyone individually and the same simultaneously (Moore-Brown, Powell, & Nishida, 2005).

The standard for NCLB is 100 percent proficiency, but the standard for IDEA is free appropriate public education (FAPE; Waterman, 2004). FAPE must be reasonably calculated to confer educational benefit (including progress toward standards), but does not require that students reach an expected performance level.

One additional area of conflict between NCLB and IDEA 2004 is in the area of school choice. Public school choice is available to parents if their child's school is identified as needing improvement, due to failure of the school to meet its AYP in two consecutive years. Under this provision, parents may choose to have their child attend an alternate school of their choice, and transportation must be paid for by the home district. IDEA 2004 does not provide a school choice option. However, if a student transfers as a result of NCLB, the receiving school must continue to comply with IDEA. The receiving school may adopt the IEP from the sending district, or may convene an IEP meeting to revise the IEP. In either event, the receiving school is still required to provide FAPE for the student (NEA & NASDSE, 2004).

Implications for Speech-Language Pathologists

NCLB will draw on the skills of speech-language pathologists and increase their involvement in the curriculum (Banotai, 2005). Speech-language pathologists working in schools must know and understand how the statewide assessment system works in their state. Students with disabilities represent a distinct subgroup under NCLB, which means that high stakes testing is part of the work of the school-based speech-language pathologist.

Because this testing is part of the school experience for students with speech-language disorders, speech-language pathologists should learn as much as they can about the testing experience, how the test is constructed, and what content students will be expected to know.

Academic content and performance standards are emphasized even more during intervention, since this is the information that will form the foundation of the test. This does not mean that speech-language pathologists or teachers should be teaching to the test. What it does mean is this: As related service providers, speech-language pathologists should provide services in concert with the academic expectations of the classroom. Since students are expected to learn in the classroom, speech-language pathologists are expected to support students so that they can achieve an educational benefit. Speech-language pathologists should also support students in developing learning strategies to become more effective learners by turning their academic content into a vehicle for practicing strategies (Ukrainetz, 2006a). Speech-language pathologists and all special educators should include information about statewide assessment results when preparing reports and IEPs. They should participate in all meetings at the school and district related to testing and standards to keep up on new requirements and mandates. Additionally, they must continue to actively examine their practices to provide adequate services to students to assist them in meeting the demands of their classroom. Following are five recommendations for becoming proficient in the lessons of NCLB (2001) (Moore-Brown, 2004a):

1. Understand how the statewide testing system works.

2. Understand the distinction between the statewide accountability system and the national accountability system.

3. Understand that conflicts exist in the system between NCLB and IDEA 2004.

4. Examine speech-language pathologists' practice and service delivery in relation to support of students in the climate of accountability.

5. Move quickly to adjust practices and decision making in accordance with school accountability mandates.

Table 2.3 highlights and summarizes key areas of NCLB and the implications for speech-language pathologists.

The Individuals With Disabilities Education Improvement Act of 2004

The 2004 reauthorization of IDEA took effect on July 1, 2005 although the requirements for highly qualified special education teachers went into effect immediately on December 3, 2004. Prior to the passage of the law, national debate occurred among educators, parents, policymakers, and lawmakers regarding the issues that needed to be addressed. However, the policymakers' goal for this reauthorization was to align IDEA 2004 with the provisions of NCLB. The manifestation of this goal can be seen throughout the law, but most vividly in the inclusion of the term *improvement* in the name of the law. A review of the various levels of legislation and regulation may be helpful (see sidebar on p. 51). Federal laws, or public laws, are passed by Congress and signed into law by the president. Following the passage of the public law, public hearings are held and input is sought before the Code of Federal Regulations (C.F.R.) is developed. These regulations describe how to implement the laws. After the proposed regulations are published, another round of public hearings and input is conducted. In the case of IDEA 2004, states adopt legislation for implementation of the federal law in that state. No state may provide less than is called for under the public law, but a state may exceed the federal requirements. Local education agencies (LEAs) establish local school board policy and administrative regulations for implementation in their local district, in compliance with state and federal laws. Local policy may have provisions that vary from state or federal law due to specific needs in their district.

The Individuals with Disabilities Education Improvement Act (IDEA; P.L. 108-446), was signed into law in 2004. The final code of federal regulations, which provides guidance on how states and LEAs are to implement the law, was released on August 3, 2006, with implementation required on October 13, 2006.

Table 2.3	**Selected Key Areas of NCLB Relevant to Speech-Language Pathologists**
	Students
Law	• Statement of purpose indicates that all children should have a fair, equal, and significant opportunity to obtain a high-quality education and reach proficiency on statewide assessment, including children with disabilities (§ 1001 [2]). • Emphasis on assisting low-achieving students in high-poverty schools, and also English learners, migrant children, neglected or delinquent children and young children in need of reading assistance (§ 1001 [2]). Source: NCLB (2001)
Implications for SLPs	Speech-language pathologists must recognize that since students with disabilities are now specifically included in NCLB subgroups, that achievement emphasis applies to them as well. SLPs need to understand the requirements of the classroom for students so that special education programs and IEPs are designed to confer educational benefit within the demands of NCLB. Additionally, it is noteworthy that NCLB is focusing on other underachieving groups as well, and has expectations for achievement for these groups. Speech-language pathologists may be called upon to ensure that students in these other groups are not inappropriately referred to special education, but are being provided every benefit under NCLB. *Continued*

Table 2.3 – *Continued*

	Accountability
Law	• Requires states to have a separate reporting of annual measurable objectives (AMO) for the achievement of students with disabilities (§ 1111 [b][2][C][v][II][cc]). • Requires that at least 95% of students in the subgroup of students with disabilities (as well as other subgroups) must participate in statewide assessment, and that accommodations, guidelines, and alternate assessments are provided consistent with IDEA (§ 1111 [b][2][I][ii]). • Requires that academic assessments provide for the participation of all students, including the reasonable adaptations and accommodations of students with disabilities as defined under IDEA (§ 602(3); § 1111 [b][3][C][ix][II]). Source: NCLB (2001)
Implications for SLPs	Speech-language pathologists can help prepare students for taking statewide assessment by addressing the testing experience and writing goals directed to the skills students need to master grade-level standards. The accountability requirements will cause the need for closer collaboration between classroom teachers and speech-language pathologists so that students are as prepared as possible for participation in statewide assessments. Documentation of statewide assessment results should be included as part of IEPs and individual evaluations.
	Local Education Agency (LEA) Plans
Law	• Must have a description of how LEAs will coordinate and integrate services to provide services to children with disabilities and to all other subgroups noted (§ 1112 [b][1][E][ii]). Source: NCLB (2001)
Implications for SLPs	Site and district plans must include descriptions of integrated services. Speech-language pathologists must be aware of the written requirements of the school and district. Participation in professional development activities may also be included here. *Continued*

Table 2.3 – *Continued*

	Reading Instruction
Law	• Defines the essential components of reading instruction (§ 1208 [3]). • Creates Reading First programs (§ 1202). • Defines the term *scientifically based research* (§ 1208[6][37]). Source: NCLB (2001)
Implications for SLPs	Speech-language pathologists should incorporate the essential components of reading instruction in their assessment and IEP goals. The mandates for scientifically based research parallel the evidence-based practice movement in communication sciences and disorders.

Need for Improved Outcomes for Special Education

The President's Commission on Excellence in Special Education (2002), a commission appointed by President George W. Bush to determine needs to address in the impending reauthorization of IDEA, made strong recommendations for changes in IDEA (1997) and alignment with NCLB. The commission held 13 open hearings around the nation, and then cited the following continuing needs in their report:

Although it is true that special education has created a base of civil rights and legal protections, children with disabilities remain those most at risk of being left behind. The facts create an urgency for reform that few can deny:

• Young people with disabilities drop out of high school at twice the rate of their peers.

• Enrollment rates of students with disabilities in higher education are still 50 percent lower than enrollment among the general population.

• Most public school educators do not feel well prepared to work with children with disabilities. In 1998, only 21 percent of public school teachers said they felt very well prepared to address the needs of students with disabilities, and another 41 percent said they felt moderately well prepared.

• Of the six million children in special education, half of those who are in special education are identified as having a "specific learning disability." In fact, this group has grown more than 300 percent since 1976.

Levels of Laws and Regulations

Federal
Public Law
Code of Federal Regulations

State
State Law
Education Code

Local Education Agency/School District
School Board Policy
Administrative Regulations

- Of those with "specific learning disabilities," 80 percent are there simply because they haven't learned how to read. Thus, many children identified for special education—up to 40 percent—are there because they weren't taught to read. The reading difficulties may not be their only area of difficulty, but it's the area that resulted in special education placement. Sadly, few children placed in special education close the achievement gap to a point where they can read and learn like their peers.

- Children of minority status are over-represented in some categories of special education. African-American children are twice as likely as White children to be labeled mentally retarded *[sic]* and placed in special education. They are also more likely to be labeled and placed as emotionally disturbed (pp. 1–2).

Commission members made three major (broad) recommendations that form the foundation of the report:

1. Focus on results, not on process.

2. Embrace a model of prevention, not a model of failure.

3. Consider children with disabilities as general education children first.

The Commission posed this final challenge:

The Commission is optimistic that our nation can build on the success of the past and do even better in meeting the needs of special education children and their families. But we will do so only through a focus on educational achievement and excellence, teacher quality and support, and rigorous research. We will succeed if we work to create a culture of high expectations, accountability, and results that meet the unique needs of every child. Only then can the promise of no child left behind truly be fulfilled (pp. 8–9).

Requirements of IDEA 2004

Although the reauthorized law is to be cited as the "Individuals with Disabilities Education Improvement Act of 2004," the approved acronym is IDEA 2004. IDEA 2004 modified the congressional findings that existed under IDEA (1997) (see sidebar on pp. 24–25). The revised purposes of the law are identified as follows (IDEA 2004 § 601 [d]):

(1) (A) To ensure that all children with disabilities have available to them a free appropriate public education that emphasizes special education and related services designed to meet their unique needs and prepare them for further education, employment, and independent living;

(B) To ensure that the rights of children with disabilities and parents of such children are protected; and

(C) To assist States, localities, educational service agencies, and federal agencies to provide for the education of all children with disabilities;

(2) To assist States in the implementation of a statewide, comprehensive, coordinated, multidisciplinary, interagency system of early intervention services for infants and toddlers with disabilities and their families;

(3) To ensure that educators and parents have the necessary tools to improve educational results for children with disabilities by supporting system improvement activities; coordinating research and personnel preparation; coordinated technical assistance, dissemination, and support; and technology development and media services; and

(4) To assess and ensure the effectiveness of efforts to educate children with disabilities.

Under IDEA 2004, the six principles that have historically guided special education law remain the same. According to Villa (2005), these include:

1. Free Appropriate Public Education

2. Full Educational Opportunity (Zero Reject Philosophy)

3. Child Find

4. Procedural Safeguards

5. Least Restrictive Environment

6. Individualized Education Programs (p. 3)

Additionally, the members of the IEP Team remain the same with the notable change that under certain conditions a member may be excused from attending an IEP Team meeting (see Chapter 4). The basic contents of the IEP remain the same and include:

1. A statement of the student's present levels of acheivement. IDEA 2004 specifies that this include academic achievement and functional performance, including how the child's disability affects the child's progress in the general education curriculum or preschool activities.

2. A statement of measurable annual goals that meet the child's needs resulting from the disability and that enable the child to be involved in, and make progress in, the general education curriculum.

3. A description of how progress toward annual goals will be measured and when periodic progress reports will be provided.

4. A statement of special education, related services, and supplementary aids and services.

5. An explanation of the extent that the child will not participate with nondisabled peers in the regular class and activities.

6. Modifications in achievement assessments, if needed.

7. A projected date for beginning services, with anticipated frequency, location, and duration.

8. A plan for postsecondary transition.

The following themes arise from IDEA 2004:

- A focus on the general education curriculum and academic achievement for students with disabilities.

- Decisions based on scientifically based research to the extent practicable.

- Alignment with NCLB.

- Focus on prevention services, including early intervening and responsiveness-to intervention models as part of eligibility determination for specific learning disability.

These themes will be noted in the implementation expected with this law.

Free Appropriate Public Education (FAPE) and Least Restrictive Environment (LRE)

The intent of Congress to provide FREE AP-PROPRIATE PUBLIC EDUCATION (FAPE) was set forth in 1975 under the EAHCA and has been reinforced through subsequent amendments and reauthorizations. State educational agencies (i.e., state departments of education) and local educational agencies (i.e., school districts) are required to establish policies and procedures to ensure that each child with a disability has available FAPE through both procedural and regulatory conditions. These are designed to avoid the possibility of functional exclusion when students are unintentionally excluded from services or "fall through the cracks."

The Code of Federal Regulations defines FAPE as follows:

Free appropriate public education or FAPE means special education and relates services that—

(a) Are provided at public expense, under public supervision and direction, and without charge;

(b) Meet the standards of the SEA;

(c) Include an appropriate preschool, elementary school, or secondary school education in the State involved; and

(d) Are provided in conformity with the individualized education program (IEP) that meets the requirements of § 300.320 through 33.324 (34 C.F.R. § 300.17).

Fundamentally, the provision of FAPE is what special education is all about. Special education is intended to meet a child's unique educational needs, and the requirements for FAPE have been litigated, argued, and debated since the inception of P.L. 94-142. The *Rowley* decision described in the next section is a Supreme Court decision which sets the standard for IEP teams in the decision of FAPE. As will be seen, the judicial and legislative interpretation of FAPE continues to evolve. Nevertheless, each day across our country IEP teams set out to conduct the business of designing an IEP that will satisfy the requirements of the law, but this is not always easy due to the complexities of student needs, limited or constrained

resources or differing opinions of parents and educators, and sometimes even between the educators themselves. The obligation of the IEP team is to first identify the student's needs in all areas of suspected disability either through assessment or through updating information on the student's functioning level, establishing goals for the student, and then recommending supports and services that will enable the student to meet those goals. The standard of *Rowley* requires that the IEP be designed to confer educational benefit. How this is done will be further discussed in Chapter 4. Functionally, FAPE means that students receive the services they need but not more than they need. One way to think about FAPE is as the umbrella under which all other requirements stem, or all requirements exist in order to lead to a FAPE for the student.

Like FAPE, the interpretation of least restrictive environment (LRE) has varied widely. The regulations require:

(i) That to the maximum extent appropriate, children with disabilities, including children in public or private institutions or other care facilities, are educated with children who are not disabled; and

(ii) That special classes, separate schooling, or other removal of children with disabilities from the regular education environment occurs only when the nature or severity of the handicap is such that education in regular classes with the use of supplementary aids and services cannot be achieved satisfactorily (34 C.F.R. § 300.114 [2]).

The underlying principle of LRE is that children with disabilities will be, to the fullest extent possible, educated alongside their peers who are not disabled. Before federal legislation, it was common practice to segregate children with disabilities from their nondisabled peers. The findings of Congress in IDEA 2004 strongly emphasized the intention of Congress to have students with disabilities in the general education classroom through specific referent.

The requirements for LRE call for a continuum of alternative placements (34 C.F.R. § 300.115) for children who are in need of special education and related services. Under the provisions of FAPE, these program options, if needed, would be provided at no cost to children or their families. The LRE requirements also outline what is meant by "placement" and define the responsibilities of the IEP team to ensure this provision.

In determining the educational placement of a child with a disability, including a preschool child with a disability, each public agency must ensure that—

(a) The placement decision—

(1) Is made by a group of persons, including the parents, and other persons knowledgeable about the child, the meaning of the evaluation data, and the placement options; and

(2) Is made inconformity with the LRE provisions of this subpart...

(b) The child's placement—

(1) Is determined at least annually;

(2) Is based on the child's IEP; and

(3) Is as close as possible to the child's home.

(c) Unless the IEP of a child with a disability requires some other arrangement, the child is educated in the school that he or she would attend if nondisabled;

(d) In selecting the LRE, consideration is given to any potential harmful effects on the child or on the quality of services that he or she needs; and

(e) A child with a disability is not removed from education in age-appropriate regular classrooms solely because of needed modifications in the general education curriculum (34 C.F.R. § 300.116).

The Code of Federal Regulations includes clarification about the extension of LRE into nonacademic settings as established by IDEA 2004 as follows:

In providing or arranging for the provision of nonacademic and extracurricular services and activities, including meals, recess periods, and the services and activities set forth in § 300.107 (nonacademic services), each public agency must ensure that each child with a disability participates with nondisabled children in the extracurricular services and activities to the maximum extent appropriate to the needs of that child. The public agency must ensure that each child with a disability has the supplementary aides and services determined by the child's IEP Team to be appropriate and necessary for the child to participate in nonacademic settings (34 C.F.R. § 300.117).

Often, one section of the code refers to another section. In this case, section 300.117 refers to section 300.107 which defines nonacademic services. It is clear that it is the intent of Congress and the USDE to extend the provisions of LRE to these settings and activities. This section states the following:

(a) Each public agency must take steps, including the provision of supplementary aids and services determined appropriate and necessary by the child's IEP team, to provide nonacademic and extracurricular services and activities in the manner necessary to afford children with disabilities an equal opportunity for participation in those services and activities;

(b) Nonacademic activities and extracurricular services and activities may include counseling services, athletics, transportation, health services, recreational activities, special interest groups or clubs sponsored by the public agency, referrals to agencies that provide assistance to individuals with disabilities, and employment of students, including both employment by the public agency and assistance in making employment available (34 C.F.R. § 300.107).

The standards and interpretation of how to design and provide FAPE in the LRE are continually evolving along with educational practice, legal mandates, and judicial decisions. The evolution of special education has been described. Initially, the intent of special education, which focused on access, has evolved to inclusion and

now mandates results (Fulfrost, 2007). As students with disabilities are now required to pass the same statewide tests as their nondisabled peers, the practice of removing students with disabilities from the general education classroom to receive supports and services is increasingly under scrutiny. It is recognized that the delivery of the core curriculum and instruction occurs in the general education classroom, and that special education has not demonstrated that it is able to replicate this delivery of information in separate settings. The change in expectations of the educational system and the laws ultimately changes the meaning of FAPE and LRE.

> It is recognized that the delivery of the core curriculum and instruction occurs in the general education classroom, and that special education has not demonstrated that it is able to replicate this delivery of information in separate settings.

Landmark Court Decisions Regarding FAPE and LRE

The Rowley Standard

The first special education case heard by the United States Supreme Court was a 1982 case out of New York: *Board of Education of Hendrick Hudson Central School District v. Rowley*, 458, U.S. 176. This case set the standard for defining an appropriate program. Amy Rowley was a student who was deaf and attending a general first grade class, following a successful kindergarten year. School authorities provided Amy with an FM wireless ASSISTIVE LISTENING DEVICE for amplification of the teacher's voice in the classroom. She was to receive additional support from tutors and her parents. Amy's parents requested that the school also provide Amy with a sign language interpreter. The school district denied their request because a trial period with a sign language interpreter had demonstrated to the district that this service was unnecessary since Amy learned just as well without the interpreter. The Supreme Court ruling in this case held that Congress set the standard for FAPE that is still considered and followed. In *Rowley*, the court established that:

- A "free appropriate public education" consists of educational instruction specially designed to meet the unique needs of the handicapped *[sic]* child, supported by such services as are necessary to permit the child "to benefit" from the instruction (III A).

- ...the requirement that a State provides specialized educational services to handicapped *[sic]* children generates no additional requirement that the services so provided be sufficient to maximize each child's potential "commensurate with the opportunity provided other children" (III A).

- Assuming that the [Education for All Handicapped Children Act] was designed to fill the need identified in the House Report—that is, to provide a "basic floor of opportunity" consistent with equal protection—neither the Act nor its history persuasively demonstrate that Congress thought that equal protection required anything more than equal access. Therefore, Congress' desire to provide specialized educational services, even in furtherance of "equality," cannot be read as imposing any particular substantive educational standard upon the States (III B ii).

- Implicit in the congressional purpose of providing access to a "free appropriate public education" is the requirement that the education to which access is provided to be sufficient to confer some educational benefit upon the handicapped *[sic]* child (iii).

- When the language of the Act and its legislative history are considered together, the requirements imposed by Congress become tolerably clear. Insofar as a State is required to provide a handicapped *[sic]* child with a "free appropriate public education," we hold that it satisfies this requirements by providing personalized instruction with sufficient support services to permit the child to benefit educationally from that instruction. Such instruction and services must be provided at public expense, must meet the State's educational standards, must approximate grade levels used in the State's regular education, and must comport with the child's IEP. In addition, the IEP, and therefore the personalized instruction, should be formulated in accordance with the requirements of the Act, and if the child is being educated in the regular classroom of the public education system, should be reasonably calculated to enable the child to achieve passing marks and advance from grade to grade (iii C).

The *Rowley* case reinforced the importance of the IEP process in defining appropriate education. The standard for educational benefit, and not maximum development, has continued to be upheld by the courts in subsequent rulings. States establish their standards for FAPE. The *Rowley* interpretation of a floor, not ceiling, of opportunities is upheld in all states.

The importance of the *Rowley* decision has grown and expanded over the years. Initially, lower courts strictly applied the *Rowley* standard to other court cases. However, later courts struggled with the distinction between "some" educational benefit being more than just "trivial" benefit. Courts later moved to a less strict interpretation and extended the *Rowley* standard to that of "meaningful" educational benefit. Special educators must understand that the IEP should be designed so that it results in educational advancement or meaningful educational benefit that the student can reasonably be expected to achieve. The standards for FAPE have also changed according to the times and the new requirements under each reauthorization, specifically as related to where students are provided an education (Zimmerman, 2002; Fulfrost, 2007).

While the Regular Education Initiative (REI) and the Inclusion Movement may have advocated for normalizing the setting and methods for providing services to children with disabilities (see "General and Special Education Reforms" in Chapter 1), the courts are where clarification occurred in terms of what would be acceptable settings and methods. The procedural safeguards afforded to parents allowed for either parents or school districts to request a due process hearing or mediation if there was a disagreement on any issue dealing with the identification, evaluation, educational placement, or provision of FAPE to a child, including issues arising in the IEP process (see "Resolution Sessions, Mediation, Due Process Hearings, and State IDEA Complaints" in Chapter 8 for full discussion). The ruling of an administrative law judge or impartial hearing officer stands as the final decision, unless the decision is appealed. Appeals in these cases may be heard as a civil action in federal court or may be heard in a state court of competent jurisdiction. As in most other legal proceedings, complainants in due process proceedings are required to exhaust administrative remedies before filing a court action.

Following *Rowley*, court actions have defined LRE in terms of "inclusion," or placement of a child with disabilities into a general education classroom. These cases were all heard first at the level of due process hearing, and then worked their way to the court system.

Daniel R. R. v. State Board of Education (Fifth Circuit, 1989)

Daniel was an elementary school student with Down syndrome. His parents wanted Daniel included in a regular classroom, but the school district denied the placement. Noting a strong congressional preference for mainstreaming, in 1989 the Fifth Circuit Court created a two-part inquiry for determination of placement:

First, the school must determine whether placement in the regular classroom, with supplementary services, could be achieved satisfactorily. To make that determination, the school must ask the following questions:

- Has the school taken steps to provide supplementary aids and services to modify the regular education program to suit the needs of the disabled child?

- Once modifications are made, can the child receive an educational benefit from regular education?

• What effects will the disabled child's presence have on the regular classroom environment, and thus, on the education the other students are receiving?

Second, if the decision is made to remove the child from the regular classroom for all or part of the day, then the school must also ask whether the child has been mainstreamed (spending some time in the regular classroom) to the maximum extent possible (located at http://kidstogether.org/right-ed_files/daniel.htm).

Oberti v. Board of Education of Borough of Clementon School District **(Third Circuit, 1993)**

In *Oberti v. Board of Education of Borough of Clementon School District* (1993), the Third Circuit Court ruled that the school district bore the burden of proof in LRE cases and that mere token attempts at inclusion on the part of the district were not satisfactory to meet the requirement. Rafael Oberti was a student with Down syndrome placed in a developmental

kindergarten class in New Jersey school district. He was reported to show disruptive behaviors and was difficult for the teacher to manage. The Findings of Fact in this case chronicled that the school district did not provide enough support, or even effort, to make the placement work. The court concluded that the preference for mainstreaming was so strong that the argument in favor of the placement could be rebutted only if the school district could prove any of the following: (1) the student would receive little or no benefit from the inclusion placement, (2) the student would be so disruptive that other students' learning would be impaired, or (3) the cost of providing services in the regular classroom would have a negative effect on other students. The court found that, in this case, additional teacher training might have eliminated any potential disruption to the classroom and that the necessity to modify the curriculum was not a reason for exclusion (located at http://www.kidstogether.org/right-ed_files/oberti.htm).

Sacramento City Unified School District v. Rachel H. **(Ninth Circuit, 1994)**

Sacramento City Unified School District v. Rachel H. (1994) case involved a child with mental retardation whose parents wanted her fully included in a regular classroom (located at http://www.kidstogether.org/right-ed_files/rachel.htm). In the *Rachel H.* case, the Ninth Circuit Court established the following four-factor balancing test to consider in determining appropriate placement:

1. The educational benefits of full-time placement in a regular class.

2. The nonacademic benefits of such a placement.

3. The effects of the student on the teacher and other children in the class.

4. The cost of a regular education placement with appropriate supplementary aids and services.

In these referenced cases, the courts set forth criteria that subsequently assisted IEP teams in making decisions about placement in the least restrictive environment. School districts bear the responsibility of demonstrating that a less restrictive environment cannot work, rather than arguing for more restrictive placement without first attempting the less restrictive.

Poolaw v. Bishop (Ninth Circuit, 1995)

Poolaw v. Bishop (1995) was a Ninth Circuit Court decision that affirmed an Arizona District. In this particular case, the courts set forth criteria that subsequently assisted IEP teams in making a decision in favor of placing a 13-year-old student with significant communication needs requiring intensive instruction in American Sign Language at the state school for the deaf. Notably, the Ninth Circuit Court commented on IDEA's LRE requirement:

In some cases, such as where the child's handicap *[sic]* is particularly severe, it will be impossible to provide any meaningful education to the student in a mainstream environment. In these situations, continued mainstreaming would be inappropriate and educators may recom-

mend placing the child in a special education environment.

McWhirt by McWhirt v. Williamson County School (Sixth Circuit, 1994)

McWhirt by McWhirt v. Williamson County School (1994) is a Sixth Circuit Court inclusion decision that a fourth-grade student with multiple disabilities be placed appropriately in a comprehensive special education class with partial mainstreaming rather than in the less restrictive resource room desired by her parents. The Sixth Circuit found that the severe nature of the student's disabilities prevented her from "functioning constructively in regular education."

Kari H. v. Franklin Special School District (Sixth Circuit, 1995)

The Sixth Circuit Court later relied on its authority in *McWhirt by McWhirt v. Williamson County School* in its ruling on *Kari H. v. Franklin Special School District* (1995). In this case, the inappropriate behaviors of the student in previous mainstream placements, as well as the functional gains she could realize in a special education classroom, were determined by the court to outweigh any minimal benefit she might realize from placement in the regular classroom.

A series of cases since the late nineties have dealt with questions of what school districts were required to provide and fund under special education law. In these cases the courts focused on how failure to follow procedural requirements can be interpreted as a denial of FAPE.

Cedar Rapids Community School District v. Garret F. (U.S. Supreme Court, 1999)

In the case of *Garret F.*, the U.S. Supreme Court was asked to consider whether a school district was required to fund necessary nursing services for a ventilator-dependent student, Garret F. The district argued that the nursing services were medical in nature, and therefore should not be the responsibility of the school district to fund. The Court of Appeals disagreed, finding that these services would fall in the range of "related services" under the IDEA. In their ruling, affirming the Court of Appeals, the U.S. Supreme Court stated:

> This case is about whether meaningful access to the public schools will be assured, not the level of education that a school must finance once access is attained. It is undisputed that the services at issue must be provided if Garret is to remain in school.

> Under the statute, our precedent, and the purposes of the IDEA, the district must fund such "related services" in order to help guarantee that students like Garret are integrated into the public schools.

Cronkite v. State of California and Long Beach Unified School District, 25 IDELR 947 (C.D. Calif. 1999) *White v. School Board of Henrico City,* 549 S.E. 2d 16 (Va. Ct. app. 2001)

In *Cronkite* and *White* the courts ruled that the district's proposed offer was designed to provide the student an opportunity to make educational progress, and therefore met FAPE standards.

Nein v. Greater Clark County School Corp., 95 F. Supp. 2d 961 (S.D. Ind. 2000) *R. R. v. Wallingford Board of Education,* 35 IDELR 32 (D. Conn. 2001)

In *Nein* and *R. R.*, the students received special education and related services and did not make progress after several years. Parents unilaterally placed their children in private schools and the districts were ordered to reimburse the families for costs of the private placement.

Kevin T. v. Elmhurst Community School District No. 205 (U.S. District Court for the Northern District of Illinois, 2002)

This case involved the denial of FAPE to a 19-year-old student with a learning disability, ADHD, and bipolar disorder. Throughout his educational career, his skills declined, and he achieved failing grades. The analysis of the case involves an examination of the credibility of the witnesses, and although the teacher and case carrier were found to be credible witnesses, it was determined by the court that the school psychologist's testimony was evasive and inconsistent. Problems with the IEPs included the following: (1) the goals and objectives were the same for three years; (2) the IEP team ignored the recommendations of an independent evaluator; (3) the district failed to review and revise the IEP; (4) the district did not address the student's reading difficulties; (5) the district did not change the IEP when the student had increasing academic problems; (6) the district did not consider if the student needed assistive technology; (7) the district failed to appropriately address the required provisions for statewide assessment and how the student would participate; and (8) the transition plan was not appropriate. Despite all of Kevin's difficulties in school, the district decided to issue a standard diploma to him. The Court found that he was inappropriately graduated and ordered compensatory education until the time he reached age 21.

M. L. by C. D. and S. L. v. Federal Way School District (Ninth Circuit, 2003)

In this case, school district's failure to include a general education teacher in the IEP meeting for a student who was being transferred to a special day class created a structural defect so significant that it resulted in an automatic denial of FAPE.

Court cases may seem like they are remote and removed from the daily work of speech-language pathologists and audiologists in public schools. These cases do, however, strongly influence the direction given by administrators to IEP teams so that current rulings are reflected in decision making. Table 2.4 and Table 8.2 on pp. 320–321 illustrate the effect of the outcome of cases on the practice of speech-language pathologists and audiologists.

Educational Benefit

The *Rowley* standard has long established that IEPs must confer educational benefit upon the student. What is educational benefit under this standard? In general, it means that there is evidence that a FAPE was provided in the LRE and resulted in educational advancement for the student due to the provision of special education and related services needed to address the stu-

dent's unique educational needs. The educational benefit standard is being given increasing attention under IDEA 2004. Under the standards of *Rowley* and educational benefit, process and procedures are critical, in addition to being able to demonstrate that the student made progress in the general education curriculum and on IEP goals.

Under IDEA 2004, the Congress established that special education must prepare students to lead productive and independent adult lives. IDEA 2004 also aligns academic demands with those of general education, increasing expectations for academic success. Both of these impact how FAPE will continue to be defined and challenged.

Application of FAPE and LRE to Speech-Language and Hearing Services

Educators feel the impact of legislative and judicial decisions on their daily work. Speech-language and hearing programs must comply with FAPE and LRE guidelines. To ensure that all children receive FAPE, the child's evaluation must be "sufficiently comprehensive to identify all of the child's special education and related services needs, whether or not commonly linked to the disability category in which the child has been classified" (34 C.F.R. § 300.304 [6]). To ensure that LRE is achieved, states are required to provide a "continuum of alternative placements to meet the unique needs of each child with a disability" (34 C.F.R. § 300.303). Speech-language

Table 2.4

A Summary of Key Court Cases and Their Effect on the Practice of Speech-Language Pathologists

Court Case	Court Direction	Effect on Speech-Language Pathologists' Practice
Board of Education v. Rowley (1982) (State of New York; Supreme Court Decision)	• Set standard for determination of FAPE • Ruled a goal of special education is not to maximize potential • Ruled a goal of special education is access to educational benefit	Influences decisions for recommendations for therapy
Daniel R. R. v. State Board of Education (1989) (State of Texas; Fifth Circuit Court of Appeals)	• Set guidelines for determination of provision of supplementary aids and services to modify the regular classroom in order for the child to receive educational benefit • Considered the influence of the child with a disability on the education of other children in the class	Influences the need for speech-language services to be provided either in the general education classroom or in conjunction with the work of the classroom (i.e., the curriculum)
Oberti v. Board of Education of Borough of Clementon School District (1993) (State of New Jersey; Third Circuit Court of Appeals)	• Placed the burden of proof on the school district to demonstrate that the student would receive no educational benefit from educational placement in a regular classroom • Recommended teacher training to deal with potential problems • Ruled a need to modify the curriculum was not a reason for exclusion	Influences the need to work with families and requests for services in the regular classroom; must attempt and prove a type of service delivery does not work
Sacramento City USD v. Rachel H. (1994) (State of California; Ninth Circuit Court of Appeals)	• Established four-factor balancing test to determine FAPE • Considered educational and nonacademic benefits	Means educational and nonacademic benefit must be basis of placement considerations
Poolaw v. Bishop (1995) (State of Arizona; Ninth Circuit Court of Appeals)	• Found that in certain cases, the severity of the student's disability may require a more restrictive environment to provide the child educational benefit	Allows for consideration of specialized communication needs
McWhirt by McWhirt v. Williamson County School (1994) (State of Tennessee; Sixth Circuit Court of Appeals) and *Kari H. v. Franklin Special School District* (1995) (State of Tennessee; Sixth Circuit U.S. District Court)	• Determined that the severe nature of a student's disability can prevent the student from receiving educational benefit in a regular classroom	When working as part of an individualized education program team, one considers the complexities of the disability for program service decisions

pathologists and audiologists need to provide a continuum of services using several different service delivery models, which may include collaboration, co-teaching, direct/pull-out services, consultation, and others. A one-size-fits-all model might have been typical of service delivery in the early 1970s, but is not in the spirit of FAPE and LRE.

The continuum of special education programs in schools must also be broad. This means that not only will the continuum of placements be extensive (i.e., resource room, special class, related services, special school), but also that the service delivery models of each will be varied. In working with other members of the IEP team, speech-language pathologists and audiologists will need to coordinate their services with the continua and delivery models of other service providers. These new and evolving applications of FAPE and LRE can provide rich rewards for students and service providers (see Chapter 5 for a further discussion of service delivery).

CHAPTER 3

Referral and Assessment

IN THIS CHAPTER

This chapter describes the process that results in a student being identified as requiring special education services. The chapter examines prereferral requirements, including the response to intervention (RtI) process; the referral and assessment process; as well as highlights assessment methods that are considered to be good practice for speech-language services. The importance of procedural timelines are discussed.

1. Discuss the speech-language pathologist's role in assessment.

2. How does response to intervention (RtI) affect speech-language assessment in the schools?

3. What are the various types of assessment methods that may be used by the speech-language pathologist or audiologist, and when would each method be appropriate?

4. Outline the requirements for assessment and eligibility determination under IDEA 2004.

Child Find Obligations

Under the federal requirements of special education, school districts are obligated to conduct CHILD FIND, a system to locate, evaluate, and serve children with disabilities.

The Code of Federal Regulations (C.F.R.) requires the following:

(a) *General.* (1) The State must have in effect policies and procedures to ensure that—

(i) All children with disabilities..., including children with disabilities who are homeless children or are wards of the State, and children with disabilities attending private schools, regardless of the severity of their disability, and who are in need of special education and related services, are identified, located, and evaluated (34 C.F.R. § 300.111 [a]).

The history of the requirements of Child Find date back to the enabling legislation of special education, P. L. 94-142, when children with disabilities were not being consistently served in our public schools. In the preamble to the INDIVIDUALS WITH DISABILITIES EDUCATION ACT (IDEA) 1997, Congress stated that public schools had realized the intent of finding and serving children with disabilities under this act, but now needed to focus the law on producing results for children served under special education. IDEA 2004 makes it clear that Child Find obligations also apply to homeless children, children in private schools, as noted above, but that Child Find obligations also apply to:

Children who are suspected of being a child with a disability... and in need of special education even though they are advancing from grade to grade; and (2) Highly mobile children, including migrant children (34 C.F.R. § 300.111 [c] [1][2]).

Child Find obligations are an integral part of the special education process. The avenues by which children are referred for evaluation to determine special education eligibility are sophisticated and sometimes complicated processes. Special education processes and procedures are important because failure to follow these processes may lead to a denial of the child's rights and protections under special education laws.

The processes and procedures referred to in the C.F.R. vary from state to state and from local school district to local school district, but in essence encompass the same basic processes, which will be defined in the rest of this section. These procedures are necessary and important to follow for many reasons, but most importantly so that children receive the assistance they need and that their rights are not violated.

Avenues to Referral

Not all children come to school having the same background and opportunities. Children come to school from homes in which English is the primary language and homes in which English is not the primary language; homes with hundreds of books and homes with no books; homes in which bedtime stories are read every night and homes in which no one has the LITERACY skills to help children with homework. Regardless of their background, public education in the United States greets all of these children and more.

Teachers and other educators are under a considerable amount of pressure at the beginning of the twenty-first century to provide high-quality education to students, in order to develop future workers for an economy that promises to be dramatically different from that which the teachers knew. Children who do not successfully develop skills in math, language, reading, and problem solving will have great difficulty securing employment in the Digital Age. The economic reality of the widening gap between what is

needed in the future work world and the potential for success for individuals who do not secure a solid education is cause for concern. Educators must face the weighty burden of dealing with each and every child who does not bring to the classroom the tools and circumstances that typically spell success. This situation is not new to schools. What is new is the high-profile focus on school reform, the keen societal interest in test

scores and student performance, and the reality of an economic future that will not have vocational jobs for an unskilled labor force.

How students will be referred to speech, hearing, and special education programs is undergoing a dramatic shift from what it was in the first 30 years of special education. The reason for this shift is a combination of legislative, research, and policy practices that represent a new way of thinking about what constitutes a disability as well as clearly identify the responsibilities of both general and special education. Traditionally, students were referred to the Special Education Assessment Team either from a STUDENT STUDY TEAM (SST) or through a direct referral to the speech-language pathologist or audiologist for testing. This older model of referral reflected a fundamental belief in the educational system that if a child was struggling, there must be something "wrong" with the child. Student Study Teams and Special Education Assessment Teams then, in essence, went in search of what was "wrong" with the child, oftentimes with little consideration for the environment in which the child was being taught, the child's educational history, or the competence of the instructor. Within the focus of NO CHILD LEFT BEHIND (NCLB) and IDEA 2004 underlies a belief that the system needs to adjust to the needs of the learners, and must support learners when they struggle. The application of this belief is demonstrated in the ways that we now use to determine who receives and does not receive speech and language or special education services.

There is another reason why the referral and assessment process has changed under IDEA 2004. Policymakers and local school districts have been suffering under the financial burden that has been placed upon them by special education costs and the underfunding of special education (see Chapter 9). Additionally, the increase in the number of students in special education has been staggering in recent years, adding to the costs (see Chapter 1 and Chapter 9).

IDEA 2004 and NCLB are meant to work together, as are general and special education. Children with educationally disabling conditions are identified for service under strict eligibility categories defined by law. The rest of this chapter discusses how students are referred and assessed to determine eligibility for services under IDEA 2004.

Response to Intervention and Early Intervening Services

Preventing Students from Needing Special Education: How We Conceptualize Disability

The movement toward EARLY INTERVENING SERVICES and RESPONSE TO INTERVENTION (RtI) represents clear congressional intent to change the way special education services are delivered in this country, beginning with the identification and eligibility phase of the process. This change represents a need for broad system revision in our educational system for both general and special education. As this change is occurring, speech-language pathologists and other special educators will need to remember the new premise of our identification system: Students cannot be identified for special education services if they have not been instructed.

The basis of the change represents an evolution in the philosophical base of our concepts of disability, specifically learning disability, as well as concerns over the rising costs of special education, consequently leading to policy changes in operational procedures. Since 2001, with the new requirements of NCLB in place, a national effort has been underway to make schools accountable for the learning of every student. What all of these efforts have in common is addressing student learning needs quickly and efficiently. Making a struggling student "wait to fail" before providing special attention or instruction was not an effective way to provide students with assistance.

Response to Intervention (RtI)

Response to intervention (RtI) programs are those which provide short-term interventions to determine how struggling students respond before assuming they must have a disability and referring them for special education assessment. The premise of RtI emphasizes a process whereby we look at how the system addresses student needs before we look at "within learner" challenges to explain why students are struggling. RtI allows for multiple attempts to provide assistance to students before identifying them as students with disabilities. RtI programs are typically operated within a tiered model of school support designed to have multiple ways to assist students.

RtI programs are intended to address learning and behavioral needs of students. IDEA 2004 established that students may not be called disabled if they have not been instructed. This specifically applies to students with learning disabilities and speech-language disorders, which are considered "high incidence disabilities," as they are the most frequently occurring educational disabilities. Criticism of the way the educational system previously dealt with students who had academic or behavioral issues was that they were: (1) not helped early, and (2) placed in special education after long periods of school failure.

The National Association of State Directors of Special Education (NASDSE; Batsche et al., 2005) defines RtI as "the practice of providing high-quality instruction and intervention matched to student need, monitoring progress frequently to make decisions about changes in instruction or goals, and applying child response data to important educational decisions" (p. 3). NASDSE identifies the following as the core principles of RtI:

- Effectively teach all children.

- Intervene early.

- Use a multi-tier model of service delivery.

- Use a problem-solving method to make decisions within a multi-tier model.

    1. Is there a problem and what is it?

    2. Why is this happening?

    3. What are we going to do about it?

    4. Did our intervention work?

- Use research-based, scientifically validated interventions/instruction to the extent available.

- Monitor student progress to inform instruction.

- Use data to make decisions. A data-based decision regarding student response to intervention is central to RtI practices.

- Use assessment for three different purposes:

    1. Screening applied to all children to identify those who are not making academic or behavioral progress at expected rates.

    2. Diagnostics to determine what children can and cannot do in important academic and behavioral domains.

    3. Progress monitoring to determine if academic or behavioral interventions are producing desired effects (pp. 19–20).

IDEA 2004 promotes the use of special education funds for early intervening services to assist students who are not yet eligible for special education. Under IDEA (1997), special educators were *allowed* to work with nonidentified students; but IDEA 2004 *encourages* special educators to work with nonidentified students.

The Code of Federal Regulations describes how special education can do this:

- An LEA may use up to 15 percent of its funds to develop and implement coordinated early intervening services. Agencies may blend funding to coordinate programs for students in kindergarten through Grade 12 (with particular emphasis on students in kindergarten through Grade 3) to provide additional academic and behavioral supports that promote success in a general education environment (C.F.R. § 613 [f][1]).

• Funds may be used for professional development for teachers and other school staff to learn scientifically based academic instruction and behavioral interventions. Topics may include scientifically based literacy instruction, use of adaptive and instructional software, and providing educational and behavioral evaluations, services, and supports (C.F.R. § 613 [2]).

• May coordinate IDEA-funded activities with those being carried out under NCLB (C.F.R. § 613 [f][5]).

Speech-language pathologists should become actively involved in the development of early intervening service models at their schools. Early intervening services are intended to prevent students from requiring special education and related services. Shifting to these models is part of school reform efforts. Early intervening services may include RtI programs.

A Tiered System of Support for All Learners

Struggling students in our educational system have traditionally had few resources available to them which could address their issues. With the advent of NCLB and the movement of the educational system to provide systemic supports to struggling learners, a new configuration of support systems is developing within our schools. A TIERED SYSTEM of supports allows learners to receive assistance when they begin to demonstrate difficulties, and do not have to

"wait to fail," as happened under the old model of special education.

Under the tiered model of supports, intensity of interventions is heightened as students need more intervention (McCook, 2006).

Tier I = General education core instruction

Tier II = Strategic; targeted group instruction

Tier III = Intense, individual or group instruction

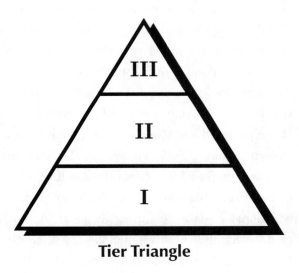

Tier Triangle

General education is responsible for these interventions; however, special education staff may be involved at all levels. IDEA 2004 formalized the working of special education staff with non-IDEA identified students who are struggling and may need assistance or intervention from staff with specialized expertise. This involvement of special education staff in providing assistance to general education struggling learners may be provided through early intervening services, which can be utilized at any of the tiers.

The concept of a tiered system of supports has become a clear way to describe a systemic approach to assist struggling learners. This model is seen not only in the literature on RtI (Batsche et al., 2005), but also in the model on professional and small learning communities (DuFour, DuFour, Eakert, & Karhanek, 2004). The model represents a system of supports for all learners in each classroom.

The use of scientifically based instruction, as mandated under both NCLB and IDEA 2004, begins at Tier I. When effective core instructional strategies and principles are utilized, it is expected that the majority of the learners in the classroom (80–90 percent) will benefit. Students who struggle in the general education classroom (10–20 percent) may need to be moved to Tier II for targeted assistance. Within Tier II, it is expected that 80–85 percent of the students will benefit from that program, leading either to returning the student to Tier I or perhaps additional assistance through Tier II. A much smaller number of students, then, will continue to struggle and require intensive assistance through Tier III. Each of these tiers involves interventions provided through general education resources, including Title I or other categorical programs. Special education staff may provide early intervening services for students in any of the tiers, but it is most likely that intense services are provided at Tier III. See Table 3.1 for the instructional characteristics and methods that may be used at each tier.

Critical to the implementation of a tiered model of instructional supports is an Instructional Support Team. (See "Instructional Support or Instructional Consultation Team" on p. 83 for more information.) Under the INSTRUCTIONAL SUPPORT TEAM (IST) or INSTRUCTIONAL CONSULTATION TEAM (ICT) model, the team is charged with looking at factors external to the student rather than deficits within the student. Importantly, the first step to assistance is not special education.

According to Rosenfield and Gravois (1996):

First, how learning problems are understood is important; they may be defined as internal deficits within children or as a mismatch between how student abilities and the school's attempts to meet the student needs. Each of these assumptions reflects different attitudes and beliefs. As long as individual student disability is perceived as the dominant cause of school failure, public education will be able to avoid undertaking the kind of reforms needed for all students to succeed (Skrtic, 1991, p. 4).

The second underlying issue is that of administrative support for educating all students—administrators and policymakers must demonstrate a commitment to funding appropriate, restructured services. Also required are guarantees to maintain special education and pupil personnel services (albeit in a restructured form), adequate student-teacher ratios, and evaluation of outcomes…Ultimately, change will be impossible unless there is a basic trust that resources will not be withdrawn as the number of labeled handicapped *[sic]* students decreased and administration will not place students with special needs into a classroom setting without adequate support to the classroom teacher (p. 4–5).

Table 3.1	**Instructional Characteristics and Methods of a Tiered System**	
Tier	**Instructional Characteristics**	**Methods**
I	Methodologies that enhance the likelihood of learner success for ALL learners	Universal Instruction Universal Design Differentiated Instruction Universal Screening
	Progress is monitored for all students	
II	Methodologies are targeted to address learner needs and enhance likelihood of learner success	Targeted Instruction
	Intervention provided for a specified period of time	Selected interventions utilizing scientifically based instructional strategies that may not be available through general education
	Progress is monitored to determine response to intervention	Increased intensity
		Smaller group size
III	Methodologies that are specialized to address learner needs and enhance likelihood of learner success	May use programs and strategies previously reserved for special education
	Intervention provided for a specified period of time	May be provided by special educators as early intervening services
	Progress is monitored to determine response to intervention	May be small group or individualized instruction

Source: Moore-Brown (2006). Reprinted with permission.

Scientifically Based Research

"....research that involves the application of rigorous, systematic, and objective procedures to obtain reliable and valid knowledge relevant to education activities and programs" (NCLB § 9101 [37]).

Working within a tiered system provides opportunities for all students to learn, benefits English learners and other students in need of intense language experiences due to linguistic deficits that are not due to a disability, and allows for progress monitoring to determine students' response to intervention.

Under this type of system, speech-language pathologists and other special educators will be working "inside" and "outside" of special education. The philosophy of this approach is to allow students access to specialists so that we might prevent students from becoming identified for special education.

According to Trioa (2005), speech-language pathologists may play these different roles in each of the tiers:

Tier I – Assist in providing professional development to teachers

- Provide strategies for teaching literacy-based skills such as alphabetic principle, strategies for decoding and spelling, and how to deliver instruction.

- Provide instruction in later vocabulary development, roots and prefixes, and how to select scientifically validated materials.

- Consult on how to deliver effective universal instruction, set up screening, and monitor progress.

- Monitor and assist school teams.

Tier II – Consultant for teams delivering targeted instruction/interventions

- Provide directed instruction for diagnostic/therapeutic instructional purposes.

- Make recommendations for interventions that prevent long term problems. (If the student does not respond to the interventions, then a comprehensive assessment may be indicated.)

Tier III – Provide direct and/or indirect intervention

- Provide specialized treatments for poor readers with language deficits who have not responded to universal instruction and targeted interventions.

- Consult with special educators to help them make their services maximally beneficial.

Early Intervening Services

The focus of both NCLB and IDEA 2004 is to intervene early with struggling students. Districts may use IDEA 2004 funds to develop policies and procedures to assist students who are not currently identified for special education but may be in need of additional academic assistance (Norlin, 2005). Early intervening services can be developed for use at all levels, but the law encourages emphasis on students in kindergarten through Grade 3 who need additional academic or behavioral supports (IDEA 2004, § 613 [f][1]). Early intervening services may be either professional development activities or evaluation services and supports, including scientifically based literacy instruction (IDEA 2004, § 613 [f][2]).

Speech-language pathologists will recognize that early intervening services, along with appropriate identification and intervention procedures, and the use of EVIDENCE-BASED PRACTICE and a WORKLOAD analysis approach, will reshape their model for service in a positive way. As early intervening service models develop throughout the country, they will likely be based upon RtI models that have proven successful, as well as the development of new RtI-type models in the future (Montgomery & Moore-Brown, 2005).

One comprehensive model that has been successful is the Iowa Problem Solving Model that will be discussed later in this chapter (Area Education Agency 6, 2000; Tilly, 2003). (See Figure 3.2 on p. 87 and Figure 3.3 on p. 88.) Many local districts have been establishing models that have been successful, including one model using a nine-week intense literacy instruction program co-taught by resource specialists and speech-language pathologists (Moore-Brown, Montgomery, Bielinski, & Shubin, 2005), as well as an expanded screening model for providing articulation intervention prior to identification, and a clinical reading model where the speech-language pathologist instructs first and second graders in phonemic awareness for 20 minutes three times a week, for three months. All of these models have proven successful in preventing students from ultimately requiring special education (Montgomery & Moore-Brown, 2005).

School districts are required under IDEA 2004 to document their early intervening services and report how many students avoided special education. It is important for speech-language pathologists to communicate with administrators when developing these programs, to be sure of the documentation necessary and to provide appropriate notice to parents.

Early intervening services have both funding and practice implications. These are discussed in Chapter 9, but are featured in the sidebar on pp. 76–78 as well. Early intervening services are not limited to speech-language intervention. Audiologists may also be able to consult or provide interventions in auditory training, acoustic modifications, or consultation services for students with hearing issues.

Screening Procedures

In some school districts, speech-language pathologists engage in individual or mass screenings annually or periodically to identify students with communication difficulties who may not be referred by teachers, other professionals, or parents. Screening refers to a rapid pass/fail procedure used by speech-language pathologists to record communicative behaviors of all students of a particular grade level, category, or class and identify candidates for formal evaluation. The speech-language pathologist may, for example, screen all kindergartners, all third graders, all new students, all children at risk, or all children in the first quartile of reading achievement. This practice, while still evident in some school districts, is gradually being eliminated in most systems for a variety of reasons.

Screening for communication impairments based upon a direct referral to the speech-language pathologist is discouraged under current practice, although screening is still included in the ASHA PREFERRED PRACTICE PATTERNS in assessment. The key is distinguishing between screening, assessment, and observation. If the purpose of the screening is to determine whether or not a student has a disability, then the

Early Intervening Services
Funding Implications

The Individuals with Disabilities Education Improvement Act (IDEA 2004) includes a new provision for the use of up to 15 percent of Part B funds for early intervening services. Part B is the portion of IDEA which requires special education services for identified students ages 3 to 22. Early intervening services allow for the use of these funds for programs and services to nonidentified students who are struggling academically and/or behaviorally, and who could benefit from the resources normally reserved for students in special education. Permissive use of funds for prereferral activities was allowed under IDEA (1997). The specific provisions for Early Intervening Services in IDEA 2004 make it very clear that Congress intends for special education to be engaged in activities which will prevent students from ultimately needing special education identification.

The early intervening services provision addresses concerns about the much criticized "wait to fail" model of special education identification, specifically in the area of learning disabilities. Through the use of early intervening services and adoption of response to intervention (RtI) models, struggling students can receive academic and behavioral supports prior to being special education eligible. The intent of this provision is to prevent ultimate special education identification by supporting and assisting these students early.

The section of the Code of Federal Regulations (C.F.R. § 300.226 [b]) which outlines early intervening services indicates that these services may include:

(1) Professional development (which may be provided by entities other than local education agencies (LEAs) for teachers and other school staff to enable them to deliver scientifically based academic instruction and behavioral interventions, including scientifically based literacy instruction and, when appropriate, instruction on the use of adaptive and instructional software; and

(2) Providing educational and behavioral evaluations, services, and supports, including scientifically based literacy instruction.

Commentary by the U.S. Department of Education (USDE) to the C.F.R. clarifies the following about early intervening services:

- Not to delay an evaluation of a student suspected of having a disability
- Recipients do not have the rights and protections of special education
- Intended for students in grades K–12
- Emphasis on K–3

Continued

Early Intervening Services – *Continued*

- Cannot be used for preschool
- May be used to purchase instructional materials to support these efforts
- May include related services personnel in the development and delivery of educational and behavioral evaluations, services, and supports

The following comment is made by USDE in relation to the funds and the rationale for allocating special education funds in this way:

"The authority to use some Part B funds for early intervening services has the potential to benefit special education, as well as the education of other children, by reducing academic and behavioral problems in the regular education environment and reducing the number of referrals to special education interventions. Therefore, we believe the use of Part B funds for early intervening services should be encouraged, rather than restricted" (C.F.R., Commentary, pp. 46626–46627).

School districts with significant disproportionality of students in special education based on race and ethnicity will be required to utilize 15 percent of their Part B funds for early intervening services to serve children in the LEA particularly, but not exclusively, children in those groups that were significantly overidentified.

States will be required to identify the specifics of how early intervening services will be provided, including who will be involved. The C.F.R. Commentary provided by the USDE states, "Nothing in this Act or regulations prevents States and LEAs from including related services personnel in the development and delivery of educational and behavioral evaluations, services, and supports for teachers and other school staff to enable them to deliver coordinated early intervening services" (C.F.R. Commentary, pp. 46627–46628).

Early Intervening Services and Speech-Language Pathologists

Using special education funds to provide early intervening services to nonidentified, but struggling, students is an example of funding flexibility. Special education personnel have historically limited their work exclusively to students with identified disabilities in most situations. With early intervening services provisions under IDEA 2004, the resources of special education, including personnel time, can and should be spent in part on attempting to prevent struggling students from needing special education identification.

Through this new avenue, speech-language pathologists have a unique opportunity to engage in prevention activities, including collaboration and consultation, professional development for teachers, and direct and indirect services through RtI programs for struggling students.

Continued

Early Intervening Services – *Continued*

Because this is a shift in how the speech-language pathologist's time is spent, coordination at the school and district level will be needed. New reporting requirements will require tracking which students receive early intervening services, so the process for referral and the type of services provided must be clearly identified.

Practice Implications

The clear intent of Congress is to utilize the expertise of special education professionals, including speech-language pathologists, to begin to work with students who are struggling academically, in order to prevent the need for such students from becoming IDEA 2004 eligible. In doing so, caseload counts will decrease. However, while this concept is readily understood by both general and special education, a shift in practice will be required. Speech-language pathologists and other special educators who engage in early intervening services must account for their time, so that it is recognized as part of the 15 percent (early intervening services) Part B funding. Additionally, general and special education staff must look at their current model of referral and supports for students to ensure that old methods which are not consistent with this intent are updated.

Some speech-language pathologists are concerned about new requirements or trends to work with nonidentified students for the following reasons: (1) they imagine that this work will be in addition to already demanding workloads, and (2) the funding formula in their state counts identified students, so may result in a decrease in funds for the school district.

Some specialists are also concerned that if they reduce their caseloads, positions will be cut or eliminated. Again, because the new requirements encourage the use of special education funds to serve nonidentified students, this concern should not be realized. However, it is important for all parties, particularly administrators and business staff, to understand that the funding of positions should not be established on caseload counts.

Maintenance of Effort requirements for special education also prevent such reductions in staffing when reduction in caseload counts is realized.

Some people are excited when they hear about "the 15 percent" of funds that can be allocated to early intervening services. It is important to remember that this is 15 percent of the Part B funds, not a new pot of money. Accessing and tracking these funds is important. By providing early intervening services speech-language pathologists can not only positively affect student performance for all students, but also begin to implement workload management efforts. Speech-language pathologists in schools are encouraged to be a part of local planning and implementation.

screening can be construed as an assessment, and therefore would need parental consent. A good rule of thumb is that anything that is done for an individual student versus the whole group (e.g., classroom) of students, likely would need parental consent, even for an observation or screening.

Screening usually employs a short face-to-face interview with the child, but screening may also include a teacher interview. The speech-language pathologist engages each child in a series of questions, a conversation, or both, to decide if more in-depth observation or assessment is necessary. If the speech-language pathologist conducts a screening program, his or her responsibilities are as follows:

- Select screening measures with technical adequacy.

- Administer and/or interpret a speech-language screening.

- Administer and/or interpret a hearing screening in accordance with state and local policy, procedures, and staffing patterns (ASHA, 2004e).

The main reason that screening is not indicated as a preferred practice in the public schools is that students must be considered in the instructional environment in which they are achieving or not achieving and that all areas of suspected disability must be considered if a child is having difficulty in school. Under the tiered model of interventions, screening of a different kind occurs. This screening is known as Universal Screening and applies to all children in the general education classroom. Through universal screening, the progress of all children in the educational system is monitored and considered closely. This type of screening is not the responsibility of special education personnel, but of general educational personnel. When students are not progressing in the manner in which they should, appropriate interventions should be applied. However, this does not mean that these children may require special education, only that they may require intense instruction in their areas of need. (See "To Screen or Not to Screen" in Appendix B for further discussion on the screening process.)

The Code of Federal Regulations does clarify that screening for instructional purposes is not evaluation:

> The screening of a student by a teacher or specialist to determine appropriate instructional strategies for curriculum implementation shall not be considered to be an evaluation for eligibility for special education and related services (34 C.F.R. § 300.302).

Instruction and Interventions in a School Reform Environment

Schools across the United States are concerned with student learning in ways that are previously unprecedented. Throughout this book, speech-language pathologists and audiologists who work in schools are encouraged to understand and participate in school reform efforts. Understanding the issues and pressures of public education will help in adjusting to the demands placed upon the educational system. "Public school educators in the United States are now required to do something they have never before been asked to accomplish: ensure high levels of learning for all students" (DuFour et al., 2004).

In order to address the requirements of NCLB and meet the mandates demanding high achievement, many schools have embarked upon initiatives to strengthen the teaching/learning connection. Many schools are establishing systems which support student learning needs and are now addressing these needs systematically and routinely as part of their school operations. Professional Learning Communities (PLC) (DuFour et al., 2004) represent one way that schools are attempting to work collaboratively to create a school system which is designed specifically to address student learning needs. PLC schools focus on learning—not teaching—and create a positive environment for these learners and teachers (DuFour et al., 2004). A community of learners assures that the whole school has a culture of wanting to help as well as provides established interventions. For many years in education, students who struggled have had few opportunities for extra or specialized instruction outside of special education or Title I programs. In the current reform movement, and

within the context of accountability, school programs are now being designed to support learners who struggle.

Most efforts to improve student achievement in our schools involve total school restructuring and examining how the processes in our schools are designed to address student learning needs for all students. The focus of these efforts is to design an educational system that will focus on learning and provide supports and processes for those learners who struggle. These processes may involve special education personnel, but will not necessarily mean that all students will be identified as special education eligible.

The first step in creating schools that effectively meet the needs of all students is to begin with instruction in the general education classroom. Under the framework of the tiered approach, this is Tier I, but should also be considered "Job One" for all educators. In the era of accountability and a reform culture, schools are responsible for the learning of all students, so systems need to be in place which can address each student's learning needs. This is far different than sending a student somewhere other than the general education classroom for assistance if the student is not mastering the curriculum in the classroom. Manthey (2007) points out that students are sent out for "intervention," but that "instruction" occurs in the classroom.

The type of school system described here ties together all of the educational reform movements, specifically meeting mandates of NCLB to account for the learning of all students, addressing the needs and "accepting responsibility" for educational equity, referring to improving educational results for all diverse learners, including students of poverty, students of color, and students with special needs (Barron & Sanchez, 2007). In addition, the criticisms of the special education system also point to the need to enhance the general education program to support student learning, and not promulgate a system whereby struggling students are sent to a different place.

At the heart of this approach is defining what educators believe about students' learning struggles and the capability of the educational system to respond to these struggles. The focus on improving student achievement ties together several initiatives including the mandates of NCLB and IDEA 2004 to use scientifically based research practices, also known as evidence-based practice. Strong, powerful, proven instructional strategies are at the center of what general education needs to provide to all students, but educators also need to believe that all students can learn, and then act accordingly.

Research in school-based speech-language pathology has directed the field to curriculum, reading, and collaboration for the last 15 years. The new requirements for identification and accountability mean that speech-language pathologists working in schools must be well versed in standards and curriculum. The value added feature that speech-language pathologists can bring to the school environment lies in utilizing their expertise in considering how the language demands of the curriculum creates challenges for learners. The speech-language pathologist may be the only expert in the school who can understand this disconnect and generate solutions for struggling learners.

The Prereferral Prevention/Intervention Process

Long before a specialist becomes involved with a student for consultation or service, a teacher typically encounters the student in his or her prevention classroom. Observant general education teachers immediately assist students if they begin to struggle with classroom demands. Such assistance may include providing individualized instruction, assigning the student an instructional aide, changing or modifying the materials or mode of presentation, using peer or cross-age tutoring, changing the student's seating position in the classroom, or making a variety of other adjustments to the classroom instructional program. All of these approaches constitute good teaching and are usually appropriate and effective, though such strategies may need to be reintroduced several times during the year when progress or motivation is lacking. Students receiving such support are not likely to need outside assistance. However, if left unassisted, these students may continue to struggle and eventually be referred to the special education system.

Traditionally, speech-language pathologists in public schools only dealt with identification of and remediation for students with communication disorders. Today, however, speech-language pathologists are also engaged in prevention and prereferral activities. (See Figure 3.1 for the procedures for providing early intervening services for specific language impairment (SLI), which may be applied to intervention for other impairments as well.)

Figure 3.1

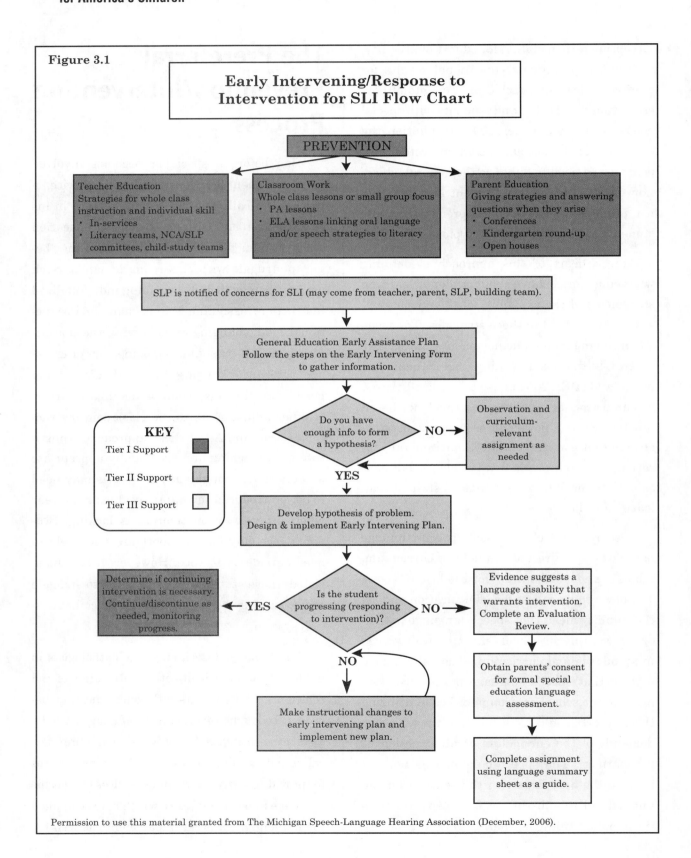

Early Intervening/Response to Intervention for SLI Flow Chart

PREVENTION

Teacher Education
Strategies for whole class instruction and individual skill
- In-services
- Literacy teams, NCA/SLP committees, child-study teams

Classroom Work
Whole class lessons or small group focus
- PA lessons
- ELA lessons linking oral language and/or speech strategies to literacy

Parent Education
Giving strategies and answering questions when they arise
- Conferences
- Kindergarten round-up
- Open houses

SLP is notified of concerns for SLI (may come from teacher, parent, SLP, building team).

General Education Early Assistance Plan
Follow the steps on the Early Intervening Form to gather information.

Do you have enough info to form a hypothesis?

NO → Observation and curriculum-relevant assignment as needed

YES

KEY
Tier I Support
Tier II Support
Tier III Support

Develop hypothesis of problem.
Design & implement Early Intervening Plan.

Is the student progressing (responding to intervention)?

YES → Determine if continuing intervention is necessary. Continue/discontinue as needed, monitoring progress.

NO → Evidence suggests a language disability that warrants intervention. Complete an Evaluation Review.

NO

Make instructional changes to early intervening plan and implement new plan.

Obtain parents' consent for formal special education language assessment.

Complete assignment using language summary sheet as a guide.

Permission to use this material granted from The Michigan Speech-Language Hearing Association (December, 2006).

#TP-29703 Making a Difference - 2nd Ed. • ©2008 Thinking Publications® • www.thinkingpublications.com • 1-800-277-8737

Instructional Support or Instructional Consultation Team

Nearly all schools have some type of formalized process to support students who are struggling, which is critical to the implementation of a tiered model. In the past, many schools utilized a Student Study Team (SST) model. The name of this team varied in different parts of the country (e.g., Student Success Team, Child Study Team, Student Assistance Team). Typically, these teams would analyze a student's strengths and needs, make recommendations, and follow-up. As a whole, the SST model was not proven successful for students, and was often criticized as being just a delay or precursor to special education. With the shift in focus from referring struggling learners for special education to providing more timely assistance within the realm of general education, this model has been replaced by Instructional Support Teams (ISTs) or Instructional Consultation Teams (ICTs). Using this approach, the team looks first at possible external factors, such as lack of instruction, rather than deficits within the student. In other words, the first step to assistance is not special education but providing assistance to the student, as determined by the team. The IST provides help to any student in the school who is having difficulties in the classroom, as well as his or her teachers and family, by using a problem-solving process to examine the instructional environment and how it is or is not assisting the student. The team usually consists of general education teachers from different grade levels, an administrator or counselor, a special education representative, and possibly the school psychologist or speech-language pa-

thologist. The parents, and student, if appropriate, are invited to the instructional support meeting. Under this model, the team facilitator leads the team in a problem-solving discussion about the student, following a familiar, two-part process, such as:

1. Gathering known information

   • What are the student's strengths?

   • What do we know about the student?

   • What are the concerns?

   • What intervention strategies (i.e., accommodations and modifications) have been attempted?

   • What were the results?

2. Troubleshooting

   • Brainstorm ideas for assistance.

   • Select what to try next and assign responsibility.

   • Schedule when to meet again to report on progress.

Strengthening general education programs to be able to address the learning needs of all students is central to improving all aspects of the overall educational system. Rosenfield and Gravois (1996) recommend developing a problem-solving culture within schools in order to accomplish this reform. Central to this culture is the concept that both students and teachers need to be learning all the time. This problem-solving approach allows a collaborative team to consult regarding students' learning needs, and then learn new ways to address the difficulties exhibited by students:

To increase student achievement toward the goal of producing learners and thinkers, we must in some way increase teacher learning and thinking. In this context, resolving problems regarding a student's difficulty in learning simple math processes implies that learners be able to learn and think about math processes in different ways. The bottom line is that looking for deficits within a student benefits neither the teacher nor the student in reaching the ultimate goal. To create learners and thinkers means that teachers need the support and resources to move themselves and their students toward this target (p. 8).

Again, a fundamental concept within this type of model is to first consider how the learning environment can be adjusted to address student learning needs, versus first assuming, or searching for needs within the student.

New concepts in expanding the resources available for students and teachers will reshape the way schools are structured. Under the system of Professional Learning Communities (PLC), these three critical questions drive how teachers, parents, and administrators work together to ensure that all students succeed:

1. Exactly what is it we want all students to learn?

2. How will we know when each student has acquired the essential knowledge and skills?

3. What happens in our school when a student does not learn (DuFour et al., 2004)?

According to NASDSE (Batsche et al., 2005), implementation of RtI requires three essential components:

1. Multiple tiers of intervention service delivery.

2. A problem-solving method.

3. An integrated data collection/assessment system to inform decisions at each tier of service delivery (p. 21).

Bradley, Danielson, and Doolittle (2007) cite the work of the National Research Center on Learning Disabilities (2006), which identified the following features of schools successfully implementing RtI:

- Students receive high-quality, research-based instruction from qualified staff in their general education setting.

- General education staff members assume an active role in student's assessment in the curriculum.

- School staff conducts universal screening of academics and behavior.

- School staff implements specific, research-based interventions to address the student's difficulties.

- School staff conducts continued progress monitoring of student performance (i.e., weekly or biweekly) for secondary and tertiary interventions and less frequently in general education.

- School staff uses progress monitoring data and explicit decision rules to determine interventions' effectiveness and necessary modifications.

- Systematic assessment is made regarding the fidelity or integrity with which instruction and interventions are implemented.

- RtI model includes, as required, provisions for referral for comprehensive evaluation, free appropriate public education, and due process protections (p. 10).

Fuchs and Fuchs (2007) outline decisions that schools must make regarding six components of RtI and offer the following recommendations.

1. **Decision**: How many tiers of intervention to use?

   Recommendation: Three tiers

   Tier I - Primary prevention: general education, universal core instructional program

   Tier II - Secondary prevention: small group tutoring in reading and math

   Tier III - Tertiary prevention: individualized programming and progress monitoring

2. **Decision**: How to target students for preventative intervention?

   Recommendation: Use universal screening and progress monitoring completed weekly for the first five weeks of the Tier II intervention.

3. **Decision**: What will be the nature of the preventative intervention?

   Recommendation: Use a combination of a problem-solving approach for behavioral problems and a standard treatment protocol for academic difficulties. The problem-solving approach includes preventative interventions that are individually designed for the student while the standard treatment protocol uses standard methods that have been shown to promote new skills in academic, behavioral, and attentional areas.

4. **Decision**: How to classify the response?

   Recommendation: Use a dual-discrepancy method which considers both the slope of improvement made by the student as well as the final level of the student, considering that both are at least one standard deviation below the mean.

5. **Decision**: What will be the nature of the multidisciplinary evaluation prior to special education?

   Recommendation: Conduct an "instructionally focused multidisciplinary evaluation designed to answer specific questions that arise during general education instruction and previous rounds of prevention, and that the special education multidisciplinary evaluation include a process for distinguishing among the high-incidence disabilities" (e.g., learning disabilities, speech-language impairment, mental retardation, emotional/behavioral disorders; p. 18).

6. **Decision**: What will be the function and design of special education?

   Recommendation: Special education should be "an important tier," designed to deliver intense instruction designed to address individual student needs, and flexible enough to allow students to move in and out of the tier as "needs change in relation to the demands of the general education curriculum" (p. 18).

A collaborative culture is a key component to designing schools that have a problem-solving approach (Rosenfield & Gravois, 1996; DuFour et al., 2004). Within these cultures, instructional support teams are built upon these three assumptions:

1. All students are learners.

2. When students struggle, we need to find an instructional match, not a place to send them.

3. A problem-solving learning community should exist in the school.

On the whole, the old SST process was not always successful in terms of providing supports that students needed. Instead, school systems should provide an environment where all resources and personnel are focused on addressing student learning needs, and everyone works together toward this goal. An example of this type of system change is highlighted by Vermont's Educational Support System (ESS):

> The ESS is conceptualized as an "umbrella" of preventative approaches, including effective, standards-based instructional practices for all students and individualized services and interventions for those students requiring more intensive levels of support. A key component of the ESS is the Educational Support Team (EST), which functions as a multidisciplinary problem-solving team designed to support students with academic or behavioral challenges. EST members collaborate to identify and monitor the implementation of classroom-based academic and behavioral interventions or to refer students when appropriate to additional supports and services, including special education (Shepard, 2006, p. 30).

A key finding in Shepard's study was the significance of the role of school principals in creating conditions within the school which advance the effectiveness of the EST. In these schools, "the participation of the principals on ESTs advanced the use of collaborative and data-based decision-making processes, and helped link team processes and outcomes to broader professional development and school improvement efforts" (p. 36).

The problem-solving process (see Figure 3.2) is recommended at every level or tier, and consists of the following steps:

- Define the problem (What is the problem and why is it happening?)

- Develop a plan (What are we going to do?)

- Implement the plan (Carry out the intervention)

- Evaluate (Did our plan work?) (Tilly, 2003; Batsche et al., 2005)

The problem-solving model and the speech-language pathologist's potential role was discussed in a presentation by Mills at the 2005 ASHA Convention in San Diego. Using the same basic four steps identified by NASDSE (Batsche et al., 2005) and Tilly (2003), Mills (2005), in Figure 3.3, illustrates how the problem-solving model increases the amount of resources allocated to match the intensity of the problem.

As models evolve to incorporate the above premises and operations, old practices will improve or be abandoned. The function of an Instructional Support Team (IST) is necessary to focus on individual student learning needs. However, these teams will have new and expanded obligations including suggesting and assisting in developing interventions within the tiers (e.g., Pyramid of Interventions) (DuFour et al., 2004), monitoring the effectiveness of the

---

Figure 3.2

Problem-Solving Process

• **Define the Problem**
(Screening and Diagnostic Assessments)
What is the problem and why is it happening?

• **Evaluate**
(Progress Monitoring
Assessment)

Did our plan work?

• **Develop a Plan**
(Goal Setting
and Planning)

What are we going to do?

• **Implement Plan**
(Treatment Integrity)

Carry out the intervention

Tilly, D. (2003, December). Heartland Area Education Agency's evolution from four to three tiers: Our journey - our results. Paper presented at the National Research Center on Learning Disabilities Responsiveness-to-Intervention Symposium, Kansas City, MO. Reprinted with permission.

---

general education instructional program, and recreating a special education program that better meets the needs of individual students.

The Speech-Language Pathologist's Role in the IST and in RtI

The speech-language pathologist can contribute in several ways to the prevention/intervention process, including in-service training, consultation with parents and teachers, ideas for prereferral interventions, and screenings (ASHA, 1999b). Being an active member of the intervention team may also serve to prevent inappropriate referrals for speech-language

services, but also allows the speech-language pathologist to contribute to the overall school program. Participation on this team can have collateral benefits of marketing the skills of speech-language pathologists, as they demonstrate their knowledge and expertise to parents, teachers, and administrators.

Speech-language pathologists should function as regular members of a prereferral/referral committee. Decisions are made within this committee that directly affect their caseload, but more importantly, if speech-language pathologists are to be seen as vital members of the school community, they need to be involved when decisions are being made about student achievement. Speech-language pathologists are uniquely

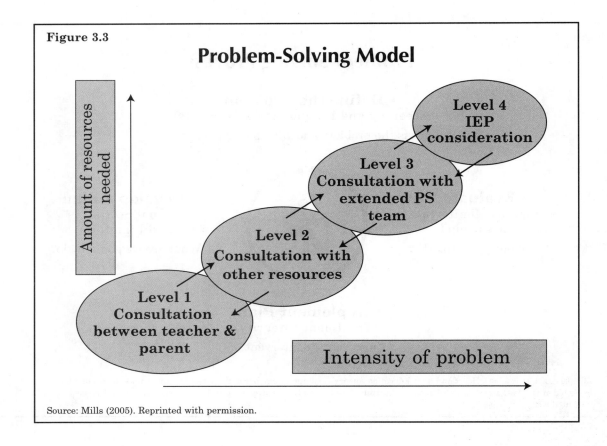

Figure 3.3

Problem-Solving Model

Amount of resources needed

Level 4
IEP consideration

Level 3
Consultation with extended PS team

Level 2
Consultation with other resources

Level 1
Consultation between teacher & parent

Intensity of problem

Source: Mills (2005). Reprinted with permission.

qualified to assist the IST members in their functions. In the document *Responsiveness to Intervention: New Roles for Speech-Language Pathologists* (Ehren, Montgomery, Rudebusch, & Whitmire, 2006), the authors suggest the following:

As a schoolwide prevention approach, RtI includes changing instruction for struggling students to help them improve performance and achieve academic progress. To meet the needs of all students, the educational system must use its collective resources to intervene early and provide appropriate intervention and support to prevent learning and behavioral problems from becoming larger issues.

Speech-language pathologists can play a number of important roles in using RtI to identify children with disabilities and provide needed instruction to struggling students in both general education and special education settings. But these roles will require some fundamental changes in the way speech-language pathologists engage in assessment and intervention activities (p. 1). (For ASHA's full document entitled *Responsiveness to Intervention: New Roles for Speech-Language Pathologists*, see Appendix A.)

Mills (2005) outlines the following implications for speech-language pathologists in

Problem Solving/RtI and Instructional Support Teams:

- Recognizes the speech-language pathologist as having a role in early intervening services.

- Gives the opportunity for speech-language pathologists to intervene with children and youths early, without having to go through the special education process.

- Provides speech-language pathologists with increased opportunities to work collaboratively with classroom teachers.

- Provides an opportunity for some speech-language pathologists to be employed under the 15 percent funding for intervening services.

- Challenges speech-language pathologists to consider their role in the elusive and not-so-well defined area of prevention.

- Increases opportunities for speech-language pathologists to become more accepted as a member of the school team responsible for student achievement.

- Has potential for reducing paperwork associated with referrals to and eligibility determination for special education.

- Provides speech-language pathologists with opportunities to co-teach students with general education teachers, allowing the speech-language pathologist to model good "language of instruction" for the teacher, and to learn from the teacher as well.

- Provides speech-language pathologists with opportunities to help teachers be-

come more knowledgeable about listening, speaking, reading, and writing.

- Provides speech-language pathologists with the opportunity to become increasingly familiar with the State's standard course of study/learning standards.

- Expects speech-language pathologists to conduct authentic/classroom-based assessments, reducing reliance on and the need for standardized testing.

- Gives speech-language pathologists an opportunity to learn more about behavior management and positive behavior supports.

- Increases opportunities to become more accepted as a member of the school team responsible for student achievement.

- Provides opportunities for the speech-language pathologist to help classroom teachers learn how to "language load" their instruction.

- Needs to be included in the curriculum of the communication science and disorders preservice program at institutions of higher education" (pp. 98–102).

Children with perceived "speech only" problems, such as articulation, fluency, or voice disorders, may be referred directly to the speech-language pathologist, bypassing the IST process. The benefit of using the IST process, instead of going directly to referral for assessment, is to ensure that other academic or social issues are not also affecting the student. Whether the need is speech or language, concern about academic impact must be considered. For example, as knowledge of the impact of phonemic awareness on literacy development has become more evident, a student with an articulation disorder should also be considered by the team in terms of reading skills. Utilizing the IST guarantees that the team reviews the student's progress in all learning areas. As a result of the speech-language pathologist's participation on the IST, other team members will develop awareness about the relationship of speech-language skills to academic performance.

The Referral Process

Most referrals for speech and language evaluations will come from within the school setting, either from teachers or the IST; however, some other outside professionals who work with children are legally required to refer a child with a suspected disability to the school district. These professionals include physicians, nurses, teachers at state or county residential facilities, psychologists, social workers, or administrators of social agencies. Before making the referral, the professional must inform the parent that the referral will be made. The referral must be in writing and must include the reason(s) why the child is believed to have a disability. Classroom behaviors that may be indications of possible communication problems and lead to referral include the following:

- Difficulty with reading
- Difficulty with spelling and writing
- Difficulty being understood when speaking in class
- Vague or evasive answers
- Frequent absences or avoidance of school

- Inability to attend or stay focused
- Rubbing ears or complaining of pain in ears
- Unusual vocal quality or recurrent hoarseness
- Avoiding making eye contact with teachers or others (not culturally based)
- Unwillingness to speak in front of the class
- Social skills difficulties

Speech-language pathologists and audiologists often find it useful to conduct in-service training for teachers regarding communication behaviors and learning patterns that might be indicators of a communication disorder. As has been mentioned, the best way for teachers to know and understand the work of speech-language pathologists or audiologists is to work together on specific cases, consulting in the classroom and work together on problem-solving teams. These opportunities will create natural situations where teachers and speech-language pathologists or audiologists have an opportunity to learn from each other for the benefit of children.

Referrals for assessment may come from many sources: parents, teachers, school psychologists, physicians, and students themselves. If parents ask the school to assess their child, the speech-language pathologist or audiologist, as members of the team, must address this request immediately. Referral by a teacher or a parent will need to go through the IST process in most states, and will generally require general education interventions before a formal assessment is undertaken. Written permission from parents is necessary to continue further in the formal assessment process for determination of special education eligibility.

Assessment for Speech, Language, and Hearing Disabilities

Backward Planning: What Does the Law Require?

In a school system, students must qualify to receive special education, including speech-language or audiological services. A great deal of emphasis is currently being placed legislatively and operationally on trying to provide assistance to students who are struggling in order to prevent them from requiring special education services. However, some students who go through the RtI process and receive assistance in various intervention programs, and who fail to respond to these interventions, will ultimately be referred for special education assessment. Because the law requires a MULTIDISCIPLINARY ASSESSMENT TEAM (MDAT), the speech-language pathologist will not be working in isolation when a referral is received (34 C.F.R.§ 300.308).

Assessment in schools is for the following purposes:

- Determining eligibility.

- Identifying strengths and areas of need.

- Identifying how the student's disability impacts their ability to succeed in the general education curriculum.

- Identifying how the student performs compared to their nondisabled peers.

- Generating recommendations for goals, programs and services.

The terms assessment and evaluation are often used interchangeably (Shipley & McAfee, 2004), although assessment mostly refers to the process of gathering diagnostic information, while evaluation refers to the decision-making process involved in determining the diagnosis or eligibility for services.

Assessment is defined in the following ways:

- A process of collecting data for the purpose of making decisions about individuals and groups (Salvia & Ysseldyke, 2004, p. 4)

- A process of collecting valid and reliable information, integrating it, and interpreting it to make a judgment or a decision about something; the process of measuring communicative behaviors of interests...; the outcome of assessment is usually a diagnosis, which is the clinical decision regarding the presence/absence of a disorder and, often, the assignment of a diagnostic label (Shipley & McAfee, 2004, p. 4)

- Clinical procedures implemented to understand a client's communicative problem and his or her personal and family history, along with existing and nonexisting communicative skills; includes measurement of communicative skills and related behaviors (Hedge & Davis, 2005)

In schools, there are several types of assessments, including classroom assessments, statewide or high-stakes assessments, school or district assessments, program assessments, chapter assessments, or common assessments. For the purposes of special education eligibility, assessments are individual assessments, which also need to consider and include information on the other types of assessments completed by the school in other arenas.

ASHA (2004e) Preferred Practice Patterns lists the following as expected results from an assessment:

- Diagnosis of a speech, language, cognitive communication and/or swallowing disorder.

- Clinical description of the characteristics of speech, language, cognitive-communication and/or swallowing impairments.

- Identification of a communication difference, possibly co-occurring with a speech, language, cognitive communication and/or swallowing disorder.

- Prognosis for change (in the individual or relevant contexts).

- Recommendation for intervention or support.

- Identification of the effectiveness of intervention and supports.

- Referral for other assessments or services (p. 10-11).

The Code of Federal Regulations (C.F.R.) outlines what is required to include in an evaluation of a student who is suspected of having a disability.

Initial Evaluation

The processes mandated for initial evaluations are set out in C.F.R. § 300.301, and require the following:

(a) The public agency must conduct a full and individual evaluation in accordance with § 300.305 and § 300.306, before the initial provision of special education and related services.

(b) A parent or a public agency may initiate a request for an initial evaluation to determine if a child is a child with a disability.

(c) Procedures for initial evaluation. The initial evaluation—

(1)(i) Must be conducted within 60 days of receiving parental consent for the evaluation; or

(ii) If a state establishes a timeline within which the evaluation must be conducted, within that timeframe; and

(2) Must consist of procedures—

(i) To determine if the child is a child with a disability under § 300.8, and

(ii) To determine the educational needs of the child.

Speech-language pathologists and audiologists should be familiar with the requirements for conducting evaluations as identified in the C.F.R. § 300.304. This section identifies the procedures the public agency must follow:

(b)(1) Use a variety of assessment tools and strategies to gather relevant functional, developmental, and academic information about the child, including information provided by the parent that may assist in determining:

(i) Whether the child is a child with a disability under § 300.8, and

(ii) The contents of the child's IEP, including information related to enabling the child to be involved in and progress in the general education curriculum (or for preschool child, to participate in appropriate activities).

(2) Not use any single measure or assessment as the sole criterion for determining whether a child is a child with a disability and for determining an appropriate educational program for the child, and

Child With a Disability (§ 300.8)

(a) General. (1) Child with a disability means a child evaluated in accordance with §300.304 through §300.311 as having mental retardation, a hearing impairment (including deafness), a speech or language impairment, a visual impairment (including blindness), a serious emotional disturbance (referred to in this part as "emotional disturbance"), an orthopedic impairment, autism, traumatic brain injury, an other health impairment, a specific learning disability, deaf-blindness, or multiple disabilities, and who, by reason thereof, needs special education and related services.

(2)(i) Subject to paragraph (a)(2)(ii) of this section, if it is determined, through an appropriate evaluation under §300.304 through §300.311, that a child has one of the disabilities identified in paragraph (a)(1) of this section, but only needs a related service and not special education, the child is not a child with a disability under this part.

(ii) If, consistent with §300.39 (a)(2), the related service required by the child is considered special education rather than a related service under State standards, the child would be determined to be a child with a disability under paragraph (a)(1) of this section.

(b) Children aged three through nine experiencing developmental delays. Child with a disability for children aged three through nine (or any subset of that age range, including ages three through five), may, subject to the conditions described in §300.111 (b), including a child—

(1) Who is experiencing developmental delays, as defined by the State and as measured by appropriate diagnostic instruments and procedures, in one or more of the following areas: Physical development, cognitive development, communication development, social or emotional development, or adaptive development; and

(2) Who, by reason thereof, needs special education and related services.

(c) Definitions of disability terms. The terms used in this definition of a child with a disability are defined as follows:

(1)(i) Autism means a developmental disability significantly affecting verbal and nonverbal communication and social interaction, generally evident before age three, that adversely affects a child's educational performance. Other characteristics often associated with autism are engagement in repetitive activities and stereotyped movements, resistance to environmental change or change in daily routines, and unusual responses to sensory experiences.

(ii) Autism does not apply if a child's educational performance is adversely affected primarily because the child has an emotional disturbance, as defined in paragraph (c)(4) of this section.

(iii) A child who manifests the characteristics of autism after age three could be identified as having autism if the criteria in paragraph (c)(1)(i) of this section are satisfied.

Child With a Disability – *Continued*

(2) Deaf-blindness means concomitant hearing and visual impairments, the combination of which causes such severe communication and other developmental and educational needs that they cannot be accommodated in special education programs solely for children with deafness or children with blindness.

(3) Deafness means a hearing impairment that is so severe that the child is impaired in processing linguistic information through hearing, with or without amplification that adversely affects a child's educational performance.

(4)(i) Emotional disturbance means a condition exhibiting one or more of the following characteristics over a long period of time and to a marked degree that adversely affects a child's educational performance:

(A) An inability to learn that cannot be explained by intellectual, sensory, or health factors.

(B) An inability to build or maintain satisfactory interpersonal relationships with peers and teachers.

(C) Inappropriate types of behavior or feelings under normal circumstances.

(D) A general pervasive mood of unhappiness or depression.

(E) A tendency to develop physical symptoms or fears associated with personal or school problems.

(ii) Emotional disturbance includes schizophrenia. The term does not apply to children who are socially maladjusted, unless it is determined that they have an emotional disturbance under paragraph (c)(4)(i) of this section.

(5) Hearing impairment means an impairment in hearing, whether permanent or fluctuating, that adversely affects a child's educational performance but that is not included under the definition of deafness in this section.

(6) Mental retardation means significantly subaverage general intellectual functioning, existing concurrently with deficits in adaptive behavior and manifested during the developmental period, that adversely affects a child's educational performance.

(7) Multiple disabilities means concomitant impairments (such as mental retardation-blindness or mental retardation-orthopedic impairment), the combination of which causes such severe educational needs that they cannot be accommodated in special education programs solely for one of the impairments. Multiple disabilities does not include deaf-blindness.

(8) Orthopedic impairment means a severe orthopedic impairment that adversely affects a child's educational performance. The term includes impairments caused by a congenital

Continued

Child With a Disability – *Continued*

anomaly, impairments caused by disease (e.g., poliomyelitis, bone tuberculosis), and impairments from other causes (e.g., cerebral palsy, amputations, and fractures or burns that cause contractures).

(9) Other health impairment means having limited strength, vitality, or alertness, including a heightened alertness to environmental stimuli, that results in limited alertness with respect to the educational environment, that—

(i) Is due to chronic or acute health problems such as asthma, attention deficit disorder or attention deficit hyperactivity disorder, diabetes, epilepsy, a heart condition, hemophilia, lead poisoning, leukemia, nephritis, rheumatic fever, sickle cell anemia, and Tourette syndrome; and

(ii) Adversely affects a child's educational performance.

(10) Specific learning disability—(i) General. Specific learning disability means a disorder in one or more of the basic psychological processes involved in understanding or in using language, spoken or written, that may manifest itself in the imperfect ability to listen, think, speak, read, write, spell, or to do mathematical calculations, including conditions such as perceptual disabilities, brain injury, minimal brain dysfunction, dyslexia, and developmental aphasia.

(ii) Disorders not included. Specific learning disability does not include learning problems that are primarily the result of visual, hearing, or motor disabilities, of mental retardation, of emotional disturbance, or of environmental, cultural, or economic disadvantage.

(11) Speech or language impairment means a communication disorder, such as stuttering, impaired articulation, a language impairment, or a voice impairment, that adversely affects a child's educational performance.

(12) Traumatic brain injury means an acquired injury to the brain caused by an external physical force, resulting in total or partial functional disability or psychosocial impairment, or both, that adversely affects a child's educational performance. Traumatic brain injury applies to open or closed head injuries resulting in impairments in one or more areas, such as cognition; language; memory; attention; reasoning; abstract thinking; judgment; problem-solving; sensory, perceptual, and motor abilities; psychosocial behavior; physical functions; information processing; and speech. Traumatic brain injury does not apply to brain injuries that are congenital or degenerative, or to brain injuries induced by birth trauma.

(13) Visual impairment including blindness means an impairment in vision that, even with correction, adversely affects a child's educational performance. The term includes both partial sight and blindness.

(Authority: 20 U.S.C. 1401 [3]; 1401 [30])

§ 300.15 Evaluation

Evaluation means procedures used in accordance with § 300.304 through § 300.311 to determine whether a child has a disability and the nature and extent of the special education and related services that the child needs.

(3) Use technically sound instruments that may assess the relative contribution of cognitive and behavioral factors, in addition to physical or developmental factors.

Additionally, the law requires that during the course of an evaluation:

(c) (1) Assessments and other evaluation materials need to assess a child under this part—

(i) Are selected and administered so as not to be discriminatory on a racial or cultural basis;

(ii) Are provided and administered in the child's native language or other mode of communication and in the form most likely to yield accurate information on what the child knows and can do academically, developmentally, and functionally, unless it is clearly not feasible to so provide or administer;

(iii) Are used for the purposes for which the assessments or measures are valid or reliable;

(iv) Are administered by trained and knowledgeable personnel; and

(v) Are administered in accordance with any instructions provided by the producer of the assessments.

Both initial evaluations and reevaluations (e.g., triennial evaluations; requested evaluations) must include the following components:

(a) As part of an initial evaluation (if appropriate) and as a part of any reevaluation...the IEP team or a team of other qualified professionals, as appropriate, must—

(1) Review existing evaluation data on the child, including:

(i) Evaluations and information provided by the parents of the child;

(ii) Current classroom-based, local, or State assessments, and classroom-based observations; and

(iii) Observations by teachers and relates services providers; and

(2) On the basis of that review, and input from the child's parents, identify what additional data, if any, are needed (34 C.F.R. § 300.305).

Becoming familiar with the requirements of the law in terms of evaluations is necessary in order to plan what needs to be done as part of the evaluation process. Another section of the law that is critical is § 300.306 which outlines the special rule for eligibility determination, or what needs to happen in the instructional area prior to referral for initial assessment. The following requirements are critical for planning in the IST process:

§ 300.306 (b) Special Rule for Eligibility Determination. A child must not be determined to be a child with a disability under this part—

(1) If the determinant factor for that determination is—

(i) lack of appropriate instruction in reading, including the essential components of reading instruction (as defined in section 1208 [3] of the ESEA);

(ii) Lack of appropriate instruction in math; or

(iii) Limited English proficiency.

(2) If the child does not otherwise meet the eligibility criteria under § 300.8 (a);

§ 300.306 (c) Procedures for determining eligibility and educational need. (1) In interpreting evaluation data for the purpose of determining if a child is a child with a disability under § 300.8, and the educational needs of the child, each public agency must—

(i) Draw upon information from a variety of sources, including aptitude and achievement tests, parent input, and teacher recommendations, as well as information about the child's physical condition social or cultural background, and adaptive behavior; and

(ii) Ensure that information obtained from all of these sources is documented and carefully considered.

The most significant changes in eligibility determination process are the changes allowed under IDEA 2004 in the area of specific learning disability (SLD). The processes identified in this area are changing the way that school districts operate in eligibility determination. The impact will be widespread and consequently will be applied to all other disability conditions. In terms of instruction needed prior to referral for special education assessment, the Code of Federal Regulations outlines the following procedures for identifying students with specific learning disabilities. These procedures lay the foundation for RtI:

§ 300.307 (a)(2) Must permit the use of a process based on the child's response to scientific, research-based intervention.

To determine the existence of a specific learning disability, the multidisciplinary assessment team may determine the existence of a learning disability if:

§ 300.309 (a)(1) The child does not achieve adequately for the child's age or to meet State-approved grade-level standards in one or more of the following areas, when provided with learning experiences and instruction appropriate for the child's age or State-approved grade-level standards:

(i) Oral expression.

(ii) Listening comprehension.

(iii) Written expression.

(iv) Basic reading skill.

(v) Reading fluency skills.

(vi) Reading comprehension.

(vii) Mathematics calculation.

(viii) Mathematics problem solving.

§ 300.309 (a)(2)(i) The child does not make sufficient progress to meet age or State-approved grade-level standards in one or more of the areas identified in paragraph (a)(1) of this section when using a process based on the child's response to scientific, research-based intervention; or

(b) (1) Data that demonstrate that prior to, or as part of the referral process, the child was provided appropriate instruction in regular education settings, delivered by qualified personnel;

(2) Data-based documentation of repeated assessments of achievement at reasonable intervals, reflecting formal assessment of student progress during instruction, which was provided to the child's parents.

Additionally, the Code of Federal Regulations lays out requirements for conducting observation as part of the evaluation process:

§ 300.310 (a) The public agency must ensure that the child is observed in the child's learning environment (including the regular classroom setting) to document the child's academic performance and behavior in the areas of difficulty.

Reevaluation

The requirements for conducting reevaluations are as follows: (1) Must be conducted at least every three years (known as the three-year or triennial evaluation), or (2) Parent, teacher, or IEP team may request a reevaluation (34 C.F.R. § 300.300). The procedure for the reevaluation is the same as for the initial evaluation, with these exceptions: (1) The MDAT reviews existing data and determines that additional assessment is not needed; the team decides whether or not the child continues to need special education and related services based on this existing data; or (2) The MDAT reviews the existing data and determines that additional data is needed, which may not include formal or standardized testing. Checking on the local procedures for implementation is important, but this provision allows for a more meaningful process to gather data about what the child needs as opposed to conducting testing and evaluation using measures that might not be as meaningful (34 C.F.R. § 300.305).

If the IEP Team, parent or student's teacher requests a reevaluation for the purpose of changing the student's eligibility, then a full evaluation must be completed (34 C.F.R. § 300.3052 [e]).

Moving into Action on an Assessment

Once a referral is received, the speech-language pathologist or audiologist gathers information from the referring source, consults with the parents, observes the student according to outlined procedures, and then decides what diagnostic testing is necessary. Written parent permission is required before the formal evaluation process begins. Much of this may have already been completed during the IST process or as part of the RtI tiered interventions. (See "Parental Consent" on p. 102.) Several team members' activities depend upon the speech-language pathologist's or audiologist's actions. In some cases, parents need reassurance. Psychologists may need corroborating data for a diagnosis that includes a communication component. General educators may be unaware of the academic impact of a hearing loss or auditory processing problems and will need guidance during this information-collection stage.

A child may be referred for a speech-language or hearing evaluation in a variety of ways. Most typically, the student will be referred from either the IST or the child's parents. Referrals may also come directly from classroom teachers, mass-screening coordinators, and medical or mental health professionals. Some school districts have received referrals from judges who order assessments to be completed in child custody cases, juvenile justice courts, or other types of situations. If a referral of this nature is received, special education administration should be consulted by the team or individual receiving the referral. Districts and states may choose a variety of ways to respond to such a referral. While the majority of referrals for assessment will come through the IST, the speech-language pathologist or audiologist and other educators should never ignore any request for assessment. These professionals must have a complete understanding of the process and procedures for dealing with any referral.

No child may be provided special education and related services until an evaluation is completed (34 C.F.R. § 300.301). This is a critical part of the law. "Comprehensive assessment (data collection) and evaluation (interpretation

of that data) enable the speech-language pathologist to identify students with significant communication disorders that are educationally relevant" (ASHA, 1999b, p. 32). As RtI and a variety of tiered interventions become more established in the schools, this information will be part of the assessment process and eligibility determination. The requirements laid out, regarding instruction prior to assessment, further reinforce the need for speech-language pathologists and audiologists in schools to know about and understand curriculum and instruction.

Conducting an evaluation before providing services is a logical course of events. The potential difficulty for a speech-language pathologist

may arise if a parent, teacher, or administrator tries to pressure the speech-language pathologist by saying "Just put Johnny in speech class. He only needs a little bit of help with his speech." This may potentially be a real problem under an RtI system. Regardless of whether a student is involved in a tiered intervention that is being provided by the speech-language pathologist or audiologist or if the student is involved in an assessment, there is always a process involved that must not be violated. Students must be evaluated and then determined eligible due to meeting criteria and requiring special education services. Any attempt to circumvent this process is considered a violation of the student's due process rights. Additionally, evaluation allows for a thorough assessment of the student's learning strengths and needs.

The importance of an accurate and thorough evaluation cannot be overstated. The evaluation is the key to detecting the existence of a student's disability or disabilities, and it sets the parameters for the course of special education and related services that will follow if the student is determined to be eligible. Knowing the legal requirements will help the both the IST and the MDAT know what needs to be done before and during a formal assessment process. Table 3.2 provides a summary of the requirements for Evaluations and Eligibility Determinations under IDEA 2004.

Team Approach

Assessments to determine eligibility must be conducted by trained and knowledgeable personnel (34 C.F.R. § 300.304 [b][3][c][iv]). Speech-language pathologists and audiologists will work as members of a multidisciplinary assessment team (MDAT). No one person determines whether or not a child has a disability. Children must be assessed in all areas of suspected disability (34 C.F.R. § 300.304 [4]) and the assessment must be "sufficiently comprehensive to identify all of the child's special education and related services needs, whether or

not commonly linked to the disability category in which the child has been classified" (34 C.F.R. § 300.304 [c][6]).

Working together as assessment team members means that all personnel must have knowledge each others' areas of expertise and evaluation, in addition to being familiar with the assessment instruments and processes that each professional discipline will use.

The Code of Federal Regulations gives guidance as to who should be a part of the multidisciplinary assessment team when considering a child as potentially having a specific learning disability. The C.F.R. indicates the team should consist of the child's parents and a team of qualified professionals, including the child's teacher, and "at least one person qualified to conduct individual diagnostic examinations of children, such as a school psychologist, speech-language pathologist, or remedial reading teacher" (34 C.F.R. § 300.308 [3][b]). The commentary to the C.F.R. by the U.S. Department of Education (USDE) indicates that in all assessments for the purposes of determining eligibility, flexibility is granted so that the teams can use the people whose expertise are needed for each different type of assessment in any disability area (Martin, 2006).

Consultation with other team members is essential when conducting assessments and determining eligibility. The synergy that is created when professionals of various disciplines work together is important to the inquiry process of evaluation. Individual team members should not work in isolation but should collaborate to ensure that all aspects of the student's functioning is examined and considered.

Table 3.2	**IDEA 2004 Evaluation and Eligibility Determination**
Law	• If a parent refuses to consent for an initial evaluation, districts may file for a due process hearing. If the parent refuses services following an initial evaluation, the district may not file for due process and is not responsible for providing FAPE (§ 614 [a][1][D][ii]). • Parents and districts may agree that a three-year reevaluation is unnecessary (§ 614 [a][2][A][ii]). • Districts are required to use a variety of assessment tools and strategies to gather relevant functional, developmental, and academic information, including information provided by the parent (§ 614 [b][2][A]). • Districts must coordinate with the previous school districts when students transfer during an evaluation (§ 614 [b][3][D]). • A child may not be determined eligible for special education if the determining factor is lack of appropriate instruction in reading, including the essential components of reading instruction as defined in NCLB (§ 614 [b][5][A]). • IEP Teams determining whether a child has a specific learning disability are not required to consider a severe discrepancy between achievement and intellectual ability in several performance areas (§ 614 [b][6][A]). • IEP Teams determining whether a child has a specific learning disability, may use a process that determines if the child responds to scientific, research-based interventions. (§ 614 [b][6][B]). • As part of initial and reevaluations, the IEP Team and others shall review existing evaluation data including local and state assessments (§ 614 [c][1][A][ii]). • Eligibility determination and determinations of whether the child continues to have a disability must include consideration of the educational needs of the child (§ 614 [c][1][B][i]). • Eligibility determination and determinations of present levels of performance must include academic achievement and related developmental needs (§ 614 [c][1][B][ii]). • LEAs are not required to conduct an evaluation if the reason for termination in service is due to graduation or aging out of the program (§ 614 [c][5][B][i]). • Upon graduation or aging out of the program, LEAs shall provide to the parent and/or child a summary of performance of the child's academic achievement and functional performance, including recommendations on how to assist the child in meeting post-secondary goals (§ 614 [c][5][B][ii]).

Source: IDEA (2004), § 614

Continued

Table 3.2 – *Continued*

	Speech-language pathologists should note the emphasis on both academic achievement and functional performance when conducting evaluations and making eligibility determinations. Also notable is the change in the criteria for specific learning disability (SLD) which removes the requirement for a discrepancy between academic achievement and intellectual performance, and allows for the use of a response-to-intervention process as part of the eligibility determination for SLD. Review requirements for evaluations carefully and follow district and state guidance on reporting.
Implications for SLPs	Source: IDEA (2004), § 614

Speech-language pathologists and audiologists need to learn the skills and competencies of their fellow team members. When planning to conduct an evaluation, sharing information with other team members about which assessment instruments will be used during an assessment is helpful. Some team members may also choose to conduct their assessments simultaneously, as in an arena assessment, which is common with infant/toddler assessments, but may also be useful for other types of assessments. Another valuable process is to have one member of the assessment team observe while another conducts testing or other assessment processes (Moore-Brown, Huerta, Uranga-Hernandez, & Peña, 2006). Most importantly, each professional member of the assessment team must be respectful of the knowledge and skills that other team members bring to the process. Each team member has a different perspective, and it is the combination of each of these perspectives that will complement and complete the picture of the student's learning needs (see also "Types of Teams" in Chapter 6).

Parental Consent

Parental participation is one of the cornerstones of special education. Informed parent consent is one of the most important procedural safeguards afforded to parents, ensuring their involvement in the process and that they have been informed that their child is suspected of having a disability. (Chapter 8 provides a full discussion of procedural safeguards in "Parental Involvement.")

According to 34 C.F.R. § 300.9 consent means that—

(a) The parent has been fully informed of all information relevant to the activity for which his or her consent is sought, in his or her native language, or other mode of communication;

(b) The parent understands and agrees in writing to the carrying out of the activity for which his or her consent is sought, and the consent describes that activity and lists the records (if any) that will be released and to whom; and

#TP-29703 Making a Difference - 2nd Ed. · ©2008 Thinking Publications® · www.thinkingpublications.com · 1-800-277-8737

(c) (1) The parent understands that granting of consent is voluntary on the part of the parent and may be revoked at anytime.

(2) If a parent revokes consent, that revocation is not retroactive (i.e., it does not negate an action that has occurred after the consent was given and before the consent was revoked).

Under the requirements of 34 C.F.R. § 300.504 (a)(1), a copy of the procedural safeguards notice must be given to parents upon the initial referral or parent request for evaluation. Districts are also required to provide written notice to parents when the district:

C.F.R. § 300.503 (a)(1) Proposes to initiate or change the identification, evaluation or educational placement of the child or the provision of FAPE to the child; or

(2) Refuses to initiate or change the identification, evaluation, or educational placement of the child or the provision of FAPE to the child. These provisions are included in what is known as Prior Written Notice.

An initial assessment must not begin until a parent returns a consent form. Informed parent consent must be obtained before conducting an initial evaluation (34 C.F.R. § 300.300 [a][1][i]) or reevaluation (34 C.F.R. § 300.300 [a][4][c][i]). Consent to an initial evaluation cannot be construed as consent to provide special education and related services to the child with a disability (34 C.F.R § 300.300 [a][ii]).

The speech-language pathologist may know the child through membership on the IST or because of serving the student in an RtI model. When the consent form is sent to a parent or guardian, notification of procedural safeguards or parent and child rights must be sent as well. As stated, the parent must agree in writing to the assessment. During the assessment, parents should be interviewed by the speech-language pathologist, as IDEA 2004 requires parent input in the assessment process. Teacher interviews are also necessary in order to get a complete picture of how the student's needs are impacting the potential for classroom success. Interviews provide essential information for the diagnostic process (Haynes & Pindzola, 2004).

The initial assessment is the first of several times that parents must be informed of their procedural rights. Members of the evaluation team must make sure that parents and students understand their rights. The speech-language pathologist is often responsible for providing a copy of the rights to parents, and it is important to document that the parents received a copy of the parent rights. (See Chapter 8 for a further discussion of parent and child rights.)

Parents sometimes refuse to give their consent for assessment. If school district personnel believe that a child has a disability, the school district may need to request mediation or a DUE PROCESS hearing on the issues (34 C.F.R. § 300.506 [b]), depending on state law. In California, for example, state law requires that school districts file for (i.e., request) a due process hearing if the parent's actions do not afford the child access to FAPE. The C.F.R. also directs school districts that "A public agency may not use a parent's refusal to consent to one service or activity...

to deny the parent or child any other service, benefit, or activity of the public agency" (C.F.R. § 300.300 [c][3]). Generally, school districts are not allowed to simply agree to or ignore a refusal of consent because it may not be in the best interest of the child. Speech-language pathologists should always consult a special education administrator when these questions or issues arise.

The majority of the time, parents consent to the proposed assessment. The CASE MANAGER should always note on the assessment plan the date that the signed plan was returned to school. Sometimes parents forget to return the paper. If this should happen, a phone call or note home is generally enough of a reminder.

Timelines

Once the assessment plan is received, the MDAT has a certain period of time in which to complete the assessment. IDEA 2004 requires that the district complete the evaluation and make services available within 60 days of receiving the parental consent for assessment (34 C.F.R. § 300.301 [c][1][i]). Specific timelines can vary from state to state, but no state can have a timeline that is beyond 60 days to complete an assessment. The only exceptions to this timeline are if a child moves or if the parent refuses to make the child available for the evaluation (34 C.F.R. § 300.301).

Diagnostic testing may take upwards of six hours, a scheduling challenge for many busy speech-language pathologists. Timelines for the assessment process, such as the sample in Table 3.3, are designed by many states and school districts to aid special educators in meeting the

IDEA 2004 requirements. Note that the speech-language pathologist must respond to the parents within 15 days when an assessment is requested, and have the results of the assessment within 60 days after the date of permission to assess is received. In some school districts, one or more speech-language pathologists rotate from school to school to assist with testing so that timelines can be maintained. It is important for the speech-language pathologist to notify a supervisor if help is needed, as violations of timelines are considered serious problems with repercussions at local, district, and state levels.

State-imposed timelines refer to the number of calendar days (not school or work days) the MDAT has between the time the family returns the assessment plan and an IEP meeting is convened. A one- or two-month wait for a team decision and the possible start of services can be difficult for parents, students, and teachers. Table 3.4 illustrates critical timelines for evaluation and IEP activity.

The regulations, timelines, documentation, and procedures of special education are all tightly regulated and extremely important. While timelines may seem to be just another rule, it is important to remember that these timelines are part of the procedural safeguards provided to the family. Violations of timelines can be construed as a denial of the child's FAPE if services were delayed in being implemented. Timelines are critical.

Timelines and Diversity

Families who are from cultures other than that of mainstream America, or who are struggling with issues of daily living, may not always be responsive to the important timelines and

Table 3.3

Procedural Timelines for Special Education Programs to Meet IDEA 2004 Requirements

Identification, Referral, Assessment, Planning, Instruction, Review

Time Frame	Task
10–15 calendar days	Referral of individual with exceptional needs and parents contacted. Assessment plan developed. Parents receive written rights and safeguards. Notification of assessment is written.
15 calendar days	Parents have this amount of time to decide and provide written consent if they wish to proceed.
20–30 calendar days	Students who transfer into a district may be placed in a comparable program for this length of time before additional assessment or previous records are obtained.
60 calendar days	Assessment is conducted by a multidisciplinary assessment team. Parent receives written notice of IEP team planning meeting. Meeting is held and eligibility is determined (34 C.F.R. § 300.323 [c][1]).
30 calendar days	Initial IEP for the purpose of determination and provision of services (34 C.F.R. § 300.323 [c][1]).
30 calendar days	An interim placement determined by the IEP team for a student who moves into the LEA.
Immediately or within a few days	Parent consents in writing to the IEP. The plan is implemented.
One year (sooner if requested)	Review of the IEP is completed.
Three years (sooner if requested)	Reassessment, as needed or at parent request, and determination if student continues special education services.

Table 3.4	Evaluation Action Timelines	
Action	**Timelines**	**Notes**
Request for assessment received	10–15 days to present parent with an assessment plan (AP)	If parent does not return AP signed, follow-up is needed
Signed assessment plan received	Team has specified days (30–60) to complete assessment	All days indicated are calendar days
IEP meeting held	Meeting notice sent 1–15 days prior to meeting date	Completed reports presented

deadlines in special education. Some speech-language pathologists and audiologists have experienced working with refugee families who are fearful of authority, due to the oppression in the countries they fled. In other situations, cultural parameters value oral, not written, communication, so meeting notices go unheeded, but visits to the home are welcomed. Individuals may also operate on a different value system regarding time. The team may find that the family arrives for a meeting (sometimes with many family members) either several hours early or several hours late. Transportation issues may also prevent families from coming to a meeting; for example, a family may not have the resources to access transportation services that might be available to them.

Sometimes, issues arising as a result of cultural differences become the responsibility of the IEP team. Helping families with these issues, and respecting their challenges, will help the student in the long run. Speech-language pathologists and audiologists must utilize their own cultural competence to know and understand

when paperwork and compliance with the legal parameters of the special education process are overwhelming or outside of the purview of the student's family. In these situations, assistance of a very different nature may be necessary.

Selecting the Appropriate Speech-Language Measurement Instruments

This section is specific to the selection of speech and language assessment tools. Audiological assessment instruments are more standardized to their specialized diagnostic procedures.

Selecting appropriate assessment tools is the next step in the process. Speech-language disabilities may be assessed using many different methods or a combination of methods. There are basically three methods for assessing students: STANDARDIZED TESTS; performance-based measures, including curriculum-based measures; and dynamic protocols. Each method helps speech-language pathologists gather information in a different way. Speech-language pathologists need to know each method, appropriate tools for that method, and when to use them.

ASHA's (2004e) Preferred Practice Patterns describes the clinical process for a comprehensive speech-language assessment:

Assessment may be static (i.e., using procedures designed to describe structures, functions, and environmental demands and supports in relevant domains at a given point in time) and/or dynamic (i.e., using hypothesis testing procedures to identify potential for change and elements of successful interventions and supports).

A thorough assessment may include the following:

- Relevant case history, including medical status, education, vocation, and socioeconomic, cultural, and linguistic backgrounds.

- Review of auditory, visual, motor, and cognitive status.

- Patient/client and family interview.

- Standardized and/or nonstandardized measures of specific aspects of speech, spoken and nonspoken language, cognitive-communication, and swallowing function.

- Analysis of associated medical, behavioral, environmental, educational, vocational, social, and emotional factors.

- Identification of potential for effective intervention strategies and compensations.

- Selection of standardized measures for speech, language, cognitive-communication

and/or swallowing assessment with consideration for documented ecological validity.

- Follow-up services to monitor communication and swallowing status and ensure appropriate intervention and support for individuals with identified speech, language, cognitive-communication, and/or swallowing disorders (p. 10–12).

The Schwab Learning Foundation (Baumel, 2003) describes assessment as a process of collecting information from several sources including the following:

- Review of records
  ✓ Health and developmental history
  ✓ Vision and hearing testing
  ✓ Prior school placements and educational history
  ✓ Group test results and report cards
  ✓ Attendance and discipline records
  ✓ Diversity issues, such a primary language, culture, etc.
  ✓ Information from other professionals who have worked with the child

- Interviews
  ✓ Structured (i.e., rating scales) and informal discussions
  ✓ With parent
  ✓ With child
  ✓ With other school staff

- Observations
  ✓ Classroom
  ✓ Playground
  ✓ During testing

- Testing

  ✓ Standardized

    - Provides norms which allow comparison of the child's performance to peers

  ✓ Criterion-referenced

    - Provides information about the mastery of specific skills

  ✓ Informal assessment

    - Miscue analysis

    - Classroom tests

    - Common assessments

    - Homework

    - Classroom participation

    - Teacher-made tests

As the speech-language pathologist and the MDAT consider how to assess the student, consideration must be given to IDEA 2004 requirements for initial assessment conducted by the LOCAL EDUCATION AGENCY (LEA):

- Use a variety of assessment tools and strategies to gather relevant functional, developmental, and academic information, including information provided by the parents.

- Gather information related to enabling a child's involvement and progress in the general curriculum. If a child is of preschool age, the LEA must gather information related to enabling the child's participation in appropriate activities.

- Do not use any single procedure, measure, or assessment as the sole criterion for determining whether a child is a child with a disability or determining an appropriate educational program for the child.

- Use technically sound instruments that may assess the relative contribution of cognitive and behavioral factors, in addition to physical or developmental factors.

- Ensure that test or other evaluation materials are selected and administered, so as not to be discriminatory on a racial or cultural basis.

- Ensure that tests or other evaluation materials are provided and administered in the language and form most likely to yield accurate information on what the child knows and can do academically, developmentally, and functionally, unless it is not feasible to do so.

- Ensure that tests and other evaluation materials are used for purposes for which the assessments or measures are valid and reliable.

- Ensure that tests and evaluation materials are administered by trained and knowledgeable personnel and are administered consistent with any instructions provided by the producers of such tests.

- Ensure that the child is assessed in all areas of suspected disability.

- Provide assessment tools and strategies yielding reliable information that directly assist persons in determining the child's educational needs (Manasevit & Maginnis, 2005, pp. 26–27).

The other consideration when planning an assessment is how eligibility determination is different with RtI. According to the National Association of State Directors of Special Education (NASDSE; Batsche et al., 2005), in-depth assessment is not required unless there is a "likelihood that serious impairment in a specific domain is a significant factor in the student's poor achievement, behavior, or both" (p. 28). Instead, in RtI, eligibility determination for special education services occurs when a student's response to both core instructional and supplemental interventions does not result in movement toward achieving benchmarks and peer performance level.

Eligibility determination can be made using the convergence of data from multiple sources to document each of the following four eligibility criteria:

- Level difference, such as large performance differences compared to peers and benchmark expectations in relevant domains of behavior.

- Rate of learning difference, such as large differences in rate of learning compared to peers and trajectories toward benchmarks when provided with high-quality interventions implemented over a significant period.

- Documented adverse impact on education and need for special education.

- Exclusion factors: (1) rule out sensory impairments and absence of instructional opportunities; and (2) depending on SEA disability categories, rule out mild mental retardation, emotional behavioral disorders and speech/language and other disabilities as the primary cause of the significant achievement deficiency (p. 28).

Guidelines for assessment can be found in professional documents, graduate school textbooks (Shipley & McAfee, 2004; Paul, 2001; Haynes & Pindzola, 2004; Salvia & Ysseldyke, 2004; Larson, & McKinley, 2003; Justice, 2006b),

and state departments of education regulations. IDEA 2004 defines each eligible disability category including a speech-language disability (see Chapter 4 "Federal Eligibility Criteria for Special Education"). This section discusses what constitutes GOOD PRACTICE in communication assessment, and gives guidance in identifying a speech-language disability. States may specify what instruments to use, and local school districts may also specify particular approaches and tools for the speech-language pathologist. The sidebar on p. 110 provides examples of methods of assessment, which are commonly used in school settings.

Standardized Tests

Norm-referenced tests are produced by commercial publishers and are standardized on large populations of students. Such tests divide language and speech into components that are probed with a series of questions or tasks. Examiners must administer the tests in a standardized format, and only readminister a test in the prescribed manner. The student's correct answers are tallied and this raw score is converted to a score on a statistical scale, which can be compared to the table of norms or average scores for other children of the same age. If the student's score is significantly lower than age expectations, he or she is judged to have a deficit in that area. Standardized tests are static measures. They are administered in a prescribed way using one set of criteria, and take a "snapshot" of the student at one point in time.

Speech-language pathologists use standardized tests primarily to identify speech impairments, language disorders, auditory perceptual problems, and academic achievement. There is

Methods of Assessment Commonly Used in School Settings

I. Standardized tests for each ability area

- Speech
- Language
- Voice
- Fluency
- Reading and writing skills

- Vocabulary
- Memory
- Word retrieval
- Perception
- Statewide achievement tests

II. Performance-based measures, including curriculum-based tests

- Video- or audiotaping
- Physiological functioning—vital capacity, oral motor examinations
- Checklists and scales of learning
- Local proficiency tests
- Unit tests
- Fine motor skills
- Self-help skills
- Social-emotional skills

III. Dynamic tests

- Cognitive tasks in nonstandardized format
- Floortime™
- Checklist with levels of support

Additional Methods of Assessment

I. Screening tests
- Speech-language
- Hearing

II. Observations
- Classroom
- Playground
- Home

III. Interviews
- Parents
- Teachers
- Other educators

IV. Review of student products
- Oral
- Written
- Technology based

#TP-29703 Making a Difference - 2nd Ed. · ©2008 Thinking Publications® · www.thinkingpublications.com · 1-800-277-8737

a norm, or expected performance, for each tested skill at different ages. Students' abilities can be compared to other students of the same age across the country. In other related areas, such as psychological testing, standardized tests are also used.

Standardized tests are constructed to account for the amount of growth expected within a year for a typical student, reflected in the scaled or standard score. After a student has taken a standardized test, retesting a year later is likely to show approximately the same standard score or lower. If a student made one year's growth in one year, his or her standard score would stay the same. If he or she made less than one year's growth—common for many students with disabilities who learn at a slower rate—his or her standard score would be lower than the initial testing because the standard score compares his or her growth with the expected growth for that period of time for students in the sample.

This statistical representation of growth is the reason that many thoughtful speech-language pathologists do not use standardized tests to measure change. If a student is making month-for-month progress, there will be no apparent improvement in the score. If a student makes less than one year's progress in one year, his or her skills will appear to decline because of the lower score. A student's standard score will increase only if he or she makes exceptionally fast progress and surpasses the rate of growth in the norming sample. Therefore, standardized tests are the most useful the first time they are given, especially for identification and initial assessment purposes, and they become less useful each time they are given thereafter. In some cases, students will show improvement on a standardized test, but the next two types of assessment procedures discussed are more reliable for this purpose.

Items on standardized tests are assumed to be appropriate for all children, though they are often normed on a population sample that does not reflect the cultural and linguistic diversity found in today's schools. Many of these tools are biased toward children in the economic, cultural, and linguistic mainstream. They assume that all students have the same experiences, language opportunities, and styles of learning. For this reason, such tests must be selected and interpreted with care.

A standardized test should always be given in its entirety. Using subtests, or parts of tests, invalidates standard scores, and therefore these scores cannot be reported. Subtest tasks are viewed as performance indicators, not test scores. A few standardized tests are actually a battery of tests, and those subtests may be given independently. Speech-language pathologists need to be completely familiar with the administration and technical manuals of the standardized tests they use. It is unwise to use standardized tests in nonstandardized ways at any time. Doing so prevents speech-language pathologists from administering a valid test at a later date, since the student's performance would be affected by familiarity with the items.

Reading the test manual must be standard practice before administering a standardized assessment to any student in order to ensure that the test is appropriate for the student's age, and cultural and linguistic background, and that the test will assist in answering the diagnostic questions of the assessment. Using standardized measures on populations that do not meet the norming sample (e.g., using a preschool test to evaluate a developmentally disabled adolescent with limited language skills) is an inappropriate practice. An excellent resource for professional behavior in assessment is the Code of Fair Testing Practices in Education (2004), available on the ASHA Web site.

In the environment of RtI, it has been mentioned that standardized, in-depth assessments will not be necessary in order to determine eligibility or even baseline functioning. Standardized instruments will likely always have a place in the assessment battery of speech-language pathologists and audiologists in schools, as well as in other disciplines. In the past, there was a heavy reliance on these instruments. ASHA (2007a) annually publishes a directory of speech-

language pathology assessment instruments, which is a useful resource for speech-language pathologists. This document offers the following regarding the role of standardized tests in the assessment process:

Results of standardized tests provide the speech-language pathologist with valuable information regarding the communication abilities in specific areas. However, ASHA recognizes that standardized tests are only one component of a comprehensive assessment process. Nonstandardized or informal assessment procedures, including behavioral and pragmatic observations in natural contexts and spontaneous and structured language sampling, provide valuable information that standardized tests alone may not (p. 1).

Wiig and Secord (2006), the authors of several standardized measures, explain the balance that is necessary between standardized measures and other approaches, and offer that "A test provides a lens for examiners to observe

> behavioral segments of language and communication within a narrow, wide-angle, or panoramic view. A test lens is not intended to provide a picture of the world of language and communication in its complexity" (p. 1). They indicate that new information in our field has expanded what we, as a field, believe about the functions of standardized measures. Knowledge about brain-behavior relationships and the necessity to include contextualized information from the student's social behavior and academic performance have broadened

the lens of the examiner so that in our evaluations "performance and assessments should serve to verify one another" (p. 2).

Just as speech-language pathologists and audiologists need to ensure that the assessment results from standardized testing match the actual communication performance of a student, likewise, psychologists and teachers need to ensure that standardized test results match a student's skills and abilities. One concern about standardized assessments in these areas is that they may be culturally or linguistically biased, as in the case of intelligence testing, which may result in lower scores. Another concern is that the academic tests do not match the curriculum that is taught in the classroom. Speech-language pathologists in particular, should become familiar with the instruments that their allied professional colleagues use so that a profile of the student's skills, abilities, strengths, and deficits can be accurately described (Salvia & Ysseldyke, 2004).

Performance-Based Assessments

Performance-based assessments are another form of static testing. Students are required to demonstrate knowledge and skills in either artificially created or authentic situations. Speech-language pathologists may engage students in conversation to assess, for example, topic maintenance, focus, vocabulary, fluency, or degree of dysarthria. Students may be asked to write, draw, explain, persuade, summarize, read a passage in a book, or retell a story. The process of collecting and analyzing a language sample is an example of performance-based assessment (Miller, 1999). The tasks are in real time and reveal the actual performance of the student.

Student products, rather than student behavior, may also be analyzed in performance-based testing. Speech-language pathologists may look at journal writing, artwork, term pa-

pers, homework, or school projects. Students may be observed participating in class or communicating with peers. Some speech-language pathologists use video- or audiotape to record the performance of a student for later, often team, analysis.

Recording physiological functioning—vital capacity, oral peripheral examinations, hearing acuity tests, monitoring of throat clearing—are other examples of performance-based assessments familiar to speech-language pathologists. Assessing a person with highly dysarthric speech, swallowing problems, a hearing loss, or English as a second language requires a speech-language pathologist to interact with the individual rather than to ask questions from a formal test (Arvedson, 2000; Homer, Bickerton, Hill, Parham, & Taylor, 2000; Ukrainetz, Harpell, Walsh, & Coyle, 2000). AUGMENTATIVE AND ALTERNATIVE COMMUNICATION (AAC) users should be assessed on performance-based measures, because speech-language pathologists are interested in how well the AAC users communicate their ideas, and how they physically and linguistically create and transmit their messages. Speech-language pathologists often want to determine if a student initiates and responds to communication in a natural setting, or want to measure communicative intent. Roles and responsibilities for assessing in the area of AAC are outlined in an ASHA position statement (ASHA, 2005f).

Performance-based measures are not typically prepared commercially, although speech-language pathologists may be familiar with some tools that require students to make, create, or do something that is suggested on a checklist. Generally, performance-based assessments are either portfolios, performances, or projects. The examiner is instructed to watch the child perform the activity and record how a problem is solved, an object is described, or a barrier is surmounted. Speech-language pathologists commonly use protocols to record the performance when instrumentation is used (e.g., audiometers, nasometers, or tape recorders). Speech-language pathologists may begin or end an assessment with performance-based tasks, making notes on students' SYNTAX, fluency, word choice, or eye contact without the restrictions of standardized questions, time limits, or uniform administration of items.

Performance-based testing is not informal assessment, although it is conducted in a nonstandardized manner. This manner of assessment is based on what students do in various situations, not on how they respond to an examiner's topic through standardized questioning, and is more reflective of how the student's communication skills impact progress toward learning and mastering curricular goals. A student's skills are not compared to other students' skills, or found superior, average, deficient, or lacking. Rather, student performance is described, recorded, analyzed, and evaluated as a way of understanding what a student has learned and how he or she communicates.

Curriculum-based evaluations (CBE) (may be called curriculum-based assessments [CBA] or curriculum-based measurements [CBM]) are a common type of performance assessment used in schools that are directly linked to the student's curriculum. They can be helpful in identifying where the student is compared to classroom expectations and peers. The use of CBE/CBA/CBM is increasing due to the C.F.R. requirements for demonstrating response to interventions (Hall & Mengel, 2002; Rogers, 2005; Stecker, 2007).

Justice (2006b) identifies two rationale for using performance-based or authentic assessments: (1) because communication skills are highly influenced by context and vary across situations, performance-based assessment allows the assessor to document the student's communication performance across settings; and (2) standardized results are not useful in planning treatment.

Dynamic Testing

Dynamic testing is the observation of language or learning during the mediation or learning process (ASHA, 2005c; Cole, Dale, & Thal, 1998; Lidz & Peña, 1996). Dynamic testing is not a static method of assessment. Rather than taking a snapshot of performance (as standardized tests do) or analyzing a student's behavior, work, or functioning (as performance-based assessments do), dynamic testing looks for a description of behavior under varying conditions. The examiner is actively engaged in the task with the student, using a process-oriented approach that looks at the child as a learner (Ukrainetz et al., 2000; Justice, 2006b). "Dynamic assessment is an interactive approach to the assessment process based on intervention, and it yields information that typically is limited in traditional (static) testing: predictive and prescriptive information" (Peña, 1996, p. 281).

Dynamic testing uses a test-teach-retest approach. A task is presented to the student who is then supported by the speech-language pathologist, in all manner of ways, to accomplish

Requirements for Initial Evaluations

- Evaluation materials are selected and administered so as not to be discriminatory on a racial or cultural basis.

- Evaluation materials are in the child's native language or mode of communication as much as feasible.

- Materials and procedures minimize the effect of English language skills for students with limited English proficiency.

- A variety of tools and strategies gather relevant functional and developmental information.

- Information from parents must be included.

- Information must be included related to enabling the child to be involved in and progress in the general curriculum or appropriate preschool activities.

- Information must assist in determining whether this is a child with a disability and what the contents of the IEP should be.

- Standardized tests are valid for the purpose, and administered by trained and knowledgeable personnel according to directions.

- Any nonstandard uses of tests are reported.

- Evaluation materials include those tailored to assess specific areas of educational need, not just a single general intelligence quotient.

- Tests are selected and administered to minimize effects of impaired sensory, manual or speaking skills.

- No single procedure is used as the sole criterion for determining if this is a child with a disability or determining an appropriate program.

- The child is assessed in all areas related to the suspected disability including, if appropriate, health, vision, hearing, social and emotional status, general intelligence, academic performance, communicative status, and motor abilities.

- Comprehensive assessment identifies all special education and related service needs, whether or not these are commonly linked with the disability area identified with the child.

- Technically sound instruments are used which may assess the relative contribution of cognitive and behavioral factors, in addition to physical or developmental factors.

Source: 34 C.F.R. § 300.304

the task. In this way, the speech-language pathologist can ascertain what type and degree of assistance is needed for the student to be successful. "One important assumption of dynamic testing is that all children are capable of learning" (Peña, 1996, p. 282). The examiner continues to provide assistance to the student until the student can perform. The examiner's role is interactive, not passive as it is in static testing. DYNAMIC ASSESSMENTS emphasize the learning process the child is using, not the products of past learning (Peña, Miller, & Gillam, 1999; Wetherby & Prizant, 1998).

Known as process-oriented testing, dynamic assessment is based on the work of Vygotsky (1978), who demonstrated that children achieved more when their teachers varied the learning tasks in deliberate ways. He considered intellectual development as a socially created phenomenon that could be manipulated by the adults in a child's world. Dynamic testing is used as the method to find out what types and amount of manipulation are helpful to student learning. This assessment information leads directly to intervention planning. Student success is measured by how much less mediation is needed to get the same result after intervention. Dynamic approaches are a most valuable tool in an RtI environment.

Dynamic testing does not result in scores. Instead, this method requires speech-language pathologists to record the student's level of performance, along with the type and degree of assistance that was most helpful as a starting point for the intervention process. *Modifiability* is the term used to describe the degree of assistance the student needs to be successful (Peña, 2000; Ukrainetz et al., 2000; Gutierrez-Clellen & Peña, 2001). Dynamic protocols can be used for assess-

ing reading difficulties, articulatory behaviors, voice abnormalities, pragmatics, and stuttering. Determining a student's specific phoneme stimulability is a dynamic assessment technique. There are no set items or materials needed to conduct the assessment, and any conducive environment may be used. Dynamic assessment is particularly useful in an RtI environment.

Successful applications of dynamic assessment have included the assessment of preschool children (Moore-Brown, 2000; Peña, Quinn, & Iglesias, 1992; Schraeder, Quinn, Stockman, & Miller, 1999; Lidz & Peña, 1996), children who are CULTURALLY/LINGUISTICALLY DIVERSE (CLD) (Moore-Brown et al., 2006) and students with severe disabilities (Blackstone, 2000; Erickson & Koppenhaver, 1995; Wetherby, 1998). Speech-language pathologists in some school districts with culturally diverse populations have been taught to use dynamic assessment methods. Preliminary investigations of the assessment of Native American kindergartners have provided support for the further development of dynamic assessment as a less biased evaluation procedure than other testing protocols (Ukrainetz et al., 2000). Speech-language pathologists who have been trained to use dynamic assessment have reported increased confidence in their ability to diagnose difference from disorder in second-language learners (Peña et al., 1992; Gutierrez-Clellen & Peña, 2001, Moore-Brown et al, 2006; Haynes & Pindzola, 2004).

Criterion-Referenced Testing

Criterion-referenced tests examine a student's mastery of particular skills or information according to absolute standards (Salvia &

How Dynamic Assessment Differs from Static Assessment

Static	Dynamic
Passive participants	Active Participant
Examiner observes	Examiner participates
Identify deficits	Describe modifiability
Standardized	Fluid, responsive

Source: ASHA (2005c). Reprinted with permission.

Ysseldyke, 2004). The individual's performance is judged against a set standard or criterion. Justice (2006b) indicates there are three important qualities which define criterion-referenced testing:

1. Clear standard of performance (p. 124)

2. Design of specific tasks that reliably document individual performance against the standard (p. 125)

3. Clear guidance for interpreting performance and determining whether an individual has achieved the standard (p. 125)

Because the criterion-referenced test gives detailed information about how the student is performing, and consequently how the student is learning, the results of this testing may be more useful to parents, teachers, and students (Bond, 1996). In the area of speech-language-hearing assessment, criterion measures may be used to determine hearing levels, swallowing skills, and rate of dysfluencies (Justice, 2006b). Criterion-referenced instruments are also often used in academic settings to measure mastery of early cognitive concepts and mastery of academic standards.

Quality-of-Life Issues

Speech-language pathologists have few outcome measurements to help identify a student's level of participation in their life activities. FUNCTIONAL OUTCOMES refer to meaningful activities in one's life, which is a very large territory to assess. According to the World Health Organization (1980), quality of life should be measured using scales, inventories, and even wellness measures. For example, secondary-level students with speech-language challenges might be asked to respond to such questions as:

· Are you happy about your life?

· Do you enjoy what you are doing?

· Do you have friends? Can you communicate with them when you wish?

- Can you practice your religious faith or spiritual beliefs?

- Do you have a meaningful job?

- Are you making money for yourself and others? Are you paying taxes?

Elementary-level students might have a more limited range of quality-of-life statements. They could appear as:

- Are you happy almost every day?

- Do you enjoy school? Can you get what you need and want each day?

- Do you have friends? Can you talk to them easily?

- Can you receive help if you need it at school? At home?

- Do you have a hobby or favorite thing to do? Can you do it in your leisure time?

Students with communication disabilities should be able to have a typical quality of life. School-based speech-language pathologists are responsible for determining if students' communication disabilities impede their learning, so assessments should always include functional outcomes. It is important to know the differences among *impairment, disability*, and *handicap* and how each is assessed to assure that eligibility is determined by both impairment and disability. These three terms are discussed in detail in Chapter 4 under "Federal Eligibility Criteria for Special Education." The term handicap is generally unacceptable for use when referring to individuals with disabilities or limitations they may experience because of their disabilities. Besides "people first" language, the references in spoken and written language should refer to participation and/or accommodations in an inclusive and accepting society. Using the framework of the IST/ICT process in schools, consider how can the environment be adapted to include the individual.

A student's year-to-year growth is measured functionally in interpersonal, emotional, and academic disability areas, not by retesting to see if the impairment remains. In some cases, an impairment will not change, while a disability will be drastically reduced. For example, a child had a hearing loss that resulted in significant academic, social, and language disabilities. After two years of therapy, she made notable growth in academic, conversational, and discourse skills. Her hearing loss was no longer a disability, but she still had the same impairment—a hearing loss. Likewise, students with cerebral palsy or AUTISM SPECTRUM DISORDERS who make great communication strides during therapy will be less disabled, but will have the same impairment. Again, it is important to measure the year-to-year growth in the disability area, not solely in the impairment area.

Preferred Practice Patterns in Assessment

The methods of assessing youngsters described use the principles of assessment found in ASHA's *Preferred Practice Patterns for the Profession of Speech-Language Pathology* (ASHA, 2004e). (See sidebar on p. 120 for the fundamental components and guiding principles of preferred practice patterns according to ASHA.) School-based speech-language pathologists should follow these guidelines in their work setting. Although school districts' or states' criteria for determining eligibility for services may differ, the elements of a professional speech-language assessment remain constant.

Following ASHA's *Preferred Practice Patterns* helps ensure that speech-language and audiology assessments performed in schools will be qualitatively similar to those performed in other settings. These guidelines may also be used as an educational tool for related professionals, consumers, and policymakers. ASHA's *Preferred Practice Patterns for Speech-Language Pathologists* (ASHA, 2004e) and *Preferred Practice Patterns for the Profession of Audiology* (ASHA, 2006f) are available on the ASHA Web site (www.asha.org).

> The speech-language assessment should give an overall picture of the child as a communicator in the school setting.

The Assessment Report

The speech-language or hearing assessment should give an overall picture of the child as a communicator in the school setting. Framing statements about the child as a student in his or her class is very important. If terms like *pragmatics, syntax,* or *lexicon* are used, the speech-language pathologist should give curriculum-related examples so that educators and family members can comprehend the impact of problems in these areas.

Student assessment is conducted during the school day, through arrangements with the teacher, for suitable periods of time that the student may leave class. The student needs to be assessed in the areas identified by the referral. Testing, observation, checklists, and other forms of assessment can take many hours to complete, depending on the child's age, attention, and skill level. With very young children, especially if autism spectrum disorder is a consideration, discussions with parents or caregivers and communication development checklists can provide more information for diagnosis than interactions with the child can (Wetherby, 1998).

The speech-language pathologist or audiologist should meet with other team members to compare and validate his or her findings. The report should describe the presenting problem, describe the nature of the assessment including purpose and results of tests, and include recommendations for intervention or support services. In some districts, the team will write one comprehensive report, with each member contributing rather than having several separate reports from each assessor. Predetermining placement and services is a violation of the procedural safeguards under IDEA 2004; however, professional staff should be prepared to make recommendations, and know in advance if there are going to be disagreements among team members at the IEP. Most importantly, the staff should know if another assessor has information salient to the findings and the recommendations being made.

**Fundamental Components and Guiding Principles of the
Preferred Practice Patterns for the Profession of Speech-Language Pathology**

- Individuals who Provide the Service(s)

- Expected Outcomes

- Clinical Indicators

- Clinical Process

- Setting, Equipment Specifications, Safety and Health Precautions

- Documentation

- ASHA Policy Documents and Selected References

Source: ASHA (2004e)

Speech-language pathologists and audiologists should use good judgment when interpreting behaviors or interactions and have sufficient documentation for conclusions. Ideally, the report should be approximately two pages or less in length and available at the meeting to all team members. "The public agency provides a copy of the evaluation report and the documentation of determination of eligibility at no cost to the parent" (34 C.F.R. § 300.306 [2]). Parents may request to see the report before the IEP meeting. This is generally a good idea and good practice, especially if the parent is concerned. A prompt short report is often much more helpful to the team than a long comprehensive one that may take much longer to compose and be read. School-based speech-language pathologists and audiologists need to become skilled at writing brief but complete reports, using descriptions understood by team members representing other disciplines. Speech-language pathologists

may need to write a longer, more comprehensive report if there are extenuating circumstances, such as a due process situation or a complicated case.

Speech-language pathologists may be able to use a comprehensive format to present all the information about a student's assessment and functioning level. Using one format is particularly helpful for students with complex medical needs or developmental disabilities in which large amounts of evidence and observational information must be conveyed to the team. This approach is particularly helpful for recording observations and comments to use as an assessment report. The profile form can streamline the efforts of all team members when students have complicated behaviors.

As the speech-language pathologist works with a group of educators over time, team members are likely to learn speech-language or audiology terminology, diagnoses, and corresponding interventions. In schools, unlike health-care or private practice settings, the speech-language pathologist is often the only person in the building who is a professional in this field. Speech-language pathologists and audiologists should consider how to increase the knowledge base of all the other team members each time they assess a student, write a report, or work with an educator or family.

Assessment is a critical aspect of working in the school setting. Unlike intervention, which may be carried out by teachers, aides, family members, assistants, bus drivers, and others under the supervision or direction of the speech-language pathologist or audiologist, assessment is carried out solely by the speech-language pathologist or audiologist. Finding a baseline of student abilities, recognizing the value and limitations of standardized tests, and determining present levels of communication performance allows the educational team to make the best decisions about the student's eligibility for services. A well-crafted report is vital to the family, the student, the team, and the school district.

Assessment reports provide the legal documentation that the school district and family need regarding completion of the requirements laid out above. Clearly documenting the processes and procedures followed, results, and conclusions provides the district with a legally defendable report that will allow everyone to follow what happened during the assessment process should there be a challenge to the decisions. The importance of accuracy and timeliness of the assessment report cannot be overstated.

Independent Educational Evaluation

From time to time, a parent may disagree with the school team's findings and feel that an outside evaluator would arrive at a different conclusion or recommendations. Typically, the parent is seeking a conclusion that includes an intervention program at school different from the one that is desired or recommended by the school IEP or MDAT team members.

If parents do not agree with an evaluation completed by school district personnel, they have the right to have an independent educational evaluation conducted by a qualified examiner at public expense. In these types of cases, the school district will generally present the parents with a list of two or three choices of qualified evaluators. Parents choose from this list, and the district is responsible for the cost, as well as for reconvening an IEP meeting to consider the results of the independent assessment.

In situations where parents seek or present the school district with an independent evaluation that they obtained at their own expense, the school district must consider the results of the evaluation (34 C.F.R. § 300.502 [c]). Parents who seek reimbursement for an evaluation obtained at their own expense should be referred to the administrator in charge of the special education program, as this would not be determined by the speech-language pathologist. Immediate attention to such requests is required, however, so the speech-language pathologist or audiologist should contact the special education administrator immediately upon receiving such a request.

Needless to say, speech-language pathologists and audiologists in schools try to avoid these confrontations whenever possible. If the state's eligibility criteria are adhered to, and the speech-language pathologist's assessment is complete and well administered, the school district should be on solid ground. School-based speech-language pathologists and audiologists must know and agree to work within the federal, state, and local parameters of a "speech, language or hearing disability," as defined by IDEA 2004, rather than the broader definitions that might be available within other work settings. Working with legal and procedural safeguards, setting and maintaining timelines, and making team decisions are all part of the daily experience of a speech-language pathologist or audiologist and can require great flexibility. Working closely with one's mentors and supervisors in the schools is advisable should any conflicts arise. (See also Chapter 8, "Independent Educational Evaluation (IEE).")

CHAPTER 4

The IEP Process and Procedures

This chapter explains the who, when, and what of the IEP meeting. It highlights federal and state eligibility criteria for speech-language and audiology services in schools. Finally, the chapter integrates the procedures for determining a student's need for services with procedures for determining successful completion of services. This integrated approach increases accountability and assists families. This chapter pertains to the IEP meeting process required by IDEA 2004, not to be confused with the methodologies involved in speech-language assessments described in Chapter 3.

1. Examine a text from any core subject and consider the information about universal design. Does this text lend itself to the precepts of universal design? How could you use this text for individuals with speech or language impairments?

2. What is the difference between eligibility and placement? Why is this distinction important?

3. Describe the World Health Organization (WHO) categories in Figure 4.1 (p. 140) in your own words and why it is so valuable in the school setting.

4. Explain the educational relevance of a communication disorder and why the federal government requires that "adverse educational affect" must be documented for speech and language services.

5. Discuss why you think that definitions and criteria for language impairment and services vary so much from state to state. Is this an advantage or a disadvantage? Explain your answer.

6. Examine content and performance standards from your state or district. Select areas that could be used as benchmarks or objectives for students with communication disorders.

7. Describe the precautions you must take in documentation and recordkeeping.

8. What is the purpose of triennial assessment?

9. When should a speech-language pathologist decide on dismissal criteria? Why?

10. Contact a speech-language pathologist in your area or study your own caseload. How many students are culturally linguistically diverse (CLD)? What percentage of the entire caseload is CLD? Is there a disporportionality of students with communication disabilities on this caseload? Why did it occur? Is it justifiable? Why or why not? What can be done about this?

The IEP Meeting Process

The language that describes INDIVIDUALIZED EDUCATION PROGRAMS (IEPs) is sometimes confusing due to the acronyms and dual meanings for some of the terminology used. An IEP may refer to "a written statement for a child with a disability that is developed, reviewed, and revised" (34 C.F.R. § 300.22). Common vernacular also uses IEP to refer to the process of the meeting or to the meeting itself.

For children 2 years, 11 months of age and younger, an INDIVIDUALIZED FAMILY SERVICE PLAN (IFSP) is developed in place of an IEP as the written document resulting from the IEP meeting. For children 3–5 years, the INDIVIDUALS WITH DISABILITIES EDUCATION IMPROVEMENT ACT (IDEA 2004) permits states to use an IFSP to meet IEP requirements if using that plan is agreed by the LOCAL EDUCATION AGENCY (LEA) and the parents (34 C.F.R. § 300.323 [b][ii]). See Chapter 6 for further discussion of preschool-age children.

Printed IEP forms include all the required components of the IEP. These components are more than just lines on a page or an intent to create burdensome paperwork. Each of these areas relates to a specific requirement of the federal or state special education law. The forms guide the IEP team through the steps of the IEP meeting process. The sections that follow describe this process.

Who Comprises the IEP Team?

The Code of Federal Regulations (34 C.F.R. § 300.321 [a]) specifies that the members of the IEP team include the following:

(1) The parents of the child;

(2) Not less than one regular education teacher of the child (if the child is, or may be, participating in the regular education environment);

(3) Not less than one special education teacher of the child, or where appropriate, not less then one special education provider of the child;

(4) A representative of the public agency who—

(i) Is qualified to provide, or supervise the provision of, specially designed instruction to meet the unique needs of children with disabilities;

(ii) Is knowledgeable about the general curriculum; and

(iii) Is knowledgeable about the availability of resources of the public agency;

(5) An individual who can interpret the instructional implications of evaluation results, who may be another member of the team described in paragraphs (a)(2) through (a)(6) of this section;

(6) At the discretion of the parent or the agency, other individuals who have knowledge or special expertise regarding the child, including related services personnel as appropriate; and

(7) Whenever appropriate, the child with a disability.

Others may also attend the IEP meeting. Parents or the district may bring anyone to an IEP meeting whom they determine has knowledge or special "expertise" regarding the child. Often a friend or relative can give parents some support for the meeting. A notable exception is if a parent intends to bring an attorney to the IEP meeting. (See "Impartial Due Process Hearings" in Chapter 8.) School district participants may only be individuals who have a legitimate educational interest in the purpose of the IEP meeting. The confines of confidentiality apply to such meetings. (See "Recordkeeping and Documentation" on p. 159 for a discussion on confidentiality.) Individuals such as union representatives or secretaries may not attend IEP meetings if their purpose for being there is not related to the development of the IEP for the child. Individuals attending IEP meetings must possess the required "knowledge or special expertise" about the child. Under this provision, the party who invites the individual with "knowledge or special expertise" is responsible for that determination (34 C.F.R. § 300.321 [a][6]).

The expectations of the regular education teacher's participation in the development of the child's IEP, specifically with regard to positive behavioral supports and supplementary aids and services, program modifications, and support for school personnel, are set forth. The support for school personnel is intended to be directed so that the child can advance toward his or her IEP goals, be involved in the general education curriculum, and be able to participate in the regular class and activities like nondisabled children (34 C.F.R. § 300.324 [a][3]).

Note that the members of the MULTIDISCIPLINARY ASSESSMENT TEAM (MDAT) may also be members of the IEP team. Certain MDAT members, such as a psychologist, may not be able to attend all IEP meetings. Table 4.1 compares the types of teams and potential members of each. Team responsibilities are an important part of the speech-language pathologist's role in schools.

Parent participation in IEP meetings was given renewed emphasis under IDEA 2004 (see sidebar on pp. 128–129). Lack of parent interest or the inconvenience of scheduling IEP meetings are common frustrations for school personnel. School-based professionals need to pay particular attention to the requirements for involving families, including the requirements for documenting attempts at scheduling the IEP meeting at a mutually agreed upon time and place (34 C.F.R. § 300.322 [a][2]), which may be a conference call if attendance is not possible (34 C.F.R. § 300.322 [c]). Holding meetings before or after the speech-language pathologist's work hours may have legal, safety, and union ramifications. These considerations can be arranged with the administrator and require flexibility on everyone's part.

Requirements for parent participation in meetings are set forth in 34 C.F.R. § 300.501:

(b) (1) The parent of a child with a disability must be afforded an opportunity to participate in meetings to inspect and review all educational records to—

(i) The identification, evaluation, and educational placement of the child; and

(ii) The provision of FAPE to the child.

Table 4.1

School Team Members

Instructional Support Team (IST)	Multidisciplinary Assessment Team (MDAT)	IEP Team
General Ed Teacher(s)	Speech-Language Pathologist	Parent
Special Ed Teacher	Psychologist	Local Education Agency Representative (Administrator)
School Administrator	Nurse	General Ed Teacher
Counselor	General Ed Teacher	Special Ed Teacher
Parent	Special Ed Teacher	Members of the MDT (if reviewing assessment results)
Student (if appropriate)	Parent	Student (if appropriate)
Specialist(s) (optional)	Specialists* (if necessary)	Individuals invited by parent or school district
* Psychologist	* Occupational therapist	
* Speech-language pathologist	* Physical therapist	
* LD Teacher	* Teacher of hearing impaired	
School counselor (MS/HS)	* Teacher of visually impaired	
Nurse (if necessary)	* Behavior specialist	

*Specialists who potentially might be team members

IDEA 2004 has some new provisions regarding meeting attendance and excusal of team members. These provisions must be utilized with caution, as the purpose of the IEP meeting is to ensure that the whole team is aware of the child's needs and programs. However, Congress recognized that sometimes there is a need to have a meeting and some team members may not be able to be in attendance.

34 C.R.F. § 300.320 (e) IEP Team attendance.

(1) A member of the IEP Team described in paragraphs (a)(2) through (a)(5) of this section is not required to attend an IEP Team meeting, in whole or in part, if the parent of a child with a disability and the public agency agree, in writing, that the attendance of the member is not necessary because the member's areas of the curriculum or related services is not being modified or discussed in the meeting.

(2) A member of the IEP Team described in paragraph (e)(1) of this section may be excused from attending an IEP Team meeting, in whole or in part, when the meeting involves a modification to or discussion of the member's area of the curriculum or related services, if—

Parent Participation in IEPs

(a) Public agency responsibility—general.

Each public agency shall take steps to ensure that one or both of the parents of a child with a disability are present at each IEP meeting or are afforded the opportunity to participate, including—

(1) Notifying parents of the meeting early enough to ensure that they will have an opportunity to attend; and

(2) Scheduling the meeting at a mutually agreed on time and place.

(b) Information provided to parents.

(1) The notice required under paragraph (a)(1) of this section must—

(i) Indicate the purpose, time, and location of the meeting and who will be in attendance; and

(ii) Inform the parents of the provisions in Sec. 300.344 (a)(6) and (c) (relating to the participation of other individuals on the IEP team who have knowledge or special expertise about the child).

(2) For a student with a disability beginning at age 14, or younger, if appropriate, the notice must also—

(i) Indicate that a purpose of the meeting will be the development of a statement of the transition services needs of the student required in Sec. 300.347 (b)(1); and

(ii) Indicate that the agency will invite the student.

(3) For a student with a disability beginning at age 16, or younger, if appropriate, the notice must—

(i) Indicate that a purpose of the meeting is the consideration of needed transition services for the student required in Sec. 300.347 (b)(2);

(ii) Indicate that the agency will invite the student; and

(iii) Identify any other agency that will be invited to send a representative.

(c) Other methods to ensure parent participation.

If neither parent can attend, the public agency shall use other methods to ensure parent participation, including individual or conference telephone calls.

(d) Conducting an IEP meeting without a parent in attendance.

A meeting may be conducted without a parent in attendance if the public agency is unable to convince the parents that they should attend. In this case the public agency must have a record of its attempts to arrange a mutually agreed on time and place, such as—

Continued

Parent Participation in IEPs – *Continued*

(1) Detailed records of telephone calls made or attempted and the results of those calls;

(2) Copies of correspondence sent to the parents and any responses received; and

(3) Detailed records of visits made to the parent's home or place of employment and the results of those visits.

(e) Use of interpreters or other action, as appropriate.

The public agency shall take whatever action is necessary to ensure that the parent understands the proceedings at the IEP meeting, including arranging for an interpreter for parents with deafness or whose native language is other than English.

(f) Parent copy of child's IEP.

The public agency shall give the parent a copy of the child's IEP at no cost to the parent.

Source: 34 C.F.R. § 300.322

(i) The parent, in writing, and the public agency consent to the excusal; and

(ii) The member submits, in writing to the parent and the IEP Team, input into the development of the IEP prior to the meeting.

The U.S. Department of Education (USDE) cautions school districts to use this provision with reserve. The intent is to provide school districts with flexibility but not to deny participation of the team members, nor to deny parents access to these members.

An LEA may not routinely or unilaterally excuse IEP Team members from attending IEP Team meetings as parent agreement or consent is required in each instance. We encourage LEAs to carefully consider, based on the individual needs of the child and the issues that need to be ad-

dressed at the IEP Team meeting whether it makes sense to offer to hold the IEP Team meeting without a particular IEP Team member in attendance or whether it would be better to reschedule the meeting so that person could attend and participate in the discussion...An LEA that routinely excuses IEP Team members from attending IEP Team meetings would not be in compliance under the Act..." (71 Fed. Reg. 46674).

Using the excusal provision must be done with concern regarding the provision of FAPE. Several due process cases and court decisions have held that the absence of certain teachers constituted a *de facto* (e.g., automatic) denial of FAPE for the child (see Chapter 8).

Team members are allowed to meet and confer outside of an IEP regarding students without parents being present:

(3) A meeting does not include informal or unscheduled conversations involving public agency personnel and conversations on issues such as teaching methodology, lesson plans, or coordination of service provision. A meeting also does not include preparatory activities that public agency personnel engage in to develop a proposal or response to a parent proposal that will be discussed at a later meeting.

When Are IEP Meetings Held?

An IEP meeting must be held at least once each year (known as an annual review) and when a reevaluation is completed. Reevaluations can be completed for different reasons: because it is time for a triennial reevaluation (also known as a three-year evaluation) as required by IDEA 2004, because of requests from the student's parents or teachers, or because the school district determined reevaluation was warranted (34 C.F.R. § 300.305). (See "Annual and Triennial Assessments" on p. 163 and "Reevaluations" in Chapter 3 for more details.) IDEA 2004 requires that an IEP meeting must be held within 30 days of an initial determination that a student needs special education and related services (34 C.F.R. § 300.323 [c][1]).

An IEP meeting should also be held any time new factors that affect the student's program occur. Such examples include the following: (1) the student is not making anticipated progress on goals; (2) the student is having difficulties in school (e.g., behavior problems or failing a class); (3) a new service is being considered; or (4) any member of the IEP team, including the parent or teacher, requests a meeting. At the IEP meeting, the team develops the student's IEP, which

constitutes the basics of the student's specially designed program. Additional meetings held during the year to revise the IEP may be held as an addendum to the existing program. Local practice dictates how this process is handled.

Who Is Responsible for Sending the IEP Meeting Notice?

The responsibility for sending out the notice of an IEP meeting varies from district to district and may depend on the nature of the meeting. Generally, a CASE MANAGER is responsible for sending the IEP meeting notice, since he or she coordinates the special education program for the student. Most often, the case manager is the person who is the student's primary service provider. If the speech-language pathologist is the only service provider, then he or she is likely to be the one responsible for sending out the meeting notice. Federal regulations require that parents be notified of the meeting early enough to ensure that they will have an opportunity to attend and that the meeting will be held in a mutually agreeable time and place (34 C.F.R. § 300.322 [a][1][2]). States and local education agencies vary in terms of accepted practice for the amount of time to notify a parent of a meeting. Generally, a week to ten days is required.

What Must Be Considered at an IEP Meeting?

In developing each child's IEP, the IEP team shall consider—

(i)   The strengths of the child;

(ii)   The concerns of the parents for enhancing the education of their child;

(iii) The results of the initial evaluation or most recent evaluation of the child; and

(iv) The academic, developmental, and functional needs of the child (34 C.F.R. § 300.324 [a]).

The same section of the code (34 C.F.R. § 300.324 [2]) specifies that the IEP team must also consider special factors, such as:

- The need for positive behavioral supports for the child whose behavior is impeding the child's learning or the learning of others.

- Language needs for a child with limited English proficiency.

- Instruction in Braille and the use of Braille for a child who is blind or visually impaired, as well as the need for appropriate reading and writing media.

- The communication needs and academic instructional needs of a child who is deaf or hard of hearing.

- ASSISTIVE TECHNOLOGY (AT) devices and services (including an intervention, accommodation, or other program modification needed by the student in order to learn or use the device or service).

When the IEP team considers the language needs of children with limited English proficiency, as those needs relate to the child's IEP, speech-language pathologists may be called upon to differentiate between a language difference and a language disorder. Speech-language pathologists must have knowledge and expertise in the normal developmental process for second language acquisition, since some of these processes may present like a language disorder. The sidebars below and on p. 132 highlight other skills needed by speech-language pathologists working with diverse student populations.

Federal and state laws for special education specifically deny eligibility if the reason for the child's learning problem is due to "environmen-

---

Skills Needed by Speech-Language Pathologists
Serving Diverse Student Populations

- Skills for diagnostics; intervention
- Ability to provide differential diagnosis
- Understanding of new roles in team membership
- Ability to use and supervise support personnel (e.g., speech-language pathology assistants)
- Assurance of appropriate provision of services
- Flexibility in service delivery model

- Ability to serve multicultural student populations in an environment of school reform
- Demonstration of treatment outcomes
- Application of the role of the speech-language pathologist in literacy
- Knowledge of the curriculum
- Ability to advocate for students and the professions

From *Multicultural Issues for the Professions,* by B. Moore-Brown, 1999a. Presentation at the Fourth Annual Communication Disorders Multicultural Conference of the National Student Speech-Language-Hearing Association, Fullerton, CA. ©1999 by B. Moore-Brown. Adapted with permission.

Information Needed by Speech-Language Pathologists
Serving Diverse Student Populations

Speech-language pathologists in public schools need to know the following to best serve all students, but particularly students from diverse backgrounds.

The curriculum, including requirements for:
- High school exit exam
- Social promotion and retention
- Statewide assessment
- Multiple measures

The other categorical programs, including:
- Federal program: Title I
- State program: Economic Impact Aid/Limited English Proficient (EIA/LEP)

The district/county/state resources:
- Watch for training sessions and attend them with a general educator

The processes for helping/assisting students in your school/district:
- Student Success Teams
- Local intervention programs
- Other categorical programs
- Alternative education programs (including adult education)

From *Multicultural Issues for the Professions,* by B. Moore-Brown, 1999a. Presentation at the Fourth Annual Communication Disorders Multicultural Conference of the National Student Speech-Language-Hearing Association, Fullerton, CA. ©1999 by B. Moore-Brown. Adapted with permission.

tal or economic disadvantage; or limited English proficiency" (34 C.F.R. § 300.309 [a][3][v][vi]). The demands of a student population that is increasingly diverse necessitates that speech-language pathologists be culturally competent (Wolf & Calderon, 1999; ASHA, 2004d; 2005b) and aware of the issues outside of school (e.g., mobility, poverty, literacy, access to education, access to health care, variability of language/cultural upbringing, and parental participation in the child's education) that may be affecting the school performance of students from diverse backgrounds (Moore-Brown, 1999a, 1999b). The need for trained, competent, fully certificated staff will continue to permeate the work world of schools to deal with this population (ASHA, 2004d).

There are many sources of guidance for serving students from diverse backgrounds (Roseberry-McKibbin, 2007). The AMERICAN SPEECH-LANGUAGE-HEARING ASSOCIATION'S (ASHA's) Office of Multicultural Affairs may be of assistance to members. State departments of education may also offer resources or handbooks (e.g., *Guidelines for Language, Academic, and Special Education Services Required for Limited-English-Proficient Students in California Public Schools, K–12* (California Department of Education, 1997). State association projects and reference books in the field will also provide guidance for serving students from diverse backgrounds, for example, the California Speech-Language-Hearing Association's Diversity Committee sponsors a Web page which lists numerous links to sites with information on diversity issues. The Texas Speech-Language-Hearing Association has a Diversity Issues section on their Web site featuring the CLD Corner with Frequently Asked Questions, as well as a document *on Linguistically Diverse Populations: Considerations And Resources For Assessment and Intervention* (See sections on "Disproportionality" (on p. 146) and "Language Minority Students" (on p. 149) later in this chapter.)

What Are the Steps in the IEP Meeting Process?

IEP forms should guide the IEP team through the procedural requirements of the IEP. When developing an IEP, following a particular process is very important. The recommended process will not only guarantee that the requirements of IDEA 2004 are followed, but will also ensure that each member of the team can follow along and assist in building a program for the child that will provide FREE APPROPRIATE PUBLIC EDUCATION (FAPE).

When developing an IEP, think of the process and resulting document as a road map to the student's education. The IEP meeting process has three parts: (1) determination of present levels of educational achievement; (2) development of goals and short-term objectives or benchmarks; and (3) determination of program, placement, and services. Following this three-step process at every IEP meeting will allow for information to be shared and the resulting decisions to be made based on the requisite information. (Table 4.2 highlights important changes under IDEA 2004 and their implications for speech-language pathologists.)

Determination of Present Levels of Educational Achievement

The first step in the IEP meeting process is determining present levels of educational achievement. Depending on the type of meeting being held, present levels of educational achievement are considered by any and all of the following methods:

- Reviewing assessment(s), including statewide, schoolwide, or classroom, as well as specialist or psychoeducational assessments.

- Reviewing classroom work.

- Reviewing grade reports.

- Teacher or specialist report (oral or written).

- Parent and student information and interests.

- Review of the previous year's goals and the progress made.

- Consideration of new information brought forth by any member of the team.

- Report on student progress and behavior by service providers.

Table 4.2	**IDEA 2004 IEP Processes and Procedures**
Law	• Present levels of performance statements include the child's present levels of academic achievement and functional performance (§ 614 [d][A][i][I]). • For students who take alternate assessments, include benchmarks or short-term objectives aligned to alternate achievement standards on the IEP (§ 614 [d][A][I][cc]). • IEPs must include statements of measurable annual academic and functional goals designed to meet the child's needs that result from the child's disability. Goals must support the child's progress in the general education curriculum and meet each of the child's other educational needs resulting from the child's disability (§ 614 [d][B][II][aa][bb]). • Periodic reports of the child's progress toward the annual goals are to be provided concurrent with report cards (§ 614 [d][A][i][III]). • To the extent practicable, statements of special education, related services and supplementary services will be based on peer-reviewed research (§ 614 [d][1][A][i][IV]). • Special education, related services, modifications, and supports will be planned to help the child advance toward attaining annual goals, be involved in and make progress in the general education curriculum, participate in extra-curricular and other nonacademic activities, and participate with other children with and without disabilities (§ 614 [d][1][A](i)[IV]). • The IEP must include a statement of accommodations necessary on State and districtwide assessments (§ 614 [d][1][A](i)[VI][aa]). • Transition goals and services must be included in the IEP by the time the child is age 16 (§ 614 [d][A][VIII]). • Language regarding IEP Team members notes that "not less than one" general education teacher and "not less than one" special education teacher or service provider are to be included in the composition of the IEP Team. The representative of the LEA must be knowledgeable in the general education curriculum (§ 614 [d][B]). • Attendance at the IEP meeting is not necessary for a member of the IEP Team whose area of curriculum or related service is not being modified or discussed at the meeting, and if the parents and LEA agree that person does not need to be in attendance (§ 614 [d][1][C][i]). • Attendance at the IEP meeting is not necessary for a member of the IEP Team if that area of curriculum or related service is being modified or discussed when the parent and LEA agree to the excusal and the member submits input to the IEP Team in writing prior to the meeting (§ 614 [d][1][C][ii]). • Parent consent to excusal of IEP Team members must be in writing (§ 614 [1][d][C][iii]). • In addition to considering the strengths of the child, the concerns of the parent for enhancing the education of their child, and the results of initial evaluation or reevaluation of the child, the IEP Team must also consider the academic, developmental, and functional needs of the child (§ 614 [d][3][A]). • After the annual IEP meeting, parents and LEAs may make agreements not to reconvene an IEP meeting to amend or modify the child's current IEP. Instead they may develop a written document to agree on the amendment(s) (§ 614 [d][3][D]). • Upon request, parents will receive a revised copy of the IEP with the amendments incorporated (§ 614 [d][3][F]). • LEAs are encouraged to consolidate reevaluation meetings and other team meetings (§ 614 [d][3][E]).

Source: IDEA (2004)

Continued

Table 4.2 – *Continued*

Implications for Speech-Language Pathologists	IEP development and meetings emphasize consideration of the child's academic achievement and functional performance. This underscores the need for speech-language pathologists to have goals that are curriculum related, and to understand and address how the child's communication disorder impacts the child's ability to both access and meet the goals of the general education classroom. This also includes considering adaptive or functional skills that interfere with academic performance. Note that the former language, "at least one" general education teacher and "at least one" special education teacher or service provider, has changed to "not less than one." Allowances for IEP amendments and excusal of certain participants from IEP meetings should be reviewed carefully. Guidance should be sought at the local level on these requirements. Make sure parent agreement is documented in writing.
	Now, even more than before, speech-language pathologists should develop and maintain strong, compassionate, and professional relationships with parents. These relationships can result in important contributions from parents during the evaluation and IEP planning processes.

• Discipline and behavioral information.

• Consideration of statewide assessment results.

When writing present levels of achievement, use positive rather than negative statements (see sidebar on p. 136). IDEA 2004 regulations require that all IEPs include:

(a) (1) A statement of the child's present levels of academic achievement and functional performance, including—

(i) How the child's disability affects the child's involvement and progress in the general curriculum (i.e., the same curriculum as for nondisabled children); or

(ii) For preschool children, as appropriate, how the disability affects the child's participation in appropriate activities (34 C.F.R. § 300.320).

Conducting intervention with curriculum goals in mind is not a new concept in the field of speech-language pathology (Hoskins, 1990; Montgomery, 1994; Moore-Brown, 1992; Nelson, 1990; 1992), but the IDEA 2004 requirement puts the conceptual practice into law (Brannen et al., 2000). Speech-language pathologists in public schools must be able to integrate knowledge of COMMUNICATION DISORDERS with knowledge of the scope and developmental sequence of curriculum.

Classroom curriculums are built on taxonomies that reflect the developmental levels of children in each grade. Children who are delayed or disordered will most certainly have challenges with the curriculum of the classroom. State or local standards for learning describe the instructional concepts that must be mastered at each grade level. These documents must be available to all teachers in a school district, and are also available to specialists. If speech-language pathologists do not have a copy of the district's adopted standards, they should contact the princi-

Writing Positive Statements of Present Levels of Educational Achievement

Present levels should be stated in terms of what the student is able to do. When describing present levels of educational performance, discuss the student's strengths and state needs in positive terms.

Negative	Positive
• Cannot understand speech	• Able to produce five single words intelligibly
• Does not use words	• Uses gestures to communicate intent
• Does not know alphabet	• Able to distinguish between letters and numbers
• Has not mastered sound/symbol relationships	• Identifies words that begin with the same sound sixty percent of the time

pal or the district's administrator of educational services. Speech-language pathologists must know what the expectations are for students in each grade in order to assist the child in his or her interaction with the curriculum and to develop the IEP with standards in mind.

As an IEP team member, the speech-language pathologist will need to go beyond sharing the results of standardized or nonstandardized assessments of communication skills. He or she must be able to interpret how those results are related to what happens in the classroom and design intervention to meet curriculum-based goals or outcomes.

These requirements reflect the connection between NO CHILD LEFT BEHIND (NCLB, 2001) and IDEA 2004. The present law extends the emphasis on post-school outcomes as being a primary responsibility of IDEA 2004. The IEP is the document that ties together the goals of both laws—including children with disabilities in the general education accountability system while still ensuring attention to a student's individual learning needs.

The Office of Special Education Programs (OSEP, 2005) comments:

IDEA is now aligned with the important principles of NCLB in promoting accountability for results, enhancing the role of parents and improving student achievement through instructional approaches that are based on scientific research. While IDEA focuses on the needs of individual students and NCLB focuses on school accountability, both laws share the goals of improving academic achievement though high exceptions and high-quality programs.

Through these efforts we are reaching beyond physical access to the education system toward achieving full access to high-quality curricula and instruction to improve education outcomes for children and youths with disabilities (pp. 1–2).

This focus on outcomes, results, and accountability is the essence of the law—higher than access and higher than inclusion (Fagan, Friedman, & Fulfrost, 2007). The mandate to make a statement about the student's academic achievement and have a discussion about how the disability impacts the student's ability to succeed in the general education curriculum again directs the IEP Team and service providers to the curriculum and the general education program. To ensure access to the general education curriculum, IDEA 2004 suggests the use of UNIVERSAL DESIGN principles.

To meet the mandate for mastering the general education curriculum, curricula that have students' specialized learning needs in mind need to be developed, as described by Orkwis and McLane (1998):

> Access to the curriculum begins with a student being able to interact with it to learn...The curriculum must be delivered with an array of supports for the student. The barriers to access must be removed, but importantly, the curriculum has to continue to challenge them [students] (pp. 6–7).

The method for removing barriers is universal design. According to Orkwis and McLane (1998):

> In terms of learning, universal design means the design of instructional materials and activities that allows the learning goals to be achievable by individuals with wide differences in their abilities to see, hear, speak, move, read, write, understand English, attend, organize, engage, and remember. Universal design for learning is achieved by means of flexible curricular materials and activities that provide alternatives for students with disparities in abilities and backgrounds. These alternatives should be built into the instructional design and operating systems of educational materials—they should not have to be added on later (p. 9).

For school districts and local curriculum committees, the U.S. Department of Education (USDE, 1999) recommended the following considerations to guide curriculum selection:

- Does the curriculum provide multiple means of presentation of content?

- Does the curriculum provide multiple and flexible means of student engagement or participation?

- Does the curriculum provide multiple means of student responses (p. I-26)?

Universal Design for Learning (UDL) is often paired with DIFFERENTIATED INSTRUCTION (DI) as methods which can effectively provide curriculum support for students with disabilities. UDL curriculum is intended to be "innately flexible" (Hall, Strangman, & Meyer, 2003). UDL operates on the following three principles:

1. To support recognition, learning; provide multiple, flexible methods of presentation.

2. To support strategic learning, provide multiple, flexible methods of expression and apprenticeship.

3. To support affective learning, provide multiple, flexible options for engagement (Hall et al., 2003, p. 7, 23).

The USDE was concerned that special educators were often not involved in the development of curriculum, at either a state or local level. Additionally, the USDE noted that standards and universal design would only be effective if educators were trained in pedagogy, which could lead to an understanding of how to make the curriculum concepts meaningful to all students. A need for instructional materials that are accessible to students through a variety of formats and in multiple presentation modes was identified by the USDE.

Finally, instructional strategies must be intense, frequent, explicit, and individually referenced for the student(s) so that students will "acquire skills that will better prepare them for life after school" (USDE, 1999, pp. I-30). California is one example of a state that has included information on universal design in its framework in order to assist educators in developing curriculum (California Department of Education, 1999e). Further, IDEA 2004 requires that the LEA representative on the IEP team is knowledgeable about the general curriculum (34 C.F.R. § 300.321 [a][4][ii]) to direct the linkage between the special education program and the general education curriculum and setting.

Federal Eligibility Criteria for Special Education

If the purpose of the IEP meeting is to review initial assessments (see Chapter 3 for a discussion of the initial assessment process), then present levels of academic achievement and functional performance will be determined when eligibility is considered. If the purpose of the IEP meeting is part of a triennial reevaluation (see "Annual

and Triennial Assessments" on p. 163), continuing eligibility will be considered.

In either case, a child may not be determined to be eligible if:

(b) (1) The determinant factor for that eligibility determination is—

(i) Lack of appropriate instruction in reading, including the essential components of reading instruction (as defined in section 1208 [3] of the ESEA);

(ii) Lack of appropriate instruction in math; or

(ii) Limited English proficiency; and

(2) The child does not otherwise meet the eligibility criteria under Sec. 300.8 (34 C.F.R. § 300.306).

If it is determined that a child is not eligible for special education, the next two steps in the IEP meeting process—development of goals and short-term objectives or benchmarks and determination of program, placement, and services—do not occur. The IEP team may instead do any of the following: (1) make some general recommendations to the classroom teacher for assisting student in the classroom, (2) refer the student back to the IST or a tiered program, or (3) refer the student to the 504 team for eligibility determination under Section 504 (see Chapter 8 "Section 504 and the Americans with Disabilities Act [ADA]"). In these situations, IEP teams should ensure that some form of assistance is provided so that the child does not continue to struggle and fail in school.

If a child is determined to be eligible for special education, the next two steps in the

IEP process do take place. The MDAT can determine that a student is eligible if the student has one or more disabilities that require special education and related services because of the disability(ies). The 13 eligibility categories identified under IDEA 2004 appear in the sidebar below. Notice that the terms *impairment* and *disability* occur. The World Health Organization (WHO) developed a helpful way to conceptualize the terms *impairment, disability*, and *handicap*, which were embraced by ASHA in 1995 (see Figure 4.1). Although these terms have been used interchangeably over the years, they have distinctly different meanings.

Impairment refers to the existence of an abnormality of the structure or function of the student's communication at an organic level (e.g., vocal nodules, a tongue thrust, a distorted /r/ phoneme, hearing loss, repetition of the initial phoneme in words, or cognitive limitations). The presence of an impairment can be ascertained with the traditional instruments and STANDARDIZED TESTS that are common to the field. These tools will help determine if the person's communication deviates from the norms for age and ability. Traditional diagnostic measures can and should be used to determine impairment in any setting the student is seen for assessment. Impairment can be determined by comparing the child's standard score with age-appropriate norms (i.e., percentiles or similar measures from a nondisabled population).

Disability refers to the functional consequence of the known impairment. Speech-language pathologists must use functional status measures to determine the communication problems that impede the student's daily life activities. In school, the broadest educational environment is used to determine functional status: class grades, class participation, self-esteem,

Federal Eligibility Categories for Special Education

Autism	Multiple Disabilities
Deaf-Blindness	Other Health Impairment
Developmental Delay (state option)	Orthopedic Impairment
Emotional Disturbance	Speech or Language Impairment
Hearing Impairment	Traumatic Brain Injury
Learning Disability	Visual Impairment
Mental Retardation	

States may also authorize school districts to include the condition of "developmental delay" for children aged 3 through 9, or a subset of this age group.

Source: 34 C.F.R. § 300.7 (a)(1)

Figure 4.1

World Health Organization (WHO) Categories
(Adapted for Communication Disabilities)

Impairment	Disability	Handicap
An abnormality in a person's structure or physical function	Actual effect an impairment has upon a person's life activities	Society's views of persons with disabilities
Examples: Autism, dysarthria, hearing loss, voice disorder, stuttering, etc.	**Examples:** Difficulty hearing conversation, reading problems, hard for others to understand, memory problems, etc.	**Examples:** Limited social life and career options; less likely to make high income, attract desirable partner, become well educated
Measured by: Standardized, norm referenced tests in the discipline	**Measured by:** Functional outcomes in one's actual life activities; changes that occur due to interventions	**Measured by:** Quality of life indicators, society's beliefs and pre-conceptions, violation of laws
Use to decide eligibility if adverse effect on learning	Use for progress reports, year-to-year changes	Use to determine possible violations of civil rights

Source: WHO (1980)

oral and written work, school leadership, parents' concerns, peers' reactions, and so on. There are almost no functional status tests in common use for speech-language, so speech-language pathologists must rely on reports from teachers, parents, peers, the student, and a review of class performance, including grades. If functional status does not appear to be affected by the identified impairment, the student is not disabled and therefore not eligible for speech-language services under IDEA 2004. A preliminary set of functional status measures were made available by ASHA in 1998(e). See "Functional Outcomes and the School-Based Speech-Language Pathologist" in Chapter 5 for samples of these statements.

Handicap refers to society's perception of what an individual can or cannot do based on what persons without disabilities believe is possible. There may be many genuine social consequences of a disability: joblessness, isolation, fewer friends, fewer educational opportunities, and other limitations on how one communicates with others. Although an impairment causes a disability, it is the failure to ameliorate that disability that leads to a handicap. Because communication is such a vital activity of daily living, a communication impairment is usually disabling, but when remediated or modified to no longer limit a student's ability to learn or interact successfully, an impairment may not be a handicap.

In 2001, the WHO family of international classifications added the International Classification of Functioning, Disability and Health (ICF), a standard language and framework for the description of health and health-related states. Like the first version, the ICF is intended for a wide range of uses in different sectors. This classification of health-related domains helps us describe changes in body function, structure, activity and participation. Each list includes voice, speech, language, and communication aspects. The ICF accounts for social aspects of disability and serves as a mechanism to determine functioning levels without regard to diseases or health conditions. Researchers in communication disorders have proposed innovative ways to use the new ICF framework (Gallagher, 2007; Threats, 2000; Westby, 2007).

In determining eligibility and placement, IDEA 2004 directs the IEP team to:

(i) Draw upon information from a variety of sources, including aptitude and achievement tests, parent input, and teacher recommendations, as well as information

about the child's physical condition, social or cultural background, and adaptive behavior; and

(ii) Ensure that information obtained from all of these sources is documented and carefully considered (34 C.F.R. § 300.306 [c]).

There is a distinct and important difference between ELIGIBILITY and PLACEMENT. Eligibility refers specifically to considering the student's assessment results as they compare to the outlined eligibility criteria, to determine if the student has a disability and if, because of that disability, the student requires special education and related services.

Any of the 13 listed eligibility categories for special education (see sidebar on p. 139) can have speech-language issues involved with the presenting exceptionality. For example, when the IEP team determines that a student qualifies as a child with ASDS or traumatic brain injury, such students likely present with speech or language disorders as well. The IEP team should identify speech and language as an area of need and subsequently discuss goals and services to address this need as part of the student's special education program.

Speech-language services in schools are part of special education and must meet the requirements of IDEA 2004. Students are determined to be eligible for such services by following a two-step process. First, the student is assessed using the procedures described in Chapter 3. If the student scores significantly below expected levels, speech-language pathologists must go to the second step—determining if these identified communication deficits impede the student's educational performance. IDEA 2004 regulations state: "Speech or language impairment means a communication disorder, such as stuttering, impaired articulation, a language impairment, or a voice impairment, that adversely affects a child's educational performance" (34 C.F.R. § 300.8 [c][11]). The key to this definition is the requirement that the impairment "adversely affects a child's educational performance." When asked "Does a speech impairment always trigger eligibility under the IDEA or § 504?" Gorn (1997b) answered "No," pointing to the requirement for adverse affect. Speech-language pathologists may identify, for example, that a student has a myofunctional disorder resulting in a tongue thrust without a frontal lisp. Such a student is not considered eligible under IDEA 2004 because there is no adverse educational impact.

ASHA sought guidance from the Office of Special Education Programs (OSEP) regarding the limitations, if any, to the requirements on adverse affect, as well as other items. In response to ASHA's query, OSEP Director's letter (Posny, personal communication, 2007) clarified "that the determination of whether or not a child is a child with a disability is not limited to academic performance" (p. 1).

Under IDEA 2004, speech-language services (and all special education services) may be provided to students in school only if both conditions are satisfied—a disability exists and it adversely affects the child's educational performance. The adverse effect may be shown in one or more areas: academic, social, or vocational. This second step is a distinct departure from similar services in health care and private practice.

This two-step process is frequently misunderstood. Nonschool agencies and parents may not understand the restriction that the educational system has in terms of providing special education services. Speech-language pathologists in school systems must abide by the eligibility criteria set forth in state and federal law. Students with mild impairments may not qualify to receive services in schools. Although services may assist the student, it is not the responsibility of the education system to assume the cost of such services since there is no adverse educational effect. Federal regulations require that parents receive a copy of the team's evaluation report and documentation of the eligibility determination (34 C.F.R. § 300.306 [a][2]).

Increasingly, some milder speech-language impairments may be treated under a RESPONSE TO INTERVENTION (RtI) model and never require an IEP. As this model of service delivery is expanding, speech-language pathologists in schools are discovering a way to provide services without the cumbersome processes required for students served under IEPs. (See Chapter 5 for more information on RtI as a service delivery.)

State Eligibility Criteria for Speech-Language Services

The definition of a speech or language impairment is interpreted by each of the states in their own special education laws. The combination of tests needed for a valid assessment, the number and types of tests, plus the "cut-off" points on standardized tests are determined by each state. Consequently, a student could have an educationally related communication disorder identified in one state, but not in another. This does not happen often, but it is possible.

Issues in determining eligibility for language disorder are complicated by several factors including what constitutes a significant level of language disability, as well as regulations imposed by government agencies and local school districts. Since IDEA's inception in the mid-1970s (then known as the EAHCA), language disability has been a confusing entity for states and regulatory agencies to define. Defining *language* and *language disorder* has been equally problematic for researchers, scholars, and speech-language pathologists in the field. Over the years, child language has grown from a simple notion of expressive and receptive vocabulary development to a sophisticated interplay of phonology, morphology, syntax, semantics, and pragmatics. These three categories—content, form, and use—are employed in some states. Students with literacy difficulties may also be in need of language intervention. (See Chapter 6 for a discussion of how language now also encompasses reading and writing as the functional outcomes of language intervention that are related to academic success [ASHA, 2000c].)

Historically, according to ASHA (1989), to determine a language disability, STATE EDUCATIONAL AGENCIES (SEAs) may adopt pre-existing eligibility criteria based on one or more of these four categories:

1. Approved lists of norm-referenced tests.

2. Mandated use of a discrepancy formula.

3. Predetermined age equivalent, standard deviation, or minimum percentile rank units.

4. Exclusionary regulations for populations that are not considered.

State-by-state variations in speech-language eligibility criteria have been investigated for several decades, resulting in little change (Apel, 1993; Nye & Montgomery, 1989). Apel (1993 compiled a unique profile of language impairment criteria by state into the categories of:

- General definition of communication disorders.

- Five-aspect definition of language (semantic, syntactic, pragmatic, phonological, morphological) or three-aspect definition (content, form, and use).

- Definitions of language that included oral, oral/written, or no mention of either.

- Descriptions of speech production errors for articulation, phonology, or both.

- Qualifications for service based on units (standard deviation, severity, chronological age).

- Measure of severity ratings for language (mild, moderate, severe).

States also determine which children with language impairments (and a corresponding adverse educational effect) are eligible for services. Many states have updated their eligibility documentation for speech-language services since the passage of IDEA 2004. These updates also reflect changes in the professional literature regarding language disorders. Many states include some component of RtI in their documentation, but many are still evolving in this area.

Two of the more widely used approaches to determining eligibility are normative reference points and severity ratings. These approaches are discussed in the sections that follow.

Normative Reference Points

Several normative reference points for expected language development have been used by states to determine eligibility. Two are most common: MENTAL AGE (MA) and CHRONOLOGICAL AGE (CA). If language performance matches MA, some states declare the child ineligible for speech-language services. (This approach is referred to as cognitive referencing.) In other states, if language performance matches MA but still falls below CA expectations, the child may still be eligible for speech-language services. Researchers disagree on the relative value of these two methods and conclude that neither is clearly superior (Fey, 1996; Singer & Bashir, 1999). A speech-language pathologist needs to know the issues involved in MA referencing versus CA referencing (i.e., cognitive referencing) and what his or her state requires (ASHA, 1989; Butler, 1999; Cirrin, 1996; Issakson, 2000; Krassowski & Plante, 1997; Nelson, 1999).

The relationship of language to intellect is complex. Some educators try to separate the two; others believe there is a causal relationship between language and intelligence. Arguments in support of cognitive referencing contend that language skills can never exceed a student's intellectual capability; therefore, language intervention is not warranted if performance on language tests is equivalent to performance on intellectual measures. Determining intellectual capability is problematic, however, since most intelligence tests rely on students' verbal skills. Additionally, cognitive referencing emphasizes scores on static norm-referenced assessments and tends to overlook the potential of intervention to improve functional outcomes. Cognitive referencing is no longer a recommended practice (ASHA, 1991c; 2005c). Eligibility criteria for language disorders remain controversial (Secord, 1998) and the speech-language pathologist is advised to closely follow the dictates of his or her state department of education.

Severity Ratings

State severity ratings were reviewed by Nye and Montgomery (1989) and continue to be of interest to SEAs to manage the potentially large number of children who could qualify for services. There is considerable variation in the types of severity ratings used, and each year a few states will alter their eligibility criteria or coding process to some degree. This alteration can take several years to implement in large or heavily regulated states. Severity ratings are suggested by ASHA as useful tools for the school-based speech-language pathologist to manage CASELOAD and student needs (ASHA, 1999b; 2000a). Currently, 16 states refer to severity ratings for determining eligibility (Apel, 1993; ASHA, 1999b). These states may use scales with one to six levels and/or the terms mild, moderate and severe.

Once a child is found to meet eligibility criteria, GOALS and SHORT-TERM OBJECTIVES or BENCHMARKS are established in the identified area(s) of need. Following eligibility determination and establishment of goals in the area(s) of need, consideration is given to program placement and services (e.g., speech-language services). Placement may be thought of as the description of the program that meets the student's individual educational needs. After reviewing the student's present levels of achievement and making an eligibility determination (if necessary), the next consideration is which skills and abilities the student needs to develop.

Special Considerations in Eligibility Determination

Severe Communication Needs

One of the hallmarks of services to students with disabilities is the dramatic increase in the numbers of children with more significant disabilities, which also means an increase in the intensity of their needs and requisite services. Approximately two million individuals in the United States would be considered persons with severe disabilities, which include "persons with severe to profound mental retardation, autism, and other disorders that result in severe socio-communicative and cognitive communication impairments" (National Joint Committee for the Communication Needs of Persons with Severe Disabilities, 1992; pp. 3, 18). The statistics are staggering in some cases: 1 in every 150 children in the United States is diagnosed with ASDs according to the Centers for Disease Control (Autism Society of America, n.d.), affecting 1.5 million families at a cost of $35 million annually. The National Dissemination Center for Children with Disabilities (NICHCY, 2004) relates that the reference to individuals with severe disabilities traditionally has indicated that these individuals have severe to profound mental retardation, and require extensive supports to participate in integrated activities in the community. Characteristics of these individuals include limited speech or communication, difficulty in basic physical mobility, the tendency to forget skills through misuse, trouble generalizing skills from one situation to another, and a need for support in major life activities. Table 4.3 illustrates categories of severe disabilities and the number of students served in these categories in the Fall of 2002 (OSEP, 2004).

When speech-language pathologists and audiologists are part of assessment teams for students with severe disabilities, the question is typically not whether or not the student will meet eligibility criteria for special education, but whether or not the student has needs in the areas of speech, language, or hearing which will require speech and language or audiological support services. The 1992 National Joint Committee guidelines suggest current BEST PRACTICES at the time to view focus on human communication as a social

Table 4.3

Categories of Severe Disabilities					
Fall 2002	**Mental Retardation**	**Emotional Disturbance**	**Multiple Disabilities**	**Autism**	**Traumatic Brain Injury**
Ages 6–21	580,375	480,187	130,443	118,092	21,384
Ages 6–21	9.9%*	8.1%*	2.2%*	2.0%*	0.4%*

*Reflects disability distribution for students served in this age group under IDEA.

Source: USDE (2004a)

behavior and not simply on the linguistic structure of speech in communication acts. The focus of intervention should be on developing a functional communication system and attaining socially effective communication repertoires. The guidelines recommend that assessment practices involve assessing the form and function of communicative interactions, examining the environmental and partner interactions, and considering the appropriateness of the communication attempts made by the individual.

In terms of eligibility for services, how and when services occur, as well as the nature of the services to students with severe communication impairments, is a challenge to school-based personnel. Cognitive referencing is a practice which has often been used to determine that a student with a severe intellectual disability would not be entitled to speech and language services. This method of service determination is not appropriate for students with both severe and nonsevere disabilities (McGrew & Evans, 2003). A more current statement from the National Joint Committee for the Communication Needs of Persons with Severe Disabilities (2002) provides specific

guidance regarding historical practices that denied individuals with severe disabilities access to services due to the utilization of criteria that were not appropriate to make such determinations (see sidebar on p. 147). Speech-language pathologists in schools need to be familiar with these position statements and why older methods of determining who may and may not be eligible for service (e.g., cognitive referencing) are not appropriate for students although these methods may have previously been perceived to be a method of caseload management.

Disproportionality

Prior to the reauthorization of IDEA 2004, President George W. Bush commissioned a group to hold public hearings and make recommendations to Congress to improve IDEA and align it with NCLB. The report of the President's Commission on Excellence in Special Education (2002) outlined several concerns about how special education was operating in this country, including the ongoing concerns about the overrepresentation of ethnic minority students in special education.

Children of minority status are over-represented in some categories of special education. African-American children are twice as likely as White children to be labeled mentally retarded and placed in special education. They are also more likely to be labeled and placed as emotionally disturbed (pp. 1–2).

Concerns about overrepresentation of minority students has been long-standing since the inception of special education (Harry & Klinger, 2007; McLaughlin, Pullin, & Artiles, 2001). In the reauthorization of IDEA 2004, Congress identified this problem as one of the most important issues to be addressed in the implementation of the law. Of concern, Congress cited:

- Minority children are identified as having an emotional disturbance at rates greater than their White counterparts.

- In the 1999–00 school year, African-American children represented just 14.8 percent of the population age 6 through 21, but comprised 20.2 percent of all those with disabilities.

- Studies have found that schools with predominately White students and teachers

National Joint Committee's Position on Eligibility for Communication Services and Supports

It is the position of the National Joint Committee for the Communication Needs of Persons with Severe Disabilities that eligibility for communication services and supports should be based on individual communication needs. Communication services and supports should be evaluated, planned, and provided by an interdisciplinary team with expertise in communication and language form, content, and function, as well as in augmentative and alternative communication (AAC). Decisions regarding team composition, types, amounts, and duration of services provided, intervention setting, and service delivery models should be based on the individual's communication needs and preferences. Eligibility determinations based on a priori criteria violate recommended practice principles by precluding consideration of individual needs. These a priori criteria include, but are not limited to: (a) discrepancies between cognitive and communication functioning; (b) chronological age; (c) diagnosis; (d) absence of cognitive or other skills purported to be prerequisites; (e) failure to benefit from previous communication services and supports; (f) restrictive interpretations of educational, vocational, and/or medical necessity; (g) lack of appropriately trained personnel; and (h) lack of adequate funds or other resources.

Source: National Joint Committee (2002). Reprinted with permission.

have placed disproportionately high numbers of their minority students into special education (Gamm, 2007; p. 2).

Even with the increased focus on this area in the reauthorization of IDEA 1997, the national data continued to be "alarming":

For example, in 1994, African-American students were 2.2 times more likely than other students to be identified as having MR [mental retardation]; in 2002, they were 3.04 times more likely to be so identified, an increase of 38 percent from 1994; the increase of risk for African-American students in the area of ED [emotionally disturbed] in 2002 from 1994 was even greater (41 percent). Even with the heightened awareness of this issue, the risk ratio for African-American students to be identified as MR and ED increased in 2002 from the previous year (Gamm, 2007, p. 2).

The national data does not find disproportionality in disability categories that are more obvious, such as hearing, vision, or orthopedic impairments. In these categories, students from minority groups are represented in proportion to their representation in the general population. The areas of disproportionality appear in the categories considered "judgmental," or "those areas usually identified after a child starts school and by school personnel rather than by a medical professional" (Gamm, 2007, p. 4).

Solving the problems of overidentification and disproportionality are complex at best, beginning with how deficits are viewed (Harry & Klinger, 2007). In order to begin to address the issue, the Code of Federal Regulations requires each state to collect data with regard to the identification, placement, and discipline of children in these groups. If the state does find that a LEA is disproportionate in these areas, they must require the LEA to reserve the maximum amount

of funds (i.e., 15 percent) to provide comprehensive early intervening services to these students. Additionally, the LEA must publicly report how they have revised their policies, practices, and procedures in this area (34 C.F.R § 303.646).

Speech-language pathologists may be involved in eligibility determination, providing early intervening services, or assisting with developing policies and improved practice to address the needs of students from racial and ethnic minority groups. While system change will be necessary to improve practices and change how a system can assist students without making special education identification, the important influence that any individual member of the team can make in these situations cannot be overstated. Most likely, assessment of students from racial and ethnic minority students who may be referred for eligibility determination will require performance or dynamic measures in order to ensure that a student receives an objective evaluation. Documentation of early intervening services provided to these students, including RtI programs, will need to be documented. Cultural competence will be required to create successful solutions for students.

Language Minority Students

In addition to the concerns about overrepresentation of students from racial and ethnic minority groups, Congress also raised concerns about appropriateness of identification and services to students who are English learners (EL). For this population, the concern is both the possible overidentification as well as possible underidentification. In terms of eligibility determination, limited English proficiency is one of the exclusionary factors for specific learning disability. In other words, a student may not be identified as having a specific learning disability if the reason for the determination is due the limited English proficiency. The ASHA documents, *Cultural Competence* (2004) and the *Knowledge and Skills Needed by Speech-Language Pathologists and Audiologists to Provide Culturally and Linguistically Appropriate Services* (2004), can assist speech-language pathologists and audiologists in approaching these cases appropriately.

One of the major factors in eligibility determination is considering whether a child has a language disorder or a language difference. Professional associations may provide helpful documents and other resources to ensure appropriate practices in this area (i.e., *Perspectives on Language Learning and Education*, July 2007, themed issue on Evidence-Based Practice and English learners [ASHA, 2007]).

The Texas Speech-Language-Hearing Association (TSHA) document, *Linguistically Diverse Populations: Consideration and Resources for Assessment and Intervention,* for example, addresses appropriate practices which may be helpful to professionals working with linguistically diverse students.

Once a student is identified, providing appropriate services is vital. The Office of Special Education Program (OSEP, 2000) suggests the following culturally relevant instructional principles:

- Link assessments of student progress directly to the instructional curricula rather than to abstract norms for standardized tests.

- Examine not only the individual child but also his or her instructional environment, using direct observational data.

- Create classroom environments that reflect different cultural heritages and accommodate different styles of communication and learning.

- Develop and implement family-friendly practices to establish collaborative partnerships with parents and other caregivers, including those who do not speak English.

Development of Goals and Short-Term Objectives/Benchmarks

The second step in the IEP meeting process is to develop GOALS and SHORT-TERM OBJECTIVES/BENCHMARKS. At least one goal should be established for each identified area of need. Goals are written in only the identified area(s) of need and not for curricular or developmental areas that will be addressed in the scope of the classroom instruction at the student's grade level or above. (See sidebar below for information on goal setting.) IDEA 2004 regulations require each IEP to include:

(i) A statement of measurable annual goals, including academic and functional goals designed to—

(A) Meet the child's needs that result from the child's disability to enable the child to be involved in and progress in the general curriculum; and

(B) Meet each of the child's other educational needs that result from the child's disability.

(ii) For children with disabilities who take alternate assessments aligned to alternate achievement standards, a description of benchmarks or short-term objectives (34 C.F.R. § 300.320 [a][2]).

IDEA 2004 requires annual goals for students with disabilities, and only requires short-term objectives/benchmarks for students who are taking alternate assessments. The rationale for dropping benchmarks for most students in special educa-

Practical Application of Goal Setting

During the IEP process, goals and short-term objectives or benchmarks are developed based on the student's present levels of educational achievement.

Sequence

1. The IEP team identifies the area of need by examining present levels of performance.

2. The IEP team identifies a goal area.

3. The IEP team develops either short-term objectives or benchmarks or both to contribute to attainment of the goal.

Application for Kara, a 4th Grader

1. Kara uses less than 100 words in free-write activities.

2. Kara will use second-grade vocabulary in spoken and written language.

3. Short-Term Objective: Use 10 new vocabulary words each week in reading and writing.
Benchmark: During second semester, read and use vocabulary from a book written at the 2.5 level.

Reading/Language Arts Content Standards

Reading

Word Analysis, Fluency, and Systematic Vocabulary Development (Grade 1)

Concepts About Print

> • Match oral words to printed words

Phonemic Awareness

> • Distinguish initial, medial, and final sounds in single-syllable words

Comprehension and Analysis of Grade Level Appropriate Text

> • Respond to who, what, when, where, and how questions

> • Retell the central ideas of a simple expository or narrative passage

Source: California Department of Education (1998)

Language Arts

Demonstrates competence in general skills and strategies of the reading process (Grades 6–8)

> • Generates interesting questions to be answered while reading

> • Represents abstract information (e.g., concepts, generalizations) as explicit mental pictures

> • Understands stories and expository texts from the perspective of the attitudes and values of the time period in which they were written

Source: Kendall & Marzano (1996)

---

tion, is that the goals need to be standards driven, so benchmarking is not necessary. Because students who take alternate assessments are working on more functional goals, short-term objectives or benchmarks are needed. It should be noted that in some school systems, local practice is to still include benchmarks for all students in special education.

The emphasis on standards, curriculum, and educational results direct the course of what IEP Teams need to do in their goal setting for students. School districts across the country have adopted standards that students are expected to master, so there should be no doubt what students are expected to learn. Many electronic IEP programs have pull-down menus to assist IEP teams in developing standards-based goals. The IEP team, however, still must be sure that the goals are individually determined. The academic orientation of the standards might be limiting for students whose goals must include functional or social-emotional skills. However, for the majority of students on the speech-language pathologist's caseload, using standards as a guide for IEP goal development should be an everyday practice.

Speech-language pathologists in public schools have expertise in speech and language acquisition, development, and disorders. Curriculum and standards are constructed based on the developmental levels (e.g., cognitive, linguistic, and social-emotional) that children are expected to have reached at any given grade level. When writing a goal or developing short-term objectives/benchmarks for students working on either academic or functional curriculum, the speech-language pathologist will need to examine the learning expectations and classroom instructional environment to determine how the student's identified disability or delay will impact his or her achieving such expectations. From this information, goals and short-term objectives/benchmarks can be developed. (See the sidebar on pp. 153–154 for an example of how speech-language services can be integrated within the curriculum using annual goals and benchmarks.)

Consider an example taken from California's content standards (California Department of Education, 1999d):

Reading Comprehension: Students will identify the basic facts and ideas in what they have read, heard, or viewed, drawing on such strategies as generating essential questions and comparing information from several sources.

Comprehension and Analysis:

Grade 1: Respond to who, what, where, when, and how questions (1.2.2);

Grade 2: Ask clarifying questions concerning essential textual elements of stories (why, what-if, how) (2.2.4).

Speech-language pathologists have written goals for *wh-* questions for many years. There is evidence of when such a skill is needed not only for oral language communication, but also to facilitate reading comprehension. The speech-language pathologist might consider writing the following goals and benchmarks for a second-grade student who has difficulty answering and asking *wh-* questions:

Goal: Manuel will answer and ask *wh-* questions about narrative stories and about stories read in class from the grade-level text.

Benchmarks (if being used):

- By the first reporting period, Manuel will answer *who, what*, and *where* questions about narrative stories told to him by his teacher or speech-language pathologist.

- By the second reporting period, Manuel will answer *who, what, where, when*, and *how* questions about stories read aloud to him from the first-grade text.

- By the third reporting period, Manuel will ask clarifying questions about narrative stories told to him by his teacher or speech-language pathologist.

- By the fourth reporting period, Manuel will ask clarifying questions concerning essential textual elements of stories read to him from his grade-level text.

Consider another example in which the identified area of need is vocabulary with the goal for vocabulary development to enhance spoken and written comprehension. Following is an example of goals that could be set for Sarah, an eighth grader:

How Speech-Language Services Can Be Integrated Within the Curriculum Using Annual Goals and Benchmarks

A. Measurable Annual Goal: Theresa will produce her target phonemes correctly in initial and final position in words when practicing the passages selected for her third-grade oral-reading rate exercises.

Benchmarks:

- She will recognize her target phonemes in the words that contain them in a third grade reading passage. (first report card)

- She will produce her target phonemes correctly in single words selected from the books used in class. (second report card)

- She will self-correct when reading for the weekly check of Words Read Correctly Per Minute (WRCPM) in class and in therapy. (third report card)

- She will correctly produce target phonemes in initial and final positions in words in third-grade oral-reading rate exercises. (fourth report card)

Note:

The fourth report card should show Theresa reaching the goal in one school year. A percentage correct at each stage is not required as long as she continues to make progress toward the goal, and this is reported meaningfully to parents at each reporting period. While oral-reading rate is a general education benchmark, age-appropriate articulation skill is a speech and language standard. One supports the other. Progress in speech links to academic performance. Average oral-reading rate is the child's age $\times$ 10. Reading passages aloud will be the next step toward complete carryover to conversation which the speech-language pathologist may write as the next goal. With continual practice on the classroom material, students frequently generalize on their own. Concurrently, they become better readers because they are reading more.

B. Measurable Annual Goal: Tuan will demonstrate phonological awareness skills needed to succeed in the second-grade reading program in his classroom.

Benchmarks:

- He will recognize spoken word boundaries by stating correctly the number of words in an utterance. (first report card)

Continued

How Speech-Language Services Can Be Integrated – *Continued*

- He will correctly count the number of syllables in multisyllabic words read to him from his textbooks. (second report card)

- He will say aloud at least three words that rhyme with a given word presented orally. (third report card)

- He will accurately match a spoken word with its corresponding graphemes selected from his reading workbook. (fourth report card)

- He will be able to decode five unfamiliar words presented in therapy and in class as well as any three other students in his grade. (last report card)

Note:
Tuan's IEP benchmarks represent the developmental sequence for phonological awareness skills for reading, plus they are typical auditory processing skills presented in therapy. Combined, they enable Tuan to acquire both emergent reading skills and language and communication skills in his speech and language program. The speech-language pathologist would likely use many therapeutic strategies to help Tuan develop these auditory processing skills, however the IEP goals and objectives would reflect the functional use or generalization of those skills into the school curriculum.

Standard: Vocabulary and concept development

Goals:
Analyze idioms, analogies, metaphors and similes to infer the literal and figurative meanings of phrases (8.1.1).

Use word meaning with the appropriate context and show ability to verify those meanings by definition, restatement, example, comparison, or contrast (8.1.2).

The goals, which simply need to address the standards, were taken directly from the reading/language arts content standards. By examining the standard for her grade level, and the skills that Sarah will need to pass the California High School Exit Exam (CAHSEE), the speech-language pathologist can ensure that the interventions provided for Sarah will address her progress in the core content area. At the same time, the activities necessary are consistent with language intervention. If the speech-language pathologist and classroom teacher, as well as Sarah's parents, begin to systematically address these areas, Sarah will not only develop her vocabulary, but also will be mastering skills identified as necessary to be successful in the curriculum. As Sarah develops these skills, the members of the IEP team can look to the next benchmarks for ninth and tenth graders, so that Sarah can develop skills identified for her same-age peers.

When writing goals and short-term objectives/benchmarks for the general education curriculum, remember the concept of universal design, which organizes curriculum into tasks that can be performed by students with a wide range of skills using a variety of modalities:

Ideally, effective universal design does not result in lowered expectations or watered-down instruction. Rather, it calls for multiple ways of expressing competency in regards to a given standard. Universal design also results in blending of different types of standards (USDE, 1999, pp. I-25).

Universal Design helps speech-language pathologists and educators understand that demonstration of knowledge attainment may vary, and will help support the alternatives for achieving and measuring goal attainment.

Goals are intended to set the course for progress, which also means that the progress must be measurable. When considering which goals to write for a student, the IEP team should consider which standard(s) can connect the IEP to the general education curriculum that the student needs to master. Goals help to guide the student's instructional program, but are not intended to be a daily instructional plan. Goals also are intended to define what types of special education and related services a student will receive in order to meet the goals (Association of California School Administrators [ACSA], 2006).

Local guidelines or forms will give the speech-language pathologist direction in how each LEA requires measurement to be reflected for the goals or objectives/benchmarks. IEP goals should always describe in measurable terms what the team determines the student is expected to achieve one year from the date of the IEP meeting. Goals and short-term objectives/benchmarks should never identify what adults (i.e., teachers, instructional assistants, or parents) do; they should always have the "who" identified as the student. Additionally, they should always be written in positive language, not in a way that reflects a decrease in negative behavior. If the desired behavior is identified, then the competing negative behavior will correspondingly decrease or disappear. According to the ACSA (2006), a good format for writing IEP performance goals and objective/benchmarks is to answer these six questions: who, does what, when, given what, how much (criteria/mastery), and how will it be measured (see sidebar on p. 156).

IDEA 2004 has a reporting requirement that aligns reporting on IEP goal progress to the reporting periods of general education. This requirement mandates that IEPs include a statement of:

(i) How the child's progress toward the annual goals will be measured; and

(ii) When periodic reports on the progress the child is making toward meeting the annual goals (such as through the use of quarterly or other periodic reports, concurrent with the issuance of report cards) will be provided (34 C.F.R. § 300.320 [a][3]).

Six Questions to Answer When Writing IEP Goals and Objectives

Who: ....the student

Does what: ....observable behavior

When: ....by reporting date

Given what: ....conditions

How much: ....mastery or criteria

How will it be measured: ....performance data

Source: ACSA (2006), p. 42

How school districts demonstrate and document progress is central to documenting the provision of FAPE. The legal standard for progress is "educational benefit," or the *Rowley* standard. In the *Rowley* case (see Chapter 2), the Supreme Court provided a two-prong test to show educational benefit: (1) procedural compliance, and (2) designing the IEP so that it is reasonably calculated to enable the student to achieve passing grades and advance from grade to grade.

Advancing from grade to grade may be considered evidence of educational benefit, but not necessarily exclusively so. The law requires IEP teams to meet at least annually to review the IEP, but it is important to note that the law also requires the IEP team to address a lack of expected progress, which means if a student is not making progress, the team should reconvene and address the issue. Fagen, Friedman, and Fulfrost (2007) provide the following practice pointer:

Goals must be based on past data showing need. Have objective data available (e.g., test results, classroom portfolio work, teacher observations) to support expectations. In addition, the IEP must specify how progress toward goals will be measured. Work on writing concise, clear, measurable goals.

Additionally, Fagen, Friedman, and Fulfrost (2007) offer the following "practitioner's guide to demonstrating progress in special education":

1. Fully understand the *Rowley* standard as it applies to educational benefit and FAPE.

2. Clearly identify at the IEP meeting the methods that will be utilized to measure progress.

3. Review past progress in relation to the student's performance in the general curriculum.

4. Discuss lack of progress, based on objective data, at the IEP meeting.

5. If grades are one element in noting progress, know your district's policy regarding how grades are awarded.

6. For students with severe disabilities, goals may provide the best way to measure progress.

7. Understand the importance of using standards-based goals to measure progress.

8. Be aware that progress can extend beyond academics (pp. 120–121).

Determination of Program, Placement, and Services

Once a student has been identified as being eligible for special education by meeting eligibility criteria, that student is entitled to receive any service that the IEP team determines is needed. The IEP team must follow the require-

ments and philosophy of LEAST RESTRICTIVE ENVIRONMENT (LRE) when determining placement and services, and ensure that:

(i) To the maximum extent appropriate, children with disabilities...are educated with children who are nondisabled; and

(ii) Special classes, separate schooling or other removal of children with disabilities from the regular educational environment occurs only if the nature or severity of the disability is such that the education in regular classes with the use of supplementary aids and services cannot be achieved satisfactorily (34 C.F.R. § 300.114 [2]).

One of the most important considerations for IEP teams in making determinations of placement is to keep children in the neighborhood school, or as close to home as possible, and attending the school that they would attend if they did not have a disability, unless their IEP requires some other arrangement. IDEA 2004 regulations specifically direct the following about placement:

Additional Resources for Standards-Based IEPs:

A Seven-Step Process to Creating Standards-Based IEPs (2007, June) (www.projectforum.org)

Holbrook, M.D. (2007, August). Standards-Based Individualized Education Program Examples. ProjectForum at NASDSE. Alexandria, VA: NASDSE.

Association of California School Administrators (ACSA). (2006). Handbook of goals and objectives related to state of California Content Standards. Sacramento, CA: Author.

(a) The placement decision—

(1) Is made by a group of persons, including the parents, and other persons knowledgeable about the child, the meaning of the evaluation data and the placement options; and

(2) Is made in conformity with the LRE provisions...

(b) The child's placement—

(1) Is determined at least annually;

(2) Is based on the child's IEP; and

(3) Is as close as possible to the child's home.

(c) Unless the IEP of a child with a disability requires some other arrangement, the child is educated in the school that he or she would attend if nondisabled;

(d) In selecting the LRE, consideration is given to any potential harmful effect on the child or on the quality of services that he or she needs; and

(e) A child with a disability is not removed from education in age-appropriate regular classrooms solely because of needed modifications in the general curriculum (34 C.F.R. § 300.116).

For children with "speech only" disorders (e.g., articulation, fluency, or voice disorder), speech services may be the only special education provided to the student. For children with language impairments that have an academic impact, support from the resource teacher or learning disabilities specialist may be provided. As the nature of the student's disability becomes more complex, it is more likely that the student will receive additional services. Sometimes the speech-language pathologist will be the only provider of special education services. Similarly, the audiologist may only be monitoring a student's amplification if the student is older and well managed in terms of his or her hearing loss. Other times, the speech-language pathologist or audiologist will be a member of a larger team. The service provider who is with the student the most usually assumes case management responsibility. Service delivery and how to make these decisions is discussed in Chapter 5.

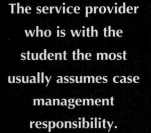

The service provider who is with the student the most usually assumes case management responsibility.

Both speech-language pathology services and audiology services are identified as a related service (i.e., a service necessary for the student to benefit from special education) under federal law. Speech-language services can be also be identified as special education if they are considered so under state guidelines.

Speech-language services are defined as:

(i) Identification of children with speech or language impairments;

(ii) Diagnosis and appraisal of specific speech or language impairments;

(iii) Referral for medical or other professional attention necessary for the habilitation of speech or language impairments;

(iv) Provision of speech and language services for the habilitation or prevention of communicative impairments; and

(v) Counseling and guidance of parents, children, and teachers regarding speech and language impairments (34 C.F.R § 300.34 [c][15]).

Audiology services are defined as:

(i) Identification of children with hearing loss;

(ii) Determination of the range, nature, and degree of hearing loss, including referral for medical or other professional attention for the habilitation of hearing;

(iii) Provision of habilitative activities, such as language habilitation, auditory training, speech reading (lip reading), hearing evaluation, and speech conservation;

(iv) Creation and administration of programs for prevention of hearing loss;

(v) Counseling and guidance of children, parents, and teachers regarding hearing loss; and

(vi) Determination of children's needs of for group and individuals' amplification, selecting and fitting an appropriate aid, and evaluation of the effectiveness of amplification (34 C.F.R § 300.34 [c][1]).

The determination of the services a student requires to meet his or her identified goals and receive educational benefit is a most important function of IEP teams. Issues such as caseload management and service delivery options are also tied to placement determination but should only be discussed at the IEP meeting if the issues pertain to the student. In other words, caseload size is an issue for the speech-language pathologist, but is not an IEP issue. Figure 4.2 recaps the IEP meeting process.

Recordkeeping and Documentation

In keeping with accountability requirements and to clearly explain the course of intervention to parents, teachers, the student, and others, documentation is critical to the work of public school speech-language pathologists. To verify which activities were completed with the student and how these activities were designed to meet IEP goals, it is recommended that speech-language pathologists and audiologists maintain records for each student. The following are suggestions of what might be recorded in this documentation:

1. Schedule of when students were seen for service and for how long.

2. Log of intervention activities and outcomes.

3. Portfolio of student performance/student work.

4. Records of communication with parents, teachers, and others regarding the student.

5. Student file with all IEP and assessment information, as well as IEP procedure documentation and progress report cards.

Speech-language pathologists and audiologists should be aware that if parents request their child's records, copies of all documentation, in addition to the typical school records, must be provided to them. For this reason, all professionals must be cautious and prudent about the notes they include in files. Speech-language pathologists should also have records of the intervention strategies being used, the

---

Figure 4.2

IEP Meeting Process

Determination of Present Levels of Educational Achievement

- Review evaluation data
- Review classroom performance
- Review other related information
- Consider input from parents, teachers, and specialists

↓

Development of Goals and Short-Term Objectives or Benchmarks

- Based on identified areas of need
- Designed to enable the child to progress in the general education curriculum
- Must be measurable

↓

Determination of Program, Placement, and Services

- Includes services needed in order for goals to be achieved
- Designed to confer meaningful educational benefit

---

success they are having with them, the modifications being made, and the conditions in which the intervention is taking place. Not only must goals be measurable, but the service provider must also document when and how those measurements are taken. Data sheets and logs need to be readable and complete.

Langdon (2000) provided excellent suggestions for enhancing interactions with families of English learners. Langdon's suggestions are generally good practices:

- Avoid using professional jargon and provide examples instead.

- Ensure that the parents understand the assessment procedures and reason(s) why the student may have a language-learning difficulty.

- Invite the parent to offer their perspective about their child.

- Respect the parents' comments about their child's problem. Also, understand how various handicapping *[sic]* conditions can be viewed by various cultures and individuals within a culture.

- Offer suggestions that are realistic.

- Provide as many examples as possible from the school setting.

- Avoid insisting that the parents use English.

- Invite the parents to attend and participate in the intervention process. (pp. 382–383)

Participating as a member of the IEP team, writing and developing an IEP, and conducting intervention based on the plan outlined in the document is a complex process. Speech-language pathologists and audiologists who are new to the field or new to a school system should seek a mentor to learn the specifics of the IEP process for the system in which he or she works. If the speech-language pathologist or audiologist is a Clinical Fellow (CF), then his or her CF supervisor may be able to serve in this capacity. Other non–speech-language pathology and audiology professionals in the school district may also be able to assist a new staff member learning the way.

Confidentialilty

All educators must be aware of the confidentiality requirements under the FAMILY EDUCATIONAL RIGHTS AND PRIVACY ACT (FERPA, 1974, § 513 of P. L. 93-380 [The Education Amendments of 1974]), which applies to IDEA 2004 and all school records. Under FERPA, students' and parents' rights to privacy are protected with regard to personally identifiable information in education records. An IEP is an education record, therefore, to disclose improperly the contents of an IEP would be a violation of FERPA (Gorn, 1997a).

Speech-language pathologists, audiologist and other special educators need to be aware of the interface between IDEA 2004, FERPA, and the Health Insurance Portability and Accountability Act (HIPAA) of 1996. HIPAA regulations required compliance by April of 2003. HIPAA covers protected health information (PHI), which is individually identifiable health information, both oral and recorded. Under HIPAA, records, such as educational records, that are protected under FERPA are excluded under HIPAA. Shorter (2004) advises professionals to be clear as to which records are considered educational records and which ones are not. Guidelines to help make this distinction are as follows:

Educational records covered by FERPA and IDEA 2004:

- Include the following:

  1. Records directly related to the student.

  2. Records maintained by an educational agency or institution or party acting for the agency or institution.

- Exclude the following:

  1. Personal notes.

  2. Employee records.

  3. Law enforcement records.

  4. Certain adult student treatment records.

  5. Records not maintained by the registrar.

In practical terms, this means that all educators must be extremely careful when they discuss cases. Revealing the names of children and parents would be considered a violation of their rights, if the receiver of the information is not involved in the case by virtue of their position with the LEA. Make it a personal rule not to reveal the names of children or families to anyone who does not have direct involvement in the case and never to use the names of children on your caseloads in public, even when discussing a case with a team member. If speech-language pathologists and audiologists make this their personal habit, they will not have to worry about being overheard by a child's relative or family friend. Professionals need to be vigilant about not engaging in conversations in the lunchroom or around the teacher's break room regarding children or their families when the other faculty members do not have a legitimate interest in the case. School-based personnel must also be cautious not to unintentionally leave documentation with children's names on it laying in common areas of the school. All documents need to be kept in a secured locked location.

Parental Access to School Records

Parents also have the right to access and examine school records as part of their procedural safeguards ensuring participation (34 C.F.R. § 300.501 [a]). If a parent requests to review their child's records, the LEA must respond without reasonable delay, which is typically defined in state law and is often five (5) school or business days. Additionally, if parents need someone to interpret the records for them, the district must

> Make it a personal rule not to reveal the names of children or families to anyone who does not have direct involvement in the case.

provide someone to do so. Districts must also allow a parent's representative to review the records if so requested (34 C.F.R. § 300.613). School districts must provide parents with copies of school records if requested, but can charge a fee. Parents are typically provided copies of IEPs and reports at IEP meetings, and, of course, there is no charge for that. However, when a parent requests a full copy of the student's educational records, then school districts often have a school board policy outlining the procedures for this. It would be unlikely that the service provider, such as the speech-language pathologist or audiologist, would be required to gather the fees.

Two points are important with regard to student records. One is that if a parent does request records from the speech-language pathologist or audiologist or classroom teacher, an immediate response is required because of the timeline. Additionally, it is important to remember that all records are considered part of a student's record, so confidential, cumulative, student discipline, health records, and teacher files will all need to be copied or available for inspection. One additional point is that sometimes parents request that letters or documentation be generated by the service provider for some purpose. A general rule is that no record that is not a student record should be generated without consulting with a district administrator. This would prevent the record from being used inappropriately, such as in a child custody situation or other court action that was not the intended purpose for the document. School district personnel should be very cautious about generating any records that are not part of the typical documentation.

Sometimes parents request to have documentation changed or removed from a school district file. The procedures for responding to this type of a request are outlined in the district's school board policy. Again, this type of a request requires administrative attention, and should be referred to the appropriate personnel.

When creating documents for the student's records, such as evaluation reports or IEPs, school district staff can and should be open to input from the family, especially in terms of developmental history and the child's level of functioning from the family's perspective. However, if there is a disagreement in terms of professional opinion, the speech-language pathologist or audiologist as well as other school district personnel should always report their findings and interpretation according to their professional judgment. If there is a disagreement about interpretation, conclusion, and recommendations, then the parent can dissent, submit a document to be attached to the IEP, or use procedural methods to challenge the interpretation. If there is a disagreement of this nature, and it is discussed in the IEP, of course, this should be documented in the minutes of the IEP meeting.

Speech-language pathologists, audiologists, and other special education personnel often complain about paperwork demands. Paperwork can be overwhelming, however, all requirements are procedurally driven. In order to comply with the law, documentation must be completed. In addi-

tion to completing forms correctly and following appropriate procedures, timelines must be kept. Teams that work closely together find the process moves along smoothly, assuring compliance and quality.

Annual and Triennial Assessments

IDEA 2004 requires that students who are eligible for special education services have their progress reviewed at least annually by the IEP team. This is called the ANNUAL REVIEW, and the intended date is written on a student's current IEP. Every three years, the IEP team needs to decide if a TRIENNIAL ASSESSMENT is needed to determine if the student should remain in special education. Because "comprehensive evaluation is the critical foundation for developing an educationally relevant IEP" (Brannen et al., 2000, p. 20), each type of evaluation will be discussed below.

An annual review of the student's IEP is conducted each year in order to measure and record the amount of change that occurred for each of a student's written annual goals. In addition, goals and objectives are reviewed to determine if they are needed and remain relevant to the general education curriculum. Although a speech-language pathologist may choose to reassess a student using some standardized tests, these tests are not required, not recommended, and, in fact, may be less effective. The results of standardized tests are useful for qualifying students for services, since these tests compare the abilities of a student with the expected abilities of other students his or her age, usually nationwide. However, these tests do not offer results in functional terms. When used to measure change, test scores offer a numerical value of how a student responded to a testing probe, but not his or her actual performance in the classroom, with peers, or in other true-life situations. The FUNCTIONAL COMMUNICATION MEASURES (FCMs) described at the end

of Chapter 5 are more useful. Speech-language pathologists use nonstandardized tests, observations, checklists, portfolios, and other formal and informal measures to determine progress toward the goals in a year. IDEA 2004 requires that IEPs report on the results of statewide assessments. The results of any districtwide administered assessments should also be reported on an IEP. Because IDEA 2004 focuses on the general education curriculum, report-card-type grades, progress toward standards or periodic narratives should be part of both annual and triennial reports. Therefore, all student evaluations should be conducted and interpreted using multiple means of assessment.

Every three years, an IEP team must determine if a student continues to meet criteria and require special education. In some cases, standardized testing may be used. The same evaluation measures used for annual assessments may be used at the triennial assessment with the same cautions. IDEA 2004 allows the IEP team to determine if additional data are actually necessary to make the determination of the student's continued disability. If it is judged not necessary, the district must notify the parents and the parents have the right to request an assessment.

The district is required to assess all students whose parents request these services. Since parents are a part of all decision making for their child's program, they are involved in the discussion of which, if any, triennial assessments are needed. At times, student needs are clear without formal testing. For example, a child making year-to-year progress on speech-language goals for communication disabilities related to cognitive impairment would not need to have a triennial assessment to determine if he or she still has a cognitive impairment. The disability would not have to be reaffirmed unless parents specifically request that to be done.

The school district must administer the tests and other evaluation materials needed to produce the data identified by the IEP team. Parents are asked to help define the data needed for their child. The IEP is the vehicle that links this vital evaluation information to the desired outcomes for each child. These outcomes become the basis for determining the particular services that the student needs, which professionals can best provide them, and in what setting they should be offered. Annual reviews and triennial reevaluations, whenever needed, serve this purpose for students and families. Local policy directs procedures for assessments (see also discussion on assessments in Chapter 3).

Some school districts require a report for the annual review, however, others just have the documentation information on the IEP. Sometimes, the dates for the annual and the triennial become misaligned. IDEA 2004 encourages IEP teams to consolidate these meetings when a reevaluation occurs (34 C.F.R. § 300.324 [a][5]). In fact, it only makes sense to revise the IEP when new evaluation information is available.

Exit or Dismissal Criteria

Although this chapter emphasizes how to place children with communication disorders into intervention programs, of equal importance is to describe the criteria for successfully completing that intervention. It is good practice to think about exit criteria at the beginning of the intervention cycle, because the criteria should serve as the "beacon" that guides the intervention process.

Evaluation updates of a student is required by IDEA to make a dismissal decision (34 C.F.R. § 300.305 [e][2]). The student should be dismissed when his or her communication no longer has an adverse effect on education. This can be difficult to ascertain unless functional outcomes have been collected throughout the intervention. Focusing on reducing the effect of the impairment (i.e., the disability) will provide the information needed to decide on dismissal. The data that have been gathered while the student was receiving speech-language services can be used for the dismissal decision.

Intervention should not continue until a student is "perfect" or "100 percent." This is often not realistic. Goals generally should be written to 75 or 80 percent. If an individual is able to complete tasks at that level, he or she no longer needs intervention to master the skill, simply practice.

Dismissal may occur before a student demonstrates complete mastery of all targeted skills. Reassessment for dismissal requires the speech-language pathologist to revisit the options of standardized, performance-based, and DYNAMIC ASSESSMENT (as discussed in Chapter 3) to determine which will provide the most useful information. Dismissal criteria should be functionally based, not test-based.

States have been slower to design exit criteria than eligibility criteria. Some have more exacting statements than others. Some school districts have developed their own dismissal criteria to help support their statements to parents and teachers that a student has made sufficient progress, or may benefit more from a different service. In a few instances, a decision to terminate speech-language services may be based on mutually agreed on circumstances such as the student's interest, motivation, or available time.

The ASHA (2004a) document *Admission/Discharge Criteria in Speech-Language Pathology* provides guidance to the field in this area. Speech-language pathologists and audiologist should also check with their local agencies to see if state or local guidelines exist.

CHAPTER 5

Service Delivery Options in Schools

1. What are the components of service delivery in speech-language programs in schools today? How have they changed in the last decade? Why did they change?

2. What are the essential features of ASHA's position statement on inclusion (see sidebar on p. 178)? How do you think the position statement has shaped the design of service delivery systems in schools? If you worked in an elementary school, describe a role you could play to support inclusion of a six-year-old student with Down syndrome.

3. How did speech-language pathologists attempt to answer the four basic questions that center on functional outcomes (see Figure 5.5 on p. 195) before considering a functional approach? What resources can you use to respond to the four questions?

4. Review the section on functional outcomes beginning on p. 189, and write three outcome statements for each of the students described in the case studies (see sidebar on p. 203). What elements do you need to address to make the outcomes functional?

5. Use Figure 5.4 on p. 183 to make up a school schedule for a speech-language pathologist who does any nine of the activities in the bulleted list. Write the schedule to account for a month of his or her time in the school.

6. What program characteristics may be used to show consumers that a student will receive appropriate benefit from an IEP? Give examples of measures that would demonstrate student benefit.

7. Use the sample functional communication measures (FCMs) in the sidebar on p. 202 to project a one-year goal for a student performing at Level 3 for language comprehension. Design assessments or probes to use in gathering data for quarterly progress reports to parents.

8. Review the concept of clinically significant change. Design a graphic that shows the three basic elements and their relationship to each other and to the process of evaluating students who are receiving speech and language interventions.

Concept of Service Delivery

Traditionally, speech-language pathologists scheduled students for intervention based on physical factors, such as what type of disorder a student presented, the age of the student, the size of the speech room, the school's academic schedule, and the number of days per week the speech-language pathologist was at that site. While these are all factors in a school-based program, they are not critical to obtaining the best FUNCTIONAL OUTCOMES for the student. (See "What Are the Steps in the IEP Meeting Process?" in Chapter 4 for a discussion of the importance of functional outcomes related to disability instead of impairment.) With increasing emphasis on using research-based strategies, the intent is to improve the efficiency and functionality of all special education intervention programs. Service delivery will need to be based on which approach provides the most appropriate treatment for the student, requiring speech-language pathologists to adjust models and time constraints to fit. Blosser and Kratcoski (1997) stated that the current "concept of unique and discreet options has in effect limited, instead of expanded, clinician's thinking about how to develop appropriate treatment programs" (p. 101).

New ways to think about and plan for school-based speech-language service delivery, including direct and indirect intervention, have been posed over the years. Early textbooks urged "speech correctionists" to use "forms of practice" such as "singing, perceptual reorganization, naming, oral reading, radio speaking, choral speaking, catharsis" and other "adjustive techniques." Public school interventions were described with four models for service delivery:

> (1) schools for exceptional children, (2) itinerant remedial speech correction, (3) speech improvement, and (4) classroom teachers who felt the need to know something about speech handicaps [sic], and in the process of professional preparation for teaching, have taken one or more courses dealing with speech disorders (Johnson, Brown, Curtis, Edney, & Keaster, 1956, p. 413).

An Overview of Special Education Services

Perhaps the best way to understand how speech-language services fit into the fabric of special education services begins with a review of the interventions common to that part of public education. The INDIVIDUALS WITH DISABILITIES EDUCATION IMPROVEMENT ACT (IDEA) Amendments of 1997 and 2004 were discussed in detail in the first three chapters of this book; however, the actual delivery of school-based services requires further description. With the possible exception of assessment, service delivery is the most visible part of IDEA. While there are some differences among states, the general practice of assisting struggling learners identified with exceptional needs in the public education system is applied in all 50 states.

Prevalence of Speech-Language Disorders

The prevalence of speech-language disorders in public school populations has consistently been reported to be 3 to 4 percent of students enrolled in general education, but was 2.2 percent of the general population in 2002 (USDE, 2005d). This number can be misleading, however, as it does not take into account all the students who have communication disorders secondary to medical or educational disabilities. Students identified as having special education needs represent approximately 10 to 12 percent of the school population. Within this special education school-age population, about 18.7 percent are students with speech-language impairments (not those with hearing disorders or students in other groups who commonly also have communication disorders, such as traumatic brain injury, developmental disabilities, and LEARNING DISABILITIES). The U.S. Department of Education (USDE; 2005d) reports that all of the students receiving special education, the category of specific learning disability represents the largest group (48.3 percent) and speech-language impairment represents the second largest (18.7 percent). However, many students in special education receive speech and language services due to the communication disorder resulting from their disabling condition.

The largest proportions of special education students served primarily in general education classrooms are those students with communication disorders (see Table 5.1). Of the students with speech-language impairments, 88 percent are served primarily in the general education classroom (USDE, 2005d). This practice meets the letter and the spirit of the federal law, assisting states to meet federal guidelines for least restrictive enviroment.

The breadth of service delivery expected of speech-language pathologists in school programs is evident from states' plans for educational relevancy written to meet federal guidelines (Brannen et al., 2000). These usually include all services delivered, not simply intervention services. Looking at Figure 5.1, it is obvious that service delivery encompasses much than the small "Implementation" box in the center implies. This box may be thought of as the "hub" of the schematic since intervention to assist the learner is also the reason we engage in all the other activities. Figure 5.1 includes the dimensions addressed in the next three chapters of this book.

Levels of Special Education Services

The classic diagram of seven levels of service delivery in special education, presented in Figure 5.2, was introduced in 1976 after the passage of the EDUCATION FOR ALL HANDICAPPED CHILDREN ACT (EAHCA) and credited to Deno (1970). It shows that the greatest number of students are in the LEAST RESTRICTIVE ENVIRONMENT (LRE) of Level One (general education classroom), cascading down to the most restrictive, Level Seven (nonpublic school). Most students with speech-language disabilities, even those with multiple needs, are served in Levels 1–4. They spend most, if not all, of their school day in the general education classroom with their peers. The general education curriculum, taught by classroom teachers, is the

Table 5.1

Percentage of Time Students With Disabilities Are Served Outside the General Education Classroom

Disabilities	Time outside the regular class			
	<21 percent of the day	21-60 percent of the day	>60 percent of the day	Separate environments[a]
	Percent			
Specific learning disabilities	48.8	37.3	13.0	0.9
Speech/language impairments	88.2	6.8	4.6	0.4
Mental retardation	11.7	30.2	51.8	6.3
Emotional disturbance	30.3	22.6	30.2	16.9
Multiple disabilities	12.1	17.2	45.8	24.9
Hearing impairments	44.9	19.2	22.2	13.7
Orthopedic impairments	46.7	20.9	26.2	6.2
Other health impairments	51.1	30.5	15.0	3.5
Visual impairments	54.6	16.9	15.6	12.8
Autism	26.8	17.7	43.9	11.6
Deaf-blindness	22.2	13.9	33.6	30.3
Traumatic brain injury	34.6	29.9	27.1	8.4
Developmental delay	51.2	28.2	18.6	2.0
All disabilities	49.9	27.7	18.5	3.9

Source: U.S. Department of Education, Office of Special Education Programs, Data Analysis System (DANS), OMB #1820-0517: "Part B, *Individuals with Disabilities Education Act*, Implementation of FAPE Requirements," 2003. Data updated as of July 31, 2004. Also table 2-2 in vol. 2 of this report. These data are for the 50 states, District of Columbia, BIA schools and four outlying areas. Puerto Rico did not submit 2003 data on educational environments.

[a]Separate environments include public and private *residential facilities*, public and private *separate schools* and *homebound/hospital* environments.

most prevalent form of education for students that speech-language pathologists serve. This is the single most important factor in the creation of speech-language service delivery models in schools today. The identification, focus, frequency, intensity, purpose, and progress monitoring of students with speech-language disabilities is predicated on their general education program.

Levels 5, 6, and 7 of Figure 5.2 refer to self-contained classrooms in which MAINSTREAMING

(i.e., including a student with his or her typically developing peers) is the only way a student has access to same-age students. In these settings, students are frequently grouped by disability within an age span of four to six years due to the lower incidence of such conditions. This is even more likely to be the case in rural or low population areas. Educational and social time with peers needs to be arranged for most of these students. This can be difficult logisti-

Figure 5.1

Flowchart for Provision of Services

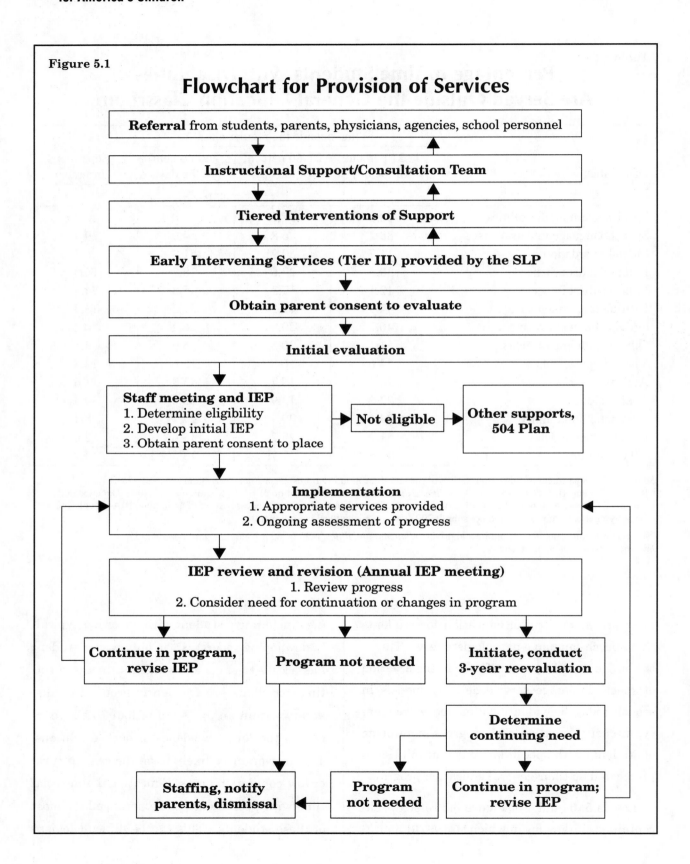

#TP-29703 Making a Difference - 2nd Ed. · ©2008 Thinking Publications® · www.thinkingpublications.com · 1-800-277-8737

Figure 5.2

Application of the Seven Levels of Service in Special Education to Communication Disabilities

Level One
General education classroom—the greatest number of
options are available here, especially in inclusive settings nationwide.

Level Two
General education classroom with consultation—
students are supported by speech-language pathologist/teacher
teams in collaborative ways.

Level Three
General education classroom with designated instruction
and services—pull-out types of sessions are typical here.

Level Four
General education classroom with resource
assistance—speech-language pathologists and resource
teachers work together to offer greater support.

Level Five
Full-time special education classroom—
classes may be taught by speech-language
pathologists or other qualified teachers.

Level Six
Special school—larger numbers
of students with communication
disabilities are grouped together.

Level Seven
Nonpublic school—a
clinical or educational
setting in the community.

From "The Cascade of Special Education Services," by E. Deno, 1970, *Exceptional Children, 39*, p. 495. ©1994 by the Council for Exceptional Children. Adapted with permission.

cally, and may be overlooked, resulting in few age-appropriate speech and language models. Students might even be on segregated sites, where only students with special needs are educated. These sites make peer contacts even more awkward to manage. In some cases, speech-language sessions might provide the only contact with age-appropriate peers. Students identified with speech-language needs could receive services in a pull-out program with same-age peers and a grade-appropriate curriculum. (Highly innovative speech-language pathologists do make a difference for these students!) Speech-language services for students in these service levels often lack the range of options available on other levels. Thoughtful planning and implementation are needed to assure that all students' services are not lessened by the restrictions of the setting.

Types of Special Education Services

Speech and Language as a Primary Disability

Speech or language impairment is one of the 13 federal eligibility categories for special education (see sidebar in Chapter 4 on p. 139). Therefore, students may receive services if this condition has an adverse educational impact on their ability to learn and make academic progress. Some schools refer to these students as "speech only" since the speech-language pathologist is the only service provider.

Related Services

Students may be eligible to receive FREE APPROPRIATE PUBLIC EDUCATION (FAPE) through special education alone or with corresponding related services that support the special education services for the primary disability area and enable a child to benefit from his or her special education program. According to the Code of Federal Regulations:

The term related services means transportation and such developmental, corrective, and other supportive services as are required to assist a child with a disability to benefit from special education, and includes speech-language pathology and audiology services, psychological services, physical and occupational therapy, recreation, including therapeutic recreation, early identification and assessment of disabilities in children, counseling services, including rehabilitation counseling, orientation and mobility services, and medical services for diagnostic or evaluation purposes. The term also includes school health services, social work services in schools, and parent counseling and training (34 C.F.R. § 300.34 [a]).

Students with speech-language disabilities may also have other cognitive, educational, behavioral, emotional, or health challenges. In fact, speech-language disabilities may be manifestations of other congenital or acquired conditions, such as developmental delays, Down syndrome, head trauma, AUTISM SPECTRUM DISORDERS, and cerebral palsy. Speech-language development plays an integral part in the educational success of children with such conditions, so speech-language services may be recommended as a related service when a student meets the criteria for one of the other 12 special education eligibility categories. Speech-language pathologists would then provide related services that would allow a student to benefit from a special education program. For example, developing an AUGMENTATIVE AND ALTERNATIVE COMMUNICATION (AAC) system may be a related service that would allow a student with cerebral palsy to participate more effectively in his or her special education instruction. The most frequently requested and provided related service is speech-language assessment and intervention (USDE, 2004b).

Mainstreaming and Inclusion

Congress always intended for children with disabilities to be educated with their nondisabled peers. Some early programs for special education placed students in separate classrooms for most of their school day and then scheduled selected activities or other academic experiences for these students with typically developing peers. The practice was known as mainstreaming. The REGULAR EDUCATION INITIATIVE (REI; Will, 1986) was critical of the practice of separating students receiving special education and advocated for greater integration and involvement of general education in the education of students with disabilities. The REI eventually evolved into the INCLUSION MOVEMENT and ultimately had a far-reaching effect on the delivery of all instructional services in schools (Biklin, 1992; Hoskins, 1990; Stainback & Stainback, 1996; Friend &

Bursuck, 2002; Hardman, Drew, & Egan, 1999). Speech-language pathologists have described the profound differences that inclusion brought to service delivery in schools (Creaghead, 1999; Hoskins, 1995; Power-deFur & Orelove, 1997; McGinty & Justice, 2006; Ritzman, Sanger, & Coufal, 2006; Montgomery & Hayes, 2005). "The movement toward inclusionary education for children with special needs has dramatically changed the professional roles of special educators working in schools. A remedial framework, previously the cornerstone of intervention for special education services, has been challenged" (Merritt & Culatta, 1998, p. ix). All school and community-based services for children with disabilities have been influenced by the Inclusion Movement.

Educators have used the term mainstreaming to refer to students with exceptional needs who are served in self-contained special education classrooms but join their same-age peers in recess, lunch, art, music, and classroom academics for perhaps 10 to 40 percent of their day (Biklin, 1992; Mastropieri & Scruggs, 2000).

This part-time program has been gradually replaced in many schools with inclusion. In the inclusive environment, students are with same-age peers for the majority of the school day but may leave from time to time for services outside the classroom. Speech-language intervention is one of those services. The Inclusion Movement "has also challenged the manner in which speech-language pathologists plan and deliver services to children with communication impairments" (Merritt & Culatta, 1998, p. ix). All service providers have already altered their programs to include children with and without disabilities (Hoskins, 1995; Mastropieri & Scruggs, 2000; Montgomery, 1997a, 1997b; Moore-Brown, 2007a). Many national organizations—including the AMERICAN SPEECH-LANGUAGE-HEARING ASSOCIATION (ASHA) and others with large numbers of members who are speech-language pathologists in schools—have issued policy and position statements on inclusion (see sidebar below for a list of organizations available online). These organizations' statements range from strongly worded opposition (e.g., the American Federation of Teachers (AFT) to cautious support (e.g., the National Association of School Psychologists) to enthusiastic endorsement (e.g., TASH). Individual state education departments often have official statements on inclusive schooling for their states. It is wise for speech-language pathologists to know the philosophy of various professional organizations, educators, parent organizations, and the communities involved in the school.

Parents and educators have had strong feelings on both sides of the theory and practice of inclusion. Some felt that students needed to

Position Statements on Inclusion

Many organizations have published positions on inclusion practices. Samplings of viewpoints are available online.

American Federation of Teachers (AFT)

www.aft.org/about/resolutions/1994/inclusion.htm

TASH

http://www.tash.org/IRR/inclusive_education.html

National Association of School Psychologists (NASP)

www.schoolhousedoor.com/media/teacher/haggart-inclusiveprog.txt

National Education Association (NEA)

http://www.nea.org/specialed/inclusionpolicy.html

be with same-age peers as much as possible to make friends and to help all students learn social roles (Stainback & Stainback, 1996). Others have complained that the amount of modification necessary for some children is disruptive to the students with disabilities and their peers without disabilities (Kauffman & Hallahan, 1995; National Joint Committee on Learning Disabilities [NJCLD], 2001). Many parents and professionals, especially those in the field of hearing loss and deafness, believe each student is so highly individualistic that the exact same set of learner characteristics could indicate inclusion in one case, but not in another (Seal, 1997).

Speech-language pathologists have relied on ASHA's (1996b) *Inclusive Practices for Children and Youths with Communication Disorders* to help clarify service delivery for students with disabilities who receive their support in general education classrooms. This position paper supports an array of settings for students but recognizes the powerful effect that peer interactions have on the development of communication skills. (See sidebar on p. 178 for the full text of ASHA's position statement, which falls in the range of cautious support with a strong focus on individual needs.)

A large percentage of students with communication disorders are educated in inclusive settings. Those students with communication disorders in addition to another special education condition are likely to be in more restrictive environments using the mainstreaming concept of "visiting their peers' classrooms" (Mastropieri & Scruggs, 2000, p. 23). This practice continues to change. When successful, students with more significant disabilities gradually spend a larger portion of their day with same-age peers. However, greater amounts of time in inclusive environments require more targeted modifications for students, especially as they reach the secondary level (Montgomery, 1997a; Seal, 1997). Seal (1997) suggests that differentiated classes for deaf students, or those with severe hearing loss, might include deaf culture, ASSISTIVE TECHNOLOGY, self advocacy, and others. Montgomery (2000b) lists three guidelines for successfully beginning the inclusion process. An INDIVIDUALIZED EDUCATION PROGRAM (IEP) team should ensure that students reentering an inclusive classroom after special class placements should initially be supported to:

- Make one or more friends.

- Have a job or responsibility in the classroom.

- Follow a schedule based on what the rest of the class is learning and doing.

Each of these guidelines relies heavily on a student's functional communication and, if warranted, becomes a goal on the child's IEP. These supports have been found to be valid for elementary- and secondary-level students (Montgomery, 1997a).

Creating and participating in an inclusive educational system is vital for both social and academic achievement for students with disabilities. Legally, the courts have shown a preference for a more inclusive educational environment (see Chapters 2 and 8). Academically, educators are increasingly aware that for students to participate in the accountability system, it is important that they have access to the core curriculum in the general education environment. Speech-language pathologists and audiologists

ASHA's Position Statement on Inclusion

It is the position of the American Speech-Language-Hearing Association (ASHA) that an array of speech, language, and hearing services should be available in educational settings to support children and youths with communication disorders. The term "inclusive practices" best represents this philosophy. The inclusive-practices philosophy emphasizes serving children and youths in the least restrictive environment that meets their needs optimally. Inclusive practices consist of a range of service-delivery options that need not be mutually exclusive. They can include direct, classroom-based, community-based, and consultative intervention programming. Inclusive practices are based on a commitment to selecting and designing interventions that meet the needs of each child and family. Factors contributing to the determination of individual need include the child's age, type of disability, communication competence, language and cultural background, academic performance, social skills, family and teacher concerns, and the student's own attitudes about speech, language, and hearing services.

ASHA recognizes that the provision of speech, language, and hearing services in educational settings is moving toward service-delivery models that integrate intervention with general educational programs, often termed inclusion. Inclusion has numerous strengths, including natural opportunities for peer interaction, and available research suggests cautious optimism regarding its effectiveness in promoting communication abilities and skills in related developmental domains. ASHA believes that the shift toward inclusion will not be optimal when implemented in absolute terms. Rather, the unique and specific needs of each child and family must always be considered.

The broad goal of inclusive service delivery should be compatible with continued recognition of the individual's unique needs and concerns. Inclusive practices are recommended as a guide in the development of intervention programming for children and youths with communication disorders.

From "Inclusive Practices for Children and Youths with Communication Disorders" [Position statement], by the American Speech-Language-Hearing Association (ASHA), 1996b, *ASHA, 38*(Suppl. 16), p. 35. ©1996 by ASHA. Reprinted with permission.

must be prepared to support students in inclusive settings in order to assist them in accessing the information they need to learn.

Choosing a Service Delivery System

Speech-language service delivery in schools is a synthesis of the inclusive education philosophy and IDEA 2004's mandate for universal access to the general education curriculum. Models of service delivery presented here were selected from a review of the current literature in school-based practice, surveys of school-based speech-language pathologists (Peters-Johnson, 1998), and experiences of both authors as school-based speech-language pathologists. Service delivery models are described using ASHA's *Preferred Practice Patterns for the Profession of Speech-Language Pathology* (2004), school realities, and the most appropriate student outcomes. Speech-language pathologists perform many activities on behalf of students from birth to age 21 nationwide, and to age 25 in Michigan. The diversity of these activities is illustrated in Figure 5.3. Some of these activities have already been discussed in preceding chapters and others will be addressed later in this book (see Chapters 6 and 7). To do their jobs successfully, speech-language pathologists need to carefully schedule their time and duties, especially if they are working at multiple sites. These services are all used in school-based programs, though speech-language pathologists will not necessarily conduct them all.

Components of Service Delivery

Service delivery models, or how a speech-language pathologist delivers service to students is dynamic and ever evolving. In the era of accountability, service delivery should be "effective, efficient, economical and evidence-based" (Moore-Brown, 2007a). Blosser and Kratcoski (1997) posed a framework for designing service delivery models that would take into account all the conventional criteria and allow speech-language pathologists to embrace new models as they became necessary. They felt that a speech-language pathologist's role was continually evolving with an increased understanding of individuals with communication disorders and the effects on learning and daily living tasks. Throughout the field, consumers of speech-language services have become more involved in their own treatment. In schools, partnerships are formed with parents and community agencies, technology has made the improbable likely, and documentation of student outcomes drives education and rehabilitation. Speech-language pathologists need a framework that encompasses all service delivery models, not a proliferation of more and more models. Blosser and Kratcoski's framework (see Table 5.2) appears to conclude at the year 2000, but the three foci of treatment dominate decision making for the foreseeable future.

Every service model should address four ideas: overall effectiveness, coordination with other programs and services, commitment of all parties, and resources available. A student should receive services that are matched to his or her needs at that point in time and are flexible to changing conditions. According to Blosser

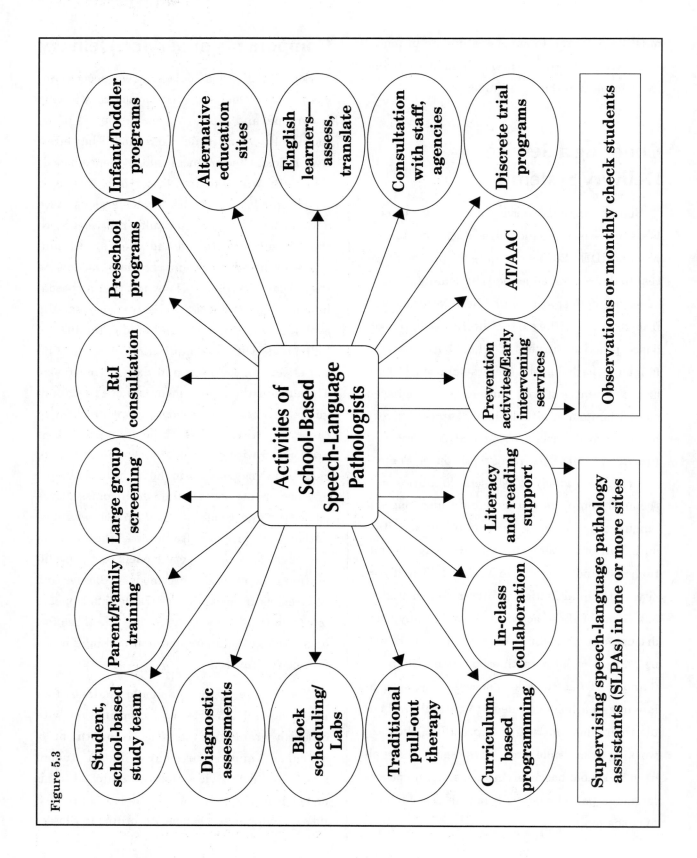

Figure 5.3

Infant/Toddler programs

Alternative education sites

English learners—assess, translate

Consultation with staff, agencies

Discrete trial programs

Preschool programs

AT/AAC

RtI consultation

Activities of School-Based Speech-Language Pathologists

Prevention activites/Early intervening services

Observations or monthly check students

Large group screening

Literacy and reading support

Parent/Family training

In-class collaboration

Supervising speech-language pathology assistants (SLPAs) in one or more sites

Student, school-based study team

Diagnostic assessments

Block scheduling/ Labs

Traditional pull-out therapy

Curriculum-based programming

#TP-29703 Making a Difference - 2nd Ed. · ©2008 Thinking Publications® · www.thinkingpublications.com · 1-800-277-8737

and Kratcoski (1997), this requires flexing the provider, the activities, and the context. In the following descriptions, the provider arrangement changes, the range of activities is broad but primarily curriculum-centered, and the contexts are school-related. Flexibility among provider, activities, and context is important in the following models, as in the curriculum models in Chapter 6 and the expanded and specialized service delivery models presented in Chapter 7. Whitmire (2002, p. 71) encapsulates the "contemporary vision of school-based practice" as converging on three fundamental elements of school-based speech and language therapy: contextually based assessment, educationally relevant intervention plans, and increased collaboration and consultation.

The Concept of Good Practice

The term GOOD PRACTICE is used in school-based programs (and other settings) to denote the use of research-based, effective, and measurable techniques to provide intervention or in-

---

Table 5.2

The Evolution of Speech-Language Pathologist Service Delivery Models

	1970s	**1980s**	**1990s**	**2000**
Focus for treatment	Mechanistic view of language	Pragmatics	Functional, interactive communication Preparation for learning, living, and working	Outcomes
Speech-language pathologist's role	Specialist model	Expert model	Collaborative-consultative model	Facilitator of the service delivery
Emerging issues	Language use is important	Language and learning are linked	Inclusion, transition, efficacy, accountability, outcomes	To be decided
	syntax / semantics / phonology	content / form / use	communication / learning / collaboration	context / providers / activities

From "PACs: A Framework for Determining Appropriate Service Delivery Options," by J.L. Blosser and A. Kratcoski, 1997, *Language, Speech, and Hearing Services in Schools, 28,* p. 100. ©1997 by the American Speech-Language-Hearing Association. Reprinted with permission.

struction for students who experience communication disorders and disabilities. In contrast to BEST PRACTICE, which establishes one intervention as better than all others, good practice can be defended successfully in legal proceedings and mediations. What is best for one student's circumstances may not be best for another. Professionals in speech and language, and other educational pursuits, are ethically bound to apply good practice principles to all their responsibilities, maintaining vigilance for new evidence and research. "To use only one [approach]...is not malpractice. To use more than one is merely enriched practice" (Rosenbek, 1984, p. 361).

Some speech-language pathologists teach classrooms of students with communication disorders; some may co-teach with RESOURCE TEACHERS; and others use multiple approaches of pull-out therapy (i.e., removing children from a classroom for speech-language services), co-teaching, and classroom support. There are many models based on the needs of students, the culture of school districts, and the innovative ideas and skills of speech-language pathologists everywhere.

Good practice in schools requires speech-language pathologists to recognize the commonalities and differences among three macrodelivery systems—CLASSROOM INSTRUCTION, CONVENTIONAL THERAPY, and COLLABORATIVE INTERVENTION—and to choose the system or combination of systems most likely to result in progress for a student. Progress in speech-language skills was initially the goal of school-based speech-language pathologists, but with the reauthorization of IDEA 2004, this progress must be linked to academic achievement at a student's appropriate level (Brannen et al, 2000).

Speech-language pathologists may choose one or more of the macrodelivery systems, or may alternate from one to another over the period of time a student receives speech-language services. "Service delivery is a dynamic concept and should change as the needs of the students change. No one service delivery model should be used exclusively during treatment" (ASHA, 1999b, p. 58). STATE EDUCATION AGENCIES (SEAs), through their consultant staff and committees of speech-language pathologists from the field who volunteer their time, publish guidelines for assessment, eligibility, and service delivery for speech-language and hearing services in their states (see "Who to Ask When You Have a Question on the Job" in Chapter 9). These comprehensive manuals specify the school service delivery models encouraged in a particular state. They help speech-language pathologists select an appropriate assessment procedure followed by one or more intervention programs. Figure 5.4, the schematic from the Indiana Speech-Language-Hearing Association (ISHA, 1997), has been included to illustrate the breadth and variety of services the school-based speech-language pathologist may provide. The service delievery options in a school service area in Illinois (see sidebar on p. 184) and the generic model for schools (see Table 5.3, p. 185) provide further examples of the guidance available regarding service delivery.

Classroom instruction is typically delivered by a classroom teacher, a supervised instructional aide, or a subject-area specialist (e.g., music, art, or biology).

Figure 5.4

Indiana's Overview of Good Practice in Schools

Public School Speech-Language Pathologists Provide a Continuum of Services for

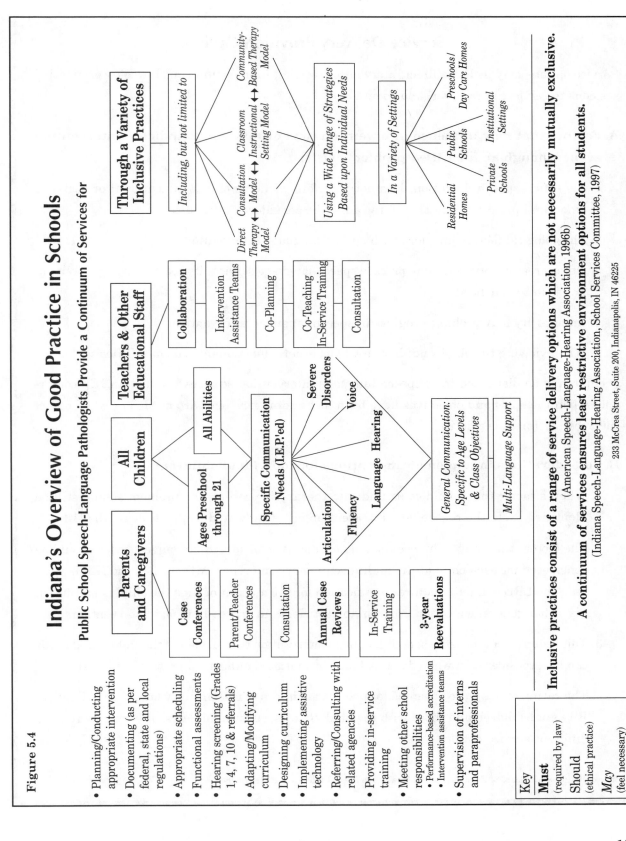

From *Indiana's Overview of Good Practice in Schools*, by the Indiana Speech-Language-Hearing Association (ISHA), 1997, Indianapolis, IN: Author. ©1997 by ISHA. Adapted with permission.

Service Delivery Provision Options

Service options may include: direct intervention, consultation, monitoring, biweekly or monthly sessions to reinforce carryover, and so on.

A. Factors that may influence intervention time or may contraindicate intervention events though an identified problem exists:

1. Identified speech deviation does not interfere with the child's educational or social or emotional progress, and therefore cannot be considered a handicap.

2. Physiological factors interfere with speech-language intervention.

3. Other areas of service need to precede speech-language services if speech-language intervention is to be beneficial.

4. Immaturity may prohibit progress in speech-language intervention.

5. When viewing the child's needs as a whole, other educational needs have priority.

A child may be dismissed from speech-language intervention services through an IEP conference when the goals and objectives have been met and no new ones are needed or when one of the above factors has priority.

B. Considerations in implementing options for individual children:

1. When a factor that would contraindicate therapy is present, the problem should still be identified. Note the reason why intervention is not indicated at this time on the IEP.

2. The factors that may influence the amount and type of speech-language service should be considered for each child at the multidisciplinary conference (MDC) when the IEP is written. The LRE mandate requires justification for the amount of time the child is missing in his or her general education program to participate in speech-language intervention.

3. This requirement to justify speech-language intervention time in view of the child's total needs can be a consideration when dismissal may be indicated although a problem still exists.

4. The rating scales were designed for use with children whose primary language is English. Bilingual children and those with regional dialects, cultural dialects, or both may require different service options.

Source: Illinois State Board of Education, Black Hawk Area Special Education District (1993)

Table 5.3

Service Delivery Model for Speech-Language Pathologists

	Itinerant Program (Direct Service)	Resource Room Program (Direct Service)	Self-Contained Program (Direct Service)	Consultation Program (Indirect Service)
Cases Served	• All communicative disorders. • All ranges (mild to severe).	• All communicative disorders (moderate to severe).	• Severe and/or multiple communicative disorders. • Primary handicapping condition is communication regardless of etiology.	• All communicative disorders. • All ranges (mild to severe).
Services Provided	• Program development, management, coordination and evaluation. • Direct services. • Provision of speech-language services in coordination with classroom teacher and/or other special educators.	• Program development, management, coordination and evaluation. • Direct service and/or self study. • Provision of speech-language services in coordination with classroom teacher and/or other special educators. • Primary responsibility for academic instruction rests with classroom teacher.	• Program development, management, coordination and evaluation. • Direct speech-language services plus academic instruction provided by speech-language pathologist with SEA Guidelines.	• Program development, management, coordination and evaluation. • Indirect services: Develops clinical program to be carried out by others.
Group Size	• Individual or small group. • Up to 3 students per session.	• Individual or small group. • Up to 5 students per session.	• Up to 10 students per speech-language pathologist. • Up to 15 students per speech-language pathologist and aide.	• Individual or group (through indirect service).
Time Per Day	• Variable: ½ hr. (mild) to 2 hours per day for (severe).	• 1 to 3 hrs. per day.	• Full school day.	• Variable: Possible range ½ hr. (mild) to 3 to 4 hrs. per day.
Time Per Week	• 2 to 5 times per week.	• 4 to 5 times per week.	• Full-time placement.	• 1 to 5 times per week.
Rationale for Caseload Size	• Moderate-severe cases require more service. • Increased clinical time required to produce change. • Amount and type of service needed is considered in determining caseload numbers.	• Moderate-severe cases may require more intensive services. • Consistent with some state regulations for classes of special education.	• Consistent with some state regulations for classes of special education. • Provides for intensive services.	• Amount of time necessitated by organizational and structural variety of personnel/agencies involved. • Variability of student needs and of the needs of those being trained.
Caseload Maximums	• Up to 25 severe. • Up to 25–55 maximum.	• Up to 15–25 students.	• Up to 15 students with aide. • Up to 10 students without aide.	• 10–15 severe. • 15–55 mild moderate. • As needed.

Sources: ASHA (1998d); Peters-Johnson (1998)

- In self-contained classrooms for students with special needs, this person can be a special education teacher or a speech-language pathologist.

- The intent in this setting is to teach students the grade- or age-level curriculum.

- Speech-language skills are directly or indirectly taught by a teacher as part of the subject area (e.g., auditory attention skills, opposites, descriptive labels, public speaking, oral book reports, noun-verb agreement in written discourse, vocabulary, or narrative scripts).

- The instruction is directed to the ability level of the middle of the class, and although students earn individual grades on report cards, whole class improvement is sought. Individual instruction is planned; however, an entire class is taught subject matter together. This is challenging when students present a wide range of skills and abilities.

Conventional therapy is typically delivered in individual or small-group pull-out sessions in a small room or area designated for intervention.

- A speech-language pathologist or a supervised SPEECH-LANGUAGE PATHOLOGY ASSISTANT (SLPA) presents a task, introduces the directions, and often interacts directly with a student during the session.

- The intent in this setting is to modify a student's specific deficient communication skills. Some groups are composed of students who all have the same type of deficiency while others may have different areas of need.

- The skills are selected from developmental hierarchies, standardized testing levels, and expectancies for children at various ages. Speech-language skills are directly modeled, encouraged, and reinforced using a wide range of materials and interest areas (e.g., toys, games, books, cards, practice workbooks, and kits).

- The therapy is designed for a particular student, and only that individual's improvement is measured and recorded.

Collaborative intervention is typically delivered in a classroom in a co-teaching arrangement with a teacher or in a less distracting environment or pull-out session using materials from the classroom.

- A speech-language pathologist or SLPA (using tasks from the classroom) modifies the presentation or scaffolds a student's responses, or both to assure success.

- The intent is to increase the amount of interaction a student has with the curriculum, and thereby address deficient speech-language skills in a way that will rapidly impact grade-level work. New skills are taught using the student's areas of strength.

- Speech-language skills are directly modeled by a speech-language pathologist and peers, and then encouraged, facilitated, and reinforced by a student's successful completion of some or all of the assigned curriculum. Examples include:

  ✓ Class plays

  ✓ COOPERATIVE LEARNING group assignments

✓ Question-and-answer sessions

✓ Journal writing

✓ Recalling facts from a textbook

- The intervention is directed at the juncture of a student's deficient communication skills and the requirements of the curriculum.

- Although advancement of the whole class is the focus, an individual student's progress on predetermined communication goals is also monitored and recorded.

Whitmire (2002) addresses service delivery options focused on functional intervention which is based on students' needs:

All social, political, and professional influences shaping the practice of speech-language pathology in schools have emphasized the consideration of the array of service delivery options when designing an intervention plan that will best meet the individual needs of a child. These options may be combined and should be seen as flexible, depending on changing student needs (ASHA, 1996b; NJCLD, 1991). Regardless of the service delivery model(s) deemed appropriate for any given student, the focus of the interventions should be functional and content-based, integrating intervention with the meaningful activities of the child's educational experience (p. 73).

The Role of a Case Manager in Service Delivery

Decisions regarding the nature (direct or indirect), type (individual, group, or class), and location (resource room, classroom, home, or community) of service delivery are based on the need to provide FAPE for each student in the LRE which is consistent with a student's individual needs as documented on an IEP. The role of a speech-language pathologist is to assist an educational team in selecting, planning, and coordinating appropriate service delivery using various scheduling options throughout the duration of services. This begins with the initial placement decisions, extends through all reevaluations and special circumstances, and culminates when the student is dismissed from the speech-language program.

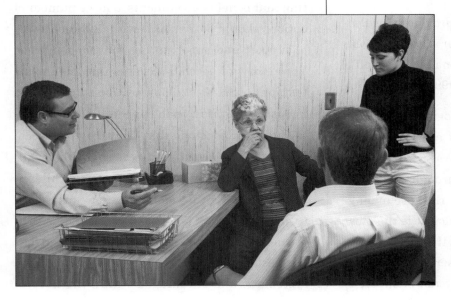

Speech-language pathologists serve as CASE MANAGERS for students whose primary need is communication or whose program is constructed around speech-language goals.

They may also serve as case managers for students who are included in a general education program and monitored by one or more special educators. As a CASE MANAGER, a speech-language pathologist may:

- Serve as the point of contact for a student's special education services.

- Schedule and coordinate both school-based and community-based assessments.

- Assume a leadership role in developing an IEP or INDIVIDUALIZED FAMILY SERVICE PLAN (IFSP).

- Assist families in identifying available service providers and advocacy organizations within a community.

- Coordinate, monitor, and ensure timely delivery of special education services, related services, or both.

- Schedule and coordinate any requested re-evaluation processes.

- Facilitate the development of IDEA-required transition plans at any level.

- Coordinate services or provide consultation for students in charter schools, private schools, or other educational agencies off a school campus (ASHA, 1999b).

If a speech-language pathologist is not a case manager, he or she remains an active team member, providing appropriate services to identified students and following through on all joint responsibilities coordinated by the case manager. The speech-language pathologist is the most knowledgeable person to select the service delivery model for speech-language services; however, input from parents and other team members is always considered. According to ASHA (1999b), when choosing the most promising service delivery model, the speech-language pathologist acting as case manager must give consideration to a student's:

1. Strengths, needs, and emerging abilities.

2. Need for peer modeling.

3. Communication needs as they relate to the general education curriculum.

4. Need for intensive intervention.

5. Effort, attitude, motivation, and social skills.

6. Disorder(s) severity.

7. Disorder(s) nature.

8. Age and developmental level .

In the *Twenty-Sixth Annual Report to Congress on the Implementation of the Individuals with Disabilities Education Act* (USDE, 2005d), the continuing need for a full continuum of services for students with disabilities was stressed. Because there is no single special education setting that benefits all students, a large number of options should be available with different levels of support and opportunities for independence. The review of special education models in this text, plus ASHA's (1996b) position statement on inclusive practices, enables speech-language pathologists to conclude that "an array of speech, language, and hearing services should be available in educational settings to support children and youths with communication disorders" (ASHA, 1996b, p. 35). This further underscores the need for a variety of possible settings, so that the best match can be made and changes are systematic and encouraged within the natural environments of school, home, and community. During the course of his or her intervention, a student might participate in many different service delivery models. Three important concepts that drive all service delivery model decisions include the following:

1. Service delivery is a dynamic concept, and it changes as the needs of the student change.

2. No one service delivery model is to be used exclusively during intervention.

3. For all service delivery models, it is essential that time be made available in the weekly schedule for collaboration/consultation with parents, general educators, special educators, and other service providers (ASHA, 1996b).

Preferred Practice Patterns for Intervention

PREFERRED PRACTICE PATTERNS are generic and universally applicable for all service delivery models. They are based on the *Classification of Speech-Language Pathology and Audiology Procedures and Communication Disorders* (ASHA, 2005a). The practice patterns were developed and periodically updated as a guide to enhance the quality of professional services, as an educational tool for persons outside the profession, and as a method to help ensure uniformity of service delivery across settings. Therapeutic practices provided in schools, for example, will be essentially the same in a nonschool agency.

The principles of ASHA's (2004e) preferred practice patterns for screening, assessment, and intervention services have been used to describe the models chosen throughout this book. Visit ASHA's Web site (www.asha.org) for a complete list of preferred practice patterns.

Functional Outcomes and the School-Based Speech-Language Pathologist

FUNCTIONAL OUTCOMES are defined as "the results of care" in health-care circles and the "results of intervention" in educational settings They can be considered evidence of progress. The bottom line for all service delivery programs is contained in this question: When you provide services for a student with COMMUNICATION DISORDERS, how do you determine that the intervention has made a meaningful difference in that student's life? This may seem like a straightforward question, but in determining the tools and procedures speech-language pathologists need to find the answer, several other questions are raised:

- Can speech-language pathologists rely on standardized test scores to capture the improvement?

- Is it more authentic if persons other than speech-language pathologists report the changes they observe?

- Do others besides the student know if the intervention was helpful?

• Do speech-language pathologists know if most students with similar diagnoses make similar improvements? How can this be found out? If students do not, why not?

• Does the student's rate of improvement change with different speech-language pathologists?

• Does one service provider see results more quickly or more slowly than another? How can speech-language pathologists alter that rate?

Speech-language pathologists have responded to questions about individual effectiveness (Enderby & Emerson, 1995). For example, researchers and speech-language pathologists have investigated the efficacy of one clinical approach over another (Bain & Dollaghan, 1991; Kamhi, 1991). Speech-language pathologists have asked if clients receiving a certain type of intervention scored higher on the same battery of tests at the end of a cycle of treatment (ASHA, 1999a; Enderby & Emerson, 1995). The profession has queried itself about whether clients actually had less communication difficulty at the conclusion of therapy, if clients regressed or maintained their skills, or if clients received direct assistance from a speech-language pathologist a second time (Crawford, 1998; Enderby & Emerson, 1995). These were closely related and interesting questions, but they did not adequately address an underlying concern in health care and education posed in the twenty-first century: Is there a research base to show that speech-language pathology services are valuable and necessary for persons with communication disorders?

According to Enderby and Emerson (1995), the answer is a strong yes. Measuring and reporting that value and then linking it directly to a speech-language pathologist's intervention process is the purpose of functional outcomes (Campbell, 1999; ASHA, 2007d). (See also "Evidence-Based Practice" on p. 198.) Moore-Brown et al., (1998) emphasized how critical it was for school speech-language pathologists to "make sure the goals are well written and truly reflect the outcomes desired for this child…We need to be able to provide this information and answer questions as to what it is we're doing, what difference it makes, how long it takes, and what it costs" (p. 11).

Functional Outcomes Defined as Results of Intervention

The employers, agencies, insurance companies, school boards, legislators, and clients who pay for speech-language services want to know when meaningful change can be attributed to speech-language pathologists. These payers want to know consumers' functional outcomes. Because speech-language pathologists are most often employees of a school district or a regional system, the idea of these agencies as service payers may seem out of place at first glance. Speech-language pathologists and all professionals who work in school systems must remember that taxpayers support all educational services. "Documentation of accountability in schools is important to assist in developing reasonable cost/benefit ratios for program planning purposes. Effective utilization of this documentation can be a highly persuasive tool" (Ferguson, 1994–1995, p. 8). Cost/Benefit ratios and similar methods of accountability determine whether school-based speech-language pathologists are hired, receive the respect of fellow professionals, and how responsibilities are assigned.

Functional outcomes are not student scores on STANDARDIZED TESTS. Nor are they a list of the OBJECTIVES an individual has mastered. Instead, they are an accounting of the cost, time, and resulting restoration (or newly acquired performance) of the client (Rao as cited in Crawford, 1998; Wolf, 1997) and a treatment tool that shows close relationship to reimbursement in all work settings. While the use of functional outcomes is a relatively new concept for some speech-language pathologists, it has been noted in the professional literature for several decades (Montgomery, 1997b).

Functional outcomes for adults are measured in terms that reflect a life context beyond therapy. An adult may return to work or previous social activities, interact with family and friends, and be independent at selected tasks again after treatment for a communication disorder. These changes are called RESTORATIVE. For children and youth, functional outcomes are framed in broader educational standards—progress in academics or a life-skills curriculum, friendship development, and age-appropriate interdependence and interaction with family members and care providers. Functional outcomes for children are HABILITATIVE, or newly acquired performances. An exception to this might be a traumatic brain injury where the focus of therapy would be to restore previous functioning and learn new academic information at the student's grade level. (See Table 5.4 for a list of ASHA's functional status measures for students.)

Functional Outcomes: Relationship to Health Care

School administrators watched the evolution of functional outcome measures in health care during the early 1990s. Speech-language pathologists providing services through health care were jarred by the sudden restrictions on reimbursement imposed by HEALTH MAINTENANCE ORGANIZATIONS (HMOs) and fee capitation (Wolf, 1997). In an even tighter managed care system introduced in 1998, speech-language pathologists were expected to share the risk of habilitation or rehabilitation of a client with parties paying for the intervention services. Significant change in patient-functioning level was required in a prescribed amount of time to receive a maximum payment. If it took longer to reach the expected level of function, in most cases, there were no additional payments (Crawford, 1998).

The restrictions required health-care administrators to accurately estimate the time it would take for speech-language pathologists to meet patients' goals; otherwise, speech-language pathologists or health-care facilities found it was not cost-effective to offer services. Insurance companies did not deny services, but they did deny payment. Speech-language pathologists were expected to know how many sessions would be needed for a client to reach a certain performance level. Conversely, they had to decide how much patient progress was reasonable in the amount of intervention time that was covered by insurance. Speech-language pathologists also needed to recognize clients who could not be expected to make meaningful change and judiciously not schedule them for therapy reim-

---

Table 5.4

ASHA Functional Status Measures

For each statement, indicate on a scale of 0–7 how much assistance is needed for a student to function in each area within the educational environment.

> 0 = No basis for rating
> 1 = Does not do
> 2 = Does with maximal assistance
> 3 = Does with moderate to maximal assistance
> 4 = Does with moderate assistance
> 5 = Does with minimal to moderate assistance
> 6 = Does with minimal assistance
> 7 = Does independently

a. The student's speech is understood.

b. The student responds to questions regarding everyday and classroom activities.

c. The student produces appropriate phrases and sentences in response to classroom activities.

d. The student communicates wants, needs, ideas, and concepts to others either verbally or by use of an augmentative communication system.

e. The student uses appropriate vocabulary to function within the classroom.

f. The student describes familiar objects and events.

g. The student knows and uses age-appropriate interactions with peers and staff.

h. The student initiates, maintains, and concludes conversations with peers and staff within classroom settings.

i. The student initiates, maintains, and concludes conversations with peers and staff in non-classroom settings.

j. The student indicates when messages are not understood.

k. The student completes oral presentations.

l. The student demonstrates the ability to give directions.

Continued

Table 5.4 – *Continued*

m. The student demonstrates the ability to follow directions.

n. The student demonstrates the ability to recall written information presented in the educational environment.

o. The student demonstrates the ability to recall auditory information presented in the educational environment.

p. The student demonstrates the ability to use verbal language to solve problems.

q. The student demonstrates appropriate listening skills within the educational environment.

r. The student recognizes and demonstrates comprehension of nonverbal communication.

Definitions for Evaluating the Functional
Status Measures on the Scale of Independence

0	No basis for rating	Includes circumstances in which a behavior is not observed, directly tested, and/or the information is not available from other sources.
1	Does not do	Child does not perform the communication behavior, even with maximal assistance or prompting.
2	Does with maximal assistance	Child performs the communication behavior with constant assistance and prompting only.
3	Does with moderate to maximal assistance	Child performs the communication behavior but frequently needs assistance and prompting.
4	Does with moderate assistance	Child performs the communication behavior, often needing assistance and prompting.
5	Does with minimal to moderate assistance	Child performs the communication behavior, occasionally needing assistance and/or prompting.
6	Does with minimal assistance	Child performs the communication behavior, rarely needing assistance and/or prompting.
7	Does independently	Child performs the communication behavior, needing no assistance and/or prompting.

From *User's Guide Phase I—Group II, National Treatment Outcome Data Collection Project,* (pp. 41–44), by the American Speech-Language-Hearing Association (ASHA), 1995, Rockville, MD: Author. ©1995 by ASHA. Adapted with permission.

bursed by a particular payer. New MEDICARE fee schedules, PROSPECTIVE PAYMENT, and a SHARED CAP on rehabilitation services intensified the treatment/reimbursement issues for the profession (ASHA, 1998a). While many speech-language pathologists decried this health-care environment as fiscally driven, it was apparent that this fiscal pressure fueled the need for accurate outcome data in speech-language pathology and audiology (Baum, 1998; Grimes, 1997).

Functional outcomes have been measured therapeutically, fiscally, and emotionally in adult health care before the terms reached the schools. Slightly tongue in cheek, Rao (as cited in Crawford, 1998) noted that success in adult rehabilitation in speech-language services was formerly measured with the six Ds: death, disease, dollars, disability, discomfort, and dissatisfaction. School-based speech-language pathologists, pressed to demonstrate success in their programs, might also have selected five Ds: dollars, departure, dissatisfaction, diploma, and dismissal!

Functional Outcomes as Reflected in IDEA 2004

According to IDEA 2004, all special educators are mandated to link intervention with a student's core curriculum and proficiency in core subject areas. Further, special educators must report student progress to parents on a similar schedule as general educators as well as address curriculum BENCHMARKS on an INDIVIDUALIZED EDUCATION PROGRAM (IEP). IDEA 2004 states that educators write comprehensive goals for students; they do not have to write short-term objectives or benchmarks. Some states continue to write both goals and objectives/benchmarks.

Speech-language pathologists may write short-term objectives for increasing a child's AUDITORY PROCESSING skills to build a foundation for other skills, or they may write goals to show the level of spelling and literacy skills that comprise the educational standards the child needs to reach. Goals which relate to academic or school behaviors identify functional outcomes while those that relate to processing deficits usually do not. Benchmarks and short-term objectives serve as points along a path to a goal. If the early parts of intervention are focused on changing underlying skills only, a speech-language IEP may not appear to be connected with the student's use of these new skills. Speech-language pathologists need to link skills with daily functional activities from the beginning (Moore-Brown et al., 1998; Moore-Brown, 2007a). If speech-language pathologists use a method of sampling improvements called progress monitoring, it is not necessary to write lengthy statements of objectives the student will "touch" along the path toward his or her goal. Examples of functional outcomes written as measurable annual goals can be found in Chapter 4.

Four Basic Questions for Functional Outcomes

The systematic search for practical intervention benchmarks has pushed speech-language pathologists in all settings to begin to explore and use functional outcomes. Four basic questions, like the borders of a picture frame illustrated in Figure 5.5, characterize these functional outcomes. Side 1 asks "How many sessions does it take to show meaningful change?" Side 2 queries "How will each assessment streamline the costs of serving this student?" Side 3 poses the question "Is this the most cost-effective way to provide this service?" Side 4 asks "Can you prove that the services you provide make a difference for the student?" (Montgomery, 1997b).

When an individual speech-language pathologist answers one or more of these questions with confidence, he or she has ventured that much closer to restructuring services around a student's and payer's expectancies, which leads to greater customer satisfaction and more consistent remuneration for speech-language pathologists. While tying speech-language services so closely to the payment system has been considered crude or commercial in some circles, or lacking in professionalism by others, it is precisely this results-based approach that demonstrates the speech-language pathologist's value in the health workplace. Keeping track of the client's functional outcomes, instead of reporting more

Figure 5.5

Four Essential Questions for Functional Outcomes in School-Based Service

2. How will each assessment streamline the costs of serving this student?

1. How many sessions does it take to show meaningful change?

3. Is this the most cost-effective way to provide this service?

4. Can you prove that the services you provide make a difference for the student?

From "Using Functional Outcomes in the Schools," by J.K. Montgomery, 1997b, *CSHA Magazine, 26*(2), pp. 7–8. ©1997 by the California Speech-Language-Hearing Association. Adapted with permission.

trivial changes in discrete communication skills or comparing scaled scores on a pre- and post-test, demonstrates that the speech-language pathologist is applying resources wisely (Larson & McKinley, 1995a; Mullen, 2000).

Speech-language pathologists in schools must align their intervention with students' academic or developmental progress. Results must document increased functional performance levels of students who receive speech-language services. Increasingly, the functional outcome that is needed is academic achievement. For students with more significant disabilities, other types of functional outcomes will be needed and can be measured by FCMs; but for most students ,their functional outcome will be realized in terms of grades, advancing from grade to grade, participating in the academic curriculum, passing a high school exit exam and earning a high school diploma. As the goals of NO CHILD LEFT BEHIND (NCLB) and IDEA 2004 become more closely aligned, these real life outcome measures will become dominant for students with disabilities and those who serve them.

Clinically Significant Change

Functional outcomes must be the paramount product of speech-language pathologists' planned intervention for students. Speech-language pathologists must design measurable goals and select meaningful benchmarks that truly mat-

ter to students, families, and systems educating students. Speech-language pathologists want to be sure that their work results in clinically significant change for individuals with communication disorders. The criteria for clinically significant change from Bain and Dollaghan (1991) is widely cited in the field. They propose that clinically significant change must be:

1. Due to intervention, not maturation.

2. Real, not random.

3. Important, not trivial.

Bain and Dollaghan's (1991) guidelines assist speech-language pathologists in selecting consumer-driven goals. "The documentation of clinical significance is useful in prospective, on-line, and retrospective decision making" in service delivery in schools (Ferguson, 1994–1995, p. 8), and IEPs must be designed to confer educational benefit. What better way to do this than to use functional outcomes?

Unlike the fiscally based decisions of cost and length of speech-language services, functional outcomes (also called PERFORMANCE OUT-COMES) evolve directly from a speech-language pathologist's assessment of a student's functioning level. Functional or performance outcomes are the best estimate of the student's anticipated communicative status. Functional outcomes for students actually vary little by practice setting since all the statements focus on how individuals will have more effective and satisfying lives. In education, curricular goals are the focus; in health care, life or workplace expectancies are emphasized. Eventually the use of functional outcomes may actually draw together education and health care, and private- and public-sector speech-language pathologists in common benchmarks and even common agreement of termination points for therapy. Functional outcomes have a universal appeal to multidisciplinary teams, families, and payers (i.e., insurance agencies and state taxpayers). When students' IEPs are designed to confer educational benefit, functional outcomes are easier to document.

> Eventually the use of functional outcomes may actually draw together education and health care, and private- and public sector speech-language pathologists.

Direct Versus Indirect Outcomes

Outcomes can be viewed as either direct or indirect (Montgomery, 1997b). DIRECT OUTCOMES are behavioral changes that are planned. For example, if Felicia learns to convey accurate information to another person during a telephone call by practicing telephone dialogues, it would be a direct outcome. INDIRECT OUTCOMES

may occur if a new and appropriate behavior emerges that was not anticipated (Blackstone & Pressman, 1996). If Felicia, while practicing telephone dialogues, learns to use acceptable telephone etiquette, the indirect outcome is Felicia using appropriate social language and pragmatics over the telephone. This acquisition of pragmatic skills should be documented as a functional outcome even if it was not specifically planned in the IEP. Speech-language pathologists need to be alert to the manifestations of improved communication skills beyond those directly targeted.

Outcomes may also be categorized as intended versus unintended. When Connie learns to write statements about a character's feelings, using adjectives and adverbs, in her collaborative speech and language sessions, writing such statements about a novel read in class is an intended outcome. Another time, if Connie uses her writing skills to write notes to a friend in her class about an argument with her boyfriend, her text is an unintended outcome. The unintended outcome, though a personally valuable activity, demonstrates the skill even if she did not write the class assignment correctly (Montgomery, 1999b). Though learning the playground game and writing notes to friends may not have been these students' predicted outcomes, their emergence may be credited to intervention. Although we plan for direct, intended skill development, speech-language pathologists need to identify the indirect, unintended outcomes that signal progress as well!

An example of this phenomenon is the incidental learning of sight words by students during articulation therapy (Stewart, Gonzalez, & Page, 1997). Changes in academic behavior occurred that no one expected when students were found able to read the words they used in each speech session to practice their target phonemes. Students increased their reading skills because the words were printed on the picture cards, and students read the print repeatedly during their speech-language sessions.

When communication events are related to the anticipated new or restored skills, they should be recorded as outcomes. Speech-language pathologists may need to look beyond direct intended skill acquisition to unexpected indirect outcomes with their students. In schools, academic expectancies may be the driving force behind the majority of intended outcomes; however, the achievement of social or interpersonal goals, even though these goals may be set more conservatively, may result in more unintentional outcomes because of the unlimited opportunities to use these skills in daily activities. Speech-language pathologists should anticipate recording both intended and unintended outcomes when measuring student progress. Both types of outcomes are examples of clinically significant change as defined by Bain and Dollaghan (1991).

Evidence-Based Practice (EBP)

Evidence-Based Practice (EBP) has been defined as "the conscientious, explicit, and judicious use of current best evidence in making decisions about the care of individual patients... *[by]* integrating clinical expertise with the best available external clinical evidence from systematic research" (Sackett et al., 1996; Dollaghan, 2004). EBP derives from evidence-based medicine, and has been the standard in the medical field for over ten years.

The use of EBP in the delivery of services is deemed necessary and ethical by ASHA (2005f). (See sidebar on p. 199 for ASHA's position statement on EBP.) EBP reflects the current trend in clinical and educational decision making.

Both NCLB and IDEA 2004 have requirements for the use of scientifically based research, also known as evidence-based practice (NCLB § 9101 [37]; 34 C.F.R. § 300.35). ASHA (2004b) supports the use of EBP suggesting that it "has the potential to improve the quality of the evidence base supporting clinical practice in speech-language pathology and audiology, and ultimately improve the quality of clinical services to patients with speech, language, and hearing disorders (p. 1).

The use of EBP by school-based speech-language pathologists and audiologists requires attention to systematic change in the institutional decision-making processes in schools on one level, but ultimately is about how and why clinical decisions are made. It means knowing how to decide what approach to use in treatment (Justice & Fey, 2005; Apel & Wolter, 2004b).

Nye, Schwartz, and Turner (2005) outline a seven step approach for EBP:

1. Ask an EBP question.

2. Identify the source for best evidence.

3. Evaluate the quality of the evidence.

4. Analyze the evidence.

ASHA's Position Statement on Evidence-Based Practice

It is the position of the American Speech-Language-Hearing Association that audiologists and speech-language pathologists incorporate the principles of evidence-based practice in clinical decision making to provide high quality clinical care. The term *evidence-based practice* refers to an approach in which current, high-quality research evidence is integrated with practitioner expertise and client preferences and values into the process of making clinical decisions.

In making clinical practice evidence-based, audiologists and speech-language pathologists—

- recognize the needs, abilities, values, preferences, and interests of individuals and families to whom they provide clinical services, and integrate those factors along with best current research evidence and their clinical expertise in making clinical decisions;

- acquire and maintain the knowledge and skills that are necessary to provide high-quality professional services, including knowledge and skills related to evidence-based practice;

- evaluate prevention, screening, and diagnostic procedures, protocols, and measures to identify maximally informative and cost-effective diagnostic and screening tools, using recognized appraisal criteria described in the evidence-based practice literature;

- evaluate the efficacy, effectiveness, and efficiency of clinical protocols for prevention, treatment, and enhancement using criteria recognized in the evidence-based practice literature;

- evaluate the quality of evidence appearing in any source or format, including journal articles, textbooks, continuing education offerings, newsletters, advertising, and Web-based products, prior to incorporating such evidence into clinical decision making; and

- monitor and incorporate new and high-quality research evidence having implications for clinical practice.

Source: ASHA (2005f). Reprinted with permission.

5. Check for chance meaning of the evidence.

6. Average the meaning of the evidence.

7. Interpret the meaning of the evidence.

8. Move from best evidence to best practice.

Gierut (2001) distinguishes the following important concepts in the consideration of EBP:

- Treatment effectiveness – whether or not a treatment works.

- Treatment effects – the behavioral changes that occurred following treatment.

- Treatment efficiency – whether one treatment method was better than another; clinically, the most important of the three.

School-based speech-language pathologists do not have to be concerned that EBP will take too much of their time. Increasingly, professional journals and other resources are focusing on the EBP topic, such as:

- "Clinical Forum on Combining Research and Reason to Make Treatment Decisions." *Language, Speech, and Hearing Services in Schools*, October 2006 issue of Vol. *37* (4)

- "Clinical Forum on Understanding Children Who Have Been Affected by Maltreatment and Prenatal Alcohol Exposure." *Language, Speech, and Hearing Services in Schools*, April 2007 issue of Vol. *38* (2)

Evidence-based practice briefs on the following topics include:

- *Classroom-Based Versus Pull-Out Language Interventions: An Examination of the Experimental Evidence* (McGinty & Justice, 2006)

- *Improving Communication for Children with Autism: Does Sign Language Work?* (Schwartz & Nye, 2006)

- *Evidence-Based Vocabulary Instruction for Elementary Students Via Storybook Reading* (Johnson & Yeates, 2006)

- *Parent-Implemented Interactive Language Intervention: Can it be Used Effectively?* (Justice & Pence, 2007)

- *English Literacy Development for English Language Learners: Does Spanish Instruction Promote or Hinder?* (Thomason, Gorman, & Summers, 2007)

These collections examine the evidence base on specific topics, such as outlined by Nye, Schwartz, & Turner (2005).

Moore-Brown (2005) suggests that there are several reasons for using EBP in schools, including:

1. Accountability – EBP means conducting therapy which can assist students in meeting standards and functional goals.

2. Due Process – Using EBP makes the work legally defensible.

3. Student/Clinician Time – Being efficient in our treatment means that everyone's time is maximized and that students are not in therapy longer than they need to be, and that the clinician is available for the next student or project that needs his or her attention.

4. Challenges from the outside – EBP builds a response to questions and challenges.

5. Parent/Teacher/Student Satisfaction – EBP will mean increased satisfaction with speech-language pathology services and increased consumer satisfaction.

6. Enhanced Professionalism – Since EBP is the standard for the field, the evidence will be there that the speech-language pathologist is conducting him or herself according to the highest professional standards.

Linking Services to Consumer Satisfaction

Consumer satisfaction is a fitting conclusion to a discussion of functional outcomes. Speech-language pathologists may be unaware of how their services appear to consumers. In infant and preschool services provided by schools, children and families are primary consumers. For school-aged consumers, we add their teachers, peers, and state legislatures. They are all seeking satisfaction, often for diverse outcomes.

When a speech-language assessment indicates the need for an intervention program, a parent wants to know the best program available for his or her child. Finding what is best for each client means focusing on consumer satisfaction. "Best" is a thoughtful combination of what functional outcomes are desired, when and where services are provided, and the amount of time and resources needed. IDEA 2004 requires schools to provide intervention that is of educational benefit for a student. It does not require that the best or maximum intervention be sought. IDEA 2004 and SEAs require HIGHLY QUALIFIED personnel to use research-based practices and adequate resources to ensure that all students have access to the curriculum and can benefit from their education. Speech-language pathologists recognize that this may translate into good practice instead of best practice.

Selecting more effective interventions, with some individual variance, will become easier if we use the academic outcome data being gathered on elementary and secondary level students (Gillon, 2000; Larson & McKinley, 1995a). What is best for one student may not be best for another. For speech-language pathologists, "there is a continuing problem of specifying which treatment is likely to work with which child" (Enderby & Emerson, 1995, p. 126). All students in special education should receive appropriate services resulting in clinically significant change and educationally functional outcomes. A parent/guardian observation of student change subsequent to services showed 97 percent satisfaction with speech-language services in schools, and 92 percent believed there was improvement (Whitmire, Karr, & Mullen, 2000).

Even though more data are needed to reach conclusions (Whitmire, Karr, & Mullen, 2000), speech-language pathologists who respond to the four basic questions in the picture frame of Figure 5.5, for students on their caseload or in their classroom, will be able to address consumer satisfaction. There is a great need for outcome data for school-age children that is collected nationwide from school-based speech-language pathologists serving individuals with communication disorders (Mullen, 2000). This is an immense undertaking and efforts will continue into the future.

Functional Communication Measures (FCMs)

Pilot studies or comprehensive data collection based on functional outcomes have been conducted yearly in schools since 1995 (ASHA, 1999a). A seven-point rating scale of functional communication measures (FCMs) was designed and field tested in K–12 settings by school-based speech-language pathologists (ASHA, 1999a) (see sidebar on p. 202). ASHA's FCMs are the most comprehensive set of functional outcomes for school-based speech-language pathologists available. There are statements of student abilities in 15 areas: articulation/phonology, AAC comprehension, AAC production, cognitive communication, dysphagia, fluency, language comprehension, language production, central auditory processing, hearing sensitivity, hearing loss, hearing gain from amplification, hearing aid use, hearing aids, and assistive listening device (ALD) operation and management. The sidebar below includes a description of the seven levels for language comprehension. FCMs enable speech-language pathologists to rely less on standardized test scores to determine pres-

ent levels of achievement by defining performance at a particular level (1–7) as a baseline. Speech-language pathologists can probe many times during the intervention sessions to record improvements, and speech-language pathologists, teachers, and families can observe changes. FCMs resemble the process of dynamic assessment discussed in Chapter 3. They keep the intervention process linked to the functional activities of students at any developmental level. Students who were judged to be performing at a Level 1 or 2 on the FCM might have short-term objectives (or benchmarks) written to reach a

Functional Communication Measures for Language Comprehension

CNT/DNT	An aspect of communication that one could not test (CNT) due to the level of functioning or should have tested but did not test (DNT) due to time or other factors.
Level 1	Profound impairment: No understanding of verbal language.
Level 2	Severe impairment: 10–20 percent comprehension of single words in restricted contexts; cannot participate in conversations.
Level 3	Moderate to severe impairment: 30–40 percent comprehension of words and phrases in restricted contexts; minimal response as a conversational participant.
Level 4	Moderate impairment: 50 percent comprehension of phrases and sentences in typical contexts; moderate response as a conversational participant to one or two topics.
Level 5	Moderate to mild impairment: 60–70 percent comprehension of sentences and conversation in familiar contexts; good participation in conversations for a limited number of topics.
Level 6	Mild impairment: 80–90 percent comprehension of conversation in broad contexts; full participant in most conversations.
Level 7	Normal comprehension of language.

Clinically Significant Change: Two Cases

Sara, a 6-year-old, had dysarthric, mostly unintelligible speech due to cerebral palsy. Although she was able to learn in her inclusive classroom, few of her peers or teachers knew her abilities until she began to use a powerful augmentative communication system with voice and print output. Finally, she could demonstrate what she knew, participate in class, and become a reader and writer. The speech-language pathologist taught Sara the AAC methods she needed, and the educational successes followed.

Matthew, a 9-year-old, experienced severe stuttering behavior in the classroom and in most social situations. He was thought to be—and even considered himself—a slow learner with poor organizational skills, low self-esteem, and a limited grasp of new concepts in the curriculum. He rarely participated in his noisy, highly interactive fourth-grade classroom. After successful speech intervention reduced his disfluencies and gave him new strategies to compete in the classroom, he took greater responsibility for learning, began to feel successful, participated more often, and lifted his grades from mostly Ds to mostly Bs.

In both cases, change was clinically significant.

Level 3, while students at initial Level 4 or 5 could be expected to reach Level 6 or 7 in one year or less. Students who perform at Level 6 should not be enrolled in speech-language intervention unless there are extenuating circumstances (e.g., recurrent otitis media or adverse educational impact), since they are most likely to improve without it (ASHA, 1998e).

According to IDEA 2004, all special education service providers, including speech-language pathologists, must measure student progress in a functional and educationally relevant way. Functional measurement is a critical part of the reforms in general and special education that require increased accountability of all educators and related services professionals. Stating how the child's disability limits educational performance, and then how the student has responded to the instructional adaptations and supports put in place, must be functionally described and measured. FCMs make this possible in the schools of the twenty-first century (Brannen et al., 2000).

Using the FCM levels discussed in this chapter, preliminary data from a three-year study have shown that 87 percent of speech-language students on caseloads of 40 or less made progress in a year while only 64 percent of those on caseloads of 60 or more did so (Whitmire, Karr, & Mullen, 2000). This has far-reaching implications for all school-based speech-language pathologists. Once a student is identified with an impairment that results in a disability and is found eligible for services in school, a speech-language pathologist can use the FCMs to ascertain the student's functional level and plan the expected outcome in one year of services. The FCMs can also help an IEP team decide if particular communication goals are reasonable for the student. If the student has a FCM of Level 2, the team could examine the likelihood that the student will achieve an FCM of Level 3 by the end of the year. An IEP team should not recommend an intervention plan for a change in level if progress is not anticipated within a year. Some students with physical or cognitive limitations may not be able to advance past a certain communication level. Stability at one FCM level could be one of the indicators for dismissal as discussed in Chapter 4.

It is possible for a student to make progress toward more functional communication in a form that cannot be recorded with available FCMs. These behaviors may fall in the unintended outcomes previously discussed in this chapter under "Direct Versus Indirect Outcomes" (see p. 197). More work on FCMs in the next decade will help to close this gap.

Academic Standards

Because school-based interventions occur within the educational system, they must align with educational standards. As we noted above, therapy that exists within a health-care system aligns with health-care expectations. Therefore, it is the responsibility of the speech-language pathologist to know the academic standards—or learning expectations—for the students receiving services. The focus on standards and accountability may be exceedingly challenging for students with significant communication difficulties. Their IEP goals must incorporate both measurements—significant clinical change and progress toward academic standards.

Standards are brief statements of the sequential steps of content learning that students should acquire at each grade level. They are typically written by state curriculum committees and used by school districts to monitor and quantify student learning. IDEA 2004 requires that students make progress when receiving special education services. These content area standards are convenient ways to link therapy with curriculum. In fact, therapy and curriculum often overlap. The sidebar on pp. 205–206 shows examples of how state content standards are used in speech and language interventions for vocabulary development, written language, and English learners.

Response to Intervention as a Service Delivery Model

RESPONSE TO INTERVENTION (RtI) was briefly sketched in NCLB (2001), proposed under the concept of EARLY INTERVENING SERVICES in IDEA 2004, elaborated upon in the 2006 CODE OF FEDERAL REGULATIONS, and linked general and special education in the reauthorization of NCLB (proposed wording as this book goes to press). (See Chapter 5 for a full discussion of RtI.) RtI is a model that provides intervention for struggling students *before* they are considered for special education. It usually incorpo-

Examples of English Language Arts Standards Frequently Used by Speech-Language Pathologists

English Language Arts Standards from all 50 states and District of Columbia, U.S. Territories, and U.S. Department of Defense Schools. These are used in a vocabulary intervention program called *The Bridge of Vocabulary* by Montgomery, 2007.

- Identify and sort common words into conceptual categories. (Massachusetts English Language Arts Curriculum Framework)

- Identify the initial sound of a word. (Curriculum Guide to the Alabama Course of Study- English Language Arts Reading Addendum)

- Read and comprehend unfamiliar words using root words, synonyms, antonyms, word origins and derivations. (Illinois Learning Standards for English Language Arts)

- Elaborate and enhance the central idea with descriptive and supportive details. (Louisiana English Language Arts Achievement-Level Descriptors)

- Imitate patterns of rhythm, rhyme and figurative language in communicating. (Literacy for All: The Rhode Island English Language Arts Framework)

- Determine word meanings through restatement or synonym. (Utah Secondary Core Curriculum-Language Arts.)

- Analyze idioms to infer the literal and figurative meanings of phrases. (Indiana's Academic Standards-English Language Arts)

Source: Montgomery, J.K. (2007)

English Language Arts Standards Selected from the McREL Standards (2004)
Used in a Written Language Intervention Called *Ten Steps to Writing Better Essays* by Montgomery, 2007.

- Uses listening and speaking strategies for different purposes (Grades 6–8)

- Uses the general skills and strategies of the writing process (Grades 6–8)

- Asks questions in a way to broaden and enrich classroom discussions (Grades 9–12)

- Uses a variety of prewriting strategies (e.g., develops a focus, plans a sequence of ideas, uses structured interviews, speed writing, diagrams (Grades 9–12)

- Draws conclusions and makes inferences based on explicit and implicit information in texts (Grades 6–8)

Continued

Examples of English Language Arts Standards – *Continued*

- Organizes information and ideas from multiple sources in systematic ways (e.g. time lines, outlines, notes, graphic representations) (Grades 6–8)

- Formulates questions, refines topics, develops a plan for seeking information (Grades 9–12)

Source: McREL, Content Knowledge: A Compendium of Standards and Benchmarks for K–12 Education as cited in Montgomery & Kahn (2007). Reprinted with permission.

English Language Development Standards for English Learners (California, 2006)

- Make oneself understood when speaking by using consistent standard English grammatical forms and sounds; however, some rules are not followed such as third person singular and male and female pronouns.

- Retell stories by using appropriate gestures, expressions and illustrations.

- Demonstrate understanding of most idiomatic expressions (e.g., "Give me a hand") by responding to such expressions and using them appropriately.

- Negotiate and initiate social conversations by questioning, restating, soliciting information, and paraphrasing the communication of others.

*The ELD standards must be applied appropriately for students in each grade level from kindergarten through Grade 12.

Source: California Department of Education (1999d). Reprinted with permission.

---

rates three tiers of support for general education students. Speech-language pathologists are frequently involved in the following aspects of RtI at the school level:

- Serving on the Instructional Consultation Team.

- Supporting students in the classroom who need assistance with language and literacy skills.

- Providing teachers with appropriate interventions for Tiers II and III.

- Providing interventions for Tier II or III.

- Providing materials for teachers.

- Monitoring progress for students on RtI plans.

- Placing students on short-term, focused, intensive RtI programs to determine if they need to be considered for special education speech and language services.

- Preventing students from unnecessary special education labels by providing some speech and language services within general education.

School districts have reported success with RtI approaches in speech and language services (Mire & Montgomery, in press; Moore-Brown et al., 2005; Kuhn, 2006; MSHA, 2006; Taps, 2006). Speech-language pathologists may provide materials, advice, consultation, or direct services to general education students and their teachers. Early intervening services are strongly recommended at the K–3 grade level, however, speech-language pathologists have reported their effectiveness in preventing special education at Grades 3–8 as well (Montgomery & Moore-Brown, 2006). Focused, intensive services at the middle school and high school level have assisted students in written language and academic skills such as narrative and expository text (Montgomery & Kahn, 2007).

To the outside observer, service delivery in RtI looks the same as it does in special education. It is highly clinician-directed, evidence-based, related to content standards, and is usually conducted in small groups. It differs from special education intervention in some ways by using vigorous progress monitoring, a more intensive format, and has a specified ending time. The speech-language pathologist provides the service to determine the stimulability of students in some cases and/or if they are high or low responders. High responders do not need special education—they need more instruction. Low responders may have specific learning disabilities and need special education. Thus, RtI is an expanded assessment process that offers intervention to students rather than a waiting period. Moore-Brown et al. (2005) found that

85 percent of fourth and fifth grade struggling learners made a year's progress in 45 hours of explicit, systematic instruction.

There are numerous advantages to providing speech and language services in both the traditional format (special education) and the new format (general education). First, it encourages a WORKLOAD versus CASELOAD approach to service delivery. Instead of counting the number of students served (caseload), speech-language pathologists count the number and type of services provided at the school (workload). Second, if RtI is successful for students, they will not need to be placed in special education speech and language services. In the case of speech sound disorders, they will have achieved speech normalization with the assistance of a speech-language pathologist, reducing the extra time out of class and the paperwork of the IEP process. When students suspected of language disabilities are found to be high responders to RtI, their instruction can be quickly adjusted to improve reading and writing skills. Third, fewer children in the special education subgroup helps the school reach its adequate yearly progress (AYP) each year. Finally, the speech-language pathologist becomes a more integral member of the school site team to help *all* students achieve. Determining students' response to intervention for speech sound disorders, language impairments, voice, and fluency problems can facilitate more effective, efficient service delivery.

Speech-language pathologists utilizing the wide range of service delivery models that occur in school-based programs will realize greater success with their students. Speech-language pathologists must be prepared to design and implement services that match the needs and expectations of their school assignments. Due to the impact of new federal laws that address the needs of all students, speech-language services are a part of both special education and general education. We reviewed the exciting roles for school-based speech-language pathologists in defining and implementing inclusive education, models of speech-language intervention, good practice issues, working with a school team, functional outcomes, linking services to consumer satisfaction, functional communication measures, the importance of content standards, and the potential of response to intervention (RtI) approaches. Speech-language pathologists must choose from evidence-based practices, prepare themselves to intervene using these practices appropriately, and carefully match them to student learning styles and their school culture. Successful models will result in more effective, efficient services, enabling more students to have access to and achieve in the core curriculum.

Service delivery in speech-language services includes a combination of practices to assure an appropriate intervention for identified students. Reviewed in this chapter, these practices include the following: (1) Planning the intensity and frequency of intervention, (2) Scheduling intervention that is sensitive to classroom programs, (3) Using evidence-based practices, (4) Operating in inclusive settings, (5) Being aware of functional outcomes, (6) Using clinically significant change, and (7) Linking intervention with content standards. While good decisions at the service delivery level are critical to therapeutic success, the resulting improved communication skills for students are key to academic success.

CHAPTER 6

Providing Successful Intervention and Access to Curriculum

IN THIS CHAPTER

This chapter introduces issues that surround and compound service delivery. One section focuses on managing caseloads and workloads. Service delivery is discussed in the form of specific intervention models that are based on ASHA guidelines, incorporate both direct and indirect forms of contact with students, and link to the curriculum. Helpful grouping strategies and specific models for consultation and collaboration are described. Examples of literacy support from the speech-language pathologist in schools and preschool programs, plus a focus on secondary students are included.

1. Discuss the ASHA position statement on reading and writing in light of what you know about the important role of reading in being a successful student. Find the list in this chapter of roles and responsibilities in promoting reading and literacy (see p. 244), and compare yourself to the expectancies for speech-language pathologists. Where can you get more information to be prepared?

2. Why is there a feeling of urgency when working with preschoolers? How does that urgency affect the delivery of services? Plan a series of questions to ask a parent to help you understand how the child communicates at home.

3. Should high school students receive speech-language services if they have had more than three years of service in the elementary grades? Defend your answer.

4. From your viewpoint, discuss the effect of year-round education (YRE) on all students, students with disabilities, and the professionals who work with them, especially speech-language pathologists. Would YRE affect functional outcomes? In what way?

5. What factors would you consider when deciding how to group students for intervention? Select one grouping arrangement described in the text and plan a lesson utilizing it.

6. Collaborative consultation assumes cooperativeness among professionals. Cooperation does not always occur in schools. Why is it important to have a plan to handle resistance? What are some of the causes of resistance to new service delivery models? Suggest what might be done when resistance to the process exists.

7. Practice writing a speech and language goal that is linked to a child's general education curriculum. If you do not know how, what resources might you tap to locate the curriculum?

Caseloads and Service Delivery

Speech-language pathologists in schools have the same responsibilities as all employees in a school district. They must enforce the academic standards of STATE EDUCATION AGENCIES (SEAs) and LOCAL EDUCATION AGENCIES (LEAs) while they enable students with communication disabilities to be successful in school. Fortunately, the AMERICAN SPEECH-LANGUAGE-HEARING ASSOCIATION (ASHA), researchers, and speech-language pathologists have developed many effective service delivery methods that speech-language pathologists may use with confidence.

Service delivery takes on many forms in the school environment. Speech-language pathologists should not only use a variety of methods and delivery models, but they should be able to categorize or describe them to fellow professionals to build administrative support at the school or district level. Using and advocating for a range of service delivery models promotes new ideas and gains support for speech-language pathologists as school team members (Montgomery, 1990; Ehren, 2000). These models also guide speech-language pathologists in becoming an integral part of their school team, enabling them to apply their expertise to the goals of the school and the curriculum. Speech-language pathologists base most of their clinical decisions on information they were taught in three places—their graduate programs, their clinical experience, and the opinions of their colleagues (Zipoli & Kennedy, 2005). This is contrary to the principles of EVIDENCE-BASED PRACTICE (EBP), in which professionals should utilize research evidence, sound theory, and client needs (Gillam & Gillam, 2006). The effective school-based clinician must give careful thought to service delivery.

ASHA Service Delivery Options

ASHA has issued guidelines for seven service delivery options that help speech-language pathologists become more effective members of a total school team (see sidebar on p. 212). Note that they revolve around the good practice options summarized in Chapter 5: CLASSROOM INSTRUCTION, conventional intervention, and COLLABORATION. ASHA's *Guidelines for the Roles and Responsibilities of the School-Based Speech-Language Pathologist* (1999b) includes service delivery options and offers a valuable list of service delivery models for use in schools. These options provide speech-language pathologists with great flexibility to address the needs of students on their CASELOAD.

These options are simply frameworks within which students of any age, disability, or learning situation can receive services. After an assessment and identification process is completed and an INDIVIDUALIZED EDUCATION PROGRAM (IEP) meeting is held, the team, the parents, and many times the student, determine what arrangement of time, resources, and location will serve that individual best. Voice, articulation, fluency, language, and other communication disabilities can be served in any of these configurations. The authors encourage "think-

Service Delivery Options

Monitor: The speech-language pathologist sees the student for a specified amount of time per grading period to monitor or "check" on the student's speech and language skills. Often this model immediately precedes dismissal.

Collaborative Consultation: The speech-language pathologist, regular and/or special education teacher(s), and parents/families work together to facilitate a student's communication and learning in educational environments. This is an indirect model in which the speech-language pathologist does not provide direct service to the student.

Classroom-Based: This model is also known as integrated services, curriculum-based, transdisciplinary, interdisciplinary, or inclusive programming. There is an emphasis on the speech-language pathologist providing direct services to students within the classroom and other natural environments. Team teaching by the speech-language pathologist and the regular and/or special education teacher(s) is frequent with this model.

Pull-Out: Services are provided to students individually and/or in small groups within the speech-language resource room setting. Some speech-language pathologists may prefer to provide individual or small group services within the physical space of the classroom.

Self-Contained Program: The speech-language pathologist is the classroom teacher responsible for providing both academic/curriculum instruction and speech-language remediation.

Community-Based: Communication services are provided to students within the home or community setting. Goals and objectives focus primarily on functional communication skills.

Combination: The speech-language pathologist provides two or more service delivery options (e.g., provides individual or small group treatment on a pull-out basis twice a week to develop skills or preteach concepts and also works with the student within the classroom).

From *Guidelines for the Roles and Responsibilities of the School-Based Speech-Language Pathologist* (p. 37), by the American Speech-Language-Hearing Association (ASHA), 1999c, Rockville, MD: Author. ©1999 by ASHA. Reprinted with permission.

ASHA Position Statement on Workload

It is the position of the American Speech-Language-Hearing Association (ASHA) that the total workload activities required and performed by school-based speech-language pathologists must be taken into account to set caseload standards. A workload analysis approach to setting caseload standards is necessary to ensure that students receive the services they need, instead of the services speech-language pathologists have time to offer or services based on administrative convenience. The following principles underlie this position:

Each student added to the caseload increases the time needed, not only for direct and indirect services and evaluations, but also for mandated paperwork, multidisciplinary team conferences, parent and teacher contacts, and related responsibilities.

Caseloads must be of a size to allow speech-language pathologists to provide appropriate and effective intervention, conduct evaluations, collaborate with teachers and parents, implement best practices in school speech-language pathology, carry out related activities, and complete necessary paperwork and compliance tasks within working hours.

Education agencies must implement a workload analysis approach to setting caseload standards that allow speech-language pathologists to engage in the broad range of professional activities necessary to meet individual student needs.

From *A Workload Analysis Approach for Establishing Speech-Language Caseload Standards in the School: Position Statement*, ASHA (2002). Reprinted with permission.

ing outside the box" when designing intervention services and schedules. A list of models is helpful to speech-language pathologists and school teams in the same way a menu encourages one to consider new choices. Although models may be helpful in this way, it is important to remember that intervention can be provided in any form that speech-language pathologists can show are effective and efficient for students.

ASHA Workload Approach

In 2002, ASHA promoted a new concept in caseload and service delivery management: WORKLOAD. Central to this approach is the understanding that while providing services to students is the main function of a speech-language pathologist, there are many other duties and responsibilities that are demanding, necessary, and time consuming. (See the "ASHA Position Statement on Workload" in the sidebar on p. 213.) These activities are accounted for in the workload clusters of the model in Figure 6.1.

This position statement does not include a recommended maximum caseload number. Any arbitrary caseload maximum is inconsistent with a workload analysis approach to setting caseload standards. Instead, it is necessary for education agencies to consider how the amount of time available in each school day, week, or month can be divided across services to children. It is also important to consider that the expanding responsibilities required of school speech-language pathologists reduce the time available for face-to-face services to students. Furthermore, setting a caseload maximum number may be misused as a caseload minimum. Speech-language pathologists who work with students with high needs may be functioning at capacity yet serve significantly fewer students than an arbitrary maximum number, due to the array of intensive direct and indirect services their students need.

Figure 6.1

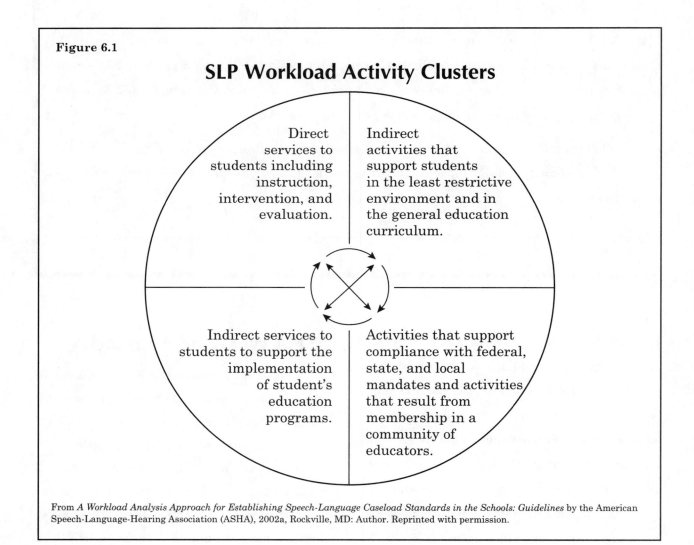

SLP Workload Activity Clusters

Direct services to students including instruction, intervention, and evaluation.

Indirect activities that support students in the least restrictive environment and in the general education curriculum.

Indirect services to students to support the implementation of student's education programs.

Activities that support compliance with federal, state, and local mandates and activities that result from membership in a community of educators.

From *A Workload Analysis Approach for Establishing Speech-Language Caseload Standards in the Schools: Guidelines* by the American Speech-Language-Hearing Association (ASHA), 2002a, Rockville, MD: Author. Reprinted with permission.

Traditionally, the workload of school speech-language pathologists has been conceptualized as being almost exclusively synonymous with caseload. Caseload is more accurately conceptualized as only one part of speech-language pathologists' total workload. The term caseload typically refers to the number of students with INDIVIDUALIZED EDUCATION PROGRAMS (IEPs) or INDIVIDUALIZED FAMILY SERVICE PLANS (IFSPs), who school speech-language pathologists serve through direct and/or indirect service delivery options. In some school districts, speech-language pathologist caseloads may also include students who do not have identified disabilities, and who receive prereferral intervention and other services designed to help prevent future difficulties with language-learning and literacy. Speech-language pathologists may also serve as CASE MANAGERS for all or some students on their caseload, which adds significant responsibilities and time for writing and managing IEPs, as well as assuring compliance with special education regulations. Workload refers to all activities required and performed by school-based speech-language pathologists. Speech-language pathologist workloads include considerable time for direct services to students. Workloads also include many other activities necessary to support students' education programs, implement BEST PRACTICES for school speech-language services, and ensure compliance with IDEA and other mandates.

ASHA members report that large caseloads (i.e., caseloads exceeding the maximum numbers recommended by ASHA in 1993) constrain the speech-language pathologist's ability and capacity for engaging in the expanded roles that are necessary to meet the individual needs of today's diverse and complex student population. Recent research indicates that large speech-language caseloads are related to poorer student outcomes and to the availability of fewer service options for students with disabilities (Mullen, 2000). This suggests that large caseloads impede the intent of IDEA from being fully implemented, given that federal legislation mandates the use of a continuum of services tailored to students' individual needs, and collaboration between special education and regular education teachers.

Workload and caseload size issues for school speech-language pathologists are difficult to resolve because of the complex interaction of the many factors that influence the number of children and adolescents speech-language pathologists serve. Speech-language pathologists, teachers, administrators, union representatives, parents, and others should work in partnership to ensure that caseload size does not negatively affect speech-language pathologists' ability to meet the needs of their students. Setting caseload standards on the basis of an analysis of speech-language pathologists' total workload activities can help ensure students with disabilities receive the services they need to support their education programs.

The documents that accompany the position statement, including the technical report (ASHA, 2002b) and guidelines (ASHA, 2002a), as well as the implementation document (ASHA, 2002d), review important concepts regarding the relationship to caseload and workload. In the period of time since this document was published, the workload concept has been well received and also adopted by other professional organizations (e.g., National Association of School Psychologists [NASP]). Caseload size remains the biggest influence on the work that a speech-language pathologist does, but through the workload approach, the other activities are also recognized as being part of what needs to occur during the work day, not at night or on the weekend.

Speech-language pathologists around the country have adopted this model and adjusted it to what works for them. Their success stories are also available on the ASHA website: http://www.asha.org/members/slp/schools/resources/districtworkloadchart.

Caseload Size

Examining school-based speech-language pathologists' typical caseloads by day and by week has long been considered a factor in choosing models of service delivery. The authors believe that this factor should not be the focus. Caseload size will vary greatly across the country with lows of 35 to 40 students per speech-language pathologist (e.g., Nebraska and Iowa) and reported highs of 90 or more students per speech-language pathologist (e.g., Illinois, New York, and California). In 1999, a nationwide survey found even greater ranges of 3 to 145 students per speech-language pathologist (Council for Exceptional Children [CEC], 1999). States, not federal law, determine their caseload minimums and maximums, thus the extremely wide variations. Caseload size and management was the number one issue for speech-language pathologists in schools on an ASHA (1998d) survey and was selected as the first priority issue for the ASHA Legislative Council in 2000 (Whitmire, 2000a) and again in 2006. Advocating for a reduction in the size of caseloads for public school speech-language programs is a politically and economically volatile issue because of competing needs and limited resources.

GOOD PRACTICE and good service delivery, however, are not based on political and economic issues. Regardless of caseload size, consumers expect speech-language pathologists to make professional decisions that must include choosing interventions wisely, matching students' performance levels with available services, and measuring progress with functional outcomes (see "Functional Outcomes and the School-Based Speech-Language Pathologist" in

Chapter 5). Nevertheless, speech-language pathologists do need to advocate for reasonable caseloads so that they can perform their duties. As will be discussed in "Professional Organizations" in Chapter 9, maintaining a political voice through membership in professional organizations and being on alert for proposed legislation is a responsibility of speech-language pathologists. Vigilance and tenacity in reshaping state caseload maximums does reap benefits for students and their families.

Although maintaining a lower caseload may allow speech-language pathologists to schedule more frequent or intensive services for some children (ASHA, 2006a), data on improved outcomes in these circumstances have not been collected in a standardized manner (Mullen, 2000). Such data have not yet been used to convince lawmakers to reduce caseload size (Moore-Brown, Montgomery, Biehl, Karr, & Stein, 1998; Whitmire, Karr, & Mullen, 2000). Speech-language pathologists also need to be vigilant in the management of their caseloads by ensuring that they are using current practices and service delivery models, and exiting students who no longer need services in order to do what can be done proactively (Moore-Brown, Nishida, & Laverty-Reeves, 2003).

Scheduling the Caseload

Caseload size can significantly influence the service delivery choices that speech-language pathologists make, however, individual student needs must be the overriding factor. This can cause anxiety and require great flexibility from everyone involved. It is important to remember that no single method of delivering services is appropriate for the entire intervention period. Model changes are inherent in the scheduling process and should be based on students' needs, not on the time of year, space, or other external factors. Practically, of course, all these factors must be worked into a schedule. For example, a student may need one-to-one service for a phonological disorder for six weeks, then an in-class model to begin the generalization process with meaningful classroom-based cues for eight weeks, and finally a once a month "drop-in group" (i.e., checkup) for reinforcement for the remainder of the school year.

Speech-language pathologists need to be able to make adjustments whenever necessary. As long as a student is making steady progress toward IEP GOALS, the existing service model may be maintained. Lack of progress mandates a need for change in one or more aspects of service delivery. One of the advantages of a school-based service model is the many options available that are not found in hospital programs, day clinics, or private practice settings. In these other settings, the pool of typical peers is simply not there, and the learning environment provides limited opportunities for naturalistic practice.

Table 6.1 offers ideas for how to schedule programs in elementary and secondary schools as well as programs for speech-language pathologists who serve multiple school sites. Schedules must allow for some assessment and meeting time and use every available minute of the school day to serve students. Most school days allow about 6 to 6½ hours of student contact time, so time is at a premium. Almost 60 percent of

Table 6.1

Creating Schedules for Service Delivery

There are several different types of schedules that must be created by speech-language pathologists each year. They serve as the evidence of delivery of services as specified in student IEPs. Each schedule has a distinct purpose, a different audience, and a corresponding format. Some features will be found in every schedule while others are unique to a specific format. Schedules with student names on them are considered a part of confidential records and are not shown to unauthorized persons. Types of schedules used in school programs are outlined below.

Type of Schedule	Purpose	Audience(s)	Format
Daily	Used to record daily activities at a specific location	Education team, site administrator	By time and names
Daily with Assistant	Used to record daily activities of speech-language pathologist and assistant(s) at a specific location	Education team, site administrator, assistant(s), supervisor(s)	By time and names
Weekly	Used to track weekly locations for services if more than one location, week at a glance if one location. Important for block scheduling and monitoring students	SLP, education team, district administrator(s), parents	By time and activity
Weekly with Assistant	Same as above with assistant(s) added where appropriate	Same as above, classified staff administrators(s), assistant(s)	By time and activity
Monthly	Kept for documenting monthly responsibilities, such as school staff meetings, out-of-district or agency meetings, district meetings, professional growth conferences, CEUs, and so on. Important if using block scheduling, curriculum-based instruction (off-campus), or monthly monitoring and checking	Same as above	By month and activity; usually includes contact information such as names and phone numbers
Yearlong	Primarily used for documenting long-range planning, evidence of contacts with agencies, out-of-district commitments, and so on. May have screening dates, IEPs, triennial reevaluations, school-based teams for prereferral, and special education interventions	Administrators, hearing officers, court orders, subpoenaed records	By activity and contact time expended; may include names of others at meetings

#TP-29703 Making a Difference - 2nd Ed. · ©2008 Thinking Publications® · www.thinkingpublications.com · 1-800-277-8737

speech-language pathologists' days are spent in direct intervention (ASHA, 1998d). Despite the pressure to use every available minute for intervention, speech-language pathologists must wisely allocate time for lunch, breaks, meetings, and required assigned duties that are expected of all school personnel.

Year-Round Education (YRE)

Traditional school calendars were established to meet the needs of an agrarian society in which entire families needed to devote uninterrupted time to harvest crops each year. Although we are no longer driven by crop harvests, YEAR-ROUND EDUCATION (YRE) may provide an alternative to the traditional 180-day, September through June schedule.

Year-round education sites are reorganizing the school year to provide more continuous learning by breaking up the long summer vacation into shorter, more frequent vacations throughout the year. It does not eliminate the summer vacation, but reduces it and redistributes it as vacation or intersession time during the school year. Students attending a year-round school go to the same classes and receive the same instruction as students on a traditional calendar. The year-round calendar is organized into instructional periods and vacation weeks that are more evenly balanced across 12 months than the traditional school calendar. The balanced calendar minimizes the learning loss that occurs during a typical three-month summer vacation (National Association of Year-Round Education [NAYRE], 2001, ¶ 2).

The *Encyclopedia of American Education* (Unger, 1996) defines year-round school as follows:

A school that operates a 12-month-a-year academic program to ensure maximum utilization of school facilities and accommodate a larger number of students without investing in plant expansion (p. 1095).

During the 2006–2007 school year, 387 school districts in 44 states used a YRE schedule. This equated to 2,764 public schools serving over 2 million children through this type of alternative scheduling (NAYRE, 2007). YRE schools use several calendar variations that typically schedule three quarters of the students to attend "on-track," while one quarter of the students are "off-track." Although YRE was begun, in part, to maximize facility usage in crowded buildings, academic benefits may be realized for students, especially those in need of SPECIAL EDUCATION, due to shorter nonschool breaks.

Teachers generally follow the same track or schedule as their students, but scheduling becomes more difficult for support services providers (e.g., speech-language pathologists) on a YRE schedule. Special education services must be provided across all tracks throughout the entire 246 or 247 days that school is in session. Speech-language pathologists need a work calendar that provides service to students throughout the school year. Some solutions include:

- Speech-language pathologists' contracts and salaries are extended, covering between 200 and 230 days of the school year.

- Certain days of the year are identified as "no speech" days and are nonwork days for speech-language pathologists, such as the first week of school, the three days before the Thanksgiving holiday, the week before the winter holiday break, or the last week or two of school.

- Speech-language pathologists coordinate schedules to provide coverage for each other during others' off-track time.

- Speech-language pathologists work a four-day work week.

Other creative solutions have been used to assure students receive speech and language services, and that speech-language pathologists receive either pay or vacation within the YRE schedule.

Once a work calendar is established for speech-language pathologists, the challenge of how to serve students must be tackled. The most significant difference for speech-language pathologists in a YRE school is the fact that the groupings of students can change every month (if on a multitrack YRE schedule). Although this may sound like a daunting task (and it is at first), skilled scheduling may allow speech-language pathologists to realize greater variation and effectiveness in service delivery. The changing mix of students on the caseload will allow for greater intensity at times with certain groups and will also allow children greater opportunities to work with different peers.

Speech-language pathologists working in YRE schools must learn how to calculate special education procedural timelines according to the various tracking systems in the schools. Mandated timelines are on hold when students are off-track, but not when speech-language pathologists are. Most YRE school districts publish

a timeline calendar in order to make this calculation easier for staff.

Other members of a team may not have the same vacation schedule as a speech-language pathologist, so planning forward and backward is a good idea when working in a YRE school. Scheduling meeting dates when everyone will be available should be done at the beginning of the year. Some assessments may need to have plans signed early to accommodate vacation schedules. Moving a timeline up is always acceptable practice, but being late on completing an assessment or IEP, especially due to vacation schedules, is never acceptable and would be considered non-compliant with IDEA 2004. Team coordination takes exceptional planning in a YRE school, but it is possible.

Tables 6.2 and 6.3 show schedules for a speech-language pathologist who serves a multitrack YRE school. There are four tracks: A, B, C, and D. One track is always "off," and three are always "on." Table 6.2 shows A, B, and D on and Table 6.3 shows B, C, and D on. When A track students are on vacation, C track students replace them on the schedule. For example, in Table 6.2 in the 11:00 to 11:30 a.m. slot on Monday, four children in kindergarten are seen for intervention. In Table 6.3, two of the children, Matt and Chris, continue in the second schedule, while Jason and Gabriel, who go on vacation, are replaced by Tabitha and Adam.

There is great potential in YRE for positive effects for students and greater flexibility in service delivery models. Remember that although the YRE schedule may seem like a greater amount of time, it is really the same amount, spread over a 12-month period.

Table 6.2

YRE Schedule for Speech-Language Services—Part 1
Calle Lakeview School

Tracks A, B, D

	Monday	Tuesday	Wednesday	Thursday	Friday
9:00–9:40 Response to Intervention	Austin Casey Chase Andrew Nadia	Austin Casey Chase Andrew Nadia	Austin Casey Chase Andrew Nadia	Austin Casey Chase Andrew Nadia	Austin Casey Chase Andrew Nadia
9:45–10:15 Primary-level class	Artesia Andrea Denise Rebecca	Steven Mattie	Chrissy Missy	Andrew	Assessments ↓
10:30–11:00 Pull-out	Denise	Daniel Andrew	Chrissy Mikla Ennis	Daniel Nikki Alex	
11:00–11:30 Kindergarten	Matt Chris Jason Gabriel	Travis	Matt Chris Jason Gabriel	Travis	
11:30–12:00 Pull-out/Class	Darren Brian	Special ed class	Darren Chris	Natalie Juan	Will Emily
1:00–1:30 Primary-level class	Andrew Kevin Bura	Bernice Joanna Nick Kristine	Andrew Kevin Brian	Lonnie Joanna Kevin Nick Kristine	Instructional Support Team Meeting ↓
1:30–2:00 Co-teach upper-level class	Sofia Bryan Dereck Robert Jimmie	Justin Tearah Christine	Sofia Bryan Dereck Robert Jimmie	Justin Tearah Christine	
2:00–2:30 In-class	Courtney Heather Darryl	Gabriel	Courtney Heather Darryl	Jill Toya	Consultation ↓
2:30–3:00 Pull-out	Kristin Matt Ashlee	Kevin Andrea Marlie Cody	Kristen Matt Ashlee	Andrea Marlie Cody Kevin	

Table 6.3

YRE Schedule for Speech-Language Services—Part 2
Calle Lakeview School

Tracks B, C, D

	Monday	Tuesday	Wednesday	Thursday	Friday
9:00–9:40 Response to Intervention	Jose Griffin Travis Hunter Nadia	Jose Griffin Travis Hunter Nadia	Jose Griffin Travis Hunter Nadia	Jose Griffin Travis Hunter Nadia	Jose Griffin Travis Hunter Nadia
9:45–10:15 Primary-level class	Artesia Andrea Denise Rebecca	Steven Mattie Kennisha	Andrew	Chrissy Missy	Assessments ↓
10:30–11:00 Pull-out		Daniel Mikla Ennis Kelly		Daniel Mikla Ennis Kelly	
11:00–11:30 Kindergarten	Matt Chris Tabitha Adam	Travis	Off Campus Head Start Collaborative Program	Home Visits, Curriculum Team Meetings	
11:30–12:00 Pull-out/Class	Brian Chris	Special ed class			
1:00–1:30 Primary-level class	Andrew Kevin Bura	Bonnie Kyle Zachary			Instructional Support Team Meeting
1:30–2:00 Co-teach upper-level class	Sofia Bryan Dereck	Justin Eric Taylor			↓
2:00–2:30 In-class	Courtney Tony Nate Barstow	Adolfo Sarah Darryl			Consultation ↓
2:30–3:00 Pull-out	Kristin Matt Ken	Kristin Matt Ken	↓	↓	↓

#TP-29703 Making a Difference - 2nd Ed. · ©2008 Thinking Publications® · www.thinkingpublications.com · 1-800-277-8737

There are two keys to ensuring successful implementation of alternative scheduling. The first is to remain open and creative. School-based speech-language pathologists have met numerous challenges with patience, understanding, and creativity. The second key is to stay involved and be proactive (Bland, 1998). YRE may provide time for intensive interventions that are more efficient for some students, reducing their overall time receiving services.

Should You Organize by Disability?

Organizing service models by communication disability has been reported in several sources (ASHA, 1998d; Neidecker, 1987). The authors believe this approach restricts creativity in service delivery for speech-language pathologists and students. PREFERRED PRACTICE PATTERNS do not indicate that particular service models are reserved for certain disabilities (ASHA, 1997b). In fact, the IDEA 2004 requirements for IEPs preclude the use of a one-size-fits-all program.

The ASHA (2006a) Schools Survey used a disability-based model to organize questions about service delivery. Survey data reflected the numbers of students served in each "disorder," instead of numbers served with various service delivery models. The use of disability categories awarded some implied validity to this organizational framework. In the future, analysis of functional outcomes for each service delivery model might reveal more interesting and useful data on effective service delivery for America's school children.

Support Personnel Model

Using support personnel in a school speech-language program is a recent innovation. Although support personnel have been routinely used in other special education settings since the early 1970s, they have had little involvement with speech-language services. Some states established special training and employment categories for speech-language support personnel early, but many states were hesitant to start until the field formally embraced the idea of trained support personnel in 1995 through its national professional organization, ASHA (see "Speech-Language Pathology Assistants [SLPAs] and Aides in Schools" in Chapter 9).

The SPEECH-LANGUAGE PATHOLOGY ASSISTANT (SLPA) is typically regulated in a school program through at least two levels: the state licensing or CERTIFICATION of training level and the local school district employment level. States were concerned with meeting IDEA (1997, 2004) requirements to use qualified providers and trained and supervised SLPAs. Local districts were concerned with hiring practices, salary, benefits, seniority issues, and a new category of instructional staff that was more highly trained and costly than previous ones. Trained and supervised SLPAs can be very helpful to speech-language pathologists, especially if caseload numbers are high or spread over several sites per week. SLPAs allow greater numbers of children to be seen for more intensive services.

Using SLPAs dramatically changes the way speech-language pathologists manage the intervention schedule and organize service delivery. A short list of the roles and responsibilities of SLPAs shows the potential parameters of this expanded model:

- Conduct speech-language SCREENINGS.

- Provide direct intervention to students.

- Follow documented intervention plans and IEPs.

- Document student progress.

- Assist during student assessments.

- Assist with informal documentation, prepare materials, perform clerical duties.

- Schedule activities; prepare charts, records, graphs, or otherwise display data.

- Perform checks and maintenance of equipment.

- Participate in research projects, in-service training, and public relations programs (ASHA, 1996a).

The support personnel model enables speech-language pathologists to provide a greater range of services to students on the caseload, but SLPAs cannot maintain their own caseload. They must serve students who are identified by a speech-language pathologist and an IEP team only. They must be directly supervised 10–30 percent of the time they are working with students. Initially, SLPAs will require greater amounts of supervision to assure that intervention and other activities are conducted accurately and uniformly. However, SLPAs can provide services to students using all available models and may work simultaneously with speech-language pathologists. This allows daily intensive therapy for some students, in-

class support for some students, and discrete trial sessions for others. Carryover and generalization sessions can be set up on a routine basis for students about to be dismissed.

The support personnel model is actually a cluster of models that can be managed by a communication team (e.g., the speech-language pathologist and one, two, or three SLPAs). Speech-language pathologists are responsible for the complete program but may delegate tasks to SLPAs. SLPAs are the trained eyes and ears of speech-language pathologists when they are in the classroom and are equally effective at using the therapy room for small groups when speech-language pathologists are team-teaching in the classroom. SLPAs are also able to monitor students who need to be checked each week for hearing aid batteries, oral motor exercises, and written journal entries.

> SLPAs are the trained eyes and ears of speech-language pathologists when they are in the classroom and are equally effective at using the therapy room for small groups.

Schedules should remain flexible throughout the year. One method that facilitates flexibility is to use cards with students' names on them in a pocket chart, so that assignments can be moved around as conditions change. A master schedule of all students seen for speech-language intervention may be necessary to share with other team members who need to coordinate with an ever-changing schedule that involves several speech-language service providers on the communication team. This model increases the visibility of the speech-language pathologist and connects him or her more closely with the life and mission of the school.

Articulation Resource Centers

Due to the expanded service delivery possible with RESPONSE TO INTERVENTION (RtI) (discussed in depth in Chapter 5), speech-language pathologists can now serve some students within general education. If students have impairments, for example, speech sound errors that do not have an adverse impact on their academic performance, they can be served for brief periods of intense intervention without an IEP. A third grader with a frontal lisp who gets As and Bs in her class does not have a disability. She does have a speech sound error. She deserves the services of a speech and language pathologist to improve her communication. IDEA 2004 makes it possible to serve these students in a wide range of general education venues, one of which is an articulation resource center. Students who need direction for the specific placement of articulators, intensive supervised practice, and a strong home to school generalization program can be served in the resource center. Resource centers serving larger groups of children, aided by SLPAs, have reported significant reductions in the caseload size and overall effectiveness in schools (Taps, 2006). Using a complexity approach to articulation intervention (Morrisette & Gierut, 2002), requiring 150 correct productions of a target sound or word in a session, a large urban district reported that students remediated speech sound errors in 20 hours or less (Taps, 2006).

Sometimes the resource center concept is literally brought to the students for one-on-one intervention in either general or special education. Kuhn (2006) reported on a highly intensive program for speech sound errors in which the clinician saw the student 3 to 4 times a day for 5–10 minutes at a table in the hall. Students missed only short portions of the school day, responded rapidly to intensive, explicit intervention, and 69 percent of students reached their goal in 16 weeks or less.

Variations on the resource center concept hold promise as a new service delivery option since IDEA 2004. Students with IEPs may also be served in these settings, however, the resource center holds the greatest promise for those on 504 plans (see Chapter 8) or those with relatively mild articulation impairments who do not meet eligibility criteria for a special education disability label. This model results in a dramatic reduction in paperwork and meetings, and an equally dramatic increase in the number of students who can be rapidly dismissed from the caseload as corrected after intensive services.

A recent meta-analysis of phonological treatment studies concluded that the research provides little guidance for clinicians seeking the best clinical practice (Weston & Bain, 2003). Normative data indicate that the majority of young students have limited explicit knowledge of phonemes and may gain little from work on sound awareness (Locke, 1997). Service delivery is determined by clinicians' theoretical perspectives on correcting speech sound errors. Thus, service delivery changes as perspectives change. If one uses the current literature reviews and "facts about normal speech development to determine service delivery, clinicians would not target any unit smaller than the syllable, and the primary focus of treatment would be on acquiring words" (Kamhi, 2006b, p. 273). If we want to demonstrate that change in an individual's communication behaviors are due to our interventions, as evidence-based practice would dictate, a range of service delivery options will be required.

Grouping Strategies

Scheduling, professional collaboration, and efficiency can be enhanced by using thoughtful grouping strategies. A body of research on the effectiveness of grouping strategies exists, linking cooperative learning groups to academic success (Johnson & Johnson, 1989; Kagan, 1994; Slavin, 1990). Children learn in groups throughout their school years. Recognizing that groups are the natural context of the classroom can help speech-language pathologists build collaborative working relationships with teachers and other education professionals. Students learning in groups have several overall benefits.

Grouping students for intervention can occur in traditional PULL-OUT models, classrooms, resource centers and collaborative teams. Three types of groups are used in schools—SKILL GROUPS, FRIENDSHIP GROUPS, and RANDOM/PURPOSE GROUPS. Speech-language pathologists can use all three.

Skill Groups

Skill groups are composed of any children who cannot independently do an assigned task or lack an underlying skill necessary to complete a task. Educators and speech-language pathologists commonly group children with similar skill levels together. These professionals need to work intensively with skill groups because there are no peer models in these groups who can do the task. If a whole class is divided into skill groups, as is often done for reading, instructors must move rapidly from group to group to provide teaching.

Speech-language pathologists frequently use skill groups, assigning children with peers who have the same perceived or tested deficits. Perhaps a student does not demonstrate a skill, such as conversational turn-taking or consistent production of a phoneme. All students near that student's age who have the same difficulty would be placed together in a skill group. Skill grouping is labor-intensive for speech-language pathologists who do all the modeling, facilitating, and reinforcing. Students must wait, not always patiently, for professionals to provide cues and evaluation. Skill grouping often results in teaching isolated communication skills in an unnatural communication context, which can limit generalization.

Skill groups are easy to assemble and plan. Progress can be easily measured using only one probe for the group. Once a student shows improved skills, he or she is likely to be moved to another skill group. Then students are reassigned to join a new group of students who also need assistance with the next task that they need to learn. As frustrating as it might seem for speech-language pathologists, students have been known to seek out ways to stay in their skill group. If improvement in the target skill means leaving the comfort and routine of a group of friends, students sometimes choose to not demonstrate that they can do the task. Progress dissipates when some students conclude that they like to attend speech sessions just to be with their group, even though they can already perform the expected task successfully. Speech-language pathologists need to observe their skill groups conscientiously to assure that students are moving ahead at a steady pace.

Friendship Groups

Friendship groups are comprised of students who choose to be together or who are assigned together by adults because they are friends. In these groups, students may be highly motivated and often quite social. They enjoy each other's company and will often work much harder just to keep all their friends together. Educators find these groupings to be full of energy and surprisingly productive. Much work can be accomplished quickly in a friendship group.

Speech-language pathologists rarely group this way since they are less aware of the social groupings of their students or may not be able to place classmates, let alone friends, together. However, when social groups are possible, speech-language pathologists remark on how exciting the activities are and how supportive the students are of each other, especially considering the variety of target goals a group may have. Friendship groups often get an extra boost in their effectiveness because students genuinely like each other, enjoy the opportunity to practice together, and are powerful models for each other. The targeted need of one student is a strength of one or more of the other students, providing peer facilitation, social rewards, and motivation. Natural contexts provide many opportunities for practice and generalization of communication skills. These groups can be exuberant and noisy or require the speech-language pathologist to monitor the social conversation that occurs.

Methods for Enhancing the Grouping Process

Educators often assign students who are to be in a random/purpose group (also referred to as "flexible grouping" or "heterogeneous grouping") through some type of matching task. Speech-language pathologists might enhance this grouping process by using language-oriented sorting methods, such as passing out cards with words, phrases, or pictures printed on them. Speech-language pathologists might ask students with picture cards to move around the room and talk to other students to determine what "scene" they belong in, such as a rain forest, a desert, a grassy plain, or a mountain. The picture card belongs to one of the scenes. Content from the classroom can be used, such as recent books read, science words, or adjectives that go with nouns. The process of finding one's group is an authentic language and communication experience. Speech-language pathologists may want to assure that caseload students receive cards that will place them in the appropriate group. Speech-language pathologists who work in collaborative classrooms use these types of activities often.

Random/Purpose Groups

Random/purpose groups are the most time consuming to assemble but result in the most facilitative learning environment for children. Even though they appear random, speech-language pathologists have a purpose for putting them together. Educators group children by selecting students who can do various aspects of a task, so that they must join together to get it done. In the classroom, this usually means a group composed of some students who read easily and some who struggle, some students who write well and some who avoid it, some students who have artistic talent, and some students who can organize others. A group of five to six students can pull together and accomplish something that none of them can do alone. They may or may not be friends, but they recognize that together they can accomplish the task. The term COOPERATIVE LEARNING is often used for this type of group in variations known as jigsaw learning, pinwheels, or share pairs.

In speech-language intervention, a group of students with various phonological disabilities can operate like a random/purpose group. Children with multiple articulation errors, sometimes unintelligible, are grouped together and cycled through many phoneme productions. Different phonemes are targets for different children. This enables some students to be models for others in the group rather than depending on an adult model, who is often less motivating than peers. In random/purpose groups, speech-language pathologists structure services to accommodate the strengths and needs of all children. Montgomery and Bonderman (1989) found that random/purpose groups of four to nine un-intelligible children were very successful in phonological remediation programs, with 85 percent of the students demonstrating significant change in 17 weeks or less of therapy. Groups of this type take considerable time and effort to organize. Changes in the group can upset instructional goals and activities.

Educators have reported to the authors that they often keep effective random/purpose groups together for several subject areas as students become more and more productive and eventually learn to blend and multiply their skills. Speech-language pathologists can use this strategy also, moving previously unsuccessful students into already functioning groups without the limitations of matching a child's specific area of need as is done in skill groups. One speech-language pathologist found success in grouping students according to grade level. She commented that because the students brought their various needs to and from the classroom, working in a group on various need areas built a support network for the students when they were back in the classroom and the speech-language pathologist was not there.

Successful grouping of students on school caseloads is an important and easily overlooked responsibility of speech-language pathologists. The effectiveness of group therapy lies in the thought behind the grouping, which can result in greater effectiveness and motivation in students.

Using wise grouping strategies is an important component of COLLABORATIVE CONSULTATION. Flexible grouping of children provides services for vastly different communication needs. Purpose grouping can be a great assistance to teachers and can bring speech-language pathologists into classes for a wide variety of communication intervention activities.

Consultation and Collaboration

Consultation and collaboration, distinctly different approaches, evolved as models for all aspects of service delivery nationwide in the 1990s as a consequence of the REGULAR EDUCATION INITIATIVE (REI) and a focus on the general education curriculum (Montgomery, 1992; Whitmire, 2002; Moore-Brown, 2007a). When deciding to work in a consultative/collaborative environment, focus on the student and ask: What is it about the student's learning/language disability that is preventing the student from performing the function needed to achieve standards? It is important to remember he purpose of the intervention is to assist the student in achieving the goals of school (Moore-Brown, 2007a).

In response to these concerns about the effectiveness and efficiency of individualized and small pull-out groups, districts attempted to integrate their special education services into the mainstream of education and combine some of the specialized intervention with grade-level academic activities. This integration promoted the idea of professionals working with each other to support students, rather than each professional always working directly with each student. Such speech-language school services have been enthusiastically described in the literature (e.g., Creaghead, 1999; Ehren, 2000; Ferguson, 1991; Miller, 1989; Montgomery, 1992; Moore-Brown,

2000; Nelson & Hoskins, 1996; Prelock, 2000; Secord, 1999; Secord & Damico, 1998; Whitmire, 2002; Moore-Brown, 2007a; Roth & Worthington, 2001).

Broadly speaking, speech-language intervention services may be provided in three forms—direct, indirect, or collaborative/consultative.

- A student can be served directly by a speech-language pathologist individually or in a group of students, either separately from the classroom or in the classroom.

- A student can be served indirectly by a speech-language pathologist individually, in a small group, or with the whole class in the student's classroom.

- A student can be served by a trained person, who is directed by a speech-language pathologist, in any relevant setting. This collaborative/consultative arrangement can be with a SLPA, a classroom teacher, another special educator, a peer, a parent, a bus driver, and so on (Montgomery, 1992).

IDEA 2004 requires that service delivery be directed by qualified professionals (e.g., speech-language pathologists), but it does not have to be administered directly by these professionals. In some cases, intervention is much more effective if it is not directly administered. The support personnel model reviewed earlier in this chapter (see p. 223), for example, can be an effective consultative model. It is another way to structure meaningful intervention services for students and release speech-language pathologists for assessment, consultation, or work with families. For another example of indirect services through consultation, see "Infants and Toddlers" in Chapter 7. Service delivery can happen wherever it is arranged to happen. The essential component is that services are planned, supervised, measured, and evaluated for their effectiveness by speech-language pathologists.

Delivery models can be differentiated between consultation, collaboration, and collaborative/consultation approaches:

Consultation is a *voluntary process* in which one professional assists another to address a problem of a third party. It is a process rather than a style. It is voluntary and entails an indirect relationship. It involves shared participation, effective communication, teamwork, sharing, and problem solving.

Collaboration is a *style* in which two co-equal parties engage voluntarily in shared decision making as they work toward a common goal. It involves shared participation, resources ownership, accountability, and rewards (Secord, 1999, p. 7).

Collaborative-consultation is an *interactive process* that enables teams of people with diverse expertise to generate creative solutions to mutually defined problems. The outcome is enhanced and altered, and produces solutions that are different from those that the individual team members would have produced independently (Idol-Maestas, Paolucci-Whitcomb, & Levin, 1986, p. 1).

All of these service delivery approaches constitute the way speech-language pathologists function as support professionals in an educational setting. Speech-language pathologists in medical settings are often referred to as allied-health professionals. In the same way, speech-language pathologists in schools are allied-education professionals. They provide services in an array of direct and indirect ways to meet student needs.

It is no longer appropriate for speech-language pathologists to provide their services independently. The classroom teacher is the expert on curriculum. The speech-language pathologist is the expert on language acquisition. Putting those two together will facilitate the most efficacious treatment for the student (Shulman, as quoted in Campbell, 1999, p. 7).

ASHA's 2006 Schools Survey revealed that most speech-language pathologists in schools still use the traditional pull-out model as their primary method of providing service. On a weekly basis, the speech-language pathologist spent 21 hours providing services in a traditional pull-out model; 4 hours a week in classroom-based/curriculum-based and self-contained classrooms; 2 hours per week in collaborative/consultation and in prereferral or response to intervention activities, and 1 hour per week in a resource room. In one of a few studies comparing the three service delivery models, the collaborative model was the most effective in teaching curricular vocabulary for students receiving speech-language services (Throneburg, Calvert, Sturm, Paramboukas, & Paul, 2000). The same was found in the EVIDENCE-BASED PRACTICE (EBP) brief comparing classroom to pull-out intervention models (McGinty & Justice, 2006).

Using any of these consultative constructs with deliberative planning allows speech-language pathologists to work in conjunction with classroom teachers, resource specialists, occupational therapists, social workers, and others. The curriculum is incorporated into therapy and therapy into the curriculum. Solutions to taxing service delivery issues present themselves when more than one individual assumes ownership for services, and when entire schools assume ownership for all of their students. This assures more functional interventions, reduces the fragmentation of students' days, and enables speech-language pathologists to take a more active part in the schools. Collaboration begets more collaboration as team members begin to rely on each other, meet more often, and get pleasure from each others' successes.

Types of Teams

IDEA 2004 requires the use of a group of qualified professionals representing different disciplines and parents, often called a MULTIDISCIPLINARY TEAM (MDT), to plan and implement a student's IEP. Appropriate service delivery (i.e., planning and implementing the IEP) for the student with communication disabilities is directly linked to how well the MDT functions. The MDT differs from an INTERDISCIPLINARY TEAM (IDT) and a TRANSDISCIPLINARY TEAM (TDT) in important ways (Secord, 1999). The limited degree of cross-disciplinary work found in the MDT gives rise to the need for consultation and collaboration in schools to create effective ways to support students throughout their school days and their

school career. This collaborative work can be accomplished by using the interdisciplinary and transdisciplinary methods described in Table 6.4. Both these teams extend the effectiveness of service delivery for children and families and enhance generalization to other contexts (Montgomery, 1992).

It is obvious that although an MDT is identified in IDEA 2004, it is the least collaborative of the three types. Effective service delivery rests on a TDT model that functions well. Therefore, the collaboration and consultation concepts inherent in TDT need to be formally taught to members of school MDT teams. Speech-language pathologists who are aware of this mismatch can promote and participate in cross-discipline training that makes service delivery models outside of traditional pull-out therapy feasible in schools. Some long-standing school teams have evolved into IDT or TDT models, and collaborative service delivery is less stressful for them. Speech-language pathologists need to appraise their teams' methods of interaction and expand their comfort levels in sharing expertise to encourage collaborative models.

Writing Goals Together

An effective way for speech-language pathologists and other educators to begin collaborative/consultative service delivery is to write and implement shared goals for students with

> **Collaboration begets more collaboration as team members begin to rely on each other, meet more often, and get pleasure from each others' successes.**

Table 6.4			
Team Methods			
	Multidisciplinary Team (MDT)	Interdisciplinary Team (IDT)	Transdisciplinary Team (TDT
Definition	This is either a generic term for coordinated services or a specific term for a group of professionals who play their traditional roles with little coordination of services (Donahue-Kilburg, 1992; Wilcox, 1989).	Members work together on the evaluation and treatment team but evaluate and treat the student and family separately. They often have formal channels for communication and a functioning case manager (Donahue-Kilburg, 1992).	Members divide their work into direct and indirect student services. Not everyone works with every student, but all members consult with each other to carry out the service delivery plans the group, including parents and caregivers, designs together (Donahue-Kilburg, 1992).
Typical Activities	Work independently and make decisions regarding their areas of expertise; review findings at a team meeting with all the other disciplines in attendance; conduct assessments, establish objectives independently, and then share assessments and goals; work together for implementation of goals	Have members with an area of expertise who are aware of the other team members' expertise; designate a team leader to coordinate all activities; develop two-way communication channels to exchange ideas often; conduct assessments, establish objectives independently, and then share assessments and goals; work together for implementation of goals	Engage in role release and move across discipline boundaries, teaching, learning, and sharing with each other; design goals based on what a student and family believe is important, add their ideas, agree to carry out the plan that evolves; conduct assessments together, observe students functioning while another team member works with them, work closely with and rely on reports from families; work together for implementation of goals

disabilities. Teams in a suburban school district have used the following methods to write shared goals by using transdisciplinary planning even though their IEP process was still basically multidisciplinary:

- The speech-language pathologist and two special educators meet and plan their actions together, resulting in three joint goals rather than a series of goals from each specialist.

- For some children, only one common goal is most effective. All the team members responsible for the child's program contribute to the writing of this statement and rotate the responsibility for monitoring it throughout the year.

- Educators write goals and objectives in their own areas of expertise (e.g., speech and language; academic areas such as English-Language Arts; adaptive physical education), however, other adults or peers are assigned to carry them out.

- Speech-language goals are written which require the parents to carry out one objective at home and the speech-language pathologists to carry out one objective at school. Both objectives need to be met to reach the goal. The parent has to agree to do this at the meeting.

- Parents and educators write goals and objectives together, using a single monitoring system carried back and forth by the child each night in his backpack. A separate monitoring system in each setting can be used and routinely compared to measure progress in different settings.

- Teams write embedded skill goals, where all objectives lead to a single goal such as functional communication. For example, Theresa will use her communication board to meaningfully respond to an adult greeting once a day. Occupational therapy and physical therapy have embedded motor goals, while the teacher has embedded cause and effect cognition goals and the vision therapist has embedded left to right sequencing goals.

- The student's school day is viewed through life domains (e.g., homeroom, hallways, bus stop, scouts, cafeteria, etc.) and service plans and objectives written by the team are taught to the nonspecial education personnel in each setting or domain. Data are kept on a large chart by eight adults and one peer (Montgomery, 1993b, p. 23).

Modifying Instructional Language

Students in general education classes with language and learning problems often cannot benefit from the curriculum presented by their teachers without some significant modifications in the instructional language. This can be accomplished in the collaborative model of service delivery. Rather than have the student leave the classroom to receive remedial services, the speech-language pathologist can co-teach the actual curriculum using the most effective strategies (e.g., listen, repeat, listen, code, and read). In this way, the strategies are taught along with the curriculum, and it is less time consuming than learning strategies in one place and content in another. High levels of success have been reported using this model for struggling readers and writers (Nelson, 2006; Toner & Helmer, 2006).

Figure 6.2

Collaborative Consultation Form

Student _____ DOB _____ Grade _____

School _____ Parent(s) _____

Speech-Language Pathologist _____ Date of Meeting _____

Team Members _____

_____

How was student involved in consultation?_____

_____

Describe problem in behavioral terms: _____

_____

Describe outcome and how it will be measured:_____

_____

Brainstorm strategies to assist student in reaching outcome: _____

_____

Develop action plan:_____

Date of Follow-up Meeting: _____

Who	Action	Timeline	Desired Student Outcome

Sources: Merritt & Culatta (1998); Secord (1999)

Recordkeeping Is Critical

Recordkeeping is important with all service delivery models and often serves useful functions for many team members involved with indirect service models. When speech-language pathologists act as consultants, the use of a recordkeeping form helps to structure the discussion and keep it focused on positive problem solving. The form can also guide a team in setting expectations for each team member's activities and examining results. The "Collaborative Consultation Form" (see Figure 6.2) is one example of a recordkeeping form (Merritt & Culatta, 1998; Secord, 1999).

Records of a consultative meeting should include identification information regarding a student, family, and team participants. A clear description of any difficulties or challenges should be stated in terms that are observable and measurable along with a statement of the desired behavior or outcome. A review of past attempts to resolve the problem can be helpful. A range of options to address the issue may be listed, and the action that is agreed on should be clearly identified. The consultative meeting should never adjourn without first setting a date to check on progress or results.

Consultative forms should be used to clearly identify action plans, including persons responsible, what they will do, and timelines for implementation. These actions should be clearly tied to the functional outcomes desired for a student. (See "Functional Outcomes and the School-

> When speech-language pathologists act as consultants, a form helps to structure the discussion and keep it focussed on positive problem solving.

Based Speech-Language Pathologist" in Chapter 5 for a discussion of functional outcomes.)

Consultants need to display empathy and support for staff members, but that is not the purpose of the meeting. When acting as consultants, speech-language pathologists will guide team members to focus on problems, identify successes as well as concerns, and clearly state the desired functional outcomes for a student. A well-designed form helps draw the discussion away from frustrations and toward a vision of what is desired for the student.

Action plans should clearly identify responsibilities, deadlines, and expected outcomes. This format helps reinforce the concept of teamwork and avoids the assumption that consultants have taken on the responsibility of solving problems independently. Consultants may use consultation forms to check back with team members to monitor their progress toward deadlines. When teams meet at their assigned follow-up sessions, they will have the information needed to determine the success of intervention and any adjustments that need to be made.

Peer Tutors as Part of Service Delivery

Once planning is focused on the environment of a student, peers take on greater significance in the delivery of services. Some students respond much more favorably to peers than adults and can demonstrate faster progress if the work is connected to peer interactions. This is a distinct advantage of school-based intervention that many speech-language pathologists may overlook. Speech-language pathologists can gradually shift responsibilities for monitoring to peer tutors or cooperative learning groups using the collaborative/consultative approach. This is also effective with adolescents (Larson & McKinley, 2003). Speech-language pathologists need to make the shift gradually, select peer models carefully, orient and train peers, have supports readily available for peers, and monitor and follow up with students and peers conscientiously. The advantages to peer tutoring are numerous and match many overall communication and academic goals designed for target students by speech-language pathologists. Some of these advantages include the following:

- Increases time for support and assistance for target students.

- Increases the number of contexts in which target students can be supported.

- Provides more natural intervention as most students learn with peers not with adults.

- Supports a "give and take" interaction between target students and peer tutors.

- Models collaboration without directly involving other professionals, which can serve as a first step in a resistive school environment.

- Provides opportunities for incidental learning and social and academic scripts that serve target students well in school and beyond (German, 1992; Larson & McKinley, 2003; Hardman, Drew, & Egan, 1999; Friend & Bursuck, 2002).

Building Relationships With General Educators

General educators may be valuable resources in helping identify and serve children who may need services since children with language disabilities often exhibit concomitant problems with grammar, vocabulary, or effective conversation skills (Secord, 1999). Speech-language pathologists should team with teachers to jointly observe a student's interactions in class and other school settings. Teaming facilitates all types of service delivery, especially collaboration. Successful collaboration means all professionals involved with the child's services will attend referral and IEP meetings together. "Teachers can augment the speech-language pathologist's observations with their own anecdotes or test results" (Campbell, 1999, p. 8). IDEA 2004 requires that each child's IEP team must include "not less than one regular education teacher of the child (if the child is, or may be, participating in the regular education environment)" (34 C.F.R. § 300.321[a] [2]). This should be someone who teaches or would have taught the student in a general education class. This person may be a grade-level teacher, a subject-area teacher, or a teacher at the home school of a student placed in a specialized school. The grade-level educator keeps the conversation grounded in general education instruction, curriculum, and expectancies. If the student has significant educational needs, it may be difficult for specialists to recall what students at that age and grade are doing in the classroom. This person's role should add a realistic and thoughtful appraisal of the student in the natural environment.

General Educators at the IEP Meeting

General educators can make great contributions to the development of a student's IEP. Speech-language pathologists will find that "language of the classroom" issues are indeed relevant to educators, and therapy is more successful when the whole team is aware of and working on the student's communication goals (Throneburg et al., 2000, p. 13).

There are specific actions that general educators can take prior to or during meetings to provide the other team members with information as to the academic expectations and instructional methods of his or her classroom (see the sidebar below for suggestions). Speech-language pathologists can share ideas with general education peers as appropriate for the age and grade of a student. General educators have a unique perspective on education that is often unfamiliar to special education teams. Appropriate decisions for a student's level of inclusion or support can be made at subsequent meetings if facts and opinions are shared early in the process. Again, it is important to have a classroom teacher be aware of the speech-language goals for a student by joint planning.

Speech-language pathologists and audiologists can and should take a leadership role in the area of communication with and about students on their caseloads. General educators make im-

---

What General Educators Can Do As Required Members of IEP Teams

- Listen carefully to the discussion of a student's strengths and needs without undue concern about the label or diagnosis the student may carry.

- Bring a copy of the age-appropriate curriculum to the meeting. Be sure it is the one actually used to create that class.

- Describe a project or product students produce at your grade level.

- Bring or name a few books that are read to students at this grade level.

- Describe how supplies and materials are acquired and stored by students in your classroom.

- Bring a list of what you believe are the five most important concepts your students will learn that year.

- Be prepared to answer questions about instructional methods that you use frequently.

- Give examples of the type of instructional support that is provided to students in your class.

- Describe the technology used by you and students in your class.

- Discuss the teaming activities of teachers at your grade level.

- Think about and share experiences you have had with paraprofessionals or other support personnel.

From *Funnel Toward Phonics*, by J. K. Montgomery (2004). ©2004 by Super Duper® Publications. Reprinted with permission.

portant contributions when accommodations and modifications are discussed. It is the responsibility of classroom teachers to ensure that all students in their classrooms learn. Special education teams support general educators to meet that expectancy based on each student's present level of performance.

Linking Services to the Curriculum

Speech-language intervention services gradually evolved from clinically based therapy to broader-based educationally and developmentally related intervention services. Individual or small group sessions with speech-language pathologists were once the norm. Larger student groupings with technology-assisted, curriculum-related sessions conducted in classrooms are used in many districts. Descriptions of these exciting models are available in the literature and several will be discussed in this chapter.

Several models have been developed to compare purposes and characteristics of therapy versus instruction. One such model (see Table 6.5) has been observed by the authors in numerous schools and follows the spirit and letter of IDEA 2004. It links all the communication services to a student's educational goals and includes roles for speech-language pathologists to provide CONVENTIONAL THERAPY and classroom instruction. This approach has been used by many speech-language pathologists who use the student's curriculum as the vehicle for practicing targeted communication skills.

Some states tap the expertise of speech-language pathologists to work as communication teachers in self-contained classrooms. These professionals teach the content of the curriculum, guided by a strong language component, to children who have pervasive communication disabilities. This reduces the fragmentation that occurs with pull-out services. A thorough description of service delivery in schools must include speech-language pathologists who apply all the therapeutic practice directly to the teaching of a content area. This position may require additional coursework or another credential in some states (California Department of Education, 1999e).

In the environments of classroom instruction, conventional therapy, and COLLABORATIVE INTERVENTION, speech-language pathologists blend therapeutic goals and methods with educational standards, so that generalization of common skills is enhanced. Compatible with IDEA 2004, this model shows how educators and parents can be made aware of the impact of students' evolving communication skills.

These three macrosystems, presented in Table 6.5, may use many broad-based instructional strategies. A service delivery model is similar to the outside walls of a house or the fence around a yard. Each occupant can furnish or plant it to fit his or her tastes, interests, and resources. Once the parameters of service are established, numerous therapeutic strategies will fit. As noted in the many previous examples in this chapter, using evidence-based practices, a wide range of theoretical perspectives will fit comfortably within service delivery models in schools (Gilliam & Gilliam, 2006; Justice, 2006a; Kamhi, 2006a; Taps, 2006).

Table 6.5	**Blended Therapeutic/Educational Role for Collaboration in the Curriculum**		
Factors to Consider	**Classroom Instruction**	**Conventional Therapy**	**Collaborative Intervention**
Learning	Deals with learning new information and skills in the normal course of development	Deals with remediating or compensating for deficient skills that have not developed or that have been lost	Focuses on a combination of learning new information plus research-based intensive strategies using individualized instructional accommodations with a sensitivity for different learning styles and varying levels of student support
Student Engagement	Involves a captive audience with varying degrees of active engagement at different times	Depends on a student's ongoing, active participation in a self-help process	Combines the advantages of students working in multi-skilled groups of same-age peers with individual empowerment possible with effective scaffolds
Planning	Uses a teaching sequence based on external criteria, curriculum standards, and progression	Uses a sequence of activities based on individual needs and progress	Uses a sequence based on individual needs and progress within the larger framework of curricular expectations for students at a particular grade level
Needs of Learners	Is oriented to group goals and uses a standard approach	Incorporates selection of individual goals and uses a diagnostic approach	Incorporates a selection of individual, measurable annual goals but encourages use of state or local standards as benchmarks under those goals
Pace	Is determined by the majority of group and average ability	Is determined by a student's mastery and the speech-language pathologist's judgements	Demands more intense efforts and adjusted pace to promote mastery; actions of all members of the team, including the general education teacher, are contingent on the actions of the student
Interaction	Has teachers teach the planned lesson and students provide feedback after specific tasks	Incorporates the speech-language pathologist's actions contingent on a student's reactions; informative and corrective feedback are essential and ongoing	Uses informative and corrective feedback provided in both formal and informal ways from educators, speech-language pathologists, peers, and support personnel

From *Inclusive Practices in the Middle School* [Handout], by J.K. Montgomery, 2000b, presentation at Hewes Middle School, Tustin Unified School District, Tustin, CA. ©2000 by J.K. Montgomery. Adapted with permission.

Literacy, Reading, and Writing

ASHA Position Statement

The American Speech-Language-Hearing Association (2000d) makes the following statement concerning the role of speech-langauge pathologists with respect to reading and writing:

> Speech-language pathologists play a critical and direct role in the development of literacy for children and adolescents with communication disorders, including those with severe or multiple disabilities. Speech-language pathologists also make a contribution to the literacy efforts of a school district or community on behalf of other children and adolescents (p. 1).

This forthright statement acknowledged the strong connection between spoken and written language, asserting that speech-language pathologists would play a major role in supporting students with reading and language difficulties. It was motivated by the national interest in promoting literacy for all individuals, the acknowledgement that speech-language pathologists serve students whose language difficulties involve reading and writing, the role of speech-language pathologists as advocates for these students, the benefits of collaborative partnerships between educators, and the questions that speech-language pathologists had regarding their role in literacy (ASHA, 2000c). There is a considerable body of research that confirms the connection between language and reading from the communication disorders, linguistics, and education fields (Catts & Kamhi, 2005; Sand-

ers, 2001; Stone et al., 2004). Reading, language arts, and communication skills are linked and interdependent in the educational process.

Reading and Reading Disabilities

Literacy is defined by Section 3 of the National Literacy Act of 1991 as "an individual's ability to read, write, and speak in English and compute and solve problems at levels of proficiency necessary to function on the job and in society, to achieve one's goals and to develop one's knowledge and potential." Literacy encompasses reading, writing, speaking, listening, and thinking. Literacy is the purpose of schooling in this country (Goldsworthy, 1996). "Of all school learning, nothing compares in importance with reading; it is of unparalleled significance" (Bettleheim & Zelan, 1982, p. 5).

Some descriptions of reading explain the reading event but are not helpful to explain why some students struggle to learn to read. Each definition seeks to include the two basic elements of reading: comprehension and decoding. Catts and Kamhi (2005) call reading "thinking guided by print" (p. 3). Snow, Burns, and Griffin (1998) combined the ideas of a national panel of 17 reading experts into a definition of reading:

> Reading as a cognitive and psycholinguistic activity requires the use of form (the written code) to obtain meaning (the message to be understood), within the context of the reader's purpose (for learning, for enjoyment, for insight) (p. 33).

Goldsworthy (1996), in one of the early texts on intervention for reading disabilities for speech-language pathologists, indicated some simple definitions were misleading if reading was defined as an event rather than a process:

> During the reading process, information extracted from the printed page, whether at the level of decoding and word recognition or comprehension of text, is analyzed and compared with previously stored information. If it were a simple matter of learning a set of associations between sounds of the spoken language and printed squiggles on a page, learning to read would be relatively easy because it would involve little that is new to the would-be reader with the exception that language will now be presented through the visual modality. The process involved in reading acquisition, however, is far more complex than a simple transfer of meaning from oral to written language (p. 33).

The National Reading Panel Report (2000) outlined five elements of reading instruction. A review of over 10,000 studies led the panel to conclude that a complete reading program needed to include instruction in these areas:

- Phonemic awareness
- Phonics
- Fluency
- Vocabulary
- Text comprehension

Most researchers would agree that 80 percent of children in elementary schools learn to read adequately (Catts & Kamhi, 2005; Fey, 1999; Lyon, 1998). The 20 percent who struggle do so for many reasons—they may have sensory impairments, developmental or language disabili-

ties, or be English learners to name a few common situations (Snow, Burns, & Griffin, 1998; August & Shanahan, 2006). These students require explicit systematic instruction in the areas outlined by Lyon (as cited in Snow, Burns, & Griffin, 1998) to be successful (see sidebar on p. 242). "Reading proficiency is an important goal for virtually all students who receive special education" (California Department of Education [CDE], 1999b, p. 7) and students with moderate to severe disabilities can benefit from literacy instruction (Kliewer & Landis, 1999; Koppenhaver & Yoder, 1993; ASHA, 2005d). Students who have developmental disabilities that affect cognitive organization, memory, language processing, and physical manipulation of print are often not taught reading in their self-contained classrooms (Erickson & Koppenhaver, 1995; ASHA, 2005d). Developing their literacy skills is often a challenge for speech-language pathologists and an important focus of intervention programs (ASHA, 2000c; Goldsworthy, 1996; van Kleeck, 1998; Yoder & Koppenhaver, 1993; ASHA, 2005d; Ehren, 2007; Justice, 2007).

Roles and Responsibilities in Reading

The roles and responsibilities of speech-language pathologists in literacy development are identified in three sources: (1) national literacy recommendations, (2) state guidelines in special education and reading, and (3) ASHA guidelines for roles and responsibilities for speech-language pathologists in facilitating literacy.

The National Council on Preventing Reading Difficulties in Young Children noted in its find-

Areas of Instruction for Successful Readers

In testimony to the U.S. House of Representatives, Committee on Education and the Workforce, July 10, 1997, G. Reid Lyon, Chief, Child Development and Behavior Branch of the National Institute of Child Health and Human Development (NICHD) said: "To learn to read, a child must integrate phonemic skills into learning phonic principles, must practice reading so word recognition is rapid and accurate, and must learn how to actively use comprehension strategies to enhance meaning" (as quoted in Snow, Burns, & Griffin, 1998, p. 41).

ings that identification of and service to children with language problems by speech-language pathologists was second in a long list of critical recommendations for prevention (as cited in Snow et al., 1998). It reported that identification of preschool children who were at risk for learning to read was based on these research-derived indicators:

1. In infancy or during the preschool period, significant delays in expressive language, receptive vocabulary, or IQ

2. At school entry, delays in a combination of measures of readiness, including:

   • Letter identification

   • Understanding the functions of print

   • Verbal memory for stories and sentences

   • Phonological awareness

   • Lexical skills, such as naming vocabulary

   • Receptive language skills in the areas of syntax and morphology

   • Expressive language

   • Overall language development

Many states have robust literacy programs that address the issues of prevention of reading difficulties, philosophies of reading acquisition, the selection of reading books and educational materials, and university teacher education programs. States have documented that 80 percent of the children referred for special education programs exhibited reading problems (President's Commission, 2002). The vast majority of goals and objectives on IEPs address needs in reading and writing. Poor reading skills were preventing these children from accessing meaningful instructional content in their classrooms. For 85 to 90 percent of poor readers, effective prevention and early intervention can increase their reading skills to within average levels (Lyon, 1998; Justice, 2007). Speech-language pathologists and other special educators have a role to play in service delivery to students with reading and language disabilities as described in *The California Reading Initiative and Special Education in California: Critical Ideas to Focus Meaningful Reform* (CDE, 1999b). Service delivery in reading was heralded as "professionally exciting for all special education teachers and specialists, including school psychologists and speech and language specialists (p. 3).

The ASHA (2000c) guidelines for speech-language pathologists' roles and responsibilities in promoting reading and literacy in school-age children (see sidebar on p. 244) expand the initial technical report and the profession's position paper on reading and writing. These guidelines are intended to clarify that speech-language pathologists have the expertise and responsibility to play important roles related to literacy. Collaborative approaches with other school-based professionals are urged throughout the ASHA guidelines, along with close adherence to state and local policies, procedures, and regulations on the subject of reading and literacy. Service delivery for children with a combination of reading difficulties and language disabilities should include prevention, identification, assessment, intervention, coordination with other professionals, and contributions to future research and information. The ASHA document that outlines each of these areas in highly practical detail is almost 60 pages long, which attests to the importance of service delivery in this expanded model (ASHA, 2000c). This document will likely serve as a major resource for graduate courses in speech-language pathology. The guide is available on the ASHA Web site (www.asha.org).

Speech-language pathologists can ensure that all children gain access to instruction that helps them learn to read and write as well as to communicate orally, manually, or with augmentative and alternative techniques and devices. The fact that language problems are both a cause and a consequence of reading disabilities, and that written language capabilities are critical to academic success, makes it not only appropriate, but essential, that speech-language pathologists accept responsibility for these roles.

Special educators, including speech-language pathologists, have investigated the myths and misconceptions that have revolved around teaching reading to students with mild, moderate, and severe disabilities. Many have concluded that a large number of these students were never taught to read using explicit, systematic instruction or effective books and materials. Special techniques, often lacking in empirical validation, were thought to be necessary because students were labeled "special" or experienced significant disabilities (Simmons & Kame'enui, 1998). Special educators involved in literacy instruction need to:

- Have a comprehensive knowledge of spoken and written English.

- Understand the process of reading as both comprehension and decoding.

- Know the early indicators of reading difficulty.

- Intervene using research-based strategies.

- Encourage all children to read often in authentic situations.

> Service delivery should include prevention, identification, assessment, intervention, coordination with other professionals, and contributions to future research and information.

ASHA Guidelines for Speech-Language Pathologists' Roles and Responsibilities in Promoting Reading and Literacy

1. Prevention
Joint book reading
Environmental print awareness
Concepts of print
Concepts of phonology
Alphabetic letter knowledge
Sense of story
Adult modeling of literacy activities
Experiences with writing materials
Other activities

2. Identification
Children at risk for reading
  and writing problems
Individual and cultural differences
Early identification
Older students

3. Assessment
Formal assessment
Emergent level
  Family literacy
  Phonological awareness
  Print awareness
  Oral language

Early elementary level
  Phonological awareness
  Rapid naming
  Letter identification
  Invented spelling
  Reading
  Writing
  Oral language

Later level (4th grade and up)
  Reading
  Writing
  Curriculum-based assessment
  Metacognitive functioning
  Oral language

Using published tools

4. Intervention
Targeting literacy
  Individual plans
  Individual implementations
  Expectations of the curriculum

Research-based interventions
  Strategic literacy goals
  Knowing the literature
  Characteristics of good and
    poor readers

Balanced intervention

Culturally appropriate intervention

Developmentally appropriate
  Early childhood programs
  Early elementary programs
  Later elementary and secondary
    programs
  Students with multiple or severe
    developmental impairments

Needs-based curriculum-relevant
  intervention
  Basic principles of curriculum
    planning
  Modifications for special needs

5. Other roles and responsibilities

Assistance to general education teachers

Curricular responsibilities on behalf
  of all students

Extending the knowledge base for
  students and colleagues

From *Roles and Responsibilities of Speech-Language Pathologists with Respect to Reading and Writing in Children and Adolescents,* by the American Speech-Language-Hearing Association (ASHA), 2000c, Rockville, MD: Author. ©2000 by ASHA. Adapted with permission.

- Know how to measure progress and make instructional adjustments when needed (Simmons & Kame'enui, 1998).

Comprehension and decoding may affect students' reading behaviors in different ways. One skill group without the other is not true reading; however, students with special needs will often acquire skills unevenly. Balancing the teaching of comprehension (e.g., listening, narrative, and retelling skills) with decoding (e.g., sound-symbol matching and pattern-recognition skills) must be a collaborative effort between speech-language pathologists and other educators. Speech-language pathologists provide intervention services in both components of reading (ASHA, 2000c).

Readers of this text are urged to expand their knowledge and skills in literacy instruction. Many excellent literacy Web sites are available. Periodic articles in Special Interest Division 1 and Division 16 newsletters from ASHA and ASHA's *Roles and Responsibilities of Speech-Language Pathologists with Respect to Reading and Writing in Children and Adolescents* (2000c) are also informative (see sidebar on p. 244).

Phonological Awareness

PHONOLOGICAL AWARENESS is critical to the development of reading (Adams, 1999; Catts & Kamhi, 2005; Gillon, 2000; Goldsworthy, 1996; Snow, Burns, & Griffin, 1998; Torgeson, 2001).

Instructional and Therapeutic Strategies

Speech-language pathologists report using similar instructional and therapeutic strategies in all settings. Frequently, these are strategies created by speech-language pathologists working with students in schools. Although this list could be considerably longer, we chose only a few to highlight. *Communication Lab* (Pritchard Dodge, 1994) is a total class activity, addressing individual goals as well as general classroom discourse. It develops pragmatic skills and useful classroom social skills and interactions. Interventions for narratives and expository text development include *The Story Grammar Marker* (Rooney-Moreau & Fidrych-Puzzo, 1994), *ThemeMaker* (Rooney-Moreau & Fidrych, 1998), and *Brady (Moreau, 2005). The Magic of Stories* (Strong & Hoggan North, 1996) uses classic children's literature for teaching text comprehension and narrative skills. *Conversations* (Hoskins, 1996) allows speech-language pathologists to target and monitor planned discourse for students in small groups. Successful strategies are available to speech-language pathologists in many forms, including audiotapes (e.g., Nelson & Hoskins, 1997) and software, *Literacy Links* (Wilson, 2007).

Yopp (1995) concluded that this overall awareness of how sounds are separate, yet connected to each other in the speech stream, is necessary to learn to read and the result of learning to read. Speech-language pathologists have highly relevant training and clinical experience in this area and can incorporate it into their service delivery (ASHA, 1999b; Gillon, 2000; Goldsworthy, 1996, 1998).

Phonological awareness can be defined as sensitivity to the patterns of spoken language that recur and can be manipulated without regard to their meaning (Snow et al., 1998). Goldsworthy (1998) offers a very useful hierarchy of skill development from less difficult sentence-level phonological activities, to word-level skills, and finally phoneme-level skills. Using this three-level approach, speech-language pathologists reported immediate changes in students' reading skills confirmed by classroom teachers. Developing phonological awareness skills in students with significant language disabilities has become an effective service delivery approach for speech-language pathologists (Gillam, 1999b; Montgomery, 2005; van Kleeck, 1998).

Collaborative partners need to use each other's professional vocabulary with ease and be able to explain standards and BENCHMARKS to parents and policymakers. Sometimes confusion exists if reading terms seem to overlap with speech-language terminology. For example, terms in phonological awareness may be confusing. To share information accurately, speech-language pathologists need to know general education, special education, and speech-language terminology for phonological awareness. Figure 6.3 provides some clarification for speech-language pathologists who follow their state guidelines to provide support in phonological awareness as an extension of their speech-language interventions with struggling readers.

Serving Students in Preschool

Assessing and providing therapy for children under 5 years of age was a permissive program under the EDUCATION FOR ALL HANDICAPPED CHILDREN ACT (EAHCA) of 1975. A permissive special education program is one that federal law approves to be funded but does not mandate. Some states immediately began serving very young children, with Michigan offering programs in schools, preschools, and day care settings for children age 2 years. In other states, parents of children with long-standing conditions, such as hearing loss, cerebral palsy, developmental delays, or syndromes, waited for their children's fifth birthdays to have them assessed by the school district, so that they could receive services free and in the vicinity of their neighborhood school. Unfortunately, lack of intervention through the formative preschool years only made the task of appropriate programming that much more difficult in kindergarten.

School districts without preschool intervention found a need to know the number of children with disabilities, and which disabilities would arrive in their kindergartens each year. Once they knew the children and families, they could prepare suitable programs and have staff hired or trained when necessary. The best reason for early intervention programs was, of

Figure 6.3

Phonological Terms Used in Reading

Phonological Processing is using information about the sound structure of speech to process oral and written language (Hodson & Edwards, 1997). These skills are used in aural and oral modalities.

Phonological Awareness is the general ability to attend to the sounds of language distinct from its meaning, including rhyming, counting syllables, segmenting words, and recognizing onset and rime in words (Snow et al., 1998). Skills are used in aural and oral modalities.

Phonemic Awareness is the explicit understanding that words are composed of segments of sound smaller than a syllable (phoneme), plus the knowledge that these individual phonemes have distinctive features (Torgesen, 1999). These skills are used in aural and oral modalities.

Phonics are instructional practices that educators use to emphasize how spellings are related to speech sounds in systematic ways (Snow, Burns, and Griffin, 1998). These skills are used in aural, oral, and graphemic modalities.

(Phonological) Decoding is a method to derive a pronunciation for a printed sequence of letters based on knowledge of spelling-sound correspondence (Adams, 1999). These skills are used in aural, oral, graphemic, and motoric modalities.

From *Inclusive Practices in the Middle School* [Handout], by J.K. Montgomery, 2000b, presentation at Hewes Middle School, Tustin Unified School District, Tustin, CA. ©2000 by J.K. Montgomery. Adapted with permission.

course, that successful ones ameliorated children's disabilities and enabled them to be a part of a general education class sooner. Since these youngsters would spend the next 12 to 16 years in the school system, schools had a big stake in early and effective intervention.

With the amendments to the EAHCA (1975) in P.L. 99-457 (1986), preschool programs became a part of the full special education spectrum offered by schools. Preschool programs were included in Part B of the EAHCA, to include services for children with special needs beginning at age 3. Districts sought space to set up classes and offer center-based services (i.e., children come to a school facility to receive services), sometimes nudging out privately run preschools that were leasing empty classrooms in schools. In the late 1980s, large preschool programs were created in many states (e.g., Texas, California, and Maryland), including transportation systems for very young children and a full staff of specialists to assess children; counsel families; and provide occupational, physical, and speech-language therapy. Communication disorders quickly became the most commonly identified disability and its intervention the most frequently requested service in preschools. Most preschool children with identifiable impairments and disabilities demonstrate some type of communication disorder (Polmanteer & Turbiville, 2000; Paul, 2001). Preschool services were not altered by the 2004 reauthorization of IDEA (see Chapter 3 for details).

Since children are still developing their language throughout preschool, delayed communication development can masquerade as simple immaturity. Children's communication skills are not yet stabilized, and many children are still acquiring the last few motorically complex sounds of their first or second languages. Researchers have described the literal explosion of new vocabulary that a child acquires between the ages of 4 and 5, when school begins for most of them (van Kleeck, 1998; Vygotsky, 1978). In the preschool setting, it is particularly important for speech-language pathologists to thoroughly know these two principles:

1. Normal acquisition of speech and language, so that children are not overidentified.

2. Appropriate intervention models for this age group that are not merely scaled-down versions of similar services for school-age children.

Assessment and Eligibility for Preschoolers

Children aged 3 to 5 with suspected communication disabilities must be assessed by speech-language pathologists. Preschoolers are referred by parents, community agencies, physicians, private preschool administrators, or others outside the school. There is no cost for the assessment even if a child has not previously been known to the school. The assessment may take place at the neighborhood school, a central assessment center, or a child's home.

Young children should be assessed informally as well as formally using tools that are designed for their age group only. If a child's language or culture is different from that of a speech-language pathologist, the professional needs to be sensitive to the child-rearing practices of the family, listen carefully to the family's concerns, and use an interpreter if needed. For example, a speech-language pathologist must be cautious not to mistake a 3-year-old's shyness while speaking to a stranger for a communication problem. Family members are often the best resource for the speech-language pathologist to learn about a child's typical performance.

There are separate preschool eligibility criteria in most states because of the importance of early intervention. The paucity of standardized tests at this level, the difficulty getting responses from a young child on demand, and the interplay of cognition and language at this age are accounted for in less stringent criteria at this level. Most criteria refer to developmental levels of children rather than test scores. States and school districts recognize the relatively short amount of time available to reach students during this critical stage of development and do not wish to delay or deny services by setting strict entrance criteria.

Individual Family Service Plans (IFSPs)

If a child is found to have a speech-language disability, services may be provided in a variety of places, such as a daily preschool for children with disabilities, the typical preschool the child already attends, a day care center, a HEAD START PROGRAM, a typical public school, or in the child's home. An IEP or, as it is called at this age, INDIVIDUAL FAMILY SERVICE PLAN (IFSP)

is developed by the team that has assessed the child, plus parents and any other adults who know the child well. Usually, the child is too young to attend this meeting; although it does bring a sense of authenticity for all participants when the child attends.

An IFSP states all the services needed, the person responsible for each, the location of the services, and the specific roles and responsibilities parents or caretakers will have. In this way, the IEP for preschoolers differs from the conventional IEP for school-age children. Preschoolers cannot be authentically discussed or planned for outside of the strong network of their families. Often parents have specific questions about how to communicate with their child that should be addressed in the assessment and the service plan (Polmanteer & Turbiville, 2000). The IFSP is written for a year or less, whichever is appropriate for a particular child. Functional outcomes are incorporated into the planning, and accommodations for the language and culture of the family are integrated into the IFSP (see "Functional Outcomes and the School-Based Speech-Language Pathologist" in Chapter 5 for a discussion on functional outcomes). Some of these are family outcomes rather than direct child outcomes. The use of lay language rather than professional jargon is a marker of a family-responsive plan (Polmanteer & Turbiville, 2000).

Caseloads and Scheduling

The models of service delivery and corresponding samples of speech-language pathologists' schedules discussed earlier in this chapter have some application for preschoolers. However, preschool models and schedules often include a wider variety of settings and models. Home-based programs are appropriate for some children, while center-based ones may be more effective for others. Natural environments for preschoolers vary depending on their families' child-rearing practices and preferences. Caseloads and scheduling of services for preschoolers in either setting should follow child-directed guidelines.

Speech-language pathologists need to devote larger blocks of time to serve preschoolers, maintain close contact with caregivers and teachers, and allow for children's regular recharging through naps, snacks, and a mixture of fine- and gross-motor activities. Speech-language pathologists work directly and indirectly in the preschool classroom, meet with teachers and parents, use recess, snack time, and animal-petting time, and incorporate children's interests and friends to generalize new skills.

Preschoolers may have high energy one moment and be too tired to keep their eyes open ten minutes later. Usually, mornings are better times for teaching and learning new skills; however, afternoon preschools can be equally beneficial if time is used wisely. Center-based programs often run a morning and an afternoon class. Some speech-language pathologists serve students in preschool classrooms; other preschool-age students are brought to centers for therapy only; some students are served in inclusive neighborhood child or preschool programs. Some preschool classes are taught by speech-language pathologists, enabling these professionals to thread language activities throughout the curriculum.

Preschool Schedules

Preschool schedules need to incorporate some elements that differ from school schedules due to the children's young age, the role of families, and the types of services offered. Frequently, the following elements are on preschool schedules:

- 10–15 minute individual treatment sessions

- Joint sessions with parent and child

- Group activities scheduled at the playground, art area, water table, clay sink, animal cages, and so on, that integrate gross- and fine-motor skills with language

- Snack or nutrition time

- Bathroom schedules

- Parent meetings

- Home visits

- Nap or rest time if more than 1½ hours of instruction

- Travel time to agency preschool sites, Head Start programs, or private facilities

Not all speech-language pathologists will need to schedule all these options. Some speech-language pathologists work exclusively with preschoolers; others work with preschoolers, infants, and toddlers; and others work with preschoolers along with a school-age population.

ASHA (2000a) recommends a caseload of 24 preschoolers for a speech-language pathologist working exclusively in this setting. This is a guideline that many schools have followed, however, caseloads are determined by state agencies, so there are wide variations among states (e.g., Ohio, Florida, and Kentucky vary greatly).

Providing comprehensive preschool services to 24 young children, their families, and other support personnel is a challenge. Keeping up-to-date on educational, therapeutic, and legal issues when dealing with families is equally important. Speech-language pathologists also need to be culturally competent (see "Students Who Are Culturally/Linguistically Diverse [CLD]" in Chapter 7) and sensitive to families' interests and preferences (ASHA, 2005b; ASHA 2004d; Brice, 2000; Cheng, 1999). Even though these children are enrolled on speech-language pathologists' caseloads, working with families is the key to success.

Developmentally Appropriate Programs for Children 5 & Under

Too many early intervention programs have been operated like school pull-out programs. It is inappropriate for a 3-year-old child to sit across a table from a speech-language pathologist in a room separate from a preschool environment and attempt to learn new skills through drill. This situation offers virtually no opportunity for the preschooler to incorporate speech-language acquisition into play, experimentation, or ongoing physical and cognitive trial-and-error efforts. Therefore, artificial environments should be avoided.

Despite the predominance of the pull-out model with preschoolers (ASHA, 1998d; Paul-Brown & Caperton, 2002), speech-language pathologists have also used classroom-based and collaborative/consultative models. Advantages to these models include greater relevancy, generalization, frequency of intervention, and op-portunity to assist other children who are at-risk but not receiving services (Cirrin & Penner, 1995). Initially, educators and families wanted children to be served in disability-focused programs. Administrators found it more cost-effective to serve all preschoolers in one building or complex. More speech-language pathologists were being trained as experts in working with children under 5 years of age, and they often chose to work with other similarly trained professionals exclusively. There were some advantages to having the expertise all in one place, but public policy and public pressure began to create a demand for programs that remained within the general education environment, including the natural environment for children not yet in formal schooling (Power-deFur & Orelove, 1997).

Effect of Inclusive Practices

INCLUSIVE PRACTICES for educating all children, including those under age 5, have not been defined in IDEA (1997, 2004) legislation. Instead, organizations have published statements about the effects of including students in general education environments. ASHA (1996b) produced a position statement on inclusive practices that, although it addressed all children, had a dramatic effect on the service provision for 3- to 5-year-olds with speech-language disabilities. Paul-Brown and Caperton (2002) provide an overview of the compatibility of service delivery models with features of inclusive practice in Table 6.6. (See the sidebar on p. 178 in Chapter 5 for the full text of ASHA's inclusive practice statement). Inclusive practices in preschools for children with communication disabilities set the tone for subsequent interventions in school.

Table 6.6

Compatibility of Service Delivery Models
With Features of Inclusive Practices

	Features of Inclusive Practices	Features of Service Delivery Models		
		Pull-Out	Collaborative/ Consultative	Classroom-Based
Service Setting	Provides services in typical educational setting	Separate intervention room	Classroom	Classroom
Manner of Service Delivery	Uses the natural environment to provide opportunities for peer interactions	Speech-language pathologist and child interact	Teacher and peer interactions in classroom	Teacher, speech-language pathologist, and peer interactions in classroom
Content/ Curriculum for Service	Integrates speech-language intervention within the classroom curriculum and activities	Uses classroom curriculum or separate content	Infuses speech-language goals with classroom curriculum and activities	Infuses speech-language goals with classroom curriculum and activities
Service-Provider Roles	Fosters collaboration among speech-language pathologist, teachers, parents, and others	Direct service by speech-language pathologist; could coordinate with teachers, parents, and others	Indirect service by speech-language pathologist; collaborative consultation (in contrast to unidirectional expert consultation)	Direct service by speech-language pathologist and teacher in classroom; ongoing collaboration
Direction of Service	Brings speech and language services to a child rather than taking the child to a separate treatment room	Brings child to services	Brings services to child	Brings services to child

From *Treatment Settings and Service Delivery Models for Children with Communication Disorders in the Context of Early Childhood Inclusion* (p. 441), by D. Paul-Brown and C.J. Caperton (2001), in M.J. Guralnick (Ed.), *Early Childhood Inclusion: Focus on Change*, Baltimore: Brookes. ©2001 by Paul H. Brookes. Adapted with permission.

Speech-language pathologists played a vital role in integrating communication skill building into children's days—a big departure from pull-out sessions or therapy isolated from the normal activities of children's days.

The ASHA (1996b) document was philosophically situated between the liberal and conservative positions of other organizations. TASH (2000), formerly known as The Association for Persons with Severe Disabilities, concluded that all students should be included while others suggested very few children with LEARNING DISABILITIES could be educated full-time in the classroom (e.g., Learning Disabilities Association of America [LDA], 1993; CEC, 1997a; National Center for Learning Disabilities [NCLD], 1994). This vision had a great impact on preschool services at a time when preschools were being closely examined to determine functional outcomes and whether these programs were successful and enabled the children they served to enter general education programs (Justice, 2006b; Valdez & Montgomery, 1997).

Paul-Brown and Caperton (2002) identified several service delivery factors that either supported or prevented inclusive practices in preschools. They compared the features of three service delivery models—pull-out, collaborative/consultative, and classroom-based—described elsewhere in this chapter with five aspects of service delivery for children ages 3 to 5 (see Table 6.6). The features were service setting, manner of service, content/curriculum for service, service-provider roles, and direction of service. Parents requested maximum direct service plus maximum peer contact (inclusion). Table 6.7 summarizes factors that support and inhibit in-

clusive preschool activities. It is a tool that could be shared with parents of preschoolers and, perhaps, the school IEP team. It is relatively jargon free and points out service differences without making value judgements. Objectivity can be hard to maintain when families request less intrusive services to allow their youngsters to enjoy childhood but still have maximum results. Speech-language pathologists recognize how little time there is to try one model after another.

Paul-Brown and Caperton (2002) concluded that segregated settings do not offer any advantages in terms of frequency of social interactions or other aspects of peer relations. They also suggested that limited research funds not be spent on comparing the effectiveness of various settings but rather used to improve services to young children who have communication disorders in inclusive settings.

Preliteracy and Literacy Acquisition

PRELITERACY and literacy skills develop in preschool. Many children who exhibit later reading problems had speech-language disabilities identified in preschool (Boudreau & Hedberg, 1999; Catts & Kamhi, 2004; Center for the Improvement of Early Reading Achievement [CIERA], 2000). Speech-language pathologists need to know how reading is acquired and how children begin to acquire PRINT MEANING and print form between the ages of 3 and 5 (van Kleeck, 1998). Phonological awareness skills are informally taught and reinforced by parents in this time period (Torgeson, 1998). These are important precursors to reading and are frequent-

Table 6.7		
Factors Supporting or Inhibiting Inclusive Preschool Activities		
Factors:	**Supporting Inclusion**	**Inhibiting Inclusion**
	Legislation Society and public policy Social-interactive theory of language Child outcomes in research View of language as social acts	Resistance to change Professionals' limited skills Little administrative support Family preferences Lack of planning time Little efficacy data available
Settings:	**Classroom Models**	**Therapy Models**
	Which ones? For how long? For which children? With which other professionals?	Which ones? For how long? For which children? With which other professionals?

From *Treatment Settings and Service Delivery Models for Children with Communication Disorders in the Context of Early Childhood Inclusion,* by D. Paul-Brown & C.J. Caperton (2001), in M.J. Guralnick (Ed.), *Early Childhood Inclusion: Focus on Change,* Baltimore: Brookes. ©2001 by Paul H. Brookes. Adapted with permission.

ly delayed in children who struggle with reading (Boudreau & Hedberg, 1999). Speech-language pathologists have an important role to play in literacy development since it includes reading, writing, speaking, listening, and thinking skills (Montgomery, 1998). The breadth of print-related activities that young children need is staggering (van Kleeck, 1998), and literally all of these activities can be used by speech-language pathologists as language-based activities and objectives for preschoolers with communication disabilities. Models of reading that emphasize

balanced reading and literacy instructional programs, such as those described by van Kleeck (1998), Adams (1999), or Justice and Skibbe (2005), are advocated by many state departments of education.

Typical preschools are often rich in early auditory and visual patterning skills connected to reading, and children who have communication disabilities need to have the same opportunities to learn these patterns as their peers. They probably need even more exposure to and reinforcement of the patterns to be successful (Boudreau & Hedberg, 1999). Working with preschoolers requires speech-language pathologists to be constantly looking forward to the next stage of learning, no matter what the current performance level of a child might be. Low expectations at this early point can impede a child's ability to learn and grow in the mainstream of education. A disability or label does not indicate how much the child can achieve. Research has shown that diagnosis cannot be correlated with the child's ability, socialization, eventual employment, or motivation (Centers for Disease Control [CDC], 1999). Many professionals believe that preschool is the time to keep all the future academic options open (Paul, 2001; van Kleeck, 1998). All preschool children should be considered potential readers and writers, so speech-language pathologists who provide services to preschoolers must acknowledge and plan for this eventuality.

Feeding and Swallowing Problems in Preschool Populations

Children under 5 years of age who have feeding and swallowing problems may be eligible for services in preschool programs (O'Toole, 2000; Whitmire, 2000b) and usually present with fragile medical health, neurological disorders and syndromes, or related etiologies that place them at risk (Kurjan, 2000). An IFSP or IEP may have goals and objectives with a school team and family members that address a child's nutrition, eating habits, and skills at home and in a school program or center. Speech-language pathologists have been responsible for these

specialized issues in preschools, using an MDT approach, including cross-training and co-treatment (Kurjan, 2000). Homer, Bickerton, Hill, Parham, and Taylor (2000) found that a large suburban school district in Louisiana needed to have specially trained speech-language pathologists, called a swallowing action team (SWAT), to ensure that preschoolers and school-age students had safe nutrition and hydration during school hours. Preschool programs often require speech-language pathologists to have skills, such as working with swallowing problems, that extend beyond the education traditionally received in undergraduate or graduate programs plus an understanding of scope-of-practice statements for state licensure and ASHA certification (Kurjan, 2000; O'Toole, 2000; Whitmire, 2000b). For a full description of the scope of practice for speech-language pathologists, go to www.asha.org/policy (ASHA, 2001c).

The Clock Is Ticking!

One of the troubling realities of working with preschoolers is the brief time available. All the assessment and intervention with children and families must be accomplished within a mere 24 months because, of course, the ages of 3 to 5 have an established beginning and ending time. One cannot continue preschool services for just a few more weeks or months. The clock starts running immediately at age 3 and stops when children are old enough for kindergarten. From time to time, there may be a 5-year-old in preschool, but it is unusual and not encouraged. Assessment must be prompt and accurate, contacts with other service providers must be ongoing, and intervention must be targeted and results driven. It is clear that speech-language pathologists who wish to work in preschool settings will need to know all the service delivery models and intervention techniques, be well versed in the development of 3- to 5-year-olds, be innovative and flexible to meet family and child needs, and devote their energies to assuring that a majority of the children who are served in preschool programs do not need continued communication services once they start school. Creating and maintaining preschool programs focused on maximum outcomes in 24 months or less is a major responsibility and an exciting area for speech-language pathologists.

Services for Secondary Students

IDEA 2004 mandates special education services for individuals from birth to age 21, but adolescents are "a population of students who have long been ignored," and few speech-language pathologists have attempted to support "the language they need to achieve academic and social success" (Apel, 1999, p. 229). As previously mentioned, however, there is an increased national focus on adolescents, specifically in the area of reading (Biancarosa & Snow, 2004; Snow & Biancarosa, 2003a; Cassidy & Cassidy, 2007; Kamil, 2003; Education Trust, 2005). Although speech-language services for secondary students may not typically be organized by the age of clients, the interaction between a speech-language pathologist and a student may be strongly influenced by the student's classes, schedule, and physical location on a high school campus.

Characteristics of Adolescents

As students get older, they spend greater amounts of time with their peers and often appear to dislike or be uncomfortable in the company of adults. Intervention programs need to align with the interests, tastes, and motivation of a consumer to be effective in any setting (Larson, McKinley, & Boley, 1993; Nelson, 1992; Singer & Bashir, 1999; Larson & McKinley, 2003). Students age 13 and older frequently have well-defined interests and motivations (Apel & Swank, 1999). Their academic programs are typically departmentalized, including walking from class to class; working under several teachers; and increased personal responsibility for rules, regulations, homework, time schedules, and deadlines. They have more unscheduled time before and after school and are often exploring student groups, competitive athletics, clubs, service activities, and social time.

Apel and Swank (1999) reminded speech-language pathologists working with older students that "the self-concept and motivational level of these students must be recognized and addressed in their intervention program or success may be unattainable" (p. 239). Planning a service delivery program at middle and high schools must take these factors into account.

Adolescents with communication disabilities also experience related academic difficulties. Their language deficits may adversely affect their comprehension skills, attention, organization, and writing ability. Speech-language pathologists should recognize some of the unique characteristics of older students who have LANGUAGE DISORDERS as described by Larson and McKinley (1995b) in Table 6.8.

Table 6.8	\multicolumn{2}{c}{**Characteristic Problems of Older School-Age Students with Language Disorders**}
Category	**Expectations**	**Problems**
Cognition	To be at the formal operational level	They often remain concrete operational thinkers.
	To observe, organize, and categorize data from an experience	They make chaos out of order.
	To identify problems, suggest possible causes and solutions, and predict consequences	They may not recognize the problem when it exists; if they do, they do not know how to develop alternative solutions.
	To place concepts into hierarchical order	They often cannot place concepts in a hierarchy.
	To find, select, and utilize data on a given topic	They have limited strategies for finding, selecting, and utilizing data.
Metalinguistics	To demonstrate conscious awareness of linguistic knowledge	They have difficulty bringing to awareness categories and relations in all aspects of language.
	To talk about and reflect on various linguistic forms	They do not know the labels for talking about language during formal education.
	To assess communication breakdowns and revise them	They do not have awareness of breakdowns and, if they do, they lack repair strategies.
Comprehension and Production of Linguistic Features	To comprehend all linguistic features and structures	They misunderstand advanced syntactical forms.
	To follow oral directions of three steps or more after listening to them one time	They may not realize that they are being given directions and/or have difficulty following them.
	To use grammatically intact utterances	They often use sentences that are fragmented and that do not convey their messages.
	To have a vocabulary sufficient for expressing ideas and experiences	They have word-retrieval problems as well as a high frequency of low-information words.
	To give directions with clarity and accuracy	They often leave their listeners confused.
	To get information or assistance by asking questions and to respond appropriately to questions asked of them	They may know what questions or answers to give, but they do not know how to do so tactfully.
	To comprehend and produce the slang and jargon of the hour	They do not comprehend or produce slang/jargon, thus they are ostracized from the group to which they most desire to belong.

Continued

Table 6.8 – *Continued*

Category	Expectations	Problems
Discourse	To produce language that is organized, coherent, and intelligible to their listeners	They use many false starts and verbal mazes.
	To follow adult conversational rules for speakers	They consistently violate the rules (e.g., maintaining a topic, initiating a topic).
	To be effective listeners during conversation without displaying incorrect listening habits	They often have poor listening skills.
	To make a report, tell or retell a story, and explain a process in detail	They often leave their listeners confused.
	To listen to lectures and to select main ideas and supporting details	They often do not grasp the essential message of a lecture.
	To analyze critically other speakers	Their judgments are arbitrary, illogical, and impulsive.
	To express their own attitudes, moods, and feelings and to disagree appropriately	They have abrasive conversational speech.
Nonverbal Communication	To follow nonverbal rules for kinesics	They violate the rules and misinterpret body movements and facial expressions.
	To follow nonverbal rules for proxemics	They violate the rules for social distance.
Survival Language	To comprehend and produce situational phrases and vocabulary required for survival in our society	They do not have the necessary concepts and vocabulary needed in places such as banks, grocery stores, and employment agencies.
	To comprehend and produce concepts and vocabulary required across daily living situations	They do not have the necessary concepts and vocabulary needed across daily living situations such as telling time, using money, and understanding warning signs.
Written Language	To comprehend written language required in various academic, social, and vocational situations by organizing, planning, composing, and editing.	They do not consistently and/or efficiently process information obtained through reading.
	To produce cohesive written language required in various academic, social, and vocational situations	They do not consistently and/or efficiently generate written language that conveys their messages.

From *Language Disorders in Older Students* (pp. 78–79), by V. Lord Larson & N. McKinley, 1995b, Eau Claire, WI: Thinking Publications®. ©1995 by Thinking Publications. Reprinted with permission.

Academic-Centered Goals for Adolescents

Many students with communication disorders need continued assistance from speech-language pathologists and other special educators to be successful in upper grades. The TRANSITION process (i.e., preparation for postsecondary employment or education) for students with special education needs must be carefully planned and implemented. On average, a student age 13 or older who is receiving services has been in speech-language programs for several years. The goals and objectives have changed for the student, but he or she continues to need support to be successful and access the curriculum. There is a close connection between intervention and academic achievement in middle school, and by high school, therapy is often completely integrated into academic standards. In secondary schools, students are no longer learning underlying skills; instead, they must apply strategies to increase their comprehension, retain needed information, and produce acceptable written work. Spelling, constructing sentences, expanding vocabulary, developing and describing ideas, plus locating pertinent information and writing about it dominate the intervention process at this level (Graham & Harris, 1999). In addition, many students need assistance with pragmatics and social language to engage in the reciprocal friendships and working relationships so critical at the secondary level (Donahue, Syzmanski, & Flores, 1999).

Transition Plans

IDEA 2004 requires that for all students with disabilities, beginning at age 16 (or younger, if appropriate), an IEP include a statement about the transition service needs of a student that focuses on his or her course of study (34 C.F.R. § 300.320 [b][1]). Transition services is a coordinated set of activities that:

> "...is designed to be within a results-oriented process, that is focused on improving the academic and functional achievement of the child with a disability to facilitate the child's movement from school to post-school activities, including postsecondary education, vocational education, integrated employment (including supported employment), continuing and adult education, adult services, independent living, or community participation" (34 C.F.R. § 300.43 [a][1]).

INDIVIDUALIZED TRANSITION PLAN (ITP) development is often a part of an IEP process but may be a separate assessment and meeting in a given school or district. The purpose of an ITP is to begin planning for a student's integration into the world of work and independent living. For many students, communication skills are critical to be successful in a job situation. Speech-language pathologists may find themselves designing role-plays of job interviews or working collaboratively with job coaches to help students achieve ITP goals (Montgomery, 1997a).

Functional outcomes are the best tool for evaluating adolescent services. The model chosen by speech-language pathologists and school teams is appropriate if students learn to function at a higher level on meaningful school-based or quality-of-life indicators. In middle and high school, these indicators should be a part of an IEP and be observable beyond the speech room. Transition goals may help all educators focus on functional outcomes instead of limiting their focus to helping students earn credits for graduation. Older students can help keep track of their own progress in many secondary school environments (Montgomery, 1997a). Apel and Swank (1999) were convinced that programs for older students could be successful when speech-language pathologists were strongly committed to "second chances" (p. 231). Eger (as cited in Bland, 1999)—an audiologist, speech-language pathologist, and administrator in a large urban cooperative school district—offered the following summative statement:

> If we focus on outcomes or end products, our intervention strategies will be much more integrated into the rest of the child's educational program. For example, teaming and having the educational team, not the speech-language pathologist alone, set communication priorities for each student will be the routine. Success will be judged by how well the student communicates in class, in the lunchroom, on the playground, and at home, not in the therapy room (p. 10).

Making a Difference at the Secondary Level

Larson and McKinley (1995b) have presented educational, social, ethical, and fiscal arguments for providing services to adolescents in unique and meaningful ways. Reversing patterns of failure and refocusing previously undirected students toward finishing high school and pursuing career or job opportunities become important functional outcomes for adolescents

(Nelson, 1996). Students, with the assistance of speech-language pathologists and other IEP team members, can develop highly practical, personally motivating IEPs for themselves. IDEA 2004 lists students as members of IEP teams, if appropriate. The law requires that students be invited to IEP meetings whenever transition services are considered, and if students do not participate in meetings, the district must take other steps to ensure that students' preferences and interests are considered. It is hard to imagine how an effective IEP for an adolescent, transition-related or not, could be written without that student's input.

Some students with significant disabilities will continue to receive speech-language services in middle and high school if an IEP team agrees that improvement or progress is expected for a student within a year. Maintaining the student's functional level does not require intervention; it requires practice with the skill in an authentic setting. This type of practice may be carried out by other educators. All intervention should be directly tied to an observable improvement in the students' daily activities. An IEP for students in Grade 6 or above should include one or more of the following goals written in measurable terms:

- Increased literacy (i.e., reading, spelling, and writing) skills
- Increased social language skills
- More appropriate peer interactions
- Progress on a transition plan
- Progress toward a vocational goal
- Improved organization, attention, or study skills

- Progress toward emotional control and stability

- Greater independence or interdependence than the previous year

With greater emphasis on accountability for all students' success (IDEA, 2004; NCLB, 2001), secondary schools have focused on their disabilities subgroup to determine why many of these students are not graduating. One such obstacle to graduation has been written language skills (Montgomery & Kahn, 2005). Speech-language pathologists working with a team of secondary educators may instruct identified students to write both narrative and expository text to meet the grade level

standards needed for graduation (Montgomery & Kahn, 2007). This service may be effectively provided in pull-out or co-teaching settings.

Models That Match Students and School Settings

Selecting one or more service delivery models to encourage these important outcomes will depend on the factors presented in Chapter 5 plus the ages and interests of adolescents. Larson and McKinley present several models in Figure 6.4 that speech-language pathologists can use to structure service delivery at the secondary lev-

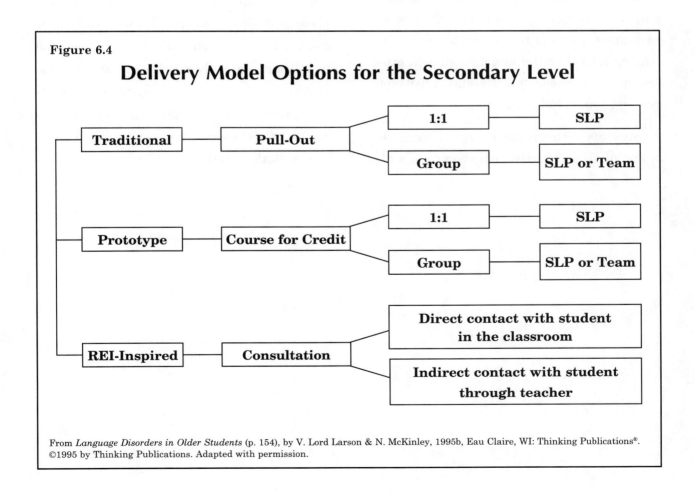

Figure 6.4

Delivery Model Options for the Secondary Level

From *Language Disorders in Older Students* (p. 154), by V. Lord Larson & N. McKinley, 1995b, Eau Claire, WI: Thinking Publications®. ©1995 by Thinking Publications. Adapted with permission.

el. Of these, the prototype model (i.e., offering speech-language service as a course for credit) is usually the most palatable to adolescents (Larson & McKinley, 1995b).

Older students are more likely to be grouped, seen for periods of time that mirror the academic schedule, and held accountable for their own progress. Many speech-language pathologists teach a class called Communication Skills, so that students can receive academic credit for working on IEP goals. Others arrange to award grades, so that student work can be figured into the grade-point average. A class must be approved by a school board for students to receive credit. Other speech-language pathologists report that co-teaching is the most effective way to support students in classes that have challenging subject matter and high student expectations (Creaghead, 1992; Hoskins, 1995; Montgomery, 1997a; Nelson, 1996).

Students with various types of special education needs will receive attention from a high school IEP team. Service delivery models will need to be changed from time to time during the school year to accommodate students' changing needs or to intervene, to avert, or to recover from a crisis situation (Sanger & Moore-Brown, 2000). Students who are fully included in high school may need speech-language pathologists' support. These students often fall into one of two categories: students with mild to moderate learning disabilities who require ongoing assistance to succeed or students with severe disabilities who require extensive supports—one-to-one aid, ASSISTIVE TECHNOLOGY, modified physical environment, and other communication skills—to flourish in a general education placement (Montgomery, 1997a; Wallach & Butler, 1994). Students who are fully included do not automatically require speech-language intervention; however, adequate communication skills often determine whether students are successful socially and academically (Wallach & Butler, 1994).

CHAPTER 7

Specialized Services

Public schools are committed to educating *all* students, many of whom bring unusual circumstances or needs with them. This chapter addresses students—both general and special education—who may need the services of speech-language pathologists.

Some individuals will be English learners, some will use assistive technology or augmentative and alternative communication, and still others may be infants or toddlers who were identified at birth with a hearing loss. Students with communication disorders may present characteristics on the autism spectrum. Some students must be temporarily educated at home or in hospitals, rehabilitation units, or detention facilities. Increasing numbers of these students with special needs are served in school-based programs, necessitating highly flexible service delivery models to accommodate their temporary location and/or unique needs. Speech-language pathologists must be prepared for expanded or specialized practice in the schools.

1. Describe the important elements of working with the families of students with communication disorders whose culture or language is different than the speech-language pathologist's. Contact a local school and ask how many different languages are spoken by their students. Find out how English learners are assured access to the general education curriculum. What does this school do to prevent English learners from being inappropriately referred for special education services?

2. Contact your state speech-language and hearing association and ask if they have a list of speech-language pathologists in the state who can assess and provide intervention in languages other than English. What languages are represented? How do speech-language pathologists qualify for this list?

3. Explain the difference between accent and dialect and how the speech-language pathologist can help other educators and administrators to differentiate both from communication disorders.

4. Why is it important to know the various definitions of autism spectrum disorders (ASDs) to provide the services parents and administrators request in the schools? What role does the speech-language pathologist's professional judgment play in the decision-making process?

5. Compare and contrast assistive technology (AT) and augmentative and alternative communication (AAC). Arrange to meet and converse with a student who uses a communication system as well as his or her speech-language pathologist.

6. Explain the universal newborn hearing screening (UNHS) mandated by law, and how it has an impact on the school service delivery programs for speech and language. Does your state have UNHS? Find out what hospitals in your area are doing to provide not only universal screening but also follow-up services for families. Interview an audiologist in the program if possible.

7. What are the educational rights of students who are serving time in prison during their school years? What impact does this have on the speech-language pathologist?

8. Locate a speech-language pathologist in the schools who has responsibilities as a lead speech-language pathologist. Interview this person about the advantages and disadvantages of this type of service delivery. Examine his or her weekly and monthly schedule to appreciate the increased and varied responsibilities.

Students Who Are Culturally/Linguistically Diverse (CLD)

Students whose culture or language differs from the mainstream English of public schools in this country are defined as CULTURALLY/ LINGUISTICALLY DIVERSE. Not all of these students are English learners (EL), however, over half of them are. When the culture of home and school are distinctly different, children may experience social and academic challenges. Students who are culturally diverse may be having academic issues (due to cultural or second language learning) that are impacting their mastery of the language needed to master curriculum. Speech-language pathologists must be vigilant in ensuring that their assessments and involvement with these students reflect cultural competence and sensitivity. Service delivery for students with identified communication disabilities who are culturally/linguistically diverse (CLD) has five distinct aspects: (1) using non-biased assessment, (2) selecting the language of instruction—including special factors to consider from the INDIVIDUALS WITH DISABILITIES EDUCATION IMPROVEMENT ACT (IDEA) 2004, (3) using interpreters in intervention, (4) being aware of accents and dialects, and (5) working with families who are culturally/linguistically different from the speech-language pathologist. (See also "Disproportionality," Chapter 3.)

The number of students who are English learners (EL) more than doubled between 1979 (6 million) and 1999 (14 million). It is estimated that by the year 2020, more than 40 percent of the students in public schools will come from a home whose primary language is other than English (August & Shanahan, 2006). These students represent the fastest growing population in our nation, and some of them will need special education, including speech-language services. Special education referrals of students who are English learners have been reported to be inappropriately high in some parts of the country (Ortiz & Yates, 2002; August & Shanahan, 2006; IDEA 2004). Students learning English frequently struggle with academics until their English language skills are more highly developed. (See the discussion on the increase in diverse populations in schools under "Children and Families in the Twenty-First Century" in Chapter 1 and "English Learners" in Chapter 10). Prevention of school failure and early intervention for English learners is the key to reducing the number of students who are inappropriately referred for special education. Ortiz and Yates (2002) identify three types of English learners: Type I need positive school climate, academically enriched curriculum, and effective instruction in the general education program. Type II need early intervening, clinical teaching, and teacher assistance teams to prosper. Type III students need culturally sensitive assessment, family involvement, and special education.

For over three decades, speech-language pathologists and audiologists have believed: "Multicultural research and continued development of techniques and materials for assessment and intervention need to be priorities of professionals who provide services to these populations" (American Speech-Language-Hearing Association [ASHA], 1985, p. 32). These needs are ongo-

Making a Difference
for America's Children

ing. To serve the needs of children who are CLD and have communication disabilities, approaches to assessment and intervention must incorporate culturally sensitive approaches (Quinn, Goldstein, & Peña, 1996; Roseberry-McKibbin, 2007). A sample of approximately 4,500 ASHA constituents responded to the 2001 Omnibus Survey, indicating the percentage of students on their caseloads in ethnic and racial categories (see Table 7.1).

In the 2006 ASHA School Survey, 54 percent of the respondents reported that services were provided in English to English learners on their caseloads. In a nationwide sample, almost a third of the children served in speech-language programs were CLD, not in just a few border states as once thought (ASHA, 2006a).

How to best serve students who struggle is an ongoing theme in schools under NCLB and

Table 7.1	**ASHA Survey Results**		
	Questions Related to Students' Race or Ethnicity		

Approximately what is the percentage of individuals in your typical monthly caseload who are in each of the following ethnic categories?

Total (n = 350)	CCC-SLP (n = 159)	CCC-A (n = 121)	Ethnicity
12.9	13.1	13.3	Hispanic or Latino
80.8	80.8	79.2	Not Hispanic or Latino
6.3	6.1	7.6	Don't Know

Approximately what is the percentage of individuals in your typical monthly caseload who are in each of the following racial categories?

Total (n = 289)	CCC-SLP (n = 133)	CCC-A (n = 102)	Race
1.2	1.1	1.3	American Indian or Alaskan Native
1.7	1.5	3.5	Asian
20.0	20.9	14.2	Black or African American
0.5	0.4	0.9	Native Hawaiian or Other Pacific Islander
73.3	73.2	74.9	White
3.7	3.3	6.1	Don't Know

From *2001 Omnibus Survey Results*, ASHA (2001). Reprinted with permission.

#TP-29703 Making a Difference - 2nd Ed. • ©2008 Thinking Publications® • www.thinkingpublications.com • 1-800-277-8737

IDEA 2004. Students from diverse cultural and linguistic backgrounds pose significant challenges for schools that do not have the capacity or personnel to appropriately address this population (McLaughlin, Pullin, & Artiles). Because of the specific knowledge in language development and disorders that speech-language pathologists have, their role will be important to ensure that speech-language pathologists, along with other leaders in the school, serve English learners with disabilities appropriately (Thurlow, Barrea, & Zamora-Duran, 2006). This means that all educators, and especially those addressing language needs, must understand current research and thinking in the field in these matters.

One area of emerging research pertains to the linguistic development of second language learners. Thordardottier (2006) reminds us that growing up bilingual is normal and positive, and should not be treated as a problem. Research on bilingual language development is consistently demonstrating that bilingualism facilitates language development and vocabulary growth. Recommended intervention approaches, therefore, should promote the use of both languages, and not be limited to one language. Similarly, code-switching (going back and forth between languages) is also typical in bilingual speakers and should not be discouraged. Code-switching, in fact, should be considered an emerging skill, because it occurs so frequently in the general bilingual population (Thordardottir, 2006).

Research in reading and language impairment is also gaining information from studying English learners. In the past, much of the research in reading and English learners has focused on phonological awareness, but research now points to how language development, the definition of language impairment, and reading all impact normal language and the development of disorders in reading. More importantly, the research provides new guidance in facilitating rather than harming through the therapeutic approaches chosen (Silliman & Scott, 2006a; Gerber & Durgunoglu, 2004; McCardle, Mele-McCarthy, Cutting, & Leos, & D'Emilio, 2005; August and Shanahan, 2006).

IDEA 2004 is highly concerned with appropriate services to minority students and students who are English learners (EL). Because of the tracking of the EL subgroup and the Disability Subgroup under No Child Left Behind (NCLB), academic achievement is paramount. However, what this really means is that implementing the current evidence base in the field is imperative in order to achieve the greatest success for the student.

Nonbiased Assessment

While it is beyond the scope of this chapter to discuss formal and informal assessment tools, important general principles are listed:

1. English learners should be assessed in both English and their native language.

2. Whenever possible, equivalent procedures and instruments should be administered in English and the student's native language.

3. Establish the student's level of English proficiency and amount of English instruction the student receives in academic settings.

4. Use valid and reliable instruments with culturally and linguistically appropriate sample procedures to establish their norms.

5. Seek alternative assessments of academic and language skills.

6. Use language assessment data (oral and written) that is no more than six months old.

7. Obtain culturally and linguistically sensitive assessment of intelligence and achievement.

8. A team of professionals must rule out all factors that may appear to be causing the students' learning difficulties (Ortiz & Yates, 2002).

Comprehensive school reform is needed to assure that students in the process of learning English are not placed in special education if what they actually need is support in the general education classroom to be academically successful. Policies, programs, and practices need to be dramatically adjusted in many schools to assure that speech-language disabilities are not declared in order to provide students with English instruction.

Choosing the Language of Instruction

When choosing the language of instruction and service delivery for a child, the IEP team must consider where on the continuum the student's language skills are within both his or her primary language and English. Speech-language pathologists play a role in this decision for the team and must consider the student's pragmatic, social, or interpersonal communication skills instead of the structural accuracy of the language. The key is to distinguish between errors made because of lack of exposure to the curriculum and insufficient opportunity to master the language. Although English may be the language of instruction in the school, the child may have more advanced skills in a primary language used for social interaction. This would suggest that the home language should be used for instruction initially or concurrently.

Consideration of special factors is necessary for the assessment, eligibility, and IEP phases of the special education process. A communication limitation can make it very difficult to determine if a student is struggling primarily with learning a second language or has one or more disabilities. Once eligibility is determined, the speech-language pathologist may work with the student because of communication disabilities related to a disorder or condition. Selecting the language for service delivery cannot be based on the skills the speech-language pathologist possesses, but rather on the skills the student needs, and in which language. Suggestions from Ortiz and Garcia (1988) to determine language proficiency were used to create these questions that may guide the IEP team in their decision making:

- What is the student's dominant language in various settings?

- What is the student's level of proficiency in both the primary language and English for social and academic language?

- What are the styles of verbal interaction used in the primary language and English?

- How much exposure has this student had to styles of verbal interaction in English?

- What is the extent and nature of exposure in each language (e.g., family, peers, TV, stories, etc.)?

- Are the student's language behaviors characteristic of second language learners?

- What types of language intervention has this student already had and for how long?

"The literature in bilingual education of the last two decades suggests that children who are learning two languages may benefit from a bilingual approach in intervention" (Gutierrez-Clellen, 1999, p. 299). Gutierrez-Clellen (1999)

> Service delivery for students who are CLD must be grounded on what they need for academic success.

emphasized that no studies were able to show that English-only was a preferable intervention approach for students with communication disabilities. She stated that achievement and performance were maximized when the student's first language was used as an organizational framework. In addition, speech-language pathologists need to help students identified with special needs learn pragmatic and social-cultural aspects of language (e.g., eye contact, facial expression, nonverbal messages, and tone) that will enable them to participate in the activities of the classroom (Cheng, 1999; Fung & Roseberry-McKibbin, 1999). Service delivery for children who are CLD must take the form of multidimensional, interspersing sessions in the therapy room, in the classroom, and in small interactive groups that encourage conversation (Battle, 1998). The speech-language pathologist will need to move easily from one setting to another to encourage the adaptation necessary to fit into the dominant culture (Brice, 1993).

Using Interpreters and Translators in Intervention

When the child's primary language is not English, speech-language pathologists must either speak the child's language or use an interpreter/translator. (Note: *Interpretation* refers to oral language and *translation* refers to written language.) Less than 4 percent of the professionals belonging to ASHA report speaking a language in addition to English (ASHA, 1999c). Some states have many more bilingual speech-language pathologists than others. In some large states and some border states (e.g., Florida, Texas, California, and New York), bilingual speech-language pathologists are in great demand and can command salary bonuses, previously unheard of in most school settings.

Using an interpreter/translator is the method of choice for those who are not fluent enough to provide therapy in both languages (ASHA, 1999c; Langdon, 1999). Langdon (1999) and others have pointed out both the cautions and the value of working with interpreters and translators when serving students. A resource titled *Collaborating with Interpreters and Translators* (Langdon & Cheng, 2002) describes effective service delivery and gives guidance specific to the speech-language pathology field.

Accents and Dialects

Accents and dialects, used both by speech-language pathologists and by students who speak languages in addition to English, have been controversial in the field of speech-language pathology. Although bilingual or multilingual speech-language pathologists have been in great demand in this country, many of them have reported facing bias in graduate education programs and in the job market (Montgomery, 1999a). Public school students with accents or dialects that are different from that of the mainstream culture of their school have been referred for special education services, speech services, or viewed as low achievers (Roseberry-McKibbin & Eicholtz, 1994). In the late 1990s, an effort to dispel these misguided concerns and avoid potential discriminatory behaviors resulted in a position statement and supporting technical report entitled *Students and Professionals Who Speak English with Accents and Nonstandard Dialects: Issues and Recommendations* (ASHA, 1998c). In this statement, accent was defined as a phonetic trait from one's first language that was carried over to one's second language (Wolfram, 1991). The listener can hear some of the patterns of sound production found in the person's first spoken language that are not in the second language. Persons who use English as their second (or third or fourth) language may have accented English, depending on their age and the circumstances under which they learned English.

Dialect was defined as a set of differences, wherever they may occur, that make one English speaker's speech different from another's (Wolfram & Fasold, 1974). Each dialect has distinguishing linguistic characteristics (phonological, morphological, semantic, syntactic, and pragmatic), although the majority of linguistic features of the (American) English language are common to each of the varieties of (American) English (Montgomery, 1999a).

The concluding statement of ASHA's (1998c) position statement issues a clear directive:

All individuals speak with an accent and/or dialect; thus, the nonacceptance of individuals into higher education programs or into the professions solely on the basis of the presence of an accent or dialect is discriminatory. Members of ASHA must not discriminate against persons who speak with an accent and/or dialect in educational programs, employment, or

service delivery, and should encourage an understanding of linguistic differences among consumers and the general population (p. 28).

Speech-language pathologists working in the schools must recognize that "no dialectal variety of English is a disorder or pathological form of speech or language. Each social dialect is adequate as a functional and effective variety of English" (Cole, 1983, p. 25).

Dialects and accents are often called language varieties to emphasize that they are accepted differences in speech (Cole, 1983). The educational, emotional, political, and economic controversies related to these language varieties continue in many settings. Service delivery for students who are CLD must be grounded on what they need for academic success, not on accent or dialect differences falsely perceived as disabilities. School-based speech-language

pathologists must provide appropriate service delivery options for these students along with information for colleagues and families. Reasoned judgments based on current research should guide decision making and service delivery. Speech-language pathologists must model respect for the children who offer the richness and variety of their accented speech.

Working With Families

Families are often the basic social unit for students who are CLD, and they should be included in the context of the child's intervention program as much as possible for best results (Roseberry-McKibbin, 2007; Wyatt, 1999). For example, according to Seymour, Bland-Stewart, and Green (1998), determining difference versus deficit in children's use of African-American English is more accurate, and more appropriately treated, when there is family contact. Including the family in the intervention process shows respect, increases carryover, and knits the school and community together in the same cause.

Family literacy is a common school-related activity for children, parents, and extended families. The read-aloud aspect of family literacy has considerable appeal and effectiveness for families that are CLD. The speech-language pathologist may consider taking an active part in organizing such communication-related programs as Family Reading Night, Grandparents Read-Aloud Program, or Everybody Read Together. These activities are especially meaningful to families, encourage respect, and are extensions of the collaborative service delivery process described in Chapter 6.

Roseberry-McKibbin (2007, 2008b) offers specific ways to include multiculturalism into speech and language intervention when the practitioner does not speak the student's native or dominant language. A few examples include the following: showing interest in the student's home country, language, and culture; learning and using a few words of the student's first language.

Infants and Toddlers

IDEA 2004 and state special education programs provide intervention for identified infants and toddlers in collaboration with developmental disability services, mental health agencies, or similar health-care entities. Programs for infants and toddlers in schools are covered in Part C of IDEA 2004, which attempts to link families, communities, and schools with a program for children birth to 3 that is qualitatively different than Part B. Section 631 describes an urgent and substantial need:

1. To enhance the development of infants and toddlers with disabilities and to minimize their potential for developmental delay.

2. To reduce the educational costs to our society…by minimizing the need for special education and related services after infants and toddlers with disabilities reach school age.

3. To minimize the likelihood of institutionalization…

4. To enhance the capacity of families to meet the special needs of their infants and toddlers with disabilities.

5. To enhance the capacity of State and local agencies and service providers to identify, evaluate, and meet the needs of historically underrepresented populations, particularly minority, low-income, inner-city, and rural populations.

Each state must have a statewide system for services to infants and toddlers which meets all the requirements of Section 635 of IDEA 2004. Each state has developed systems with different kinds and numbers of agencies involved, their own guidelines, and service delivery that matches that state's infrastructure. They all share the concept of the individualized family service plan (IFSP) in place of the IEP for children under age 3. An IFSP may be also used for children ages 3 through 5 if agreed to by the family and school. (See Chapter 6, "Individual Family Service Plans [IFSPs].")

Settings for Infant and Toddler Programs

One of the qualitatively different aspects of serving infants and toddlers is the setting; they are typically served in their homes or day-care settings. Speech-language pathologists and other specialists work directly with families in these settings, showing them methods to encourage speech and language development and coaching families as they work with their infants.

To be effective, speech-language pathologists need special training to work with infants, toddlers, and families. This training is available from some graduate education programs, many state personnel development grants, some employers, and every major annual state speech-language association conference or ASHA convention. Journals that focus on the communication needs of infants and toddlers are available (e.g., The National Association for the Education of Young Children publishes *Young Children and the Council for Exceptional Children*, Division for Early Childhood publishes *Journal of Early Intervention and Young Exceptional Children*), as are videotaped continuing education courses and teleconferences offered by experts in the field.

Speech-language pathologists must work closely with medical staff, counselors, other therapists, and families when infants have multiple health and medical needs in the first two years of life. This is facilitated in center-based rather than home-based programs. While some school districts hire speech-language pathologists for these positions, others contract with county agencies, state Early Start or Even Start programs, or university clinical programs. Due to fewer families and reduced resources overall, smaller districts often assign the speech-language pathologists at K–12 schools responsibility for the infants and toddlers in their own communities. Although not ideal, this arrangement is financially feasible and helps prepare the school staff for some children's needs years before the children enter school.

If babies are served in a center, the family members, who must come with them for training, support one another, and get new ideas from professionals. Direct therapy with a baby for prespeech development is highly unusual

> Direct therapy with a baby for prespeech development is highly unusual and not considered a preferred practice pattern.

and not considered a PREFERRED PRACTICE PATTERN. ASHA has many documents and publications to assist the speech-language pathologist with family-focused therapy (ASHA, 1990, 1997a).

Unique Aspects of Infant Programs

A program conducted in an infant's home with the family is the most common service delivery model (U.S. Department of Education [USDE], 2005d). Speech-language pathologists travel to the home weekly or monthly, often followed up by an assistant or support person for a later visit. The family is taught communication support techniques and encouraged to integrate them into their daily routines. The speech-language pathologist has the responsibility to be culturally competent, recognize and appreciate the child-rearing approaches the family uses, include all the relevant family members, and not present knowledge or techniques that may offend care providers or make them feel uncomfortable (ASHA, 1991b, 1997a; Paul, 2001).

When assessing infants, readiness for communication is first considered, including the concept of reciprocity, which will indicate whether the child is ready for communicative interaction. Additionally, the speech-language pathologist will need to assess parent communication and family functioning (Paul, 2001). The speech-language pathologist recognizes that the child is a product of how the parents have raised him or her, and the way the baby has influenced the parents. It is a constant give-and-take relationship. Each time that parents interact with babies, the baby learns; babies in turn shape parent responses. The speech-language pathologist goes into the home to help the baby develop communication skills with the parents, but also to help the parents develop a communication system with their child. Each must change and react to the other. Lewis (1984) outlined the following typical Infant Development Principles used to reach this goal:

1. Infants are active—They participate in their own development and act on their own environment. As early as 10 weeks, infants show interest and increased activity when their movements cause audio-visual stimuli to occur.

2. Infants are competent—Babies come well equipped. They are able to see, hear, smell, and respond to touch. They are very ca-

pable of signaling their caregivers through crying to provide them what they want.

3. Infants are social—Babies come with systems in place for carrying out interaction. At birth, their visual acuity is greatest at 8½ inches, which allows them to focus on a parent's face when feeding. They prefer the configuration of a face over random figures, and they prefer the higher pitch of a female voice.

Assessment of Infants and Toddlers

Speech-language pathologists and audiologists use vastly different measures to assess for communication delays in infants and toddlers compared to school-age or even preschool children. There are a few standardized tests, but most are rating scales, family inventories, structured observations, caregiver reports, and medical histories (Sparks, Clark, Erickson, & Oas, 1990; Paul, 2001). In the hands of competent and experienced speech-language pathologists, these are fine tools. The speech-language pathologist who has not worked extensively with infants, toddlers, and families, who has not taken appropriate coursework, or who has not been mentored by an experienced professional team is advised to seek out the many excellent resources in the communication field (e.g., Paul, 2001; Woods & Weatherby, 2003; Crais, 2000; Retherford, 1996; Rosetti, 1993;

Wetherby & Prizant, 1992; Wilcox, 1997) before performing assessments. They should also be guided by ASHA's (2004) Preferred Practice Patterns for assessment.

Increasingly, assessment of infants and toddlers is conducted through arena assessment using a dynamic assessment approach (see Chapter 3, "Dynamic Assessment"). One of the primary assessment measures for this population is to find the category of risk for a condition evident at birth, as listed in the sidebar on p. 276. Assessment might begin at any of these risk categories, and may or may not lead to a diagnosis of a disability that requires special education support from the speech-language pathologist. The condition of at-risk does not immediately translate into identification or services (Sparks et al., 1990).

Whenever intervention is planned for babies and young children, the speech-language pathologist will be working closely with a variety of individuals who care for and are a part of the child's life besides the parents. Those involved in a child's care, and therefore the intervention plan, can include grandparents, aunts, uncles, siblings, partners of parents, babysitters, nannies, and neighbors. Any one of these individuals may serve as the caregiver in a center-based program or participate in the assessment or intervention activity. They must all be taught to facilitate the child's development. Rather than being frustrated or annoyed at having many different family members involved, the speech-language pathologist should appreciate the richness that many care providers can bring to the child's program.

Impact of Universal Newborn Hearing Screening on Infant and Toddler Programs

Screening of babies at birth is a long established method of identifying risk conditions as soon as possible, which allows medical or other intervention to begin before the baby starts to develop. Disabilities that would have materialized later can be prevented at birth. Infants have been screened for PKU, Tay-Sach's disease, and Rh incompatibility for many years. Hearing loss has typically not been discovered until age 2½ to 3 years, an age when auditory behavioral testing was more dependable. This has meant that hearing loss in babies could go undetected during the critical first years of their lives (Herer & Glattke, 2000; Smith Lang, 2000).

This wait-and-see situation changed dramatically in 1997 when the National Joint Committee on Infant Hearing in conjunction with the National Institutes of Health Consensus Panel agreed that all newborns in this country should have their hearing screened before they leave the hospital. Now, screening a baby's hearing can occur as early as nine hours after birth (Herer & Glattke, 2000). Relatively new technology, called otoacoustic emissions (OAE), has allowed sleeping babies to be tested in about three minutes using a small ear probe to record the "echo" of the cochlea's response on a computer. The OAE procedure is often used in newborn hearing screening programs in conjunction with a screening version of auditory brainstem response technology. Data from seven years of screening indicate that these technologies are reliable, relatively inexpensive, and can identify babies with hearing loss at birth (Herer, 2007).

Categories of Risk for Communication Disorders in Newborns and Infants

Conditions of established risk:

1. Chromosomal disorders, Fragile X, Down syndrome
2. Single gene disorders—Hunter/Hurler syndrome, Tay-Sachs disease
3. Environmental disorders—fetal alcohol syndrome, AIDS

Conditions of unknown expectations of risk:

1. Congenital hearing loss
2. Cerebral palsy
3. Neural tube defects
4. Clefting

Conditions that may result in a disability:

1. Anoxia
2. Maternal infections—syphilis, rubella, herpes
3. Maternal diabetes
4. Blood group incompatibility
5. Maternal alcohol and drug ingestion
6. Lack of prenatal care
7. Prematurity
8. Low birth weight
9. Respiratory distress syndrome
10. Hyperbilirubinemia
11. Anesthetic intoxication
12. Neonatal medications
13. Acute or chronic disease of the central nervous system
14. Failure to thrive
15. Otitis media
16. Seizures
17. Head injury, accidents, abuse
18. Neglect
19. Iatrogenic disorder
20. Exposure to toxic agents

Conditions of care-giving that have implications for disorders:

1. Mentally, physically or drug-impaired parenting
2. Mother under 19 years old
3. Parents with very little education
4. Parents who have experienced recent loss of infant or loved one
5. Parents with low self-esteem
6. Parents with unrealistic expectations for an infant
7. Parents who abuse or neglect
8. Parents who did not want the pregnancy
9. Single parent without a support system
10. Parents experiencing grief for an existing risk condition
11. Poverty
12. High stress
13. Separation of parents from infant

Source: Sparks et al. (1990)

#TP-29703 Making a Difference - 2nd Ed. • ©2008 Thinking Publications® • www.thinkingpublications.com • 1-800-277-8737

Infant hearing screening has a profound effect on families, early intervention programs, and school-based infant and toddler programs. Speech-language pathologists must develop the skills to work with 3-month-old babies using hearing aids, teach parents multiple communication systems, and help parents choose educational interventions for their child during the critical early years when speech and language skills are acquired. Early intervention services play a unique role supporting families during a child's first three years. Hopefully, the child will not have to catch up or receive services later. There is great potential for these children to be in fully inclusive settings, working at grade level with appropriate supports by the time they enter the school system (Herer & Glattke, 2000). Prevention is the essence of IDEA 2004 philosophy. Communication disorders may be one of the first disciplines to demonstrate the value of preventive intervention.

A universal newborn hearing screening (UNHS) program, designed and supervised by an audiologist, is implemented by trained technicians in a birthing hospital. Protocols for universal programs do not screen only at-risk babies or those with familial histories of deafness or hearing loss. Rather a UNHS program screens all newborns. Babies who are not screened face the potential of reduced auditory input as their speech, language, and cognition develop (Herer, Knightly, & Steinberg, 2007).

Herer (2007) reports results based on 47,920 newborns tested in a UNHS program from 1997 to 2004. He shows that: (1) the prevalence rate for hearing loss in newborns from the Well-Baby Nursery is 1.8 per 1000, but significantly greater, 7.4 per 1000, for those in the Newborn Intensive Care Unit (NICU); (2) babies with conductive hearing losses can also be identified early for medical interventions; (3) almost half of the babies identified with a hearing loss, 47.7 percent, did not have risk factors and would not have been reported to a High Risk Registry, and (4) if only infants from the NICU had been screened, as some have suggested, 72 percent of the babies with hearing loss born during the seven years of the study would have been missed. (See Table 7.2 on p. 278 for more information.)

The impact on services that speech-language pathologists provide in school districts has just begun. Audiologists and speech-language pathologists work with their school districts to develop appropriate IFSPs for toddlers who were identified at birth with moderate to severe sensorineural hearing losses. Many of these babies use hearing aids, and are developing speech and language skills within normal limits. The toddlers use hearing aids, attend typical preschools, and receive family-centered therapy from their local school districts. There are great changes ahead in these programs as audiologists and speech-language pathologists work closely with families of infants and toddlers with hearing loss identified at birth. Functional outcome data have confirmed that evaluation requires a number of different strategies to examine impact, outcome, and the overall effectiveness of early intervention (Mullen, 2000). Sometimes changes in babies can be measured. Effectiveness is often judged most authentically by families, the consumers of services for infants and toddlers. Perhaps the most cogent source of evaluation is family satisfaction with the program. If families

Table 7.2	Prevalence Rates of Hearing Loss for 47,920 Newborns 1997–2004	
Overall Rates		
Well-Baby Nursery	80 of 43,749 Newborns, 1.8 per 1000	
NICU*	31 of 4171 Babies, 7.4 per 1000	
Rates by Type of Hearing Loss	**WBN**	**NICU**
Bilateral Sensorineural	.731 per 1000	2.158 per 1000
Bilateral Conductive	.343	1.918
Unilateral Sensorineural	.503	1.678
Unilateral Conductive	.251	1.678
Total Incidence Rate	1.828	7.432

*Newborn Intensive Care Unit

Source: Herer & Glattke (2007). Reprinted with permission.

feel that they have been supported in their efforts to provide the best possible environment for child development, the program has had a positive impact (Donahue-Kilburg, 1992, p. 273).

Children With Autism Spectrum Disorders (ASDs)

One of the most challenging areas of school-based speech-language service delivery is meeting the needs of students identified with AUTISM SPECTRUM DISORDERS (ASDs). The awareness of ASDs as an educational problem has skyrocketed in recent years, with research indicating that it is being diagnosed in 1 in 500 children (Centers for Disease Control, 2007). Communication is a primary issue for children with ASDs and speech-language pathologists play a prominent role in programming in school and home. School districts in every state have added comprehensive professional development courses for their special education staff, and many districts have identified and trained speech-language pathologists and other team members as experts in the area. Most school districts have comprehensive programming for children with ASDs, including services that are unique to this population.

The focus on services and specialized programming for children with ASDs has dominated special education services since the mid-1990s. Specialized services vary from placements in private or state-administered schools, to 40-hour-a-week intensive behavior modification discrete trial training sessions, to general education placements with pull-out sessions with the speech-language pathologist, to full inclusion programs with one-to-one aide support in the general education classroom (Winner, 2006). Perhaps educational and therapeutic programming for children with ASDs is so diverse because ASDs are so diverse, presenting in so many different forms and degrees of ability.

The National Research Council's (2001) report addresses the question of what are considered appropriate educational services for young children with ASDs:

> At the root of questions about the most appropriate educational interventions for autistic spectrum disorders are differences in assumptions about what is possible and what is important to give students with these disorders through education. The appropriate goals for educational services for children with autistic spectrum disorders are the same as those for other children: personal independence and social responsibility. These goals imply progress in social and cognitive abilities, verbal and nonverbal communication skills, and adaptive skills, reduction of behavioral difficulties, and generalization of abilities across multiple environments (p. 5).

Speech-language pathologists need to be well informed on this topic through coursework, independent study, reading recent literature, and experience working with children who present with ASDs. Wetherby (2000) has stressed the great need to examine the efficacy of interventions being used across the nation. Speech-language pathologists and their multidisciplinary colleagues in school programs are expected to be well versed in several methodologies specific to this population and to know what combination of services are best for a child and then make continual adjustments for age and progress (Greenspan & Wieder, 1999; National Research Council, 2001; Bevilacqua & Norlin, 2004; Diehl, 2003). Speech-language pathologists in the schools must be well acquainted with ASDs and the wide range of service delivery options that schools and parents request. In a school-based intervention program, a comprehensive approach to treatment is expected. Approaches that are both developmental and behavioral will intersect to build a program that will provide functional, developmental, behavioral, and academic improvement.

Defining Autism Spectrum Disorders

ASDs have been defined several ways in medical and educational literature. Definitions and the perceived nature of a disability may affect how services are delivered in schools. For the purposes of this book, three definitions will be briefly examined: the mental health/psychology definition from the *Diagnostic and Statistical Manual of Mental Disorders,* Fourth Edition, Text Revision (DSM-IV–TR, 2000), the classic definition from the Autism Society of America (2007), and the definition according to IDEA 2004.

ASDs are defined in section 299.00 of the *Diagnostic and Statistical Manual of Mental Disorders* (2000) as:

A. A total of six (or more) items from (1), (2) and (3), with at least two from (1), and one each from (2) and (3):

(1) qualitative impairment in social interaction, as manifested by at least two of the following:

(a) marked impairment in the use of multiple nonverbal behaviors such as eye-to-eye gaze, facial expression, body postures, and gestures to regulate social interaction

(b) failure to develop peer relationships appropriate to developmental level

(c) a lack of spontaneous seeking to share enjoyment, interests, or achievements with other people (e.g., by a lack of showing, bringing, or pointing out objects of interest)

(d) lack of social or emotional reciprocity

(2) qualitative impairments in communication as manifested by at least one of the following:

(a) delay in, or total lack of, the development of spoken language (not accompanied by an attempt to compensate through alternative modes of communication such as gesture or mime)

(b) in individuals with adequate speech, marked impairment in the ability to initiate or sustain a conversation with others

(c) stereotyped and repetitive use of language or idiosyncratic language

(d) lack of varied, spontaneous make-believe play or social imitative play appropriate to developmental level

(3) restricted repetitive and stereotyped patterns of behavior, interests, and activities, as manifested by at least one of the following:

(a) encompassing preoccupation with one or more stereotyped and restricted patterns of interest that is abnormal either in intensity or focus

(b) apparently inflexible adherence to specific, nonfunctional routines or rituals

(c) stereotyped and repetitive motor mannerisms (e.g., hand or finger flapping or twisting, or complex whole-body movements)

(d) persistent preoccupation with parts of objects

B. Delays or abnormal functioning in at least one of the following areas, with onset prior to age 3 years: (1) social interaction, (2) language as used in social communication, (3) symbolic or imaginative play.

C. The disturbance is not better accounted for by Rett's Disorder or Childhood Disintegrative Disorder.

The Autism Society of America (2007) defines autism in the following way:

Autism is a complex developmental disability that typically appears during the first three years of life and is the result of a neurological disorder that affects the normal functioning of the brain, impacting development in the areas of social interaction and communication skills. Both children and adults with autism typically show difficulties in verbal and non-verbal communication, social interactions, and leisure or play activities. One should keep in mind however, that autism is a spectrum disorder and it affects each individual differently and at varying degrees—this is why early diagnosis is so crucial. By learning the signs, a child can begin benefiting from one of the many specialized intervention programs (¶ 1).

Autism is one of five disorders that falls under the umbrella of Pervasive Developmental Disorders (PDDs), a category of neurological disorders characterized by "severe and pervasive impairment in several areas of development."

The five disorders under PDDs are:

- Autistic Disorder

- Asperger's Disorder

- Childhood Disintegrative Disorder (CDD)

- Rett's Disorder

- PDD-Not Otherwise Specified (PDD-NOS)

Each of these disorders has specific diagnostic criteria which been outlined in the *American Psychiatric Association's Diagnostic & Statistical Manual of Mental Disorders* (APA, 2000).

The term *spectrum,* used in the context of autistic spectrum disorders, suggests a range of related qualities or activities. The same term used in reference to pervasive developmental disorders (PDDs) means that each specific PDD disorder, although different, shares some related chararcteristics. ASDs are a class of related developmental disorders that overlap but are clinically distinct and separately diagnosed. It is generally conceded that autistic disorders (AD), or classic autism, is the prototypical and most severe form of any of the ASDs. With careful assessment, PDDs can be differentially diagnosed (APA, 2000).

The IDEA 2004 definition (34 C.F.R. § 300.8) is as follows:

(c)(1)(i) Autism means a developmental disability significantly affecting verbal and nonverbal communication and social interaction, generally evident before age three, that adversely affects a child's educational performance. Other characteristics often associated with autism are engagement in repetitive activities and stereotyped movements, resistance to environmental change or change in daily routines, and unusual responses to sensory experiences.

(ii) Autism does not apply if a child's educational performance is adversely affected primarily because the child has an emotional disturbance, as defined in paragraph (c)(4) of this section.

(iii) A child who manifests the characteristics of "autism" after age three could be diagnosed as having autism if the criteria in paragraph (c)(1)(i) of this section are satisfied.

The National Research Council (2001) suggests:

"Autism is a developmental disorder of neurobiological origin that is defined on the basis of behavioral and developmental features...Autism is best characterized as a spectrum of disorders that vary in severity of symptoms, age of onset, and associations with other disorders (e.g., mental retardation, specific language delay, epilepsy) (p. 11). Within the definitions and description of autism, the "verbal and nonverbal communication are considered a core deficit in the diagnostic criteria for autism spectrum disorders" (p. 48).

Assessment of ASDs

Assessment of children with ASDs requires a highly skilled multidisciplinary team due to the complexities and pervasiveness of the condition (National Research Council, 2001; Prelock, Beatson, Bitner, Broder, & Drucker, 2003). The National Research Council (2001) indicates: "Difficulties in communication are a central feature of autism, and they interact in complex ways with social deficits and restricted patterns of behavior and interests in a given individual. Accurate assessment and understanding of levels of communicative functioning is critical for effective program planning and intervention" (p. 29). The following recommendations are made in terms of communication assessment:

- Communication skills should be viewed in the broad context of overall development and documented in a natural context.

- Standardized tests should constitute only one component of the assessment.

- Language comprehension skills are important to determine in addition to expressive skills; communicative intent and the functions of delayed and immediate echolalia, if present, should be noted.

- Oral motor difficulties should be noted.

- Checklists and parent interviews can be used (National Research Council, 2001).

Prelock (2001) offers:

The diagnostic parameters that are particularly relevant to speech-language pathologists and audiologists include:

- examination of family prevalence and patterns of decreased cognitive skills, specifically verbal and adaptive function.

- observation of verbal and nonverbal communication, and specific deficits in speech and language.

ASHA (2006h) defines the roles and responsibilities of speech-language pathologists in diagnosis, assessment, and treatment of ASDs, indicating that in both assessment and intervention:

Embracing a broad view of communication, speech-language pathologists should assess and enhance the following:

- The initiation of spontaneous communication in functional activities across social partners and settings.

- The comprehension of verbal and nonverbal communication in social, academic, and community settings.

- Communication for a range of social functions that are reciprocal and promote the development of friendships and social networks.

- Verbal and nonverbal means of communication, including natural gestures, speech, signs, pictures, written words, functional alternatives to challenging behaviors, and other augmentative and alternative communication systems.

- Access to literacy and academic instruction and curricular, extracurricular, and vocational activities (p. 7).

The core characteristics of ASDs will be the focus of the communication assessment, which include:

- Impairments in aspects of joint attention (e.g., social orienting, establishing shared attention, monitoring emotional states, and considering another's intentions).

- Social reciprocity (e.g., initiating bids for interaction, maintaining interactions by taking turns, and providing contingent responses to bids for interaction initiated by others).

- Language and related cognitive skills (e.g., understanding and using nonverbal and verbal communication, symbolic play, literacy skills, and executive functioning—the ability to problem solve and self-monitor future, goal-directed behavior).

- Behavior and emotional regulation (e.g., effectively regulating one's emotional state and behavior while focusing attention to salient aspects of the environment and engaging in social interaction) (ASHA, 2006h).

Prelock et al. (2003) describe a model for the assessment of children with ASDs, known as the Vermont Rural Autism Project (VT-RAP) that both involves families and leads to intervention decisions. The theoretical foundation of the model incorporates family-centered care, cultural competence, and a strengths perspective. The steps outlined in this interdisciplinary (e.g., multidisciplinary) assessment process are listed in Table 7.3.

Planning for Long-Term Services

Because ASDs and PDDs all include specific speech-language characteristics, the speech-language pathologist is always involved in the assessment, planning, and intervention for students who are so identified. The condition is pervasive, long lasting, and disruptive to learning requiring professionals to consider many service delivery approaches over time to be sure that the programming remains suited to the student (Scott, Clark, & Brady, 2000; National Research Council, 2001; Prelock, 2001; Winner, 2006). It is important to weigh program options, work closely with families, and be exceptionally creative, while mindful of Blosser and Kratcoski's (1997) premises for service delivery in the 2000s (see Table 5.2 in Chapter 5 on p. 181). The sidebar (on p. 285) provides guidelines for school service teams serving students with ASDs.

In ASHA's document, *Principles for Speech-Language Pathologists in Diagnosis, Assessment, and Treatment of Autism Specturm Disorders Across the Life Span (2006)*, the following six principles are outlined to guide speech-language pathologists in their work with individuals with ASDs:

Principle 1. Speech-language pathologists play an important role in promoting social communication skills that further the independence and self-advocacy of individuals with ASDs (p. 18).

Principle 2. Due to the pervasive nature of social communication impairment, individuals with ASDs should be eligible for speech-language pathology services (p. 19).

Principle 3. Speech-language pathologists play a critical role in the screening and diagnosis of individuals with ASDs, as early intervention is a critical variable associated with positive long-term outcomes (p. 20).

Table 7.3

Steps in the Interdisciplinary Assessment Process for Children with Autism Spectrum Disorders

1. Assignment of an assessment coordinator: Ensures that one individual has been identified as responsible for facilitating the elements of the assessment process.

2. Intake: Face-to-face meeting with the family in the home or a location of the family's choice to gather background information on the child and family that will be used to guide the assessment.

3. Preassessment planning meeting: Meeting held with the interdisciplinary team, the family, and community team members to collaborate on the preparation of the assessment plan.

4. Assessment: Visit by the interdisciplinary team members to the child's community (e.g., home, school, child care) to observe and interact with the child, interview family and community providers, and review records, following the assessment plan developed at the preassessment planning meeting.

5. Post assessment planning meeting: Meeting held with the interdisciplinary team, the family, and community providers to review the assessment findings and brainstorm key recommendations to address the priority needs of the child and family.

6. Report writing: Development of a working draft based on the input of the interdisciplinary team that is reviewed with the family and community providers for accuracy and assurance that questions raised have been answered.

7. Community follow-up meeting: Meeting held in the community to review the final report and create action plans for implementing the recommendations.

8. Resource notebook development: Binder of selected resource materials prepared for the family and community providers to increase their knowledge base around the diagnosis of autism spectrum disorders, intervention strategies with and without a research basis, and available community contacts.

Prelock et al. (2003), p. 196. Reprinted with permission.

Guidelines for the Service Planning Process
for Students With Autism Spectrum Disorders

1. Have timelines been met? Was staff responsive to referral or request for service?

2. Has team planning been thorough and coordinated?

3. Was the multidisciplinary assessment team qualified and knowledgeable in all areas?

4. Did the report document determination, behavior implications, assessment in all areas of suspected disability, and child's developmental levels?

5. Are required components of IEP, IFSP, and transition plans documented?

6. Have services addressed all areas of need?

7. Are service options provided by qualified, specifically trained personnel?

8. Does the program provide for coordination, collaboration, ongoing training, and supervision of providers and parents?

9. Does the documentation include all necessary information and data collection?

10. Are timelines and decision-making criteria established?

11. Have all responsibilities been assigned?

12. Are there dates set for further program planning and evaluation?

Source: California Department of Education (1999a)

Principle 4. Speech-language pathologists should prioritize assessment and intervention approaches that are related to improvements in social COMMUNICATIVE COMPETENCE, that is, the ability to form relationships, function effectively, and actively participate in natural routines and settings (p. 22).

Principle 5. Speech-language pathologists should form partnerships with families of individuals with ASDs in assessment and intervention, while incorporating family pref-

erences, honoring cultural differences, and respecting the challenges associated with limited resources (p. 23).

Principle 6. Speech-language pathologists should collaborate with families, individuals with ASDs, other professionals, support personnel, peers, and other invested parties, as this supports the identification of critical priorities that will lead to functional outcomes across social partners and contexts (p. 24).

Intervention Approaches

Intervention for ASDs generally fall within either a behavioral (e.g., functional) or a social-communication (e.g., developmental) approach. The approach that works best for the child with an ASD is the one that is the most specific to a given child's needs. Children with ASDs demonstrate highly individualized learning styles (Schreibman, Koegel, Charlop, & Egel, 1990; Prelock et al., 2003).

Functional/behavioral approaches and developmental/social-communication approaches need not be mutually exclusive nor competitive (Greenspan & Wieder, 1999; National Research Council, 2001; Diehl, 2003). Behavioral techniques include applied behavioral analysis (ABA), discreet trial training (DTT), and, more recently, positive behavioral supports. Some children may respond best to applied behavior analysis methods, which are highly structured teaching and speech-language intervention in a controlled environment (Lord, Bristol, & Scholper, 1993; Palacio, 2000). Recently, the blending of these methods have combined functional communication and positive behavioral supports to examine and intervene in social contexts while considering the communicative function of the behavior (National Research Council, 2001; Diehl, 2003). Because problem behavior is a hallmark of ASDs, and because it can create challenges for educators and interventionists, speech-language pathologists should be well versed in the positive behavioral supports (Buschbacher, 2005; Dunlap, 2005; Buschbacker & Fox, 2003).

Some children with ASDs benefit from play therapy (Wolfberg & Schuler, 1993) using socio-drama, peer interaction, and child-led interactions. Still others chiefly have pragmatic language disorders and respond well to social scripts (Gray & White, 2002; Winner, 2006). Most often, intervention related to social-communication establishes goals for joint attention, gaze regulation, gestural communication and communicative function. Language goals are mapped onto this social-communication approach (National Research Council, 2001; Woods & Weatherby, 2003).

One area of increased attention is the area of social skills intervention for students with ASDs, and in particular students who are older and have been diagnosed with Asperger syndrome. Related to this area is consideration of a construct called "Theory of Mind", or perspective taking, which is typically absent or impaired in the individual with an ASD (DeCurtis, Schryver-Stahly, & Ferrer, 2003; Silliman, Diehl, Huntly Bahr, Hnath-Chisolm, Bourchard Zenko, & Friedman, 2003). Social-skills training and groups are increasingly being incorporated into intervention approaches for this population (Attwood, 2003; Strulovitch & Tagalakis, 2003). Because students with Asperger Syndrome are impacted with severe pragmatic and social communication deficits, speech-language pathologists have a direct and critical role in providing intervention in the following areas: conversational skills, narrative skills, speech/voice (e.g., prosody), academics, self-regulation, and understanding the hidden curriculum of school (Paul & Sutherland, 2003). Although this area of practice has increased, lack of clear evidence leading to evidence-based practice (EBP) in this area is still lacking (Burgess & Turkstra, 2006) and needs to be developed (Paul & Sutherland, 2003; Burgess & Turkstra, 2006).

The obvious deficits in behavior and social skills can often overshadow the actual language impairment experienced by children with ASDs. Some children experiencing ASDs may exhibit some of the same deficits as children with SLI (Botting & Conti-Ramsden, 2003). Narrative abilities have been found to be deficit in both lower functioning and higher functioning individuals with ASDs (Losh, 2003). This language skill is essential to learning, and the speech-language pathologist's role in intervention is evident in this area (Koegel & Vernon, 2005). Language intervention methods such as social stories (Gray & White, 2002), priming (Koegel & Vernon, 2005; Koegel, Koegel, Frea, & Green-Hopkins, 2003) and pivotal response treatment (PRT) (Koegel & Koegel, 2006) occurring in natural language contexts can support language and learning development and also assist in controlling problem behavior (National Research Council, 2001).

The speech-language pathologist's professional philosophy regarding therapy for children with ASDs may or may not mesh with the team's or parents' ideas. Because intensive speech-language intervention with the child and training for the family may be viewed as the core of the program when children are under 3 years of age (Greenspan, 1992), the way communication services are provided is a critical decision. Several approaches that school-based speech-language pathologists have used successfully in different circumstances are summarized in Table 7.4. Speech-language pathologists must have knowledge of the entire range of choices the parent(s) may be considering, enabling different approaches to be introduced, advocated, or discontinued when progress is slow or change is needed. Additionally, knowing when to change approaches due to a child's developmental level, age, and educational needs is important. It is tempting to continue to use an approach that has been successful, but may not be appropriate for advancing to the next skill level. Continuing with an approach such as discrete trial training may be appropriate for a younger child in order to establish some behavior controls, but can actually limit skill development in other areas such as social communication, and generalization of skills to other environments as the child gets older (National Research Council, 2001).

The intervention approaches for children with ASDs stress the functionality of language for these students. In addition to balancing the providers, activities, and contexts of service delivery decisions, the speech-language pathologist will need to consider the belief system of the educational team and parents, and the availability of comprehensive training for all service providers (Crais, 2000). Due to the nature of ASDs, and its overwhelming impact on language and social development, these students will need comprehensive communication intervention (Scott et al., 2000; National Research Council, 2001).

Information on effective intervention with ASDs continues to develop (Wetherby, 2000; Diehl, 2003). Screening for ASDs should routinely be part of "well-child" checks-ups according to the National Institutes for Mental Health (2007). There are many speculations regarding what is responsible for the increase in ASDs. Whether the cause is related to environmental conditions such as vaccines or chemicals in the environment or improved public and professional awareness, the "epidemic" of ASDs is a na-

Table 7.4	
Intervention Methods for Students With ASDs	
Method	**Description**
TEACCH Treatment and Education of Autistic and Related Communication Handicapped Children	Highly structured teaching and accommodations in the learning environment, includes parents as teaching assistants. Picture schedules are posted for children, and visual cuing is used in instruction. Applies to many settings. Source: Lord et al. (1993)
IBI Intensive Behavior Intervention	One to five years of structured learning opportunities for 37–40 hours per week address all significant behaviors in all of child's environments by all significant persons. Emphasizes speech and language in early years, and one-to-one training sessions are most effective. Requires specialized training. Source: Lovaas (1996)
Natural Language Intervention	Using procedures similar to those for typically developing children, language targets are taught in a variety of social settings using natural reinforcers with a communication partner. Useful in pull-out and classroom-based settings. Source: Camarata (1996)
PRT Pivotal Response Training	Based on IBI approach, teaches a cluster of stimulus cues that will trigger simple or complex behaviors (like speech). Increases motivation of students, broadens opportunities for child to respond, increases generalization. Useful in many settings. Source: Koegel, Schreibman, Good, Cerniglia, Murphy, & Koegel (1989)
PECS Picture Exchange Communication System	Teaches children to initiate communication in a social context by giving pictures to adults to request an object or action. Useful in many settings. Source: Bondy & Frost (1994)
AAC Augmentative and Alternative Communication	Using an AAC system suited to child's cognitive and academic level facilitates social interaction and communication. Useful in many settings. Source: Williams (2000)
DIR Developmental, Individual-Difference, Relationship-Based Approach	Emphasizes the differences between students with ASDs, and the relationships that can be built with the child and the family. Source: Greenspan & Wieder (1999)

tional crisis, which severely taxes families and the educational system. There is no doubt that continued research and resources will need to be directed to this area

Appropriate Benefit

Parents and teachers of students with ASDs are brought into contact with many medical and educational professionals. Some are brief encounters while others are ongoing. Speech-language pathologists must be aware of the ongoing controversy when schools serve students with ASDs. School programs can be effective interventions for students; however, their underlying treatment premise can vary at times from the private sector. Families and school teams can disagree heartily on what the school can or should do for students with ASDs. Speech-language pathologists need to understand why service delivery recommendations appear to clash.

Since appropriate (not best or maximally feasible) benefit remains the federal standard for students with disabilities, a fairly modest set of expectations is fostered in special education. This frequently comes into conflict with the culture of ASDs. Many parents of children with ASDs are well aware of and believe they should expect the best education and related services shown to be effective. Perhaps it is the pervasiveness of ASDs, coupled with the startling progress some students make under optimized programs, that drives families to seek best practices rather than settling for less. In response to the advocacy efforts of families and professionals, several states have gone beyond the federal minimum and have raised their standards and commitments to all students with disabilities

in their state constitutions (Scott et al., 2000; Mandlawitz, 2002; Bevilacqua & Norlin, 2004).

Professionals in COMMUNICATION DISORDERS continue to play a very active role with the treatment of ASDs, including the development of interdisciplinary clinical practice guidelines for ASDs (Interdisciplinary Council on Developmental and Learning Disorders [ICDL], 2000). This approach uses a cross-disciplinary, comprehensive, and functional developmental intervention system for students and families. Developmental Individual-Difference Relationship-Based (DIR) approach is designed to meet the unique needs of children and families. The model is built on research that shows that while students with ASDs have common characteristics, they are not all alike. Their interventions must be matched to personal characteristics, interests, and family strengths. The speech-language pathologist is required to build a relationship with the student and experience the world the way he or she does (Greenspan & Wieder, 1999). For example, the ICDL guidelines state that 45 percent of the sample of 200 children with ASDs use limited speech, while 55 percent have virtually no speech. Speech-language pathology proponents of the ICDL intervention guidelines question how any communication program can be prescribed for students with ASDs if half of the population is known to have highly contrasting speech and language behaviors (ICDL, 2000).

DIR is based on building a relationship with each child and working on "all essential functional developmental capacities (regulation and attention, engagement, two-way purposeful interaction, problem solving, interactions, the creative uses of ideas, and logical thinking), individual processing differences (auditory, language, visual spatial, motor planning, and sensory modulation), and child-caregiver interactions and family functioning as well as additional cognitive and learning skills" (ICDL, 2000, p. 26). DIR has ten major principles: (1) Floortime™, semistructured, and structured learning; (2) all-day and evening programs; (3) intensive individual therapies; (4) integrated play opportunities; (5) appropriate IEPs; (6) tailored biomedical approaches; (7) technology-based learning matched to the child's potential; (8) mental health consultations; (9) no delays or waiting periods if a child is found to have interruptions in relating, communicating, or thinking; (10) continuity of programming as the child grows. Speech-language intervention, conducted by qualified and specifically trained speech-language pathologists, plays a major role in carrying out each of the ten principles (ICDL, 2000).

Contrasting Perspectives

Some interventions for students with ASDs that were considered highly controversial in the 1990s continue to be the focus of carefully constructed and appropriately controlled research (Biklin & Cardinal, 1997; Creaghead, 1999). Facilitated communication, auditory integration training, sensory integration therapy, and intensive, computer-assisted auditory temporal processing programs have all been interventions difficult to validate using conventional procedures (Calculator, 1999; Creaghead, 1999; Duchan, 1999; Gillam, 1999a; Griffer, 1999; Madell, 1999; Mauer, 1999; Tharpe, 1999; Veale, 1999). The speech-language pathologist has the educational background and the professional resources to make valid communication intervention decisions for students with ASDs. Whitmire (1999) offered the following systematic series of questions the speech-language pathologist should use to evaluate treatment procedures, products, or programs in school settings:

- What are the stated uses of the procedure, product, or program?

- To which client/patient population does it apply?

- To what other populations does it claim to generalize?

- Are outcomes clearly stated?

- Are there publications concerning this procedure, product, or program?

- Is there peer-reviewed research that supports or contradicts the stated outcomes or benefits?

- What is the professional background of the developers?

- Are there similar procedures, products, or programs currently available? How do they compare in performance and cost?

- Is it within my profession's scope of practice?

- Have you checked to see if there are any ASHA statements or guidelines on this topic?

- Is the cost reasonable and justifiable?

- Is the use justifiable?

- What are potential risks/adverse consequences?

- What is recommended as sufficient training to be considered a qualified user (pp. 427–428)?

Students Who Use Assistive Technology (AT) and Augmentative and Alternative Communication (AAC)

In 1992, Congress recognized the importance of ASSISTIVE TECHNOLOGY (AT) devices and services as tools to assist students with disabilities to lead more independent and productive lives (Rehabilitation Act Amendments). AT was used in schools before this time (ASHA, 1991a), but use was sporadic and often overlooked by busy school special education teams. At times, knowledge about AT was minimal, and staff did not feel confident about what equipment was available, how it was used, and how it could augment the communication and/or education of a child. Concerns about cost and lack of funds also caused teams to avoid the AT discussion. Speech-language pathologists and others lobbied Congress heavily to include specific wording in IDEA (1997) to assure that these service delivery problems would be addressed and resolved. Many students with severe physical and neurological disabilities could not communicate with speech and they needed alternative, often technological, methods to communicate and learn. The addition to the law in 1992 was crucial to the field, and further refinements occurred in the reauthorization of IDEA in 1997: "Assistive technology device means any item, piece of equipment, or product system, whether acquired commercially off the shelf, modified, or customized, that is used to increase, maintain, or improve functional capabilities of a child with a disability" (34 C.F.R. § 300.5).

Assistive technology service means any service that directly assists a child with a disability in the selection, acquisition, or use of an assistive technology, including the following:

(a) The evaluation of the needs of a child, including a functional evaluation of the child in the child's customary environment.

(b) Purchasing, leasing, or otherwise providing for the acquisition of assistive technology devices by children with disabilities.

(c) Selecting, designing, fitting, customizing, adapting, applying, maintaining, repairing, or replacing assistive technology devices.

(d) Coordinating and using other therapies, interventions, or services with assistive technology devices, such as those associated with existing education and rehabilitation plans and programs.

(e) Training or technical assistance for a child with a disability, or, if appropriate, that child's family.

(f) Training or technical assistance for professionals (including individuals providing education or rehabilitation services), employers, or other individuals who provide services to, employ, or are otherwise substantially involved in the major life functions of that child (34 C.F.R. § 300.6).

IDEA (1997) required that technology be considered at every IEP meeting. Schools must consider, on a case-by-case basis, the use of school-purchased assistive technology devices in the child's home or other settings if the IEP team determines a device is needed to ensure FREE APPROPRIATE PUBLIC EDUCATION (FAPE). To comply with IDEA requirements, many school districts have hired or trained personnel to be AT specialists and have provided in-service education for special education staff. Some professionals embraced the concept easily, while others have remained somewhat intimidated by technology and reliant on other team members to handle this part of special education.

Many speech-language pathologists are well equipped by education and experience to become AT specialists in their districts. Some have been using AT systems for many years and are able to "think outside the box" to support a student who struggles with the motoric aspects of reading, writing, speaking, and listening. Hearing aids and other ASSISTIVE LISTENING DEVICES (ALD) are well known to speech-language pathologists, and many have used communication boards or computer software as intervention strategies (Glennen, 2000). IDEA 2004 prevented school

districts from purchasing medically implanted assistive technology, likely targeting the proliferation of costly cochlear implants for children with severe hearing loss.

AT and AUGMENTATIVE AND ALTERNATIVE COMMUNICATION (AAC), though closely related, are not the same. Assistive technology can be used to support students with many types of disabilities. AAC may be a type of AT for students who need to have their communication supported so they can access the curriculum and take part in their daily life activities. AT and AAC can be either low-tech or high-tech.

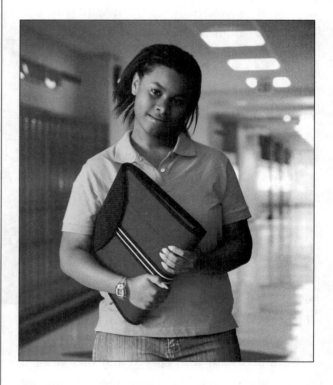

Low-tech examples include equipment and other supports readily available in schools, including off-the-shelf items to accommodate the needs of students that can be provided by general or special education through the student study team or IEP process. Low-tech items also include calculators, tape recorders, pencil grips, school constructed language boards, and TV captioning.

High-tech examples encompass specialized equipment and support services beyond basic AT and require more in-depth assessment and customizing. These are often needed by students with low incidence or severe disabilities. Examples of high-tech items include closed circuit television, FM systems, augmentative communication devices, sound field systems, computer access devices, and specialized software.

When considering AT, teams should begin by considering low-tech adaptations that may be appropriate for the student and easily obtained. The term technology suggests highly sophisticated equipment, but that was not the intent of the law. A team needs to be sure the student needs it and will use it. Table 7.5 lists AT devices organized by the academic task that could be adapted or modified for the student. AAC is listed under the activity of speaking, however, there is considerable overlap with writing, reading, and other curriculum-based school tasks since communication intersects with so many daily activities. For medical insurance coverage, the term speech generating device (SGD) is often used to denote high-end AAC equipment that produces simulated speech.

The awareness and use of technology has greatly increased in the general population in the last few years, making it easier for necessary technology to reach students in schools. Computers are an expected part of every classroom and school. A student's curriculum and learning strategies incorporate computers as learning tools, providing better access for students

with severe speech disabilities to use AT for literally all of their communication. In some cases, a student with learning disabilities may use AT for writing (spell-checker) or mathematics (calculator) unrelated to his or her communication skills, and the speech-language pathologist will simply incorporate this technology into speech services if needed. In other cases, communication will be such a critical component of the child's needs that the AAC will dictate all the other parts of the education program. Training teachers, family members, peers, and communication partners to use the AAC with the child is also the responsibility of the speech-language pathologist and is listed on the IEP as a related service necessary for the child to benefit from special education.

Other texts (e.g., Buekelman & Miranda, 1998; Church & Glennen, 1992; Romski & Sevcik, 1996) are available to provide greater detail about the assessment and intervention services for students who need AAC. This section was designed to help speech-language pathologists recognize the scope of AT and AAC and the role that speech-language pathologists play in team decisions, parent training, equipment upgrading, and curriculum matching. See sidebar on pp. 295–296 for additional resources and sidebar on p. 297 for FAQs on AT and AAC.

Intervention using AAC is a big task that speech-language pathologists should not do alone. It is always more successful when the full team is involved (Blackstone, 2000), widening the circle of potential communication partners for the student and vastly increasing the number of daily opportunities for practice and reinforcement.

Table 7.5

Assistive Technology Organized by Academic Task

Academic Area or Task	Sample Assistive Technology Devices
Speaking	Communication boards Picture Exchange Communication Symbols, Bliss symbols Speech-to-speech telephone access Speech output augmentative devices
Listening	Assistive listening devices Variable speech control tape recorder/player Conventional tape recorder Loop amplification system
Writing	Word processor, spell-checker Proofreading programs Outlining software Abbreviation expanders Speech synthesis screen reading programs Word prediction programs
Reading	Optical character recognition speech synthesis Speech synthesis for books on tape Variable speech control tape recorders Audio-taped books Picture Story software
Organization and Memory	Classroom schedule frame on wall Personal data organizer software Free form data base, calendar programs Tape recorder/player
Mathematics	Talking calculators, conventional calculator Onscreen computer-based calculator Drill and practice software programs with scoring
Daily Activities	Adaptive eating devices Adaptive drinking devices Adaptive dressing devices
Mobility	Walker, grab rails, manual wheelchair Power chair, powered mobility toys and appliances Easy access switches to operate equipment

From *Assistive Technology for Children with Learning Difficulties* (p. 25), by M. Raskind, (2000), San Mateo, CA: Schwab Foundation for Learning. ©2000 by M. Raskind. Adapted with permission.

Successful AT and AAC services in schools can generally be examined by using five critical elements. Speech-language pathologists are not responsible for all the elements, but they frequently play a large role in the coordination of this effort and the linkage with parents and other agencies. If the AT is an AAC system, the speech-language pathologist usually functions as the team leader or CASE MANAGER and will likely be involved the following five elements:

1. Assistive technology evaluation

2. Training and technical assistance

3. Acquisition and use of devices

4. Maintenance of devices

5. Coordination of services

The following sections describe each element as it relates to an AAC device, mindful that the same would be true of any other AT device. Use of low-tech devices may take less time to implement, since they are easier to obtain and their effectiveness can be evaluated more quickly. Training and technical assistance are important, even for low-tech devices, as an appropriate tool can be rejected if the professionals do not know how to implement the technology, or if the student's use is inconsistent. High-tech devices require a slower pace for decision making and have greater consequences for the student and the school's resources if found unsuccessful. Assessments do not have to entail long test batteries or trips to a distant rehabilitation center. Teams who are willing to work with AT and

Resources for the Speech-Language Pathologist Using AT and AAC

The Alliance for Technology Access (ATA)

1304 Southpoint Blvd, Suite 240

Petaluma, CA 94954

707-778-3011 • 707-778-3015 (TTY) • 707-765-2080 (Fax)

Email: *atainfo@ataccess.org* • Web site: *www.ataccess.org*

This is a national network of technology resource centers and technology vendors.

Assistive Technology Funding and Systems Change Project

1660 L Street NW, Suite 700

Washington, DC 20036

202-776-0406 • 202-776-0414 (fax)

Email: *atproject@ucpa.org*

This project provides training, information, and technical assistance on AT issues through a consortium of six national organizations led by United Cerebral Palsy Associations.

Continued

Resources for the Speech-Language Pathologist Using AT and AAC – *Continued*

State Tech Act Programs

1700 North Moore Street, Suite 1540

Arlington, VA 22209-1903

703-524-6686 • 703-524-6630 (fax) • 703-524-6639 (TTY)

Email: *resnata@resna.org* • www.resna.org

This is a technical assistance project funded by IDEA and operated by the Rehabilitation Engineering Society of North American (RESNA) to help you reach the project located in your state.

State Protection and Advocacy Agencies

202-406-9514 • 202-408-9520 (fax)

Email: *napas@earthlink.net*

This agency will help parents and others with legal questions about technology and other education issues. There is a contact agency in each state, which can be located through this central number in Washington, DC.

United States Society for Augmentative and Alternative Communication (USSAAC)

P.O. Box 21418

Sarasota, FL 34276

877-8USSAAC • 410-296-5710 (fax)

Email: *info@ussaac.org*

This is a national organization of professionals, consumers, and families who are experienced with AAC devices of all types. They provide technical assistance, advocacy, and training for users, their families, and their service providers and have national and regional conferences and newsletters.

International Society for Augmentative and Alternative Communication (ISAAC)

49 The Donway West

Suite 308

Toronto, ON M3C 3M9

Canada

Tel: 416-385-0351 • Fax: 416-385-0352

www.isaac-online.org

The International Society for AAC works to improve the life of every child and adult with speech difficulties by increasing awareness around the world about AAC.

#TP-29703 Making a Difference - 2nd Ed.   • ©2008 Thinking Publications® • www.thinkingpublications.com • 1-800-277-8737

Frequently Asked Questions about AT and AAC

Q. Are schools required to pay for AT and AAC devices?

A. Yes, school districts have the responsibility under IDEA 2004 to provide equipment, services, training, and programs for students with an IEP who need AT in order to increase, maintain, or improve their functional capabilities. Other funding resources may include insurance companies, foundations, fraternal organizations, businesses, and individuals.

Q. Do students have access to AT or AAC if they are eligible for extended-year services?

A. Yes, if the IEP team decides that the student needs AT to access the curriculum in summer school or extended-year programs.

Q. Is a school district required to provide state-of-the-art equipment for a student?

A. No. The equipment needs to be appropriate for the student's needs to ensure FAPE. The IEP is guided by the assessment and is under no obligation to select a more or less expensive or sophisticated device.

Q. Under what conditions may AT or AAC be considered a related service?

A. AT equipment is a related service if it is a complementary service necessary for the student to benefit from his or her special education. Instruction or technical assistance for family members or staff to communicate with a student using AAC would also be an example of a related service.

Q. How can school districts use Medicaid funds to purchase AT or AAC?

A. Medicaid regulations vary in each state, but the parent must always give permission to access the funds. Funds can be used according to Medicaid regulations which are based on medical necessity.

Q. How can school personnel locate AT and AAC resources?

A. Working with AAC resources requires more than the usual materials and supply catalogs. Many states have technology centers that may also function as assessment centers in some regions. The sidebar on pp. 295–296 lists six national contacts that will put the speech-language pathologist in touch with state resources as well. AAC is available in every state and many countries around the world. Local manufacturing representatives have been known to visit schools, join planning teams if requested, or bring loaner equipment for students to try.

learn what to do will become accomplished at making all low-tech decisions. Some teams can also handle high-tech decisions or make them in conjunction with another agency or regional support center which has access to equipment for trials.

Assistive Technology Evaluation

States have regulations and procedures for assessment, and districts may have selected resources to use for this purpose. The assessment must be both developmental and functional and at least partially conducted in the student's customary environment. A series of questions may be asked at the IEP meeting to determine what types of technology would be helpful. A speech-language pathologist within the district, or a technology center outside the district, could be used. Technology centers may be set up by nonprofit agencies to enable families to try out various systems, which are often too expensive to rent or buy outright. Usually an occupational or physical therapist assists with seating and positioning if that is an issue. There should be a written report and recommendations based on the student's trial with a device or devices. A student has changing needs, so the evaluation may need to be updated from time to time, either by the educational team or by an outside team. Newer technology is constantly becoming available, so reevaluation will allow the team to focus on better interventions as they become available.

> Technology centers may be set up by nonprofit agencies to enable families to try out various systems, which are often too expensive to rent or buy outright.

Training and Technical Assistance

Training is a critical key to success with all AT. Training is an organized, scheduled event with specific goals and topics for the participants (e.g., educators, the AAC user, parents, and peers). Technical assistance, on the other hand, is more informal, involving an ongoing relationship between the persons on the team and the family, including troubleshooting, discussions, and moral support.

The speech-language pathologist typically provides student instruction during therapy or collaborative sessions in the classroom. The speech-language pathology assistant (SLPA) often continues this instruction until the next level of skills is needed. The classroom teacher may assist with AT instruction that is connected to the curriculum. All three of these people may need training to be proficient enough on a device to teach the student. Sometimes, the classroom aide or a personal assistant assigned by the school will help to encode new vocabulary to expand a device, teach new access skills, or practice an oral or written report with a child. When more people are involved in the instruction phase, the AAC user will have more skilled communication partners such as the teacher, peers, and paraprofessionals (Blackstone, 2000).

Technical assistance for the speech-language pathologist will likely be needed if the device malfunctions or if adjustments or modifications need to be made. Some of these can be done by the speech-language pathologist or assistants, but many are time-consuming or require special tools. The technical support person must be a part of the team and easy to reach. Technical assistance may be listed on the IEP as a support for either the trainer or the trainee.

Both training and technical assistance need to be set up ahead of time so that the student can begin using the communication system without long delays or interruptions. There are some costs involved here, and the speech-language pathologist needs to be sensitive to how they are handled. IDEA 2004 requires that a member of the IEP team, called the LOCAL EDUCATION AGENCY (LEA) representative, be a person who is authorized to commit the district's resources as needed to carry out the IEP. If an AAC device is written into the IEP, the costs for training and technical assistance are absorbed by the school district. In some cases, the family or another agency will step in to assist with costs. Teams should discuss these training and technical assistance requirements at the IEP so that all team members are aware of them. Technical support may be included in the purchase of a device, or it may involve an additional fee. The speech-language pathologist should encourage the team to arrange for such services to make the AT choice successful.

Acquisition and Use of Devices

An AAC device is used by students to communicate, and thereby participate in and benefit from their educational program. This condition of educational benefit is necessary for assistive technology to be identified on the IEP as a related service. The AAC device often enables a student to engage in academics for the first time, have increased control of his or her school environment, and have access to more personal choices. All of these lend themselves to a less restrictive environment, greater access to the general education curriculum, and improved academic progress and functional outcomes. AAC must be tied to these educational expectancies or the family becomes responsible for providing AAC through other funding sources.

Devices can be purchased, leased, loaned, or received as a gift or donation. They are listed either generically or specifically on the IEP with other related services. When school systems are responsible for acquiring the AAC system, devices purchased by the LEA remain the property of the school. At times, the family may choose to purchase the device instead of the school, so that the student has sole access to the device in all settings. Regulations state that the equipment must be procured in a timely manner, not delaying the implementation of the signed IEP. Insurance companies and Medicaid may also purchase equipment if it is found medically necessary for the student. The school makes AAC decisions based on what is educationally beneficial for the student. These two ideas can be in conflict at times, and the speech-language pathologist may be the only team member who can differentiate between health-care requirements and educational standards.

Students use their AAC device in school, but the IEP team may also determine that it can be taken home for educational purposes that allow the child to receive a FREE AND APPROPRIATE PUBLIC EDUCATION (FAPE). A device may be used by more than one student at school, as long as it is available to each student whenever it is needed according to each student's IEP.

When students move from school to school, or from school to post-school environments, the ideal situation is for customized AAC equipment to follow them. As noted previously, the equipment is often the property of the school district. Ownership of a customized piece of equipment must be addressed in state and local policies, but the issue is often neglected at the local level until there is a relocation. The U. S. Department of Education issued a policy guidance statement on June 28, 1998, encouraging this transfer of devices to the person's new setting, but this guidance is not stated in IDEA (1997). The speech-language pathologist is in a pivotal position to be sensitive to the user's need for a personal communication system, yet recognize the financial commitments of the school district. The policy guidance statement may be helpful to avoid the public relations disaster likely if a school attempted to reclaim its device from a graduating student with disabilities. With the rapid turnover in high technology, most AAC systems have extremely limited resale value. Speech-language pathologists should seek advice from their supervisor early in the process to assure that an equipment transition will be smooth.

Maintenance of Devices

AAC devices are rarely ready for use right out of the box. They must be designed, fitted, programmed, customized, adapted, maintained, repaired, and replaced. The school may need to use technical assistance for fitting or customizing. The speech-language pathologist, teacher,

and student may personalize the AAC system with identification, photos, taped messages using a friend's voice, and so on. The school district is responsible for maintenance and repairs of student-owned equipment if it is used at school.

A list of approved repair vendors is invaluable. The speech-language pathologist may be the person who arranges for a substitute AAC device while the main one is being repaired. Substitute devices must allow students to maintain their communication skills and not jeopardize their educational activities or grades during a lengthy repair period. Though few states have specific qualifications for those who repair AAC equipment, the repair person should be knowledgeable and experienced with that equipment. The speech-language pathologist is rarely qualified to be the repair person.

Coordination of Services

AT needs to be coordinated with all other interventions or services the student receives. For example, typically one team member works directly with the student and AAC device, knows the technology well, and has contact with all the other members of the team, including the parents. This coordinator is usually not the AT specialist who is responsible for AT support for the entire district or region. The AT specialist serves the team better in technical assistance than in day-to-day coordination of services for each AT or AAC user.

Occupational therapists, physical therapists, or teachers may coordinate a student's IEP, but experience has shown that it is often speech-language pathologists who coordinate the AAC user's overall program because of their education and skills and also because communication is so central to these students' school lives. The entire team will contribute to any brainstorming or problem solving necessary for the AAC user, but one team member has to see that the plan is completed, that each person follows through, and that parents and students have an informed role in the process. Misunderstandings between team members are common as the program is implemented.

The IEP should identify roles and persons to carry out these tasks. When AAC is coordinated, the IEP goals and objectives will reflect how the technology serves as a support to the student's education program.

Has Technology Been Considered?

Figure 7.1 illustrates the steps a school district could take to select an AT service or AAC device when the team responds affirmatively to the IEP question "Has technology been considered?" and determines that AT or AAC is appropriate for the student. Notice how each step leads to one of the five elements of AT. Selection of functional outcomes and writing of goals and short-term objectives or benchmarks leads to the expected progress. If the student shows lack of progress, the team returns to the decision-making process and tries again. All AAC decisions are complex and have many possible results, largely because communication is a very personal act and because any method of communication must take multiple factors into account.

Working with AT can be a challenging part of the speech-language pathologist's job that re-

quires use of many diagnostic, negotiation, prediction, therapeutic, educational intervention, and coordination skills. Since speech-language pathologists are often key IEP team members for AAC, they must learn techniques for working with students with significant communication needs, coordinating large numbers of people, obtaining and maintaining a relatively costly intervention device, and directing ever-changing sets of student skills and emerging technologies.

Home-Bound, Home-Schooled, Hospital-Bound, Suspended/Expelled, or Incarcerated Children and Youth

Students who are eligible for special education services, including speech-language services, may need to receive this support in locations other than the school for periods of time. This can occur for various reasons.

A student may be restricted to home due to a medical condition, such as severe allergies or autoimmune disorders, with education provided by a home-based teacher assigned by the school district. Students hospitalized for a period of time (the amount of time varies from state to state) may receive general and special education services from either their home district or the school district in which the hospital or rehabilitation facility is located. If they were eligible for speech-language services before the

Figure 7.1

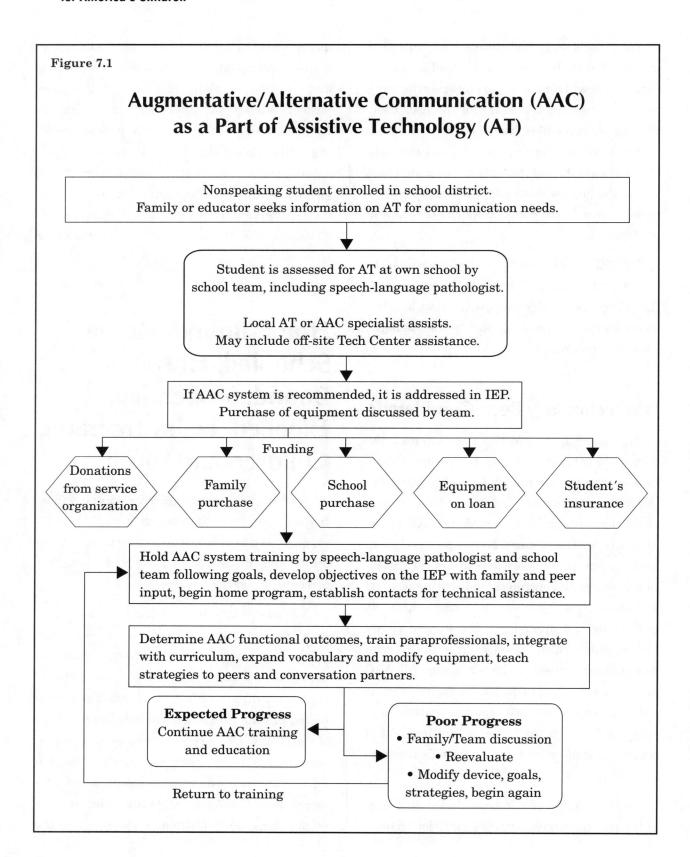

Augmentative/Alternative Communication (AAC) as a Part of Assistive Technology (AT)

Nonspeaking student enrolled in school district.
Family or educator seeks information on AT for communication needs.

Student is assessed for AT at own school by school team, including speech-language pathologist.

Local AT or AAC specialist assists.
May include off-site Tech Center assistance.

If AAC system is recommended, it is addressed in IEP.
Purchase of equipment discussed by team.

Funding

Donations from service organization

Family purchase

School purchase

Equipment on loan

Student's insurance

Hold AAC system training by speech-language pathologist and school team following goals, develop objectives on the IEP with family and peer input, begin home program, establish contacts for technical assistance.

Determine AAC functional outcomes, train paraprofessionals, integrate with curriculum, expand vocabulary and modify equipment, teach strategies to peers and conversation partners.

Expected Progress
Continue AAC training and education

Poor Progress
• Family/Team discussion
• Reevaluate
• Modify device, goals, strategies, begin again

Return to training

#TP-29703 Making a Difference - 2nd Ed. • ©2008 Thinking Publications® • www.thinkingpublications.com • 1-800-277-8737

protracted hospitalization, students are entitled to continued services if they are physically able to participate. This is usually coordinated with the provision of academic instruction. Speech-language pathologists who are employees of the hospital or rehabilitation facility may provide services, but there are often complicated fiscal issues to resolve between the school district, other funding sources, and service providers.

In the previously described cases, the school speech-language pathologist would provide speech-language services according to the specifications on the IEP. The IEP may be revised, however, to accommodate the student's medical situation. IEPs for students who are off-site are written to provide adequate progress in the curriculum. Students typically spend much less time with a teacher providing home-bound services than they would spend at school, since they are receiving intensive one-to-one support. Some districts require the speech-language pathologist from the student's school to travel to the home or hospital. Others have a home or hospital special education team that serves all students at temporary home or medical sites.

Students with an IEP for speech-language services who are suspended for more than ten days or expelled from school may need to receive these services at home until another school can be found. Even after expulsion, students retain their right to FAPE, and the IEP goals must be pursued. Other students may receive special education services at a neutral site, usually due to safety or discipline concerns present at the school site. Special educators are expected to carry out such assignments, with adequate safety precautions provided.

Students who are incarcerated during their school years typically receive their special education at their youth detention site. The assessment and appropriate intervention for speech-language services can be done by the home district, but more densely populated areas or larger penal institutions usually have speech-language pathologists employed by the state's corrections agency. Incarcerated persons 21 years of age and younger are entitled to special education services if they were identified with a disability, had an IEP before their incarceration, and have not yet received a regular high school diploma.

IDEA 2004 requires that all school-age children who reside in a district must be included in Child Find activities. This includes children who are home-schooled or who are enrolled in private education facilities. Schools must make parents and professionals aware of the availability of special education services and how children may be referred for evaluation. Speech-language services, as one of those programs, are frequently requested.

Under IDEA 2004, students who are enrolled by their parents in private school, are entitled to evaluation for suspected disabilities, but they may not be entitled to the full continuum of special education services provided to children in public schools. SLPs should inquire how their school district deals with this regulation.

Schools may provide special education services to some of these children in a variety of locations. If the child is transported to a special location for services, including the public school, the school district is responsible for the transportation cost. From time to time, school-based SLPs may need to travel to a distant site to serve a student or have a student transported for services. Working in a school may require the practitioner to negotiate the best way to offer services or create a delivery model that includes an adjusted compensation for time or travel.

All children in America must develop communication skills as they are vital to their success in life. Through the models described in this chapter, school-based SLPs have added several new dimensions to their work that have been well received by educators and communities. "Current perspectives propose an expansion of service delivery options based on a commitment to serving all children in the environment that best fits their individual needs" (Blosser & Kratcoski, 1997, p. 99).

CHAPTER 8

Procedural Safeguards and Other Protections for Children in Special Education

IN THIS CHAPTER

This chapter focuses on the procedural safeguards afforded to parents and children under IDEA 2004. In addition, the processes of resolution sessions, mediation, due process hearings, and complaint procedures will be discussed. These processes are designed to ensure the due process rights of individuals with exceptional needs. Legal requirements are an important component of working within special education. The chapter also addresses strategies for working with families to increase parent involvement and for dealing with difficult situations, including student discipline, which has specialized regulations for students with exceptional needs.

Making a Difference
for America's Children

1. Review the rights and protections outlined in this chapter. Why do you think these specific rights were developed? What are the implications of implementing these rights? (Recall that Chapter 2 discussed the foundations of due process in the development of the (Education of All Handicapped Children Act [EAHCA]).

2. Why is it important for speech-language pathologists to be familiar with student discipline codes?

3. What role might speech-language pathologists take in dealing with the prevention of student violence? How might this role assist students on a speech-language caseload?

4. Locate and review a parental-rights document. Discuss the presentation of the rights. Is it understandable to the general reader? Would the reader know what to do if a disagreement develops? Where would the reader go for help in understanding these rights?

5. What procedures would a school-based speech-language pathologist want in place to ensure proper preparation in the event a case goes to mediation or due process hearing?

6. Reflect on how you handle conflict. How might your reactions help or hinder a contentious interaction with a family? What skills might you need to learn?

7. What are the similarities and differences among the provisions of IDEA 2004, Section 504, and the Americans with Disabilities Act (ADA)?

Parental Notification and Involvement

Special education laws, including the EDU-CATION FOR ALL HANDICAPPED CHILDREN ACT (EAHCA) of 1975 and the INDIVIDUALS WITH DISABILITIES EDUCATION IMPROVEMENT ACT (IDEA 2004) are considered civil rights laws (see Chapter 2). Congress enacted legislation in 1975 that prevented situations in which parents were left out of the educational decision-making process for their child. Subsequently, the rights and protections afforded to parents and children through special education laws have been strengthened. Procedural safeguards that are written into these laws are the means by which parent involvement is ensured and defined. These safeguards are designed under constitutional principles known as due process of law. The requirements for DUE PROCESS of law are also applied in school discipline requirements for all students, with specialized requirements for students receiving special education. Turnbull (1993) explained due process passionately in his work *Free Appropriate Public Education: The Law and Children with Disabilities:*

> For those who pioneered the right-to-education doctrine, the procedures for implementing the right were as crucial as the right itself. Procedural due process is a means of challenging the multitude of discriminatory practices that the schools had habitually followed...Without due process, the children would have found that their right to be included in an educational program and to be treated non-discriminatorily (to receive a free appropriate education)

would have a hollow ring. Procedural due process—the right to protest—is a necessary educational ingredient in enforcing every phase of the disabled child's right to an education.

> Procedural due process is also a constitutional requisite under the requirement of the Fifth and Fourteenth Amendments that no person shall be deprived of life, liberty, or property without due process of law. In terms of the education of disabled children, this means that no disabled child can be deprived of an education without the opportunity of exercising the right to protest what happens to him or her (p. 207).

The legal requirements under IDEA 2004 can seem overwhelming to educators. Knowing the ramifications of these legal requirements is critical to the practice of special education and to the assurance of FREE APPROPRIATE PUBLIC EDUCATION (FAPE) for students. Violations can hold serious consequences for public agencies and the individuals IDEA 2004 was designed to protect.

Procedural compliance questions have historically focused only on whether procedures had been followed correctly. Although the focus of special education is now on educational results, procedural compliance and the assurance of due process of law remains an essential cornerstone of IDEA 2004.

IDEA 2004 describes the processes and procedures that agencies and staff must follow to protect the rights of parents and children when delivering special education programs. Procedural safeguards are found in Title 20 § 1415 of the United States Code (U.S.C.) and in Title 34, Subpart E – *Procedural Safeguards Due Process Procedures for Parents and Children* of the Code of Federal Regulations (C.F.R.). These regulations include the following due process procedures: records examination and participation in meetings, INDEPENDENT EDUCATIONAL EVALUATION (IEE), notice requirements, and parental consent.

Records Examination and Participation in Meetings

Parents have a right to review all educational records and participate in all meetings that deal with their child's identification, evaluation, educational placement, and FAPE provision. However, regarding parent involvement, Title 34 C.F.R. § 300.501 (b)(23) states that:

> A meeting does not include informal or unscheduled conversations involving public agency personnel and conversations on issues such as teaching methodology, lesson plans, or coordination of service provision if those issues are not addressed in the child's IEP. A meeting also does not include preparatory activities that public agency personnel engage in to develop a proposal or response to a parent proposal that will be discussed at a later meeting.

Parents must be involved in special education placement decisions about their child. It is critical that educators understand the provisions of this requirement. If parents are unable to participate, "the public agency must use other methods to ensure their participation, including individual or conference telephone calls or video

conferencing" (34 C.F.R. § 300.501 [c][3]). An INDIVIDUALIZED EDUCATION PROGRAM (IEP) team can make placement decisions about a student without the parent(s) only after several attempts have been made to involve the parents. These attempts must be documented according to standards set in 34 C.F.R. § 300.322 (d):

1. Detailed records of telephone calls made or attempted and the results of those calls.

2. Copies of correspondence sent to the parents and any responses received.

3. Detailed records of visits made to the parent's home or place of employment and the results of those visits.

Independent Educational Evaluation (IEE)

The parents of a child with a disability have the right to obtain an IEE at public expense if they disagree with an evaluation obtained from a public agency (34 C.F.R. § 300.502 [b][1]). If parents request that the school pay for the IEE, the district must inform them of the criteria for an acceptable evaluation and recommended service providers (34 C.F.R. § 300.502 [e]). If parents obtain a private evaluation that meets agency criteria and submit results to the school, an IEP team must consider the results of the evaluation as part of the IEP (34 C.F.R. § 300.502 [c][1]). If parents submit a report from an evaluation they obtained, an IEP team meeting should be called to consider this information.

All special educators must know the rules regarding IEE. If parents request an IEE, educators must be cautious not to give any impression that such a request might not be honored. Such requests must be honored by the school team, and the resulting report must be discussed by an IEP team. Learning the appropriate protocol for the LOCAL EDUCATIONAL AGENCY (LEA) is necessary in the event that such a request is made. When parents request an IEE, notification of a supervisor, administrator, or program manager is highly advisable. Procedures will vary among school districts regarding the approval of and payment for an IEE. (See also Chapter 3, "Independent Educational Evaluation.")

Notice Requirements

The process whereby public agencies notify parents about proposed actions or refusals to act is highly regulated. Every time an action is being considered by IEP team members, written notice must be given to parents, including the items described in 34 C.F.R. § 300.503:

1. Parents must receive prior written notice whenever an agency proposes, refuses, or initiates a change regarding:

   • Identification.

   • Evaluation.

   • Educational placement.

   • Provision of FAPE.

2. The prior written notice must:

   • Be in language understandable to the general public.

   • Be in the native language of the parents or translated orally for them.

   • Describe the action proposed or refused.

   • Explain why the agency is proposing or refusing the action.

   • Describe other options considered and the reasons why those options were rejected.

   • Describe the information used as a basis for the action.

   • Include any other relevant factors used in making the decision.

   • Include a statement that the parents have protection under the procedural safeguards of IDEA 2004 and, if the notice is not an initial referral for evaluation, include how a copy of the procedural safeguards can be obtained.

   • Include sources of information to assist parents in understanding IDEA.

Usually, LEAs have booklets for parents or have the notice of rights written on the back of an IEP document. Under IDEA 2004, LEAs are allowed to post copies of the procedural rights on their agency's Web site (34 C.F.R. § 300.504 (4)(b). The list of procedural safeguards is very long and complex under IDEA 2004 and may be daunting to parents attempting to understand it. Speech-language pathologists and other educators must be aware of their responsibilities under school policies for notifying parents of their rights and may be called on by parents to help explain the notice.

IDEA 2004 requires that parents be given notice (i.e., provided with written documentation and a verbal explanation) of their rights at each of the following times: when a student is initially referred for evaluation to determine eligibility for special education; when a student is reevaluated; upon receipt by the public agency of a state complaint or filing of a due process action; when a student is being considered for removal

Parental Consent

Congress intended that decisions or actions never be taken with regard to a child's education without parent involvement. IDEA 2004 requires that parental consent be obtained before conducting an initial evaluation or a reevaluation. To comply with this requirement, most agencies have a Consent to Assess form, also known as an ASSESSMENT PLAN or something similar. (See Chapter 3 for a discussion about when an assessment plan is needed.) The requirements for parental consent do not apply to reviews of files or data as part of an initial evaluation or a reevaluation (34 C.F.R. § 300.300 [c] [2][i]) or to the administration of testing done with all students in the school, such as group tests, unless consent is required from all parents (34 C.F.R. § 300.300 [a][2][ii]).

that constitutes a change of placement due to a disciplinary incident according to the discipline procedures of the Code of Federal Regulations (34 C.F.R. § 300.530 (h); or upon request by the parent. Responsibility for preparing the notice documents (i.e., parental-rights booklets or notice-of-meeting forms) belongs to educational agencies; however, under school policy, it may be the responsibility of special education service providers to ensure that parents receive and understand these rights and protections.

Speech-language pathologists who are new to public agencies should ask for assistance to learn how their employers want procedural safeguards to be explained to parents. Speech-language pathologists should review the procedural-safeguards-notice document, ask for clarification of questions they may have from administration in their agency, and be able to explain the document to families. Some LEAs may require that copies of procedural safeguards are given to parents other than the mandated times outlined in the Code of Federal Regulations (C.F.R.). Local agency policies should always be followed and documented in this regard.

If parents refuse to sign an assessment plan (i.e., decline to have their child assessed to determine if the child has special needs), a public agency may choose to or may be required to pursue a due process action to proceed with an evaluation, depending on state law (34 C.F.R. § 300.300 [3][i]). (See "The Mediation Process" on p. 315 and "Impartial Due Process Hearings" on p. 316 for a discussion on mediation and due process.) Reevaluations may proceed if parents do not respond to requests for consent, but only after documentation of numerous attempts to secure the consent (34 C.F.R. 300.300 § [c][ii]). This section of the C.F.R. now gives the public agency the ability to conduct a reevaluation without parental consent if reasonable steps to obtain these consents have been taken and the parents have not responded. State law will vary in procedures to be taken under these circumstances. A speech-language pathologist or audiologist should never make a decision to conduct an evaluation in the absence of a consent without first consulting with their special education administrator and seeking direction in such a matter. Documentation of such contacts and conversations with school officials is also advised.

IDEA 2004 prohibits denial of other services to a student based on parental refusal to consent (34 C.F.R. § 300.300 [c][ii][3]). An example of this would be a student who is receiving resource-room services in addition to speech-language services. At the time of the triennial evaluation, the parents may agree to give the speech-language pathologist access but not the resource-room teacher. In such a situation, all services to the child must continue, but the team should consult the supervisor or administrator for guidance on how to proceed.

Resolution Sessions, Mediation, Due Process Hearings, and State IDEA Complaints

Due process of law is an element in both the FIFTH and FOURTEENTH AMENDMENTS of the U.S. Constitution. Due process guarantees civil rights through procedural safeguards designed to protect individual rights. Due process tends to be a phrase that is used in a variety of contexts in special education. Due process procedures include mediation, impartial due process hearings, and state IDEA complaints. Procedural safeguards are part of due process. Due process also refers to the hearing process available when parents and LEAs disagree on issues related to a student's identification, evaluation, educational placement, or receipt of FAPE. Table 8.1 compares the procedures for resolving procedural complaints.

Resolution sessions, mediation, and due process hearings are utilized for disputes related to a student's special education—that is, anything that deals with evaluation, goals and objectives, program, placement, and services. The complaint process is designed for violations of procedural safeguards, such as timeline or implementation violations. These processes are available to parents and public agencies.

Most often, requests for hearings or investigations through the complaint process are actions taken by the parents. However, states are increasingly holding school districts accountable for ensuring a child's FAPE when there is a disagreement with parents. "FAPE belongs to the child, not the parent," advised attorney Melinda Maloney (1997). An LEA may later be held responsible for compensatory education for the student if a hearing officer finds that the school district failed to aggressively pursue the student's FAPE despite the disagreement on the part of the student's parents. It is for this reason that speech-language pathologists and other special educators must be very cautious when there are disagreements with parents regarding the recommendations and implementation of IEP procedures.

Table 8.1

IDEA Dispute Resolution Processes Comparison Chart

	MEDIATION	DUE PROCESS COMPLAINT	RESOLUTION PROCESS	STATE COMPLAINT
Who can initiate the process?	Parent or LEA/Public Agency, but must be voluntary for both	Parent or LEA/Public Agency	LEA schedules the resolution meeting upon receipt of a due process complaint unless the parties agree to waive or use mediation	Any individual or organization, including those from out of state
What is the time limit for filing?	None specified	2 years of when the party knew or should have known of the problem (or a State law specified timeline) with limited exceptions	Triggered by a parent's due process complaint	1 year from the date of the alleged violation
What issues can be resolved?	Any matter under Part 300, including matters arising prior to the filing of a due process complaint (there are exceptions)	Any matter relating to the identification, evaluation or educational placement or provision of a free appropriate public education (there are exceptions)	Same as the issues raised in the parent's due process complaint	Alleged violations of Part B of IDEA or Part 300
What is the timeline for resolving the issues?	None specified	45 days from the end of the resolution period unless specific extensions to the timeline are granted	LEA must convene a resolution meeting within 15 days of receipt of the parent's due process complaint, unless the parties agree in writing to waive the meeting or agree to use mediation Resolution period is 30 days from receipt of the parent's due process complaint unless the parties agree otherwise or the parent or LEA fails to participate in the resolution meeting or the LEA fails to convene the resolution meeting within 15 days of receipt of the parent's due process complaint	60 days from receipt of the complaint unless an extension is permitted

   #TP-29703 Making a Difference - 2nd Ed.   ©2008 Thinking Publications®   •   www.thinkingpublications.com   •   1-800-277-8737

Table 8.1 – *Continued*

	MEDIATION	DUE PROCESS COMPLAINT	RESOLUTION PROCESS	STATE COMPLAINT
Who resolves the issues?	Parent and LEA/Public Agency with a mediator The process is voluntary and both parties must agree to any resolution	Hearing Officer	Parent and LEA/Public Agency Both parties must agree to any resolution	SEA

Source: OSEP (n.d.)

The Resolution Session

IDEA 2004 added a new step in the due process procedures in order to allow LEAs and parents one more opportunity to resolve differences outside of the constraints of an IEP meeting. This step is known as a RESOLUTION SESSION PROCESS (34 C.F.R. § 300.510). Under this section, the LEA arranges a meeting with the parent within 15 days of receiving the due process complaint. The meeting should include a representative of the LEA (i.e., typically a district level administrator) who has decision-making authority, significant members of the IEP team (which means that not all members of the IEP team need to be present), and the parent (34 C.F.R. § 300.510 [a][i]). Attorneys for the school district are prohibited from attending these meetings unless the parent brings an attorney (34 C.F.R. § 300.510 [a][ii]). The C.F.R. outlines that—

The purpose of the meeting is for the parent of the child to discuss the due process complaint and the facts that form the basis of the due process complaint, so that the LEA has the opportunity to resolve the dispute that is the basis for the due process complaint (34 C.F.R. § 300.510 [a][ii][2]).

The resolution session process is intended to give parents and school districts one more opportunity to resolve the disputes between them. A binding written settlement agreement is developed if an agreement is made during this session (34 C.F.R. § 300.510 [d]). Often these sessions can be productive in not only resolving the disputes, but also allowing families and districts to work together in a more nonadversarial manner and preserve the relationships between them. Depending on their role in the case, the speech-language pathologist or audiologist may or may not be part of the resolution session itself, and may or may not be involved in implementing an agreement reached in the session.

Litigation and Legal Ramifications

Procedural safeguards afforded to parents and students under IDEA 2004 provide for a system to resolve disputes arising from special education evaluation or the contents of the IEP. Collectively, the dispute processes are referred to as due process, which typically implies actions and processes that occur following a filing on behalf of one party requesting a due process hearing. Litigation, or due process, is of ongoing concern to public school personnel.

IDEA 2004 encourages dispute resolution and mediation processes prior to actual hearings. Due process hearings are held if resolution cannot be reached during dispute resolution or mediation. Each state has a somewhat different system for managing due process hearings. Because IDEA 2004 is a federal law, any appeal of a due process hearing decision goes to a federal trial court at the U.S. District Court for that judicial region. There are 94 judicial districts in the U.S. District Court System. Appeals from the U.S. District Court go to one of 12 regional U.S. Circuit Courts of Appeal. Any appeal from the U.S. Circuit Court system goes to the U.S. Supreme Court (Understanding the Federal Courts, n.d.). Understanding the appeal system in the United States judiciary system is necessary, first because trends can be seen in the rulings, and secondly because decisions made at the U.S. Court of Appeals level apply to all school districts in that region and, of course, decisions made at the U.S. Supreme Court level apply to all districts in the country. Figure 8.1 below illustrates this progression of the judicial system.

Figure 8.1

Procedural Appeal System for Due Process

Resolution Session
▼
Mediation
▼
Due Process Hearing
▼
Appeal to U.S. District Court
▼
Appeal to U.S. Circuit Court
▼
Appeal to U.S. Supreme Court

Continued

Litigation and Legal Ramifications – *Continued*

There are 12 U.S. Regional Circuit Courts. They are divided as follows:

1st Maine, Massachusetts, New Hampshire, Puerto Rico, Rhode Island

2nd Connecticut, New York, Vermont

3rd Delaware, New Jersey, Pennsylvania, U.S. Virgin Islands

4th Maryland, North Carolina, South Carolina, Virginia, West Virginia

5th Louisiana, Mississippi, Texas

6th Kentucky, Michigan, Ohio, Tennessee

7th Illinois, Indiana, Wisconsin

8th Arkansas, Iowa, Missouri, Nebraska, North Dakota, South Dakota

9th Alaska, Arizona, California, Guam, Hawaii, Idaho, Montana, Nevada, Northern Mariana Islands, Oregon, Washington

10th Colorado, Kansas, New Mexico, Oklahoma, Utah, Wyoming

11th Alabama, Florida, Georgia

The Mediation Process

Under IDEA 2004, mediation is a voluntary process that at a minimum must be available whenever a hearing is requested (34 C.F.R. § 300.506). Mediation is a process of formal discussion with a neutral third party to resolve differences. At the point that due process procedures are being used, emotions may be running high on either side of the case, and the mediator can help parties refocus on the issues. Many states had mediation available prior to 1997, but the reauthorization of IDEA (1997) made the availability of this process mandatory, and this process continued in the reauthorization of IDEA 2004.

Mediation is a state-level process. Each state maintains a list of qualified mediators. LEAs may establish procedures to encourage mediation for parents who elect not to participate in mediation after requesting a due process hearing. Such procedures might include arranging a meeting for parents with a neutral party, so that the benefits of mediation are explained and parents are encouraged to use the process. Most states now have information regarding due process procedures available on their state department of education's Web site, easily available to parents and educators.

To attempt to resolve issues prior to entering into a mediation process, some regional and local agencies provide ALTERNATIVE DISPUTE RESOLUTION (ADR). This follows a win-win type of process, acknowledging desires and limitations on both sides. This is a local-level process that occurs before a state-level mediation agency is involved. Mediation and ADR procedures may never be used to delay or deny the right to a due process hearing. Useful information about ADR and other dispute resolution processes may be found on the Consortium for Appropriate Dispute Resolution in Special Education (CADRE) Web site, www.directionservice.org/cadre/.

The mediation process involves parties from the school district and parties from the family meeting with a mediator. Depending on agency procedures and the case, a speech-language pathologist or audiologist may or may not be involved in the mediation process. Discussions occurring during the process must be confidential and cannot be used in a due process hearing (34 C.F.R. § 300.506 [b][7]). Both sides have an opportunity to tell the mediator their perspective of the dispute and what it would take to solve the dispute. If a solution cannot be reached with both parties in the same room, the parties caucus independently with the mediator. The mediator moves back and forth between the two parties, attempting to reach a mediation agreement. Such an agreement must be put in writing (34 C.F.R. § 300.506 [b][6]). The agreement may resolve all of the issues being brought forward, or it may resolve only some of the issues. If issues are not resolved, either of the parties may choose to proceed to a due process hearing.

> **Speech-language pathologists and educators should understand that mediation may result in agreements that are highly unusual.**

Speech-language pathologists, audiologists, and other educators should understand that mediation may result in agreements that are highly unusual. These agreements should be considered individualized in all cases, not precedent setting. For example, a speech-language pathologist may be required to make up missed therapy sessions or give extra therapy sessions over and above what was previously agreed to in the IEP. Although not precedent setting, the agreement will often change the way services are offered or documented districtwide to prevent problems in the future. Implementation of a specialized program might lead to others deducing the outcomes of an agreement, but all mediation agreements are confidential.

Impartial Due Process Hearings

With or without voluntary mediation, parents, students who have reached the age of majority (age 18 in most states), and school districts are able to request an impartial due process hearing (also referred to as a fair hearing). Issues that can be resolved in a due process hearing are limited to issues involving the IEP process: identification, evaluation, educational placement, FAPE, and placement of a student in an interim alternative educational setting as a result of a disciplinary matter. School districts and parents should always work with each other to avoid going to a hearing, which is expensive and time consuming, and often contributes to agitation on both sides. In a small percentage of cases, however, a hearing will be held to decide the dispute.

A due process hearing is a formal procedure with a hearing officer who presides and listens to evidence presented by both sides. Often both sides are represented by attorneys. Unlike the mediation process, where parties have a neutral third party attempting to assist in developing a compromise, a due process hearing is like a court proceeding where evidence is presented and, ultimately, one side prevails. The general feeling about due process hearings is that, in the long run, no one really wins as there are so many hard feelings after these events.

School districts are typically reluctant to use their power to file for (i.e., request) a due process hearing against parents. In California, the education code (56346) dictates a school district's affirmative duty to file for a due process hearing if the district believes that the actions of parents are resulting in the denial of FAPE to students. As explained previously, the right to FAPE belongs to students, not parents, and cannot be denied by the school district based on parental wishes (Maloney, 1997). In California, a district's failure to take parents to a hearing in such a case may result in the district later being ordered to provide compensatory education to students. This can happen if students file for due process once they reach the age of majority and prevail in a claim that FAPE was withheld. Other states may have similar requirements.

Attorneys often become involved in cases that could lead to a hearing. All STATE EDUCATIONAL AGENCIES (SEAs) and LEAs are required to provide parents with information about low-cost legal services and other relevant services when parents request a due process hearing (34 C.F.R. § 300.507 [b]). This is the responsibility of an administrator, not a speech-language pathologist or audiologist. In any situation where parents mention an intent to seek counsel from an attorney or advocate, the speech-language

pathologist or audiologist should notify a supervisor. Such a comment is considered a "red flag," indicating that parents are unhappy about something. Hopefully, the speech-language pathologist or audiologist is aware of the specific concerns of the parent and can inform the administrator about them. In that way, once the administration is notified, attempts to resolve the issues can begin prior to the situation escalating.

Under IDEA 2004, parents cannot seek reimbursement from a school district for their attorney's fees for attendance at an IEP meeting unless the meeting is ordered by a hearing officer or administrative law judge. A court may award attorney fees to parents when the parents are the prevailing party in a due process proceeding, meaning that one or more of their issues are upheld. In such a situation, the school district will be responsible for the cost of attorneys on both sides (if both sides have attorneys) in addition to any costs involved (e.g., the costs of equipment, staff, or training that is found to be necessary) in the educational request of the parents (34 C.F.R. § 300.517).

Depending on agency procedures and the case, a speech-language pathologist or audiologist may be involved in a mediation process leading up to the hearing. If a case goes to a due process hearing, the speech-language pathologist or audiologist may be asked to testify. The situation is much like testifying in court. When school personnel are called to testify, most attorneys for the school district will prepare them prior to the hearing. This means that the speech-language pathologist or audiologist testifying will know what to expect to the best of the attorney's knowledge. Statements of training and evidentiary information about education, background, documentation on student progress, and the like will probably be a part of the testimony. This is one reason why speech-language pathologists, audiologists, and all special educators should be sure that they keep detailed records about student progress and build treatment plans that are grounded in research-based protocols. (See sidebar on p. 319 for helpful tips on testifying). The speech-language pathologist and audiologist should rely on ASHA's (2004e; 2006f) PREFERRED PRACTICE PATTERNS as a rationale for assessment and intervention methods.

Every time a due process hearing is requested by either side, the procedural safeguard known as STAY PUT goes into effect. "Stay put" means that a student will remain in the educational placement he or she was in when the due process hearing request was filed unless the parties agree otherwise (34 C.F.R. § 300.518). For example, if an IEP calls for speech-language services twice a week for 40 minutes per session and the parents request a due process hearing, the amount of service remains the same (i.e., at present educational placement) until the matter is settled unless both parties agree otherwise through a mediation agreement. IDEA 2004 regulations for "stay put" clarify that when a child transitions from Part C (infant services) to Part B (preschool and school-age services), that the LEA is not required to provide Part C services if there is a dispute regarding services (34 C.F.R. § 300.518 [c]).

Timelines apply when due process is initiated. States are required by IDEA 2004 to ensure that due process decisions are reached within 45 days of receipt of a request (34 C.F.R. § 300.515 [a]). If mediation is used, the parties may agree to an extension. The decision of the hearing officer is final unless appealed. In some states, the first appeal is to the SEA; in others, the appeal is directly to a state court of competent jurisdiction or federal court.

Dos and Don'ts of Testifying

Do	Don't
• Toot your own horn. (Be willing to talk about your accomplishments and knowledge.)	• Be modest.
	• Be tentative.
• Be affirmative.	• Volunteer information that you weren't asked.
• Answer direct questions.	
	• Guess if you don't know.
• Answer "I don't know" if you don't.	• FREAK! (Become too stressed to function)
• Ask for a break if you are feeling anxious.	• Rush.
• Take your time so you can answer accurately.	
• Set your own pace.	• Let the family's attorney set a rapid pace of questioning.
	• Be defensive.
• Tell the Hearing Officer/Judge if you are feeling hassled.	
• Check the clock and remember that it will eventually be over.	

Source: Moore-Brown (2006). Reprinted with permission.

Ultimately, due process hearing decisions, and those cases that are appealed to state and federal jurisdictions, create what is known as case law. These key cases set the courts interpretation of disputes that arise in special education. Both districts and parents monitor the court's decisions in these matters and this lays out arguments for future disputes as well as giving guidance to the field in terms of legal interpretation. Chapter 2 presents a listing of cases that have given practice guidance for speech-language pathologists and other special educators. Table 8.2 reviews additional important cases which set case law and interpretation on common issues of concerns to special educators. These decisions affect how school districts, parents, and IEP teams conduct their business.

Table 8.2

A Summary of Recent Key Court Cases and Their Effect on the Practice of Speech-Language Pathologists

Court Case	Legal Outcome	Effect on Speech-Language Pathologists' Practice
Cypress-Fairbanks Independent School District v. Michael F. (1997) (State of Texas; No. 96-20221 5th Circuit)	Court ruled that there are four factors that can serve as indicators of whether an IEP is reasonably calculated to provide a meaningful educational benefit under the IDEA: (1) the program is individualized on the basis of the student's assessment and performance; (2) the program is administered in the least restrictive environment; (3) the services are provided in a coordinated and collaborative manner by the key "stakeholders"; and (4) positive academic and non-academic benefits are demonstrated.	IEP teams need to ensure that they follow the four indicators provided by the court to ensure that the IEP is appropriately designed to confer educational benefit to the student.
Cedar Rapids Community School Dist. v. Garret F. (1999) (State of Iowa; 526 U.S. 66, 119 S.Ct. 992, 143 L.Ed.2d 154	The school district was responsible for funding nursing services for a student who was ventilator dependent.	Students who have significant medical disabilities will attend public schools and will need to be provided with services and supports designed to meet their needs in order that they can attend school.
Kevin T. v. Elmhurst Comm. School District No. 205 (2002) (State of Illinois; U.S. District Court)	A 19 year old student who had been receiving special education services since he was six years old demonstrated decreasing skills although he has received special education services for twelve years. The court found that advancing the district did not appropriately assess and inappropriately graduated the student.	The court examined witness credibility, failure to review and revise goals, the student's regression of skills and overall lack of planning as part of its consideration. IEP teams must address student's lack of progress in their IEPs, adjusting services accordingly. The consideration by the court of witness credibility is important for IEP team members to know.
Deal ex rel. Deal v. Hamilton County Board of Education (2004) (State of Tennessee; 42 IDELR 109; 6th Circuit)	A school district's predetermination of a program for a child with autism denied the parents meaningful participation in the IEP process. The district also did not consider the child's individual needs through their unofficial policy of refusing 1:1 ABA programs.	Parent input and participation in the IEP is critical. Predetermination of placement is considered a denial of meaningful participation. School district teams can meet and confer, but cannot make final decisions prior to the IEP meeting.

Continued

Table 8.2 – *Continued*

Court Case	Legal Outcome	Effect on Speech-Language Pathologists' Practice
M. L. v. Federal Way School District (2004) (State of Washington; No. 02-35547; 9th Circuit)	A school district's failure to include a general education teacher in the IEP meeting created a structural defect so significant that it resulted in an automatic denial of FAPE.	The presence of a general education teacher at the IEP meeting is required in order to ensure the student is provided FAPE.
Schaffer v. Weast (2005) (State of Maryland; U.S. Supreme Court 54 U.S. 04-698)	The burden of proof in special education cases is placed upon the party bringing the action (i.e., the party seeking relief).	School districts should always prepare their IEPs in a legally defensible manner, but the burden to demonstrate whether or not the IEP is appropriate will fall to the party (e.g., parents or school district) who made the due process request.

State IDEA Complaint Procedures

Complaint procedures can be used by families, staff, organizations, or individuals when violations of special education law occur (34 C.F.R. § 300.151–153). Examples of common reasons complaints are filed include failure to provide records when requested or failure to implement an IEP. When parents are advised of their procedural due process rights, they must also be advised of the state complaint procedures (34 C.F.R. § 300.504 [c]). This information is typically preprinted on parental-rights forms and may be available on the Internet. To file a complaint, a written letter must be sent to an SEA outlining the alleged violation. The SEA is required to respond, investigate, and issue a written decision within 60 days of receipt of the complaint. The time limit may be extended only if an exceptional circumstance exists in respect to a particular complaint (34 C.F.R. § 300.152).

Behavior and Student Discipline
Discipline Procedures

Schools safety has been one of the top concerns of citizens in America following the tragedies on school campuses that have become all too familiar news stories. Guidelines regarding the discipline of all students in a school setting are founded on the principle of due process of law:

All student discipline must be accompanied by due process (Goss v. Lopez, 419 U.S. 565 [1975]). The level of due process necessary will be determined by the severity of the sanction. But, before any sanction is imposed, the student must know what offense is charged and be given an opportunity to tell his or her side of the story. In the case of a relatively light sanction, such as detention, this entire process may take only a few minutes. But it must be complied with, to assure the school's right to impose discipline (Collins & Dowell, 1998, p. 35).

Students receiving special education can be disciplined yet must be afforded due process of law when involved in a disciplinary action (Yell, Katsiyannis, Bradley, & Rozalski, 2000). *Goss v. Lopez* (1975), referred to by Collins and Dowell (1998) above, was the U.S. Supreme Court ruling that put into law the necessary components of due process for all student discipline. *Honig v. Doe* (1988) was a later Supreme Court ruling that required a MANIFESTATION DETERMINATION for students receiving special education prior to expulsion or long-term suspension. This means that before a student in special education is subject to a district's regular discipline procedures, an IEP team must determine if the behavior for which the student is being disciplined was a manifestation of the student's disability and whether the student's placement was appropriate.

All schools, school districts, and states have a code of conduct for their students. Most are similar to California's discipline code (see sidebar on pp. 323–324). Consequences for inappropriate actions are administered at the classroom level, with consequences of increasing severity for more significant violations under the educational code or policy of a district. The goal is to shape student behavior, encouraging them to learn appropriate behavior that allows them and those around them to learn.

Two types of removals are typically common in schools: suspension and expulsion. Suspension is the removal of a student from a classroom or a school for a limited period of time, usually one to five days. Expulsion refers to removal from the educational programs of a school district for a lengthy period of time, usually two semesters or longer, and is imposed by a school board or other governing body. Suspensions can be imposed by teachers and school principals and require a minimum of due process. However, the number of days a child with a disability may be suspended without any educational services is limited to ten cumulative days in a school year (34 C.F.R. § 300.530 [b][2]). Therefore, cumulative suspensions over ten days require an IEP team meeting to respond to the change in placement and consider changes to the behavioral intervention plan. Expulsion can be imposed by a school board only and requires more extensive disciplinary due process procedures, including an expulsion hearing where evidence is heard. Children with disabilities who are expelled from school must continue to receive FAPE (34 C.F.R. § 300.530 [d]). (See "Home-Bound, Home-Schooled, Hospital-Bound, Suspended/Expelled, or Incarcerated Children and Youth" in Chapter 7 for further discussion of how to serve students who have been suspended or expelled.)

Grounds for Suspension and Expulsion

A pupil may not be suspended from school or recommended for expulsion, unless the superintendent or the principal of the school in which the pupil is enrolled determines that the pupil has committed an act as defined pursuant to any of subdivisions (a) to (q), inclusive:

(a) (1) Caused, attempted to cause, or threatened to cause physical injury to another person. (2) Willfully used force or violence upon the person of another, except in self-defense.

(b) Possessed, sold, or otherwise furnished any firearm, knife, explosive, or other dangerous object, unless, in the case of possession of any object of this type, the pupil had obtained written permission to possess the item from a certificated school employee, which is concurred in by the principal or the designee of the principal.

(c) Unlawfully possessed, used, sold, or otherwise furnished, or been under the influence of, any controlled substance listed in Chapter 2 (commencing with Section 11053) of Division 10 of the Health and Safety Code, an alcoholic beverage, or an intoxicant of any kind.

(d) Unlawfully offered, arranged, or negotiated to sell any controlled substance listed in Chapter 2 (commencing with Section 11053) of Division 10 of the Health and Safety Code, an alcoholic beverage, or an intoxicant of any kind, and either sold, delivered, or otherwise furnished to any person another liquid, substance, or material and represented the liquid, substance, or material as a controlled substance, alcoholic beverage, or intoxicant.

(e) Committed or attempted to commit robbery or extortion.

(f) Caused or attempted to cause damage to school property or private property.

(g) Stolen or attempted to steal school property or private property.

(h) Possessed or used tobacco, or any products containing tobacco or nicotine products, including, but not limited to, cigarettes, cigars, miniature cigars, clove cigarettes, smokeless tobacco, snuff, chew packets, and betel. However, this section does not prohibit use or possession by a pupil of his or her own prescription products.

(i) Committed an obscene act or engaged in habitual profanity or vulgarity.

(j) Unlawfully possessed or unlawfully offered, arranged, or negotiated to sell any drug paraphernalia, as defined in Section 11014.5 of the Health and Safety Code.

(k) Disrupted school activities or otherwise willfully defied the valid authority of supervisors, teachers, administrators, school officials, or other school personnel engaged in the performance of their duties.

Continued

Making a Difference
for America's Children

Grounds for Suspension and Expulsion – *Continued*

(l) Knowingly received stolen school property or private property.

(m) Possessed an imitation firearm. As used in this section, "imitation firearm" means a replica of a firearm that is so substantially similar in physical properties to an existing firearm as to lead a reasonable person to conclude that the replica is a firearm.

(n) Committed or attempted to commit a sexual assault as defined in Section 261, 266c, 286, 288, 288a, or 289 of the Penal Code or committed a sexual battery as defined in Section 243.4 of the Penal Code.

(o) Harassed, threatened, or intimidated a pupil who is a complaining witness or a witness in a school disciplinary proceeding for the purpose of either preventing that pupil from being a witness or retaliating against that pupil for being a witness, or both.

(p) Unlawfully offered, arranged to sell, negotiated to sell, or sold the prescription drug Soma.

(q) Engaged in, or attempted to engage in, hazing as defined in subdivision (b) of Section 245.6 of the Penal Code.

Additional Grounds: Sexual Harassment § 48900.2

§ 48900.3   Hate Violence

§ 48900.4   Harassment, Threats, or Intimidation (Grades 4–12 only)

§ 48900.7   Terroristic Threats

Mandatory Expulsion & Referral: § 48915 (c)

i. Possession, selling, or otherwise furnishing a firearm

ii. Brandishing a knife at another person

iii. Unlawfully selling a controlled substance

iv. Committing or attempting to commit a sexual assault or committing a sexual battery

Mandatory Recommendation for Expulsion: § 48915 (a)

i. Causing serious physical injury to another person, except in self-defense

ii. Possession of any knife, explosive, or other dangerous object of no reasonable use to the student

iii. Unlawful possession of any controlled substance, except for the first offense for the possession of not more than one avoirdupois ounce of marijuana, other than concentrated cannabis

iv. Robbery or extortion

v. Assault or battery

Source: California Education Code 48900 (2006)

#TP-29703 Making a Difference - 2nd Ed. · ©2008 Thinking Publications® · www.thinkingpublications.com · 1-800-277-8737

Manifestation Determination

For students receiving special education, IDEA 2004 provides protections designed to ensure that students are not penalized for behavior that is manifested as part of their disability. Discipline procedures were specifically addressed in IDEA 2004 to make clear that all special educators have responsibilities in these matters. This includes conducting a functional behavioral assessment (FBA) and implementing a behavioral assessment plan (BIP), required components of IEP meetings when a student is experiencing behavorial or discipline problems (see sidebar on p. 326).

In situations when expulsion is recommended or required (e.g., carrying a weapon into school or to a school function, or possessing or selling illegal drugs or controlled substances), a manifestation determination review must be conducted immediately, if possible, or no later than ten school days after the decision to take disciplinary action. The purpose of the review is to determine—

(i) if the conduct in question was caused by, or had a direct and substantial relationship to, the child's disability; or

(ii) if the conduct in question was the direct result of the LEA's failure to implement the IEP (34 C.F.R. § 300.530 [e][1][i] [ii]).

An IEP team and other qualified persons must consider relevant evaluative and observational data, the student's IEP, teacher observation, and information provided by the parent that is relevant. The team must use this information to make the determinations laid out in 34 C.F.R. § 300.530 (e)(1)(i) and (ii). If the answer to the questions posed under these two criteria is "yes" (e.g., the conduct was caused by or had a direct and substantial relationship to the child's disability, or the conduct in question was the direct result of the LEA's failure to implement the IEP), then the student may not be processed for general disciplinary actions. If, however, the answer to these questions is "no," then the student can be subject to the same disciplinary procedures as general education students.

If the IEP team makes a determination that the action was a manifestation of the student's disability, they must take the following additional steps:

1. If a functional behavioral analysis had not been conducted before the incident and a behavioral intervention plan did not exist, the IEP team must develop an assessment plan with the goal of developing a behavioral intervention plan (34 C.F.R. § 300.530 [b][1][i]).

2. If a behavioral intervention plan was in place at the time of a serious incident, an IEP team must review the plan and decide if adjustments are needed (34 C.F.R. § 300.530 [b][1][ii]).

Special education has been criticized for supposedly having a different discipline standard than that of general education, frustrating administrators, parents, teachers, and students. Zirkel (2006) observes that the procedures for manifestation determination under IDEA 2004 represent a shift from the focus on the IEP that was seen under the regulations of IDEA (1997) to a focus on causality; specifically, is there something about the student's disability that caused the infraction? Although the procedures of the

Functional Behavioral Assessment (FBA) and Behavior Intervention Plan (BIP)

IDEA 2004 contains specific requirements to guarantee that IEP teams and school-based personnel work to remediate problematic behavior in students with disabilities (34 C.F.R. § 300. 530). Speech-language pathologists must be aware of requirements for conducting a functional behavioral assessment (FBA) and implementation of a behavioral intervention plan (BIP), which are necessary components of the IEP when a student is experiencing behavioral and/or discipline problems. FBA is a systematic method of analyzing a student's behavior, examining when a student acts inappropriately and what circumstances precipitate the behavior. Most often, a school psychologist conducts the FBA, but the MDT is involved, especially those members who work with the student on a regular basis. The purpose of the FBA is to reveal patterns that predict the student's misbehavior. The FBA will consist of observations in a variety of settings, as well as interviews with staff and the parent(s) of the child, and, if appropriate, the student. One of the goals of the FBA is to discover situations that are reinforcing for the student. These situations will eventually become part of the BIP. When the BIP is developed, the team will identify skills and strategies that need to be learned by the student. Speech-language pathologists may feel that their training did not encompass strategies for dealing with difficult behavior. In fact, communication strategies are frequently needed by students with maladaptive behavior (Sanger & Moore-Brown, 2000).

The IEP team should conduct an FBA whenever a student's challenging behavior is persistent despite implementation of generally successful behavior management techniques. Additionally, an FBA should be conducted whenever a student's behavior is harming him- or herself or others, and if the behavior is placing him or her at risk of, or subject to, disciplinary action, such as repeated suspensions or expulsion. Once a BIP is developed, consistent implementation is critical, especially to ensure student success (Deveres & Pitasky, 1999a, 1999b).

Although FBAs and BIPs are intended for use with a student who is presenting behavioral issues, specific regulations apply for a student involved in disciplinary matters. If the student has been suspended for more than 10 days, manifestation determination provisions of IDEA go into effect. Under these circumstances, the C.F.R. directs teams to conduct an FBA and develop a BIP if one is not already in place for the student, or to review the BIP if one is in place, and determine if modifications are necessary (34 C.F.R. § 300.530).

manifestation determinations have changed between IDEA (1997) and IDEA 2004, the protections of IDEA, however, are still present for students with disabilities who violate their school's discipline code.

Educators who are called to be a part of a manifestation determination review must consider what they know about the student and what could have been predicted about his or her behavior. For example, for a student with documented attention deficit hyperactivity disorder (ADHD), which manifests in impulsive action, it may be found that his or her impulsivity was responsible for the inappropriate action. In this case, the team could determine that the behavior was a manifestation of the disability and may also decide to revise the IEP to more effectively assist the student in coping with his or her impulsivity. However, impulsivity is likely not responsible if the same student was involved in an action that was planned over a number of days. In that case, the team may determine that the behavior was not a manifestation of the disability. Zirkel (2006) specifically considers a situation of impulsivity and how it may be treated under the new requirements for manifestation determination under IDEA 2004 versus the standards of IDEA (1997):

> Under IDEA 1997, it *[the impulsivity factor]* was attached to the secondary, control, and consequences criteria, whereas under IDEA 2004, its role appears less likely within the overall causality standard (p. 11).

Examining causality might lead the IEP team to determine that a student who stutters had no prior history or anything in his profile which would have contributed to him bringing a knife to school. But a student with a pragmatic disorder may predictably be involved in an incident of disrespecting authority that might lead him or her to a disciplinary proceeding. One of the keys in the new IDEA 2004 regulations is the component of ensuring that the district's failure to implement the IEP may have contributed to the incident in question. For example, in a case where an IEP team recommends that a student with a pragmatic disorder receive counseling services or social skills training, but there is no follow-through on the part of the IEP team, the student would not be able to be disciplined.

A common complaint about special education is that students cannot be disciplined—this is not true. However, procedural violations on the part of staff will stand out glaringly when a determination is made that a student's IEP was not being implemented, and therefore the student will not be disciplined accordingly. In all situations involving student discipline, the speech-language pathologist or audiologist must work closely with administrators to ensure that laws are followed. The manifestation determination review process is summarized in the sidebar on p. 328. Speech-language pathologists and audiologists might be involved in discipline cases due to the relationship between communication and violence (Sanger, Moore-Brown, & Alt, 2000). Students with disabilities not only run the risk of being the perpetrators of misbehavior and violence but may also be victims, especially those students with cognitive impairments, learning disabilities, and emotional disturbances (USDE, 1999).

Manifestation Determination Reviews

When are manifestation determination reviews conducted?

A manifestation determination review is conducted when a student receiving special education is subject to the following disciplinary actions:

- Has been suspended for 10 school days (consecutive).
- Has been suspended for 10 school days (cumulative).
- Is recommended for expulsion.

Who conducts a manifestation determination review?

The IEP team members and other qualified personnel (34 C.F.R. § 300.530[e]).

What is the timeline for conducting a manifestation determination review?

Within 10 school days of any decision to change the placement of a child with a disability... (34 C.F.R. § 300.530[e]).

What does the review consist of?

... must review all relevant information in the student's file, including the child's IEP, any teacher observations, and any relevant information provided to the parent to determine—

(i) If the conduct in question was caused by, or had a direct and substantial relationship to, the child's disability; or

(ii) If the conduct in question was the direct result of the LEA's failure to implement the IEP.

What if the IEP team meets and determines that the behavior was related to the student's disability, or that the placement was inappropriate, or that the student was unable to determine right from wrong?

If any of the review standards are not met, the behavior is determined to be a manifestation of the disability. The student cannot be subject to the relevant disciplinary procedure. If the public agency has identified deficiencies in the child's IEP or placement, it must remedy them immediately.

What if the IEP team determines that the behavior is not a manifestation of the student's disability and that placement was appropriate and the student was able to determine the consequences of his or her behavior?

Then the student can be disciplined in the same manner as nondisabled students with the exception that FAPE must continue to be provided.

What other requirements exist?

If a behavioral intervention plan was in place at the time of the incident, then the IEP team must convene a meeting to review the plan. If a functional behavioral analysis had not been conducted prior to the incident and a behavioral intervention plan did not exist, the IEP team must develop an assessment plan toward the goal of developing such a plan.

Source: 34 C.F.R. § 300.530

Working With Families

IDEA 2004 put additional emphasis on the importance of and requirements for working with families. Speech-language pathologists and audiologists will find that the experience of working with families can vary greatly. No one will argue that parents are a critical part of the special program design and implementation of an IEP. Certain realities provide perspective and may be helpful when dealing with challenging situations. One reality is that parents and children have rights; school districts and school district personnel have legal obligations to ensure those rights (Gilyard, 1999). Another reality is that children do not choose the circumstances into which they are born. This applies to any circumstance including economic, physical, or familial. A third reality is that a positive partnership with families can be most rewarding personally and professionally, and will benefit the student greatly. Most educators and parents desire this type of relationship with families, although it is not always realized.

Speech-language pathologists and audiologists will encounter a multitude of family situations. Communication impairments affect the entire family constellation. When working with children, considering the impact of their disability on their home lives, in addition to their school lives, helps speech-language pathologists and audiologists understand the big picture of the impact of the disability. The role of school-based intervention is to improve educationally related difficulties. However, since communication is at the heart of relationships and learning, both at school and at home, expanded understandings can promote effective interventions.

Working with families can put speech-language pathologists and audiologists in some trying situations, such as being the person who confirms the presence of a disability or having to share data with parents that present a child as being more impaired than the family may be prepared to accept. When specialists are dealing with parents, the circumstances can be sensitive. Children are the most precious connection to a parent's being.

Dealing with difficult issues regarding children can be rewarding and challenging at the same time. A reality of the entire IEP process, including assessment, identification, eligibility determination, and intervention, is that educators participate in IEPs as a part of the professional team. For parents, this is a part of their personal life. Participation in this process is new, frequently confusing, and even intrusive. As a school professional, it is a speech-language pathologist's or audiologist's job to work with parents in designing and carrying out an educational program for their child. Attorney Lawrence Siegel, a special education attorney and advocate, advised parents as follows:

> Advocating for your child is easy. You want the best for her. Still, there will be bumps along the way. The IEP process is maze-like, involving a good deal of technical information, intimidating professionals, and confusing choices. For some families, it goes smoothly, with no disagreements; for others, it is a terrible encounter in which you and your school district cannot even agree on the time of day. For most people, the experience is somewhere in between (1999, pp. 1, 3).

Speech-language pathologists and audiologists may find that the circumstances in a home are not conducive to supporting education. There may be no one available to assist a child with homework or books, or other printed materials may not be available, or the parents may be illiterate or experience a disability themselves. A child's linguistic development may be adversely affected in a home where the primary language is other than English or where cultural differences exist that are dramatically different than that of the school culture or classroom expectations. These issues can be difficult for typically developing children, and may be either more or less difficult for children with disabilities. Low socioeconomic homes often also have limited or poor access to health care. This may mean that medical situations that might lead to learning disabilities or communication impairments are not treated, exacerbating the situation. These examples do not mean that all children from low socioeconomic or culturally diverse situations are at risk of developing communication disorders, but when evaluating such children, it is important to distinguish difference versus disorder versus delay, and also important to consider all aspects of the child's and family's situation. (See Chapter 3 for a discussion of dynamic assessment and Chapter 7 for further information on students who are CULTURALLY/ LINGUISTICALLY DIVERSE [CLD].)

Parent Involvement

Children have a wide range of family constellations; family can mean any number and relationship of people who are involved with taking care of a child. Regardless of the circumstances, speech-language pathologists and audiologists must remember that only parents or legal guardians assigned educational rights can sign for permission to assess or consent to placement in an IEP. Even when children have been removed from parental custody, parents may still retain educational rights. This is regulated differently in each state, so be sure to check state laws for clarification.

If children do not have a custodial parent, LEAs will assign a surrogate parent. Surrogate parents are individuals who have received specialized training and are assigned by the school district to represent children in all matters relating to children's identification, evaluation, placement, and provision of FAPE (34 C.F.R. § 300.519). When children are placed through court action in a licensed child-care institution (e.g., a group home) or a foster home, birth parents may still have educational rights, even if children do not live with these parents. These situations can become very complex for care providers, educators, children, and birth parents. Additionally, the dynamics of these situations can be trying. Speech-language pathologists and audiologists should enlist the assistance of a supervisor when questions arise regarding parental status. These situations, however, do not necessarily need to be difficult. If the approach taken by the school is that the student has many adults who care, then positive results can happen.

Parents may react in any variety of ways when asked to be involved in educational planning for their children. Speech-language pathologists and audiologists may work with parents in any of the following situations:

• Parents who do not respond to phone calls or do not come to appointments or IEP meetings. These parents may seem not to care, but may also have other demands that prevent active participation. IDEA 2004 requires holding meetings at a mutually agreed on time when parents can attend but does not require undue hardship of staff. Teleconferencing is allowed if that is the only way that parents can participate in their child's IEP.

• Parents who are grateful for the help and appreciative of the assistance of the specialists involved with their child. These parents may even be too passive in their acceptance of the information shared. The goal in all situations is to make parents partners in evaluation, planning, and treatment. Parents of this type may at first seem to be the most cooperative with which to work, but then may not follow through at home or recognize their role in their child's education.

• Parents who are active team members and bring ideas and suggestions to planning sessions. These parents are usually actively involved in home programs established for their child.

• Parents who are active team members and bring ideas and suggestions to planning sessions, but may bring ideas that are contrary to those brought forward by professionals. This type of situation may be more challenging for professionals. This can lead to a situation that may be on the path to mediation or a due process hearing. Under no circumstances should ideas brought forth by parents be dismissed or not discussed. Seek assistance as soon as a situation appears to be adversarial or one that will create dissent. In all cases, listen closely, seek more information, and document what parents are requesting.

• Parents who are adversarial or mistrustful of the IEP process and may be confrontational or uncooperative. These types of people are challenging in any walk of life; however, in special education, a federal law requires that parents and school people work together. The next section gives some suggestions on strategies to use in difficult situations.

These generalities are likely exaggerations of any situation but do represent differing types of situations that speech-language pathologists and audiologists should be prepared to encounter. In any of these situations, strategies that focus a group on the needs of children can help to improve the situation. The USDE (1999) reports that school personnel behavior can influence parental participation in either a positive or inhibiting way:

Research indicates that the overwhelming majority of parents of children with disabilities are involved in their children's education through meetings with teachers, volunteering at school, helping with homework, or other school- and home-based activities. Educators may enhance levels of parent involvement by establishing ongoing relationships with parents, teaching parents about their rights under IDEA, and using specific strategies to promote involvement (pp. I-11–I-12).

Strategies for Avoiding or Managing Conflict

Training programs and literature in the field often do not prepare speech-language pathologists and audiologists for work situations that involve conflict. Working in special education can, at times, be sensitive and perhaps even contentious due to the trying nature of the work. Parents are struggling to adjust to the nature of their children's disabilities while maintaining jobs, families and other personal situations; general educators are attempting to work with these children as students in their classrooms while attending to the needs of the other students and demands for improved student performance; and special educators are grappling with increased student needs, demands for accountability and outcomes, and paperwork that can seem overwhelming. Administrators are trying to balance all of these needs and be fiscally accountable. Stressors exist at every level.

> Training programs and literature in the field often do not prepare speech-language pathologists and audiologists for work situations that involve conflict.

In training programs, speech-language pathologists and audiologists learn how to use a scientific method to approach the disabilities presented by students. In many ways, approaching difficult situations should be viewed in much the same manner while adding heart, understanding, and patience. IDEA 2004 provides for a team approach to planning for and working with children. In the best of all possible worlds, all people come to their roles in the team equally prepared to work together and use solid, up-to-date information and research-based methods to help students. In such a scenario, the team acknowledges the importance of each person's role, including the valuable role that parents play.

IEP teams, like any other team, are made up of individuals who each bring differing backgrounds and experiences to their responsibilities. In such circumstances, difficulties can arise. Some of these are unique to the situation of special education, others are unique to education in general, and some are characteristic of working with difficult people. For the latter circumstance, speech-language pathologists and audiologists may find taking a workshop on working with difficult people useful. For the other circumstances speech-language pathologists and audiologists might be wise to watch and learn from those who have successfully worked under such situations for several years (e.g., fellow speech-language pathologists or audiologists, mentor teachers, principals, or other administrators). These people have developed skills and abilities that can be learned and applied when necessary.

#TP-29703 Making a Difference - 2nd Ed. • ©2008 Thinking Publications® • www.thinkingpublications.com • 1-800-277-8737

Chapter 4 describes the IEP as a process. Involving all parties as part of the process can help to achieve a "win-win" situation. All parties have a stake in the agreement reached with the IEP document. In an ideal scenario, all parties come to the process with something to contribute and respecting the input of others, and the process goes well. However, in some situations, this scenario does not occur. In these less than ideal cases, team members should examine issues that might confound successful teamwork to decide how to approach the process. Table 8.3 offers some possible issues that speech-language pathologists may need to respond to when administrators, special educators, and other staff bring them to the IEP process. Some of these issues are hidden, while others are quite apparent. This table is certainly not exhaustive, but it encapsulates the types of situations that might arise.

The number one way to avoid problems with parents or colleagues, however, is to be sure that the IEPs are done correctly. Many problems that districts have with IEPs are because of mistakes that could have been avoided. Fagan, Friedman, and Fulfrost (2007) identified the following ten most common IEP mistakes that can be avoided:

1. **Mistake**: No placement offer

   What to do: The placement offer should be stated clearly.

2. **Mistake:** More than one placement offer

   What to do: The district's offer must be clear; do not give parents options from which to choose.

3. **Mistake:** Absence of key teacher(s)

   What to do: Reschedule if necessary, but must have the teacher(s) at the meeting that work directly with the student.

4. **Mistake:** No transition plan

   What to do: Need to have transition plans for any school movement—from nonpublic school to a self-contained classroom, from Part C to preschool, from preschool to school-age, high school to post-secondary, etc. Failure to provide an appropriate transition plan can result in needing to provide the student with compensatory education, despite the fact that the student has earned a diploma. Also, transition plans are needed for students moving from feeder elementary districts to high school districts.

5. **Mistake:** Missing important assessment information

   What to do: Have adequate assessment information to lay the foundation for the IEP.

6. **Mistake:** No review of prior goals

   What to do: If the student has not made progress or has made limited progress, the goals should not be continued; they should be changed.

7. **Mistake:** Needs without goals

   What to do: For each area of need, there should be goals, which then drive service. Follow the process.

8. **Mistake:** Unclear service levels

   What to do: Everyone needs to have a clear understanding of the services the IEP offers.

Table 8.3	**Strategies for IEP Team Member Issues**		
Disgruntled IEP Team Member	**Possible Issue**	**Characteristic Statement**	**Suggested Strategy**
General Education Teacher	Does not want to work with the student	"You know, I have 30 other students in my classroom."	Offer consultative support with specific times to meet
	Does not believe that it is his or her job to work with special education students	"It wouldn't be fair to the other students in the class if we made exceptions for Bobby."	Discuss "fairness," discuss and problem-solve issues of concern, have in-class support services to demonstrate methodologies
	Overwhelmed by other job demands	"I'm just not sure when I would have time to do this."	Discuss and problem-solve issues of concern, outline specific requirements, offer assistance with documentation
	Scared he or she does not know what to do with the student	"I'm not really the person who would know how to work with this type of problem."	Offer training, offer consultation, demystify the disorder and expectations
	Fearful of criticism/ Lack of ownership	"We never receive any support when we do this."	Query what type of support is thought to be needed
	Cannot believe the referred student does not qualify for special education	"What am I supposed to do?"	Suggest accommodations/modifications/ instructional methods to use
Special Education Teacher	High caseload	"It's hard for me to individualize with so many students to serve."	Assist with schedule; add extra time, if appropriate; review placement of other students in class
	Burnout/Not feeling supported	"They always give me the tough kids."	Acknowledge hard work
	Not having the skills to work with student's needs	"I've never had a student like this." "No one knows how hard my job is."	Offer training/staff development/program manager's support

Table 8.3 – *Continued*

Disgruntled IEP Team Member	Possible Issue	Characteristic Statement	Suggested Strategy
Administrator	Concerned that special education takes too much time	"I have a whole campus to run."	Acknowledge how busy the administrator is
	Concerned about teachers	"I don't know how you can expect these teachers to do this."	Attempt to make concerns specific
Parents	In one of the grieving stages: shock/denial, anger (inward), anger (outward), depression, acceptance	"I don't believe you." "He can do that at home."	Remind parents that we are all on the same side, defuse the situation, remind parents that IEPs are temporary documents—they can always be rewritten
	Do not believe that anything can be done for their child	"My child doesn't belong in one of those classes." "My child is not like those children." "I'm the parent; I know my child the best."	Ask: "What part don't you believe?", discuss instructional methods and that there are different kinds of abilities/disabilities, agree that the parents are the experts on the child

9. **Mistake:** Extended school year services (ESY) – not specified, not enough, not offered

   What to do: ESY services are needed for students who may regress during long breaks and will not be able to recoup their prior levels in a short period of time. Consider ESY individually according to student need.

10. **Mistake:** Lack of professional judgment

    What to do: Professional behavior should be used at all times. This enhances relationships with parents and colleagues.

Having a global perspective of how to approach difficult situations can provide team members with a method to deal with the types of issues and statements presented in Table 8.3. Alternative dispute resolution approaches were mentioned in the section on mediation. Such strategies may be necessary in IEP meetings when the meetings necessitate negotiations. A successful business book about negotiations, *Getting to Yes: Negotiating Agreement without Giving In* (Fisher, Ury, & Patton, 1991), provides an excellent methodology for working through such situations:

Any method of negotiation may be fairly judged by three criteria: It should produce a wise agreement if agreement is possible. It should be efficient. And it should improve or at least not damage the relationship between the parties. (A wise agreement can be defined as one that meets the legitimate interests of each side to the extent possible, resolves conflicting interests fairly, is durable, and takes community interests into account.) (p. 4)

These authors were not describing IEP meetings, but they might have been. Team members need to clearly understand everyone's roles (see "Who Comprises the IEP Team?" in Chapter 4) as involvement of parents, students, and general education teachers increases. When more people become involved in the team process, more perspectives are considered, which should be an advantage. Involvement of more people should mean more people focusing on what is needed for a student. When members do not have a common focus, the method outlined by Fisher et al. (1991) will be helpful. Their method, developed at the Harvard Negotiation Project, is known as Principled Negotiations, and is comprised of four primary parts:

People: Separate the people from the problem.

Interests: Focus on interests, not positions.

Options: Generate a variety of possibilities before deciding what to do.

Criteria: Insist that the result be based on some objective standard (p. 10).

An IEP is not meant to be a contentious process. IDEA 2004 is silent on the conduct of the meeting, outlining only what should be addressed at the meeting (34 C.F.R. § 300.320–300.324). Siegel (1999) gives parents information on how to advocate for their children through an IEP process. Educators need to be equally informed on how to work through difficult issues and utilizing the Fisher et al. (1991) method may help. Failure to find ways to implement appropriate IEPs can have serious consequences for school districts, such as requiring reimbursement for the costs of private school placements, compensatory education, or damages. When team members do not agree on IEP issues, what is sacrificed is the appropriate education of students.

In order to remove barriers and develop successful parent-school partnerships, the USDE (1999) recommended the following:

- Improve communication among parents, teachers, and administrators.

- Tap *[into]* parents' expertise.

- Involve families in community-based intervention/instruction (pp. I-13–I-14).

Successful parent-school partnerships will contribute to IEPs that better identify student needs and methods to effectively meet those needs. When working through difficult IEP processes and implementing the methods of Fisher et al. (1991), speech-language pathologists, audiologists, and IEP teams may find the following strategies useful:

- Always check with participants about what is being documented. For example, if parents and school staff see a behavior differently, then document both points of view (e.g., "School staff report that Sally does not speak at school. She uses gestures to express her wants and needs. Parents report that Sally uses one- and two-word phrases at home to express her wants and needs.").

- Be sure that recommended goals and objectives or benchmarks are founded on research-based practices, so that the rationale for their recommendation can be explained to other IEP team members.

- When team members disagree on recommended services or goals, attempt to agree on a short-term solution (e.g., agree to small group services three times per week for three months rather than a full year).

- Set a meeting time for two to three months in the future to address or readdress sensitive issues.

- Keep meeting notes for all IEPs. Always document parental comments and requests.

- Always begin meetings by identifying what issues are to be discussed and what process will be used. Always ask parents what issues they would like discussed at the meeting.

- Be sure everyone is comfortable with the language used (English or other) or have interpreter services available.

- Use a flip chart or white board to write issues and illustrate discussion items. This is particularly helpful when drafting goals, illustrating students' schedules, and writing topics that need to be covered.

- Make every attempt to resolve disagreements between professionals prior to a meeting. In other words, do not engage in professional debates in front of parents.

- Begin with one or two items everyone can agree on to set a positive tone.

- Offer to have weekly or bi-monthly (i.e., every other week) meetings of one or more members of the school team to check progress. Such meetings are not IEP meetings, but are known as collaboration or team meetings.

- If there is a time constraint for the meeting, identify it at the beginning. Keep track of the time throughout the meeting, as well as what still needs to be addressed.

- Set time limits for meetings that will be contentious. Check with local administration on this. In general, lengthy IEP meetings just make people more positional, and do not contribute to building relationships. If multiple meetings need to be scheduled to work through the tough issues of the IEP, then do so. This is a preferred approach to holding IEPs that last full days.

- Write all decisions into the IEP document.

- If emotions run very high, suggest a five-minute break for fresh air, a drink of water, or a quick change of scene.

- Always thank everyone for being in attendance at the meeting.

- Remember that everyone has the student's best interests at heart. There just may be different versions of how to achieve them.

- Smile, use a sense of humor (as appropriate), and shake hands.

Federal Laws That Prohibit Disability Discrimination

Section 504 and the Americans with Disabilities Act (ADA)

Two federal laws that are not specific to education have had an effect on school programs and facilities. SECTION 504 of the Rehabilitation Act of 1973 was passed to prohibit discrimination against individuals with disabilities by any program receiving federal financial assistance. The AMERICANS WITH DISABILITIES ACT (ADA) was passed in 1990 to strengthen the access requirements of Section 504 and extend them to all public domains.

ADA (1990) and Section 504 (1973) issues frequently are related. ADA deals with access to buildings, facilities, and transportation and includes the provision of auxiliary aids and services to individuals with vision or hearing impairments. Provisions under Section 504 include anything required to enable access to an instructional program, including modifications to the learning environment and materials to meet the needs of students who have identified disabilities. ADA, Section 504, and IDEA 2004 overlap in places.

Until the 1990s, Section 504 (1973) was not commonly applied to students in schools. Since school districts receive federal assistance, however, this act applied to these agencies. Section 504 of the Rehabilitation Act of 1973 requires that:

No qualified handicapped [sic] person shall, on the basis of handicap, be excluded from participation in, be denied the benefits of, or otherwise be subjected to discrimination under any program or activity which receives Federal financial assistance (Office for Civil Rights [OCR], 1999, § 104.4 [a]).

Some children may receive speech-language services under Section 504 (1973) instead of special education. Speech-language pathologists and audiologists who work in schools need to know the legal and procedural basis for this provision of services as it is quite different from special education. Both IDEA 2004 and Section 504 protect students' civil rights. IDEA 2004, however, provides federal funding and describes the procedural requirements required to receive this funding at state and local levels. Section 504 does not provide funding, so schools must use local resources to provide any services or facilities that help students with disabilities access school programs.

A significant difference between the laws, in relation to school-age students with disabilities, is the eligibility criteria. IDEA 2004 protects only students who, by virtue of their disabilities, require special educational services. Section 504, however, prohibits discrimination against all school-age children, regardless of whether or not they require special education services (Gorn, 1997a, p. 11:2).

All individuals who are disabled under the Individuals with Disabilities Education Improvement Act (IDEA) are also considered to be disabled, and therefore protected, under Section 504/ADA. However, all individuals who have been determined to be disabled under Section 504 may not be disabled under IDEA 2004. These children require a response from the regular education staff and curriculum. With respect to most students with disabilities, many aspects of the Section 504 regulation concerning FAPE parallel the requirements of the Individuals with Disabilities Education Improvement Act (formerly the Education of All Handicapped Children Act) and state law (Council of Administrators of Special Education [CASE], 1999, pp. 1–2).

ADA (1990) deals with accessibility to public domains (including communication access) and "prohibits discrimination on the basis of disability in employment, programs, and services provided by state and local governments, goods and services provided by private companies, and in commercial facilities" (U.S. Department of Justice, 1999, ¶ 1).

In communities and employment situations, ADA (1990) issues may become part of the work of speech-language pathologists or audiologists in schools, particularly when dealing with transition to postsecondary settings. For example, a student who is deaf may need a telephone decoding device (TDD) to communicate at a work site. Recent and future advances in telecommunications provide additional accessibility for individuals with communication impairments to be successful in the workplace and these must be made available by employers as they become reasonable to acquire. Schools and public facilities must provide physical access for persons using wheelchairs or who have other mobility impairments (e.g., ramps and elevators); signs must be accessible to persons with visual impairments (e.g., Braille); safety features must be accessible to all (e.g., flashing lights on fire alarms); and facilities, such as water fountains, sinks, toilets, and light switches, must be accessible from various heights and clearances.

Responsibilities to Students Under Section 504

Coverage under Section 504 (1973) is much broader than the eligibility criteria under IDEA 2004. An individual who is considered disabled under Section 504:

- Has a physical or mental impairment that substantially limits one or more major life activities, including "walking, seeing, hearing, speaking, breathing, learning, working, caring for oneself, and performing manual tasks."

• Has a record of such impairment

• Is regarded as having such impairment (CASE, 1999b, p. 7).

To determine if a student is covered under Section 504 (1973), a data-gathering process that considers information from many available sources is used. The individuals involved with this evaluation process comprise the 504 team and are familiar with the student as well as the information considered. The team then meets and determines if the student is considered disabled under the provisions of Section 504.

Section 504 (1973) requires public agencies (i.e., school districts) to provide FAPE in the least restrictive environment (LRE) to any student with a disability that limits a major life function. "Appropriate education" means an

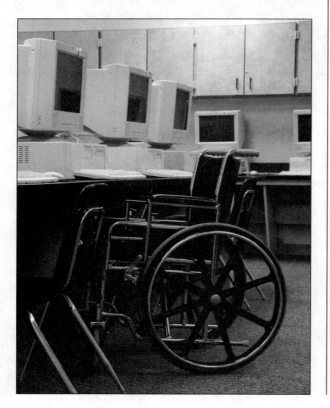

education comparable to the education provided to nondisabled students, requiring that accommodations be made" (CASE, 1999, p. 8). A written plan is not required under Section 504 but is considered "good professional practice" (CASE, 1999, p. 8). This accommodation plan should address five areas:

1. Nature of the student's disability and the major life activity it limits.

2. Basis for determining the disability.

3. Educational impact of the disability.

4. Necessary accommodations.

5. Placement in the least restrictive environment (Gorn, 1997a, pp. 11:4–11:5).

As previously stated, students identified under IDEA 2004 automatically have the protections offered under Section 504 (CASE, 1999, pp. 1–2). However, students who are identified as disabled using Section 504 procedures usually do not need the special education services offered under IDEA 2004 (Zirkel, 2000). Examples of such situations would be students with attention deficit disorder (ADD) who do not demonstrate a learning disability under IDEA 2004, or who are not found to qualify under other health impairment or other eligibility criteria considered in IDEA 2004. The accommodation plan would identify the necessary modifications and accommodations needed to allow the students to access their education (see Table 8.4 for examples).

If a student is found by an IEP team to be ineligible for special education, parents and teachers might advocate for the student to be

Table 8.4	**Section 504 Examples**	
Identified Disability	**Major Life Activity Affected**	**Accommodations Provided**
Attention deficit disorder	Learning	Shortened assignments Reminder prompts Learning center/Study carrel Timer Reinforcers Planning chart on desk Reminder binder Phone message from teacher to parent regarding homework assignments After-school tutoring Peer counseling
Asthma	Breathing	Adjusted physical education requirements, per doctor's orders Modified assignments for physical education Health plan developed for medication needs
Spinal tumor	Working, performing manual tasks	Extra time between classes Peer assistant to take notes Adjusted assignments (due to fatigue) Teacher calls at night to discuss assignments with parents, child, or both Homework club

identified as disabled under Section 504 (1973) with the goal of having the student receive special education and related services through Section 504.

Technically, students identified under Section 504 (1973) cannot be denied special education services. However, if a student's needs are so significant that special education services are required, then an IEP team should identify that student as a child with a disability under IDEA 2004. Accommodations and modifications, such as those identified in Table 8.4, do not need to meet IDEA eligibility for implementation because they can be accomplished using general education staff and resources. Gorn (1997b) explained that "a speech impairment will not always trigger eligibility under either the IDEA or the more inclusive Section 504" (p. 1:9) due to the requirements for adversely affecting educational performance (under IDEA [1997]) or substantially impairing a major life activity (under Section 504 [1973]). A child with a lisp, for example, would probably not qualify under either law, but only the school 504 team could make that determination.

CHAPTER 9

The Work World of Speech-Language Pathologists and Audiologists in Public Schools

IN THIS CHAPTER

The purpose of this chapter is to consider some of the practical and professional issues that impact school-based speech-language pathologists and audiologists, to develop an understanding of the school environment, and to describe how to work effectively in a school environment. Topics include how to obtain a position; roles and responsibilities of speech-language pathologists, audiologists, and speech-language pathology assistants; where to go for assistance; and a variety of professional and organizational issues that are characteristic of a public education system. This chapter is also intended to provide a school-based perspective to the speech-language pathologist exploring a career as an educational professional working in the child's natural environment.

1. Discuss why providing private paid therapy for students from your school caseload on Saturdays would be unethical. What policies would be violated and which speech-language pathologist certifications could be endangered?

2. What does it mean to receive Medicaid payment for speech-language and hearing services in schools? If this is a practice in your area, invite a school-based speech-language pathologist to share the way the program works and how it can be structured as a benefit for children with disabilities and for the speech-language staff in a district.

3. Review the licensing requirements for speech-language pathologists and audiologists for your state. What do you need to know about your state license to practice in the schools?

4. Do your state's licensure rules address assistants or support personnel? Why or why not? What value might they provide to a school setting? How would you utilize their skills?

5. Why should school-based practitioners belong to more than one professional organization?

6. Does your state have labor unions in the schools? Why or why not? How are the school-based speech-language pathologists and audiologists that you know represented in negotiations for salary and working conditions?

7. Practice answering the interview questions in the sidebar on p. 356.

8. Interview a speech-language pathologist from a local school system. Discuss the organizational structures in that school system. Who evaluates the speech-language pathologist? Where does the speech-language pathologist find help, assistance, and support? Report your findings.

9. Review the list of roles and responsibilities of school-based speech-language pathologists (pp. 373–374) and discuss your impression of this list. What roles do you consider particularly interesting? Are there any that seem less familiar to you?

10. Discuss why the prudent professional carries liability insurance.

Certification and Licensing

The world of schools requires a specialized understanding of how "the system" works and what it means to be an employee in a public school system. To work in an educational setting, speech-language pathologists, audiologists and SPEECH-LANGUAGE PATHOLOGY ASSISTANTS (SLPAs) must be licensed or credentialed according to the regulations of their state. There is a relationship between the requirements set at national, state, and local levels. Being familiar with these regulations is important. The AMERICAN SPEECH-LANGUAGE-HEARING ASSOCIATION (ASHA) Web site has a complete listing of the requirements for each state. Before applying for a job (see "Securing a Position" on p. 351), a candidate must make certain he or she has completed all the necessary requirements and paperwork for certification, licensing, or both, if required. With the mandates for highly qualified staff under NO CHILD LEFT BEHIND (NCLB) and the INDIVIDUALS WITH DISABILITIES EDUCATION IMPROVEMENT ACT (IDEA 2004), all of these requirements are given serious attention by the human resources departments of educational agencies. ASHA provides a comparison of ASHA and state certification featured in Table 9.1.

National Certification

The CERTIFICATE OF CLINICAL COMPETENCE (CCC) was established in 1952 by ASHA. See Table 9.2 on p. 350 for cerfication and licensing requirements for speech-language pathologists and audiologists. Although ASHA certification is voluntary, it is recommended because holding the CCC indicates to potential employers that speech-language pathologists and audiologists are committed to providing quality services, since its holders have met the standards of excellence established by this national organization. ASHA certification is typically required in health care, private practice, or other settings that receive third-party reimbursement, since Medicare and Medicaid require ASHA certification for reimbursement. At the national level, the CCC permits its holders to provide independent clinical services and to supervise the clinical practice of students studying speech-language pathology and uncertified clinicians. States have the option to require the speech-language pathologist to have the CCC and hold membership in ASHA in order to supervise SLPAs, monitor a student teacher, participate in ASHA data collection projects, or oversee a colleague completing a Clinical Fellowship (CF). In addition, those who have earned the CCC in speech-language pathology or audiology have the verified knowledge and skills to work in many settings worldwide including American schools and military schools abroad. Some countries (e.g., the United Kingdom) have reciprocity agreements that recognize the CCC.

Since the late 1990s, new reasons have emerged for holding national certification in schools. As mentioned above, such certification may be required in a given state for any third-party billing that is being done by the school system. On a professional level, the concept of national certification has received heightened attention with a recognized system for national teacher certification. As this movement

Table 9.1

Comparison of ASHA Certification Maintenance and State/Local Licensure or Education Certification

What is the difference? What is the same?

Definitions

> **ASHA Certification:** A voluntary credential that verifies an individual's achievement of rigorous, uniform, and validated standards that are nationally recognized.

> **State Licensure:** A mandatory credential that grants permission to practice in a particular state.

> **State Department of Education:** A mandatory credential that regulates individuals who work in public schools.

Comparison of ASHA Certification, State Licensure, and State Department of Education Certification		
ASHA Certification	**State Licensure/ Education Certification**	**ASHA Certification, Licensure, and Education Certification**
Voluntary professional credential	Mandatory for practice	
Based on validation studies of required knowledge, skills, and tasks for independent practice	Established by the state legislature and usually implemented by different state agencies	
Portable: national recognition of being a qualified professional	Possibly recognized by other states	Provides different levels of assurances to the public, other professionals, third-party payers, and employers
Verifies a master's degree • Accredited academic program • Supervised clinical experience and mentorship • Passing score on a national exam	Dictates minimal qualifications to practice • Job titles • Supervision of support personnel, where applicable	License and education certificate requirements differ from state to state. Requirements for a license and for an education certificate in the same state are usually different.

Continued

Table 9.1 – *Continued*

Requires continuing education/professional development to maintain. Wide range of activities and content is accepted.	Requires continuing education/professional development to renew licensure or education certification in most states; may require pre-approval of sponsor of activities.	
Accepts only official transcripts, test scores, and supervision by an individual who holds the CCC as validation to earn the credential.	Many states will accept ASHA CCCs as documentation necessary to meet some or all requirements.	
Requires 30 contact hours of continuing education every three years for maintenance of the certificate.	Continuing education required by most state licensing boards and some state education agencies; number of required contact hours and the length of renewal cycles vary from state to state and from license to education certificate.	
Accepts contact hours for CE activities offered by many respected educational agencies.	Generally requires CE contact hours be from an educational agency that is pre-approved by the state licensing board or by the state education agency; may also accept only certain content.	What is acceptable for ASHA continuing education may not be acceptable to the state and vice versa.

Source: ASHA (n.d.). Reprinted with permission.

emerged, holders of the CCC asserted that they have held such national recognition for years. Some school districts have negotiated treatment of the CCC as the same as national state teacher certification in their collective bargaining agreements. Additionally, a growing number of states and local school districts have established salary supplements and/or are now providing stipends to holders of the CCC or other types of licensure. This practice has grown as a method of retention due to the shortages of speech-language pathologists and audiologists across the country.

While certification is important to establish credibility, licensing is required in many states to legally practice speech-language pathology. In most states, ASHA certification satisfies many of the state requirements for licensure. In fact, in several states, ASHA's certification standards are the only requirement for licensure (ASHA, 2000d).

State Licensing

A school district may not use ASHA's CCC as verification that the individual is appropriately qualified if the state department of education only recognizes its state's certification(s). Some school districts do require the CCC in addition to any state requirements.

All 50 states regulate audiologists via licensure except Colorado, which regulates via registration; 47 states regulate speech-language pathologists (all states except Colorado, Michigan, and South Dakota). The District of Columbia does not regulate either speech-language pathologists or audiologists. Twelve states (CT, DE, HI, KS, IN, LA, MA, MT, NM, OH, TX, and VT) require that school-based audiologists and speech-language pathologists be licensed. Continuing education requirements are in place in 41 states.

Teacher Certification

Each STATE EDUCATIONAL AGENCY (SEA) requires a credential that shows a speech-language pathologist or audiologist has completed a course of study in a university communication disorders program with certain elements, courses, and field experiences approved by that state. These state authorizations may be called teacher permits, teaching certificates, teacher licenses, or clinical service credentials. In this way, the SEA has final approval of all speech-language pathologists and audiologists who work with students in that state.

Speech-language pathologists and audiologists must have some type of state teacher certification to work in a public school setting. Some states have reciprocity with other states (e.g., New England states have reciprocity with each other), but most states only accredit their own state universities and teaching staff. Speech-language pathologists and audiologists must have a state teaching or clinical license to bill a third party, such as an insurance company or Medicaid, for a student's services in schools.

Ideally, school-based speech-language pathologists and audiologists should possess all three credentials—ASHA's CCC, a state license, and teacher certification—in states that have licensure; however, the legal requirement is to hold whatever state certification is needed for providing speech-language services in a par-

ticular state's public schools. The requirements for the three credentials do overlap, especially academic requirements, clinical clock hour requirements, and the required professional year(s) of supervised practice. Simultaneously completing these national and state requirements early on is easier than trying to return to a university to complete one or more credentials later in one's career, since test scores often become outdated and logs of courses and hours can be misplaced or lost. Speech-language pathologists and audiologists in certain states may become frustrated with the need to hold multiple certifications and licenses. This occurs in government related systems that have overlapping oversight from various agencies. Maintaining all requisite certifications is a recommended professional practice, and may become a point of defense if credentials are challenged in any sort of due process action (see Chapter 8).

The current requirements for ASHA's CCC are available on the ASHA Web site (www.asha.org), as is an overview of teacher licensing requirements for each state and contact information for each SEA. Applications for a state teacher certificate must be requested from each SEA, and licensing applications must be requested from the state licensing panel or board, usually housed in a social services or health care department. Although the requirements for certification and licensing might initially appear confusing, Table 9.2 should help school-based speech-language pathologists and audiologists understand the details of certification and licensing.

Highly Qualified Staff

NCLB contains requirements for teachers and paraprofessionals to be HIGHLY QUALIFIED. These requirements mean that teachers must hold the appropriate state certification in the core academic area(s) they are teaching. Core academic subjects are identified as English, reading or language arts, mathematics, science, foreign languages, civics and government, economics, arts, history, and geography. Teachers may establish that they are highly qualified through a process known as HIGH OBJECTIVE UNIFORM STATE STANDARD OF EVALUATION (HOUSSE), which allows for documentation of activities considered sufficient to prepare a teacher as highly qualified. Additionally, NCLB requires that all paraprofessionals in Title I programs have two years of postsecondary education, in addition to a high school diploma or its equivalent (USDE, 2002a). The National Education Association (NEA) and the National Association of State Directors of Special Education (NASDSE, 2004) point out "it is critical to note that the new NCLB paraprofessional qualifications apply to *all* paraprofessionals with instructional duties who are employed in a school that receives schoolwide Title I program funds" (p. 24). Although NCLB requirements do not apply to special education teachers, the concept of highly qualified teachers does appear in IDEA 2004.

Speech-language pathologists and audiologists are considered related service providers under IDEA. Under IDEA 2004, related services personnel and paraprofessionals must have qualifications that are consistent with any state-

Table 9.2

Certification and Licensing Requirements

Certification	Agency	Purpose	Academic Preparation	Test	Practica	Renewal	Required for School Services
Speech-Language Pathology							
Certificate of Clinical Competence in Speech-language pathology (CCC-SLP)	American Speech-Language-Hearing Association (ASHA)	Recognize clinical competence	Graduate degree in the discipline	Praxis II® – Examination in Speech-Language Pathology	250 hours clinical practicum, and 36 weeks of supervision on the job	Pay fee every year	No
Speech-language pathology license	Designated state agency	Protect the public from untrained practitioners	Determined by the state, many mirror the ASHA guidelines for the CCC	Praxis II® – Examination in Speech-Language Pathology	1–2 years of supervision on the job	Pay fee every year or every other year plus obtain CEUs in 38 states	Only in states with universal licensure
Audiology							
Certificate of Clinical Competence in Audiology (CCC-A)	Council on Academic Accreditation in Audiology and Speech-Language Pathology (CAA) of the American Speech-Language Hearing Association (ASHA)	Recognize and validate clinical competence within the scope and sequence of the profession	Graduate degree in an audiology program accredited by CAA-ASHA	Praxis II® – Examination in Audiology	12 months of full-time supervised experience	Payment of appropriate dues and fees	No
Audiologist License	Designated by individual state agencies	Protect the public from untrained practitioners	Master's or doctoral degree with an emphasis in audiology (or 75 credit hours of study that culminates a doctoral or other recognized degree from an accredited ASHA agency)	Praxis II® – Examination in Audiology	Complete supervised clinical practicum approved by the board and delineated in the rules and regulations of that state; or complete a supervised postgraduate experience during the completion of a doctoral degree	Pay dues/fees with renewal application. Each state board determines renewal terms. Complete contact hours or CEUs of continuing education per renewal period	Typically required to work in the schools; however, each state's requirements differ

#TP-29703 Making a Difference - 2nd Ed. · ©2008 Thinking Publications® · www.thinkingpublications.com · 1-800-277-8737

approved or state-recognized certification, licensing, or registration (§ 612 [a][14][B][i]). Emergency, temporary, or provisional certification are prohibited (§ 612 [a][14][B][ii]). It should be noted that the language for highest requirements in the state found in IDEA (1997) at § 612 (a)(15)(B)(ii) was removed from IDEA 2004. Speech-language pathologists and audiologists must be vigilant in their states to monitor any attempt to reduce professional standards. ASHA will assist state associations to resist efforts to lower professional personnel standards. It is tempting for states, in times of shortages, to lower standards; however, maintaining high personnel qualification is critical for ensuring quality services for students.

An Ideal Timeline

Typically, candidates who intend to work in the public schools complete their bachelor's degree in communication disorders, become full-time graduate students, attain their master's degree, pass the national examination (i.e., Praxis II®), complete a Clinical Fellowship (CF) during their first year on the job, and meet ASHA's certification requirements by the end of their first year of work. This process may take longer for some candidates to accomplish than others. Some states do not require a master's degree in communication disorders for candidates to begin working in public schools; however, this is not endorsed by ASHA nor is it recommended by professionals in the field.

Speech-language pathologists and audiologists must realize how important it is to schedule these personal benchmarks carefully and completely, with guidance from mentors in the school district and a graduate-school advisor. This scheduling may help speech-language pathologists or audiologists avoid suddenly realizing that they cannot finish all the requirements in the first year and then losing the momentum needed to complete the academic preparation. Many candidates report that keeping the goal in sight can be hard, especially when others in the school community do not have to earn two more certifications after earning their teaching credentials. However, the CCC and the state license (in states requiring licensure) are critical steps in the preparation of a fully qualified professional. In order to work through a three- to five-year plan for completing these three certifications, speech-language pathologists and audiologists will find it imperative to keep complete and accurate records of all courses, classes, clock hours, registered supervision plans, and test scores in a personal file for solid documentation. It is always the candidate's responsibility to provide proof of meeting all requirements.

Securing a Position

The Job Market

Shortages of special education teachers and specialists have been documented since the mid-1990s (USDE, 1998, 1999). School districts throughout the country have testified particularly to the need for speech-language pathologists in the Study of Personnel Needs in Special Education (SPeNSE, 2002). In the 2000 ASHA Schools Survey, respondents noted the shortage of highly qualified personnel was cited as the largest barrier in recruiting and retaining professionals. It was also reported that the shortage was the greatest in the western part of the country.

The 2002 report from the USDE entitled *Twenty-Fourth Annual Report to the Congress on the Implementation of the Individuals with Disabilities Education Act* contains an entire chapter entitled "Ensuring An Adequate Supply of High-Quality School-Based Speech-Language Pathologists." The information in the document is based on data from SPeNSE. This chapter examines quantity, quality, shortages, and the relationship between working conditions and speech-language pathologists' intent to stay in the profession, qualifications, and perceptions of competence. The introduction states:

In 1999–2000, 1,089,964 students had speech or language impairments as their primary disability, accounting for 19.2% of all students ages 6 through 21 with disabilities served under the Individuals with Disabilities Education Act. Many additional students had speech or language impairments as secondary or tertiary disabilities. The high incidence of speech/language impairments requires a large, highly qualified pool of speech-language pathologists to meet these student's needs.

The quality of the nation's speech-language pathologist workforce depends on having an adequate supply of qualified individuals. Should shortages occur, local districts may be forced to hire less qualified personnel or assign staff to positions for which they are unprepared (p. III-1).

It is estimated that there were 49,721 speech-language pathologists in schools in 1999–2000. The report states: "Having an adequate supply of school-based speech-language pathologists is as important as the quality of those available because shortages typically force administrators to hire less qualified individuals." When administrators can't find speech-language pathologists, the following options are typically implemented:

- Increase other speech-language pathologist's caseloads

- Hire assistants

- Utilize contract services

The report also states: "Perhaps a greater concern than current shortages is the potential for future shortages." It is estimated that 49 percent of school-based speech-language pathologists are 45 or older and will be eligible to retire over the course of the next 15 years. The eldest groups are in suburban and rural areas and the west. Another 5 percent plan to leave the field as soon as possible due to other reasons.

Working conditions impact the quality of services and retention. The report speculated that the practice of increasing CASELOAD size as a way of dealing with shortages might actually exacerbate shortages rather than actually dealing with them (USDE, 2002b).

The U. S. Department of Labor Statistics identified the following information related to shortages in the field:

- Employment rate for speech-language pathologists is expected to grow as fast as average for all occupations through the year 2014.

- Period between 2000–2010: speech-language pathology is the 25th fastest growing occupation of the 700; 11th of the 68 health care professions.

- Project more than 34,000 additional speech-language pathologists will be needed to fill the demand between 2000–2010 (39 percent increase in job opening).

- Project more than 57,000 speech-language pathologist job openings between 2000–2010 due to growth and net replacements.

- Period between 1988–2000 was projected to be faster than average, but was *much* faster than average. In 1988, 53,000 speech-language pathologists were employed; projected in 2000 there would be 68,000, but in reality there were 106,000 (ASHA, 2003e).

The reasons for the shortage is multifactoral. Among the intersecting issues are the following:

- University training programs are filled, but universities may not perceive that there is a need to expand programs and increase the number of graduates entering the field.

- Only 269 training programs exist across the country for speech-language pathologists; not all programs also train audiologists.

- Communication disorders programs are costly to operate. Universities are impacted by funding issues, just as funding issues impact K–12 public education.

- In an expanded job market for young people, there is competition as universities are looking for the best and the brightest candidates to enter their programs.

- Virtually no data exist regarding retention of speech-language pathologists and audiologists in the field.

- Poor working conditions likely contribute to shortages.

ASHA has begun to undertake a more active role in trying to create solutions to the problem. In the meantime, existing speech-language pathologists and those entering speech-language pathology university programs are much needed, so their negotiating power is increased.

> Speech-language pathologists and those entering speech-language pathology university programs are much needed, so their negotiating power is increased.

The Application

Obtaining a job in a school setting is a formal process. Schools typically have an application process for all prospective employees that can be obtained from the personnel or human resources department, although increasingly job applications are available online. Often these are available through the agency's Web site. Some districts join with other school districts for centralized job applications. Before submitting an application to a LOCAL EDUCATIONAL AGENCY (LEA), the applicant may wish to determine if that agency has a speech-language opening. Such information may be found by calling the agency's personnel or human resources department, calling the special education department, searching for job postings on agency Web sites (e.g., ASHA, state speech-language-hearing associations, the Council for Exceptional Children, state departments of education, local school districts, regional service agencies, or Web sites that specialize in posting employment opportunities), looking at job postings at a local university, or reviewing national or regional publications with classified advertisements.

Include a cover letter with all applications. In this letter, state what type of position is being sought, how your qualifications match the desired qualifications for the position (i.e., certification and licensure), and why you are interested in that particular agency. This letter should be short (no more than one page), but should allow readers to see qualifications that might interest them as an employer. Emphasize interest and eagerness to work with children. Identify any specialized training received while in graduate school or any other unique experiences that show involvement with education or children.

In addition to the cover letter, most applications include an essay question. Such questions will typically be broad in scope, for example, "Describe your belief system about education," or "Describe some noteworthy experience you have had in the last three years," or "Who was the person who most influenced your decision to become a teacher?" Time and consideration should be taken in answering any essay question. The response is a prime opportunity to communicate interests, energy, and beliefs about education, special education, and speech-language pathology in the schools to the potential employer. The essay plays an important role in forming the first impression for those who are screening applications, so details such as organization, clarity of ideas, spelling, and legibility should not be overlooked.

The Interview

Applications will be screened by one or more persons at the school district or agency prior to an invitation to interview. The interview process will vary from agency to agency, but candidates should expect to be interviewed by individuals who do not have expertise in speech and language or audiology. Candidates should expect a panel of two to five people to interview them. Additionally, there may be several different panels or meetings with various individuals. For example, the first-level interview might be with a building principal and staff members from a school site. Other special educators, including

speech-language pathologists or audiologists, may or may not be included. Usually someone from the district special education department, such as the director or program manager, will participate as a member of the first interview panel. Second- and third-level interviews may be part of the process and may include other professionals, administrators, parents, PTA members, or teacher organization representatives.

Questions will vary depending on who is conducting the interview. Be prepared to answer questions of a technical nature about speech and language, including questions regarding service delivery and student eligibility. Questions about student discipline and classroom management are likely to be included. It is also advisable to know something about the current educational issues in the local school or in the nation. Reading articles in recent issues of state speech-language-hearing association newsletters or ASHA publications or checking the agency's Web site are effective ways to prepare.

Personal presentation is very important in an interview. Practice responding to interview questions posed by familiar people a few days before the actual interview. Practice answering questions that are likely to be asked, such as, "Tell us about yourself, your background, and your educational training." The culture of schools can be very "student friendly" and interviewers will also want to know if you can provide this level of concern. Educators seek a caring and kind speech-language pathologist who is interested in students first, wants to be a member of their school team, and has a solid knowledge base in the profession so as to be a good resource for them. These traits should be communicated in an interview. With current requirements for access to curriculum, it is also critical that a candidate can explain the role of the speech-language pathologist working with a curriculum.

When interviewing for a school position, especially for the first time, do not be surprised if there are questions which are unfamiliar. Do not try to make up answers. Feel free to say "I do not know" or "I am not familiar with that area." When in an interview, remember that someone in the room wrote the question and does know the answer, so fabricating an answer is usually not successful. Another good answer is usually, "I don't know, but I am willing to learn." The most important advice for an interview is to relax and let personality and experience be guides. An example of possible interview questions can be found in the sidebar on p. 356. Use these as a starting point for practice.

There is usually a time in an interview when the candidate may ask questions. It is not advisable to ask questions about money or benefits at that time. That information, especially salary, can be obtained either through the agency's Web site or through the human resources department. It is considered appropriate to ask questions about working conditions, caseload size, continuing education opportunities, and budget.

Accepting the Position

When an offer of employment is made, make sure all questions about employment conditions are asked and answered fully. Now is the appropriate time to ask questions about the following:

Possible Interview Questions for Speech-Language Pathologists

1. Please begin by telling us about your professional training and experience, including your job-related experiences and education.

2. Describe how a student qualifies to receive special education services. What are the specific criteria to determine if a student is eligible to receive speech and language services?

3. A fourth-grade student has been referred for a language evaluation. How will you conduct the assessment? What tools and procedures will you use?

4. Describe your experience working with bilingual students. Discuss the issues related to students who come from a monolingual Spanish-speaking home but have received English-only instruction.

5. Review for us your experience with the following disorders. Discuss both assessment and intervention: Fluency

    Voice

    Articulation/Phonology

6. Describe your experiences with the following:

    Alternative and Augmentative Communication

    Assistive Technology

    Students with significant disabilities, including ASDs

    Oral motor disorders

    Literacy

7. Discuss the various types of service delivery models that you might use and how you would determine what is appropriate.

- Salary

- Payment schedule (10 months or 12 months)

- Work calendar

- Benefits (including health, dental, vision, and other insurance)

- Union membership (required or optional)

- Site assignment(s)

If a candidate is in the enviable position of having two or more viable offers, he or she may be able to negotiate. However, be cautious so as not to lose both offers. It is acceptable to be straightforward and tell the prospective employer that another offer is being considered, describe the pros on that side, and see what each district will offer. Due to shortages, some districts are offering signing or incentive bonuses to entice candidates to sign on with their system. It is important to note that sign-on bonuses typically require an agreement to stay in the position for a specific time and may ask for the return of all or a portion of the money if a decision is made to leave the position before the time period has expired.

Another option for working in school-based settings that some speech-language pathologists and audiologists may increasingly consider is the option of working for a contract company. Such companies may offer flexibility and benefits that may be enticing, especially to candidates who do not anticipate committing to a full career with a specific educational system. In some cases, the salary may be higher than in the school district itself. Other advantages of working for a contract company may be that the company provides moving costs or certain living expenses.

School districts look to contract companies when they are unable to fill open positions on their staff. There may be pros and cons to working for a contract company that speech-language pathologists and audiologist wish to consider. Salaries and flexibility may be among the pros as well as other benefits such as the payment of association dues and licensing fees. Working directly for a school district also has its benefits. Security in terms of tenure earned in the school system, paying into a retirement system that has strong benefits after a full career, and earning seniority which comes with a broader say in assignments may be among some of the advantages of working directly for a school district. As a member of the school district staff, speech-language pathologists and audiologists will also be involved with the reform efforts in that district and have influence in the role that special education takes. Most contract individuals will not be asked to sit on committees or to contribute in a decision-making manner to school issues.

Organizational Structures

Schools in the United States are created under many different types of organizational structures. Schools themselves usually are part of a district, with names that may sound familiar: Jefferson County Public Schools (Louisville, KY); Los Angeles Unified School District (Los Angeles, CA); and Sunnybrook School District (Lansing/Lynwood, IL). School districts vary by size, organizational structure, geography, historical events, and state fiscal procedures. The Los Angeles Unified School District encompasses a massive area, not only in terms of land, but also in the more critical responsibility of educating nearly 800,000 children (nearly as many students as in the entire state of Wisconsin). The state of North Dakota has approximately 130 school districts for slightly over 101,000 students enrolled in their entire state's school system. And in Hawaii, the entire state encompasses only one school district, serving approximately 184,000 children.

The organizational structures that provide services to children with disabilities vary greatly from district to district and from state to state. Throughout this book, reference has been made to local, regional, and state services. Local usually refers to a school district, but not always. For example, in a rural or smaller suburban district, special education services may be provided on a regional basis. Regional systems are typically cooperatives of smaller school districts that join resources together to provide services to children with specialized needs. State systems typically support schools for students who are blind or deaf, and who require highly specialized forms of instruction. States may also run diagnostic centers. The federal law frequently refers to the LEA to denote the organizational entity that has responsibility for the provision of services to students with exceptional needs. Table 9.3 provides an overview of the organizational structures in 16 states and overseas.

Special education services may be provided through a variety of organizational structures. In some circumstances, the services are provided by speech-language pathologists, audiologists, and other service providers employed by the school district. In other circumstances, a regional area system may be the employing agency for speech-language pathologists and audiologists or other support personnel. In these situations, the service providers are then assigned to schools or districts in the surrounding geographical area. When services are provided through a regional system, it may be that the school district is too small to support a full-time specialist staff, or there may be a belief that a higher level of expertise can be maintained by supporting specialist staff through a regionalized service area. Both district and regional systems will have administrative and program support personnel. Depending on the size of the agency and the administrative structure within the local school system, the speech-language pathologist or audiologist may

or may not have much contact with the administrative regional and support staff.

Funding

Before trying to understand how funding occurs for special education, the prudent employee should have a basic understanding of how public education is funded in the United States. Education is compulsory for children through age 15, 16, 17, or 18, depending on the state. Each state constitution requires that a comprehensive educational program exist and be funded for either kindergarten or Grade 1 through Grade 12. Some states have state-operated preschool programs, and some states have two-year post-secondary educational programs that are open to all high school graduates at little or no charge. Sometimes such systems articulate with a statewide university or technical college system.

School Finance

The massive K–12 educational system is free to the citizens of all states, a concept found in few nations in the world. Revenue for school districts comes from a combination of local, state, and federal sources (see sidebar on p. 360). Federal funds for education are quite limited and targeted to specific programs with strict usage guidelines. State taxes for education are derived from revenue sources that are relatively constant—income, property, and sales. These revenue sources are identified in the state constitution. Local funding is typically generated through levies on property values and sales tax charged in addition to state-mandated taxes.

Table 9.3

Public Education Organizational Structures
Responses of Council of State Association Presidents to November 1999 Survey

State	Organizational Systems for Public Schools
California	School Districts, County Agencies, Special Education Local Plan Areas (SELPAs)
Delaware	School Districts, Intermediate Units, County and Charter Schools
Georgia	School Districts, Regional Offices (Georgia Learning Resource Systems)
Hawaii	School District
Indiana	Special Education Planning Districts, Partners for Assistive Technology in Indiana (PATINS), Institute for Developmental Disabilities (ISDD at Indiana University)
Iowa	School Districts, Area Education Agencies (AEAs)
Louisiana	State Department of Education, Parish School Systems
Montana	School Districts, Private Cooperatives (provide contract services and serve rural areas)
Nebraska	School Districts, Educational Service Units
New York	School Districts, Board of Cooperative Educational Services Programs
North Carolina	Local Education Agencies, Raleigh Department of Public Instruction, Local County Units
North Dakota	School Districts, Local Education Co-operative
Ohio	School Districts, County Programs, Supervisory Network, Ohio Ohio School Speech Pathologists Educational Audiologists Coalition Education Resource Centers
Oregon	School Districts, Educational Service Districts
Overseas/ Department of Defense	Local District Superintendent's Office (DSO), Early Developmental Intervention Services (EDIS)
Pennsylvania	School Districts, Intermediate Units
South Dakota	School Districts, Educational Cooperatives

Source: Moore-Brown & Montgomery (1999)

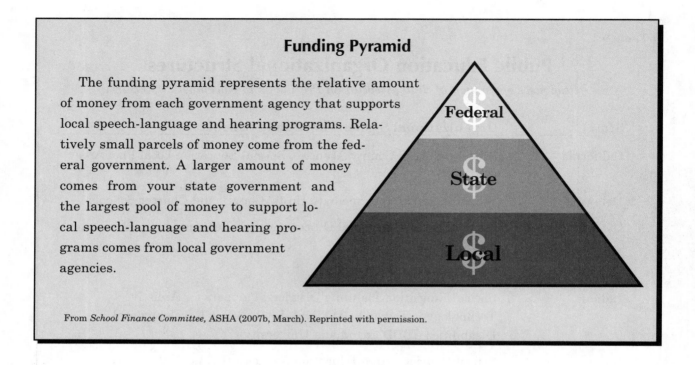

Funding Pyramid

The funding pyramid represents the relative amount of money from each government agency that supports local speech-language and hearing programs. Relatively small parcels of money come from the federal government. A larger amount of money comes from your state government and the largest pool of money to support local speech-language and hearing programs comes from local government agencies.

From *School Finance Committee,* ASHA (2007b, March). Reprinted with permission.

The actual dollars realized from each different revenue source can vary dramatically across states. In some states, city or county taxes are utilized for education, contributing to great variations between affluent and low income areas, urban and rural districts, and districts where property values are high versus low. Since the late 1970s, equity in state educational funding between school districts has been a controversial issue and the topic of many legal challenges. See Figure 9.1 for the ASHA School Finance Committee's illustration of how funding flows to school districts for special education programs.

Funding for Special Education

Since the inception of the EDUCATION FOR ALL HANDICAPPED CHILDREN ACT (EAHCA) of 1975, the funding of special education has been one of the more controversial aspects of the whole school funding picture. When EAHCA was enacted, federal funding for this program was originally promised by Congress at 40 percent of the total cost of special education in each state. This level of funding has never been realized. Parents, professionals, and politicians have been advocating for full funding of special education for many years. Special education is an example of an unfunded mandate of the federal government, meaning that state and local entities are required to implement programs legislated by Congress for which they do not receive adequate federal funding.

In spirit, the concept of full funding has bipartisan support. In the reauthorization of IDEA 2004, Congress built in a formula designed to bring the allocation for special education to full funding within ten years. In this formula, there are recommendations for the funding levels needed to be reached each year in order to

#TP-29703 Making a Difference - 2nd Ed. • ©2008 Thinking Publications® • www.thinkingpublications.com • 1-800-277-8737

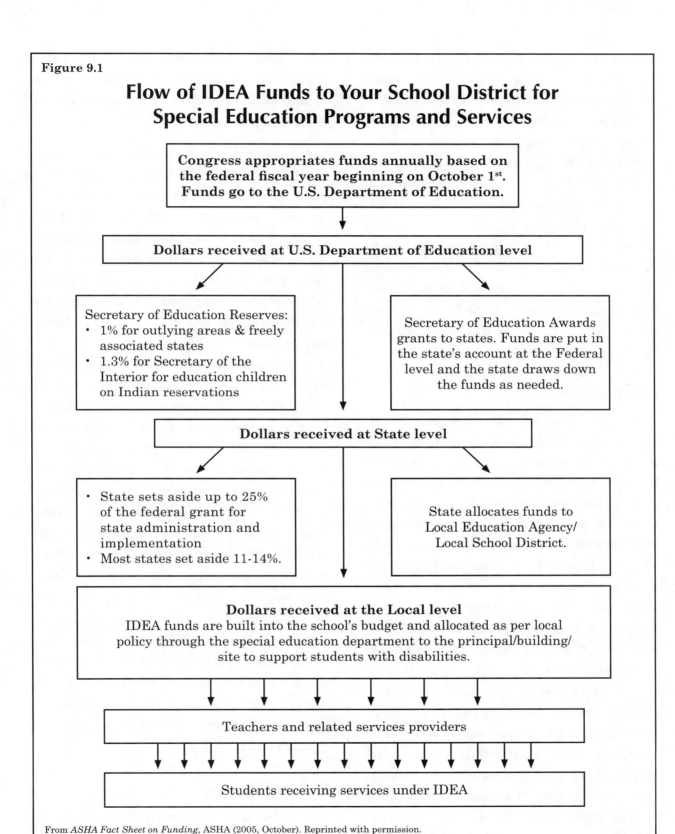

Figure 9.1

Flow of IDEA Funds to Your School District for Special Education Programs and Services

Congress appropriates funds annually based on the federal fiscal year beginning on October 1st. Funds go to the U.S. Department of Education.

Dollars received at U.S. Department of Education level

Secretary of Education Reserves:
- 1% for outlying areas & freely associated states
- 1.3% for Secretary of the Interior for education children on Indian reservations

Secretary of Education Awards grants to states. Funds are put in the state's account at the Federal level and the state draws down the funds as needed.

Dollars received at State level

- State sets aside up to 25% of the federal grant for state administration and implementation
- Most states set aside 11-14%.

State allocates funds to Local Education Agency/ Local School District.

Dollars received at the Local level
IDEA funds are built into the school's budget and allocated as per local policy through the special education department to the principal/building/ site to support students with disabilities.

Teachers and related services providers

Students receiving services under IDEA

From *ASHA Fact Sheet on Funding*, ASHA (2005, October). Reprinted with permission.

achieve the full funding goal. Unfortunately, each year since the reauthorization, the recommended allocations have been cut by the finance committee. Although the recommended levels are stated in the law, IDEA funding continues to be discretionary and not mandatory, so Congress, although it states support, still can put other priorities ahead of full funding for IDEA. When federal funding does not meet its intended level, state and local contributions need to be increased in order to cover the costs of special education. These funds come from the general fund, depleting funds available for other education programs and purposes, and creating tension between general and special education.

Categorical Funding

Special education funding is considered categorical, or restricted, meaning that the dollars in the special education fund are restricted to being spent on that category of services and related costs only. General education funding is considered unrestricted since those dollars can be spent on any program in the schools. The costs of special education programs represent approximately 13.9 percent of total spending on elementary and secondary education in the United States (Chambers, Perez, Harr, & Shkolnik, 2005). The money allocated to fund special education typically falls short of the true cost of the programs. There is an expectation applied to most state special education funding formulas that the general education fund will contribute to the cost of special education programs. Rising costs and inequitable formulas for special education programs have created the need to increasingly draw on the general fund of most local education agencies. General edu-

cators, school board members, and parents may blame special education costs for the inability of their system to provide items for the students in general education.

Per pupil cost provides a more dramatic example of the cost of special education, especially in comparison to general education. In 1999–2000, the cost of educating students in special education was 1.9 times higher than the cost of educating general education students. However, in the period from 1968–69 to 1999–2000, the estimated cost of educating general education students actually increased at a faster rate than that of special education students. It should be noted that the percentage of students receiving special education services increased from 8.3 percent in 1977–1978 to 12.1 percent in 1999–2000, indicating that the increase in special education spending may be related to an increasing number of students served (Parrish et al., 2004). Increases in the special education population may be due to a variety of factors including an increase in the number of infants and preschoolers served, the possibility that demographic indicators such as poverty and low-birth weight infants (see Chapter 1) may be contributing to learning needs, and higher accountability. The Center for Special Education Finance (CSEF) observes "...The percentage of students in special education has risen steadily since the passage of the IDEA. It is this steady, uninterrupted growth across the nation that may be of greatest concern to policymakers" (Parrish et al., 2004).

Funding Systems

The National Association of State Boards of Education (2002) reports that, historically, states have used one of the following approaches to fund special education:

- Pupil Weights—Funding is allocated on a per student basis, with the amount(s) based on a multiple(s) of regular education aid. Weights are generally differentiated on the basis of student placement (e.g., pull-out, special day class), disability category, or a combination of these two factors.

- Resource-Based—Funding is based on allocation of specific education resources (e.g., teachers or classroom units). Classroom units are derived from prescribed staff/student ratios by disabling condition or type of placement.

- Percent Reimbursement—Funding is based on a percentage of allowable or actual expenditures. That is, the amount of state special education aid a district receives is directly based on its expenditure for the program. Districts may be reimbursed for 100 percent of their program expenditures, or some lesser percentage.

- Flat Grant—Funding is based on a fixed funding amount per student or per unit. A variation of this approach, called a census-based approach, is based on the total number of students in a district, rather than the number of special education students.

Special education funding is complex and changing. When EAHCA (1975) was enacted, many children with disabilities were not receiving education (see Chapter 2). As a result, great efforts were required to locate children in the community to bring them into the educational system and provide them with needed services.

The emphasis on CHILD FIND resulted in a funding model structured to pay districts and states for the numbers of children who were identified. As the numbers of children served in special education increased, the late 1980s saw state funding systems being revised to move from child count systems to census-based systems, with the latter being considered "incentive-free" (CSEF, 1999, ¶ 4; NASBE, 2002).

A census-based approach allocates funding using a fixed formula that is calculated according to the number of students in a school district, rather than providing funding based on the number of special education students served. In a census-based system, a school district will receive the same allocation regardless of the number of students identified. A census-based system should eliminate incentives to identify students for special education when the district can use prevention and intervention methods to reduce the severity of students' needs, and thereby reduce the need for special education services.

In the year 2000–2001, the federal funding formula for a FREE APPROPRIATE PUBLIC EDUCATION (FAPE) changed from a child count formula to a formula based on total resident population (85 percent) and student poverty (15 percent). Although the federal portion of special education funding is the smallest portion of the allocation, this change reflected the trend to eliminate the incentives of funding based on identified students.

State funding formulas are variable, leading to vast differences in the percentage amount contributed by the state, and consequently the local government for special education. The type of funding formula at the state level can influence practice. For example, states who still maintain a child count formula may be reluctant to move to a RESPONSE TO INTERVENTION (RtI) method of identification. States also are variable in their base funding for general education, which contributes to great disparity among states for the base level of per pupil expenditures (Parrish et al., 2004).

Speech-language pathologists, audiologists, and other special educators need to understand how funding systems work for their state and local entity. Providers of special education services are frequently frustrated by the seeming lack of support or funding for the programs in which they work. Questions about why staff is not added or why supplies and materials or conference budgets are tight or nonexistent frequently plague service providers. In addition, pressures may be put on speech-language pathologists and audiologists by parents and other educators to provide services when the resources to do so are not available. In these instances, speech-language pathologists and audiologists may find themselves caught in the middle of the unfunded mandate quandary. Solving this quandary is clearly not the responsibility of speech-language pathologists or audiologists, but understanding the issues may help deal with the questions.

Growth in Identification: Costs and Funding Issues

The *Twenty-Sixth Annual Report to Congress* (USDE, 2005d) reports the following trends in the numbers and percentage of students served under IDEA (1997) in Fall 2002:

Infants and Toddlers (IDEA, Part C):

• On December 1, 2002, 268,331 children ages birth through 2 received early intervention services under IDEA, Part C [includes the 50 states, DC, Puerto Rico and four outlying areas]. Of these, 265,145 received services in the 50 states and the District of Columbia; this number represents 2.2 percent of the birth-through-2 population in the 50 states and District of Columbia (p. 5).

• Between 1994 and 2002, the total number of children served under IDEA, Part C has increased steadily (with the exception of one year) from 165,351 to 268,331—an increase of 62.3 percent. The apparent decline in the number of children served in 1998 was the result of a data reporting problem in one state that year (p. 5).

• The risk ratio for all racial/ethnic groups are clustered around 1.0 (no difference between the groups). Children in all racial/ethnic groups were about equally as likely to be receiving early intervention (p. 8).

• Between 1996 and 2001, the percentage of infants and toddlers served primarily in the home increased from 56.0 percent to 77.6 percent. In the same time period, the percentage of infants and toddlers served primarily in programs for children with developmental delays or disabilities decreased from 22.5 percent to 8.5 percent. The percentage of infants and toddlers served primarily in a service provider location decreased from 14.0 percent to 7.7 percent (pp. 8–9).

- Overall, 82 percent of infants and toddlers received their early intervention services primarily in the home or in programs designed for typically developing children. Thirty-two states and outlying areas met or exceeded this national figure (p. 9).

- About two-thirds (66 percent) of Part C infants and toddlers were eligible for Part B services when they turned age 3 (p. 9).

- At entry to early intervention, infants and toddlers receiving Part C services were in poorer health than children in the general population. Parents reported 16 percent of children receiving early intervention to be in poor to fair health compared to just over 2 percent of the general population (p. 13).

Children Ages 3 Through 5 (IDEA, Part B)

- In 2002, Part B served 647,420 children ages 3 through 5 (p. 16).

- In 2002, more than one-third (35.4 percent) of all children ages 3 through 5 with disabilities received special education and related services in early childhood environments (p. 19).

- Around one third (32.0 percent) of all children ages 3 through 5 with disabilities received special education and related services in early childhood special education environments (p. 19).

- Only 3.1 percent of children ages 3 through 5 with disabilities received special education and related services in home environments (p. 19).

Students Ages 6–21 (IDEA, Part B)

- In 2002, 6,606,702 children and students ages 3 through 21, were served under IDEA, Part B in the United States and outlying areas (USDE, 2005d, Vol 2).

- In 2002, 46.3 percent of students (2,904,282) receiving special education and related services under Part B were ages 6 through 11, 48.7 percent (2,759,522) were ages 12 through 17 and 5.0 percent (295,478) were ages 18 through 21 (p. 20).

- In 2002, the largest disability category was specific learning disabilities (48.3 percent). The next most common disability category was speech or language impairments (18.7 percent) followed by mental retardation (9.9 percent), serious emotional disturbance (8.1 percent) and other health impairment (6.6 percent) (p. 21).

- For a few disability categories, the relative percentages of the general population receiving special education and related service increased between 1992–2002. These categories are specific learning disabilities (4.1 percent vs. 4.3 percent), other health impairments (0.1 percent vs. 0.6 percent) and autism (0.03 percent vs. 0.2 percent) (p. 21).

- For all racial/ethnic groups, the largest disability category is specific learning disability (p. 26).

- The percentage of the population receiving special education and related services varies by race/ethnicity. The risk for special education is largest for Black students (12.2 percent), followed by American Indian/Alaska Native (12.0 percent), White (8.7 percent),

Hispanic (8.0 percent), and Asian/Pacific Islander (4.4 percent) students (p. 28).

- Asian/Pacific Islander students were 1.20 times more likely to receive special education and related services for hearing impairments and 1.24 times more likely to receive special education and related services for autism than all other racial/ethnic groups combined (p. 29).

- Black students were 3.04 times more likely to receive special education and related services for mental retardation and 2.25 times more likely to receive special education and related services for serious emotional disturbance than all other racial/ethnic groups combined (p. 29).

- Hispanic students were 1.20 times more likely to receive special education and related services for hearing impairments and 1.10 times more likely to receive special education and related services for specific learning disabilities than all other racial/ethnic groups combined (p. 29).

- In 2002, 96 percent of students with disabilities were educated in regular school buildings. However, the time they spent in regular classrooms varied (p. 30).

- Almost half of all students with disabilities (48.2 percent) were educated for most of their school day in the regular classroom; that is, they were outside the regular classroom for less than 21 percent of the school day (p. 30).

- Students with speech or language impairments were more likely than students with other disabilities to be educated in regular classes for most of the school day (p. 33).

Special education enrollments have increased steadily since the enactment of EAHCA in 1975. In 1976–77, special education students represented 8.33 percent of the total public enrollment; by 1987–88 this percentage was 11.09 percent and in the year 2000–2001 it was 13.83 percent for all students ages 0 to 21. In terms of students served under Part B (ages 6 through 21) the percentage has increased 17.57 percent between 1988–89 and 2000–2001 (Parrish et al., 2004).

This overall growth has provided stressors to the total funding system for education, with programs competing for the limited resources within the system as well for resources from external funding sources. At the same time, the special education population will continue to grow not only in numbers but in intensity of needs. Such factors will certainly impact the level of competence and skill required of school-based speech-language pathologists and audiologists in order to be prepared to serve students in new and creative ways. (See "Speech-Language Pathologists' Roles and Responsibilities" on p. 372.)

Changes in Funding Systems

Federal funding for special education comes to states in a number of different types of grants. These are allocation grants, not competitive grants, meaning that the states automatically receive the funds. These grants are distributed to states, which then distribute the funds to local education agencies. The grant funds are to cover various costs such as personnel development, direct and support services to children in various age categories, administrative costs, and other related activities. In 2002–2003, just over $7 billion was spent on Part B grants, which provide funding for direct and support services to students.

IDEA 2004 funding builds on the intentions set in IDEA (1997) to give greater flexibility in the use of special education funds, and also to blend funds with other categorical programs, specifically Title I and other programs under NCLB. These funding changes mean that schoolwide plans may be developed that assign speech-language pathologists and audiologists

as a part of prevention or intervention programs. Speech-language pathologists and audiologists may include nondisabled student peers in groups when working in class, and joint services may be provided to students who qualify for several programs. Speech-language pathologists and audiologists in schools must know and understand local restrictions and allowances since each state and LEA will interpret these new regulations in slightly different ways.

Early Intervening Services

In an effort to encourage flexibility and also to move away from the "wait to fail" model of special education identification, IDEA 2004 includes a new funding mechanism for the use of up to 15 percent of a local education agency's (LEA) allocation to develop and implement EARLY INTERVENING SERVICES (EIS). This provision encourages the coordination with other funding structures (i.e., ESEA/NCLB/Title I) to provide these services (34 C.F.R. § 300.226 [e]), but are not intended to deny or delay the provision of FAPE or an evaluation for a student who is suspected of having a disability (34 C.F.R. § 300.226 [c]). These funds are intended to be directed at students who are not currently identified under IDEA, but who are "in need of additional academic and behavioral supports to succeed in the general education environment" (34 C.F.R. § 300.226). While these services can be directed at all students in kindergarten through twelfth grade, the Code calls for specific emphasis to be placed on students in kindergarten through third grade.

For school districts where significant disproportionality has been identified (i.e., the overrepresentation of minority students in special education), early intervening services must be reserved and utilized to the maximum extent possible (OSEP, 2006).

The activities allowed to implement coordinated, early intervening services (34 C.F.R. § 300.226 [b]) include:

(1) Professional development (which may be provided by entities other than LEAs) for teachers and other school staff to enable them to deliver scientifically based academic instruction and behavioral interventions, including scientifically based literacy instruction and, when appropri-

ASHA Documents on Medicaid

Introduction to Medicaid
http://www.asha.org/members/issues/reimbursement/medicaid/medicaid_intro.htm

Medicaid FAQs
http://www.asha.org/members/issues/reimbursement/medicaid/medicaid_faqs.htm

Medicaid Guidance for Speech-Language Pathology Services:
Addressing the "Under the Direction Of" Rule (Position Statement)
http://www.asha.org/docs/html/PS2004-00098.html

Medicaid Guidance for Speech-Language Pathology Services:
Addressing the "Under the Direction of" Rule (Technical Report)
http://www.asha.org/docs/html/TR2004-00142.html

ate, instruction on the use of adaptive and instructional software.

(2) Providing educational and behavioral evaluations, services, and supports, including scientifically based literacy instruction.

The provisions for early intervening services (EIS) are where the development and utilization of some RtI programs may be realized. This component of the law, then allows speech-language pathologists and audiologists, as well as other special educators, to support and work directly with students who may be struggling in general education without waiting until the students are identified through a formal assessment as meeting criteria under special education law. The language of the law emphasizes the concept that prior to any identification for special education, students need to be provided with scientifically based instruction.

States and local districts will establish guidelines for the implementation of these provisions, as there are reporting requirements under the law (34 C.F.R. § 300.226 [d]), in addition to the necessity to ensure that misuse of the provision does not occur.

EIS and the utilization of RtI programs are examples of the system response to implementing program and practice changes which should not only result in more immediate assistance for struggling learners, but also result in financial savings. As has been illustrated, special education enrollment has climbed, significantly straining and impacting the overall system. The utilization of funding and resources of special education to provide interventions prior to identification is a blend of current research, policy, and fiscal solutions. As Parrish et al. (2004) note: "Stemming the tide of special education enrollments appears to be the real answer to special education cost containment—a task that will require more holistic education remedies and enhanced cooperation between regular and special educators" (p. 30).

Medicaid

One way that many school districts increase available revenue to support special education programs is through Medicaid reimbursement. This program is authorized under the administration of the Centers for Medicare and Medicaid Services (CMS). The Medicaid program authorizes payment for speech-language pathology services provided in schools under IDEA Part B when the following criteria are met:

- Services are provided to Medicaid-eligible children.

- Services are medically necessary.

- Services are delivered and claimed in accordance with all other federal and state guidelines.

- Services are included in the state plan.

Under the Early and Periodic Screening, Diagnosis, and Treatment (EPSDT) Program, a child health component of Medicaid, speech-language pathology and audiology services are covered for:

1. The identification of children with speech or language impairments.

2. Diagnosis and appraisal of specific speech or language impairments.

3. Referral for medical or other professional attention necessary for rehabilitation of speech or language impairment.

4. Provisions of speech and language services.

5. Counseling and guidance of parents, children and teachers.

6. Medicaid may also pay for augmentative devices, hearing aids and services.

ASHA provides numerous documents which give guidance to school-based professionals who are billing Medicaid. These documents are available to members on the ASHA Web site and include general information about the Medicaid program, Medicaid frequently asked questions (FAQs), and both a position statement and technical report on the "under the direction of" rule (see Web sites in sidebar on p. 368).

Figure 9.2 illustrates how Medicaid dollars flow to school districts. Under this program, the revenue generated through the cost of medical assistance is intended to go back to the programs that provided these services. Decisions about how this happens at the local level are made by a collaborative, as required under the program. Speech-language pathologists and audiologists who participate in billing for Medicaid services should inquire about participating on the collaborative, or at least ensure that there is representation of the professional group.

The Center for Special Education Finance (CSEF) reports that 44 percent of school districts recovered funds through the Medicaid program representing an estimated $648 million in 1999–2000. While this only represents 1.3 percent of the funds spent on special education, utilization of these funds at the local level provide dollars that otherwise are not available.

Figure 9.2

Flow of Medicaid Funds to Your School District

> **Congress appropriates funds annually based on
> the federal fiscal year beginning on October 1ˢᵗ.
> Funds go to the U.S. Department of Health and Human Services**

↓

> **Dollars are received at U.S. Dept. of Health and Human Services
> and are administered by the Centers for Medicare and Medicaid (CMS)**

↓

> **Funds are put in the state's account at the Federal level
> and the state draws the funds as needed.**
>
> - Funds are allocated to each state to match state expenditures for the cost of medical assistance (i.e., Medicaid is a federal-state matching system.)
>
> - Medicaid's federal matching rates, or Federal Medical Assistance percentages (FMAPs), are determined by a formula tied to state per capita income. According to the Kaiser Commission on Medicaid and the Uninsured, on average the federal matching rate is 57% of the costs of Medicaid benefits (Medicaid Resource Book, July 2002)

↓

> **Dollars Received At State Level**
>
> - State may or may not require LEAs or school districts to bill for Medicaid services.
>
> - If schools do participate, a system for billing is established: (Example: state regional agency; private vendor; local education agency)
>
> - States are not required to return all money generated by the schools back to the schools. It depends on state laws and regulations. (For example, a state may retain a percentage for administrative costs; a private vendor may retain a percentage.)

#TP-29703 Making a Difference - 2nd Ed. · ©2008 Thinking Publications® · www.thinkingpublications.com · 1-800-277-8737

Figure 9.2 – *Continued*

Dollars Received At the Local Level

- Medicaid revenue, if received by the school district (see above) is placed into the school budget and allocated as per state and/or local policy. Some states have specific requirements for how a local district must use funds.

- Examples of how local school districts use Medicaid revenue: special education; general fund; health services; equipment/supplies; professional development; hiring staff; return funds to program that generated the revenue; purchase of technology for staff; creation of new special education programs.

- Some states place restrictions on how local school districts may use Medicaid revenue. Examples: may only be used for educational purposes and shall not be made available to local communities for purposes other than education; may not be used to supplant funds currently being spent on health and social services; must be used within the special education program; may not be transferred to the district's general fund.

Teachers and Related Services Providers

Funding reaches teachers and related service providers based on how local school district allocates the Medicaid revenue (see above)

Students

Students benefit based on how district allocates Medicaid revenue.

Source: ASHA (n.d.). Reprinted with permission.

Speech-Language Pathologists' Roles and Responsibilities

Primary Roles

The speech-language pathologist is responsible for a wide range of duties that vary from school district to school district but appear essentially similar in 50 states, the District of Columbia, and the Department of Defense Schools (DODS) for the U.S. military stationed in other countries. For this reason, ASHA was able to develop a fairly generic list in their *Guidelines for the Roles and Responsibilities of the School-Based Speech-Language Pathologist* (1999c), that has guided states as well as assisted individual ASHA members. The list is represented in the sidebar on pp. 373–374.

Some states have guidelines which are the state department officials' interpretations of federal laws within the funding and political structure of their state, and consequently are more flexible and subject to more frequent changes than federal regulations. ASHA's guidelines are only suggestions from a national professional organization and are not binding in any state. Local school districts, consortiums, and regional areas can also assemble such lists to guide their speech-language pathologists and audiologists in a particular area. Many times, school-based speech-language pathologists and audiologists and their state professional organizations will help to write these lists so that they accurately reflect the professional aspects of the position that may not be known to education officers who are assigned these tasks (see "State Consultants," p. 402).

Lists of roles and responsibilities may cast a longer shadow in school districts than they do in health-care or private practice environments because of employee unions. The conditions of work, the demands made on management on behalf of an employee, and most importantly, the relative fairness of one employee's job responsibilities compared to another are critical issues. Therefore, lists of assigned, primary duties are important to know and follow in public education. Additional roles and duties, and who assigns them to the speech-language pathologist, are equally important.

Additional Responsibilities

Every work environment will place additional responsibilities on speech-language pathologists. These will vary according to an interesting set of criteria inherent in the individual school or school district and determined by school characteristics, such as the size, grade levels, ages of students, location (rural, suburban, or urban), degree of security needed, discipline codes, student transportation, teacher/staff relationships, community expectations, personal interests, and an administrator's style.

The list of additional roles and responsibilities in the sidebar on p. 375 represent those that speech-language pathologists and audiologists have taken on voluntarily based on personal interests, because the previous speech-language pathologist did them, because the school was short-handed, or because everyone took on extra duties to cover the territory. It is easy to see how involved speech-language pathologists and audiologists can get in their schools.

Core Roles and Responsibilities of School-Based Speech-Language Pathologists and Audiologists

Prevention–Speech-language pathologists, as educational team members, address the prevention of communication disorders, including consultation and active involvement for both primary prevention and secondary prevention for birth through age 21.

Identification–Speech-language pathologists participate as team members in identifying students who may be in need of assessments to determine possible eligibility for special education or related services; this includes prereferral, screening, and referral.

Assessment–Speech-language pathologists conduct thorough and balanced speech, language, or communication assessments; this includes collecting data and gathering evidence using appropriate, nonbiased tools, interviews, and structured observations.

Evaluation–Speech-language pathologists interpret the assessment, giving value to the data, including the nature and severity of the disorders and the potential effect on the student's educational and social performance. Clinical judgement is required to determine the communication disorder or difference.

Eligibility Determination–Speech-language pathologists, in cooperation with the educational team, determine the student's need and eligibility for special education or related services according to the eligibility criteria of each state.

IEP/IFSP Development–Speech-language pathologists assist a team in developing an individualized education program (IEP) or an individualized family service plan (IFSP) when students are found eligible for services. Speech-language pathologists must take all special factors into account and help to design the IEP with all the required components (IDEA, 1997, § 614d [3][a][i–ii], 614d [1][a][i–viii]).

Caseload Management–Speech-language pathologists assist the team in selecting, planning, and coordinating the appropriate service delivery using an array of services and inclusive practices. Speech-language pathologists may serve as case managers for some students.

Intervention for Communication Disorders–Speech-language pathologists provide services for identified students using the most recent literature of the discipline, research-based intervention strategies, principles of effective instruction, and appropriate academic or developmental curriculum for each individual.

Intervention for Communication Variations–Speech-language pathologists must be knowledgeable about monolingual and bilingual language acquisition, the linguistic rules for social dialects and language differences, the use of interpreters and translators, and nonbiased assessment to assist the classroom teacher and others.

Continued

Core Roles and Responsibilities – *Continued*

Counseling–Speech-language pathologists participate in honest and open communication regarding the recovery from, or adjustment to, a communication impairment using effective counseling techniques and coordination with other professionals.

Reevaluation–Speech-language pathologists conduct reassessments of students receiving services at least every three years when dismissal is considered, if special circumstances arise, or if parents request such. Reevaluation is ongoing, thorough, and documented.

Transition–Speech-language pathologists participate with a team to assist students in transitioning from one setting to another, within school, or beyond school at all ages. Speech-language pathologists may work directly with students on transitional goals.

Dismissal–Speech-language pathologists begin the consideration of dismissal when services begin, with a focus on achieving functional outcomes. Speech-language pathologists weigh the factors for dismissal, including academic performance, state or local dismissal criteria, ASHA's guidelines for dismissal, or a combination of these.

Supervision–Speech-language pathologists may supervise other speech-language pathologists, support personnel, university practicum students, or volunteers. This supervision is conducted competently, ethically, and legally according to state licensing regulations and other procedures.

Documentation and Accountability–Speech-language pathologists keep clear comprehensive records to justify the need for and effectiveness of assessment/intervention. Performance appraisals, third-party billing, and risk-management records are maintained accurately, confidentially, and in accordance with federal, state, and local reporting requirements.

Additional roles and responsibilities that may be undertaken or assigned:
- Community and professional partnerships–research, grants, parent training
- Professional leadership–mentoring, specializations, school boards
- Advocacy–students, programs, legislative issues

Source: ASHA (1999c). Adapted with permission.

Although taking on extra activities may not appeal to every speech-language pathologist, the authors engaged in one or more events each year and found that doing so enhanced their speech and language service delivery in unexpected ways. Additional school roles can increase the visibility of speech-language pathologists and audiologists schoolwide, offer opportunities to observe students communicating with their peers in a generalizing environment, build staff relationships, attract administrator support, and integrate speech-language pathologists and audiologists into more aspects of the school and community.

**Additional Roles and Responsibilities of
School-Based Speech-Language Pathologists and Audiologists**

Recess duty	Bus duty	Morning duty
Play director	Bulletin board decoration	Club advisor
Athletics coach	Dance chaperone	Magazine sales coordinator
Social committee chair	Student government	Field trip assistant
Preschool monitor	Head Start read aloud	Parent education programs
Parent Teacher Organization	School accountability team	School discipline team
Curriculum committees	Triathlon coach	School newspaper
School yearbook	School Web site	Assessment team
Assistive technology	Candy sales	School store
School post office	Bilingual assessor	After-school care
Homework club	Internet pen pals	Literacy lab
Assistant principal	Department chair	Assessment Committee coordinator
Grant writer	School improvement committee	Administrator's designee
Principal's designee	Science fair mentor	

Speech-Language Pathology Assistants (SLPAs) and Aides in Schools

Extending Service With Paraprofessionals

Professionals in many fields work with paraprofessionals who support professionals and enable them to accomplish more. Physicians work with physician assistants, attorneys work with paralegals, physical therapists work with physical therapy assistants, and occupational therapists assign duties to certified occupational therapy assistants. Speech-language pathologists and audiologists can extend their services through the use of SPEECH-LANGUAGE PATHOLOGY ASSISTANTS (SLPAs) and aides.

Support personnel in school speech-language programs may be called SLPAs, aides, assistants, technicians, paraprofessionals, and other related job titles. Some positions require entry-level skills; others seek applicants with advanced training, such as a postsecondary degree or a certificate to show educational accomplishments. More skilled support personnel take a greater responsibility for the instructional program and enable speech-language pathologists to be more effective and assume some or many of the tasks necessary to implement a single-school or multi-site program. In some cases, SLPAs actually provide therapy and monitor student progress.

Although historically the use of untrained support personnel provided a valuable addition to speech and language programs, their contribution was constrained by their training, experience, and the limitations placed on them by regulations of the state or district. Today, however, SLPAs and aides are regulated by the state in which they work.

ASHA's Guidelines for SLPAs and Aides

In 2004, ASHA updated its guidelines for training, using, and supervising SLPAs and the less rigorous category of speech-language pathology aides (Paul-Brown & Goldberg, 2001). New service delivery models in health care and education demanded that support personnel be an integral part of the many new levels of service proposed to both reduce costs and compensate for the shortage of professionals. Paraprofessional support is vital to the provision of special education services in schools, including speech-language services. (See sidebar on pp. 377–378 for FAQs about SLPAs.)

Under ASHA's (2004c) guidelines, there are two levels of support personnel in speech-language pathology: the aide and the assistant (or SLPA). The complete text of the position paper establishing support personnel in all practice settings is available on the ASHA Web site. The discussion here will review the application of support personnel services in public school programs.

Aides are people with a high school diploma who have been trained by school-based speech-language pathologists or audiologists to assist with programs. Aides are able to assist with contacting parents, locating and collecting identified students, developing materials, repairing equipment, and preparing a wide range of clerical work necessary for a school-based program. Aides cannot work with students unless they are supervised, but can be very helpful to busy speech-language pathologists. Aides may work in more than one general education or special education program and extend the activities of the speech-language pathologist to more corners of the school.

SLPAs, on the other hand, are persons with a minimum of an associate's degree or equivalent course of study in speech-language pathology. They work with students under the direct supervision of speech-language pathologists. They take coursework at community colleges or universities in child development and speech-language pathology and have the recommended number of hours of field experience with a variety of communication disorders. Although a bachelor of arts or science degree in communication disorders could be used as the coursework, the person would still need to take the practicum or field experience to be registered, or licensed in some states, as an assistant.

Aides and assistants can be utilized in school speech, language, and hearing programs if they

> Paraprofessional support is vital to the provision of special education services in schools, including speech-language services.

are properly trained and appropriately supervised by a certified speech-language pathologist. Both the speech-language pathologist and assistant must follow their state licensing laws if they work in a state with licensure requirements.

Speech-language pathology assistants and aides can make a significant difference in how services are offered in many schools. Savvy speech-language pathologists and audiologists need to know how to design quality programs that include these assistants and aides.

Frequently Asked Questions (FAQs) About SLPAs

Q. Will speech-language pathology assistants be used to replace speech-language pathologists?

A. No. Assistants cannot replace qualified speech-language pathologists. Rather, they can support clinical services provided by speech-language pathologists. ASHA guidelines were developed to ensure that speech-language pathology services provided to the public are of the highest quality and that speech-language pathologists continue to be responsible for maintaining this quality of service. According to ASHA guidelines and state licensure laws, no one can employ a speech-language pathology assistant without a speech-language pathologist as supervisor. ASHA guidelines and most state laws limit the number of speech-language pathology assistants a speech-language pathologist may supervise and define boundaries for how assistants are used.

Q. What are the advantages to the speech-language pathologist in using speech-language pathology assistants in his/her practice?

A. The ASHA-certified speech-language pathologist may extend services (i.e., increase the frequency and intensity of services to patients or clients on his/her caseload), focus more on professional-level tasks, increase client access to the program, and achieve more efficient/effective use of time and resources. According to the ASHA 2000 Schools Survey, 47.3 percent of respondents indicated that the use of SLPAs led to "more time for direct service," while 23.1 percent reported that the use of SLPAs led to "more time for planning/consultation with teachers."

Q. Who is responsible for services provided by a speech-language pathology assistant?

A. The fully qualified, ASHA-certified supervising speech-language pathologist is responsible for the services provided by assistants. In states that regulate speech-language pathology assistants, speech-language pathologists who hold full, unrestricted licenses assume these responsibilities for persons working under their direction.

Continued

Questions About SLPAs – *Continued*

Q. Does ASHA credential speech-language pathology assistants?

A. Not at this time. ASHA started a voluntary registration program for speech-language pathology assistants (SLPAs) in 2003, of which one criterion for such registration required an associate degree in SLPA from a technical training program for speech-language pathology assistants. At its Spring 2003 meeting, ASHA's Legislative Council passed a resolution to discontinue the registration program for speech-language pathology assistants and the approval process for SLPA technical training programs as of December 31, 2003, due to financial reasons. ASHA no longer has a recognition process for associate degree technical training programs for SLPAs nor a registration process for SLPAs. ASHA will continue to disseminate the *Guidelines for Training, Use, and Supervision of Speech-Language Pathology Assistants*, which were revised in 2004. The revised Guidelines include recommended curriculum for training programs and a checklist for supervisors of SLPAs that can assist in the verification of technical proficiency of the assistant.

Q. How does one become a speech-language pathology assistant?

A. ASHA recommends completion of an associate's degree from a technical training program with a program of study designed to prepare the student to be a speech-language pathology assistant. Because the requirements for speech-language pathology support personnel vary across the country, persons interested in serving as speech-language pathology assistants should check with the state of intended employment for that state's specific requirements. State agencies (licensure boards) currently regulating support personnel have training requirements that range from a high school diploma to a baccalaureate degree plus graduate credit hours, as well as a variety of differing requirements for those supervising these individuals. In addition to state regulatory agencies, state education agencies may credential support personnel to work solely in schools to support service delivery provided by a qualified speech-language pathologist. ASHA's *Guidelines for Training, Use, and Supervision of Speech-Language Pathology Assistants* are national in scope and can serve to promote greater uniformity in the terms used to identify speech-language pathology support personnel, training and educational requirements, and job responsibilities.

From Frequently Asked Questions about Speech-Language Pathology Assistants, by the American Speech-Language-Hearing Association (ASHA), 2006b, Rockville, MD: Author. ©2006 by ASHA. Adapted with permission.

The Role of States in Regulating SLPAs

State licensing laws take precedence over ASHA guidelines (2004c) for the use of SLPAs. The ASHA guidelines (2004c) outline good clinical practice, responsible supervision, concern for students, and ethical conduct. Any direct conflicts between ASHA guidelines (2004c) and state laws need to be discussed at the state level with all involved agencies for the sake of students who need services. State speech-language-hearing associations often take the lead in these issues. In 2006, of the 50 states and the District of Columbia, 34 had licensure laws that recognized support personnel (ASHA, 2006b).

There is wide variation in how states regulate aides and assistants in speech-language pathology (ASHA, 2006b). According to ASHA, some states require a high school diploma (Georgia, Nebraska, and Indiana), while others require a bachelor's degree (Arkansas, Kentucky, Rhode Island, and West Virginia). Kentucky's requirements for SLPAs apply to school-based settings only, while California's SLPA program addresses all work settings. Ten states, including Maryland and California, require an associates degree. Twenty-two states require registration for assistants and 12 require licensing. Ten states require assistants to take from 5 to 20 continuing education hours every two years to maintain their position. Any listing of support personnel guidelines or state requirements may be updated at any time.

Speech-language pathologists and audiologists in schools have the responsibility of knowing their state licensing regulations as well as ASHA's guidelines for support personnel to assure that students receive the most effective services from qualified personnel. Most states do have supervision requirements. The Code of Federal Regulations requires paraprofessionals in special education programs to be trained and supervised (34 C.F.R. § 300.156 [2][iii]). This includes aides or assistants who are assigned to school districts' speech and language programs.

SLPA Responsibilities and Limitations

According to ASHA's *Guidelines for Training, Use, and Supervision of Speech-Language Pathology Assistants* (2004c), SLPAs may conduct the following tasks under the supervision of speech-language pathologists:

- Conduct speech-language screenings.

- Provide direct intervention to students.

- Follow documented intervention plans and IEPs.

- Document student progress.

- Assist during assessments.

- Assist with informal documentation, prepare materials, and perform clerical duties.

- Schedule activities and prepare charts, records, graphs, or otherwise display data.

- Perform checks and maintenance of equipment.

- Participate in research projects, in-service training, and public relations programs.

In contrast, SLPAs are not authorized to do the following tasks:

- Perform standardized or nonstandardized tests, formal or informal evaluations, or interpret test results.

- Participate in parent conferences, case conferences, or any interdisciplinary team meeting without the presence of a supervising speech-language pathologist.

- Provide student or family counseling.

- Write, develop, or modify an intervention plan.

- Assist students without following the intervention plan prepared by a speech-language pathologist.

- Sign any formal documents, reimbursement forms, or reports.

- Select students for services.

- Dismiss a student from services.

- Disclose confidential information about a student.

- Make referrals for additional service.

- Communicate with families or students without the specific consent of a supervising speech-language pathologist.

- Represent themselves as speech-language pathologists.

State laws may differ slightly from these guidelines in regard to the roles of SLPAs. How SLPAs are utilized will differ on a local or building level as well. SLPAs will be in contact with aides in the special education program who have vastly different duties. Some administrators may require greater uniformity at their schools and require that all support staff carry additional duties. SLPAs may be assigned by the princi-

pal to contribute to some of the overall activities of the school such as those listed below:

- Bus or recess duty

- Field trip assignments

- Office assignments

- Health monitoring

- Fire drill assignments

- School fundraising campaigns

- Homework correction

The primary function of SLPAs should be serving students. If schools assign SLPAs to duties that disrupt services to students on the caseload, speech-language pathologists may need to advocate for a change with the supervisor. Each SLPA's role must be managed by the supervising speech-language pathologist with appropriate attention to other educators and administrators. The value of trained SLPAs, of course, is their knowledge of communication disorders, sensitivity to child development, and availability to continue therapy when speech-language pathologists must complete evaluations or visit another site or home. The SLPA can also maximize the use of the augmentative communication system during instruction. If SLPAs speak another language besides English or have a culture different from speech-language pathologists, they can be tremendous assets to programs. Many SLPAs represent the cultural and linguistic diversity of their communities and can be powerful extensions of the speech and language program into the community (Montgomery, 2000; Moore-Brown, Cooper, & Ferguson, 1998; Moore-Brown, Robinson, Williams, Claussen, & Martinez, 1998).

ents who may be unaware of the training and skills of supervised SLPAs and may not recognize how beneficial such services can be. Speech-language pathologists need to constantly examine what all the students in a school need, how staff are attempting to meet those needs, and the possible advantages of one or more SLPAs to improve overall productivity and educational outcomes.

Both high school and elementary speech and language programs with SLPAs can provide highly effective services. As seen in the photograph above, they may assist students with moderate to severe disabilities who require close monitoring in the classroom.

Speech-language pathologists who use SLPAs report that it is "energizing," "more interactive during the day," "easier to reach more students," "refreshing," and that the speech-language pathologists role "extends into many more classrooms and increases my visibility throughout the school" (Montgomery, 2000).

School-based speech-language pathologists may need to educate their school districts, directors of special education, and other administrators about the benefits of having SLPAs. These public education officials may be unaware of the contribution SLPAs can make, as well as the way they are trained, hired, and compensated for their work in the comprehensive speech-language program. Speech-language pathologists may need to provide information on how SLPAs enhance the therapy program to par-

Roles and Responsibilities of Educational Audiologists

Educational audiologists serve a variety of functions within the school setting beyond the diagnosis and management of hearing loss. These professionals work as a member of a team that designs an educationally appropriate program for students with hearing loss (Kooper, 2005). IDEA 2004 mandates that services related to hearing conservation and hearing loss be provided in public schools. According to the Educational Audiology Association (EAA) (http://www.edaud.org) such activities and services include:

- Coordinating hearing screening programs.

- Providing community awareness about hearing.

- Conducting comprehensive hearing evaluations.

- Providing management for hearing aids and other assistive devices.

- Providing medical and community referrals.

- Assisting in program placement.

- Providing therapy in the areas of speech reading, listening, and hearing aid care.

- Participating in multidisciplinary team meetings.

- Counseling families about effects of hearing loss.

- Providing training to staff.

- Educating about noise pollution.

- Evaluating educational environment for noise.

Because educational audiologists are working as members of the multidisciplinary team for individual children and as consultants to the overall school system, their roles extend beyond that of a consulting audiologist or one who may be seeing a child through a hospital program or physician's office. While audiology services include clinical diagnostics, the Educational Audiology Association's (EAA) position statement, *Advocacy for Audiologists Working in the Schools* (2006), also contends that these services include planning and delivery of (re)habilitation services as well as counseling (Lucker, 2005). According to ASHA (2006f) and EAA (2006), comprehensive audiology services in schools include the following: prevention, identification, assessment, (re)habilitation, providing follow-up and monitoring, equipment and materials, administrative support, evaluation, and research. See the

> Because educational audiologists are working as members of the multidisciplinary team, their roles extend beyond that of a consulting audiologist or one who may be seeing a child through a hospital program or physician's office.

sidebar on p. 383 for recommended professional practices appropriate for educational audiologists according to EAA (1997).

EAA (2002) also outlines roles and responsibilities for educational audiologists in the early detection and intervention of hearing loss. The position statement makes the following assertion:

Audiologists who are employed in school settings have an opportunity as well as responsibility to promote the early detection and intervention of hearing loss. While the definition of audiology, according to the Individuals with Disabilities Act, includes identification of children with hearing loss, the responsibility of population-based screening activities are generally considered health initiatives rather than special education responsibilities.

The roles and responsibilities of the educational audiologist in this area are identified as:

1. Identification of children with hearing loss, using appropriate audiological screening techniques.

2. Determination of the range, nature, and degree of hearing loss and communication functions, by use of audiological evaluation procedures.

3. Referral for medical and other services necessary for the habilitation or rehabilitation of children with hearing loss.

4. Provision of auditory training, speech reading training, listening device orientation and training, and other services.

5. Provision of services for prevention of hearing loss.

6. Determination of the child's need for individual amplification, inclusion selecting, fitting, and dispensing appropriate listening and vibrotactile devices, and evaluating the effectiveness of those devices.

7. Counseling and guidance of children, parents and teachers regarding hearing loss.

Educational audiologists are uniquely skilled to assist with several current areas of practice, which have impacted how and to whom schools provide service due to technological advancements. One area is the treatment and management of children who are identified through universal newborn hearing screening. The same is true of the management of children and students who have been implanted with cochlear

Recommended Professional Practices for Educational Audiology

Identification and Management

- Screening/Management of Hearing Screening Programs
- Audiologic Evaluations
- Assessment of Central Auditory Processing

Amplification

- Hearing Aid Evaluation and Analysis
- Classroom Amplification

Hearing Loss Management

- Medical/Educational Referral
- Counseling and Guidance of Students/ Parents/Teachers
- Inservice Training/Consultation and Interpretation for School Personnel
- (Re)Habilitation and Instructional Services
- Individualized Education Plan (IEP)/Individualized Family Service Plan (IFSP) Planning and Writing

Conservation/Consultation

- Hearing Conservation
- Soundfield Amplification
- Classroom Acoustics

Program Management

- Training and Supervision of Support Personnel
- Calibration
- Record Maintenance
- Program Administration

Professional Leadership/Development

- Community Leadership/Collaboration
- Evaluation and Research

Recommended Professional Practices for Educational Audiology – Taken from the Position Statement of the Educational Audiology Association (1997). Adapted with permission.

devices. The mapping of these devises as well as the auditory training that is necessary is highly specialized treatment involving both speech-language pathologists and audiologists.

One other new area of practice receiving increased attention is the area of hearing conservation. ASHA's 2006 campaign, "Listen to Your Buds," is an example of consumer awareness efforts about how normal hearing can be damaged by listening to personal amplification systems, such as iPods™, too loudly. Because of the noise inherent in schools due to classroom environments, bands, and the activities of students, the educational audiologist is a wonderful resource for health conservation initiatives.

Ethics

Ethical behavior is expected of all professionals. Speech-language pathologists and audiologists in public schools will find themselves in situations that call on their ethical code of conduct. Any speech-language pathologist or audiologist who is an ASHA member with a CCC or who is in a Clinical Fellowship (CF) is bound to abide by ASHA's (2003a) Code of Ethics (see Appendix C). State speech-language and hearing associations also typically have a code of ethics that members are expected to uphold. While membership in professional associations is recommended, the code of ethics should serve as a guideline for any individual who practices as a speech-language pathologist, regardless of membership in these organizations. Under the code of ethics, speech-language pathologists and audiologists have a reporting responsibil-

ity if they are aware of unethical behavior on the part of a fellow professional. ASHA's Ethical Practices Board responds to violations that are reported against ASHA certificate holders.

In a *Communication Connection* article entitled "Professionalism and Ethics: How do you spell success? E-T-H-I-C-S," Frank C. Bucaro (2000) noted that each individual brings life experiences and moral beliefs to their daily decisions. According to Bucaro, training in ethical decision making should be addressed by employers and institutions of higher education so that instincts, emotions, and moral spirit are utilized appropriately in given situations. This is especially important because "Every decision you make affects someone else, and we must always take that into consideration before making the decision" (p. 4).

Americans generally hold honesty and integrity as important values and do not anticipate situations that would compromise such values. In the everyday work world, unfortunately, situations may arise that create uncertainty regarding appropriate behavior. In more extreme situations, a speech-language pathologist may encounter people who do not behave ethically and who put the speech-language pathologist in a compromising position. In all cases, speech-language pathologists and audiologists must follow federal and state regulations and laws. Consider Cooper's example given in the ASHA Ethics Roundtable (Moore-Brown et al., 1998) entitled "When Supervisor and Supervisee Disagree." In this case study, the speech-language pathologist makes recommendations for an intervention plan in her report and the supervisor changes the recommendations. In dealing with this type of a situation, speech-language pathologists and audiologists may find themselves in an ethical conflict between doing the right thing for the student and possibly compromising their employment position if questioning the supervisor presents a threat to employment.

Other situations that may arise in public schools include:

- A student needs a type of intervention that the speech-language pathologist does not feel competent to provide.

- A teacher or parent demands services when a student is not in need of such service.

- The speech-language pathologist believes that a student should be referred to a private speech-language pathologist for specialized treatment or evaluation services, but the school district will not pay for the referral.

- The speech-language pathologist believes that a student requires more intervention time than is available in the schedule.

If speech-language pathologists and audiologists are challenged in this way, it is wise for them to seek advice from a mentor—another colleague or an administrator (e.g., principal, program specialist, or director). Be certain that whoever is selected will keep the issue confidential. Maintaining professionalism and confidentiality in communications regarding an ethical situation are equally important. Speech-language pathologists and audiologists can also contact the state department of education or regional education agency for assistance. The ASHA Web site (www.asha.org) maintains educational resources on this issue.

State and national speech-language-hearing associations are good places to turn when situations arise that provide ethical challenges. These organizations may provide guidance to those in the field regarding a variety of professional or ethical challenges such as:

- Caseload size and management.

- What to do when a supervisor directs an evaluation be conducted when the speech-language pathologist has screened and indicated no evaluation is necessary.

- What to do when a parent demands to be present during an evaluation.

- Use of new therapy techniques that are controversial.

One legal and ethical challenge that often faces speech-language pathologists and audiologists in schools is the issue of providing services to children outside of the school setting in a private practice situation. If a speech-language pathologist is serving a student in the school setting, it would be considered a conflict of interest to provide that same student outside services that address his or her IEP goals. The reason for this is that IDEA 2004 calls for program and services to be provided to children through the IEP in order to provide FAPE. The parent would have recourse, through due process, to argue that the services provided outside the school should be provided or paid for by the school district. These are sticky situations, so it is recommended that speech-language pathologists and audiologists avoid private practice with students who are being served in their employing school system under an IEP.

Another scenario that might present itself is a request for the speech-language pathologist to serve the student during the summer, or when the student is off-track in a year-round setting. Regulations pertaining to the provision of extended-year programming do not allow school districts to categorically exclude certain students from services during break periods. Therefore, while speech-language pathologists and audiologists previously may have felt comfortable serving students on a fee-for-service basis during the summer or over school breaks, the new regulations make it clear that some children may be eligible for extended school year programs if the service is required for the child to receive FAPE (34 C.F.R. § 300.106). It is recommended that the speech-language pathologists and audiologists be very cautious about serving students in a private practice setting

if they are also providing services to these students during the school year. Some school-based speech-language pathologists and audiologist avoid any potential conflict by doing summer work in hospitals, skilled nursing facilities, or private practice offices that serve geriatrics.

Professional Organizations

Professional organizations provide a needed link to current developments in the field, legislative information, and networking with others. Speech-language pathologists and audiologists who work in schools have many professional organizations they may join. Speech-language pathologists and audiologists typically want to affiliate with organizations that will keep them in contact with at least three aspects of their employment: (1) the discipline of speech-language pathology nationally, (2) their discipline within the state, and (3) the broader field of schools and education. In many cases, speech-language pathologists will also wish to become members of an organization for a specialty area within speech-language pathology, such as fluency, ASDs, or family counseling. Audiologists may wish to join specialty organizations that focus on treatment of children with cochlear implants, aural rehabilitation, or hearing conservation. Joining several organizations will provide speech-language pathologists and audiologists with a more well-rounded view of controversial topics, more scholarly journals, access to conferences for up-to-date information, as well as a greater (or multiple) effect on regulatory agencies. Although there are some costs involved in maintaining one's membership dues and in attending conferences, professionals should view membership in more than one organization as a necessity, not a luxury. The following suggestions are designed to help speech-language pathologists and audiologists decide which are the most appropriate organizations to join.

The National Organization: the American Speech-Language-Hearing Association (ASHA)

ASHA is considered the primary association for the professions of speech-language pathology and audiology. Since CERTIFICATION and membership are separate entities, speech-language pathologists and audiologists who have a CCC need to request membership if they wish to join. Membership in ASHA should be viewed as a responsibility and a privilege of school-based speech-language pathologists. Working in a school district with many other ASHA members is a distinct advantage and increases speech-language pathologists' professionalism. A school district with speech-language pathologists on staff who hold ASHA memberships will attract new professionals to complete their CF there in order to take full advantage of the valuable mentoring opportunities. Many other professionals who work in school settings do not have the opportunity to hone their new skills in a nurturing CF environ-

> ASHA is considered the primary association for the professions of speech-language pathology and audiology.

ment their first year on the job. Related fields are seeking ways to do this, through externships for special education teachers and through state sponsored mentor-teacher positions to enable more skilled educators to help new employees learn the ropes.

Membership in ASHA provides journals, newsletters, conventions, access to important lobbying and political action committees, position papers and technical resources for service delivery, the latest information on a clinical population or new assessment tools, and a code of ethics to guide one's practice and decision making. The network of over 123,000 professionals in speech-language pathology and audiology is a tremendous resource. The interests of each state are represented in the governing body of ASHA and in the work of national committees and task forces that influence school-based practice. Attracting school-based speech-language pathologists and audiologists to ASHA committees is very important to the viability of the national organization, but it is even more important to the practice of speech-language pathology in public schools. National regulatory agencies, particularly the Office of Special Education and Rehabilitative Services (OSERS), can interact directly with ASHA on key issues. This type of access to key policymakers is nearly impossible for school district employees to get on their own. ASHA also provides its members benefits such as low-cost professional liability insurance, continuing education options to maintain a license or increase one's skills, and critical resources on functional outcomes and accountability for services.

Special interest divisions are an important part of the organizational structure of ASHA. Divisions allow for an in-depth professional connection around a particular aspect of the profession. ASHA has the following special interest divisions:

1. Language Learning and Education

2. Neurophysiology and Neurogenic Speech and Language Disorders

3. Voice and Voice Disorders

4. Fluency and Fluency Disorders

5. Speech Science and Orofacial Disorders

6. Hearing and Hearing Disorders: Research and Diagnostics

7. Aural Rehabilitation and Its Instrumentation

8. Hearing Conservation and Occupational Audiology

9. Hearing and Hearing Disorders in Childhood

10. Issues in Higher Education

11. Administration and Supervision

12. Augmentative and Alternative Communication

13. Swallowing and Swallowing Disorders (Dysphagia)

14. Communication Disorders and Sciences in Culturally and Linguistically Diverse Populations

15. Gerontology

16. School-Based Issues

Division 16 was established in December 1999 as the division dedicated to school issues and service delivery. Division 1 also addresses the language and learning aspects of students in educational settings. School-based speech-language pathologists and audiologists are likely to find that belonging to one or more divisions will provide them with a strong base of infor-

The National Student Speech-Language-Hearing Association (NSSLHA)

Prior to ASHA membership, students in communication disorders programs are eligible to become members of the National Student Speech-Language-Hearing Association (NSSLHA). Membership in NSSLHA allows students to receive journals and discounted conference rates. NSSLHA members can also belong to ASHA Special Interest Divisions and will receive a discount when they convert to full ASHA membership upon completion of their education requirements. Joining NSSLHA affords students an opportunity to meet colleagues from the discipline, become knowledgeable about national issues, gain valuable insight into clinical and professional topics, and get a head start in their first job.

mation about topics specific to their needs. Each special interest division has a newsletter and a listserve that provides both scholarly and practical information for practitioners in that area. Divisions also sponsor or co-sponsor conferences and workshops for continuing education credits that are responsive to member needs.

ASHA's School Services division is dedicated to assisting school-based personnel. Since 55 percent of ASHA's membership is school-based, the association is intimately familiar with issues in the schools and strives to provide resources and support for school-based professionals. Although holding a CCC is not required in many states, school-based ASHA members find the membership benefits valuable in their daily work, including legislative, professional and practice information, and networking. In order to establish a solid connection between ASHA and state issues, State Education Advocacy Leaders (SEALs) are appointed by state speech-language-hearing associations to work directly with ASHA on their specific state issues. The names of the SEALs for each state can be found on the ASHA Web site.

State Speech-Language-Hearing Associations

Another discipline-specific organization of interest to the speech-language pathologist in schools is the state speech-language-hearing association. Every state and the District of Columbia has such an organization, plus there is an organization for those who work overseas, mainly in American Schools and Department of Defense Schools (DODS) for dependents in the

U.S. Armed Forces. The state associations and their Web sites are listed in Table 9.4.

State associations are independent entities, not chapters of the national association. They address their members' state concerns, represent them before legislative bodies, create continuing education opportunities, and determine their own membership criteria. Nearly all state organizations have student membership at a reduced membership rate. A state organization is also discipline-specific, but carries much more weight than ASHA does with state governance, funding sources, higher education agencies, and state licensing bureaus. In fact, many times a state organization is the only entity that can address inequities for speech-language pathologists and audiologists in a school system, since public schools are state-funded enterprises. State associations vary in size from approximately 100 to 5,000 members and have a loose relationship with ASHA as "recognized associations." The state organizations can band together at times to push for federal changes, led by the Council of State Association Presidents (CSAP). (Information about CSAP is available on their Web site, www.csap.org.)

Membership in a state association greatly assists school-based speech-language pathologists and audiologists with licensing requirements, continuing education offerings, state news, and connections with a network of professionals who work under the same state regulations. Some state organizations work very closely with their state departments of education, interpreting and influencing state policy. Being part of this process is important to speech-language pathologists and audiologists and their school dis-

Table 9.4

Web Sites for State Speech-Language-Hearing Associations

State	Association		Web Site
Alabama	Speech and Hearing Association of Alabama	(SHAA)	www.alabamashaa.org
Alaska	Alaska Speech and Hearing Association	(AkSHA)	www.aksha.org
Arizona	Arizona Speech-Language-Hearing Association	(ArSHA)	www.arsha.org
Arkansas	Arkansas Speech-Language-Hearing Association	(ArkSHA)	www.arksha.org
California	California Speech-Language-Hearing Association	(CSHA)	www.csha.org
Colorado	Colorado Speech-Language Hearing Association	(CSHA)	www.cshassoc.org
Connecticut	Connecticut Speech-Language-Hearing Association	(CSHA)	www.ctspeechhearing.org
Delaware	Delaware Speech-Language-Hearing Association	(DSHA)	www.dsha.org
DC	District of Columbia Speech-Language-Hearing Assoc.	(DCSHA)	www.dcsha.org
Florida	Florida Association of Speech-Language Pathologists & Audiologists	(FLASHA)	www.flasha.org
Georgia	Georgia Speech-Language-Hearing Association	(GSHA)	www.gsha.org
Hawaii	Hawaii Speech-Language, and Hearing Association	(HSHA)	www.hsha.org
Idaho	Idaho Speech, Language, Hearing Association	(ISHA)	www.idahosha.org
Illinois	Illinois Speech-Language-Hearing Association	(ISHA)	www.ishail.org
Indiana	Indiana Speech-Language-Hearing Association	(ISHA)	www.islha.org
Iowa	Iowa Speech-Language-Hearing Association	(ISHA)	www.isha.org
Kansas	Kansas Speech-Language-Hearing Association	(KSHA)	www.ksha.org
Kentucky	Kentucky Speech-Language-Hearing Association	(KSHA)	www.kysha.org
Louisiana	Louisiana Speech-Language-Hearing Association	(LSHA)	www.lsha.org
Maine	Maine Speech-Language-Hearing Association	(MSLHA)	www.mslha.org
Maryland	Maryland Speech-Language-Hearing Association	(MSHA)	www.mdslha.org
Massachusetts	Massachusetts Speech Language Hearing Association	(MSHA)	www.mshahearsay.org
Michigan	Michigan Speech-Language-Hearing Association	(MSHA)	www.michiganspeechhearing.org
Minnesota	Minnesota Speech-Language-Hearing Association	(MSHA)	www.msha.net
Mississippi	Mississippi Speech-Language-Hearing Association	(MSHA)	www.mshausa.org
Missouri	Missouri Speech-Language-Hearing Association	(MSHA)	www.showmemsha.org

Continued

#TP-29703 Making a Difference - 2nd Ed. · ©2008 Thinking Publications® · www.thinkingpublications.com · 1-800-277-8737

Table 9.4 – *Continued*

State	Association	Abbrev.	Website
Montana	Montana Speech-Language, and Hearing Association	(MSHA)	www.mshaonline.org
Nebraska	Nebraska Speech-Language-Hearing Association	(NSLHA)	www.nslha.org
Nevada	Nevada Speech-Language Hearing Association	(NSHA)	www.nvsha.org
New Hampshire	New Hampshire Speech Language and Hearing Association	(NHSLHA)	www.nhslha.org
New Jersey	New Jersey Speech-Language Hearing Association	(NJSHA)	www.njsha.org
New Mexico	New Mexico Speech-Language, and Hearing Association	(NMSHA)	www.nmsha.net
New York	New York State Speech-Language-Hearing Association	(NYSSLH)	www.nysslha.org
North Carolina	North Carolina Speech, Hearing and Language Association	(NCSHLA)	www.ncshla.org
North Dakota	North Dakota Speech Language Hearing Association	(NDSLHA)	www.minotstateu.edu/ndslha
Ohio	Ohio Speech and Hearing Association	(OSHA)	www.ohioslha.org
Oklahoma	Oklahoma Speech-Language-Hearing Association	(OSLHA)	www.oslha.org
Oregon	Oregon Speech-Language, and Hearing Association	(OSHA)	www.oregonspeechandhearing.org
Overseas	Overseas Association of Communication Sciences	(OSACS)	www.asha.org/about/legislation-advocacy/state/info/osacs.htm
Pennsylvania	Pennsylvania Speech-Language-Hearing Association	(PSHA)	www.psha.org
Rhode Island	Rhode Island Speech-Language-Hearing Association	(RISHA)	www.risha.info
South Carolina	South Carolina Speech-Language-Hearing Association	(SCSHA)	www.scsha.com
South Dakota	South Dakota Speech-Language-Hearing Association	(SDSLHA)	www.sdslha.org
Tennessee	Tennessee Assoc. of Audiologists and Speech-Lang. Pathologists	(TAASLP)	www.taaslp.org
Texas	Texas Speech-Language-Hearing Association	(TSHA)	www.txsha.org
Utah	Utah Speech-Language-Hearing Association	(USHA)	www.ushaonline.net
Vermont	Vermont Speech-Language, and Hearing Association	(VSHA)	www.vslha.org
Virginia	Speech-Language-Hearing Association of Virginia	(SHAV)	www.shav.org
Washington	Washington Speech and Hearing Association	(WSHA)	www.wslha.org
West Virginia	West Virginia Speech-Language-Hearing Association	(WVSHA)	www.wvsha.org
Wisconsin	Wisconsin Speech-Language Pathology and Audiology Assoc.	(WSHA)	www.wisha.org
Wyoming	Wyoming Speech-Language-Hearing Association	(WSHA)	www.wsha.info

tricts. Participating in special interest groups and committee work in state associations can enhance speech-language pathologists' effectiveness. Having held state association presidencies, both authors are convinced that membership in one's state association is critical for speech-language pathologists and audiologists and for the profession.

Associations of Related Interests

Another association type is one reflecting general education, special education, or both. Some speech-language pathologists and audiologists find that they can appreciate and be appreciated by their general education colleagues if they feel a connection with the greater education environment. Organizations listed in the sidebar on p. 393 are popular choices for speech-language pathologists and audiologists because they either combine educational approaches, or give another perspective on public schools. One of the authors of this book found that joining the National Association for the Education of Young Children (NAEYC) was like looking up from the microscope and seeing a whole laboratory for first time. The central focus of the Council for Exceptional Children (CEC) is special education in the schools. CEC, like ASHA, has divisions for special interests. The Division for Communicative Disabilities and Deafness (DCDD) provides a common network for those working with children with these issues. The International Reading Association (IRA) and the Association for Supervision and Curriculum Development (ASCD) provide great resources at a time when understanding general education curriculum and instruction is necessary. These organizations are national, however, states and regions have similar organizations on smaller scales that focus on state issues. Again, these groups have great value for speech-language pathologists and audiologists because education is a state issue, and the decisions about education are made by local legislatures and school boards who listen to their constituents, not to a group that represents other states. Bigger is not necessarily better when it comes to influencing opinion makers about their personal ideas of quality.

It is important to recognize the key organizations for other school professionals even if you cannot or do not join them. A few national organizations focused on the broader view of general or special education include National Association of Secondary School Principals (NASSP), National Association of Elementary School Principals (NAESP), and National Association of School Psychologists (NASP).

As noted earlier, some speech-language pathologists and audiologists find it advantageous to join an organization that specializes in a particular disorder, approach, philosophy, or subgroup. Although special interest groups in both ASHA and state associations may have similar subgroups, these are still managed by the parent organization and have the same basic orientation and resources.

Professional organizations play an important part in the school-based speech-language pathologist becoming someone who knows the discipline within the larger context of education, plus one or two specialty areas in great depth. Membership in more than one organization allows speech-language pathologists and audiologists to hone skills in one activity and use them with another related group. The new energy

Professional Organizations Useful to
Speech-Language Pathologists and Audiologists in Schools

Examples of valuable specialization organizations outside ASHA are listed below. The ones marked with an asterisk (*) include consumers as well as professionals, an authenticity that is missing in professionals-only groups. Others are particularly valuable because they are international and bring speech-language pathologists and audiologists into contact with professionals from school systems beyond the United States. International organizations can often be recognized by their titles.

- Alexander Graham Bell Association for the Deaf and Hard of Hearing* *(www.agbell.org)*

- American Academy of Audiology *(www.audiology.org)*

- Association for Supervision and Curriculum Development *(www.ascd.org)*

- Autism Society of America* *(www.autism-society.org)*

- Council for Exceptional Children *(www.cec.sped.org)*

     - Council of Administrators in Special Education *(www.casecec.org)*

     - Division for Children's Communicative Development *(education.gsu.edu/dcdd)*

     - Division for Early Childhood *(www.dec-sped.org)*

     - Division for Learning Disabilities *(www.teachingld.org)*

- Council for Learning Disabilities (International) *(www.cldinternational.org)*

- Educational Audiology Association *(www.edaud.org)*

- International Association of Logopedics and Phoniatrics *(www.ialp.info/joomla)*

- International Reading Association *(www.reading.org)*

- International Society for Augmentative and Alternative Communication* *(www.isaac-online.org)*

- National Association for the Education of Young Children *(www.naeyc.org)*

- National Cued Speech Association* *(www.cuedspeech.org)*

- National Down Syndrome Congress* *(www.ndsccenter.org)*

- Rehabilitation Engineering & Assistive Technology Society of North America* *(www.resna.org)*

- United States Society for Augmentative and Alternative Communication *(www.ussaac.org)*

that professional organizations add to the practice of speech-language pathology and audiology in schools is a great reason to join them.

Teacher Unions

Having a professional career as a speech-language pathologist or audiologist in the schools means working in a specialized environment. The speech-language pathologist or audiologist is an employee of the school district but is not a teacher in the sense of classroom instruction. The speech-language pathologist or audiologist is a service provider who selects which students will receive speech-language or audiology services and to what extent, but typically is not an administrator. These positions exist to provide supports to students who require specialized assistance to enable them to be successful in the classroom and curriculum.

In some states, speech-language pathologists and audiologists are viewed as teachers for purposes of credentialing, union membership, and salary placements. In other states, they have all of the above-named teacher rights but are considered nonteaching employees when they apply for related credentials or mentor teacher pay. Within states, some districts will place their speech-language pathologists and audiologists on the management or support services track (i.e., nonunion) to receive additional pay but not management responsibilities.

Unions are prevalent for educators in some states and nonexistent in others. Teacher union employee groups are organized for the purpose of collective bargaining and are considered to be a "community of interest" (Webb, Greer, Montello, & Norton, 1987). Unions seek to cover fragmentation groups such as nonmanagement employees but may not always do so. Unions may have local chapters and most are aligned nationally with either the National Education Association (NEA) or the American Federation of Teachers (AFT).

When a speech-language pathologist or audiologist is hired by a school district, county agency, or regional special education unit, the local leader of the teachers' bargaining unit usually contacts the new employee to provide information on the union. If the union is a closed shop, all teaching employees—which may or may not include speech-language pathologists and audiologists—must pay dues to that union. If it is an open shop, the speech-language pathologist or audiologist may choose whether or not to join the union which bargains on behalf of the members, but can only select the currently situated union. Advantages of union membership are hotly debated, though the issue of joining is often moot for speech-language pathologists and audiologists if the employing district is a closed shop union. However, they are typically well represented by unions if they bring their issues to the attention of the union's leadership.

At times, speech-language pathologists and audiologists will bring concerns about employment conditions to the attention of ASHA or a state association and seek intervention from the professional association. These are not professional issues but rather bargaining issues that must be worked out between the parties in the employment contract (i.e., the school district and its employees), then the professional association may not be able to directly assist, but can provide advice. ASHA has resources available on their Web site for assisting speech-language pathologists and audiologists in working with their teachers unions on such issues as salaries and working conditions. Often one district will assist colleagues in a neighboring district with contract wording or work conditions that have been successfully resolved.

Liability and Insurance

General and special educators currently find they work within a highly litigious environment at times. While most professionals do not expect to be involved in litigation or to have their ethics or professional behavior questioned, in fact, this does happen. Occasionally, spurious accusations are made or, unfortunately, unprofessional conduct occurs. The vast majority of the time, if professionals conduct themselves in a professional manner, their work behavior will not be challenged. The realities of a modern society dictate, however, that speech-language pathologists and audiologists in public schools be informed and take adequate precautions regarding their own professional liability. Throughout this book, the importance of documentation and using research-based practice patterns has been emphasized. These habits will serve speech-language pathologists and audiologists well should they become involved in litigation. In addition, speech-language pathologists and audiologists should take the steps that professionals in related fields take and carry professional liability insurance.

Professional liability and related insurance has several applications in the public school setting. There are basically three aspects to the liability issue:

- Liability for one's professional conduct in assessment and treatment of students with communication disabilities.

- Liability for working as an educator of children to carry out the school district's curriculum, policies, procedures, and expectancies.

- Liability as a citizen to abide by the civil laws and regulations of the city, state, and country (including laws that protect against discrimination toward persons with disabilities).

In the first case, to protect oneself from a claim regarding the conduct of professional practice, the speech-language pathologist or audiologist needs to purchase professional liability insurance through an ASHA-approved agency or a similar service. Union membership sometimes provides this coverage. In the second case, the school district's insurance will cover an employee who is accused of negligence or incompetence if the person has operated under the district's policies and guidelines. In the third case, the person is liable for her own conduct as a law-abiding citizen.

It should be noted that being accused and being liable may be two different things. In certain circumstances the liability coverage of the school district may not be able to cover legal representation, even if the accusations are unfounded. Such is the case when criminal accusations are involved. This is one of the reasons why it is prudent to carry liability insurance. Again, no one can prevent a lawsuit from being filed, but being able to have adequate defense is very important in all situations.

After investigation, if the speech-language pathologist is found responsible for inappropriate action, reprimands can take many forms. One's certification and/or state license could be forfeited if found guilty of a violation of professional practice. One's job, credentials, or both could be forfeited for not properly carrying out district procedures, and one could face civil action for a violation of civil rights laws.

Because school district policies are understandably silent on many aspects of a communication intervention program and permit speech-language pathologists and audiologists to make their own judgments for assessment and intervention, the wise professional should carry professional liability insurance in addition to the coverage the school district provides. The scope of practice of the speech-language pathologist is an ever-changing landscape. For example, engaging in an evolving practice such as dysphagia treatment with children in a school setting is exciting but has greater liability for the speech-language pathologist (O'Toole, 2000; Homer, 2000). Speech-language pathologists and audiologists who are covered by liability insurance can be reassured that they are protected when engaging in appropriate practice, in the event that their practices are challenged.

Teacher associations and unions are also very helpful with insurance arrangements or immediate assistance if allegations of wrong-doing are brought against one of their members. Assistance with insurance and liability issues may also be available from school-based colleagues, ASHA, state associations, unions, and insurance brokers. All professions have well-structured insurance plans to protect clients against workplace hazards, such as false claims against the insured, unsubstantiated terminations, costly defense actions, and unfair treatment.

Who to Ask When You Have a Question on the Job

No matter how long someone works in the schools, questions about situations that are new and novel come up frequently. The first rule of working in public schools is "Don't be afraid to ask for help!" Where to go for that help may vary depending on the nature of the question. One thing to remember is that public school staff members are generally thoughtful and helpful, since this is the nature of people drawn to working with children. As a new person, though, seek advice from someone who has the knowledge to answer your question and has the experience to help you learn the expected methods of working within your school culture.

Support Networks

Speech-language pathologists and audiologists need to develop several networks to acquire the types of information they need. Table 9.5 provides helpful information on who may be able to provide specific information needed when working in public schools.

Table 9.5

People and Places for Finding Assistance

Level	Person	Nature of Information	Type of Question or Request
Site	Secretary	Supplies, equipment, meetings, schedules, absences	Where do I get pencils and other supplies? Can I use the copier at the school site? Where do I report my absences? Who do I report to regarding changes in my schedule? Where do I get a key for my room?
	Custodian	Furniture, cleaning, supplies	How often is my room cleaned? Could I get another chair for this room?
	Principal	Schedules, meetings, resources, books and materials, funds, families, curriculum trends	Where is my room? Where can I obtain curriculum material? Who will chair IEP meetings? When do you want those meetings scheduled? What schoolwide and district meetings should I attend? What are the special programs that I should know about?
	Special Education Teacher	Policies and procedures for special education, service delivery models used at the site, student data, strategies for instruction	Which students receive duplicated services? How can we work together to provide services?
	General Education Teacher	General education curriculum, Instructional Support Team (IST) practices, student performance information, current instructional methodology	How is a particular student doing in class? What modifications/accommodations are being used? What is the program/curricular emphasis in the classroom?

Continued

Table 9.5 – *Continued*

Level	Person	Nature of Information	Type of Question or Request
District/ Region	Secretary (Special Education)	Student database, forms, ordering/budget	Who sets up IEP meetings? What is the process for turning in paperwork? What data am I required to keep? How do I order supplies?
	Psychologist	Behavior/social issues, testing, program issues, eligibility questions	Are there characteristics being demonstrated that might be considered emotional disturbance? What is the student's performance on processing tests? What programmatic considerations should we be making? What if the student does not qualify?
	Program Specialist/ Manager	Assistance with student issues, referral to more restrictive environments, assistance with referrals to outside agencies, assistance with issues involving advocates or attorneys	Please come and observe this student. This student is not being successful. What should we consider? Parents say they will bring an advocate to the meeting. What should I do?
	Program Administrator (Coordinator; Director)	Allocations of funds and resources, assignments, assistance with student issues, due process issues, hiring, supervision, program coordination	What is my assignment? What is my budget? Can I discuss suggestions for program changes with you? Who is conducting my performance evaluation?
	Regional Administrator	Legal assistance, allocations of funds, assignments (in some organizations)	(Same as those for the Program Administrator, depending on the organizational structure.)

#TP-29703 Making a Difference - 2nd Ed. · ©2008 Thinking Publications® · www.thinkingpublications.com · 1-800-277-8737

There are other important people who can be a resource to beginning speech-language pathologists and audiologists. Such people might include:

- Other speech-language pathologists and audiologists in schools.
- Speech-language pathologists and audiologists in health care.
- District or regional resource support staff for technology, staff development, categorical programs (e.g., Title I, bilingual education, American-Indian education, or school-to-work), child welfare and attendance, and research and evaluation.
- Directors of curriculum and instruction.
- Assistant superintendents.
- Business managers.
- Superintendents (depending on the issue and size of the district).
- Parent groups.
- Advisory groups.

When seeking information, speech-language pathologists and audiologists should know the culture of the district and understand the hierarchy for gaining information or obtaining resources. While most people will be relatively friendly, some school districts are very sensitive about the ways that employees go about getting what they need. While a new person should feel comfortable asking questions, he or she should be sensitive in terms of from whom and where the information is sought. Sometimes an employee may be told they "do not need to know about that." In such a circumstance, speech-language pathologists and audiologists should simply ask who handles the matter and find out how to work with that person.

Existing structures for problem solving will also likely be in place. Examples would be department, job-alike (i.e., people with the same job titles), regional, or school site meetings. Another example of problem-solving systems is to hold lunch meetings to discuss cases, which the authors have found to be a most successful learning and team-building experience. If such a system does not exist where you work, you might set it up!

Speech-language pathologists and audiologists should also go to their state and national associations for guidance on specific issues. Such organizations often have policy and practice statements that may be useful in making decisions or communicating a position to administrators, parents, or teachers. The following helpful ASHA documents are available on the ASHA Web site (www.asha.org):

- Scope of Practice Statements: A list of professional activities that define the range of services offered within the professions of speech-language pathology.

- Preferred Practice Patterns: Statements that define universally applicable characteristics of activities directed toward individual patients/clients, and that address structural requisites of the practice, processes to be carried out, and expected outcomes.

- Position Statements: Statements that specify ASHA's policy and stance on a matter that is important not only to the membership but also to other outside agencies or groups.

- Practice Guidelines: A recommended set of procedures for a specific area of practice, based on research findings and current practice, that details the knowledge, skills, and/or competencies needed to perform the procedures effectively.

The sidebar below provides activities for the aspiring speech-language pathologists to begin engaging in professional activities common to the work world of school-based speech-language pathologists.

Local and Regional Supervisors

Speech-language pathologists and audiologists in public schools work with a variety of individuals who serve in different supervisory positions. The person who writes the speech-language pathologist's or audiologist's performance evaluations may or may not have a background in speech-language pathology or audiology, or even special education. However, speech-language pathologists and audiologists,

Activities for Aspiring Speech-Language Pathologists and Audiologists

Invite an officer of your state association to class, or interview him or her on your own. Prepare questions about the role that your association plays in legislation, recruitment, and retention of school-based speech-language pathologists and audiologists. Inquire whether there is a committee or a board position to represent school issues. Inquire whether there is a student chapter or reduced student membership fee, and how you can get involved.

Plan to attend the next state or national conference for speech-language and hearing professionals that is held in your geographic area, or plan to travel to one. Register in advance so you receive a copy of the program and note how many topics are on school-based issues. Plan to attend those sessions, especially any committee meetings or task force meetings that are open to you. Ask questions and get to know the professionals involved in these issues in your state.

Join or become more active in your campus NSSLHA chapter. Bring issues from this class or this book for discussion at the next meeting. Record the responses and keep track of the certifications, regulations, and procedures in your state for the topics discussed in this chapter.

Create a personal portfolio of your continuing education and professional development activities thus far. Begin to collect documentation of conference and course attendance that is necessary to maintain your state and national certifications. Record activities that have developed your professional skills even if they are not immediately needed for minimum requirements. List professional organizations, volunteer activities with children, leadership tasks in your school, and extracurricular activities that demonstrate your knowledge and commitment to public education.

as much as any other professional in the system, may be promoted into general or special education administration.

Building-level staff, including speech-language pathologists, are likely to report to a principal. In some systems, the supervisor is from the special education department and may have a background from either general or special education. There is not one particular career track for general or special education administrators. Audiologists are more likely to be supervised by regional or district level administrators, since they are more likely to serve several schools, although in some situations, such as a special site or program for students with hearing impairment, the audiologist may be assigned and supervised by a principal who has a specialized background.

Many special education systems have a middle management person called a program specialist or program manager. These individuals may or may not be administrators, but they have significant involvement in program development, program placement decisions, and staff development. Some also are involved in employment decisions such as making recommendations for hiring and termination. Job performance evaluations are typically conducted by individuals who are administrators, which is why a principal often performs that function for the specialist staff.

Depending on the size of the district, the special education department may also have a director or coordinator who oversees the entire operation of special education in the district. This person may also have job responsibilities other than special education, such as other pupil ser-

vices functions (e.g., health, psychological, counseling, student discipline, home study, or other services). The speech-language pathologist or audiologist may or may not interact on a regular basis with the district-level special education administrator. If the district is large, program support persons will provide guidance. A large district or consortium of smaller districts may even have one individual who oversees only the speech-language and audiology programs. In a midsize or smaller school district, the speech-language pathologist or audiologist may have regular contact with the district-level administrator.

Speech-language pathologists and audiologists who have moved into supervisory and administrative roles in public schools have access to groups such as the ASHA Special Interest Division 11, *Administration and Supervision*, and the Council for Administrators and Supervisors of Speech, Language, and Hearing Programs (CASSLHP) to provide support and collegial interaction. Supervisors who are speech-language pathologists may need input regarding program goals, the speech-language pathologist's role, and the work of the field. When sharing information with a supervisor, it is usually helpful to recognize that person's perspective and what is important to him or her. Speech-language pathologists and audiologists will find that discussing how their expertise can promote improved reading ability and academic skills is of great interest to a principal. Principals typically place high regard on the skills and training of the speech-language pathologist and audiologist who works with the students on their campus. If the principal is not knowledgeable about how the skills of the speech-language pathologist or audiologist can support academic success for the students on the campus, it is the responsibility of those professionals to provide such information to the principal. Once the principal learns the extent of skills and abilities of the speech-language pathologist or audiologist, a great partnership can occur that will be rewarding for all parties.

State Consultants

In the early days of special education, most state education agencies (SEAs) had consultant positions for all specialty areas (e.g., visual impairments, deaf/hard of hearing, preschool, and speech-language). By the end of the 1990s, several states still had consultants with a speech-language background, but these individuals had job responsibilities that extended far beyond the field of speech-language. Such responsibilities included working with the complaints and monitoring division of the SEA, working with school reform issues, and working with Medicaid billing. Despite these other job responsibilities, today's SEA consultants connect with speech-language pathologists and audiologists in the field in a variety ways. They also connect with each other through an ASHA-related organization called the Council of Language, Speech, and Hearing Consultants in State Education Agencies (CLSHCSEA). All 50 states have representatives to the CLSHCSEA group (CLSHCSEA, 2007).

The responsibilities of CLSHCSEA members include the following:

- Advise and consult with appropriate federal agencies, state agencies, and other public and private organizations and committees on philosophies, principles, practices, and needs in all areas relating to services for individuals who have language, speech, or hearing disabilities.

- Formulate and recommend policies and procedures in the field of language, speech and hearing, and disseminate them to appropriate agencies and organizations.

- Establish liaisons with other organizations and associations whose primary purpose is to promote the provision of appropriate speech, language, and hearing services to children from birth through 21.

- Network and share information, ideas, solutions, guidelines, innovative programs and practices, etc. with other CLSHCSEA members (CLSHCSEA, 1999, p. 1).

In their daily work, state consultants focus their energies in the following areas:

- Consult with university training programs, especially in the area of speech and language.

- Assist noncertified people who are working in the field.

- Assist certified speech-language pathologists and audiologists who have questions about issues, and need an outside recommendation.

- Provide recruitment connections between graduates and school systems.

- Conduct trainings.

- Serve as a liaison between county level systems and the state.

- Maintain a library of resources.

- Serve as the connection between general education and speech-language pathologists and audiologists in early literacy trainings (especially in the area of phonemic awareness).

- Work closely with state associations, and possibly conduct round table discussions or update sessions at the annual state conference (K. Knighton, personal communication, December 28, 1999).

Speech-language pathologists and audiologists in public schools are encouraged to contact their SEA and find out who is the consultant responsible for speech-language and hearing programs. This person can be one more valuable resource for answers and ideas.

Continuing Education

School-based speech-language pathologists and audiologists have a professional responsibility to maintain and update their clinical skills to meet the needs of myriad developmental levels and the ever-expanding range of disabilities presented by students. When assignments change, new skills often are needed or previously learned skills need to be updated. This might be particularly true when speech-language pathologists and audiologists encounter students in secondary school for the first time or students with specialized needs such as ASDs, cerebral palsy, augmentative communication, or perhaps a cochlear implant. In most schools, the speech-language pathologist is the only professional who can assess and implement a plan for these students' communication needs. Much of one's

graduate program in communication sciences and disorders is devoted to recognizing and serving students with these disorders, as well as identifying sources of information that the speech-language pathologist can access later to stay current with the field. Part of the allure of this profession is the steady stream of new developments in so many areas and continued expansion into new areas. School-based speech-language pathologists and audiologists also play increasingly important and expanding roles in reading instruction and classroom-based services, so continuing education in these areas is essential.

Continuing education is the vehicle to assure parents and other team members that qualified providers with state or national licensure and certification remain knowledgeable and qualified. In some states, a specific number of continuing education units (CEUs) must be reported for renewing credentials, while others rely on professional integrity, allowing professionals to be responsible for keeping track of their attendance at professional development workshops, seminars, and courses. The Continuing Education section of ASHA's Web site (www.asha.org/about/continuing-ed/) maintains a list of each state's requirements for licensure and the contact agencies for speech-language licensure and teacher certification.

ASHA has mandatory continuing education requirements for all holders of the Certificate of Clinical Competence to maintain their certification. ASHA policy requires 30 Certification Maintenance Hours (CMH) over a three year period. These hours may be accumulated through a variety of continuing education opportunities, including ASHA or other professional development events which offer CEUs for speech-language pathologists and audiologists. Although it is not required, one simple way to keep track of continuing education hours earned is to join the ASHA Continuing Education Registry. This service will automatically record and maintain hours earned, so that when necessary, the member can contact ASHA and receive a printout of approved CEUs earned. Information regarding ASHA requirements, as well as state and credential requirements, are typically included on the Web sites for the licensing or credentialing agency or organization, as well as in renewal mailings. Individuals are encouraged to always maintain a professional portfolio in order to verify and document trainings attended. (Table 9.6 is an example of a school-based speech-language pathologist's continuing education activities for two years that enabled her to maintain all of her credentials and keep her skills sharp.)

Table 9.6

A Speech-Language Pathologist's Continuing Education Log

(The personal portfolio contains notes and registration from each activity.)

Year	Action	Hours
1	Attended ASHA convention in home state	8*
	Attended one day of state convention	5*
	Attended two days of school district reading curriculum workshops (stipend)	8
	Read journals with Journal Group from the district for ASHA CEUs	10*
2	Attended three days of state convention	16*
	Took a three-day summer workshop on bilingual assessment from the SEA	18
	Completed two-day fluency seminar for school practitioners	10*
	Read the Special Interest Division newsletters and took the quizzes	6
	Responded on Special Interest Division listserv at least once a week	24
	Organized and attended the May Is Better Hearing and Speech Month all-day speaker on evidence-based practice in the schools	13 (5*)

*These hours convert to CEUs and each activity was registered with an approved CE sponsor for that credential.

State organizations for speech-language pathologists and audiologists are excellent sources of continuing education through their conferences, workshops, and professional study groups. ASHA offers the broadest array of continuing education formats, including conferences, workshops, seminars, audiotapes, video conferences, journal and newsletter read-and-test situations, study groups, special interest divisions, and refereed scholarly journals. Universities offer classes and courses, but enrolling may be difficult if one is not pursuing a degree. University courses can be more expensive and time-consuming than training offered by professional organizations, and may not have the advanced level of information the experienced professional is seeking. Continuing education offerings by school districts, state educational agencies (SEAs), and extended adult education programs are often free or low cost. These offerings can provide valuable information on general education curriculum and instruction, which may be very useful because of new IDEA 2004 requirements to work with the curriculum. These courses may also suffice for school district salary schedule advancement (a local union or school district decision in most areas), but they may not be acceptable for state licensure or mandatory CMH for ASHA.

CEUs must be approved by the certificate-granting body in order to be counted as professional growth hours. This circumstance could require the speech-language pathologist or audiologist to take multiple classes to accommodate what several boards, panels, and certification agencies require. Some states have developed arrangements that assist in coordinating these requirements. The speech-language pathologist or audiologist should keep in mind that school districts, university curriculum and instruction departments, and SEAs are the only agencies likely to offer courses that help speech-language pathologists and audiologists understand general education curriculum and instruction, a requirement of IDEA 2004. Learning the state and district curriculum frameworks and standards is a responsibility, particularly of the speech-language pathologist in schools, and can be met with teacher education CEUs. Participating and learning alongside teachers also gives insight into the expectations for teachers and helps to create partnerships.

The important factors to keep in mind regarding continuing education are:

- Maintain CCC yearly.

- Choose professional development training options carefully.

- Know state requirements for maintaining credentials.

- Know state requirements for maintenance of speech-language pathology licensure.

- Know what is needed to extend clinical skills in schools.

- Know needed additions to professional portfolio for staying viable in the job market.

- Know needed additions to professional portfolio to assist with defending your skills and training in a due process action if necessary.

- Look for continuing education providers who have received endorsement by all the certifying agencies to which speech-language pathologists must report to keep it affordable.

- Remember all continuing education brings added value to your knowledge and skills, although some is more immediately evident than others.

IDEA 2004 stipulates that if the speech-language pathologist, audiologist, or any other member of the student's educational team needs specific training to be effective with that student, the training can be written into the student's IEP (34 C.F.R.§ 300.320 [a][4]). This is referred to as "supplementary aids and services, program modifications, or supports for school personnel." If a team member needs specific training to help the child with a COMMUNICATION DISORDER (e.g., sign language, discrete trial training, or augmentative or alternative communication) this training can be listed as a supplementary support for school personnel in the IEP. This could provide specific training for the speech-language pathologist or audiologist, or might enable a paraprofessional or another team member to learn a supporting skill for the classroom. The LEA representative is present on the IEP in order to authorize this type of commitment of LEA resources. Another type of training that may occur and should be written into the IEP is the training that the speech-language pathologist or audiologist may need to provide to teachers, paraprofessionals, or parents.

Continuing education can take many forms, but it is always an important component of the school-based professional's role. Even if continuing education is not mandated, it is a professional responsibility, as is keeping track of one's continuing education growth activities each year.

CHAPTER 10

A Promising Future for School-Based Speech-Language Pathologists and Audiologists

IN THIS CHAPTER

This chapter considers the influences shaping the future work world of speech-language pathologists and audiologists. Trends and forces affecting the future are discussed and considered in terms of their impact on speech-language and audiology services in the educational setting. The twenty-first century skills needed by students are again considered as evidence of the challenge for the educational system. Trends in classroom instruction, support services, and speech and language services are all reactions to the need to prepare students with disabilities to enter into the work world able to compete with these advanced skills. Four areas influencing the change are system impacts, professional shortages, legislative mandates, and research to practice. The chapter concludes with predictions to watch for in the expanded practice and professionalism of speech-language pathologists and audiologists in schools.

1. Consider the old practice models and beliefs and the new practices models and beliefs and discuss which practices you have observed in your own school or a school where you have observed. Also discuss what the response of the speech-language pathologists and audiologists working in the school(s) has been to these transitions.

2. Examine the ten issues identified by the Council for Exceptional Children as those which most seriously impact their membership of special education teachers. How do these issues impact speech-language pathologists and audiologists in schools?

3. Review the twenty-first century skills needed by students and discuss how your school, or a school you know, is involved in developing these skills in students. How are the students on the speech and language caseload impacted by these programs?

4. Match the trends in classroom instruction, support services, and speech and language services to recommended practices for intervention in Chapters 5, 6, and 7.

5. Discuss why change is so difficult in schools and what strategies are recommended to deal with change. Give an example.

6. How will persistent vacancies of speech-language pathologists and audiologists impact the field in the future?

7. Conduct an Internet search on three of the predicted trends for expanded practice and professionalism. How do you see these trends affecting your own personal career?

Foundations for Envisioning the Future

Educational systems throughout the United States have experienced unprecedented change throughout the first decade of the twenty-first century. The impact of the requirements of NO CHILD LEFT BEHIND (NCLB) and the INDIVIDUALS WITH DISABILITIES EDUCATION IMPROVEMENT ACT (IDEA 2004) have been more than adding new forms or procedures to schools and educational agencies. A backward glance at the system changes undertaken since 2001 gives perspective to the overwhelming overhaul that education is experiencing. Speech-language pathologists and audiologists who work in schools have experienced changes in policy, procedures, roles, responsibilities, and practice. Looking backward gives perspective of how far we have come. Looking forward gives insight into how far we have to go.

The work of speech-language pathologists and audiologists in the educational system provides essential communication links to students whose needs range from the struggling reader with literacy challenges to a student with an augmentative device designed to compensate for his or her lack of usable speech. The expertise needed in schools by these professionals will directly determine how successful the student will be in his or her educational experience. Over the course of the history of special education, the roles of education professionals and specialists have evolved and changed along with political, legislative, social, and research influences. As we look to the future, the challenges facing the education system are significant. But within these challenges are opportunities for developing new methods of facing old problems and overcoming barriers that have been systemic and sometimes harmful to children.

While new programs and mandates can sometimes feel personal as individuals are asked to change how they do their job, educational reforms must always be considered within the broader context. One "old adage" that serves well in this context is the observation to "Think global and act local."

Beliefs and Actions: Thinking About Teaching and Learning

Special education services are extensions of the general education program. Examining the daily and big picture issues of the educational system is necessary in order for speech-language pathologists and audiologists to know how to approach their work in the public schools. This includes understanding the belief systems upon which legislative policy, research, and practice are built. Special education and general education programs are not separate; they are tied together. What happens in one program directly influences and impacts the other. Table 10.1 illustrates beliefs and actions under an old model versus the new model being advocated.

It is because of the evolution of new model beliefs and actions that some of the practices of the past are being eliminated: dual funding systems, the discrepancy model, and the one-way trajectory of special education referral and assessment. Special education services and personnel practices are changing to reflect updated thinking in the field. Once a belief system

Table 10.1	**Comparisons of Old and New Models in Special Education Services**
Old Model Beliefs	**Old Model Actions**
Students are somehow different internally and instructionally.	Assessment should search for within learner deficits.
	Tasks in intervention worked on processes rather than content.
Students with disabilities are not capable of learning higher level concepts.	Provide students with watered-down curriculum that does not include challenging content.
	Do not expect students to succeed academically, socially or vocationally, so there is no need to provide those opportunities (low expectations).
Programs for students with disabilities should be separate from general education.	Separate funding systems.
	Separate service delivery (e.g., pull-out, separate classes).
New Model Beliefs	**New Model Actions**
All students need good solid core instruction; students who are struggling need more.	Assessment guides how the environment should be changed to support the learner (i.e., materials, delivery of service, instructional supports, intensity of instruction).
All students should master standards and grade level curriculum.	Tasks in intervention work on learning the material of the classroom.
High expectations for all learners, including students with disabilities, English learners and those from minority and low socio-economic backgrounds.	Special education services should be designed to support students within the general education classroom where the core instruction occurs.
	Funding should be blended to support student needs; up to 15 percent of IDEA funds can/ should be spent on prereferral activities.

Source: Moore-Brown (2007b). Reprinted with permission.

changes, old practices do not fit any more. An example of how such change occurs can most dramatically be seen in the growth of RESPONSE TO INTERVENTION (RtI) models throughout the country (see Chapters 3 and 5).

Future Forces Affecting Education

KnowledgeWorks Foundation (2007), an organization focused on funding and leadership for educational initiatives, provides a global perspective to the future forces affecting education. The context in which these forces occur, according to the Foundation is a VUCA Environment, which stands for *volatile, uncertain, complex*, and *ambiguous*. The VUCA environment touches all institutions and community members, including schools. The Foundation's *Map of Future Forces Affecting Education* suggests that schools will be expected to play a leadership role in addressing the interrelated issues of learning, health, and civic intelligence and observes:

> Public education is at a critical crossroads. The knowledge economy and globalization continue to challenge the basic industrial era assumptions upon which most public schools, curricula, and evaluation mechanisms are based (p. 1).

The KnowledgeWorks Foundation believes that examining trends is important because "it is time to pay more attention to how the world is changing" in order to plan for educational excellence, which they believe is critical to our future. The trends affecting families, communities, markets, institutions, educators, learning tools, and practices will be a part of shaping the future of our educational institutions and families served. These trends set the national and global context for our schools and for the learners whom we are preparing for a work world.

Statistical Data Projections Regarding Schools

The National Center on Educational Statistics (NCES, 2007b) presents the following statistics for the school years up to 2007–2008 as well as projections until the year 2015:

- $489.4 billion is the projected expenditure for public elementary and secondary schools in the 2007–2008 school year.

- 49.6 million students are estimated to be enrolled in public elementary and secondary schools in the United States in 2007–2008.

- There were 97,000 public elementary and secondary schools during the 2005–2006 school year.

- It is anticipated that 3.2 million teachers will be employed during the 2007–2008 school year.

- 93 percent of children with disabilities, ages 3 through 5, received speech and language therapy during the 2003–2004 school year.

- 20 percent of school-age children spoke a language other than English at home during 2005.

- 27 percent of African-American preschool-age children were identified as having a speech or language impairment as their primary disability; whereas 42 percent of

Hispanic children and 51 percent of White children were identified as having a speech or language impairment as their primary disability.

• 17 percent increase in high school completion rates for students with disabilities from 1987 to 2003; Also, 17 percent increase in the proportion of students with disabilities participating in postsecondary education from 1987 to 2003.

The *Digest of Education Statistics: 2006* (NCES, 2007b) reports that enrollment in public elementary and secondary schools rose 24 percent between 1985 and 2006, and predicts record levels of total elementary and secondary enrollment each year through at least 2015, as the school-age population continues to rise.

Focus From the Curriculum Side

The Association for Supervision and Curriculum Development (ASCD) is a leader in advancing effective practices for teaching and learning. The ASCD's work has been consistent with the national directions discussed: a focus on all learners (Hanzelka, 2006) and an initiative launched in 2006 focusing on educating the whole child (Hodgkinson, 2006; Miller, 2007; Scherer, 2007). These initiatives, coming from the leaders in general education curriculum, are significant for those who work with students with disabilities and other struggling learners. These efforts reflect the melding of the interests of general and special education.

ASCD's publications reflect a focus on the importance of teaching academic language, using differentiated instruction and universal design (Tomlinson & McTighe, 2006), as well as curriculum and thinking maps (Hyerle, Alper, & Curtis, 2004) in order to address the needs of all students, particularly English learners and other struggling learners. Marzano and Pickering (2005) suggest specifically utilizing academic language in teaching and intervention. These authors note that systematic instruction in academic terms is critical for students who do not come from an academic background. Additionally, they report that direct vocabulary instruction on words related to content leads to improved academic achievement.

The use of academic language and academic English for English learners (Zehr, 2005), as well as using thinking maps (Hyerle et al., 2004) are all interventions and strategies that should be familiar to speech-language pathologists, and can help to bridge concerns that school-based personnel may have in terms of collaboration or co-teaching. These reports demonstrate that, in fact, the practices recommended to general education personnel are often

similar to what specialists may be using as part of interventions already.

As mentioned in Chapter 1 , the International Reading Association (IRA) does an annual survey of reading experts to determine "What's Hot" for the current year. For the year 2007, the following were identified:

Extremely Hot:

- Adolescent literacy

Very Hot:

- Direct/explicit instruction

- English as a second language/English-language learners

- Fluency

- High-stakes assessment

- Informational text

- Literacy coaches/reading coaches

- Scientific evidence-based reading research and instruction (Cassidy & Cassidy, 2007)

In reviewing the issues that are considered "hot" and even "very hot" by the reading community, speech-language pathologists can again see overlaps in their work, and also notably can align efforts with teachers and reading specialists to address these issues in schools. Cassidy and Cassidy (2007) noted in their reporting of the survey that the survey does not identify phonemic awareness, which had been on the list for many years.

The issues that are being discussed in the professional literature of curriculum and reading are important to review for several reasons. Not only can speech-language pathologists, audiolo-

gists, and other special educators learn from the advances in various disciplines, but this knowledge can provide a common ground for all professionals as they search for effective interventions for students who struggle in these areas. This could have implications for the types of interventions used with students, but could also impact whether or not students are ultimately referred for a special education assessment.

Focus From the Special Education Side

The Council for Exceptional Children (CEC) identified the ten issues that are most critical to their membership of special education teachers and administrators. These issues also form the foundation on which the future can be envisioned, as dealing with these issues will be part of any forward movement on behalf of students, including system change.

1. National special education policy (e.g., response to intervention (RtI), qualifications for inclusive and congregated settings, teacher retention, alternate assessment, highly qualified teachers, discipline, outcomes and transition needs, successful interventions for students)

2. Funding (e.g., adequate federal, state, and local funding for programs, services, and staff in special education and related services; education funding)

3. Professional development (e.g., need for customized knowledge related to job activity, university preparation for today's educational needs)

4. Staff shortage (e.g., personnel shortages in special education, related services, higher education, recruitment and retention of a diverse workforce)

5. Practice (e.g., transition, alternative assessment, outcomes, eligibility, discipline, collaboration, serving culturally and linguistically diverse students)

6. Research (e.g., evidence-based practice, RtI, successful interventions for students with attention to the needs of culturally and linguistically diverse learners, identification)

7. National general education policy (e.g., relation to special education, scientifically based instruction, assessment, adequate yearly progress, highly qualified teachers, time taken from teaching to complete testing, individual growth models, funding)

8. Paperwork (e.g., excessive time needed for documentation of assessment, parent notification, provision of services, time taken from students to complete paperwork)

9. Inclusion (e.g., provision of programs and services for students with exceptionalities in the regular education program, continuum of alternate placements, natural environment)

10. Disproportionate representation in special education (e.g., overrepresentation in disability areas and under-representation in gifted education)

The issues that were raised but not included in the top ten list included the following: accountability, support for special education from multiple sources, instructional resources, time shortages, and working conditions for teachers (CEC, 2007).

All of these issues lay the foundation from which speech-language pathologists and audiologists can view the future. By "thinking globally, but acting locally," they will be well positioned to consider additional information about services.

Educational Services in the Twenty-First Century

In 2005, a fascinating business book called *The World Is Flat: a Brief History of the Twenty-First Century* (Friedman, 2007) captured popular interest. In his book, Friedman proposed the concept of the "flattening" of the world based on globalization and the way that industrial countries and emerging markets can now compete in a technological world due to the accessibility that the Internet provides. While Friedman's book discusses supply chains in business, the concept has applicability to the educational workplace. According to Friedman, the flattened world means that interactions are dominated by collaboration. The application of these concepts can be rich for specialists in the educational system. Our educational world, too, is becoming flat. No longer will speech-language pathologists work in isolation or separately from the rest of the educational system. In fact, what we do in one place often affects what happens in another place, sometimes far away.

The concept is obvious in many areas of our work. In twenty-first century schools, job duties are overlapping and synergistic with other colleagues, including psychologists, other therapists, classroom teachers, and even administrators. Collaboration, consulting, and networking will be critical skills to have and develop as we work with other professionals. In schools, speech-language pathologists and audiologists will find their "value added" role by supporting students in the curriculum. Speech-language pathologists, audiologists, and other special educators will increasingly be spending their time working in prevention activities with nonidentified students and in general education classrooms with identified students.

In the "flattened" world of educational services, response to intervention (RtI) programs will change how and what speech-language pathologists and other specialists do when conducting assessments. The referral process will take on a whole new purpose. Assessment will need to reflect an academic focus in order to reflect the economic purpose of school. Assessment will be more dynamic and will need to reflect student's performance on standards, which is the currency of schools.

Twenty-First Century Skills

The twenty-first century skills needed by students to thrive in a digital economy were identified in Chapter 1 as: (1) Digital-age literacy, (2) inventive thinking, (3) effective communication, and (4) high productivity (NCREL/Metiri, 2007. (See Figure 1.1 on p. 16 in Chapter 1.)

Most anyone can look at this set of skills and agree that these represent what is necessary for future workers to be successful. Take a moment, however, and compare these skills to the old model beliefs discussed earlier in this chapter, where students with disabilities were effectively removed from learning advanced skills because of how the service delivery models were operationalized. If educators are to ensure that students with disabilities and other struggling and at-risk learners are to develop Digital-age literacy, inventive thinking, effective communication, and high productivity skills, then every opportunity must be afforded them, including the development of an educational system that has high expectations for these learners and ensures opportunities to develop these skills. For some challenged learners, their path to skill development may take new and different forms of experiences. That is the job of special education. These skills should be discussed as part of transition planning for students 16 years and older, but work on the development of these skills should begin in elementary school. The NCREL Web site (http://www.ncrel.org/engauge/) provides an engaging resource for thinking about these skills and their development.

ASCD's focus on the whole child (Azzam, 2007) identifies another set of twenty-first century skills needed by students: global awareness, self-directed learning, technology literacy, problem-solving skills, as well as time management, and personal responsibility skills. ASCD reports that virtual learning through online courses can easily incorporate these skills that students will need in work and life.

Trends Addressing Improved Student Achievement

As NCLB and IDEA 2004 focus educators to improve student achievement for all students,

each discipline reacts accordingly, and will intertwine in their work. Table 10.2 identifies some trends which reflect the work that is being undertaken in general education (e.g., the classroom), support services, and speech and language services to support students.

The Achievement Gap

Since the inception of the accountability movement, improvements have been seen in statewide testing scores. While there continues to be debate on how testing occurs and the ways that student achievement is measured and reported, most agree that overall improvements to the educational system are positive for students when they are realized. A growing and constant concern, however, is the persistent achievement gap between students from minority and disadvantaged backgrounds. Overall, the gap remains and is not closing.

Data from the National Assessment of Educational Progress (NAEP) shows that reading scores for 17-year-olds narrowed dramatically for both African-American and Hispanic students from 1975 through 1988. From 1990 to 1999, however, these gaps either remained constant or grew slightly in both reading and mathematics (National Governors Association, n.d.).

The increasing diversity of our nation's student population is evident in nearly all schools across the country. The problems are extremely complex and difficult to resolve. Specifically, issues of culture and race and the inherent biases in the educational system will need to be addressed at core levels in order to enroot new practices and beliefs and to begin to solve discrepancies within the system that prevent students in these subgroups from receiving the types of educational services they need, in both general and special education (McLaughlin, Pullin, & Artiles, 2001; Education Trust, 2007; Snow & Biancarosa, 2003b).

Resources and Funding

The difficulties with the funding system for special education were presented in Chapter 9. With the increases in educational advances and medical technology, costs will continue to rise in special education. Currently, local districts and general education funds are needed to subsidize special education at increasingly high levels. This reality creates tension between program administrators and other personnel who are required to manage budgets in the school dis-

Table 10.2	**Current Trends**

Trends in Classroom Instruction

- Literacy: still hot, but not new
- Data-driven decision making
- Closing the achievement gap
- Learning/thinking/curriculum mapping
- Evidence-based/Scientifically based practice
- Communities of learners (professional staff)

Trends in Support Services

- Assessment
  - Look for environmental supports, not within child deficits
  - Response to intervention
  - Performance-based
  - Curriculum-driven
  - Consideration of demands of statewide and classroom assessments
  - Limited use of standardized measures

- Intervention
  - Focus on assisting students master curriculum
  - Focus on outcomes and student achievement
  - Blended service delivery models
  - Networks

Trends in Speech and Language Services

- Evidence-Based Educationally Relevant Therapy
  - Need to know: curriculum
  - Need to know: standards
  - Need to know: instructional design
  - Need to know: difference between the curriculum and the standards
  - Need to know: measures of student progress in the classroom

Source: Moore-Brown (2007b). Reprinted with permission.

trict. The funding system for special education needs to be overhauled, but in the meantime, cost overages will be blamed on service providers and administrators, while the reality is that the program is underfunded. New approaches to special education funding are desperately needed and should be developed at the local and state level. At the national level, there continues to be bipartisan rhetoric in support of full funding for special education, but the reality has never been close. The funding formulas for special education and the levels of actual real dollars need to be tackled and new solutions generated in the near future.

Charting the Next 25 Years of Progress

In the year 2000, the Office of Special Education Programs (2000) offered the following in considering the work of the future for special education:

The next 25 years of the 21st century provide an opportunity to ensure that educational improvements for all children include infants, children, and youth with disabilities...

To meet this challenge, IDEA must build on its previous support for equality of access and continue to expand and strengthen its support for quality programs and services. Improving educational results for children with disabilities requires a continued focus on the full implementation of IDEA to ensure that each student's educational placement and services are determined on an individual

basis, according to the unique needs of each child, and are provided in the least restrictive environment. The focus must be on teaching and learning that use individualized approaches to accessing the general education curriculum and that support learning and high achievement for all.

We know, after 25 years, that there is no easy or quick fix to the challenges of educating children with disabilities. However, we also know that IDEA has been a primary catalyst for the progress we have witnessed. Because of Federal leadership, the people of the United States better appreciate the fact that each citizen, including individuals with disabilities, has a right to participate and contribute meaningfully to society. With continued

#TP-29703 Making a Difference - 2nd Ed. · ©2008 Thinking Publications® · www.thinkingpublications.com · 1-800-277-8737

Federal-state-local partnerships, the nation will similarly demonstrate that improving educational results for children with disabilities and their families is critical to empowering all citizens to maximize their employment, self-sufficiency, and independence in every state and locality across the country. Further, our nation's ability to compete successfully in the global community depends on the inclusion of all citizens. We cannot afford to leave anyone out of our effort (OSEP, p. 5).

Our Predicted Future: Speech-Language Pathologists and Audiologists in Public Schools

The theme throughout this book should be obvious: The changes that will impact speech-language pathologists and audiologists working in public schools are the changes that will impact everyone else in public education. To examine the predicted future, four areas should be considered: system, professional, legislative, and research to practice.

System

The educational system is changing rapidly and consistently. Michael Fullan (2001), a foremost authority on change in the educational system, offers these thoughts on educational change:

Change is a double-edged sword. Its relentless pace these days runs us off our feet. Yet when things are unsettled, we can find new ways to move ahead and to create breakthroughs not possible in stagnant societies (p. 1).

Remember that a culture of change consists of great rapidity and nonlinearity on the one hand and equally great potential for creative breakthroughs on the other. The paradox is that transformation would not be possible without accompanying messiness (p. 31).

Change is such a part of our cultural experience that the National School Boards Association (NSBA, n.d.) has developed a Toolkit to assist school districts in their change processes. NSBA recognizes that systemic reform efforts have been ongoing for over 15 years. They identify the systemic change process that stakeholders will engage in as having the following phases:

- Create a vision of what you want the system to look like and accomplish.

- Take stock of the current situation.

- Identify strengths and weaknesses of the current system in light of the vision.

- Target several priority items for improvement.

- Establish a plan for addressing these priority items and for measuring success.

- Assess progress regularly and revise actions as needed.

- Take stock again and use feedback to revisit vision and begin cycle again when the action cycle is completed (NSBA, n.d.).

Although acknowledged that change is a part of life and that conditions change constantly, schools and the organizational institutions that support the schools are slow to embrace new ways. However, the rapid acceleration and necessary response to mandates and problems is not going to slow down any time soon. The world we live in, and more importantly, the world the students will live in, defies stagnancy. NSBA's Change Toolkit sets the stage when asking the question "Why change?":

1. Every two or three years, the knowledge base doubles.

2. Every day, 7,000 scientific and technical articles are published.

3. Satellites orbiting the globe send enough data to fill 19 million volumes in the Library of Congress every two weeks.

4. High school graduates have been exposed to more information than grandparents were in a lifetime.

5. Only 15 percent of jobs will require college education, but nearly all jobs will require the equivalent knowledge of a college education.

6. There will be as much change in the next three decades as there was in the last three centuries (NSBA, n.d.).

The pressures on the educational system reflect society's pressures and needs. The sidebar on p. 421 identifies but a few of the pressures and challenges felt by public education.

So Why Change?

Change is necessary in order to address the pressures, the challenges, and the needs in the educational system. In responding to change, each individual will be asked to reexamine their role and how he or she can contribute to this improvement. New ideas and new ways of approaching emerging issues will present themselves. One example is looking to system supports, rather than within student deficits when a student has difficulty in the classroom. Another example is assisting students through an RtI model rather than referring for assessment, identifying that student as disabled, and putting the student in a pull-out special education program. A third example is continuing to work on keeping students in the general education classroom so they can receive the core content curriculum by the curriculum experts— general education teachers. Each of these ideas and

#TP-29703 Making a Difference - 2nd Ed. • ©2008 Thinking Publications® • www.thinkingpublications.com • 1-800-277-8737

Public Education Pressures and Future Challenges

Pressures on Public Education

- Extension of service
  - before school
  - after school
  - longer day/year
- Facilities
- Accountability
- Achievement gap
- Increasing complexity of student and family needs
- Staffing and highly qualified
- Discipline/Violence

- Children's issues
- Public perception of public education
- Funding
  - what money there is has strings attached
  - what money there is never quite covers the cost
  - public systems seek alternative funding sources
  - foundations, grants, and partnerships with community agencies

Future Views: Public Education System Challenges

- Provision of early intervention
- Increase of the numbers of children identified with autism
- New prevention/intervention models
- Literacy and numeracy
- Request for private services
- Lack of funding

- Professional shortages; recruitment and retention
- New models of service delivery
- Inclusive services
- Charter schools
- Increasing litigation

many others in this book are new, and are the system's response to the need for change. As the system works through the development of the approaches, it may be, as Fullan (2001) suggests "messy," but that is what needs to happen in order to develop better processes to address students' needs. The authors of this book see this context as a prime opportunity for speech-language pathologists and audiologists to be part of shaping the future.

Professional Shortages

The most significant professional issue that will be facing speech-language pathologists and audiologists in the next decade will be the consequences of shortages, including doctoral shortages. Persistent vacancies have been reported for many years, and this hardship is becoming more acute. (See Chapter 9 for further discussion). As we look to the future, again we suggest "Think global and act local." The authors and others believe that some of the "big ideas" to be addressed include:

1. There is a significant need to increase the supply of speech-language pathologists and audiologists, especially in high-need areas. High-need areas can be geographic (inner city, rural, sparsely populated regions [the west]), socioeconomic (poverty areas, culturally diverse), or treatment (autism, augmentative alternative communication, adolescent services).

2. A change is needed in training institution models so as to accommodate students and potential students who need to support themselves economically while studying communication disorders. Examples of innovative models include night and evening classes, online courses, and school-based clinic experiences.

3. Employers need to do everything they can to retain their current speech-language pathologists and audiologists, including examining compensation and benefit packages, working conditions, and other workplace issues.

4. States and local entities need to work together in ongoing and sustained efforts, including working with other stakeholders to address the systemic issues which have contributed to the shortage and blocked efforts to change the situation.

5. Partnerships with human resources, teachers' unions and school boards are critical if we are to solve the problem.

6. There should be no separation between efforts to address the shortage in schools and efforts to address health care or other settings.

7. Service delivery models need to be examined on an ongoing basis in order to ensure that services are being provided in the most efficient manner.

8. Expand the use of speech-language pathology assistants (SLPAs) in order to provide clinical services through trained paraprofessionals when appropriate.

9. Closely examine opportunities within educational reform to create roles for speech-language pathologists and audiologists that will streamline their work while capitalizing on their expertise.

10. Examine funding resources for building new programs and retaining and attracting staff.

Roles and Responsibilities

ASHA's document on the *Roles and Responsibilities of School-Based Professionals* (2001) is currently under revision as of the publication of this text. However, several documents on roles and responsibilities and knowledge and skills from ASHA since 2001 have contributed to the body of professional guidance from our national association. Included in these are documents on literacy, response to intervention, early intervention, attention deficit disorder, ASDs, cognitive impairments, audiological testing and services to infants and toddlers, augmentative communication, services to children who are deaf or hard of hearing (see sidebar on p. 423).

Web Sites Available for ASHA's Practice Policies

Response to Intervention–*Responsiveness to Intervention: New Roles for Speech Language Pathologists*
http://www.asha.org/members/slp/schools/prof-consult/NewRolesSLP.htm

Literacy–*Knowledge and Skills Needed by Speech-Language Pathologists With Respect to Reading and Writing in Children and Adolescents*
http://www.asha.org/docs/html/KS2002-00082.html

Early Intervention–*Principles and Guidelines for Early Hearing Detection and Intervention Programs*
http://www.asha.org/docs/html/PS2007-00281.html

Attention Deficit Disorder–*Roles of Audiologists and Speech-Language Pathologists Working With Persons With Attention Deficit Hyperactivity Disorder*
http://www.asha.org/docs/html/TR1997-00255.html

Autism–*Principles for Speech-Language Pathologists in Diagnosis, Assessment, and Treatment of Autism Spectrum Disorders Across the Life Span*
http://www.asha.org/docs/html/TR2006-00143.html

Cognitive Impairments–*Roles of Speech-Language Pathologists in the Identification, Diagnosis, and Treatment of Individuals With Cognitive-Communication Disorders: Position Statement*
http://www.asha.org/docs/html/PS2005-00110.html

Audiology–*Knowledge and Skills Required for the Practice of Audiologic/Aural Rehabilitation*
http://www.asha.org/docs/html/KS2001-00216.html

Audiology–*Guidelines for the Audiologic Assessment of Children From Birth to 5 Years of Age*
http://www.asha.org/docs/html/GL2004-00002.html

Services to infants and toddlers–*Communication-Based Services for Infants, Toddlers, and Their Families*
http://www.asha.org/docs/html/TR1989-00136.html

Augmentative Communication–*Roles and Responsibilities of Speech-Language Pathologists With Respect to Augmentative and Alternative Communication*
http://www.asha.org/docs/html/PS2005-00113.html

Deaf and Hard of Hearing Services–*Roles of Speech-Language Pathologists and Teachers of Children Who Are Deaf and Hard of Hearing in the Development of Communicative and Linguistic Competence*
http://www.asha.org/docs/html/TR2004-00256.html

In addition to the professional documents in the field on roles and responsibilities, legislative requirements will lead to emerging and evolving roles for speech-language pathologists and audiologists. The area of response to intervention has been mentioned throughout this text, and this emerging area of practice has been led in many districts by speech-language pathologists who have taken leadership roles to guide system change in their places of employment (Montgomery & Moore-Brown, 2006; Moore-Brown & Montgomery, 2006).

Because of the expansive training and knowledge base that speech-language pathologists and audiologists bring to the educational work setting, they are often leaders in assuming new roles. Bridging into curriculum issues, for example, is a natural for speech-language pathologists who have expertise in language and can easily conduct task analysis for differentiating instruction for struggling learners. At the same time, some speech-language pathologists feel that their "duty" should be to the "identified" students on their caseloads. In a world of RtI and inclusive settings, speech-language pathologists in particular will continue to expand and redefine their roles.

When taking on new roles, however, it is also equally important to evaluate, on an ongoing basis, existing duties and responsibilities, to see which are no longer of value to the system or the students. New roles and responsibilities emerge to address needs presented in the system. This also means that some skill sets and activities will either no longer be needed or will need to be abandoned or reshaped. Sometimes, trying to hang on to all of the old ways of doing things while adding on new responsibilities creates an untenable working situation for the professional. As we grow, we also will need to let go.

Workload Approach

The ASHA WORKLOAD model is gaining momentum throughout the country as an acceptable approach to organizing a speech-language pathologist's service delivery (ASHA, 2002a). Several models have received notoriety, including the three-in-one model developed in Oregon (Annette, 2004). The workload approach has also gained popularity in other special education arenas, as it makes sense to consider all the duties one has to complete, not just how many students are identified on a caseload. Managing and recognizing all of the duties and responsibilities of the speech-language pathologist and audiologist works well under the workload model. This method will continue to receive attention and acceptance, even as psychologists, administrators, and others apply the principles of this approach to their own workload.

Legislative

The dramatic overhaul of the educational system in the accountability era has been outlined in the discussions of NCLB and IDEA 2004. While the work of educators has been significantly impacted by these new mandates, another important perspective should be considered: the increasing federal role in education. This influence specifically addresses the need to close the achievement gap and equalize opportunities for children who have historically been underserved in public education. The increasing federal role in education reflects the national interest and importance in these issues.

While some critics of this increasing federal role oppose the role from a civics perspective, educators are often more pragmatic, asking the question "Where is the funding to support the mandates?" It appears that these questions will remain unaddressed in years to come, although the mandates for improvement and accountability will remain, and likely increase.

There can be no mistake that although the requirements of NCLB and IDEA 2004 may be difficult at times, these two laws have, indeed, changed the landscape of how services are provided to children throughout our country. There is also no doubt that the increased attention given to the disability subgroup under NCLB has resulted in special education being brought into the discussions of curriculum and instruction and that restructuring in school districts now includes special education personnel and students in an unprecedented manner.

There has been another action/reaction as a result of the legislative actions. The instructional improvements made in general education, specifically in the area of reading, were noteworthy prior to NCLB, and those improvements provided a foundation upon which NCLB was built. At the same time, however, Congress (preamble IDEA 1997; IDEA 2004) was rightfully critical of the lack of any instructional improvements in special education. The melding of practice under these two laws has caused both general and

special education to be more open about what is actually happening in classrooms. This open analysis has met some resistance from teachers and unions, as well as push back from special educators who have believed that their way of educating students in a more isolated setting was justified. The reality of the accountability era is that all educators will experience scrutiny of their practices, particularly if students are failing.

At the time of this publication, NCLB is going through the reauthorization process. Many of the proposals for improvement involve the testing programs and how accountability is measured (i.e., suggesting growth models and additional alternative measures for students with disabilities), increased access to instructional strategies that work, and increased funding for high need schools.

One area of IDEA 2004 that has not been fully discussed in this text is the expanded requirements for transition. This component of the law is being seen as a new potential area for litigation, as it adds increased responsibility for school districts to prepare students with disabilities for their postsecondary experience. Throughout the country, litigation is being filed in this area as parents are challenging the extent to which the district met their responsibility. Many school districts have historically provided transition programs for older students with significant disabilities, but school districts will again need to retool in order to be able to provide needed services for students with mild disabilities. Such services may include working with community college or preparatory schools outside of the jurisdiction of public education, which were previously not accessible. As these programs and arrangements are established, school districts may be vulnerable.

Research to Practice

The heart of the future work of speech-language pathologists and audiologists in schools is definitely in developing a greater sophistication with curriculum, assessment, and prereferral interventions. The accountability environment of schools sets forth this context, and therefore establishes the framework in which improvement needs to occur. Speech-language pathologists and audiologists need to not only stay current on the evolving practice within our own discipline, but also within general education curriculum and instruction, special education, reading, psychology, as well as health care, because children with various medical diagnoses will be attending school. The future, in fact, will find extremes in many ways that will seem to conflict, specifically between the extremes in the diagnoses and specialized treatments for students while at the same time, mandating

that all students continue to achieve or make progress toward common curriculum goals. Additionally, specialists will have the mandates to prepare students for postsecondary options, including college or work, while at the same time having experiences with mainstream peers.

Examining trends in the research base of all of the disciplines contributing to education can begin to predict where the fields will intersect. As mentioned previously, education research and practice within curriculum and instruction are moving in the direction of looking at the whole child, which must include mental and physical health, as well as living conditions, such as home language and socioeconomic status, in addition to learning needs and styles. As professionals, we must examine and promote ways to change the educational environment to meet student's needs as they relate to the curriculum and classroom instruction, rather than removing the student from a nonsupportive environment. In this, promoting differentiating strategies, thinking maps, and other ways of accommodating learner differences is an excellent place for speech-language pathologists, audiologists, and other special educators to work collaboratively with teachers.

There are several areas of research to practice that will create a new future in the work of speech-language pathologists and audiologists, many of which have been described in this text. Notably, the areas of ASDs, technological advances in augmentative and alternative communication (AAC), assistive technology and audiology, as well as early childhood interventions will see advancements which will require adjustments in how speech-language pathologists and audiologists provide services. Three other practice areas are noteworthy for the changes expected in the future, and will be highlighted here, due to their anticipated overall importance: adolescent literacy, English learners, and assessment.

Adolescent Literacy

In current educational and reading literature, the emphasis on meeting the needs of the secondary student, specifically the area of adolescent literacy, is multifaceted, including retooling our traditional educational system for children who have been raised in a technologically advanced society. As mentioned previously, adolescent literacy was top of the 2007 "What's Hot" survey of the International Reading Association, identifying this area as "Extremely Hot" (Cassidy & Cassidy, 2007). Although the reading researchers (Santa, 2006) caution to not interpret the focus on high school improvement as having the answer in high stakes testing, the lack of improvement in high school testing results, as well as drop-out statistics (USDE, 2007a; Education Trust, 2005; Biancarosa & Snow, 2004; Snow & Biancarosa, 2003b), are the reasons that high schools and adolescent learners are receiving increased focus and attention (Graham & Perin, 2007; Short & Fitzsimmons, 2007; Kamil, 2003).

The reports identified in these areas are simultaneously frightening and provocative, and again lay ground for the importance of the involvement of speech-language pathologists in the creation of classroom environments with instructional strategies that can match the needs of disabled and struggling readers (Catts

& Kamhi, 2005; ASHA, 2000c). One of the most needed areas for instruction and collaboration is in vocabulary (Bromley, 2007; Montgomery, 2007; Manzo, Manzo, & Thomas, 2006), an area familiar to speech-language pathologists and audiologists, and critical to the improvement of literacy skills in all students. Teaching academic vocabulary to English learners and other struggling students, including students with disabilities, has been identified as an important strategy for success (Marzano & Pickering, 2005).

Moore-Brown and Montgomery (2001) discussed an expanded definition of literacy as including the recognition that students will need competence in several genres, including multimedia texts. This trend continues and is important to recognize (Vasudevan, 2007). Biancarosa and Snow (2004) report that "Technology is both a facilitator of literacy and a medium of literacy" (p. 19). Technology presents innumerable opportunities for students, including programs for skill development and language and reading improvement. But mastery of the texts of technology (i.e., text messaging, email, media interface, instant messaging, etc.) will be the expectations in the future world of work. Students without these skills will be unable to compete. "Reading and writing in the fast-paced world require new skills unimaginable a decade ago" (Biancarosa & Snow, 2004; p. 19).

English Learners

Our entire nation is coming to a central and critical point in the education of the nearly 14 million English learners who attend school in the United States (Education Trust, 2007; August & Shanahan, 2006; Short & Fitzsimmons, 2007). Ortiz and Yates (2001) concisely identify the situation:

> English language learners (ELLs) have such limited English skills that they cannot profit from general education instruction without support. They are typically served in bilingual education or in English as a second language (ESL) programs. Because education professionals are generally unprepared to serve them, ELLs experience limited academic success and are disproportionately represented in special education programs (p. 72).

The Executive Summary of the report of the National Literacy Panel on Language-Minority Children and Youth (August & Shanahan, 2006) entitled *Developing Literacy in Second-Language Learners* cite additional sobering reality to the problem of failing to adequately educate these students:

> Language-minority students who cannot read and write proficiently in English cannot participate fully in American schools, workplaces, or society. They face limited job opportunities and earning power. Nor are the consequences of low literacy attainment in English limited to individual impoverishment. United States economic competitiveness depends on workforce quality. Inadequate reading and writing proficiency in English relegates rapidly increasing language-minority populations to the sidelines, limiting the nation's potential for economic competitiveness, innovation, productivity growth, and quality of life (pp. 1–2).

The good news in terms of future practice is that there is evidence that these students can learn and be successful if schools utilize instructional and systematic methods proven to enhance their skills. Additionally, some of the myths about educating English learners can now be dispelled.

The National Literacy Panel on Language-Minority Children and Youth (August & Shanahan, 2006) outlines the following major findings in their report:

- Instruction that provides substantial coverage in the key components of reading—identified by the National Reading Panel (NICHD, 2000) as phonemic awareness, phonics, fluency, vocabulary, and text comprehension—has clear benefits for language-minority students (p. 3).

- Instruction in the key components of reading is necessary—but not sufficient—for teaching language-minority students to read and write proficiently in English. Oral proficiency in English is critical as well but student performance suggests that it is often overlooked in instruction (p. 4).

- Oral proficiency and literacy in the first language can be used to facilitate literacy development in English (p. 5).

- Individual differences contribute significantly to English literacy development (p. 5).

- Most assessments do a poor job of gauging individual strengths and weaknesses (p. 6).

- There is surprisingly little evidence for the impact of sociocultural variables on literacy achievement or development. However, home language experiences can have a positive impact on literacy achievement (p. 7).

This highlights interesting information about the connection between oral language development in English and literacy skills in English learners. The report also makes the following points regarding oral proficiency:

- Well developed English proficiency is associated with English reading comprehension and writing skills for these students (p. 4).

- It is not enough to teach language-minority students reading skills alone. Extensive oral English development must be incorporated into successful literacy instruction (p. 4).

- Vocabulary and background knowledge should be targeted intensely throughout the sequence [of instruction]. The need to develop stronger English-language proficiency to become literate in English argues for an early, ongoing, and intensive effort to develop this oral proficiency (pp. 4–5).

- There is evidence that language-minority students are able to take advantage of higher order vocabulary skills in the first language... (p. 5).

- First language oral language proficiency also influences developmental patterns in second-language speech discrimination, speech production, intraword segmentation, and vocabulary, which reflect the pattern of the first language—at least until the students become more proficient in English (p. 5).

- Studies reveal that, given proper instruction, some language-minority students classified as learning disabled can achieve proper instruction, some language-minority students classified as learning disabled can achieve grade-level norms (p. 6).

In a report on English learners in California (EdSource, 2007), several schoolwide practices were identified as being significant in improving student achievement:

- Use of assessments and data to inform efforts to improve student achievement.

- Sufficient resources, in particular adequate and appropriate textbooks for every student, well-maintained facilities, and the principal's perception that the school's teaching staff has strong teaching skills, academic content knowledge, enthusiasm about teaching, and the ability to raise student achievement.

- Coherent curriculum and instruction that is aligned with state standards.

- Prioritizing of student achievement by both principals and teachers (pp. 1–2).

Advances in the research base regarding educational and instructional practices are critical to monitor. The issues are complicated, not the least of which are whether a student is a sequential bilingual (developed his/her primary language [L1] first and then later began developing his/her second language [L2]), or a simultaneous bilingual (developed both languages at the same time); or whether the student is native to the United States, but raised in a monolingual (L1) home, or if the student did, in fact, come from another country at some point in his/her educational career. Schools are just beginning to distinguish these groups.

As noted above, one important practice implication that has emerged out of the research is that proficiency in L1 is linked to proficiency in reading achievement in L2. This is true even for EL students identified with reading disabilities. A study of 1,500 Spanish-English bilingual kindergarteners through third graders were examined to see if oral language measures across languages would predict reading achievement for bilingual children. The researchers (Miller, Heilmann, Nockerts, Iglesias, Fabiano, & Francis, 2006) reported the following conclusion:

> Regardless of the model of reading disabilities used by professionals or school systems, oral language plays a key role in both the characterization and the remediation of reading disabilities, regardless of the number of languages learned. The results of this study suggest that learning more than one language does not by itself impede reading in the second language; rather it promotes reading in the second language (p. 40).

Speech-language pathologists and audiologists have a clear and important role in how schools address the needs of English learners. The work here is vital to the nation as we expect nearly 40 percent of our student population to speak a second language by the year 2030 (Roseberry-McKibbin & Brice, n.d.). Distinguishing between a language disorder and a language difference is no longer the only aspect of our involvement. Contributing to a school system that builds oral and written language proficiency for both English only and English learners is the future.

Assessment

In reviewing the changes the field is currently undergoing and those we anticipate, several overlaps appear. For example, the concept of prereferral intervention, including response to intervention, shows up in the ways that disproportionality and overidentification will be addressed. The manner in which these initiatives intertwine are important to recognize, as is evident when considering the emerging practices in assessment. Salvia and Ysseldyke (2004) consider the following in their discussion of the evolution of assessment practice:

- Assessment as a dynamic and dynamic practice – Assessment practices are dynamic as they are always evolving. Assessment practices are also dynamite, as they are potentially explosive due to their role in social decision making in schools, for funding, accountability, promotion, eligibility, and other educational practices.

- Expansion of assessment practices – Historically, special education assessment practices have centered around documentation of "defiance, deficits, and disabilities" (p. 679). Assessment practices are now expanding to document skill level for instructional purposes.

- Increased focus on prevention and early identification – The purpose of assessment and assessment practices are shifting away from assessment in order to "name the disability" to assessment which will be meaningful for the purpose of intervention and instructional planning. Assessment will be intended to provide meaning for a student's life.

- The significant push for accountability – Reflects the alignment of statewide assessments with educational standards.

- Standards for all and all for standards – Once standards are identified, they are for all students.

- Diversity and English learners: being responsive and responsible – New areas of research include developing assessments for students who are English learners (ELs) and have a disability.

- The promise of the problem-solving model – The problem-solving model of the Heartland Area Educational Agency (Tilly, 2003) described in Chapter 3 provides a sound model of how assessment and intervention will work together to solve educational challenges presented by students.

- Thinking about assessment practice – Consider and track these practices as they evolve (modified from Salvia & Ysseldyke, 2004).

Chapter 3 described how IDEA 2004 laid the groundwork to integrate new assessment and progress monitoring practices into the education system. Through eliminating the discrepancy model and encouraging the development of response to intervention programs and establishment of problem-solving models, our practice is evolving. As a consequence, we are moving away from standardized assessments and moving toward more dynamic and performance-based measures, and through this movement, our practice is evolving.

Speech-Language Pathologists' and Audiologists' Future Watch: Expanded Practice and Professionalism

The work of speech-language pathologists, audiologists, and other educators is complex and important. In the *Toolkit for Change*, the National School Boards Association (NSBA, 2007) identified critical skills needed by professionals in order to be successful in the change process. These skills include the following:

- Capacity for continued learning.

- Cooperation and team building.

- Precise communication in a variety of modes.

- Appreciation of disparate value systems.

- Problem solving with creativity and ingenuity.

- Enjoyment of resolving ambiguous, discrepant and paradoxical situations.

- Generation and organization of a lot of technologically produced information.

- Craftsmanship of a product.

- High self-esteem.

- Personal commitment to larger organizational and global values.

As the authors view the future through the myriad of influences creating the change, we predict that speech-language pathologists and audiologists will need the above identified skills as they expand their practice and professionalism in the following ways:

- Increasing use of evidence-based practice (EBP).

- Development of specializations in specific areas such as autism spectrum disorders (ASDs), fluency, literacy, AAC/AT, auditory processing, voice, phonology, etc.

- Shifting the distribution of how time is spent by increasing collaboration and consultation with teachers, parents, and paraprofessionals to train others in intervention methods for communication impairments, and decrease the amount of time spent in direct service provided to students. This change can parallel the service delivery models used by psychologists in the educational system, or by physicians in the medical field. The change will also reflect a maximization of expertise needed by the educational system in a time of shortages and limited availability of professional staff.

- Providing increased consultation and leadership to curriculum teams in regard to academic literacy, structuring instructional strategies for struggling learners, including English learners.

- Conducting more training for paraprofessionals, including speech-language pathology assistants (SLPAs), teachers and parents on specific strategies that can be provided by these individuals.

- Involvement in the development and delivery of prereferral intervention programs, including RtI programs, and consultation on Tier I and II interventions and delivery of Tier III interventions.

- Realizing an enhanced role in collaborative assessment teams, conducting arena assessments, joint observations, and dynamic procedures to more fully identify student's learning issues in relation to the curriculum requirements of the classroom.

- Greater participation in site and district teams and committees on system change initiatives, including the development of RtI models, and curriculum accommodations and adaptations.

- Increasing comfort with the "blurring of the lines" or the "flattening of the world" in terms of roles, responsibilities, and delineation of "who does what" and participating fully in tiered interventions, problem-solving models, and system changes designed to address learner needs.

- Increased competition between employers for speech-language pathologists and audiologists, leading to increases in salary supplements, bonuses, and other enticements for employment.

- Increased availability of assessment instruments appropriate for bilingual children, including instruments that have been normed on bilingual students.

• Increasing movement to expanded leadership roles within the educational system, extending the impact of the discipline. These roles will include but not be limited to program specialist, curriculum specialist, assistant principal, principal, coordinator, director, consortium director, assistant superintendent, and superintendent. These positions and leadership roles may be within special education or within general education.

The possibilities for our expanded practice and professionalism are endless and exciting. Speech-language pathologists and audiologists are experiencing a wonderful time in school services. At the same time that the field is experiencing critical shortages, the demand and need for our services and expertise is expanding. It is a challenging time for professionals as well as for the students in our country. Our goal should be to maximize our training, expertise, and resources to create a system that benefits students and stimulates professionals.

We believe that public schools are the best place to work, and that speech-language pathologists and audiologists are, indeed, making a difference every day for our country's children. In his discussion of "The Schools We Need," Fullan (2003) states:

> The best case for public education has always been that it is a common good. Everyone, ultimately, has a stake in the caliber of schools, and education is everyone's business. The quality of the public education system relates directly to the quality of life that people enjoy (whether as parents, employers, or citizens), with a strong public education system as the cornerstone of a civil, prosperous, and democratic society.

> As the main institution for fostering social cohesion in an increasingly diverse society, publicly funded schools must serve all children, not simply those with the loudest and most powerful advocates. This means addressing the cognitive and social needs of all children, with an emphasis on including those who may have not been well served in the past (p. 3).

As we cast our eyes on the future, it seems that the "I"s have it—it seems that many "I"

Speech-Language Pathologists and Audiologists "I"s on the Future

- Information
- IDEA
- Involvement
- Instruction
- Intervention
- Improvement
- Influence
- Innovation

words describe the future watch for speech-language pathologists and audiologists: information, IDEA, involvement, instruction, intervention, improvement, influence, and innovation.

Closing Thoughts

We said this before, and we will say it again —being a SLP in public schools is exciting, energizing, and rewarding. Educational reforms will continue, enabling SLPs and those concerned about children—all children—to be dramatically involved in creating a system that works for children with communication disorders. Allington and McGill-Franzen (2000) commented:

> So I guess the answer to what sort of schools will we have in the 21st century can be best stated as "It will depend." It will depend on the decisions we as a society make about what it means to teach and what it means to learn and to be literate, and whether schools are seen as important in achieving the ideals of a just, democratic society (p. 151).

The future depends on the work of many, including speech-language pathologists and audiologists, who do, indeed, make a difference for America's children.

Appendix A

**Responsiveness to Intervention:
New Roles for Speech-Language Pathologists**

Responsiveness to Intervention: New Roles for Speech-Language Pathologists

By Barbara J. Ehren, EdD, CCC-SLP, Judy Montgomery, PhD, CCC-SLP,
Judy Rudebusch, EdD, CCC-SLP, and Kathleen Whitmire, PhD, CCC-SLP

American Speech-Language-Hearing Association

The responsiveness to intervention (RtI) process is a multitiered approach to providing services and interventions to struggling learners at increasing levels of intensity. It involves universal screening, high-quality instruction and interventions matched to student need, frequent progress monitoring, and the use of child response data to make educational decisions. RTI should be used for making decisions about general, compensatory, and special education, creating a well-integrated and seamless system of instruction and intervention guided by child outcome data.

As a schoolwide prevention approach, RtI includes changing instruction for struggling students to help them improve performance and achieve academic progress. To meet the needs of all students, the educational system must use its collective resources to intervene early and provide appropriate interventions and supports to prevent learning and behavioral problems from becoming larger issues. To support these efforts, the Individuals with Disabilities Education Improvement Act of 2004 (IDEA '04) allows up to 15% of special education funds to be used to provide early intervening services for students who are having academic or behavioral difficulties but who are not identified as having a disability.

RtI also provides an alternative to the use of a discrepancy model to assess underachievement. Students who are not achieving when given high-quality instruction may have a disability. This approach was authorized in IDEA '04 through the following provisions: (a) local education agencies (LEAs) may use a student's response to scientifically based instruction as part of the evaluation process, and (b) when identifying a disability, LEAs shall not be required to take into consideration whether a child has a severe discrepancy between achievement and intellectual ability.

Speech-language pathologists (SLPs) can play a number of important roles in using RtI to identify children with disabilities and provide needed instruction to struggling students in both general education and special education settings. But these roles will require some fundamental changes in the way SLPs engage in assessment and intervention activities.

Challenges and Opportunities of the New Model

RtI requires changes in terms of assessment approaches as well as models of intervention and instructional support. Regarding assessment, there are challenges to SLPs working in districts that undertake the shift from traditional standardized approaches to a more pragmatic, educationally relevant model focused on measuring changes in individual performance over time. Such challenges include the shift from a "within child" deficit paradigm to a contextual perspective; a greater emphasis on instructional intervention and progress monitoring prior to special education referral; an expansion of the SLP's assessment "tool kit" to include more instructionally relevant, contextually based procedures; and most likely the need for additional professional development in all of the above. In addition, the use of formal evaluation procedures may still be an important component of RtI in many districts. Teams must still conduct relevant, comprehensive evaluations using qualified personnel. SLPs' expertise in language may be called upon to round out comprehensive profiles of students having academic or behavioral difficulties.

Regarding intervention and instructional support, SLPs must engage in new and expanded roles that incorporate prevention and identification of at-risk students as well as more traditional roles of intervention. Their contribution to the school community can be viewed as expertise that is used through both direct and indirect services to support struggling students, children with disabilities, the teachers and other educators who work with them, and their families. This involves a decrease in time spent on traditional models of intervention (e.g., pull-out therapy) and more time on consultation and classroom-based intervention. It also means allocation and assignment of staff based on time needed for indirect services and support activities, and not based solely on direct services to children with disabilities.

New and Expanded Roles

SLPs working in districts that choose to implement RtI procedures are uniquely qualified to contribute in a variety of ways to assessment and intervention at many levels, from systemwide *program design* and *collaboration* to work with *individual students*. SLPs offer expertise in the language basis of literacy and learning, experience with collaborative approaches to instruction/intervention, and an understanding of the use of student outcomes data when making instructional decisions.

Program Design

SLPs can be a valuable resource as schools design and implement a variety of RtI models. The following functions are some of the ways in which SLPs can make unique contributions:

- Explain the role that language plays in curriculum, assessment, and instruction, as a basis for appropriate program design

- Explain the interconnection between spoken and written language

- Identify and analyze existing literature on scientifically based literacy assessment and intervention approaches

- Assist in the selection of screening measures

- Help identify systemic patterns of student need with respect to language skills

- Assist in the selection of scientifically based literacy intervention

- Plan for and conduct professional development on the language basis of literacy and learning

- Interpret a school's progress in meeting the intervention needs of its students

Collaboration

SLPs have a long history of working collaboratively with families, teachers, administrators, and other special service providers. SLPs play critical roles in collaboration around RtI efforts, including the following:

- Assisting general education classroom teachers with universal screening

- Participating in the development and implementation of progress monitoring systems and the analysis of student outcomes

- Serving as members of intervention assistance teams, utilizing their expertise in language, its disorders, and treatment

- Consulting with teachers to meet the needs of students in initial RtI tiers with a specific focus on the relevant language underpinnings of learning and literacy

- Collaborating with school mental health providers (school psychologists, social workers, and counselors), reading specialists, occupational therapists, physical therapists, learning disabilities specialists, and other specialized instructional support personnel (related/pupil services personnel) in the implementation of RtI models

- Assisting administrators to make wise decisions about RtI design and implementation, considering the important language variables

- Working collaboratively with private and community-employed practitioners who may be serving an individual child

- Interpreting screening and progress assessment results to families

- Helping families understand the language basis of literacy and learning as well as specific language issues pertinent to an individual child

Serving Individual Students

- SLPs continue to work with individual students, in addition to providing support through RtI activities. These roles and responsibilities include the following:

- Conducting expanded speech sound error screening for K-3 students to track students at risk and intervene with those who are highly stimulable and may respond to intense short-term interventions during a prolonged screening process rather than being placed in special education

- Assisting in determining "cut-points" to trigger referral to special education for speech and language disabilities

- Using norm-referenced, standardized, and informal assessments to determine whether students have speech and language disabilities

- Determining duration, intensity, and type of service that students with communication disabilities may need

- Serving students who qualify for special education services under categories of communication disabilities such as speech sound errors (articulation), voice or fluency disorders, hearing loss, traumatic brain injury, and speech and language disabilities concomitant with neurophysiological conditions

- Collaborating with classroom teachers to provide services and support for students with communication disabilities

- Identifying, using, and disseminating evidence-based practices for speech and language services or RtI interventions at any tier

Meeting the Challenge

The foundation for SLPs' involvement in RtI has been established through the profession's policies on literacy, workload, and expanded roles and responsibilities. The opportunities for SLPs working within an RtI framework are extensive. To some, these opportunities may seem overwhelming—where in the workday would there be time to *add* all of these activities to our current responsibilities? Certainly if the traditional roles continue, it would be difficult to expand into these new roles. The point of RtI, however, is not to add more tasks but to reallocate time to better address prevention and early intervention, and in the long run serve more students up front rather than at the point of special education evaluation and service. Where RtI has been faithfully implemented, this seems to be the outcome. Some districts report reductions in special education referral and placement; even where placement rates have remained stable, staff nevertheless report a change in the way they spend their time. The reallocation of effort will hopefully lead to more effective interventions, both for students who remain in general education and those who ultimately qualify for more intensive services.

Successful RtI programs rely on the leadership of a strong principal or designated leader who has budgetary power and the ability to bring all educators to the same table to share professional development, children, time, space, money, and curriculum resources. The sharing of resources is sometimes a stumbling block, yet strong leaders can overcome these barriers by keeping the focus on the children being helped. SLPs can begin the RtI process by sharing with principals the benefits of an RtI approach and the support offered through IDEA, including the incentive that 15% of a school's special education funds can be used to launch the RtI process.

To meet this challenge, SLPs will need to be:

- open to change—change in how students are identified for intervention; how interventions are selected, designed, and implemented; how student performance is measured and evaluated; how evaluations are conducted; and how decisions are made;

- open to professional development—training (as needed) in evidence-based intervention approaches, progress monitoring methods, evaluation of instructional and program outcomes, and contextually based assessment procedures, and the implications for both preservice and in-service training;

- willing to adapt a more systemic approach to serving schools, including a workload that reflects less traditional service delivery and more consultation and collaboration in general education classrooms;

- willing and able to communicate their worth to administrators and policymakers—to educate others on the unique contributions that SLPs can make consistent with the provisions of IDEA '04.

IDEA '04 does not mandate significant change or prohibit traditional practices. Rather, it encourages the adoption of new approaches that promise better student outcomes. Such innovations in education offer numerous opportunities to enhance speech-language services to the benefit of all students.

Key Resources

Butler K., & Nelson, N. (Eds.). (2005). Responsiveness to intervention and the speech-language pathologist [Special issue]. *Topics in Language Disorders, 25*(2). (See six articles on RtI and SLPs.)

Mellard, D. (2004). *Understanding responsiveness to intervention in learning disabilities determination*. Available from www.nrcld.org/publications/papers/mellard.pdf (PDF format)

National Association of State Directors of Special Education. (2005). *Response to intervention: Policy considerations and implementation*. Available from www.nasdse.org

National Joint Committee on Learning Disabilities. (2005). *Responsiveness to intervention and learning disabilities*. Available from www.ldonline.org

Strangman, N., Hitchcock, C., Hall, T., Meo, G., & Coyne, P. (2006). Response-to-instruction and universal design for learning: How might they intersect in the general education classroom? Available from www.k8accesscenter.org/documents/RTIandUDLFinal.2.pdf (PDF format)

American Speech-Language-Hearing Association (2006). Responsiveness-to-intervention online professional consultation packet.

Source: ASHA (2006)

Authors adapted with permission from *Problem Solving and RTI: New Roles for School Psychologists* by Andrea Canter, 2006, February, *Communique, 34*(5). Available from http://www.nasponline.org.

Appendix B

To Screen or Not to Screen…That Is the Question

To Screen or Not to Screen...That Is the Question

Barbara Moore-Brown, Ed.D.
Director, Special & Alternative Education
El Rancho Unified School District, Pico Rivera, CA

Beth Nishida, M.A.
Coordinator, Special Education
Hacienda LaPuente Unified School District, La Puente, CA

In 1975, Congress passed Public Law 94-142, the Education for All Handicapped Children Act (EAHCA), which mandated educational services for children with disabilities in this country. Since that time, special education has continually evolved. Some of these changes may have seemed subtle, yet were extremely important, like changing the name of the law to the Individuals with Disabilities Education Act (IDEA). Others have seemed dramatic and have raised high levels of controversy, like the inclusion of students with significant disabilities into general education program, or including students with disabilities in statewide testing. Each change has been rooted in the fight to provide a free appropriate public education (FAPE) to students with disabilities. Additionally, the climate of special education has made us increasingly aware of our legal obligations and critical of our practices under the law. Presently, we are on the cusp of another reauthorization that may bring sweeping change to how special educators operate in schools, creating the need to examine what we do and why we do it. In some cases, these practices are held near and dear by some individuals who provide service to students with disabilities.

Child Find

In 1975, school districts in many parts of our country were denying educational services to children with disabilities. These circumstances led to a federal mandate for special education in the United States. To ensure that such denial would not occur, procedural safeguards, or rights and protections, were guaranteed to parents and children. Among these procedural safeguards were requirements regarding evaluation and identification of children as having a disability. Key to these rights and protections is parent consent for assessment. In order to ensure that all children with disabilities that might not be in school were located and provided with an education, requirements for "search and serve" or "child find" were put into the law.

The U.S. Department of Education (2000) has reported to the Congress that the original intent of special education, to locate and provide access to children with disabilities, has been met. In 1997, the focus of IDEA shifted from access to services, to a focus on educational results (IDEA, 1997, § 601[c]). As noted, many things have changed between 1975 and 1997, but one of the most noteworthy is in how we "search" for, or locate and find students with disabilities. In 1975, one of the easiest ways to find children who might have disabilities was to conduct massive classroom screenings of all children in certain groups, such as those entering kindergarten, or those at certain grade levels. This usually involved conducting a short battery of sample test items with students to check their articulation, vocabulary, language development and pre-academic skills. In 1975, some children who did not appear "school ready" would be sent home to mature for another year, while others would be tested to determine if they needed special education services.

In 2002, many children have some sort of pre-school experience prior to entering kindergarten. While there is still a great disparity of skills between children entering school for a variety of reasons, there is no "screening" for academic readiness. It is also rare to find speech-language pathologists (SLPs) who feel compelled to screen kindergarten classes for children who might need services. There are several reasons for this. One is because mass screening is extremely time-consuming, with seemingly little actual benefit in terms of identification. Since many children have attended pre-school, most children with speech and/or language difficulties would have been referred at that level. As educators, we also understand that even children with no prior school experience, need opportunities to enter school, learn the routine and have time to learn, adjust and mature in the educational environment. Children need to be given time to adjust to the learning environment of school, so conducting a screening of their skills early on in their school experience would be meaningless. At all grade levels, teachers and other support staff have a greater understanding of accommodations, modifications and techniques for adjusting the academic curriculum so that children can be successful. The current focus on literacy has resulted in a greater focus on individualized needs that can be addressed in the general education classroom. One final reason that SLPs no longer conduct mass screenings is that most of them do not need to go in search of students for their caseloads.

Child find continues to be a mandate under the IDEA, but school systems have different ways to conduct child find than existed in 1975. When individual children are having difficulties in school, they are referred to the school's Child Study Team (CST) or Student Study Team (SST). This process is a general education function, and is designed to assist teachers, students and families by identifying methods of assisting the student. If interventions are not successful, and a student continues to struggle, then the student may be referred for special education assessment to determine if s/he is a child with a disability requiring special education. Key to this process is considering all areas which might be impacting the student.

Evaluation Procedures

The IDEA is very specific in the procedures that must be followed for evaluation. The Code of Federal Regulations (C.F.R., 1999) requires that:

- No single procedure is used as the sole criterion for determining whether a child is a child with a disability and for determining an appropriate educational program for the child. (34C.F.R. § 300.532 (2)(f)).

- The child is assessed in all areas of suspected disability, including, if appropriate, health, vision, hearing, social and emotional status, general intelligence, academic performance, communicative status, and motor abilities. (34 C.F.R. § 300.532(2)(g)).

- In evaluating each child with a disability. The evaluation is sufficiently comprehensive to identify all of the child's special education and related services needs, whether or not commonly linked to the disability category in which the child has been classified. (34 C.F.R. § 300.532(2)(h)).

- Upon completing the administration of tests and other evaluation materials -- A group of qualified professionals and the parent of the child must determine whether the child is a child with a disability. (34 C.F.R. § 300.534(a)(1).

Concerns About Screening as a Prereferral Activity

Even though SLPs in schools have, for the most part, abandoned the practice of mass screenings of groups of children, a common practice is pre-referral screening of individual children. SLPs may conduct a screening as a result of a request by an individual teacher for them to "check" a child or as a result of a SST recommendation. Many SLPs believe screening is a very efficient practice. They view it as a way to prevent having to conduct a full assessment on an individual child, especially if the referral is inappropriate. They feel they can quickly determine if the child appears to require the services of an SLP or if the concern that the teacher has brought to their attention is developmental. The problem with this rationale, and practice, is that it is contrary to the requirements described above for evaluation to determine eligibility.

Screening has been an accepted practice for many years in our field, and is even outlined in the 1989 Program Guidelines for Speech-Language Hearing Specialists in California (California Department of Education, 1989), the ASHA Preferred Practice Patterns (ASHA, 1997) and the Guidelines for the Roles and Responsibilities of School-Based Speech-Language Pathologists (ASHA, 1999). Screening is also an approved activity for speech-language pathology assistants (SLPAs). Typically, a screening is used to check if the child might potentially qualify for services, and if further evaluation is warranted. The problem is that once that has been done, the team has begun conducting an evaluation, most often without parental consent. This practice is contrary to requirements for evaluation.

The practice of screening for the purpose of determining whether or not the child should have additional evaluation is problematic for several reasons. By conducting a screening in this way, a single assessor has pre-determined eligibility, violating the requirements for parental consent, assessing in all areas of suspected disability and the for a multi-disciplinary team assessment. If the student is recommended for further evaluation as a result of the screening, no other issues may be considered, possibly missing areas of need. If the student is not recommended for further evaluation, then the SLP alone has made the determination of eligibility, absent parental and multi-disciplinary team participation. One other problem is that when assessments are conducted, a meeting is required to review the evaluation and this has also not occurred when a screening is done.

SLPs may believe that nothing is wrong with going into a classroom and listening to a child, at the teacher's request. The belief holds because they are not administering any formal tests, they are listening to the child at the teacher's request, and they are protecting themselves from time-consuming, inappropriate referrals. The C.F.R. require that qualified personnel be the conductors of evaluation and providers of service (SS 300.23). When an SLP goes into a classroom and singles out a given child, and uses his/her trained ear and knowledge skill set to listen to the child, s/he has just conducted an assessment [e.g. data collection and the gathering of evidence (ASHA, 1999; p. 19)] and evaluation [e.g. bringing meaning to that data through interpretation, analysis and reflection]. Even though this assessment may not be a formal one and no formal tests were administered, it can be considered an evaluation because of the knowledge base and expertise of the SLP. However, this assessment has been done without parental consent or following the other requirements identified above. Violating these requirements can be considered a violation of the child's due process rights, and could lead to legal problems for the school district.

Legal Concerns

As early as 1986, a case regarding screening held that a school district was conducting an assessment when they used procedures for one student that they did not use for everyone in that child's class. (*Forest Park (MI) School District,* 352 IDELR 182; OCR 1986; cited in Gilyard, 2002) In this case, the procedures were used without consent from the parent. That case has implications for speech-language pathologists, as well as for other special education assessors. The outcome of this case suggests that general consultation about student difficulties is acceptable, but when the specialist interacted with the student in an attempt to determine whether more assessment was warranted, the evaluation had already begun.

A more recent 9th Circuit Court of Appeals case, in 1996, reinforced the importance of parental consent, and not having dual tracks for determining eligibility. (*Pasatiempo v. Aizawa,* 103 F.3d 796 (9th Cir.1966).) In this case, the state of Hawaii defended their use of a dual-track system of evaluation, depending on the suspicion of the school's screening committee as to whether or not the child had a disability. The 9th Circuit Court found that it is not in the purview of the school to make this determination prior to evaluation, and that parents cannot be denied their procedural rights to consent. In essence this case emphasized: 1) there need to procedures in place; 2) the procedures need to be systematic; 3) parents need to give consent prior to assessment; and 4) this consent needs to be informed consent. This case can be interpreted to apply to this discussion about screening, in that if screening is used as part of the procedures to determine whether or not a child has a disability, then such procedures need to be identified. It is noteworthy that since this case is a 9th Circuit decision, it has applicability to California.

Using Effective Procedures

Changing legal requirements, as well as increased due process cases, have forced school personnel to re-examine current practices. The good news is that by analyzing our practices, it may be possible to solve more than one problem at once. Consider for a moment, a long-time complaint of many SLPs in schools, that "they (teachers, administrators, parents, etc.) don't know what I do!" Current thinking on service delivery has suggested that the best way to solve this problem is by not separating ourselves from the functions of the classroom or school. (Moore-Brown & Montgomery, 2001). In other words, the more we are involved with the issues and concerns of teachers and principals, related to student need, then the greater the opportunity they have to learn about the skill set and knowledge base of the SLP. By extending this line of thinking to utilization of the SST process for consideration of all students with learning problems and suspected disabilities, it is possible to see how on-going discussion and participation by the SLP can help the team understand how speech and language issues impact the child's academic achievement. For example, the SLP can help the team understand how concerns about phonemic awareness and reading concerns in children may be related to their suspected phonological impairment. Through utilizing the school's problem solving process to address student need, the goal to avoid inappropriate referrals can be achieved. We may also be able to increase team members' general awareness of the role of the SLP, and how speech and language issues impact academics.

Local Decisions

Whether or not to utilize screening as a part of the protocol for prereferral is a local decision that should be addressed with the special education administration at the school district and Special Education Local Plan Area (SELPA). If it is decided to utilize screening as a pre-referral practice, then parental consent should be obtained. This is critical as a single child is being identified as being suspected as having a disability. Failure to obtain parental consent could be construed as denial of due process procedures. Should further speech and language evaluation not be conducted as a result of the screening results, and the parent had not been informed or consent received, the district could be responsible for the cost of that evaluation and services if the parent sought private evaluation and services.

ASHA Director of School Services, Sue Karr, indicated to the authors of this article that ASHA does advise members to follow procedures consistent with the parental consent requirements of IDEA and to check state and local education agency requirements. Unfortunately, the state of California Department of Education (CDE) does not yet have updated program guidelines for speech-language-hearing programs. However, justifying the use of screening procedures using the program guidelines from 1989, when no less than two major reauthorization of the law have been made since then, would not be considered advisable.

SLPs may be reluctant to use the SST as a method for determining whether a student should receive a comprehensive speech and language evaluation, due to dysfunction of the SST at their school site. However, the SLP may find that helping the school solve those problems may be more productive for students and staff in the long run. The benefits of an effective SST process may eventually outweigh the work required to revamp the system so that it is responsive to many needs.

In the long run, the answer on whether to screen or not to screen lies at the local level. Screening is a permissive activity. Mass screenings, as they are completed with large groups of children, do not require parental consent. However, any time an individual child is singled out, parental consent should be obtained.

In looking at updated procedures for child find, SLPs (and RSP teachers) should utilize the SST process of the school, which is designed to be a problem-solving vehicle for teachers, students and parents. Through this system, team members can learn about developmental milestones for speech and language, how to provide accommodations and modifications, implications for literacy concerns with children suspected of having a speech or language disorder, and how to look at the whole child, and not just one presenting issue. By training SST members in these skills, the SLP will also be training the team on how speech and language issues impact school performance, and what types of concerns would warrant an appropriate referral.

Before deciding whether to screen or not to screen, SLPs should examine what the purpose of the screening is. If it is to save time and to prevent inappropriate referrals, the problems may outweigh the perceived benefit. SLPs need to understand that legally there is no such thing as an individual screening or just popping into a teacher's classroom to listen to a child. The expertise utilized to perform that task just constituted that act as an assessment.

With mandates to consider how the child's disability affects their ability to progress in the general education curriculum, utilizing the procedures set forth for assisting students seems to be natural. But most importantly, the increasing world of litigation in special education makes examination of our practices critical. Whatever practice your local agency decides to follow, make sure that you have addressed the required components of multidisciplinary assessment, receiving informed parental consent and assessing in all areas of suspected disability.

References

American Speech-Language-Hearing Association (1999). *Guidelines for the roles and responsibilities of the school-based speech-language pathologist.* Rockville, MD: Author.

American Speech-Language-Hearing Association (1999). *Preferred practice patterns for the profession of speech-language pathology.* Rockville, MD: Author.

California Department of Education. (1989). *Program guidelines for language, speech, and hearing specialists.* Sacramento, CA. Author.

Code of Federal Regulations (1999). *Assistance to states for the education of children with disabilities and the early intervention program for infants and toddlers with disabilities; Final regulations,* C.F.R., Title 34, § 300, 301, and 303. (1999).

Gilyard, K. (2002, January). *Preparing special education assessors for I.E.P. team meetings and due process hearings. [Handout].* Presentation at the Association of California School Administrators Conference, Monterey, CA.

I*ndividuals with Disabilities Education Act (IDEA) Amendments,* 20 U.S.C. SS 1400 ed seq. (1997).

Moore-Brown, B. & Montgomery, J. (2001). *Making a difference for America's children: Speech-language pathologists in public schools.* Greenville, SC: Thinking Publications.

Pasatiempo v. Aizawa, 103 f.3D 796 (9TH Cir. 1996). Available [online]. http://caselaw.lp.findlaw.com/scripts/getcase.pl?navby=search&case=data2...9417092.htm.

U.S. Department of Education (2000). *Twenty-second annual report to Congress on the implementation of the Individuals with Disabilities Education Act.* Washington D.C.: Author.

American Speech-Language-Hearing Association (2001). *Scope of practice in speech-language pathology.* Rockville, MD: Author.

*Special Thanks to Sue Karr of ASHA and Drin Barber, Esq. of WACSEP
for their assistance with this article.*

Appendix C

ASHA's Code of Ethics

Code of Ethics

Last Revised January 1, 2003

Preamble

The preservation of the highest standards of integrity and ethical principles is vital to the responsible discharge of obligations by speech-language pathologist, audiologists, and speech, language, and hearing scientists. This Code of Ethics sets forth the fundamental principles and rules considered essential to this purpose.

Every individual who is (a) a member of the American Speech-Language-Hearing Association, whether certified or not, (b) a nonmember holding the Certificate of Clinical Competence from the Association, (c) an applicant for membership or certification, or (d) a Clinical Fellow seeking to fulfill standards for certification shall abide by this Code of Ethics.

Any violation of the spirit and purpose of this Code shall be considered unethical. Failure to specify any particular responsibility or practice in this Code of Ethics shall not be construed as denial of the existence of such responsibilities or practices.

The fundamentals of ethical conduct are described by Principles of Ethics and by Rules of Ethics as they relate to the conduct of research and scholarly activities and responsibility to persons served, the public, and speech-language pathologists, audiologists, and speech, language, and hearing scientists.

Principles of Ethics, aspirational and inspirational in nature, form the underlying moral basis for the Code of Ethics. Individuals shall observe these principles as affirmative obligations under all conditions of professional activity.

Rules of Ethics are specific statements of minimally acceptable professional conduct or of prohibitions and are applicable to all individuals.

Principle of Ethics I

Individuals shall honor their responsibility to hold paramount the welfare of persons they serve professionally or participants in research and scholarly activities and shall treat animals involved in research in a humane manner.

Rules of Ethics

A. Individuals shall provide all services competently.

B. Individuals shall use every resource, including referral when appropriate, to ensure that high-quality service is provided.

C. Individuals shall not discriminate in the delivery of professional services or the conduct of research and scholarly activities on the basis of race or ethnicity, gender, age, religion, national origin, sexual orientation, or disability.

D. Individuals shall not misrepresent the credentials of assistants, technicians, or support personnel and shall inform those they serve professionally of the name and professional credentials of persons providing services.

E. Individuals who hold the Certificates of Clinical Competence shall not delegate tasks that require the unique skills, knowledge, and judgment that are within the scope of their profession to assistants, technicians, support personnel, students, or any nonprofessionals over whom they have supervisory responsibility. An individual may delegate support services to assistants, technicians, support personnel, students, or any other persons only if those services are adequately supervised by an individual who holds the appropriate Certificate of Clinical Competence.

F. Individuals shall fully inform the persons they serve of the nature and possible effects of services rendered and products dispensed, and they shall inform participants in research about the possible effects of their participation in research conducted.

G. Individuals shall evaluate the effectiveness of services rendered and of products dispensed and shall provide services or dispense products only when benefit can reasonably be expected.

H. Individuals shall not guarantee the results of any treatment or procedure, directly or by implication; however, they may make a reasonable statement of prognosis.

I. Individuals shall not provide clinical services solely by correspondence.

J. Individuals may practice by telecommunication (for example, telehealth/e-health), where not prohibited by law.

K. Individuals shall adequately maintain and appropriately secure records of professional services rendered, research and scholarly activities conducted, and products dispensed and shall allow access to these records only when authorized or when required by law.

L. Individuals shall not reveal, without authorization, any professional or personal information about identified persons served professionally or identified participants involved in research and scholarly activities unless required by law to do so, or unless doing so is necessary to protect the welfare of the person or the community or otherwise required by law.

M. Individuals shall not charge for services not rendered, nor shall they misrepresent services rendered, products dispensed, or research and scholarly activities conducted.

N. Individuals shall use persons in research or as subjects of teaching demonstrations only with their informed consent.

O. Individuals whose professional services are adversely affected by substance abuse or other health-related conditions shall seek professional assistance and, where appropriate, withdraw from the affected areas of practice.

Principle of Ethics II

Individuals shall honor their responsibility to achieve and maintain the highest level of professional competence.

Rules of Ethics

A. Individuals shall engage in the provision of clinical services only when they hold the appropriate Certificate of Clinical Competence or when they are in the certification process and are supervised by an individual who holds the appropriate Certificate of Clinical Competence.

B. Individuals shall engage in only those aspects of the professions that are within the scope of their competence, considering their level of education, training, and experience.

C. Individuals shall continue their professional development throughout their careers.

D. Individuals shall delegate the provision of clinical services only to: (1) persons who hold the appropriate Certificate of Clinical Competence; (2) persons in the education or certification process who are appropriately supervised by an individual who holds the appropriate Certificate of Clinical Competence; or (3) assistants, technicians, or support personnel who are adequately supervised by an individual who holds the appropriate Certificate of Clinical Competence.

E. Individuals shall not require or permit their professional staff to provide services or conduct research activities that exceed the staff member's competence, level of education, training, and experience.

F. Individuals shall ensure that all equipment used in the provision of services or to conduct research and scholarly activities is in proper working order and is properly calibrated.

Principle of Ethics III

Individuals shall honor their responsibility to the public by promoting public understanding of the professions, by supporting the development of services designed to fulfill the unmet needs of the public, and by providing accurate information in all communications involving any aspect of the professions, including dissemination of research findings and scholarly activities.

Rules of Ethics

A. Individuals shall not misrepresent their credentials, competence, education, training, experience, or scholarly or research contributions.

B. Individuals shall not participate in professional activities that constitute a conflict of interest.

C. Individuals shall refer those served professionally solely on the basis of the interest of those being referred and not on any personal financial interest.

D. Individuals shall not misrepresent diagnostic information, research, services rendered, or products dispensed; neither shall they engage in any scheme to defraud in connection with obtaining payment or reimbursement for such services or products.

E. Individuals' statements to the public shall provide accurate information about the nature and management of communication disorders, about the professions, about professional services, and about research and scholarly activities.

F. Individuals' statements to the publics—advertising, announcing, and marketing their professional services, reporting research results, and promoting products—shall adhere to prevailing professional standards and shall not contain misrepresentations.

Principle of Ethics IV

Individuals shall honor their responsibilities to the professions and their relationships with colleagues, students, and members of allied professions. Individuals shall uphold the dignity and autonomy of the professions, maintain harmonious interprofessional and intraprofessional relationships, and accept the professions' self-imposed standards.

Rules of Ethics

A. Individuals shall prohibit anyone under their supervision from engaging in any practice that violates the Code of Ethics.

B. Individuals shall not engage in dishonesty, fraud, deceit, misrepresentation, sexual harassment, or any other form of conduct that adversely reflects on the professions or on the individual's fitness to serve persons professionally.

C. Individuals shall not engage in sexual activities with clients or students over whom they exercise professional authority.

D. Individuals shall assign credit only to those who have contributed to a publication, presentation, or product. Credit shall be assigned in proportion to the contribution and only with the contributor's consent.

E. Individuals shall reference the source when using other persons' ideas, research, presentations, or products in written, oral, or any other media presentation or summary.

F. Individual' statements to colleagues about professional services, research results, and products shall adhere to prevailing professional standards and shall contain no misrepresentations.

G. Individuals shall not provide professional services without exercising and inde3pendent professional judgment, regardless of referral source or prescription.

H. Individuals shall not discriminate in their relationships with colleagues, students, and members of allied professions on the basis of race or ethnicity, gender, age, religion, national origin, sexual orientation, or disability.

I. Individuals who have reason to believe that the Code of Ethics has been violated shall inform the Board of Ethics.

J. Individuals shall comply fully with the policies of the Board of Ethics in its consideration and adjudication of complaints of violations of the Code of Ethics.

Glossary

If unfamiliar terms are encountered in the following entries, the terms may be found elsewhere in the Glossary. Several sources were used to compile the Glossary and are cited in the entry or listed in the References—American Speech-Language-Hearing Association, Council for Exceptional Children, IDEA 2004, National Archives and Records Administration, Nicolosi, Harryman, & Kresheck, 1996; Turnbull, 1993, and U.S. Equal Employment Opportunity Commission.

ALTERNATIVE DISPUTE RESOLUTION (ADR): Any of a number of methods (including mediation) for settling disagreements between parents and local educational agencies (LEAs) intended to avoid the need for a due process hearing. ADR methods utilize win-win approaches.

AMERICAN SPEECH-LANGUAGE-HEARING ASSOCIATION (ASHA): The professional, scientific, and credentialing association for more than 99,000 speech-language pathologists; audiologists; and speech, language, and hearing scientists in the United States and around the world. ASHA's mission is to promote the interests of and provide the highest quality services for professionals in audiology, speech-language pathology, and speech and hearing science and to advocate for people with communication disabilities.

AMERICANS WITH DISABILITIES ACT (ADA): Public Law 101-336 passed in 1990 and protected the civil rights of Americans with physical and mental disabilities. The ADA guarantees equal opportunity for individuals with disabilities in public accommodations, employment, transportation, state and local government services, and telecommunications.

ASSESSMENT PLAN: A written plan that indicates assessment procedures and personnel to provide information to an individualized education program (IEP) team.

ASSISTIVE LISTENING DEVICES (ALD): A variety of technology devices used by students to aid them in hearing a teacher and filtering out background noise.

ASSISTIVE TECHNOLOGY (AT): Any item, piece of equipment, or product system acquired commercially off the shelf, modified, or customized to increase, maintain, or improve the functional capabilities of a child with a disability.

AUDITORY PROCESSING: The brain's complex organization of the details of an auditory stimulus to determine meaning, including speech sounds. The details are perceived, discriminated, combined, categorized, and related to recognizable or similar concepts that are stored in memory. The result is an understanding of the auditory stimulus.

AUGMENTATIVE AND ALTERNATIVE COMMUNICATION (AAC): 1. Any approach designed to support, enhance, or supplement the communication of individuals who are not independent verbal communicators in all situations. **2.** An area of clinical practice that attempts to compensate (either temporarily or permanently) for the impairment and disability patterns of individuals with severe expressive communication disorders. **3.** The use of nonvocal instruments (including picture boards and computer-assisted devices) and approaches by those who cannot communicate vocally.

AUTISM SPECTRUM DISORDERS (ASDs): Includes any of five diagnoses under the umbrella of Pervasive Developmental Disorders (Autism, Asperger's syndrome, Rett's syndrome, Childhood Disintegrative Disorder, and Pervasive Developmental Disorder-Not Otherwise Specified). Children demonstrate deficits in reciprocal social interactions, verbal and nonverbal communication, and restricted or repetitive behaviors or interests.

AUTISM: A developmental disability that is the most severe diagnosis of the Pervasive Developmental Disorders. It is generally evident before age 3, significantly affects verbal and nonverbal communication, social interaction, and adversely affects a child's educational performance. Characteristics often associated with autism are engagement in repetitive activities and stereotyped movements, resistance to environmental change or change in daily routines, and unusual responses to sensory experiences.

BENCHMARK: 1. The performance level expected at the end of each grade level. **2.** A major milestone in the curriculum.

BEST PRACTICE: A term commonly used for the most current, currently accepted educational methods; the term can be misleading because "best" depends on the individual needs of each child rather than on any particular program or method.

CASE MANAGER: A member of an individualized education program (IEP) team who coordinates the IEP services.

CASELOAD: Students (or the number of students) receiving services from a speech-language pathologist.

CERTIFICATE OF CLINICAL COMPETENCE: Recognition of professional knowledge and skills bestowed by the American Speech-Language-Hearing Association (ASHA) for speech-language pathologists and audiologists.

CHILD FIND: Activities to comply with the Individuals with Disabilities Education Act (IDEA), requirements to annually identify, locate, and evaluate all children with disabilities residing in a local educational agency (LEA) or state educational agency (SEA).

CHRONOLOGICAL AGE (CA): The actual age of an individual derived from date of birth and usually expressed in years, months, and days.

CLASSROOM INSTRUCTION: Teaching and learning interactions that are provided to a class, utilizing a variety of instructional methodologies.

CODE OF FEDERAL REGULATIONS (C.F.R.): A codification of the rules published in the Federal Register by the executive departments and agencies of the Federal government.

COLLABORATION: A category of service delivery or a work style in which coequal parties engage voluntarily in shared decision-making toward a common goal of assisting a student to experience school success. The speech-language pathologist may collaborate with another professional in the assessment, intervention, or classroom application of student skills.

COLLABORATIVE CONSULTATION: A form of service delivery in which a student receives intervention that is directed by a speech-language pathologist but may be provided by any trained and supervised person, such as a speech-language pathology assistant (SLPA), a classroom teacher, another special educator, a peer, a parent, or a bus driver, in any relevant setting. The professionals work together using a collaborative style.

COLLABORATIVE INTERVENTION: The delivery of speech-language intervention services by two or more providers, in multiple settings, designed and monitored by the speech-language pathologist.

COMMUNICATION DISORDER: An impairment in one or more of the processes of hearing, speech, or language that results in the inability to comprehend or express thoughts or concepts in oral, manual (e.g., sign language), or written form.

COMMUNICATIVE COMPETENCE: The wide scope of grammatical, cognitive, social, and cultural knowledge that underlies adequate language ability.

COMMUNICATIVE INTENT: The ability to express a range of wants and needs without necessarily using language as a means of communication. Gaze, gesture, and posture are early means of expression for very young children.

CONSULTATION: 1. A category of indirect service delivery models. **2.** A voluntary process in which one professional assists another to address a student's goals using shared participation, effective communication, teamwork, and problem solving.

CONVENTIONAL THERAPY: A category of service delivery models in which intervention is provided directly by a speech-language pathologist in a pull-out or in-class setting.

COOPERATIVE LEARNING: A set of instructional methods that include cooperative student to student interaction with subject matter by applying four principles: positive interdependence, individual accountability, equal participation, and simultaneous interaction (Kagan, 1992).

CULTURALLY/LINGUISTICALLY DIVERSE (CLD): A term applied to persons whose experiences vary in their cultural or linguistic contexts. This term does not imply a judgement of competence.

DIFFERENTIATED INSTRUCTION: A process for teaching and learning that recognizes that all learners in a classroom are not the same; the teacher uses processes and procedures that ensure effective learning for students' varying backgrounds, knowledge, readiness, and interests.

DIRECT OUTCOMES: Intended changes in behavior that result from an intervention.

DISCRETE TRIAL TRAINING: A teaching method used with children with autism that uses behavioral therapy; it is often used in intensive all-day programming at home and school.

DUE PROCESS HEARING: The opportunity for a parent, student, or local educational agency (LEA) to present complaints regarding a child's identification, evaluation, placement, or right to free appropriate public education (FAPE). Evidence is presented, and an impartial hearing officer makes a ruling. Also called a fair hearing and an impartial due process hearing.

DYNAMIC ASSESSMENT: A process-oriented approach to assessment that often uses a test-teach-retest format to analyze a child's responses in learning situations, describe the child as a learner, and determine how the child responds to intervention.

EARLY INTERVENING SERVICES (EIS): Academic and behavioral supports provided through the use of special education funds for students who are not yet identified for special education but need additional support to succeed in general education. Activities can include professional development, educational and behavioral evaluations, services, and supports including literacy instruction.

EDUCATION FOR ALL HANDICAPPED CHILDREN ACT (EAHCA): Public Law 94-142, passed in 1975, mandated that states provide free appropriate public education (FAPE) in the least restrictive environment (LRE) to meet the needs of children with disabilities from 5 to 21 years of age.

EDUCATION OF THE HANDICAPPED ACT (EHA): Public Law 91-230, passed in 1970, established minimum requirements for states to follow to receive federal assistance for special education.

ELIGIBILITY: A determination based on a child's assessment results as they compare to state or local eligibility criteria for special education. The determination looks at whether the child has a disability and whether that disability requires special education and related services.

EVIDENCE-BASED PRACTICE: The use of the best available evidence in research and individual clinical expertise in making decisions about the care of individual patients.

EXPULSION: The removal of a student from the educational programs of a school district for a lengthy period of time, generally two semesters or more, imposed by the school board or other governing body. Special education services must continue to be provided to expelled students.

FAMILY EDUCATIONAL RIGHTS AND PRIVACY ACT (FERPA): 20 United States Code (U.S.C.) § 1232 (g) passed in 1974 and protected the privacy interests of parents and students regarding educational records through standards for record keeping, protocols for parent access to records, and limits to disclosure of records without consent.

FIFTH AMENDMENT: One of two sources of due process protections in the United States Constitution requiring that no person may be deprived of life, liberty, or property, without due process of law.

FOURTEENTH AMENDMENT: One of two sources of due process protections in the United States Constitution requiring that no state may deprive any person of life, liberty, or property without due process of law.

FREE APPROPRIATE PUBLIC EDUCATION (FAPE): Special education and related services that (a) have been provided at public expense, under public supervision and direction, and without charge; (b) meet the standards of the state educational agency involved; (c) include an appropriate preschool, elementary, or secondary school education in the state involved; and (d) are provided in conformity with the individualized education program (IEP) required under § 614 (d) of the Individuals with Disabilities Education Act (IDEA).

FRIENDSHIP GROUPS: A method of grouping students for instructional purposes based on students' social relationships.

FUNCTIONAL COMMUNICATION MEASURES (FCMS): A series of seven-point rating scales designed by the American Speech-Language-Hearing Association (ASHA) to describe the different aspects of a patient's or student's abilities over the course of treatment.

FUNCTIONAL OUTCOMES: Measures of a person's actual performance following intervention. Also called performance outcomes.

GOAL: The end result toward which action, muscular or mental, is directed.

GOOD PRACTICE: Current, accepted education or intervention methods that are research-based and effectively address the needs of a student.

HABILITATIVE: Intervention intended to develop skills and abilities that a person has not previously exhibited.

HANDICAPPED CHILDREN'S PROTECTION ACT: Public Law 99-372, passed in 1986, authorized awarding attorneys' fees to families who prevailed in lawsuits under the due process provisions of the law. Also called the Attorney's Fees Bill.

HEAD START PROGRAM: Established in 1965, a federal program that provides comprehensive services to children from birth to age 5 and their families, targeting those with incomes below the poverty line. Services include education, health, social services, nutrition, and opportunity for parent involvement.

HEALTH MAINTENANCE ORGANIZATION (HMO): A type of managed care organization that provides comprehensive coverage for hospital and health-care practitioner services for a prepaid fixed fee.

HEARING IMPAIRMENT: A generic term that includes all types and degrees of hearing loss, with mild hearing loss being the lowest degree and severe-to-profound hearing impairment being the greatest degree.

HIGH, OBJECTIVE, UNIFORM STATE STANDARD OF EVALUATION (HOUSSE): NCLB allows states to develop an additional way for current teachers to demonstrate subject-matter competency and meet highly qualified teacher requirements. Proof may consist of a combination of teaching experience, professional development, and knowledge in the subject garnered over time in the profession.

HIGHLY QUALIFIED (HQ): Under No Child Left Behind (NCLB) states are required to ensure that all teachers are "highly qualified," meaning they (1) have a bachelor's degree, (2) full state certification or licensure for that state, and (3) demonstrate competency, typically through a state test.

INCLUSION MOVEMENT: An educational and social effort to bring students with disabilities into general education classes and environments.

INCLUSION: A philosophy that promotes access for children with disabilities to activities, situations, and environments that are designed for individuals without disabilities by providing the support and accommodations necessary, so the child with disabilities will derive as much benefit from the experience as children without disabilities.

INCLUSIVE PRACTICES: The American Speech-Language-Hearing Association's (ASHA's) position on inclusion that emphasizes serving children and youth in the least restrictive environment (LRE) that meets their needs optimally, taking advantage of the full range of service delivery models and settings.

INDEPENDENT EDUCATIONAL EVALUATION (IEE): An evaluation conducted by a qualified examiner who is not employed by the public agency responsible for a child's education and provided at no expense to parents.

INDIRECT OUTCOMES: Unintended changes in behavior that result from intervention.

INDIVIDUALIZED EDUCATION PROGRAM (IEP): A written statement describing the special education program and placement of each child with a disability that is developed, reviewed, and revised in a meeting in accordance with 34 Code of Federal Regulations (C.F.R.) § 300.341–300.350.

INDIVIDUALIZED FAMILY SERVICE PLAN (IFSP): A plan developed in place of an individualized education program (IEP) for children 2 years, 11 months of age and younger. For children 3–5 years of age, the Individuals with Disabilities Education Act (IDEA) permits states to use an IFSP to meet IEP requirements. The IFSP places a family in a central role as recipient, provider, or both of intervention to promote a child's development.

INDIVIDUALIZED TRANSITION PLAN (ITP): 1. A component of the individualized education program (IEP) for each student age 14 and older. **2.** A statement of a coordinated set of activities designed within an outcome-oriented process to promote movement from school to postschool activities.

INDIVIDUALS WITH DISABILITIES EDUCATION ACT (IDEA 1997): Public Law 105-17, passed in 1990, reauthorized and amended the Education of All Handicapped Children Act (EAHCA).

INDIVIDUALS WITH DISABILITIES EDUCATION ACT (IDEA) AMENDMENTS OF 1997: Revisions to IDEA 1990 that placed an emphasis on access to the general curriculum and high expectations for achievement for all students.

INDIVIDUALS WITH DISABILITIES EDUCATION IMPROVEMENT ACT (IDEA 2004): Revisions to IDEA that focus on academic achievement for students with disabilities, making decisions based on scientifically based research, alignment with NCLB, and prevention services including early intervening services and responsiveness to intervention models.

INSTRUCTIONAL CONSULTATION TEAM (ICT): A support team that operates on a stage-based, collaborative, problem-solving process among professionals; designed to address academic and behavioral issues and to plan proactively for maximum student achievement and development (Rosenfield & Gravois, 1996).

INSTRUCTIONAL SUPPORT TEAM (IST): A team from a school site, including the building principal, classroom teachers and other support staff who meet to consider how to assist students who are struggling in the educational environment. The IST focuses on asking the question, "What educational resources can be utilized to assist the student?" rather than, "What's wrong with the student?", uses a problem-solving approach to determine the best way to identify students needs, and determines what strategies and interventions might assist the student.

INTERDISCIPLINARY TEAM (IDT): A group of special educators from two or more disciplines who address the goals of an individualized education program (IEP). Members work together on the evaluation and treatment team but evaluate and treat a student and family separately. These teams often have formal channels for communication and a functioning case manager (Donahue-Kilburg, 1992).

LANGUAGE DISORDER: A condition characterized by impaired comprehension and/or use of spoken, written, and/or other symbol systems. The disorder may involve the form of language (phonology, morphology, syntax), the content of language (semantics), and/or the function of language in communication (pragmatics).

LEARNING DISABILITIES: A heterogeneous group of disorders that are intrinsic to the individual and presumed to be due to central nervous system dysfunction. These disorders are manifested in significant difficulties in the acquisition and use of listening, speaking, reading, writing, reasoning, or mathematical abilities.

LEAST RESTRICTIVE ENVIRONMENT (LRE): The appropriate educational setting that affords a student the opportunity to learn in an environment that is as close to general education as possible and allows the student as much interaction as possible with nondisabled peers.

LICENSING: The issuance of a legal permit to practice a profession within the jurisdiction of the licensing body.

LITERACY: The condition or quality of being literate, especially the ability to read and write.

LOCAL EDUCATION AGENCY (LEA): A public board of education or other local public authority legally constituted within a state. The board has administrative control or direction of, or performs a service function for, public elementary or secondary schools in a city, county, township, school district, or other political subdivision of a state. The board may also oversee a combination of school districts or counties as are recognized in a state as an administrative agency for its public elementary or secondary schools.

MAINSTREAMING: When students with disabilities are educated with typically developing peers in the same classes, activities, or buildings.

MANIFESTATION DETERMINATION: When an action is contemplated by a local education agency (LEA) in response to a student's violation of a school's code of conduct, an individualized education program (IEP) team meets to review the child's disability and the behavior subject to disciplinary action. The purpose of this meeting is to make a manifestation determination (i.e., to decide if the behavior was a manifestation of the child's disability). If the behavior was a manifestation of the disability, they must remedy deficiencies found in the student's IEP. If the behavior was not a manifestation of the disability, they must transmit education and discipline records to the disciplinary body.

MEDIATION PROCESS: A voluntary process of formal discussion with a neutral third party to resolve differences prior to a due process hearing.

MEDICARE: A program constituted under the United States Social Security Administration that reimburses hospitals and physi-

cians for health-care services provided to people ages 65 and older, those receiving social security payments more than two years, and all citizens who have end-stage renal disease.

MENTAL AGE: An expression of the developmental level of an individual, usually a younger child, that is characteristic of a particular chronological age.

MULTIDISCIPLINARY TEAM (MDT): A group of two or more qualified individuals who work together as part of a student's individualized education program (IEP) team after existing evaluation data are reviewed.

MULTIDISCIPLINARY ASSESSMENT TEAM (MDAT): A team of interdisciplinary professionals who jointly conduct an assessment with a child; each professional will assess in their area of expertise (e.g. psychology, speech-language pathology, audiology, academics, occupational therapy) and then the team will jointly determine eligibility, areas of need, and services needed for the child.

NO CHILD LEFT BEHIND ACT OF 2001 (NCLB): Public Law 107-110, a United States Federal law, signed on January 8, 2002, that reauthorized Federal programs to improve the performance of U.S. primary and secondary schools by increasing the standards of accountability for states, school districts, and schools. NCLB reauthorized the Elementary and Secondary Education Act of 1965 (ESEA), and included an increased focus on reading.

OBJECTIVES: 1. Measurable statements of performance. **2.** Short-term or intermediate steps in reaching an intervention goal.

PERFORMANCE OUTCOMES: Measures of a person's abilities following intervention; also called functional outcomes.

PHONEMIC AWARENESS: The explicit understanding that words are composed of phonemes (i.e., segments of sound smaller than a syllable) plus the knowledge that each of these phonemes has distinctive features (Torgesen, 1999).

PHONICS: Instructional practices that educators use to emphasize how spellings are related to speech sounds in systematic ways (Snow, Burns, & Griffin, 1998).

PHONOLOGICAL AWARENESS: The general ability to attend to the sounds of a language distinct from its meaning, including rhyming, counting syllables, segmenting words, and recognizing onset and rime in words (Snow, Burns, & Griffin, 1998).

PLACEMENT: The description of the program that meets a student's individual educational needs, including the amount, type, frequency, and location of special education and related services.

PREFERRED PRACTICE PATTERNS: Statements developed by the American Speech-Language-Hearing Association (ASHA) that define universally applicable characteristics of activities directed toward individual patients/clients and address structural requisites of the practice, processes to be carried out, and expected outcomes.

PRELITERACY: 1. Skills that are precursors to literacy. **2.** Foundational skills and experiences for reading and writing.

PRESCHOOL AMENDMENTS TO THE EDUCATION OF THE HANDICAPPED ACT: Public Law 99-457, passed in 1986, extended the age of eligibility for special education to include infants and toddlers (birth through 2 years of age) who qualified for services under less-intensive eligibility criteria.

PRESENT LEVELS OF EDUCATIONAL PERFORMANCE: A required component of an individualized education program (IEP), this statement serves as a baseline for functional performance in goal areas and describes how the child's disability affects involvement and progress in the general curriculum.

PRINT FORM: The shape and appearance of written symbols of language.

PRINT MEANING: The meaning represented by written symbols of language.

PROCEDURAL COMPLIANCE: The action of agents of the state correctly following the requirements of due process.

PROCEDURAL DUE PROCESS: 1. The right to challenge an action of the state through an adjudicative procedure before the action may infringe on one's life, liberty, or property. **2.** The procedures followed to protect one's due process rights.

PROSPECTIVE PAYMENT: A Medicare reimbursement system that makes a single payment to cover a defined time period of care for a patient based on a diagnosis and other factors. The payment is intended to cover the costs of all services provided during this time, including therapies.

PULL-OUT: In this traditional service delivery model, a student is served directly by a speech-language pathologist individually or in a group of students in a location separate from the classroom.

RANDOM/PURPOSE GROUPS: A method of grouping students for instructional purposes that varies the composition of groups over time based on criteria determined by a speech-language pathologist.

RECIPROCITY: The influence that each person in a relationship has on others in the course of their interactions.

REFERRAL: Written notification sent to a local educational agency (LEA) requesting assessment for a child who is believed to have a disability.

REGULAR EDUCATION INITIATIVE (REI): An educational movement initiated by the document prepared by M. Will for the United States Office of Special Education and Rehabilitation Services (OSERS) in 1986 that outlined reforms in special education, including greater opportunities to include students with disabilities in general education environments.

REHABILITATION ACT: Public Law 93-112, passed in 1973, prohibited discrimination on the basis of disability in programs receiving federal financial assistance, in federal employment, and in the employment practices of federal contractors.

RELATED SERVICE: A service necessary for a student to benefit from special education, including transportation and developmental, corrective, and other supportive services (e.g., speech-language pathology and audiology services; psychological services; physical and occupational therapy; recreation, including therapeutic recreation; social work services; counseling services, including rehabilitation counseling; orientation and mobility services; and medical services, except such medical services that will be for diagnostic and evaluation purposes only) that may be required to assist a child with a disability to benefit from special education. Includes the early identification and assessment of disabling conditions in children.

RESOLUTION SESSION: A mandatory meeting between key personnel in a school district and parents designed to attempt to resolve issues prior to mediation. The meeting must be offered following a request for due process.

RESOURCE TEACHERS: Special education or other teachers who provide specialized instruction in the classroom or in a separate location for part of the day.

RESPONSE TO INTERVENTION (RtI): The practice of providing high-quality instruction and interventions to students who are struggling prior to referral for special education services. Targeted or intense interventions are provided and then the students' progress is monitored to determine their response to intervention strategies.

RESTORATIVE: Intervention intended to restore or recover skills and knowledge lost due to injury or illness.

RESTRUCTURING: All aspects of reform, including instruction, participatory governance, site-based management, the increasing involvement of parents and communities in the development of partnerships and networks, and the redesign of curricula.

SCREENING: An abbreviated procedure to collect information on children's performance and to check for potential developmental or academic concerns that should be further evaluated for possible referral.

SECTION 504: The section of the Rehabilitation Act of 1973 that required all programs receiving federal funds to be fully accessible to employees and members of the general public who have disabilities.

SEMANTICS: The meaning of words in a language and the relationships between words. Semantics also relates to multiple word meanings, figurative language, and the underlying meanings of words in specific contexts.

SERVICE DELIVERY: The provision of educational or therapeutic services to a target population.

SHARED CAP: As part of the Balanced Budget Act of 1997 (PL105-33), Congress set a limit of $1500 per year on payment for outpatient rehabilitation services provided by skilled nursing facilities, rehabilitation agencies, public health agencies, clinics, and other facilities. The Health Care Financing Administration (HCFA) interpreted the language of this law to mean that speech-language pathology and physical therapy services must share a $1500 payment cap, i.e., total payment for speech-language pathology services, physical therapy services, or a combination of these services could not exceed $1500 per year. In November, 1999, ASHA and other professional organizations won a two-year moratorium on caps for all rehabilitation services.

SHORT-TERM OBJECTIVES: Measurable intermediate steps toward an intervention goal.

SKILL GROUPS: A method of grouping students for instructional purposes based on similar skills or performance levels.

SOUND/SYMBOL CORRESPONDENCE: A phoneme that is mapped onto a graphic symbol, such as a letter or a combination of letters

SPECIAL EDUCATION: Specially designed instruction, provided to identified students at no cost to parents, that meets the unique needs of a child with a disability, including instruction conducted in the classroom, in the home, in hospitals and institutions, and in other settings and instruction in physical education.

SPECIFIC LANGUAGE DEFICIT: A category of language disorder that is usually characterized as a language disorder that cannot be attributed to intellectual or sensory deficits but that substantially affects a child's ability to understand and express verbal and written language. Also called developmental language disorder, specific language impairment, language disorder.

SPEECH-LANGUAGE PATHOLOGY ASSISTANT (SLPA): Support personnel who provide services in a speech-language program under the supervision of a speech-language pathologist and have a minimum of an associate's degree or equivalent experience.

STANDARDIZED TEST: An assessment measure that provides information concerning the ability of a child in comparison with other children of the same specified group. A standardized test must always be administered in the same manner and under the same conditions to obtain reliability and validity. The standards of interpretation of the student's response behaviors are usually based on the norms of a similar population that has also completed the test.

STATE EDUCATION ADVOCACY LEADER (SEAL): State Education Advocacy Leaders (SEALs) are appointed by ASHA recognized state speech-language hearing associations to advocate on education issues. These issues may include caseload/workload, salary supplements, and maintenance of personnel standards in school settings. SEALs can be speech-language pathologists or audiologists. The State Education Advocacy Leaders were established in 1999 under ASHA's Priorities. The mission of the SEALs network is to enhance and perpetuate the advocacy, leadership, and clinical management skills of school-based ASHA members at the state and local levels to influence administrative and public policy decisions that affect the delivery of speech-language pathology and audiology services in school settings.

STATE EDUCATIONAL AGENCY (SEA): The state board of education or other agency or officer primarily responsible for the state supervision of public elementary and secondary schools or, if there is no such officer or agency, an officer or agency designated by the governor or by state law.

STAY PUT: The rule that prohibits a local educational agency (LEA) from changing a child's placement without parental consent while a due process dispute is going on.

STUDENT STUDY TEAM (SST): A group of school staff who meet regularly to problem solve regarding students, recommend in-class modifications, make referrals for specialized services, or refer for special education assessment.

SUBJECT AREA SPECIALIST: An educator who does not have a self-contained classroom of students for the day but sees a class or a small group for part of the day to address a specific subject (e.g., art, music, reading, and biology).

SUPPORT PERSONNEL MODEL: A model of service delivery that uses support personnel (e.g., aides, assistants, or paraprofessionals).

SUSPENSION: The removal of a student from a classroom or school for a limited period of time, generally fewer than or equal to 10 days, as directed by a teacher or principal.

SYNTAX: The part of grammar that regulates the arrangement of words to form meaningful sentences.

TIERED SYSTEM: A hierarchical model of service delivery of increasing levels of support for students who are struggling with academics or behavior. Tier I typically represents core instructional interventions; Tier II represents targeted group interventions; and Tier III represents individual, intensive interventions. Special education may be considered Tier III or Tier IV.

TITLE I: A federal program established under the Elementary and Secondary Education Act of 1965 that provided a system of remedial education for economically disadvantaged students and provided some entitlements to state-supported or state-operated schools for the "handicapped."

TRANSITION: The movement of a student from one level to another, especially the movement from preschool to elementary school or from high school to postschool.

TRANSDISCIPLINARY TEAM (TDT): A group of special educators from two or more disciplines who share skills, knowledge, and roles as appropriate to address the goals of an individualized education program (IEP). Members divide their work into direct and indirect student services. Not every member works with every student, but all members, including parents and caregivers, consult with each other to carry out the service delivery plans the group designs together (Donahue-Kilburg, 1992).

UNITED STATES CODE (U.S.C.): The written record of the laws of the United States enacted by the legislative branch of the federal government.

UNIVERSAL DESIGN: The design of instructional materials and activities that provides for goals to be achievable by individuals with wide differences in their physical or learning abilities. Alternatives are built into curricular materials and activities to provide students with flexible approaches to meeting instructional objectives.

UNIVERSAL NEWBORN HEARING SCREENING (UNHS) PROGRAM: A system of providing hearing screening for all infants, typically before discharge from the hospital nursery or within 3 months of birth.

WORKLOAD: All activities required and performed by an SLP working in the schools. An SLP's workload includes considerable time for direct services to students, but also includes many other activities necessary to support students' education programs, implement best practices for school speech-language services, and ensure compliance with IDEA and other mandates.

References

Adams, M. J. (1999). *Beginning to read: Thinking and learning about print.* Cambridge, MA: MIT Press.

Allington, R. L., & McGill-Franzen, A. (2000). Looking back, looking forward: A conversation about teaching reading in the 21st century. *Reading Research Quarterly, 35,* 136–153.

American Psychiatric Association (APA). (1994). *Diagnostic and statistical manual of mental disorders* (4th ed.). Washington, DC: Author.

American Psychiatric Association (APA). (2000). *Diagnostic and statistical manual of mental disorders: Text revisions.* (Revised 4th ed.). Washington, DC: Author.

American Psychological Association (APA). (2001). *Publication manual of the American Psychological Association* (5th ed.). Washington, DC: Author.

*American Speech-Language-Hearing Association (ASHA). (1985). Clinical management of communicatively handicapped minority language populations. *ASHA, 27,* 29–32.

*American Speech-Language-Hearing Association (ASHA). (1989). Issues in determining eligibility for language intervention. *ASHA, 31,* 113–118.

*American Speech-Language-Hearing Association (ASHA). (1990). Roles of speech-language pathologists in service delivery to infants, toddlers, and their families. *ASHA, 32*(Suppl. 2), 4.

*American Speech-Language-Hearing Association (ASHA). (1991a). Augmentative and alternative communication. *ASHA, 33*(Suppl. 5), 8.

*American Speech-Language-Hearing Association (ASHA). (1991b). *A building blocks module: Multicultural considerations.* Rockville, MD: Author.

*American Speech-Language-Hearing Association (ASHA). (1991c). *Guidelines for speech-language pathologists serving persons with language, socio-communication, and/or cognitive-communication impairments* [Guidelines]. Retrieved May 15, 2005, from http://www.asha.org/policy

*American Speech-Language-Hearing Association (ASHA). (1995). *User's guide phase I—group II, National treatment outcome data collection project.* Rockville, MD: Author.

*American Speech-Language-Hearing Association (ASHA). (1996a). Guidelines for training, credentialing, use, and supervision of speech-language pathology assistants. *ASHA, 38*(Suppl. 16), 21–34.

*American Speech-Language-Hearing Association (ASHA). (1996b). Inclusive practices for children and youths with communication disorders [Position statement]. *ASHA, 38*(Suppl. 16), 35–44.

*American Speech-Language-Hearing Association (ASHA). (1997a). *Building blocks: Preparing speech-language pathologists to serve infants, toddlers, and their families.* Rockville, MD: Author.

* ASHA documents are available from American Speech-Language-Hearing Association, 10801 Rockville Pike, Rockville, MD 20852.

*American Speech-Language-Hearing Association (ASHA). (1997b). *Preferred practice patterns for the profession of speech-language pathology.* Rockville, MD: Author.

*American Speech-Language-Hearing Association (ASHA). (1998a, September 8). Medicare: How the new payment system will affect you. *ASHA Leader Extra,* 11–14.

*American Speech-Language-Hearing Association (ASHA). (1998b). *Speech-language pathology assistants* [Information series]. Rockville, MD: Author.

*American Speech-Language-Hearing Association (ASHA). (1998c). Students and professionals who speak English with accents and nonstandard dialects: Issues and recommendations. *ASHA, 40*(Suppl. 18), 28–31.

*American Speech-Language-Hearing Association (ASHA). (1998d). *Survey of speech-language pathology services in school-based settings* [Final report]. Rockville, MD: Author.

*American Speech-Language-Hearing Association (ASHA). (1998e). *User's guide: National treatment outcome data collection project.* Rockville, MD: Author.

*American Speech-Language-Hearing Association (ASHA). (1999a, December). *American Speech-Language-Hearing Association priority issues and outcomes: 2000.* Retrieved May 21, 2000, from http://www.asha.org/about/leadership-projects/national-office/focused-initiatives/01-03-archive/final_report2000.htm

*American Speech-Language-Hearing Association (ASHA). (1999b). *Guidelines for the roles and responsibilities of the school-based speech-language pathologist. (37).* Rockville, MD: Author.

*American Speech-Language-Hearing Association (ASHA). (1999c). *1999 ASHA workforce study.* Rockville, MD: Author.

*American Speech-Language-Hearing Association (ASHA). (2000a). *IDEA and your caseload: A template for eligibility and dismissal criteria for students ages 3–21.* Rockville, MD: Author.

*American Speech-Language-Hearing Association (ASHA). (2000b, January). *Responding to the changing needs of speech-language pathology and audiology students in the 21st century: A briefing paper for academicians, practitioners, employers, and students.* Retrieved January 30, 2001, from http://www.asha.org/about/membership-certification/cert_benefits.htm

*American Speech-Language-Hearing Association (ASHA). (2000c). *Roles and responsibilities of speech-language pathologists with respect to reading and writing in children and adolescents.* Rockville, MD: Author.

*American Speech-Language-Hearing Association (ASHA). (2000d, February). *Why be certified by ASHA?* Retrieved January 29, 2001, from http://www.asha.org/member

*American Speech-Language-Hearing Association (ASHA). (2001a). *2001 Omnibus survey results.* Rockville, MD: Author.

*American Speech-Language-Hearing Association (ASHA). (2001b). *Roles and responsibilities of school-based professionals* [Position statement]. Retrieved October 22, 2007, from www.asha.org

*American Speech-Language-Hearing Association (ASHA). (2001c). *Scope of practice in speech-language pathology.* Rockville, MD: Author.

*American Speech-Language-Hearing Association (ASHA). (2002a). *A workload analysis approach for establishing speech-language caseload standards in the schools: Guidelines* [Guidelines]. Retrieved October 13, 2007, from http://www.asha.org/policy

* ASHA documents are available from American Speech-Language-Hearing Association, 10801 Rockville Pike, Rockville, MD 20852.

*American Speech-Language-Hearing Association (ASHA). (2002b). *A workload analysis approach for establishing speech-language caseload standards in the school: Position statement* [Position Statement]. Retrieved September 3, 2007, from http://www.asha.org/docs/html/PS2002-00122.html

*American Speech-Language-Hearing Association (ASHA). (2002c). *A workload approach for establishing speech-language caseload standards in schools: Technical report* [Technical report]. Rockville, MD: Author.

*American Speech-Language-Hearing Association (ASHA). (2002d). Implementation guide: A workload analysis approach for establishing speech-language caseload standards in the schools. *ASHA Desk Reference, 3*. Rockville, MD: Author.

*American Speech-Language-Hearing Association (ASHA). (2003a, b). Reprinted with permission from American Speech-Language-Hearing Association. (2003). *Code of Ethics* [Ethics]. Available from http://www.asha.org/policy. All rights reserved.

*American Speech-Language-Hearing Association (ASHA). (2003c). Code of ethics (revised), *ASHA 23*, 13–15.

*American Speech-Language-Hearing Association (ASHA). (2003d). Interdisciplinary assessment of young children with autism spectrum disorder by Patricia A. Prelock. *Language, Speech, and Hearing Services in Schools, 34*, 196.

*American Speech-Language-Hearing Association (ASHA). (2003e). *Omnibus survey caseload report: SLP*. Rockville, MD: Author.

*American Speech-Language-Hearing Association (ASHA). (2003f). Reprinted with permission from American Speech-Language-Hearing Asso-

ciation. (2002). *A workload analysis approach for establishing speech-language caseload standards in the schools: Technical report* [Technical report]. Available from http://www.asha.org/policy. All rights reserved.

*American Speech-Language-Hearing Association (ASHA). (2004a). *Admission/discharge criteria in speech-language pathology* [Guidelines]. Retrieved September 4, 2007, from http://www.asha.org/policy

*American Speech-Language-Hearing Association (ASHA). (2004b). *Evidence-based practice in communication disorders: An introduction* [Technical report]. Retrieved October 14, 2007, from http://www.asha.org/policy

*American Speech-Language-Hearing Association (ASHA). (2004c). *Guidelines for the training, use, and supervision of speech-language pathology assistants.* [Guidelines]. Retrieved September 5, 2007, from http://www.asha.org/NR/rdonlyres/2098755B-AC9C-4F81-9011-B84000043E59/0/v3GLSupervisionSLPAs.pdf

American Speech-Language-Hearing Association (ASHA). (2004d). Knowledge and skills needed by speech-language pathologists and audiologists to provide culturally and linguistically appropriate services*. Retrieved September 6, 2007, from http://www.asha.org/docs/pdf/KS2004-00215.pdf

*American Speech-Language-Hearing Association (ASHA). (2004e). *Preferred practice patterns for the profession of speech-language pathology*. Retrieved August 31, 2007, from http://www.asha.org/docs/pdf/PP2004-00191.pdf

*American Speech-Language-Hearing Association (ASHA). (2005a). *Classification of speech-language pathology and audiology procedures and communication disorders*. Rockville, MD: Author.

* ASHA documents are available from American Speech-Language-Hearing Association, 10801 Rockville Pike, Rockville, MD 20852.

*American Speech-Language-Hearing Association (ASHA). (2005b). *Cultural competence* [Issues in Ethics]. Retrieved September 4, 2007, from http://www.asha.org/docs/pdf/ET2005-00174.pdf

*American Speech-Language-Hearing Association (ASHA). (2005c). *Dynamic assessment.* Retrieved September 2, 2007, from http://www.asha.org/about/leadership-projects/multicultural/issues/da/default

*American Speech-Language-Hearing Association (ASHA). (2005d). *Early literacy.* Rockville, MD: Author.

*American Speech-Language-Hearing Association (ASHA). (2005e). *Evidence-based practice in communication disorders* [Position statement]. Retrieved August 29, 2007, from, http://www.asha.org/members/deskref-journals/deskref/default

*American Speech-Language-Hearing Association (ASHA). (2005f). *Evidence-based practice: Position statement.* Retrieved May 27, 2005, from http://www.asha.org/NR/rdonlyres/4837FDFC-576B-4D84-BDD6-8BFF2A803AD3/0/v4PS_EBP.pdf

*American Speech-Language-Hearing Association (ASHA). (2005g). *Fact sheet on funding.* Retrieved October 22, 2007, from http://www.asha.org/NR/rdonlyres/21AA45AD-D235-4FB4-85F2-5E310ECDDDF9/0/Federal_Funding_Fact_Sheet.pdf

*American Speech-Language-Hearing Association (ASHA). (2005h). *Principles for speech-language pathologists serving persons with mental retardation/developmental disabilities* [Technical report]. Retrieved May 27, 2005, http://www.asha.org/docs/html/TR2005-00144.html

*American Speech-Language-Hearing Association (ASHA). (2005i). *Roles and responsibilities of speech-language pathologists with respect to augmentative and alternative communication: Position statement* [Position statement]. Retrieved August 28, 2007, from http://www.asha.org/docs/html/PS2005-00113.html

*American Speech-Language-Hearing Association (ASHA). (2006a). *2006 Schools survey report: Caseload characteristics.* Rockville, MD: Author.

*American Speech-Language-Hearing Association (ASHA). (2006b). *Frequently asked questions about speech-language pathology assistants.* Retrieved August 31, 2007, from http://asha.org/about/membership-certification/faq_slpasst.htm

*American Speech-Language-Hearing Association (ASHA). (2006c). *Highlights and trends.* Retrieved August 26, 2007, from http://www.asha.org/about/Membership-Certification/member-counts.htm

*American Speech-Language-Hearing Association (ASHA). (2006d). *Knowledge and skills needed by speech-language pathologists for diagnosis, assessment, and treatment of autism spectrum disorders across the life span* [Knowledge and Skills]. Retrieved October 14, 2007, from http://www.asha.org/policy

*American Speech-Language-Hearing Association (ASHA). (2006e). *Listen to your buds.* Retrieved August 18, 2007, from http://www.listentoyour-buds.org/parents.php?id=21

*American Speech-Language-Hearing Association (ASHA). (2006f). *Preferred practice patterns for the profession of audiology.* Retrieved August 31, 2007, from http://www.asha.org/docs/pdf/PP2006-00274.pdf

*American Speech-Language-Hearing Association (ASHA). (2006g). *Principles for speech-language pathologists in diagnosis, assessment, and treat-

* ASHA documents are available from American Speech-Language-Hearing Association, 10801 Rockville Pike, Rockville, MD 20852.

ment of autism spectrum disorders across the life span [Technical Report]. Retrieved October 14, 2007, from http://www.asha.org/policy

*American Speech-Language-Hearing Association (ASHA). (2006h). *Roles and responsibilities of speech-language pathologists in diagnosis, assessment, and treatment of autism spectrum disorders across the life span* [Position Statement]. Retrieved October 14, 2007, from http://www.asha.org/policy

*American Speech-Language-Hearing Association (ASHA). (2006i). *Roles, knowledge, and skills: Audiologists providing clinical services to infants and young children birth to 5 years of age* [Knowledge and Skills]. Retrieved October 13, 2007, from http://www.asha.org/policy

*American Speech-Language-Hearing Association (ASHA). (2007a). *Directory of speech-language pathology instruments: 2007 ed.* Retrieved August 28, 2007, from http://www.asha.org/NR/rdonlyres/77DC6979-4945-44D7-B153-18958-B9C0320/0/Introduction.pdf

*American Speech-Language-Hearing Association (ASHA). (2007b). *Funding pyramid.* Retrieved October 2, 2007, from http://www.asha.org/about/legislation-advocacy/schoolfundadv/default#pyramid

*American Speech-Language-Hearing Association (ASHA). (2007c). *Language, speech, and hearing contacts in state education agencies.* Retrieved October 2, 2007, from http://www.asha.org/about/legislation-advocacy/state/education_agencies.htm

*American Speech-Language-Hearing Association (ASHA). (2007d). *Scope of practice in speech-language pathology* [Scope of Practice]. Retrieved September 4, 2007, http://www.asha.org/docs/html/SP2007-00283.html

*American Speech-Language-Hearing Association (ASHA). (n.d.). *Comparison of ASHA certification maintenance and state/local licensure or education certification.* Retrieved October 25, 2007, from http://www.asha.org/about/membership-certification/cert_vs_statelic.htm

*American Speech-Language-Hearing Association (ASHA). (n.d.). *Flow of medicaid funds to your school district* [Chart]. Retrieved October 25, 2007, from http://www.asha.org/NR/rdonlyres/CC0B8EB4-97F4-4359-8BDB-AD46D51E2E9E/0/MedicaidFundsFlow-Chart0906.pdf.

Americans with Disabilities Act (ADA), 42 U.S.C. § 12101 *et seq.* (1990).

Annett, M. (2004, March 2). Service delivery success: SLPs in Oregon schools tackle workload, enhance recruitment. *The ASHA Leader, 1,* 12–13.

Apel, K. (1993, November). *Index of state's definition of language impairment and qualification for service* [Handout]. Presentation at the annual convention of the American Speech-Language-Hearing Association, Anaheim, CA.

Apel, K. (1999). An introduction to assessment and intervention with older students with language-learning impairments: Bridges from research to clinical practice. *Language, Speech, and Hearing Services in Schools, 30,* 228–230.

Apel, K., & Swank, L. (1999). Second chances: Improving decoding skills in the older student. *Language, Speech, and Hearing Services in Schools, 30,* 231–242.

Apel, K., & Wolter, J. A. (2004a). ASHA and evidence-based practice. *Perspectives on Issues in Higher Education, 5*(3), 21–23.

* ASHA documents are available from American Speech-Language-Hearing Association, 10801 Rockville Pike, Rockville, MD 20852.

Apel, K., & Wolter, J. A. (2004b, December). The school-based speech-language pathologist's piece of the EBP pie. *Perspectives on school-based issues, ASHA Division 16, 5*(3), 3–6.

Area Education Agency 6, Special Education Division. (2000, February 4). *Breadth of the mandate* [draft]. Marshalltown, Iowa: Author.

Armbruster, B. A., & Osborn, J. (2001). *Put reading first.* Washington DC: National Institute for Literacy.

Artiles, A. J., & Ortiz, A. A. (Eds.). (2002). *English language learners with special education needs: Identification, assessment, and instruction.* Washington, DC and McHenry, IL: Center for Applied Linguistics and Delta Systems.

Arvedson, J. C. (2000). Evaluation of children with feeding and swallowing problems. *Language, Speech, and Hearing Services in Schools, 31,* 28–41.

Association of California School Administrators (ACSA). (2006). *Handbook of goals and objectives related to state of California content standards.* Sacramento, CA: Author.

Attwood, T. (2003, October). Social skills programs to teach friendship skills for children with Asperger syndrome. *Perspectives on Language Learning and Education, ASHA Division 1, 10*(3), 16–19.

August, D., & Shanahan, T. (2006). *Developing literacy in second-language learners: A report of the national literacy panel on language-minority children and youth.* Mahwah, NJ: Lawrence Erlbaum Associates. Retrieved August 31, 2007, from http://www.cal.org/projects/archive/nlreports/Executive_Summary.pdf

Autism Society of America. (1996, July–August). Definition of autism. *Advocate, 3,* 1.

Autism Society of America (n.d.). *Defining autism.* Retrieved October 12, 2007, from http://www.autismsociety.org/site/PageServer?pagename=about_whatis_home

Azzam, A. M. (2007, Summer). Special report: Twenty-first-century skills for the whole child. *Special Issue: Engaging the Whole Child. Educational Leadership, 64* (Online only). Retrieved September 3, 2007, from http://www.ascd.org

Bain, B. A., & Dollaghan, C. A. (1991). The notion of clinically significant change. *Language, Speech, and Hearing Services in Schools, 22,* 264–270.

Baird, M. (2004, December 9). *Reading failure: Guidance on FAPE, the IDEA, and NCLB.* LRP Publications Audio Conference.

Banotai, A. (2005, March 28). Education legislation: Impact of NCLB and IDEA '04 on school clinicians. *Advance,* 6–9.

Barron, R., & Sanchez, F. S. (2007). Fulfilling the commitment: Excellence for all students. *Leadership, 36*(3), 8–10, 32.

Batsche, G., Elliott, J., Graden, J. L., Grimes, J., Kovaleski, J. F., Prasse, D., et al. (2005). *Response to intervention: Policy considerations and implementation.* Alexandria, VA: National Association of State Directors of Special Education.

Battle, D. E. (1998). *Communication disorders in multicultural populations.* Boston: Butterworth-Heineman.

Baum, H. M. (1998). Overview, definitions, and goals for ASHA's treatment outcomes and clinical trials activities (What difference do outcome data make to you?). *Language, Speech, and Hearing Services in Schools, 29,* 246–249.

Baumel, J. (2003, March 12). *Assessment: An overview.* Retrieved September 6, 2007, from http://www.schwablearning.org/articles.aspx?r=27&f=search

Bettleheim, B., & Zelan, K. (1982). *On learning to read: The child's fascination with meaning.* New York: Vintage.

Bevilacqua, S., & Norlin, J. W. (Eds.) (2004). *Autism methodologies: Best practices and legal trends.* Horsham, PA: LRP Publications.

Biancarosa, G., & Snow, C. E. (2004). *Reading next–A vision for action and research in middle and high school literacy: A report from Carnegie Corporation of New York.* Washington, DC: Alliance for Excellent Education. Retrieved August 28, 2007, from http://www.all4ed.org/publications/ReadingNext/ReadingNext.pdf

Biemiller, A. (1999). *Language and reading success.* Cambridge, MA: Brookline.

Biklin, D. (1992). *Schooling without labels: Parents, educators and inclusive education.* New York: Teachers College Press.

Biklin, D., & Cardinal, D. N. (Eds.). (1997). *Contested words, contested science: Unraveling the facilitated communication controversy.* New York: Teachers College Press.

Blackstone, S., & Pressman, H. (1996, August). *Treatment outcomes in AAC.* Presentation at the biennial convention of the International Society for Augmentative and Alternative Communication, Vancouver, British Columbia, Canada.

Blackstone, S. W. (Ed.). (2000). AAC approaches for infants and toddlers. *Augmentative Communication News, 12*(6), 1–8.

Bland, L. E. (1998, May). School speech and language services. *Language Learning and Education, 5,* 33–35.

Bland, L. E. (1999, October). Interview with Diane L. Eger on the implications of IDEA '97 and accountability. *Language Learning and Education, 6,* 8–10.

Blosser, J. L., & Kratcoski, A. (1997). PACs: A framework for determining appropriate service delivery options. *Language, Speech, and Hearing Services in Schools, 28,* 99–107.

Board of Education of Hendrick Hudson Central School District v. Rowley, 458 U.S. 176 (1982).

Bond, L. A. (1996). Norm- and criterion-referenced testing. *Practical Assessment, Research & Evaluation, 5*(2). Retrieved August 4, 2007, from http://PAREonline.net/getvn.asp?v=5&n=2

Bondy, A. S., & Frost, L. A. (1994). The picture exchange communication system. *Focus on Autistic Behavior, 9,* 1–19.

Boswell, S. (2004, September 21). Due process: No-win system. *The ASHA Leader, 9*(17), 18, 20.

Botting, N., & Conti-Ramsden, G. (2003, Fall). Specific language impairment and autism. *CSHA Magazine, 33*(2), 8–9, 30–31.

Boudreau, D. M., & Hedberg, N. L. (1999). A comparison of early literacy skills in children with specific language impairment and their typically developing peers. *American Journal of Speech Language Pathology, 8,* 249–260.

Bradley, R., Danielson, L, & Doolittle, J. (2007). Responsiveness to intervention: 1997 to 2007. *Teaching Exceptional Children, 39*(5), 8–12.

Brannen, S. J., Cooper, E. B., Dellegrotto, J. T., Disney, S. T., Eger, D. L., Ehren, B. J., et al. (2000). *Developing educationally relevant IEPs: A technical assistance document for speech-language pathologists.* Rockville, MD: American Speech-Language-Hearing Association.

Brice, A. (1993). *Understanding the Cuban refugee.* San Diego, CA: Los Amigos Research Associates.

Brice, A. E. (2000). Which language for bilingual speakers? Factors to consider. *Communication Disorders and Sciences in Culturally Linguistically Diverse Populations, 6,* 1–7.

Brice, A., & Brice, R. (2007). School language and classroom programs for children with language impairments: Collaborating with parents and school personnel. In C. Roseberry-McKibbin (Ed.). *Language disorders in children: A multicultural and case perspective* (pp. 439–464). Boston, MA: Allyn and Bacon.

Bromley, K. (2007, April). Nine things every teacher should know about words and vocabulary instruction. *Journal of adolescent and adult literacy, 50*(7), 528–537.

Brown v. Board of Education, 347 U.S. 483 (1954).

Bucaro, F. C. (2000). Professionalism and ethics: How do you spell success? *The Communication Connection, 14*(2), 1–2, 4.

Buekelman, D. R., & Miranda, P. (1998). *Augmentative and alternative communication: Management of severe communication disorders in children and adults* (2nd ed.). Baltimore: Brookes.

Burgess, S., & Turkstra, L. S. (2006, December). Social skills intervention for adolescents with autism spectrum disorders: A review of the experimental evidence. *EBP Briefs, 1*(4), 1–21.

Buschbacher, P. (2005, March). Positive behavior support. *Perspectives on Language Learning and Education, ASHA Division 1, 12*(1), 1–2.

Buschbacher, P., & Fox, L. (2003, July). Understanding and intervening with the challenging behavior of young children with autism spectrum disorder. *Language, Speech and Hearing Services in Schools, 34*(3), 217–227.

Butler, K. G. (Ed.). (1999). Many voices, many tongues: Accents, dialects and variations. *Topics in Language Disorders, 19*(4), iv–v.

Calculator, S. N. (1999). Look who's pointing now: Cautions related to the clinical use of facilitated communication. *Language, Speech, and Hearing Services in Schools, 30,* 408–414.

California Department of Education (CDE). (1997). *Guidelines for language, academic, and special education services required for limited-English-proficient students in California public schools, K–12.* Sacramento, CA: Author.

California Department of Education (CDE). (1998). *English-language arts content standards for California public schools: Kindergarten through grade twelve.* Sacramento, CA: Author.

California Department of Education (CDE). (1999a). *Best practices for designing and delivering effective programs for individuals with autism spectrum disorders.* Sacramento, CA: Author.

California Department of Education (CDE). (1999b). *The California reading initiative and special education in California: Critical ideas to focus meaningful reform.* Sacramento, CA: Author.

California Department of Education (CDE). (1999c). *California special education programs: A composite of laws.* Sacramento, CA: Author.

California Department of Education (CDE). (1999d). *English-language development standards for California public schools. Retrieved October 24, 2007,* from http://www.cde.ca.gov/re/pn/fd/eng-langart-stnd-pdf.asp

California Department of Education (CDE). (1999e). *Reading/language arts framework for California public schools: Kindergarten through grade twelve.* Sacramento, CA: Author.

California Department of Education (CDE). (1999f). *Special education rights of parents and children.* Sacramento, CA: Author.

California education code: 48900, 2006.

Camarata, S. M. (1996). On the importance of integrating naturalistic language, social intervention, and speech-intelligibility training. In L. K. Koegel, R. L. Koegel & G. Dunlop (Eds.), *Positive behavioral support* (pp. 31–49). Baltimore: Brookes.

Campbell, D. (1999). Focus on function in the schools. *Advance, 9*(51), 7–8.

Cassidy, J., & Cassidy, D. (2007). What's hot, what's not for 2007. *Reading Today, 24*(4), 1,10.

Catts, H. W., & Kamhi, A. G. (2005). *Language and reading disabilities* (2nd ed.). Boston, MA: Pearson.

Cedar Rapids Community School District v. Garret F., 119 S.Ct. 992, 29 IDELR 966 (U.S. 199).

Center for Special Education Finance (CSEF). (1999, September). *Frequently asked questions.* Retrieved January 29, 2001, from http://csef.air.org/.html

Center for the Improvement of Early Reading Achievement (CIERA). (2001, January). *CIERA homepage.* Retrieved January 29, 2001, from http://www.ciera.org/ciera/publications/report-series/inquiry-2/2-002ann.pdf

Centers for Disease Control and Prevention (CDC). (1999). *Training manual for volunteer screening program of Special Olympics games.* Atlanta, GA: Author.

Centers for Disease Control and Prevention (CDC). (2007). *Autism information.* Retrieved October 16, 2007, from http://www.cdc.gov/ncbddd/autism/

Cernosia, A. (1999, March). *Individuals with Disabilities Education Act–1997 reauthorization* [Handout]. Presentation at the Special Education Division, California Department of Education, Sacramento, CA.

Chambers, J. G., Perez, M., Harr, J. J., & Shkolnik, J. (2005). Special education spending estimates from 1969–2000. *Journal of Special Education Leadership, 18*(1), 5–13.

Cheng, L-R. L. (1999). Moving beyond accent: Social and cultural realities of living with many tongues. *Topics in Language Disorders, 19*(4), 1–10.

Church, G., & Glennen, S. (1992). *The handbook of assistive technology.* San Diego, CA: Singular.

Cirrin, F. M. (1996, April). Discrepancy models: Implications for service in public schools. *Language Learning and Education, 3*(1), 9–10.

Cirrin, F. M., & Penner, S. G. (1995). Classroom-based consultative service delivery models for language intervention. In M. E. Fey, J. Windsor, & S. F. Warren (Eds.), *Language intervention: Preschool through the elementary years,* 333–362. Baltimore: Brookes.

Code of Fair Testing Practices in Education. (2004). Washington, DC: Joint Committee on Testing Practices.

Code of Federal Regulations (C.F.R.). (1999). *Assistance to states for the education of children with disabilities and the early intervention program for infants and toddlers with disabilities* [Final regulations]. C.F.R., Title 34, § 300, 301, and 303.

Code of Federal Regulations (C.F.R.). (2003, December). *Including children with disabilities in state assessment programs* [Final regulations]. C.F.R., Title 34 § 200; 600. Retrieved October 16, 2007, from http://www.ed.gov/legislation/FedRegister/finrule/2003-4/120903a.html

Cole, K. N., Dale, P. S., & Thal, D. J. (Eds.). (1998). *Assessment of communication and language.* Baltimore: Brookes.

Cole, L. (1983). Implications of the position on social dialects. *ASHA, 25*(9), 25–27.

Collins, M., & Dowell, M. L. (1998). Discipline and due process. *Thrust for Educational Leadership, 28*(2), 34–36.

Concerns and Questions about Alternate Assessment. Retrieved September 22, 2003, from http://www.doe.mass.edu/mcas/atl/QabdC.doc

Council for Exceptional Children (CEC). (1997a, September). CEC policy manual. Retrieved January 29, 2001, from http://www.cec.sped.org/AM/Template.cfm?Section=Policy_and_Advocacy&Template=/TaggedPage/TaggedPageDisplay.cfm&TPLID=1&ContentID=2014

Council for Exceptional Children (CEC). (1997b). A history of special education. *Teaching Exceptional Children, 29*(5), 5–50.

Council for Exceptional Children (CEC). (1999). Special educators share their thoughts on special education teaching conditions. *CEC Today, 5*(9), 1–5.

Council for Exceptional Children (CEC). (2007, July 20). *CEC identifies critical issues facing special education.* Retrieved September 6, 2007, from http://www.cec.sped.org/AM/Template.cfm?Section=Search&template=/CM/HTMLDisplay.cfm&ContentID=8598

Council of Administrators of Special Education (CASE). (1999). *Section 504 and the ADA: Promoting student access* (2nd ed.). Albuquerque, NM: Author.

Council of Language, Speech, and Hearing Consultants in State Education Agencies (CLSHCSEA). (1999). *CLSHCSEA* [Brochure]. Charleston, WV: Author.

Council of Language, Speech, and Hearing Consultants in State Education Agencies (CLSHCSEA). (2007). *Council of Language, Speech, and Hearing Consultants in State Education Agencies regular (active) members* [Membership list]. Charleston, WV: Author.

Crais, E. R. (2000). Ecologically valid communication assessment of infants and toddlers. In L. R. Watson, E. Crais, & T. L. Layton (Eds.), *Handbook of early language impairment in children: Assessment and treatment,* pp. 1–37. Albany, NY: Delmar.

Crawford, H. (1998). Applying outcomes. *Advance, 8*(35), 6–9.

Creaghead, N. A. (1992). *Classroom language intervention: Developing schema for school success.* Columbus, OH: Educom.

Creaghead, N. A. (1999). Evaluating language intervention approaches: Contrasting perspectives. *Language, Speech, and Hearing Services in Schools, 30,* 335–338.

Cronkite v. Long Beach Unified School District, State of California, 176 F.3d 482 (9th Cir. 1999).

Crowley, C., Agosto, N., & Castle, G. (2007). *Deviations from the norm: Cultural and linguistic biases in assessment materials.* Retrieved August 31, 2007, from http://www.nationalceu.com/crowley.pdf

Daniel R. R. v. State Board of Education, 874 F. 2d 1036 (5th Cir. 1989).

DeCurtis, L., Schryver-Stahly, K. A., & Ferrer, D. M. (2003, Fall). An introduction to theory of mind and its relationship to nonverbal and verbal communication. *CSHA Magazine, 33*(2), 13–15, 32.

Deno, E. (1970). The cascade of special education services. *Exceptional Children, 39,* 495.

Department of Education, 70 Fed. Reg. 35, 782 (June 21, 2005; to be codified at 34 C.F.R. pts. 300 and 304).

Deveres, L., & Pitasky, V. (1999a). *Student behavior: Intervention and prevention strategies that work.* Horsham, PA: LRP Publications.

Deveres, L., & Pitasky, V. (1999b). *Understanding student behavior: A guide to functional behavioral assessments.* Horsham, PA: LRP Publications.

Diehl, S. F. (2003, July). Prologue: Autism spectrum disorders: The context of speech-language pathologist intervention. *Language, Speech, and Hearing Services in Schools, 34*(3), 177–179.

#TP-29703 Making a Difference - 2nd Ed. • ©2008 Thinking Publications® • www.thinkingpublications.com • 1-800-277-8737

Dollaghan, C. (2004, April 13). Evidence-based practice: Myths and realities. *The ASHA Leader, 12*, 4–5.

Donahue, M. L., Syzmanski, C. M., & Flores, C.W. (1999). When Emily Dickinson met Steven Spielberg: Assessing social information processing in literacy contexts. *Language, Speech, and Hearing Services in Schools, 30*, 274–284.

Donahue-Kilburg, G. (1992). *Family-centered early intervention for communication disorders.* Gaithersburg, MD: Aspen.

Duchan, J. F. (1999). Views of facilitated communication: What's the point? *Language, Speech, and Hearing Services in Schools, 30,* 401–407.

DuFour, R., Dufour, R., Eaker, R., & Karhanek, G. (2004). *Whatever it takes: How professional learning communities respond when kids don't learn.* Bloomington, IN: Solution Tree.

Dunlap, G. (2005, March). Positive behavior support: An overview. *Perspectives on Language Learning and Education, ASHA Division 1, 16*(1), 3–6.

EdSource. (2007). *Similar English learner students, different results: Why do some schools do better?* Retrieved September 6, 2007, from http://www.edsource.org/pdf/ELlayreportfinal.pdf

Education for All Handicapped Children Act (EAHCA), 20 U.S.C. § 1400 *et seq.* (1975).

Education Amendments of 1974, 20 U.S.C. § 1703 (1974).

Education of the Handicapped Act (EHA), 20 U.S.C. § 1471 (1970).

Education of the Mentally Retarded Children Act, Pub. L. No. 85-926, § 2, 72 Stat. 1777 (1958).

Education Trust. (2005). *Gaining traction, gaining ground: How some high schools accelerate learning for struggling students.* Washington DC: Author. Retrieved September 5, 2007, from http://www2.edtrust.org/NR/rdonlyres/6226B581-83-C3-4447-9CE7-31C5694B9EF6/0/GainingTractionGainingGround.pdf

Education Trust. (2007). Education Trust Web site. Retrieved August 28, 2007, from http://www2.edtrust.org/edtrust/default

Educational Audiology Association (EAA). (1997). *Recommended professional practices for educational audiology* [Position statement]. Retrieved October 22, 2007, from http://eaa.affiniscape.com/index.cfm

Educational Audiology Association (EAA). (2002). Retrieved October 22, 2007, from http://eaa.affiniscape.com/index.cfm

Educational Audiology Association (EAA). (2006). *Advocacy for audiologists working in the schools* [Position statement]. Retrieved October 29, 2007, from http://eaa.affiniscape.com/associations/4846/files/AdvocacyPosStmt.pdf

Ehren, B. J. (2000). Maintaining a therapeutic focus and sharing responsibility for student success: Keys to in-classroom speech-language services. *Language, Speech, and Hearing Services in Schools, 31*, 219–229.

Ehren, B. (2007, March). External evidence in adolescent reading comprehension and intervention. *Perspectives on Language Learning and Education, ASHA Division 1.*

Ehren, B., Montgomery, J., Rudebusch, J., & Whitmire, K. (2006). *Responsiveness to intervention: New roles for speech-language pathologists.* Retrieved September 3, 2007, from http://www.asha.org/members/slp/schools/prof-consult/NewRolesSLP.htm

Elementary and Secondary Education Act (ESEA), 20 U.S.C. § 2701 *et seq.* (1965).

Elementary and Secondary Education Act (ESEA), *P.L. 93-380.* (1974).

Enderby, P., & Emerson, J. (1995). *Does speech and language therapy work?* London: Whurr.

Erickson, K., & Koppenhaver, D. (1995). Developing a literacy program for children with severe disabilities. *Reading Teacher, 48,* 676–684.

Evans, D., & Panacek-Howell, L. (1995). Restructuring education: National reform in regular education. In J. L. Paul, H. Rosselli, & D. Evans (Eds.), *Integrating school restructuring and special education reform* (pp. 30–42). Fort Worth, TX: Harcourt Brace.

Fagan, P., Friedman, H., & Fulfrost, H. (2007). *Ten most common IEP mistakes–And how to avoid them.* Presentation at the Special Education Symposium 2006–2007, Anaheim, CA.

Family Educational Rights and Privacy Act (FERPA), 20 U.S.C. § 1232g (1974).

Federal Funding Fact Sheet. (2005, October 14). Retrieved October 14, 2007, from http://www.asha.org/NR/rdonlyres/21AA45AD-D235-4FB4-85-F2-5E310ECDDDF9/0/Federal_Funding_Fact_Sheet.pdf

Federal Interagency Forum on Child and Family Statistics. (1999). *America's children: Key national indicators of well-being.* Washington, DC: U.S. Government Printing Office.

Federal Interagency Forum on Child and Family Statistics. (2007). *America's children: Key national indicators of well-being, 2007.* Retrieved September 3, 2007, from http://www.childstats.gov/americaschildren/edu5.asp

Ferguson, M. L. (1991). Collaborative consultative service delivery: An introduction. *Language, Speech, and Hearing Services in Schools, 22,* 147.

Ferguson, M. L. (1994–1995). Surviving the changing schools: A call for treatment efficacy research. *Tejas, XX*(2), 7–9.

Fey, M. (1999, Winter). Speech-language pathology and the early identification and prevention of reading disabilities. *Perspectives,* 13–17.

Fey, M. E. (1996, April). Cognitive referencing in the study of children with language impairments. *Language Learning and Education, 3,* 7–8.

Fisher, R., Ury, W., & Patton, B. (1991). *Getting to yes: Negotiating agreement without giving in* (2nd ed.). New York: Penguin.

Focus on Learners—All Learners: An Interview with ASCD President Dick Hanzelka. (2006, June). *Education Update, 48*(6).

Folkins, J. (1999, November). *The language used to describe individuals with disabilities.* Rockville, MD: American Speech-Language-Hearing Association. Retrieved February 3, 2001, from http://www.asha.org/publications/folkins.htm

Friedman, T. (2007). *The world is flat: A brief history of the twenty-first century.* New York, NY: Farrar, Straus and Giroux.

Friend, M., & Bursuck, W.D. (2002). *Including students with special needs: A practical guide for classroom teachers* (3rd ed.). Boston: Allyn and Bacon.

Fuchs, L. S., & Fuchs, D. (2006). Implementing responsiveness-to-intervention to identify learning disabilities. *Perspectives on Dyslexia, 32*(1), 39–43.

Fuchs, L. S., & Fuchs, D. (2007, May/June). A model for implementing responsiveness to intervention. *TEACHING Exceptional Children, 39*(5), 14–20.

Fulfrost, H. (2006). *Making general education special! The federal education revolution.* Presentation at the Special Education Symposium 2006–2007, Anaheim, CA.

Fullan, M. (2001). *Leading in a culture of change.* San Francisco, CA: Jossey-Bass.

Fullan, M. (2003). *The moral imperative of school leadership*. Thousand Oaks, CA: Corwin Press.

Fung, F., & Roseberry-McKibbin, C. (1999). Service delivery considerations in working with clients from Cantonese speaking backgrounds. *American Journal of Speech-Language Pathology, 8,* 309–318.

Gajewski, N., Hirn, P., & Mayo, P. (1998). *Social skill strategies*. Greenville, SC: Super Duper Publications.

Gallagher, T. (2007). *Using the ICF for evaluating language interventions*. Presentation at the International Association of Logopedics and Phoniatrics, Copenhagen, Denmark.

Gamm, S. (2007). *Disproportionality in special education: Where and why overidentification of minority students occurs*. Horsham, PA: LRP Publications.

Gerber, M. M., & Durgunoglu, A. Y. (Eds.). (2004). Reading risk and intervention for young English learners. Introduction to special issue. *Learning Disabilities Research & Practice, 19,* 199–201.

German, D. (1992). Word-finding intervention for children and adolescents. *Topics in Language Disorders, 13*(1), 33–50.

Gierut, J. A. (2001). Complexity in phonological treatment: Clinical factors. *Language, Speech, and Hearing Services in Schools, 32,* 229–241.

Gillam, R. B. (1999a). Computer-assisted language intervention using Fast ForWord: Theoretical and empirical considerations for clinical decision-making. *Language, Speech, and Hearing Services in Schools, 30,* 363–370.

Gillam, R. B. (1999b, May). Phonological awareness after the primary grades. *Language Learning and Education, 6*(1), 20–21.

Gillam, S. L., & Gillam, R. B. (2006). Making evidence-based decisions about child language intervention in schools. *Language, Speech, and Hearing Services in Schools, 37*(4), 304–315.

Gillon, G. T. (2000). The efficacy of phonological awareness intervention for children with spoken language impairment. *Language, Speech, and Hearing Services in Schools, 31,* 126–141.

Gilyard, K. (1999, March). *Student suspension and expulsion*. Presentation of the law firm of Atkinson, Andleson, Loya, Ruud, & Romo, Ontario, CA.

Glennen, S. (2000, January). *AAC: An historical perspective*. Presentation at the ASHA Division 12 Leadership in AAC Institute, Sea Island, GA.

Goldsworthy, C. L. (1996). *Developmental reading disabilities: A language-based treatment approach*. San Diego, CA: Singular.

Goldsworthy, C. L. (1998). *Sourcebook of phonological awareness activities*. San Diego, CA: Singular.

Goodlad, J. I. (1984). *A place called school*. New York: McGraw-Hill.

Gorn, S. (1997a). *The answer book on individualized education programs*. Horsham, PA: LRP Publications.

Gorn, S. (1997b). *The answer book on special education law* (2nd ed.). Horsham, PA: LRP Publications.

Goss v. Lopez, 419 U.S. 565 (1975).

Graham, S., & Harris, S. R. (1999). Assessment and intervention in overcoming writing difficulties: An illustration from the self regulated strategy development model. *Language, Speech, and Hearing Services in Schools, 30,* 255–264.

Graham, S., & Perin, D. (2007). *Writing next: Effective strategies to improve writing of adolescents in the middle and high schools: A report to Carnegie Corporation of New York*. Washington, DC: Alliance for Excellent Education. Retrieved August 28, 2007, from http://www.all4ed.org/publications/WritingNext/WritingNext.pdf

Gray, C. (2007). *Writing social stories* [Booklet]. Kentwood, MI: The Gray Center.

Gray, C., & White, A. L. (2002). *My social stories book*. New York, NY: Jessica Kingsley Publishers LTD.

Greenspan, S. I. (1992). *Infancy and early childhood: The practice of clinical assessment and intervention with emotional and developmental challenges*. Madison, CT: International Universities Press.

Greenspan, S. I., & Wieder, S. (1999). A functional developmental approach to autism spectrum disorders. *Journal of the Association for Persons with Severe Handicaps, 24,* 147–161.

Griffer, M. R. (1999). Is sensory integration effective for children with language-learning disorders?: A critical review of the evidence. *Language, Speech, and Hearing Services in Schools, 30,* 393–400.

Grimes, A. M. (1997). Audiology treatment outcomes. *CSHA Magazine, 26*(2), 10–11.

Gutierrez-Clellen, V. F. (1999). Language choice in intervention with bilingual children. *American Journal of Speech-Language Pathology, 8,* 291–302.

Gutierrez-Clellen, V. F., & Peña, E. (2001). Dynamic assessment of diverse children. *Language, Speech, and Hearing Services in Schools, 32,* 212–224.

Hall, T., & Mengel, M. (2002). *Curriculum-based evaluations*. Wakefield, MA: National Center on Accessing the General Curriculum. Retrieved September 4, 2007, from http://www.cast.org/publications/ncac/ncac_curriculumbe.html

Hall, T., Strangman, N., & Meyer, A. (2003). *Differentiated instruction and implications for UDL implementation*. Wakefield, MA: National Center on Accessing the General Curriculum. Retrieved September 3, 2007, from http://www.cast.org/publications/ncac/ncac_diffinstructudl.html

Handicapped Children's Protection Act/Attorneys' Fees Bill, 20 U.S.C. § 1400 P.L. 99-457. (1986).

Hanzelka, R. (2006, October). Harmonious learning for the whole child: Education perspectives from China. *Education Update, 48*(10).

Hardman, M. L., Drew, C. J., & Egan, M. W. (1999). *Human exceptionality: Society, school, and family* (6th ed.). Boston: Allyn and Bacon.

Hardman, M. L., Drew, C. J., & Egan, M. W. (2007). *Human exceptionality: Society, school, and family* (9th ed.). Boston: Allyn and Bacon.

Harris, D. M., & Evans, D. W. (1994). Integrating school restructuring and special education reform. *Case in Point, 8*(12), 7–19.

Harry, B., & Klinger, J. (2007). Discarding the deficit model. *Educational Leadership, 64*(5), 16–21.

Hart, B., & Risley, T. R. (1995). *Meaningful differences in the everyday experience of young American children*. Baltimore: Brookes.

Haynes, W. O., & Pindzola, R. H. (2004). *Diagnosis and evaluation in speech pathology* (6th ed.). Boston: Pearson Education.

Hedge, M. N., & Davis, D. (2005). *Clinical methods and practicum in speech-language pathology* (4th ed.). Clifton Park, NY: Thomson Delmar Learning.

Herer, G. R. (2007). Universal newborn screening. In *Choices in deafness: A parents' guide to communication options* (3rd ed.). S. Schwartz (Ed.). Bethesda, MD: Woodbine House.

Herer, G. R., Knightly, C. A., & Steinberg, A. G. (2007). Hearing: Sounds and silences. In M. L. Batshaw (Ed.), Children with disabilities. (6th ed.). Baltimore: Paul H. Brookes.

Herer, G. R., & Glattke, T. J. (2000, November 16). Making newborn hearing screening a reality. Presentation at the annual convention of the American Speech-Language-Hearing Association, Washington, DC.

#TP-29703 Making a Difference - 2nd Ed. · ©2008 Thinking Publications® · www.thinkingpublications.com · 1-800-277-8737

Hodgkinson, H. (2006). *The whole child in a fractured world*. Alexandria, VA: Association for Supervision and Curriculum Development. Retrieved August 31, 2007, from http://www.ascd.org/ASCD/pdf/fracturedworld.pdf

Homer, E. M. (2000). Dysphagia. In E. Pritchard Dodge (Ed.), *The survival guide for school-based speech-language pathologists* (pp. 399–421). San Diego, CA: Singular.

Homer, E. M., Bickerton, C., Hill, S., Parham, L., & Taylor, D. (2000). Development of an interdisciplinary dysphagia team in the public schools. *Language, Speech, and Hearing Services in Schools, 31,* 62–75.

Honig v. Doe, 484 U.S., 305 (1988).

Hoskins, B. (1990). Collaborative consultation: Designing the role of the speech-language pathologist in a new educational context. *Best Practices in School Speech-Language Pathology, 1,* 29–36.

Hoskins, B. (1995). *Developing inclusive schools*. Bloomington, IN: Indiana University, Smith Research Center.

Hoskins, B. (1996). *Conversations: A framework for language intervention*. Greenville, SC: Super Duper Publications.

How to address the shortage of speech and language pathologists. (1999). *The Special Educator, 14*(3), 1–10.

Hyerle, D., Alper, L, & Curtis, S. (Eds.). (2004). *Student success with thinking maps*. Thousand Oaks, CA: Corwin Press.

Idol-Maestas, L., Paolucci-Whitcomb, P., & Levin, A. (1986). *Collaborative consultation*. Austin, TX: Pro-Ed.

Illinois State Board of Education, Blackhawk Area Special Education District. (1993). *Speech language impairment: A technical assistance manual*. Springfield, IL: Author.

Indiana Speech-Language-Hearing Association (ISHA). (1997). *Indiana's overview of good practice in schools*. Noblesville, IN: Author.

Individuals with Disabilities Education Act (IDEA), 20 U.S.C. § 1400 *et seq.* (1990).

Individuals with Disabilities Education Act (IDEA) Amendments, 20 U.S.C. § 1400 *et seq.* (1997).

Individuals with Disabilities Education Act. (2004). Section 1412 [c][24]. Retrieved September 3, 2007, from http://idea.ed.gov

Individuals with Disabilities Education Improvement Act of 2004 (IDEA), 20 U.S.C. § 1400 *et seq.* (2004).

Interdisciplinary Council on Developmental and Learning Disorders (ICDL). (2000). *ICDL clinical practice guidelines: Redefining the standards of care for infants, children, and families with special needs*. Bethesda, MD: ICDL Press.

International Reading Association (IRA). (2002, May). *What is evidence-based reading instruction? A Position Statement*. Retrieved May 13, 2005, from http://www.reading.org/downloads/positions/ps1055_evidence_based.pdf

Issakson, C. (2000). Working through the complexities of cognitive referencing: Connecticut's eligibility criteria. *Language Learning and Education, 7*(1), 21–25.

Johnson, C. J., & Yeates, E. (2006). Evidence-Based vocabulary instruction for elementary students via storytelling reading. *EBP Briefs, 1*(3), 1-24. Retrieved October 24, 2007, from http://www.speechandlanguage.com/ebp/pdfs/1-3-oct-2006.pdf

Johnson, D. W., & Johnson, R. T. (1989). *Cooperation and competition: Theory and research*. Edina, MN: Interaction Books.

Johnson, W., Brown, S. F., Curtis, J. F., Edney, C. W., & Keaster, J. (1956). *Speech handicapped school children.* New York: Harper and Row.

Justice, L. & Skibbe, L. (2005). *Explicit literacy instruction during book reading: Impact on preschoolers with specific language impairment* [Manuscript in preparation]. Charlottesville, VA: University of Virginia.

Justice, L. (2007, March). Evidence based intervention approaches for three emergent literacy domains. *Perspectives on Language Learning and Education, ASHA Division 1.*

Justice, L. M. (2006a). Evidence-based practice, response to intervention, and the prevention of reading difficulties. *Language, Speech, and Hearing Services in Schools, 37*(4), 284–297.

Justice, L. M. (2006b). *Communication sciences and disorders: An introduction.* Upper Saddle River, NJ: Pearson Education.

Justice, L. M., & Fey, M. E. (2004, Sept. 21). Evidence-based practice in schools: Integrating craft and theory with science and data. *The ASHA Leader,* 4–5, 30–32.

Justice, L. M., & Kaderavek, J. (2002). Using shared storybook reading to promote emergent literacy. *Teaching Exceptional Children, 34*(4), 8–13.

Justice, L. M., & Pence, K. (2007). Parent-implemented interactive language intervention: Can it be used effectively? *EBP Briefs, 2*(1), 1–13.

Kagan, S. (1994). *Cooperative learning.* San Clemente, CA: Kagan.

Kamhi, A. (1991). Treatment efficacy: An introduction. *Language, Speech, and Hearing Services in Schools, 22,* 254.

Kamhi, A. G. (2006a). Prologue: Combining research and reason to make treatment decisions. *Language, Speech, and Hearing Services in Schools, 37*(4), 255–256.

Kamhi, A. G. (2006b). Treatment decisions for children with speech sound disorders. *Language, Speech, and Hearing Services in Schools, 37*(4), 271–279.

Kamil, M. (2003). *Adolescents and literacy: Reading for the 21st century.* Retrieved September 6, 2007, from http://www.all4ed.org/publications/ AdolescentsAndLiteracy.pdf

Kari H. v. Franklin Special School District, 23 IDELR 538 (6th Cir. 1995).

Kauffman, J. M., & Hallahan, D. P. (Eds.). (1995). *The illusion of full inclusion: A comprehensive critique of a current special education bandwagon.* Austin, TX: Pro-Ed.

Kavale, K., & Reese, B. (1992). The characteristics of learning disabilities: An Iowa profile. *Learning Disabilities Quarterly, 15*(2), 74–94.

Kendall, J. S., & Marzano, R.J. (1996). *Content knowledge: A compendium of standards and benchmarks for K–12 education.* Aurora, CO: Mid-Continent Regional Educational Laboratory.

Kent, R. D. (2006). Evidence-based practice in communication disorders: Progress not perfection. *Language, Speech, and Hearing Services in Schools, 37*(4), 268–270.

Kevin T. v. Elmhurst Community School District No. 205 (U.S. District Court for the No. District of Illinois, 2002).

Kist, W. (2000). Beginning to create the new literacy classroom: What does the new literacy look like? *Journal of Adolescent and Adult Literacy, 43,* 710–718.

Kliewer, C., & Landis, D. (1999). Individualizing literacy instruction for young children with moderate to severe disabilities. *Exceptional Children, 66*(1), 85–100.

KnowledgeWorks Foundation. (2007). *2006–2016 Map of future forces affecting education.* Retrieved October 24, 2007, from http://www.kwfdn.org/map/index.aspx

Koegel, L. K., & Vernon, T. (2005, March). Strategies to promote language acquisition and implications for learning. *Perspectives on Language Learning and Education, ASHA Division 1, 16*(1), 6–10.

Koegel, L. K., Koegel, R. L., Frea, W., & Green-Hopkins, I. (2003, July). Priming as a method of coordinating educational services for student with autism. *Language, Speech, and Hearing Services in Schools, 34*(3), 228–235.

Koegel, R. L., & Koegel, L. K. (2006). *Pivotal response treatments for autism: Communication, social, and academic development.* Baltimore, MD: Brooks Publishing.

Koegel, R. L., Schreibman, L., Good, A., Cerniglia, L., Murphy, C., & Koegel, L. (1989). *How to teach pivotal behaviors to children with autism: A training manual.* Santa Barbara, CA: University of California.

Kooper, R. (2005, May 3). Audiologists in schools: Helping students fulfill their potential. *The ASHA Leader,* 14–16.

Koppenhaver, D. A., & Yoder, D. E. (1993). Classroom literacy instruction for children with severe speech and physical impairments (SSPI): What is and what might be. *Topics in Language Disorders, 13*(2), 1–15.

Krassowski, E., & Plante, E. (1997). IQ variability in children with SLI: Implications for use of cognitive referencing in determining SLI. *Journal of Communication Disorders, 30*(1), 1–9.

Kubicek, F. C. (1994). Special education reform in light of select state and federal court decisions. *The Journal of Special Education, 28*(1), 27–42.

Kuhn, D. (2006). SPEEDY SPEECH: Efficient service delivery for articulation errors. *ASHA Perspectives on School Based Issues, Division 16, 7*(4), 11–14.

Kurjan, R. M. (2000). The role of the school-based speech-language pathologist serving preschool children with dysphagia: A personal perspective. *Language, Speech, and Hearing Services in Schools, 31*(1), 42–49.

Langdon, H. (1999). Collaborating with oral language interpreters and translators. *CSHA Magazine, 28*(2), 10–11.

Langdon, H. W. (2000). Diversity. In E. Pritchard Dodge (Ed.), *The survival guide for school-based speech-language pathologists,* 367–397. San Diego, CA: Singular.

Langdon, H. W., & Cheng, L.-R. L. (2002). *Collaborating with interpreters and translators.* Greenville, SC: Thinking Publications.

Larson, V. Lord, & McKinley, N. L. (1995a). Characteristics of adolescents' conversations: A longitudinal study. *Clinical Linguistics and Phonetics, 12,* 183–203.

Larson, V. Lord, & McKinley, N. L. (1995b). *Language disorders in older students: Preadolescents and adolescents.* Eau Claire, WI: Thinking Publications.

Larson, V. Lord, & McKinley, N. L. (2003). *Communication solutions for older students.* Greenville, SC: Thinking Publications.

Larson, V. Lord, McKinley, N. L., & Boley, D. (1993). Service delivery models for adolescents with language disorders. *Language, Speech, and Hearing Services in Schools, 24,* 36–42.

Learning Disabilities Association of America (LDA). (1993*). Inclusion: Position paper of the Learning Disabilities Association of America.* Retrieved January 30, 2001, from http://www.ldanatl.org/positions/inclusion.shtml

Lewis, M. (1984). Developmental principles and their implications for at-risk and handicapped infants. In M. Hanson (Ed.), *Atypical infant development*, 143–158. Baltimore: University Park Press.

Lidz, C. S. (1991). *Practitioner's guide to dynamic assessment*. New York: Guilford Press.

Lidz, C. S., & Peña, E. (1996). Dynamic assessment: The model, its relevance as a nonbiased approach, and its application to Latino American preschool children. *Language, Speech, and Hearing Services in Schools, 27*, 367.

Locke, J. L. (1997). A theory of neurolinguistic development. *Brain and Language, 58*, 265–326.

Lord, C., Bristol, M. M., & Scholper, E. (1993). Early interaction for children with autism and related developmental disabilities. In E. Schopler, M. Van Bourgondien, & M. Bristol (Eds.), *Preschool issues in autism* (pp. 111–129). New York: Plenum Press.

Losh, M. (2003). Narrative ability in autism: Strengths, weaknesses, and links to social understanding. *CSHA Magazine, 33*(2), 5–7, 24.

Lovaas, O. J. (1996). The UCLA young autism model of service delivery. In C. Maurice, G. Green, & S. Luce (Eds.), *Behavioral intervention for young children with autism* (pp. 241–348). Austin, TX: Pro-Ed.

Lucker, J. R. (2005, May 3). Finding the right fit: Educational audiology takes more than one counseling direction. *The ASHA Leader*, 18–19.

Luke, A., & Elkins, J. (2000a). Redefining adolescent literacies. *Journal of Adolescent and Adult Literacy, 43*, 212–215.

Luke, A., & Elkins, J. (2000b). Re/mediating adolescent literacies [Special themed issue]. *Journal of Adolescent and Adult Literacy, 43*, 396–398.

Lyon, G. R. (1998). *Overview of reading and literacy initiatives*. Testimony provided to the Committee on Labor and Human Resources, United States Senate. Bethesda, MD: National Institute of Child Health and Human Development.

Madell, J. R. (1999). Auditory integration training: One clinician's view. *Language, Speech, and Hearing Services in Schools, 30*, 371–377.

Maloney, M. H. (1997). *The seven deadly sins: Common mistakes that lead to due process hearings* [Video]. Horsham, PA: LRP Publications.

Maloney, M. H., & Pitasky, V. M. (1996). *The special educator 1996 desk book*. Horsham, PA: LRP Publications.

Manasevit, L. M., & Maginnis, A. M. (2005). *IDEA: New expectations for schools and students*. Tampa, FL: Thompson Publishing Group.

Mandlawitz, M. R. (2002). The impact of the legal system on educational programming for young children with autism spectrum disorder. *Journal of Autism and Developmental Disorders, 32*(5), 495–508.

Manthey, G. (2007). Modifying instruction so intervention isn't needed. *Leadership, 36*(4), 20.

Manzo, A. V., Manzo, U. C., & Thomas, M. A. (2006). Rationale for systematic vocabulary development: Antidote for state mandate. *Journal of Adolescent and Adult Literacy, 49*(7), 610–619.

Martin, E. W., Martin, R., & Terman, D. L. (1996). The legislative and litigation history of special education. *The Future of Children: Special Education for Students with Disabilities, 6*(1), 25–39.

Martin, J. (2006). *Making sense of LD eligibility under the 2006 IDEA regulations: New challenges and opportunities*. [Virtual seminar]. LRP Publications Audio Conference.

Marzano, R. J. (2000). 20th century advances in instruction. In R. S. Brandt (Ed.), *Education in a new era*, 67–95. Alexandria, VA: Association for Supervision and Curriculum Development.

#TP-29703 Making a Difference - 2nd Ed. · ©2008 Thinking Publications® · www.thinkingpublications.com · 1-800-277-8737

Marzano, R. J., & Pickering, D. J. (2005). *Building academic vocabulary: Teacher's manual.* Alexandria, VA: Association for Supervision and Curriculum Development.

Mastropieri, M. A., & Scruggs, T. E. (2000). *The inclusive classroom.* Upper Saddle River, NJ: Merrill.

Mauer, D. M. (1999). Issues and applications of sensory integration theory and treatment with children with language disorders. *Language, Speech, and Hearing Services in Schools, 30,* 383–392.

Maugh, T. H. (2000, May 4). Test identifies newborns likely to develop autism. *Los Angeles Times,* 4.

McCardle, P., Mele-McCarthy, J., Cutting, L., Leos, K., & D'Emilio. (2005, February). Learning disabilities in English Language Learners: Identifying the issues. *Learning Disabilities Research and Practice, 20*(1), 1–5.

McCook, J.E. (2006). *The RtI guide: Developing and implementing a model in your schools.* Horsham, PA: LRP Publications.

McREL. Copyright 2007. Reprinted with permission from *Content knowledge: A compendium of standards and benchmarks for K-12 education* (4th ed.). http://www.mcrel.org/standards-benchmarks/ All rights reserved.

McGinty, A.S., & Justice, L. (2006). Classroom-based versus pull-out interventions: An examination of the experimental evidence. *EBP Briefs, 1*(1), 1–13.

McGrew, K. S., & Evans, J. (2003). *Expectations for students with cognitive disabilities: Is the cup half empty or half full? Can the cup flow over?* (Synthesis Report 55). Minneapolis, MN: University of Minnesota, National Center on Educational Outcomes. Retrieved August 31, 2007, from http://education.umn.edu/NCEO/OnlinePubs/Synthesis55.html

McLaughlin, M. J., Pullin, D., & Artiles, A. (2001). Challenges for the transformation of special education in the 21st century: Rethinking culture in school reform. *Journal of Special Education Leadership, 14*(2), 51–62.

McWhirt by McWhirt v. Williamson County School, 23 IDELR 509 (6th Cir. 1994).

Menyuk, P. (1999). *Reading and linguistic development.* Cambridge, MA: Brookline Books.

Merced County Office of Education. (1998). *Speech and language eligibility criteria.* Merced, CA: Author.

Merritt, D. D., & Culatta, B. (1998). *Language intervention in the classroom.* San Diego, CA: Singular.

Michigan Speech-Language-Hearing Association (MSHA). (2006, December). *Michigan speech-language guidelines: Suggestions for eligibility, service delivery, and exit criteria. Revised.* Lansing, MI: Author. Retrieved October 16, 2007, from http://www.misd.net/SEConsult/Michigan%20SpeechLanguage%20Guidelines%20Revised%2012.06.pdf

Miller, J. F., Heilmann, J., Nockerts, A., Iglesias, A. Frabiano, L., & Francis, D. J. (2006). Oral language and reading in bilingual children. *Learning Disabilities Research & Practice, 2*(1), 30–43.

Miller, J. P. (2007, Summer). Whole teaching, whole schools, whole teachers. *Educational Leadership, 64* (Online only). Special Issue: Engaging the Whole Child (Online only). Retrieved August 28, 2007, from http://www.ascd.org/

Miller, L. (1989). Classroom based language intervention. *Language, Speech, and Hearing Services in Schools, 20,* 153–169.

Miller, L. (1999). *What we call smart: A new narrative for intelligence and learning.* San Diego, CA: Singular.

Mills v. D. C. Board of Education, 348 F. Supp. 866 (D.D.C. 1972).

Mills, W. D. (2005). *Response-to-intervention & instructional consultation teams: The SLP's role.* Seminar presented at the ASHA Convention. Slide no. 48, 98–102. San Diego, CA. Retrieved September 4, 2007, from http://convention. asha.org/2005/handouts/293_Mills_W.%20 David_072063_010906093936.ppt

Mire, S., & Montgomery, J. K. (in press). *Quik artic: An RTI approach to serving students with speech sound disorders.*

M. L. by C. D., & S. L. v. Federal Way School District, 341 F.3d 1052, 1061 (9 Cir. 15. th. 2003).

Moje, E. B., Young, J. P., Readence, J. E., & Moore, D. W. (2000). Reinventing adolescent literacy for new times: Perennial and millennial issues. *Journal of Adolescent and Adult Literacy, 43,* 400–409.

Montgomery, J. K. (1990). Building administrative support for collaboration. *Best Practices in School Speech-Language Pathology, 1*(1), 75–79.

Montgomery, J. K. (1992). Clinical forum: Implementing collaborative consultation: Perspectives from the field. *Language, Speech, and Hearing Services in Schools, 23,* 363–364.

Montgomery, J. K. (1993a). The law and the school professional. In R. J. Lowe (Ed.), *Speech-Language Pathology and Related Professions in the Schools* (pp. 67–85). Boston: Allyn and Bacon.

Montgomery, J. K. (1993b). Writing shared goals for special education services. *Curriculum and Instruction Update, Fountain Valley School District, 2*(1), 22–24.

Montgomery, J. K. (1994). Service delivery issues for schools. In R. Lubinski & C. Frattali (Eds.), *Professional issues in speech-language pathology and audiology,* 218–231. San Diego, CA: Singular.

Montgomery, J. K. (1997a). Inclusion in the secondary school. In L. Power-de-Fur & F. P. Orelove (Eds.), *Inclusive Education,* 181–192. Gaithersburg, MD: Aspen.

Montgomery, J. K. (1997b). Using functional outcomes in the schools. *CSHA Magazine, 26*(2), 7–8.

Montgomery, J. K. (1998). Reading and the SLP: Using discourse, narratives and expository text. *CSHA Magazine, 27*(3), 8–9.

Montgomery, J. K. (1999a). Accents and dialects: Creating a national professional statement. *Topics in Language Disorders, 19,* 78–89.

Montgomery, J. K. (1999b). Treatment outcomes and reimbursement: Aren't they related? *Communication Connection, Wisconsin Speech-Language-Hearing Association, 13*(1), 1–3.

Montgomery, J. K. (2000b, April). *Inclusive practices in the middle school.* Presentation at Hewes Middle School, Tustin Unified School District, Tustin, CA.

Montgomery, J. K. (2000, June). The Golden SLPA Project: *Training culturally competent speech-language pathology assistants in a community college* [Handout]. Presentation at 5th Biannual Head Start Research Conference, Washington, DC.

Montgomery, J. K. (2004). *Funnel toward phonics.* Greenville, SC: Super Duper Publications.

Montgomery, J. K. (2005, February/March). What SLPs might learn about EBP from reading research. *CSHA Magazine, 34*(3), 13.

Montgomery, J. K. (2007). *The bridge of vocabulary.* Bloomington, MN: Pearson/AGS.

Montgomery, J. K., & Bonderman, I. R. (1989). Serving preschool children with severe phonological disorders. *Language, Speech, and Hearing Services in Schools, 20,* 76–84.

Montgomery, J. K., & Hayes, L. L. (2005, Winter). Literacy transition strategies for upper elementary students with language-learning disabilities. *Communication Disorders Quarterly, 26*(2). 85–93.

Montgomery, J. K., & Kahn, N. (2005). *What's your story?* Greenville, SC: Super Duper Publications.

Montgomery, J. K., & Kahn, N. L. (2007). *Ten steps to writing better essays.* Greenville, SC: Super Duper Publications.

Montgomery, J. K., & Moore-Brown, B. J. (2005, May 4). *Response to intervention: An alternative to special education.* ASHA Telephone Seminar, Rockville, MD.

Montgomery, J. K., & Moore-Brown, B. J. (2006). *Response to intervention: An alternative to special education.* An Audio Seminar. Rockville, MD: American Speech-Language-Hearing Association.

Moore-Brown, B. (1992). Writing meaningful IEPs. *Clinically Speaking, 9*(2), 1–2.

Moore-Brown, B. (1998). *Individualized education programs and standards.* Unpublished doctoral dissertation, University of Southern California, Los Angeles.

Moore-Brown, B. (1999a, April). *Multicultural issues for the professions.* Presentation at the Fourth Annual Communication Disorders Multicultural Conference of the National Student Speech-Language-Hearing Association, Fullerton, CA.

Moore-Brown, B. (1999b, April). *President's address: Plenary session.* Presentation at the California Speech-Language-Hearing Association Annual State Conference, Pasadena, CA.

Moore-Brown, B. (1999c, July). *Skills and competencies needed by the school-based speech-language pathologist in the 21st century: Implications of educational trends.* Presentation at the American Speech-Language-Hearing Association Council on Professional Standards in Speech-Language Pathology and Audiology, Rockville, MD.

Moore-Brown, B. (2000, March). *Skills and competencies needed by the school-based speech-language pathologist in the 21st century: Implications of educational trends.* Presentation at the Speech-Language Pathologists of Area Education Agency 6, Marshalltown, IA.

Moore-Brown, B. (2004a, March). Becoming proficient in the lessons of No Child Left Behind. *Perspectives on School Based Issues, 5*(1), 7–10.

Moore-Brown, B. (2004b, July). *No Child Left Behind supplemental services: SLP possibilities.* Presentation at the Annual Schools Conference of the American Speech-Language-Hearing Association, Baltimore, MD.

Moore-Brown, B. (2005, February/March). How evidence-based practice is impacting school services. *CSHA Magazine, 34*(3), 14.

Moore-Brown, B. (2006). *Lessons from due process: Being prepared and legally defensible.* National CEU Online Seminar. Retrieved September 5, 2007, from http://www.nationalceu.com/Product.aspx?ProductID=11

Moore-Brown, B. (2007a, March). E-Ticket service delivery: Effective, efficient, economical and evidence-based. *Perspectives on School Based Issues, ASHA Division 16, 8*(1), 11–14.

Moore-Brown, B. (2007b, January 12). *Leading Administrative Response to RtI.* Presentation to the ACSA Special Education and Pupil Services Symposium. Monterey, CA.

Moore-Brown, B., Cooper, C., & Ferguson, M. (1998). When supervisor and supervisee disagree. *ASHA 40*(2), 56, 42.

Moore-Brown, B., Huerta, M., Uranga-Hernandez, Y., & Peña, E. (2006). Using dynamic assessment to evaluate children with suspected learning disabilities. *Intervention in School and Clinic, 41*(4), 209–217.

Moore-Brown, B., & Kreb, R. (2004, July). *How to avoid due process (and what to do if you can't)*. Presentation at the Annual Schools Conference of the American Speech-Language-Hearing Association, Baltimore, MD.

Moore-Brown B., Kreb, R., & Nishida, B. (2003, November). *How to avoid due process! But if you must...* Presentation at the Annual Convention of the American Speech-Language-Hearing Association, Chicago, IL.

Moore-Brown, B., Montgomery, J., Biehl, L., Karr, S., & Stein, M. (1998, November). *Accountability, outcomes and functional goals: Part II*. Presentation at the American Speech-Language-Hearing Association Annual Convention, San Antonio, TX.

Moore-Brown, B., Montgomery, J., Bielinski, J., & Shubin, J. (in press). Responsiveness to intervention: Teaching instead of testing avoids labels. *Topics in Language Disorders*. Hagerstown, MD: Williams and Wilkins.

Moore-Brown, B., & Nishida, B. (2002, Summer). To screen or not to screen....That is the question. *CSHA Magazine, 31*(4), 39–41. Also available online: http//:www.csha.org/Positionpapers/to_screen_or_not_to_screen.htm

Moore-Brown, B., Nishida, B., & Laverty-Reeves, R. (2003). *Best practices: Management of speech-language caseloads in California public schools*. Retrieved May 13, 2005, from http://www.csha.org/positionpapers

Moore-Brown, B., Powell, R., & Nishida, B. (2005, April). *Does anybody have an IDEA?* Presentation at the Annual Convention of the California Speech-Language-Hearing Association, Santa Clara, CA.

Moore-Brown, B., Robinson, T. L., Williams, R., Claussen, R., & Martinez, S. (1998). *Using speech-language pathology assistants in the schools: What's going on?* Presentation at the ASHA Teleseminar, Rockville, MD.

Moore-Brown, B. J., & Montgomery, J. K. (1999). Survey of Council of State Association Presidents. Unpublished raw data.

Moore-Brown, B. J., & Montgomery, J. K. (2001). *Making a difference for America's children: Speech-language pathologists in public schools*. Greenville, SC: Thinking Publications.

Moore-Brown, B. J., & Montgomery, J. K. (2005). *Making a difference in the era of accountability: Update on NCLB and IDEA 2004*. Greenville, SC: Thinking Publications.

Moore-Brown, B. J., & Montgomery, J. K. (2006, November 17). *SLPs and RtI: Your response will make a difference*. Presentation for the American Speech-Language-Hearing Association Annual Convention, Miami, FL.

Morrisette, M. L., & Gierut, J. A. (2002). Lexical organization and phonological change in treatment. *Journal of Speech, Language, and Hearing Research, 45*, 143–159.

Mulkerne, S. M. (1992). Emerging at-risk populations: Implication for special education reform. *Preventing School Failure, 36*(4), 20–23.

Mullen, R. (2000). Data report available for K–6 schools component of NOMS. *ASHA Special Interest Division 16* [Newsletter], *1*(3), 18.

Myers, R., & Sobehart, H. (1995). Creating a unified system—The road less traveled. *Case in Point, 9*(1), 1–9.

National Association of State Boards of Education (NASBE). (1999). *NASBE state profiles*. Retrieved January 30, 2001, from http://www.nasbe.org/ed-profiles.html

National Association of State Boards of Education (NASBE). (2002, July). *Special education funding. Policy Update, 10(12)*. Retrieved October 24, 2007, from http://www.nasbe.org/new_resources_section/policy_updates/PU_Special_Ed_Funding_07.02.pdf

#TP-29703 Making a Difference - 2nd Ed. · ©2008 Thinking Publications® · www.thinkingpublications.com · 1-800-277-8737

National Association of Year Round Education (NAYRE). (2001). Retrieved February 8, 2001, from http://www.nayre.org/about.html

National Association of Year Round Education (NAYRE). (2007). *Statistical summaries by state: 2006-2007*. Retrieved October 13, 2007, from http://www.nayre.org/

National Center on Educational Outcomes (NCEO). (1997). *High stakes testing for students: Unanswered questions and implications for students with disabilities.* Synthesis Report 26. Retrieved October 22, 2007, from http://cehd.umn.edu/NCEO/OnlinePubs/Synthesis26.htm

National Center for Learning Disabilities (NCLD). (1994). *Statement on inclusion.* New York: Author.

National Dissemination Center for Children with Disabilities (NICHCY). (2004, January). *Severe/multiple disabilities.* Disability fact sheet—No. 10. Retrieved September 1, 2007, from http://www.nichcy.org/pubs/factshe/fs10.pdf

National Education Association (NEA) & National Association of State Directors of Special Education (NASDSE). (2004, November). *The intersection of IDEA and NCLB.* Alexandria, VA: National Education Association.

National Governors Association (NGA). (n.d.). *Closing the achievement gap.* Retrieved September 4, 2007, from http://www.subnet.nga.org/educlear/achievement/index.html

National Institutes of Mental Health. (2007). *Autism spectrum disorders* (Pervasive developmental disorders). Retrieved October 14, 2007, from http://www.nimh.nih.gov/health/publications/autism/complete-publication.shtml#pub4

National Joint Committee for the Communication Needs of Persons with Severe Disabilities (1992). Guidelines for meeting the communication needs of persons with severe disabilities. *ASHA, 34* (Suppl. 7), 1–8. Retrieved August 29, 2007, from http://www.asha.org/NJC/njcguidelines.htm

National Joint Committee for the Communication Needs of Persons with Severe Disabilities. (2002). *Access to Communication Services and Supports: Concerns regarding the application of restrictive "eligibility" policies* [Technical report]. Retrieved August 29, 2007, from http://www.asha.org/docs/html/TR2002-00233.html

National Joint Committee on Learning Disabilities. (1991). Providing appropriate education for students with learning disabilities in regular education classrooms. *ASHA, 33* (Suppl. 5), 15–17.

National Joint Committee on Learning Disabilities (NJCLD). (2001). A reaction to full inclusion: A reaffirmation of the right of students with learning disabilities to a continuum of services. In NJCLD, *Collective perspectives on issues affecting learning disabilities: Position papers and statements*, 123–125. Austin, TX: Pro-Ed.

National Literacy Act of 1991, 20 U.S.C. § 1203 *et seq. (1991).*

National Literacy Panel. (2006). *Developing literacy in second-language learners: A report of the National Literacy Panel on language minority-children and youth.* Mahwah, NJ: Lawerence Erlbaum Associates.

National Reading Panel. (2000). *Teaching children to read: An evidence-based assessment of the scientific research literature on reading and its implications for reading instruction.* Washington, DC: U.S. Department of Health and Human Services.

National Reading Panel. (2006). Retrieved October 22, 2007, from http://www.nationalreadingpanel.org/default.htm

National Research Center on Learning Disabilities (2006). *Core concepts of RTI* [Website]. Retrieved October 16, 2007, from http://www.nrcld.org/research/rti/RTIinfo.pdf

National Research Council. (2001). Educating children with autism. Committee on Educational Interventions for Children with Autism. In Catherine Lord and James P. McGee, (Eds.), *Division of Behavioral and Social Sciences and Education*. Washington DC: National Academy Press.

National School Boards Association (NSBA). (n.d.). *Toolkit*. Retrieved September 4, 2007, from http://www.nsba.org/sbot/toolkit/edsctls.html

Neidecker, E. A. (1987). *School programs in speech-language: Organization and management* (2nd ed.). Englewood Cliffs, NJ: Prentice Hall.

Neidecker, E., & Blosser, J. (1993). *School programs in speech-language: Organization and management*. Needham, MA: Allyn and Bacon.

Nein v. Greater Clark County Sch. Corp, 95 F. Supp. 2d 961,977 (S.D. Ind. 2000).

Nelson, N. (1996, April). Discrepancy models and the discrepancy between policy and evidence: Are we asking the wrong questions? *Language Learning and Education, 3,* 3–5.

Nelson, N. (1999, February). *Building language and making connections: Opportunities of a computer supported writing lab*. Presentation at the 8th Annual Symposium on Disabilities and Literacy, Chapel Hill, NC.

Nelson, N., Cheng, L., Shulman, B., & Westby, C. (1994, November). Factors influencing speech language eligibility and service. *Language Learning and Education, 1,* 8–13.

Nelson, N. W. (1990). Only relevant practices can be best. *Best Practices in School Speech-Language Pathology, 1,* 15–28.

Nelson, N. W. (1992). Targets of curriculum-based language assessment. In W. Secord & J. Damico (Eds.), *Best practices in school speech-language pathology: Descriptive nonstandardized language assessment* (pp. 73–85). San Antonio, TX: Psychological Corporation.

Nelson, N. W., Bahr, C. M., & VanMeter, A. (2004). The Writing Lab Approach to Language Instruction and Intervention. Baltimore, MD: Brookes.

Nelson, N. W., & Hoskins, B. (1997). *Strategies for supporting classroom success* [Audiotape set]. San Diego, CA: Singular.

Neubert, D. A. (1997). Time to grow. *Teaching Exceptional Children, 29*(5), 5–17.

Neuman, S. B., Smagorinsky, P., Enciso, P. E., Baldwin, R. S., & Hartman, D. K. (2000). Snippets: What will be the influences on literacy in the next millennium? *Reading Research Quarterly, 35,* 276–282.

New Jersey Department of Education. (1999). *Parental rights in special education*. Retrieved January 30, 2001, from http://www.state .nj.us/njded/parights/prise_b_w.pdf

No Child Left Behind Act of 2001, 20 U.S.C., § 6311 *et seq.* (2002).

Nolet, V., & McLaughlin, M.J. (2000). *Accessing the general curriculum including students with disabilities in standards-based reform*. Thousand Oaks, CA: Corwin Press.

Norlin, J. W. (2005). *NCLB and IDEA '04: A side by side analysis*. Danvers, MA: LRP Publications.

North Carolina Department of Public Instruction, Division of Exceptional Children. (1985). *North Carolina public school guidelines for speech-language programs*. Raleigh, NC: Author.

North Carolina State Board of Education (2000) *Procedures governing programs and services for children with disabilities* [Microsoft Word format]. Raleigh, NC: Author. Retrieved January 29, 2001, from http://www.ncpublicschools.org/ec/policy/policies/procedures

North Central Regional Educational Laboratory (NCREL) and the Metiri Group. (2003). *enGauge 21st* century skills. Retrieved October 15, 2007, from http://www.ncrel.org/engauge/skills/engauge 21st.pdf

Nye, C., & Montgomery, J. K. (1989). Identification criteria for language disordered children: A national survey. *Hearsay, 4,* 26–33.

Nye, C., Schwartz, J., & Turner, H. M. (2005, February/March). Evidence-based practice for treating communication disorders: What helps? What harms? Based on what evidence? *CSHA Magazine, 34*(3), 6–10.

Oberti v. Board of Education of Borough of Clementon School District, 995 F. 2d 1204 (3d Cir. 1993).

O'Connell, P. F. (1997). *Speech, language, and hearing programs in schools: A guide for students and practitioners.* Gaithersburg, MD: Aspen Publications.

O'Donnell, D. G. (1999). *A guide for understanding and developing IEPs.* Madison, WI: Wisconsin Department of Public Instruction.

Office for Civil Rights (OCR). (1999). *Section 504 and education.* Retrieved January 30, 2001, from http://www.ed.gov/offices/OCR/regs/34cfr104.html

Office of Special Education Programs (OSEP). (2000). *Twenty-five years of progress in educating children with disabilities through IDEA.* Retrieved October 16, 2007, from http://www.ed.gov/policy/speced/leg/idea/history.pdf

Office of Special Education Programs (OSEP). (2004). *Data analysis system (DANS), OMB #1820-0517: Part B,* Individuals with Disabilities Education Act, *Implementation of FAPE requirements.* Data updated as of July 31, 2004. Also table 2-2 in vol. 2 of this report. Retrieved October 10, 2007, from http://www.ed.gov/about/reports/annual/osep/2005/parts-b-c/27th-vol-1.pdf

Office of Special Education Programs (OSEP). (2005). *Alignment with the No Child Left Behind Act.* Retrieved September 3, 2007, from http://www.ed.gov/about/offices/list/osers/index.html

Office of Special Education Programs (OSEP). (2006, April). *Including students with disabilities in large–scale assessment.* Retrieved October 16, 2007, from http://nichcy.org/toolkit/tk_lrgAssmnt_ES.htm

Office of Special Education Programs (OSEP). (n.d.). *IDEA dispute resolution processes comparison chart.* Retrieved October 15, 2007, from http://www.directionservice.org/pdf/IDEA%20DR%20Process%20Comparison%20Chart.pdf

Office of Special Education and Rehabilitative Services (OSERS). (1999, March). *IDEA '97.* Retrieved January 30, 2001, from http://www.ed.gov/offices/OSERS/IDEA/IDEA.pdf

Ohanian, S. (2000). Goals 2000: What's in a name? *Phi Delta Kappan, 81,* 344–355.

Ohio Department of Education. (1991). *Ohio handbook for identification, evaluation, and placement of children with language problems.* Columbus, OH: Author.

Orkwis, R., & McLane, K. (1998). *A curriculum every student can use: Design principles for student access* (ERIC/OSEP Topical Brief). Reston, VA: Council for Exceptional Children.

Ortiz, A. A., & Garcia, S. B. (1988). A prereferral process for preventing inappropriate referrals of Hispanic students to special education. In A. Ortiz & B. A. Ramirez (Eds.), *Schools and the culturally diverse exceptional student: Promising practices and future directions,* pp. 27–31. Reston, VA: Council for Exceptional Children.

Ortiz, A. A., & Yates, J. R. (2001). A framework for serving English language learners with disabilities. *Journal of Special Education Leadership, 14*(2), 72–80.

Ortiz, A. A., & Yates, J. R. (2002). Considerations in the assessment of English language learners referred to special education. In A. J. Artiles, & A. A. Ortiz (Eds). *English Language Learners with Special Education Needs.* Washington DC: Center for Applied Linguistics.

O'Shea, D., & O'Shea, L. J. (1997). Collaboration and school reform: A twenty-first-century perspective. *Journal of Learning Disabilities, 30,* 449–462.

O'Toole, T. J. (2000). Legal, ethical, and financial aspects of providing services to children with swallowing disorders in the public schools. *Language, Speech, and Hearing Services in Schools, 31,* 56–61.

Palacio, M. (2000). Distinct, not deficient: Structured teaching for children with autism. *Advance, 10*(1), 8–9.

PARC v. Pennsylvania, 334 F.Supp. 1257 (E.D. PA 1972).

Parent Advocacy Coalition for Educational Rights (PACER) Center. (1989). *It's the "person first"—Then the disability.* (Document PHP-c31). Minneapolis, MN: Author.

Parrish, T., Harr, J. Wolman, J. Anthony, J, Merickel, A., & Esra, P. (2004, March). *State special education finance systems, 1999–2000. Part II: Special education revenues and expenditures.* Palo Alto, CA: Center for Special Education Finance (CSEF). Retrieved September 4, 2007, from http://www.csef-air.org/publications/csef/state/statepart2.pdf

Paul-Brown, D., & Caperton, C. J. (2002). Treatment settings and service delivery models for children with communication disorders in the context of early childhood inclusion. In M. J. Guralnick (Ed.), *Early childhood inclusion: Focus on change.* Baltimore: Brookes.

Paul-Brown, D., & Goldberg, L. (2001). Current policies and new directions for speech-language pathology assistants. *Language, Speech, and Hearing Services in Schools, 32,* 4–17.

Paul, R. (2001). *Language disorders from infancy through adolescence: Assessment and intervention* (2nd ed.). St. Louis, MO: Mosby.

Paul, R. (2003, October). Asperger syndrome: The role of speech-language pathologists in schools. *Perspectives on Language Learning and Education, ASHA Division 1, 10*(3), 9–15.

Paul, R. & Sutherland, D. (2003, October). Asperger Syndrome: The role of speech-language pathologists in schools. *Perspectives on Language Learning and Education, ASHA Division 1, 10*(3), 9-15.

Peña, E. (1996). Dynamic assessment: The model and its language applications. In K. N. Cole, P. S. Dale, & D. J. Thal (Eds.), *Assessment of Communication and Language,* 281–307. Baltimore: Brookes.

Peña, E. (2000). Measurement of modifiability in children from culturally linguistically diverse backgrounds. *Communication Disorders Quarterly, 21*(3), 87–97.

Peña, E., & Gillam, R. (2000). Dynamic assessment of children referred for speech and language evaluations. In C. S. Lidz (Ed.), *Dynamic assessment: Prevailing models and applications.* New York: JAI.

Peña, E., Miller, L., & Gillam, R. (1999). Dynamic assessment of narrative ability. *CSHA Magazine, 28*(2), 12–18.

Peña, E., & Quinn, R. (2003). Developing effective collaboration teams in Speech Language Pathology—A Case Study. *Communication Disorders Quarterly, 24*(2), 53–63.

Peña, E., Quinn, R., & Iglesias, A. (1992). The application of dynamic methods to language assessment: A nonbiased procedure. *The Journal of Special Education, 26,* 269–280.

Pennsylvania Association for Retarded Citizens (PARC) v. Commonwealth of Pennsylvania, 334 F. Supp. 1257, 343 F. Supp. 279 (E.D.Pa. 1971).

Pennsylvania Department of Education (1999). EISC—Interpreting the educational imperative. Retrieved May 15, 2004, from http://www.pde.psu.edu/bbpages_reference/40005/40005100.html

Peters-Johnson, C. (1998). Action: School services, survey of speech-language pathology services in school-based settings national study final report. *Language, Speech, and Hearing Services in Schools, 29,* 120–126.

Pickett, J. P. (2000). In *The American Heritage Dictionary* (4th ed.), 553. Boston: Houghton Mifflin.

Picus, L. O., & Wattenbarger, J. L. (1996). *Where does the money go? Resource allocation in elementary and secondary schools.* Thousand Oaks, CA: Corwin Press.

Polmanteer, K., & Turbiville, V. (2000). Family responsive individualized family service plans for speech-language pathologists. *Language, Speech, and Hearing Services in Schools, 31*(1), 4–14.

Poolaw v. Bishop, 67 F. 3d 830 (9th Cir. 1995).

Power-deFur, L. (2004, March). No Child Left Behind: State-to-state variability. *Perspectives on School Based Issues, 5*(1), 10–12.

Power-deFur, L., & Orelove, F. P. (Eds.). (1997). *Inclusive education: Practical implementation of the least restrictive environment.* Gaithersburg, MD: Aspen.

Prelock, P. A. (2000, July). An intervention focus for inclusionary practice. *Language, Speech, and Hearing Services in Schools, 31,* 296–298.

Prelock, P.A. (2000). Multiple perspectives for determining the roles of speech-language pathologists in inclusionary classrooms. *Language, Speech, and Hearing Services in Schools, 31,* 213–218.

Prelock, P. A. (2001). *Understanding autism spectrum disorders: The role of speech-language pathologists and audiologists in service delivery.* Retrieved October 13, 2007, from http://www.asha.org/about/publications/leader-online/archives/2001/understanding_ASD.htm

Prelock, P. A., Beatson, J., Bitner, B. Broder, C., & Ducker, A. (2003, July). Interdisciplinary assessment of young children with autism spectrum disorder. *Language, Speech, and Hearing Services in Schools, 34,* 194–202.

Preschool Amendments to the Education of the Handicapped Act 20 U.S.C. § 1471 *et seq.* (1986).

President's Commission on Excellence in Special Education. (2002, July). *A new era: Revitalizing special education for children and their families.* Retrieved June 2, 2005, from http://www.ed.gov/inits/commissionsboards/whspecialeducation/index.html

President's Remarks at the Signing of H.R. 1350. (2004). Retrieved September 3, 2007, from http://www.whitehouse.gov/news/releases/2004/12/20041203-6.html

Price, B. J., Mayfield, P. K., McFadden, A. C., & Marsh, G. E. (2000). *Collaborative teaching: Special education for inclusive classrooms.* Retrieved January 30, 2001, from http://www.parrotpublishing.com/

Pritchard Dodge, E. (1994). *Communication lab.* East Moline, IL: LinguiSystems.

Pritchard Dodge, E. (Ed.). (2000). *The survival guide for school-based speech-language pathologists.* San Diego, CA: Singular.

Putnam, J. W., Spiegel, A. N., & Bruininks, R. H. (1995). Future directions in education and inclusion of students with disabilities: A Delphi investigation. *Exceptional Children, 61,* 553–577.

Quinn, R., Goldstein, B., & Peña, E. D. (1996). Cultural linguistic variation in the United States and its implications for assessment and intervention in speech-language pathology: An introduction. *Language, Speech, and Hearing Services in Schools, 27,* 345–346.

R. R. v. Wallingford Board of Education, 35 IDELR 32 (D. Conn. 2001).

Raber, S., Roach, V., & Fraser, K. (Eds.). (1998). *The push and pull of standards-based reform.* Alexandria, VA: Center for Policy Research on the Impact of General and Special Education Reform.

Raskind, M. (2000). Assistive technology for children with learning difficulties [Booklet]. San Mateo, CA: Schwab Foundation for Learning.

Rehabilitation Act of 1973. Section 504. 29 U.S.C. § 794. (1973).

Rehabilitation Act Amendments of 1992, Pub. L. No. 102–569, § 508, 106 Stat. 4430 (1992). P. L.

Retherford, K. S. (1996). Normal communication acquisition: An animated database of behaviors [Computer software]. Eau Claire, WI: Thinking Publications.

Ripich, D. N., & Creaghead, N. A. (1994). *School discourse problems* (2nd ed.). San Diego, CA: Singular.

Ritzman, M. J., Sanger, D., & Coufal, K. (2006, November). *Revisiting collaboration and inclusion: A qualitative case study.* Miami, FL: American Speech-Language-Hearing Association.

Robelen, E. W. (2005, April 13). 40 years after ESEA, federal role in schools is broader than ever. *Education Week, 24*(31), 1, 42.

Rogers, D. (2005). *An introduction to curriculum based measurement/curriculum based assessment.* Retrieved August 30, 2007, from http://www.specialconnections.ku.edu/cgi-bin/cgiwrap/specconn/main.php?cat=assessment&section=cbm/main

Romski, M. A., & Sevcik, R. A. (1996). *Breaking the speech barrier: Language development through augmented means.* Baltimore: Brookes.

Rooney-Moreau, M. R., & Fidrych H. (1998). *Theme-Maker.* Easthampton, MA: Discourse Skills Productions.

Rooney-Moreau, M. R., & Fidrych-Puzzo, H. (1994). *The story grammar marker.* Easthampton, MA: Discourse Skills Productions.

Roseberry-McKibbin, C. (1999). Service delivery to Asian-American families: Principles and practices. *CSHA Magazine, 28*(2), 17–18.

Roseberry-McKibbin, C. (2007*). Language disorders in children: A multicultural and case perspective.* Boston: Allyn and Bacon.

Roseberry-McKibbin, C. (2008a). *Increasing language skills of students from low-income backgrounds: Practical strategies for professionals.* San Diego: Plural Publishing.

Roseberry-McKibbin, C. (2008b). *Multicultural students with special language needs: Practical strategies for assessment and intervention* (3rd ed.). Oceanside, CA: Academic Communication Associates.

Roseberry-McKibbin, C., & Brice, A. (n.d.). *Acquiring English as a second language: What's normal; what's not.* Retrieved October 23, 2007, from http://www.asha.org/public/speech/development/easl.htm

Roseberry-McKibbin, C., & Eicholtz, G. E. (1994). Serving children with limited English proficiency in the schools: A national survey. *Language, Speech, and Hearing Services in Schools, 25,* 156–164.

Rosenbek, J. C. (1984). Treating the dysarthric talker. *Seminars in Speech and Language, 5*(4), 359–384.

Rosenfield, S. A., & Gravois, T. A. (1996). Instructional consultation teams. New York, NY: The Guildford Press.

Rosetti, L. M. (1993). Enhancing early intervention services to infants and toddlers and their families. *Journal of Childhood Communication Disorders, 15*(2), 1–6.

Roth, F. P., & Worthington, C. K. (2000). *Treatment resource manual for speech-language pathology* (2nd ed.). San Diego, CA: Singular Thomson Press.

Sackett, D. L., Rosenberg, W. M. C., Gray, J. A. M., Haynes, R. B., & Richardson, W. S. (1996). *Evidence-based medicine: What it is and what it isn't. Article based on an editorial in the British Medical Journal, 312,* 71–72. Retrieved October 14, 2007, from http://www.cebm.jr2.ox.ac.uk/ebmisisnt

Sacramento City Unified School District v. Rachel H., 14 F. 3d 1398 (9th Cir. 1994).

Sailor, W. (1991). Special education in the restructured school. *Remedial and Special Education, 12*(6), 8–22.

Sailor, W., & Skrtic, T. (1995). Modern and postmodern agendas in special education: Implications for teacher education, research, and policy development. In J. L. Paul, H. Rosselli, & D. Evans (Eds.), *Integrating school restructuring and special education reform* (pp. 418–432). Fort Worth, TX: Harcourt Brace.

Salvia, J., & Ysseldyke, J. (2004). Assessment in special and inclusive education (9th ed.). Boston, MA: Houghton Mifflin.

Sanders, M. (2001). *Understanding dyslexia and the reading process: A guide for educators and parents.* Boston: Allyn and Bacon.

Sanger, D., & Moore-Brown, B. (2000, November). *Advancing the discussion on communication and violence.* Presentation at the annual convention of the American Speech-Language-Hearing Association, Washington, DC.

Sanger, D., Moore-Brown, B., & Alt, E. (2000). Advancing the discussion on communication and violence. *Communication Disorders Quarterly, 22*(1), 43–48.

Santa, C. M. (2006). A vision for adolescent literacy: Ours or theirs. *Journal of Adolescent & Adult Literacy, 49*(6), 466–476.

Scherer, M. (2007). Why focus on the whole child? *Educational Leadership, 64*(8), 7.

Schnaiberg, L. (1996, January 17). *Oberti and the law.* Retrieved January 30, 2001, from http://www.edweek.org/ew/1996 /17law.h15

Schraeder, T., Quinn, M., Stockman, I. J., & Miller, J. (1999). Authentic assessment as an approach to preschool speech language screening. *American Journal of Speech-Language Pathology, 8,* 195–200.

Schreibman, L., Koegel, R. L., Charlop, M. H., & Egel, A. L. (1990). Infantile autism. In A. S. Bellack, M. Hersen, & A. E. Kaxdin (Eds.), *International handbook of behavior modification and therapy* (pp. 763–789). New York: Plenum Press.

Schwartz, J., & Nye, C. (2006). Teaching sign language to children with autism. *EBP Briefs, 1*(1). Retrieved September 3, 2007, from http://www.speechandlanguage.com/ebp/

Scott, J., Clark, C., & Brady, M. (2000). *Students with autism.* San Diego, CA: Singular.

Seal, B. C. (1997). Educating students who are deaf and hard of hearing. In L. A. Power-deFur & F. P. Orelove (Eds.), *Inclusive Education: Practical implementation of the least restrictive environment* (pp. 259–271). Gaithersburg, MD: Aspen.

Secord, W. A. (1998, Summer). *Assessment materials.* Presentation at the summer schools conferences on "Achieving Successful Outcomes in Schools" of the American Speech-Language-Hearing Association, Washington, DC.

Secord, W. A. (1999). *School consultation: Concepts, models, and procedures.* Flagstaff, AZ: Northern Arizona University.

Secord, W. A., & Damico, J. S. (1998, Summer). *Let's get practical: 49 ways to work with teachers in the classroom.* Presentation at the summer schools conferences on "Achieving Successful Outcomes in Schools" of the American Speech-Language-Hearing Association, Washington, DC.

Seymour, H. N., Bland-Stewart, L., & Green, L. (1998). Difference versus deficit in child African-American English. *Language, Speech, and Hearing Services in Schools, 29,* 96–108.

Shepard, K. G. (2006). Supporting all students: The role of school principals in expanding general education capacity using response to intervention teams. *Journal of Special Education Leadership, 19*(2), 30–38.

Shipley, K. G., & McAfee, J. G. (2004). *Assessment in speech-language pathology: A resource manual.* (3rd ed.). Clifton Park, NY: Thomson Delmar Learning.

Short, D. J., & Fitzsimmons, S. (2007*). Double the work: Challenges and solutions to acquiring language and academic literacy for adolescent English language learners–A report to the Carnegie Corporation of New York.* Washington, DC: Alliance for Excellent Education. Retrieved August 29, 2007, from http://www.all4ed.org/publications/DoubleWork/DoubleWork.pdf

Shorter, T. N. (2004). *Understanding HIPAA: A guide to school district privacy obligations.* Horsham, PA: LRP Publications.

Siegel, L. M. (1999). *The complete IEP guide: How to advocate for your special ed child.* Berkeley, CA: Nolo.com.

Silliman, E., & Scott, C. (2006a). Language impairment and reading disability: Connections and complexities – Introduction to the special issue. *Learning Disabilities Research & Practice, 21,*1–7.

Silliman, E., & Scott, C. (2006b). Language basis of literacy: Emerging evidence from second language learning and language impairment. *Learning Disabilities Research and Practice* (Issue Editors), *21.*

Silliman, E. R., Diehl, S. F., Huntley Bahr, R., Hnath-Chisolm, T., Bouchard Zenko, C., & Friedman, S. A. (2003, July). A new look at performance on theory-of-mind tasks by adolescents with autism spectrum disorders. *Language, Speech, and Hearing Services in Schools, 34*(3), 236–252.

Simmons, D. C., & Kame'enui, E. J. (1998). *What reading research tells us about children with diverse learning needs: Bases and basics.* Mahwah, NJ: Lawrence Erlbaum Association.

Singer, B. D., & Bashir, A. S. (1999). What are executive functions and self-regulation and what do they have to do with language learning disorders? *Language, Speech, and Hearing Services in Schools, 30,* 265–273.

Skrtic, T. M. (1991) The special education paradox: Equity as the way to excellence. *Harvard Educational Review, 61,* 148–206.

Slavin, R. E. (1990). *Cooperative learning: Theory, research, and practice.* Englewood Cliffs, NJ: Prentice Hall.

Smith Lang, J. (2000, May/June). Newborn infant hearing screening: A shift to prevention in dealing with hearing loss in children. *CSHA Magazine, 28*(7), 8–10.

Smith Lang, J. (2005, Feb/March). How evidence from newborn hearing screening is affecting early intervention for hearing loss. *CSHA Magazine, 34*(3), 18.

Snow, C. E., & Biancarosa, G. (2003a). *Adolescent literacy and the achievement gap.* New York: Carnegie Corporation of New York.

Snow, C. E., & Biancarosa, G. (2003b). *Adolescent literacy and the achievement gap: What do we know and where do we go from here?* Carnegie Corporation of New York. Adolescent Literacy Funders Meeting Report. Retrieved September 5, 2007, from http://www.all4ed.org/resources/Carnegie-AdolescentLiteracyReport.pdf

Snow, C. E., Burns, M. S., & Griffin, P. (Eds.). (1998). *Preventing reading difficulties in young children.* Washington, DC: National Academy Press.

Spahr, J. C. (1996, August). Outcome data prove value of SLP services. *ASHA Leader, 1,* 1–2.

Sparks, S. N., Clark, M. J., Erickson, R. L., & Oas, D. B. (1990). *The professional's role in the home or center: Infants at risk for communication disorders.* Tucson, AZ: Communication Skill Builders.

Stainback, W., & Stainback, S. (Eds.). (1996). *Controversial issues confronting special education: Divergent perspectives* (2nd ed.). Boston: Allyn and Bacon.

Stecker, P. M. (2007*). Monitoring student progress in individualized educational programs using curriculum-based measurement.* Retrieved September 31, 2007, from http://www.studentprogress.org/library/monitoring_student_progress_in_individualized_educational_programs_using_cbm.pdf

Stewart, S., Gonzalez, L. S., & Page, J. L. (1997). Incidental learning of sight words during articulation training. *Language, Speech, and Hearing Services in Schools, 28,* 115–126.

Stone, C. A., Silliman, E. R., Ehren, B. J., & Apel, K. (2004). *Handbook of language and literacy: Development and disorders.* New York, NY: Guilford Press.

Strong, C. J., & Hoggan North, K. (1996). *The magic of stories.* Greenville, SC: Super Duper Publications.

Strulovitch, J., & Tagalakis, V. (2003, October). Social skills groups for adolescents with Asperger syndrome. *Perspectives on Language Learning and Education, ASHA Division 1, 10*(3), 20–22.

Study of Personnel Needs in Special Education (SPeNSE). (2002). Key findings. Retrieved October 29, 2007, from http://ferdig.coe.ufl.edu/spense/KeyFindings.pdf

Taps, J. (2006, December). An innovative educational approach for addressing articulation differences. *ASHA Perspectives on School Based Issues, Division 16, 7*(4), 7–11.

TASH, (2000, March). *TASH resolution on inclusive education.* Retrieved January 30, 2001, from http://www.tash.org/IRR/resolutions/res02inclusiveed.htm

Technology counts '99: Building the digital curriculum. (1999). *Education Week, XIX,* 19.

Texas Speech-Language-Hearing Association (TSHA). (n.d.). *Linguistically diverse populations: Considerations and resources for assessment and intervention.* Retrieved August 28, 2007, from http://www.txsha.org/Diversity_Issues/cld_document.asp

Tharpe, A. M. (1999). Auditory integration training: The magical mystery cure. *Language, Speech, and Hearing Services in Schools, 30,* 378–382.

Thomason, K. M., Gorman, B. K., and Summers, C. (2007). English literacy development for English language learners: Does Spanish instruction promote or hinder? *EBP Briefs, 2*(2), 1–15.

Thordardottir, E. (2006, August 15). Language intervention from a bilingual mind. *ASHA Leader,* 6–7, 20–21.

Threats, T. (2000, September). The World Health Organization's revised classification: What does it mean for speech-language pathology? *Journal of Medical Speech Language Pathology, 8*(3), xiii–xviii.

Throneburg, R. N., Calvert, L. K., Sturm, J. J., Paramboukas, A. A., & Paul, P. J. (2000). A comparison of service delivery models: Effects on curricular vocabulary skills in the school setting. *American Journal of Speech-Language Pathology, 9*(1), 10–20.

Thurlow, M., Barrera, M., & Zamora-Duran, G. (2006, April). School leaders taking responsibility for English language learners with disabilities. *Journal of Special Education Leadership, 19*(1), 3–10.

Thurlow, M., & Liu, K. K. (2001, November). Can "all" really mean students with disabilities who have limited English proficiency? *Journal of Special Education Leadership, 14*(2), 63–71.

Thurlow, M. L., & Thompson, S. J. (1999). District and state standards and assessments: Building an inclusive accountability system. *Journal of Special Education Leadership, 12*(2), 3–10.

Tierney, R. J., Johnston, P., Moore, D. W., & Valencia, S. W. (2000). Snippets: How will literacy be assessed in the next millennium? *Reading Research Quarterly, 35,* 244–250.

Tilly, W. D. (2003, December). *Heartland area education agency's evolution from four to three tiers: Our journey, our results.* Paper presented at the National Research Center on Learning Disabilities Responsiveness-to-Intervention Symposium, Kansas City, MO.

Tomlinson, C. A., & McTighe, J. (2006). *Integrating differentiating instruction & understanding by design.* Alexandria, VA: Association for Supervision and Curriculum Development.

Toner, M., & Helmer, D. (2006). *Language and learning in school-age children and adolescents: When language is normal but reading isn't: Possible solutions.* Poster Board Presentation at 2006 ASHA Convention, Miami Beach, FL.

Torgeson, J. K. (1998). Catch them before they fall: Identification and assessment to prevent reading failure in young children. *American Educator, 22*(1–2), 32–39.

Torgeson, J.K. (2001). Preventing Early Reading Failure. American Educator, AFT.

Tosh Cowan, K., & Edwards, C. J. (2004). *The new Title I: The changing landscape of accountability.* Washington DC: Thomson.

Trioa, G. (2005). Responsiveness to intervention: Roles of SLPs in the prevention and identification of learning disabilities. *Topics in Language Disorders, 25,* 106–119.

Turnbull, H. R., III. (1993). *Free appropriate public education: The law and children with disabilities* (4th ed.). Denver, CO: Love.

Ukrainetz, T. A. (2006a). *Contextualized language intervention: Scaffolding K–12 literacy achievement.* Greenville, SC: Thinking Publications.

Ukrainetz, T. A. (2006b). The implications of RTI and EBP for SLPs: Commentary on L. M. Justice. *Language, Speech, and Hearing Services in Schools, 37*(4), 298–303.

Ukrainetz, T. A., Harpell, S., Walsh, C., & Coyle, C. (2000). A preliminary investigation of dynamic assessment with Native American kindergartners. *Language, Speech, and Hearing Services in Schools, 31,* 142–154.

Understanding the Federal Courts. (n.d.). Retrieved June 12, 2005 from http://www.uscourts.gov/understand03/index.html

Unger, H. G. (1996). Year-round school. In *Encyclopedia of American Education, III,* 1095. New York: Facts on File.

U.S. courts affirm the need for a full continuum of services. (1996). *CEC Today, 3(1),* 4–5.

U.S. Department of Commerce. (1993). *We the American children.* Washington, DC: U.S. Government Printing Office.

U.S. Department of Education (USDE). (1998). *Twentieth annual report to Congress on the implementation of the Individuals with Disabilities Education Act.* Washington, DC: Author.

U.S. Department of Education (USDE). (1999). *Twenty-first annual report to Congress on the implementation of the Individuals with Disabilities Education Act.* Washington, DC: Author.

U.S. Department of Education (USDE). (2000a, August). *The challenge of overcrowded schools is here to stay: Growing pains.* Retrieved January 30, 2001, from http://www.ed.gov/pubs/bbecho00/part2.html

U.S. Department of Education (USDE). (2000b). *Twenty-second annual report to Congress on the implementation of the Individuals with Disabilities Education Act.* Washington, DC: Author.

U.S. Department of Education (USDE). (2002a). *No Child Left Behind: A desktop reference.* Washington, DC: Author.

U.S. Department of Education (USDE). (2002b). *Twenty-fourth annual report to Congress on the implementation of the Individuals with Disabilities Education Act.* Washington, DC: Author.

U.S. Department of Education (USDE). (2004a). *A guide to education and No Child Left Behind.* Retrieved June 16, 2005 from http://www.ed.gov/nclb/overview/intro/guide/guide_pg13.html

U.S. Department of Education (USDE). (2004b). *Policy for inclusion of students with disabilities in standard-based assessment.* Retrieved February 8, 2006, from http://www.ed.gov/legislation/FedRegister/proprule/2005-4/121505a.html

U.S. Department of Education (USDE). (2005a, May) *Spellings announces new special education guidelines, details workable, "common-sense" policy to help states implement No Child Left Behind.* Retrieved May 13, 2005, from http://www.ed.gov/news/pressreleases/2005/05/05102005.html

U.S. Department of Education (USDE). (2005b). *Title I—Improving the academic achievement of the disadvantaged* [Final Rule]. Retrieved August 30, 2007, from http://www.ed.gov/legislation/FedRegister/finrule/2003-4/120903a.html

U.S. Department of Education (USDE). (2005c). *Title I—Improving the academic achievement of the disadvantaged; Individuals with Disabilities Education Act (IDEA)—assistance to states for the education of children with disabilities* [Proposed rule]. Retrieved August 30, 2007, from http://www.ed.gov/legislation/FedRegister/proprule/2005-4/121505a.html

U.S. Department of Education (USDE). (2005d). *Twenty-sixth annual report to Congress on the implementation of the Individuals with Disabilities Education Act., 1–2.* Washington, DC: Author.

U.S. Department of Education (USDE). (2007a). *Building on results: A blueprint for strengthening the No Child Left Behind Act.* Washington, DC: Author.

U.S. Department of Education (USDE). (2007b, March 8), personal communication from Alexa Posny, director of OSEP, to Catherine D. Clarke, director or Education and Regulatory Advocacy, ASHA. Retrieved October 22, 2007, from http://www.ed.gov/policy/speced/guid/idea/letters/2007-1/clarke030807disability1q2007.pdf

U.S. Department of Education, National Center for Education Statistics (NCES). (2003). *The condition of education 2003.* (NCES 2003-067). Retrieved September 7, 2007, from http://nces.ed.gov/pubsearch/pubsinfo.asp?pubid=2003067

U.S. Department of Education, National Center for Education Statistics (NCES). (2006). *Digest of education statistics, 2005* (NCES 2006-030), Chapter 2. Retrieved September 3, 2007, from http://nces.ed.gov/pubsearch/pubsinfo.asp?pubid=2006030

U.S. Department of Education, National Center for Education Statistics (NCES). (2007a). *Back to school statistics.* Retrieved September 10, 2007, from http://nces.ed.gov/fastfacts/display.asp?id=372

U.S. Department of Education, National Center for Education Statistics (NCES). (2007b). *Digest of Educational Statistics: 2006.* Retrieved September 10, 2007, from http://nces.ed.gov/programs/digest/d06

U.S. Department of Education (USDE), Office of Elementary and Secondary Education. (2003). *Federal Register 68698.*

U.S. Department of Justice. (1999). *Americans with Disabilities Act home page.* Retrieved November 26, 1999, from http://www.usdoj.gov/crt/ada/adahom1.htm

Valdez, F. M., & Montgomery, J. K. (1997). Outcomes from two treatment approaches for children with communication disorders in Head Start. *Journal of Children's Communication Development, 18*(2), 65–71.

van Kleeck, A. (1998). Preliteracy domains and stages: Laying the foundations for beginning reading. *Journal of Children's Communication Development, 20*(1), 33–51.

Vasudevan, L. M. (2006, 2007). Looking for angels: Knowing adolescents by engaging with their multimodal literacy practices. *Journal of Adolescent & Adult Literacy, 50*(4), 252–256.

Veale, T. K. (1999). Targeting temporal processing deficits through Fast ForWard: Language therapy with a new twist. *Language, Speech, and Hearing Services in Schools, 30,* 353–363.

Villa, R. A. (2005, Winter/Spring). IDEA 2004 and the IEP. *The Special Edge, 18*(2), 3–5, 7.

Vygotsky, L. S. (1978). *Mind in society: The development of higher mental processes.* Cambridge, MA: Harvard University Press.

Wallach, G. (2004). Over the brink of the millennium: Have we said all we can say about language-based learning disabilities? *Communication Disorders Quarterly, 25*(2), 44–55.

Wallach, G. P., & Butler, K. G. (Eds.). (1994). *Language-learning disabilities in school age children and adolescents.* New York: Merrill.

Waterman, R. (2004, May/June). No Child Left Behind: What special educators need to know. *In CASE, 45*(5), 16–18.

Webb, D. L., Greer, J. T., Montello, P. A., & Norton, S. M. (1987). *Personnel administration in education: New issues and new needs in human resource management.* Columbus, OH: Merrill.

Westby, C. (2007). *Interventions for Deaf students in schools using the ICF.* Presentation at the International Association of Logopedics and Phoniatrics, Copenhagen, Denmark.

Weston, A., & Bain, B. (2003, November). *Current vs. evidence-based practice in phonological intervention.* Paper presented at the meeting of the American Speech-Language and Hearing Association Convention, Chicago, IL.

Wetherby, A. (1998, July). *Improving early identification of communication disorders: Engaging parents in the process.* Presentation at the Fourth Biannual Head Start Research Conference, Washington, DC.

Wetherby, A. (2000, July). *Understanding and enhancing communication and language.* Two Day Institute at Northern Arizona University, Flagstaff, AZ.

Wetherby, A., & Prizant, B. (1992). Profiling young children's communicative competence. In S. Warren and J. Reichle (Eds.), *Causes and effects in communication and language intervention* (pp. 217–253). Baltimore: Brookes.

Wetherby, A., & Prizant, B. (1998). *Communication and symbolic behavior scales development profile* [Research edition]. Chicago: Applied Symbolix.

White House. (2000). *The Clinton-Gore administration: From digital divide to digital opportunity.* Retrieved May 5, 2004, from http://www.whitehouse.gov/WH/New/digitaldivide

White v. School Board of Henrico City, 549 S.E. 2d 16 (VA Ct. app. 2001).

Whitmire, K. (1999). Action: School services. *Language, Speech, and Hearing Services in Schools, 30,* 427–434.

Whitmire, K. (2000a). Action: School services: ASHA's 1999 priority issue I: Resources for school-based members. *Language, Speech, and Hearing Services in Schools, 31,* 194–199.

Whitmire, K. (2000b). Action: School services: Dysphagia services in schools. *Language, Speech, and Hearing Services in Schools, 31,* 99–103.

Whitmire, K. (2002). The evolution of school-based speech-language services: A half century of change and a new century of practice. *Communication Disorders Quarterly, 23*(2), 68–76.

Whitmire, K., Karr, S., & Mullen, R. (2000). Action: School services. *Language, Speech, and Hearing Services in Schools, 31,* 402–406.

Wiig, E. H., & Secord, W. A. (2006). Clinical measurement and assessment: A 25-year retrospective. *The ASHA Leader, 11*(2), 10–11, 27. Retrieved August 30, 2007, from http://www.asha.org/about/publications/leader-online/archives/2006/060207/060207d.htm?print=1

Wilcox, M. (1989). Families and their infants and toddlers with handicaps: Service delivery models and approaches. *Topics in Language Disorders, 10,* 68–79.

Wilcox, M. J. (1997). Considerations in promoting language-based learning readiness for children in Head Start. In J. Heller (Ed.), *Head Start university partnerships: Issues in child development research and practice* (pp. 61–79). Washington, DC: Administration for Children and Families.

Will, M. (1986). *Educating students with learning problems: A shared responsibility.* Washington, DC: U.S. Department of Education.

Williams, D. (2000). AAC interventions for children with autism. In J. Scott, C. Clark, & M. Brady (Eds.), *Students with autism* (pp. 214–215). San Diego, CA: Singular.

Williams, J. M. (2000, June 21). Bush: "The ADA is a good law." *Business Week Online.* Retrieved January 25, 2001, from http://www.businessweek.com/bwdaily/dnflash/jun2000/nf00621d.htm?chan=search

Winget, P., Boyle, S., & Reynolds, V. (1994, September/October). Courts, congress, associations debate LRE. *The Special Edge, 7,* 1:14.

Winner, M. G. (2006). *Think Social! A social thinking curriculum for school-age students for teaching social thinking and related skills to students with high functioning autism, PDD-NOS, Asperger syndrome, nonverbal learning disability, ADHD.* San Jose, CA: Think Social Publishing.

Wisconsin Administrative Code. (2000). Chapter PI 11.36 (5).

Wisconsin Department of Public Instruction. (June, 2000). *Revised sample special education forms* [Microsoft Word format]. Retrieved January 30, 2001, from http://www.dpi.state.wi.us/dpi/dlsea/een/form_int.html

Wisconsin Special Education Mediation System. (2001). Retrieved February 3, 2001, from http://www.cesa7.k12.wi.us/sped/wsems/index.htm

Wolf, K. (2005, February/March). Where did evidence-based practice come from? *CSHA Magazine, 34*(3), 5.

Wolf, K. E. (1997). Outcomes data: Quantifying accountability for the professions. *CSHA Magazine, 26*(2), 4–5.

Wolf, K. E., & Calderon, J. L. (1999). Cultural competence: The underpinning of quality health care and education services. *CSHA Magazine, 28*(2), 4–6.

Wolfberg, P. J., & Schuler, A. L. (1993). Integrated play groups: A model for promoting the social and cognitive dimensions of play in children with autism. *Journal of Autism and Developmental Disorders, 23*, 467–489.

Wolfram, W. (1991). *Dialects and American English.* Englewood Cliffs, NJ: Prentice Hall.

Wolfram, W., & Fasold, R. W. (1974). *Study of social dialects in American English.* Englewood Cliffs, NJ: Prentice Hall.

Woods, J. J., & Wetherby, A. M. (2003, July). Early identification of and intervention for infants and toddlers who are at risk for autism spectrum disorder. *Language, Speech, and Hearing Services in Schools, 34*, 180–193.

World Health Organization (WHO). (1980). *WHO: International classification of impairments, disabilities and handicaps.* Geneva, Switzerland: Author.

Wright, P. W. D., Wright, P. W., & Heath, S. W. (2003). No child left behind. Hartfield, Virginia: Harbour House Law Press.

Wyatt, T. (1999). Current clinical perspectives in the delivery of speech and language services to African-American children. *CSHA Magazine, 28*(2), 14–16.

Yell, M. L., Katsiyannis, A., Bradley, R., & Rozalski, M. E. (2000). Ensuring compliance with the discipline provisions of IDEA '97: Challenges and opportunities. *Journal of Special Education Leadership, 13*, 3–18.

Yoder, D. E., & Koppenhaver, D. A. (1993). In D. E. Yoder & D. A. Koppenhaver (Eds.), Literacy Learning and Persons with Severe Speech Impairments [Foreword]. *Topics in Language Disorders, 13*(2), vi–vii.

Yopp, H. K. (1995). A test for assessing phonemic awareness in young children. *Reading Teacher, 49*(1), 20–29.

Ysseldyke, J. E., Thurlow, M. L., McGrew, K. S., & Shriner, J. G. (1994). *Recommendations for making decisions about the participation of students with disabilities in statewide assessment programs* (Synthesis Report 15). Minneapolis, MN: National Center on Educational Outcomes.

Zehr, M. A. (2005, December 14). Academic English: Seen as key skill. *Education Week, 13.*

Zimmerman, B. J. (2002). Becoming a self-regulated learner: An overview. *Theory into Practice, 41*(2), 64–72.

Zipoli, R. P., & Kennedy, M. (2005). Evidence-based practice among speech-language pathologists: Attitudes, utilization, and barriers. *American Journal of Speech-Language Pathology, 14*(3), 208–220.

Zirkel, P. (2000, May). *Section 504 and ADA.* Presentation of LRP Publications, Irvine, CA.

Zirkel, P. A. (2006). Manifestation determinations under the Individuals with Disabilities Education Act: What the new causality criteria mean. *Journal of Special Education Leadership, 19*(2), 3–12.

Author Index

A

Adams, M. J. 220, 222, 245, 247, 254
Allington, R. L. 434
Alper, L. 412
Alt, E. 327
Annett, M. 424
Apel, K. 143, 145, 198 256, 260
Armbruster, B. A. 43, 45
Artiles, A. J. 267, 416
Arvedson 113
Attwood, T. 286
August, D. 241, 265, 427–8
Azzam, A. 415

B

Bain, B. A. 196, 198, 225
Banotai, A. 46
Barrera, M. 267
Barron, R. 81
Bashir, A. 144, 256
Batsche, G. 70, 72, 84, 86, 108
Battle, D. E. 269
Baum, H. M. 194
Baumel, J. 107
Bettleheim, B. 240
Bevilacqua, S. 279, 289
Biancaros, G. 256, 427
Bickerton, C. 113
Biehl 217
Biemiller, A. 12
Biklin, D. 175
Blackstone, S. 116, 293, 298
Bland, L. E. 223, 260, 271
Blend-Stewart 271
Blosser, J. L. 169, 179, 181, 283

C

Boley, D. 256
Bond, L. A. 22, 117
Botting, N. 287
Boudreau, D. M. 253–4
Bradley, R. 84, 322
Brady 283
Brannen, S. J. 135, 163, 170, 182, 203
Brice, A. E. 251, 269, 430
Bristol, M. M. 286
Bromley, K. 427
Brown, S. 169
Bucaro, F. C. 384
Burgess, S. 286
Bursuck, W. D. 6, 23, 25–6, 236
Buschbacher, P. 286
Butler, K. 144, 262

C

Calculator, S. N. 290, 293–4
Calderon, J. 132
Campbell, D. 190, 230, 236
Caperton, C. 251
Cassidy, D. 17, 256, 413, 427
Cassidy, J. 17, 256, 413, 427
Catts, H. W. 240–1, 245, 253, 427
Cernosia, A. 31
Chambers, J. G. 362
Charlop, M. H. 286
Cheng, L-R. L. 251, 269–70
Cirrin, F. M. 144, 251
Clark, M. 274
Cole, K. N. 114
Cole, L. 114, 271
Collins, M. 322
Coufal, K. 175

#TP-29703 Making a Difference - 2nd Ed. · ©2008 Thinking Publications® · www.thinkingpublications.com · 1-800-277-8737

Subject Index

A

accents 264–5, 270–1

accountability 6, 8, 15, 19, 31, 34, 36–8, 41, 47, 49, 52, 80–1, 123, 136–7, 190, 425

adolescents 215, 236, 240, 244–5, 256, 260–1, 423

African-American

children 51, 100, 147, 192–3

preschool-age children 411

Alternative Dispute Resolution (ADR) 316

American Federation of Teachers (AFT) 176, 394

American Psychological Association (APA) 30

American Speech-Language-Hearing Association (ASHA) 117-20, 142-5, 176-9, 187-93, 209-17, 240-1, 243-6, 265-6, 345-51, 368-9, 376-9, 384-5, 387-9, 391-6, 401-5, 422-4

Americans with Disabilities Act (ADA) 27, 138, 306, 338–9, 382

annual review 130

Applied Behavioral Analysis (ABA) 286, 320

articulation 89, 143, 158, 183, 201, 211

therapy 197

assessment

comprehensive 74, 99, 115

conducting 100, 415

formal 90, 98, 368

functional behavioral 325–6

high-stakes 17, 91, 413

in-depth 108, 112, 293

initial 97, 103, 108, 138

instruments 100, 102, 112, 432

methods 40, 66

performance-based 113–4

plan 104–6, 284, 310, 325, 328

procedures 111, 160, 182

process 65, 69, 99, 102–4, 112, 114, 121, 283–4

formal 90, 100

report 119–21

results 41, 127

standardized 111, 113, 431

teams 102, 145

tools 92, 101, 106, 108, 387

triennial 124, 138, 163–5

assistants 5, 121, 218, 273, 299, 343–4, 352, 375–9, 432

Assistive technology 30, 61, 131, 177, 183, 262-4, 291-2, 294-5, 298-9, 302, 356, 359, 375, 393, 426

Association of California School Administrators (ACSA) 155, 157

Associations for Supervision and Curriculum Development (ASCD) 392–3, 412

audiologic assessment of children 423

audiologists 3, 4, 12–5, 119–22, 161–3, 316–8, 329–32, 343–5, 347–9, 357–8, 366–9, 384–9, 391–6, 399–409, 421–4, 426–7, 430–3

audiology 3, 119, 194, 198, 345, 350, 354, 382, 387, 391, 393–4, 400, 423, 426

services 1, 3, 13, 19, 123, 158–9, 174, 369, 382, 394, 407

auditory processing skills 154

Augmentative and alternative communication 147, 175, 263-4, 282, 291-2, 296, 388, 393, 423, 426

autism spectrum disorders (ASDs) 14, 29, 31, 93, 118–9, 139–41, 145, 171, 174, 200, 264, 278–90, 320, 356, 365–6, 421–3

average yearly progress (AYP) 35, 38, 41, 45–6, 207

B

behavior 60, 84, 91, 94, 98, 109, 114, 131, 133, 146, 155, 193, 282–3, 286–8, 321–2, 325–8

Behavioral Intervention Plan (BIP) 325–6